**The McGraw-Hill
Marketing / Mid-Management Series**

Hampton and Zabin
   College Salesmanship

Gillespie and Hecht
   Retail Business Management

Troxell and Judelle
   Fashion Merchandising

Burke
   Advertising in the Marketplace

Mary D. Troxell

ASSOCIATE PROFESSOR
COORDINATOR OF FASHION MERCHANDISING
UNIVERSITY OF HAWAII, HONOLULU, HAWAII

Beatrice Judelle

RESEARCH CONSULTANT
SAN RAFAEL, CALIFORNIA

GREGG DIVISION/McGRAW-HILL BOOK COMPANY

New York   St. Louis   Dallas   San Francisco   Düsseldorf   Johannesburg   Kuala Lumpur
London   Mexico   Montreal   New Delhi   Panama   Rio de Janeiro   Singapore   Sydney   Toronto

Heidi V. Jefferson
108 Short St.
Tuskegee, Ala.
36083
727-4908

Fashion

Merchandising

FASHION MERCHANDISING

Copyright © 1971 by McGraw-Hill, Inc. All
Rights Reserved. Printed in the United States
of America. No part of this publication may be
reproduced, stored in a retrieval system, or
transmitted, in any form or by any means,
electronic, mechanical, photocopying, recording, or otherwise, without the prior written
permission of the publisher.

Library of Congress Catalog Card Number:
71-95834

    4 5 6 7 8 9 VHVH 0 9 8 7 6 5 4 3

ISBN 07–065275–9

Editor: *Georges E. Carpentier*
Editing Supervisor: *Mary Alice McGarry*
Designer: *Richard W. Stalzer*

Preface

Forty years ago the study of fashion was considered to be a glamorous but minor part of a retail merchandising program. Most educators considered fashion merchandising to be an art, too elusive and unpredictable to be reduced to teachable skills. Their position may have been reinforced by the retailers of the day, many of whom viewed fashion primarily in terms of women's apparel and accessories. Although these retailers realized the profit potential of fashion merchandising, they gave it no more than token consideration because of the accompanying risks. Others, however, felt differently. Educators like the late Paul Nystrom of Columbia University viewed fashion merchandising not as an art but as a science. In landmark studies conducted in the late twenties and early thirties, Dr. Nystrom identified the social, economic, and psychological factors that influenced the behavior of fashion consumers. He and contemporary scholars observed a definite pattern in the movement of fashion: fashions come and go in relatively predictable cycles. From their observations and research these early pioneers formulated a body of principles that govern the movement of fashion. These principles and their related concepts provide the scientific framework for the study of fashion merchandising.

Unfortunately, the economic and social conditions in the thirties and forties delayed the testing of these concepts. In the thirties consumers lacked the money to indulge their fashion tastes; in the early forties, the allocation of productive resources to the war effort severely limited the output of fashion goods. After World War II, however, neither of these retarding factors was present. Consumers had both the desire and the means to indulge tastes that had been suppressed during the wartime austerity. Moreover, students of Dr. Nystrom and his contemporaries had by this time become prominent figures in the world of retailing and were in a position to implement their principles. Those principles have proved viable, and the study of fashion merchandising has gained an acceptance in the academic world equal to that of retailing.

Nevertheless, until very recently few schools offered a separate program in fashion merchandising, and few, if any, textbooks on the subject were available. As the number of schools offering the program increased, the need for a comprehensive textbook became apparent. *Fashion Merchandising* was designed to fill this need.

Objectives

The primary purpose of *Fashion Merchandising* is to prepare the student for employment as an assistant buyer, buyer, or fashion coordinator. The selection of topics in the text was based upon the performance requirements of these jobs. But *Fashion Merchandising* goes far beyond merely describing these jobs. It enables the student to develop the skills needed to fulfill job requirements. The student is asked, for example, to identify suitable vendors, to develop merchandising plans, to collaborate in the establishment of a promotion program, and to coordinate a direct sales program.

The text also meets the needs of marketing students with other career goals. Since fashion merchandising is an important element in any marketing program, the study of it serves virtually all students majoring in marketing and retailing. *Fashion Merchandising* offers a comprehensive analysis of the field of fashion. It therefore can be used as a basic text in such courses as the history and movement of fashion, the manufacture of fashion apparel and accessories, fashion buying and planning, and fashion promotion and coordination.

Organization

Fashion Merchandising has been organized into three parts, with two appendixes, a glossary, and a bibliography. Part One, "The Dynamics of Fashion," describes the environment in which fashion thrives. In Chapter 1 the terminology and basic elements of fashion are introduced. The sociological, economic, and psychological factors that influence fashion behavior are identified and discussed in Chapter 2. In Chapter 3 the student is given a historical perspective of fashion. The movement of fashion is traced in Chapter 4, and those fashion leaders and followers who give impetus to this movement and who make mass production possible are identified in Chapter 5.

Product knowledge and the channels of distribution are discussed in Part Two, "Marketers of Fashion." Here the text explores the history and development, organization and operation, merchandising activities, and current marketing trends of each of the fashion industries. The producers of textile fibers and fabrics, leather, and fur are the subjects of Chapters 6 and 7. These firms take the raw materials and produce a product for resale to a fashion manufacturer. How the consumer product is manufactured from these materials is the subject of Chapters 8 and 9. The types of retail organizations that handle fashion merchandise are identified and classified in Chapter 10.

The buying, pricing, and promotion of fashion merchandise is the subject of Part Three, "Retail Merchandising of Fashion." Methods of measuring and of interpreting customer demand are the subjects of Chapter 11, while methods of preparing the merchandise plan—using both unit and dollar stock control—are explained in Chapters 12, 13, and 14. With the merchandise plan in hand, the student is ready to embark upon the market trip—the subject of Chapter 15. How to promote, sell, and coordinate fashion merchandise is presented in the final four chapters. Chapter 16 discusses methods of advertising and displaying merchandise. Publicity and personal selling are discussed in Chapter 17. The techniques of fashion coordination are the subject of Chapter 18, while Chapter 19 explains how to develop a fashion image.

Fashion Merchandising contains two appendixes, a glossary, and a bibliography. Appendix 1, "Career Opportunities in Fashion," will have particular guidance value for the vocational student. It identifies and explores specific jobs in fashion-related industries. Appendix 2, "Merchandising Mathematics," can be used either to review the basic principles of accounting and business mathematics or to supplement related material presented in the text. A comprehensive glossary contains definitions of fashion and merchandising terms used both in the text and in the trade. The bibliography will be especially helpful to the student because it contains an unusually complete listing of suggested fashion readings.

End-of-Chapter Activities

Each chapter in *Fashion Merchandising* concludes with three activities which are graded in terms of their complexity. The first activity, "Merchandising Vocabulary," lists those terms that have special fashion significance and need to be understood by the student. The student is asked to define each term.

The second activity, "Merchandising Review," tests the student's ability to recall the key concepts developed in the chapter. These questions, based on text content, can be answered easily.

The third activity, "Merchandising Digest," requires the student to employ his analytic skills. It presents problems that require the student to extrapolate, form abstractions, interpret data, or identify alternative solutions.

Instructor's Manual and Key

An instructor's manual and key has been prepared for *Fashion Merchandising*. The manual consists of four sections. Section 1 contains general teaching suggestions as well as methods for developing and structuring a fashion merchandise curriculum, course objectives, and recommended teaching schedules. Section 2 contains field-tested suggestions for launching, developing, and summarizing each chapter and a bibliography of relevant reference material and audiovisual aids. Section 3 provides the answers to the "Merchandising Vocabulary" and the "Merchandising Review" and suggested answers to the "Merchandising Digest." Section 4 contains ready-to-duplicate objective test items, together with a key. These items may be used in the sequence in which they appear or as a test bank from which the instructor may draw items to construct tests tailored to the needs of his class.

Acknowledgments

The authors are grateful to the many businessmen and educators who were consulted during the writing of this book; their responses were both helpful and generous. The authors are especially grateful to the several hundred students who cooperated in field-testing and validating experimental editions of this book. Their enthusiastic response provided the incentive needed to persevere in the completion of the final manuscript.

A special debt of gratitude is owed to Catherine Spurr for contributing both her editorial skill and human understanding to the development of this book. To the many other contributors whose help cannot be individually acknowledged, the authors are also deeply grateful.

Mary D. Troxell
Beatrice Judelle

CONTENTS

PART 1_____ DYNAMICS OF FASHION

Chapter 1   The Nature of Fashion   2

2   Environmental Influences on Fashion Demand   16

3   Historical Development of Fashion   30

4   The Movement of Fashion   52

5   Fashion Leaders and Followers   70

PART 2_____ MARKETERS OF FASHION

Chapter 6   The Materials of Fashion: Textile Fibers and Fabrics   88

7   The Materials of Fashion: Leather and Fur   104

8   Manufacturers of Fashion Apparel   120

9   Manufacturers of Fashion Accessories   138

10   Retail Distributors of Fashions   160

PART 3_____ RETAIL MERCHANDISING OF FASHION

Chapter 11   Interpreting Customer Demand   182

12   Budgeting the Fashion Merchandise Dollar   198

13   Budgeting the Fashion Merchandise Assortment   216

14   Managing Fashion Assortments   242

15   Selecting Fashion Merchandise for Resale   262

16   Promoting Fashion: Advertising and Display   282

17   Promoting Fashion: Publicity and Personal Selling   302

18   Fashion Coordination   318

19   Developing a Fashion Image   334

Appendix 1: Career Opportunities in Fashion   348

Appendix 2: Merchandising Arithmetic   366

Glossary   382

Bibliography   394

Index   398

PART 1 ___
Dynamics
of

FASHION

1
THE NATURE
of FASHION

A powerful force touches every facet of our lives. It influences what we wear, what we eat, where we live, what furnishings we have in our homes, how we travel, what we do for amusement. It involves each of us individually, frequently, personally; some use it to highlight personality and individuality, while others find in it an armor that builds self-confidence and assurance.

This same force has given a strong thrust to the vast expansion of industry and trade since the seventeenth century. Because of the spotlight of popularity it puts first on one product and then on another, it encourages manufacturers to produce, marketers to sell, and businesses of all kinds to hire, at an ever increasing rate. With its aid, the standard of living moves constantly higher.

The name of this potent force is fashion.

In dresses and dinner jackets, neckties and nightgowns, in automobiles and apartment houses, fashion plays an important role in product design, in sales promotion and advertising, in merchandise presentation, in every phase of marketing.

One common misconception of fashion is that all those who listen to fashion's commands are women, eager to change their skirt lengths, waist measurements, and hair colors on signal. Men are supposedly less responsive. Yet fashion is the force that directs men to adopt or abandon the wearing of vests, to grow or shave off beards, to accept or discard the gray flannel suit and the natural shoulder line.

Another misconception is that fashion is mysterious and unpredictable. Yet there are no unfathomable mysteries about the workings of fashion. Its direction can be detected and its changes can be predicted with remarkable accuracy.

Fashion touches everyone, and that touch can be measured and evaluated. Fashion merchandising is a science as well as an art.

The Terminology of Fashion

In studying the exciting and complex subject of fashion, certain words and phrases are used over and over again: high fashion and mass fashion, style, design, apparel, taste, classic, and fad. The words seem simple, but they are used differently by different people in different contexts. Their exact meanings within the field of fashion merchandising have to be understood if the field itself is to be understood.

The study of fashion merchandising as a science as well as an art is relatively new. It has required the exact definition of the fashion vocabulary so that concepts could be discussed and described without any misunderstanding of the terms. One of the major pioneers in the field was Dr. Paul H. Nystrom. The definitions in this section are those established by him, and they have become generally accepted for the academic study of fashion.[1]

Fashion

The prevailing style accepted and used by the majority of a group at any given time is a *fashion*. Full skirts, high heels, long hair, natural makeup—each has been a fashion, and no doubt each will be again when it is once more the style accepted by the majority of a group.

Different groups, however, can have different fashions, and fashions are often divided according to the group to which they appeal. *High fashion* refers to those styles or designs accepted by a limited group of fashion leaders, the elite among the consumers, those who are first to accept fashion change. In general, high fashion also is high in price. *Mass fashion* or *volume fashion* refers to those styles or designs that are widely accepted. Such fashions usually are produced and sold in large quantities, generally at moderate to low prices.

Style

A *style* is a characteristic or distinctive mode of presentation or conceptualization in the field of some art. There are styles in writing, in speaking, in home decorating, in table manners. In clothing, style is the characteristic or distinctive way a garment looks, the sum of the features that make it different from other garments. For instance, there are many styles of ladies' pants, such as tapered slacks, bell-bottoms, pantsuits, shorts, culottes, and jumpsuits, each a distinctively different presentation of the idea of pants.

Styles come and go in fashion acceptance, but a specific style always remains a style, whether or not it is in fashion. One or several styles may be in fashion at one time. Bell-bottoms and culottes may be the fashion news for one season, while the next season may see a gradual concentration on tapered slacks.

Styles are often named for the period of history in which they originated, and a style that has faded from the scene frequently returns to fashion again. This has happened with such styles as the Grecian, Roman, Renaissance, and Empire. When such styles return to fashion, their basic elements remain the same, although minor details may be altered to reflect the taste or needs of the new era in which they appear. Thus the Empire style of the early nineteenth century featured a waistline cinched high up under the bust, and that style can still be bought today. In today's version, however, the skirt length and the decorative details are modern.

Design

A specific or individual interpretation or version of a style is a *design*. A child's sunsuit is a style, but the countless variations in which it is available are designs. A man's bulky outdoor jacket with knitted bands at waist and wrist is a style, and the number of slightly varying models available are designs.

It is the use of different colors, fabrics, and trimmings that differentiate one design from another. Each manufacturer is apt to put out several designs or variations of a popular style. If chunky, low-heeled shoes are the fashion for women, each shoe manufacturer will offer several different designs of that style varying in color, material, or decoration.

In the fashion trade, however, manufacturers and retailers sometimes refer to a design as a "style" or a "style number" or a "number." Such trade usage should not be confused with the terminology that is used in academic discussions of fashion. Learn to use the word "design"—but remember that it may be called something else on the job.

Apparel

Although fashion touches almost every facet of living, this text concentrates, for the most part, on the merchandising of fashion apparel in general and on ladies' fashion apparel in particular. In its broadest sense, *apparel* means not only outerwear but all articles that woman wears or carries to complete her costume, including lingerie, shoes, jewelry, and handbags. In fashion retailing, "apparel," used without modification, applies only to outerwear—coats, suits, dresses, sportswear, etc.—for women, misses, and juniors.

Taste

The ability to recognize what is and what is not attractive and appropriate is *taste*. Taste in fashion implies a sensitivity not only to what is artistic but also to what prevailing fashion says is appropriate for a specific occasion. Styles may be artistically beautiful, but if they are not appropriate, they may not be in good taste. For example, a bathing suit that is artistically in good taste would be in good taste on the beach, which is the appropriate place for the suit. The same

1870
1900
1930
1940
1950
1960

suit, its artistic design unchanged, would be considered in abominable taste at a wedding reception.

Dr. Nystrom pinpointed the relationship between taste and fashion this way: "Good taste essentially is making the most artistic use of current fashion . . . bridging the gap between good art and common usage."[2]

Timing, too, makes a difference in what is considered good or bad taste. James Laver, the British costume authority, saw the relationship as a cycle through which a style goes. Whether or not a style is in good taste depends upon the place it has reached in that cycle. A style, he said, is thought to be:

"indecent"	10 years before its time
"shameless"	5 years before its time
"outré"	1 year before its time
"smart"	in its time
"dowdy"	1 year after its time
"hideous"	10 years after its time
"ridiculous"	20 years after its time[3]

While the actual amount of time covered may be greatly expanded or condensed for different styles, the cycle itself is a valid concept. A new style is first considered daring and often in dubious taste, then is gradually accepted, and finally is gradually discarded.

Classics

Some styles or designs remain in good taste over a long period, proving an exception to the often rather rapid movement of the fashion cycle. A *classic* is a style or design that remains in fashion for an extended period of time.

Everyone's wardrobe has some classics in it, while some wardrobes are made up mainly of classics. A classic is seldom high fashion because of the length of time it has been in fashion, but it is still considered acceptable and in good taste. The chesterfield has been a classic for many years. So has the shirtwaist dress.

"Good taste" in fashion changes—as this 90-year panorama of bathing suit fashions shows.

Fads

The short-lived fashion is called a *fad*. Fads usually affect only a narrow group within the total population and generally are concerned with some unimportant detail of design. Young people are especially susceptible to fads, but adults are not totally immune. Fads have also been called "miniature fashions," following the same cycle as a fashion but completing that cycle much more quickly. A fad can come and go in a single season.

Some fads that have followed the pattern of appeal to a narrow group and quick ascent and descent in popularity include Davy Crockett hats for small boys and intern-style blouses for teen-age girls, both of which reflected the influences of then popular television programs. Fads adopted by some segments of the adult feminine population in recent years include sunglasses worn atop the head as a finishing touch to the coiffure, the long, full-skirted "granny" dress, and industrial zippers on dresses.

Occasionally what first appears to be a fad later develops into a classic. The Bikini, a shocking Riviera fad of the early 1950s, gradually grew into an accepted beach fashion. Today the name has lost its capital letter, and the garment has lost its power to shock.

Another example is the sack or chemise dress, which flared into instant popularity in the late 1950s. Although it quickly passed from the fashion scene, it was reborn within a few years as the shift. In any study of dress history, in fact, the straight lines of the sack or shift dress, in one guise or another, show up over and over again.

Components of Fashion

Creating a fashion design is a complex process. The great designers of apparel do not produce by a hit-or-miss technique. Instead, the finished look of a fashion style or design is a blend, a composition, of four basic elements or components, each one contributing to the total effect. These four elements with which all apparel fashions are concerned are silhouette, detail, texture, and color. Any change in fashion involves a change in one or more of these elements.

Silhouette

The *silhouette* of a costume is its overall outline or contour. Silhouette is also sometimes referred to as "shape" or "form."

To the casual observer it may appear that women have worn countless silhouettes throughout the centuries. According to authorities, however, there have been only three basic types, each with many variations: the straight or tubular, the bell-shaped or bouffant, and the bustle or back-fullness.[4] Since the mid-eighteenth century, these basic silhouettes have consistently followed each other in fashion acceptance in the same sequence, each recurring once in approximately 100 years and lasting for about a 35-year period. Changes in very recent years indicate that the length of this period may be shrinking, but the sequence remains the same. Other components of apparel fashions tend to change more frequently, often with the season.

Detail

The individual parts that comprise the silhouette or make up its structure are called *details*. These include trimmings, skirt length, or shoulder, waist, and sleeve treatment.

Changes in detail, especially in the skirt, are steps leading toward a change in silhouette. Silhouettes evolve gradually, from one to another, through changes in detail. When the trend in a detail reaches an extreme, then a reversal of the trend takes place. For example, skirt lengths reached an extreme in brevity in the late 1960s, and the reversal began to show itself in the increasing number of midi-length styles available. The change was predictable, although the speed with which it took place was unusual.

Variations in detail offer both designer and consumer unlimited opportunity to express individuality within the framework of an accepted fashion silhouette. For example, for a natural-waistline silhouette a slender woman might choose a simple, wide belt, a heavily decorated belt, or a belt in a contrasting color to suit either her personality or the occasion. A woman who wants to de-emphasize a wide waist might choose either a narrow or a noncontrasting belt, or perhaps wear no belt at all, preferring seams that suggest a natural waistline.

Texture

One of the most significant components of fashion is texture. *Texture* is the look and feel of all types of material, woven or nonwoven.

Texture can influence the appearance of the silhouette by making it appear bulkier or more slender, depending on the roughness or smoothness of the materials used. A woman dressed in a rough tweed dress and a bulky knit sweater is likely to look larger and squarer than she does in a dress of identical lines executed in smooth jersey and worn with a cashmere sweater. In the early 1960s, when fashionable sportswear had a bulky look, the popular textures included shaggy tweeds, mohairs, cable-stitched and other heavily ribbed knit fabrics, and similar rough-textured materials. A few years later, when sleek lines became the fashion, rough textures yielded to smooth surfaces and simple flat weaves and knits.

Texture influences the drape of a garment because different textures of material drape differently when cut and sewn. Chiffon clings and flows, making it a good choice for soft feminine styles, while corduroy has a stiffness and bulk that make it a good choice for more casual garments.

Texture can influence the quality of color in a fabric by causing the surface either to reflect or to absorb light. Rough textures absorb light, causing the colors to appear dull; smooth textures reflect light, causing colors to appear bright. Anyone who has tried to match colors soon discovers that a color which appears extremely bright in a shiny vinyl, satin, or high-gloss enamel paint seems subdued in a rough wool, a suede, or on a wall finished in stucco. Pile surfaces like velvet both reflect and absorb light, making colors look richer and deeper than they would on flat, shiny surfaces.

Color

In women's clothing, color has always been a major consideration. In men's clothing, especially since the end of World War II, color has been regaining the importance it once had but lost for generations. Today color is a key factor in apparel selection for both sexes. It is important not only in the fashions themselves but in advertising, packaging, and general store decor.

Colors have historically been used to denote rank and profession. Purple, for instance, is the color associated with royalty, and in some areas at some periods could be worn only by those of noble birth. Black became the ordinary wear for the clergy and thence for most professional men, and ultimately, after the industrial revolution, for men of substance in the business world.

What a color denotes often varies with geographical location. White, for example, is the Western world's symbol of purity, worn by brides and used in communion dresses, whereas in India, white is the color of mourning.

Color has been affected by progress in technology. Better ways of tanning leather and processing cloth have resulted in a much wider collection of colored materials for the fashion designer to work with. In addition, these colors are more permanent, more resistant to fading or changing, and thus more acceptable to the consumer.

Today, a fashion designer's color palette changes with the customer's diverse preferences. In some seasons, all is brightness and sharp contrast, and no color is too powerful to be worn successfully. In other seasons, only subdued colors have appeal. Fashion merchants soon develop an eye for color, not just for the specific hues and values that are popular in a given season but also for possible future trends in consumer preference.

The Intangibles of Fashion

The definition of fashion, remember, is "the prevailing style accepted by the majority of a group at any given time." That style is tangible, made up of silhouette, detail, texture, and color. Fashion, however, is a matter of intangibles as well:

"Accepted" is part of the definition, for to be a fashion, a style must be accepted. Fashion, therefore, is acceptance. "Prevailing" and "at any given time" indicate the need to identify the style with a particular period of time, for fashion moves, fashion is change. "A given group" relates fashion to specific people living a specific kind of life in a specific place, for fashion is a mirror of the times.

Acceptance

The element of group acceptance or approval is implied in any discussion of fashion. A style must be adopted by a major portion of a single group or a major segment of the whole population before it becomes a fashion. An article of clothing may be breathtakingly new and aesthetically flawless, yet it may not be called a fashion until it has been accepted and used by a substantial number of consumers. Acceptance, rather than novelty or beauty, is required for a style to become a fashion.

Acceptance need not be universal, however. A style may be adopted by one group, thus becoming a fashion for that group, even though other segments of the population ignore it. Country club fashions are rarely popular with the college crowd; business wardrobes often bear little or no relationship to those accepted by either country club or college groups.

Similarly, a style may be accepted in one part of the world, becoming a fashion there, while it is ignored or rejected elsewhere. The igloo of the Eskimo, the thatched hut of the African tribesman, or the ranch house of the American suburbanite are all considered fashionable—but each by its own inhabitants. In the same way, some ethnic and religious groups have fashions that are unique. In this country, the Amish and the Mennonites are among those groups whose members still can be recognized by their clothes.

Acceptance also means that a fashion must be considered appropriate to the occasion and purpose for which it is worn. Clothes considered appropriate for classroom wear by college students, for example, would not be acceptable by the same body of students for wear to a formal dance.

The group that adopts or rejects a specific style decides what is appropriate for the time, the place, and the occasion, and determines what is therefore acceptable. The decision is not always considered sensible by others. For example, in the 1850s and 1860s, when the crinoline was in fashion, women finally were beginning to broaden their activities beyond the confines of the home. They rode in carriages and railroad trains, attended lectures, and nursed the sick in those tight-waisted dresses with skirts so full that one

fashion authority refers to them as "human balloons."

In the early years of the twentieth century, too, working women who operated typewriters or sewing machines wore a style that would scarcely be considered appropriate working attire today. This style, known as the "Gibson girl" costume, featured a cinched waist, trailing skirt, elaborate hairdo, and a high-necked blouse with a collar held stiffly in place with stays.

Men's fashions also provide many illustrations of uncomfortable styles considered appropriate in their day. When the term "white-collar class" was born, the collar that gave it its name was fashionably high and stiffly starched, and a man never removed his coat or tie in company.

Regardless of the suitability of a style from any practical standpoint, however, if it is accepted by the majority of a specific group at a given time and place for a specific occasion, it is a fashion.

Change

Fashion is subject to constant change, sometimes rapidly, sometimes slowly. As soon as a fashion is fully accepted, it is apt to begin to look too ordinary to some people, and they reach beyond it to find something different, something new. The emphasis on change, however, is neither peculiar to the fashion field nor new. More than 2,500 years ago a Greek philosopher said, "The only eternal truth in the history of the universe is change."

What is new is the speed at which fashion change takes place. There has been a marked acceleration in the rate of change, particularly in women's clothes, in the past 100 years.

The invention of the sewing machine and the development of synthetic fibers have played important parts in this acceleration, giving designers and the garment industry alike faster ways of turning out garments and a much greater variety of materials to work with. For the consumer, a mass-produced dress bought off the rack at a moderate price is much easier to discard than a hand-sewn or hand-knitted creation representing weeks or even months of work. The new fibers and fabrics encourage such discarding, too, for each new one seems to have more to offer than the last.

Another major factor in the acceleration in the rate of fashion change is modern communications. Newspapers, magazines, and television spread fashion news throughout the world in a matter of hours. Something new that an acknowledged fashion leader wore to a party one evening is pictured and described in newspapers the next day, and what is being worn by public figures is on view every time the television set is turned on. Thus even slight changes in fashion are given faster and wider publicity than ever before, and the consumers who decide they like those changes demand them from the merchants, who in turn demand them from producers.

Historically, women's apparel has always showed the most rapid rate of change. Men's fashions have changed at a much slower rate. Home furnishing fashions have changed at a still slower rate, and fashions in architecture have changed most slowly of all.

Change Demanded by the Consumer There is a general misconception that the business world forces fashion change upon the consumer, that makers of fashion create artificial obsolescence by bringing out new styles before the old ones have had time to wear out. That is not true. The consumer is the one who initiates the change. It is often only a small minority of the consumer population that reaches out for a change and puts it on view, but this minority is composed of the fashion leaders who set the trends the majority of consumers will follow.

The consumer demands change because of his changing interests, changing wants, and changing ideas of what is appropriate and acceptable. Sometimes the consumer demands change simply for the sake of change. The designer, the manufacturer, and the retailer try to chart, forecast, and meet these demands of the consumer.

The Futility of Forcing Change Since fashion changes are outgrowths of changes in the consumer's needs, it is seldom possible to force or hold back a fashion change. Efforts to alter the course of fashion have been made from time to time, but they usually end in failure. Fashion is a power, a potent force, whose very definition includes its support by the majority. Even royalty's attempts to alter fashion have been thwarted. Empress Eugénie of France and Queen Victoria of England, in 1860, each condemned the fashion of crinolines and stopped wearing them. Yet crinolines, then at the height of their popularity and at the extreme of their billowing fullness, continued in fashion, and presently the royal ladies resumed wearing them. Fashion had defeated the royal decrees.

To save fabric, World War II skirts were short, narrow, and pockets were usually slit-styled.

A recent example of the futility of trying to force a fashion is provided by the headwear industries. For several decades, men and women have shown an increasing fondness for going bareheaded on occasions for which hats formerly were de rigueur. The men's headwear industry and the women's millinery industry have consistently promoted campaigns to encourage the wearing of hats, but without any major results. Any reversal of the current hatless fashion, when it comes, will have to originate with the consumer. Whatever promotional or publicity efforts are in progress when the tide of change begins to turn will appear to be brilliantly successful, whereas those that preceded them and failed, simply because the consumer was not yet ready, may have been equally brilliant.

Occasionally, necessity and law can interrupt the course of a fashion. This happened during World War II, when the United States government controlled the kind and amount of fabric that could be used in consumer goods. One World War II regulation, for instance, prohibited anything but slit pockets on women's garments, to avoid the extra use of material that patch pockets would require. Skirts, of necessity, were short and silhouettes narrow, reflecting the scarcity of material.

Meeting the Demand for Change After the war, a reaction toward a freer line and a more feminine garment was to be expected. A new French designer, Christian Dior, caught and expressed this feeling in his very first collection and achieved instant fashion success. Using fabric with a lavishness that had been impossible in Europe or America during the war years, he created his New Look, with long, full skirts, fitted waistlines, and feminine curves.

Dior did not change the course of fashion. He simply recognized and interpreted the deep need women felt to get out of the stiff, narrow, and unfeminine clothes that a world war had imposed on them and to get into soft, free, feminine clothes again.

Failure to recognize and respond to early indications of the need for change on the part of consumers can be a costly mistake. The American automobile industry discovered this fact, for the

The soft, full, long lines of Dior's New Look reflected a release from wartime restrictions.

rule of fashion persists in fields other than apparel. During each consecutive year of the 1950s, automobiles became larger and more gaudy. Toward the end of that decade, the public started to revolt against these immense, lavishly decorated models, and began to show a preference for smaller, less ornate cars. The signs were there; change had begun.

Domestic automobile manufacturers, however, either missed their cue, misinterpreted it, or ignored it. They brought out even bigger and flashier models—and by the end of that decade, more than 10 percent of all new cars being purchased by Americans were small compacts of foreign make. During the 1960s, Detroit tried to compromise with a variety of what it considered compacts, but these still were not small enough and economical enough for the American consumer. It was not until the end of the decade that cars truly comparable with the European and Japanese models began to come out of Detroit.

A Mirror of the Times

Fashions are molded by the force of an era. Fashions are reflections of the way people think and live—or thought and lived. The modesty of the Victorian woman was reflected in her covered-up fashions with their bulk and concealment, for instance, while the sexual emancipation and equality felt by the flapper of the 1920s was obvious in her short skirts, short hair, and flattened figure.

The economist Thorstein Veblen related fashion to the stage of culture that any civilization had reached. In his famous *Theory of the Leisure Class*, he set forth the idea that cultures progress from the primitive, to what he termed the "predatory," and then to the industrial.[5] At each stage, a particular kind of fashion is prevalent.

In primitive cultures, says Veblen, women are valued for the service they can render; hence, robust and large-limbed types are considered beautiful, and fashions reflect that idea of beauty.

In "predatory" cultures, a woman's exemption from useful work becomes a symbol of her hus-

The blithe, brief miniskirts of the 1960s mirrored the social and cultural changes of the day.

band's high status. The constricted waist of the Western woman and the bound feet of the Chinese woman thereby reflected the material success of the male. The great delicacy of the handling of the faces, hands, and figures of women in medieval tapestries demonstrated that the knights of that era maintained their women in leisure, for the fashions shown placed emphasis on slenderness and delicacy, and concealed any possible bulk under full skirts and sleeves.

At higher levels of development, such as the industrial age, Veblen believes that the ideal of feminine beauty reverts, in some ways, to the primitive woman, at least in the sense that such a woman "does not disown her hands and feet, nor, indeed, the other gross material facts of her person."[6] Plunging necklines, miniskirts, and bikinis, certainly fashions that do not disown gross material facts about a person, came long after Veblen's death in 1929, but even in his late years the short skirts and sleeves of the 1920s must have reassured him about the validity of his theories.

Fashions mirror not only the period in which characteristic styles prevail, but also that segment of society in which they have won acceptance. Even in comparatively simple cultures, different social levels do not necessarily accept the same styles at the same time. For example, traditional European peasant costumes reflected the fact that strong sturdy wives were needed and admired. The characteristic puffy sleeves, laced bodices, and full skirts, which make even a slender girl look bulky and muscular, attested to this fact. European peasants wore such costumes at the same time that women of the wealthier classes had adopted fashions that emphasized their delicacy.

In today's society, many fashions exist side by side because of a flexible and increasingly mobile class structure. Those with home interests and casual hobbies are apt to live and dress casually, while those who concentrate on charity balls, the theater, opera, and other formal social occasions may adopt elegance and luxury in their dress. As a contrast, those who reject current conventions

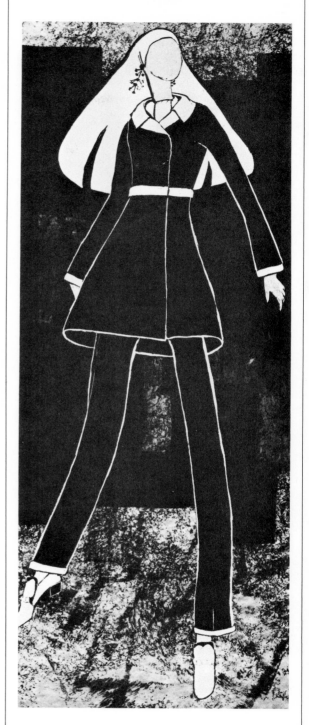

Pantsuits in the late 1960s became a symbol of more leisure and a more relaxed living style.

to form societies of their own establish their own modes and standards of dress, which are their fashions. There are typical fashions that identify the beatniks and hippies of the 1960s, just as there were fashions that identified their earlier counterparts, the Bohemians of the 1920s.

In fact, one person's wardrobe can contain elements of many fashions: slacks for gardening, an avant-garde dress for the theater, and classic styles for shopping and visiting.

Art and Fashion

Many people consider the fashion designer an artist. He develops an idea for a garment, and then he turns that idea into reality with pencil, paper, scissors, cloth, and trimmings. The resulting design may closely resemble something else already on the market, or it may be completely new, but it is his artistic creation.

The artistic elements of greatest importance in fashion are line, form, space, color, and texture. In art, these are referred to as *plastic elements*, because they can be manipulated at will to achieve various effects.

When these elements are arranged together artistically, the result is harmony. *Harmony* in fashion is the look that is pleasing and in good taste. It is therefore the look that enjoys excellent prospects for long-term acceptance by the fashion consumer.

Line

A line in art is the space between two points. It can be straight or curved or jagged. It can be narrow or wide. It can have an almost limitless number of variations.

The silhouette and details of any apparel style give it its *lines*. These lines impart definite characteristics to the garment and to the wearer of the garment. Vertical lines add height and lend dignity. Horizontal lines add width and create a feeling of repose and serenity. Diagonal lines suggest movement and animation.

The watching eye can be induced to move in any direction by line. Line can attract attention to or divert it from any particular feature. For discerning consumers, line is a key element in the choice of a fashion, for it can draw the eye of the beholder to what the wearer of the garment considers her best features and away from what she considers her worst.

Line enhances or diminishes certain characteristics of the silhouette or detail. The tubular silhouette has straight lines, but these lines can be modified if a floral print with delicately curved lines or a free-form abstract print with jagged diagonals is used. The straight lines of the tubular silhouette can be emphasized, however, by using a solid color material or a material with vertical stripes. In exactly the same way, the soft curved line of the bell silhouette will lose some of that softness or fullness if the fabric design or trim emphasizes straight lines.

Form

The sum total of the lines of a style is its form. *Form* refers to shape or contour. It is the three-dimensional whole created by the various two-dimensional lines.

In fashion, "form" is a word applied to the look of the silhouette as a whole or to any of several parts of it. The bell silhouette is a form. Leg-of-mutton sleeves are a form. The pillbox is a form. (And if some of these examples sometimes sound old-fashioned, remember that these are merely the classic ways of describing what are very common styles. The bell silhouette, for instance, describes any style that fits closely above the waist and has wide, billowing skirts.)

Because fashion form is made up of lines, changing form involves changing lines. This change can be effected either with fabric designs and trimmings, as described above, or with accessories. A plump woman in a bouffant dress will look more slender if she limits herself to a small handbag, a discreet use of jewelry, and matching rather than contrasting gloves. If she chooses instead to wear chunky earrings and heavy bracelets, and to carry a suitcase-sized handbag, the overall form may change from one that seems softly rounded to one that seems to bristle and bulge.

Space

Space refers to the background against which individual shapes or details are placed. Changing the relationship between space and the shapes placed on that space can create startlingly different artistic effects.

Big, dramatic shapes against an unrelieved background, as in a Mondrian painting, give an effect of force and power. Small shapes and spaces, as in dainty prints or fine pleating or tucking, create a delicate feminine effect. A decorative pin or monogram that blends into a large expanse of plain fabric can look unobtrusive; on the smaller background of a pocket or collar tab, the same article can dominate the immediate background and become dramatic.

Color

Color, already discussed as one of the components of the physical design of a fashion style, is also important in its role as an artistic element. Some authorities on color divide colors into two ranges. The red-yellow-orange range is considered to be "warm," with strong appeal to extroverts and people with keen appetites for innovation. The blue-green-purple range is considered to be "cool," appealing to introverts and those who are not usually found among the fashion leaders. However, in fabrics, which are the stuff of which fashion is made, pure colors are hard to find. A red may have a bluish cast, which would make it acceptable to the "cool" group of customers, while a green may have a yellowish cast, making it acceptable to the "warm" group.

Various color combinations are used in fashion and other art fields to create what the eye sees as harmonious effects. A monochromatic scheme uses varying intensities of one color or hue. An analogous color scheme uses colors that have a common connection, those that appear next to each other in a color wheel, such as yellow and orange. A complementary color scheme uses colors that are opposite one another on that color wheel, such as green and red.

In addition to selecting a color combination, the designer also has to weigh color value and intensity. These vary not only with the colors themselves but according to the type of material that has been colored. On a shiny fabric, remember, a particular tone will appear brighter and sharper than it will on a dull fabric. The designer's goal is to have some variation in both value and intensity, without having any sharp contrast in either.

The consumer may not be familiar with the science of artistic color selection, but she does know whether the designer and merchants have colors and color combinations that appeal to her—and she buys what pleases her eye and her mood.

Texture

Texture, of primary importance as an artistic element, refers to the surface appearance and feel of the material used. The finishing of the material itself may give it its texture; texture interest can also be created through tucks, pleats, seams, and other methods of construction. Trimmings, such as sequins and beads, also add texture to a material.

In handling texture, the artistic designer strives for consistency without monotony. The textures used in a costume must be interesting, and they must harmonize with the design and with one another. A certain amount of contrast is acceptable, such as a smooth leather belt on a tweed dress or a combination of smooth leather and suede in a shoe. Too much contrast, however, is jarring—a heavy leather belt with a clinging chiffon dress, for example.

Instinct and flair are important in handling texture—as they are important in handling all the artistic elements of an apparel design, when backed up by a solid knowledge of the ways those artistic elements can be used.

Instinct and flair are useful in the entire field of fashion merchandising—again, when backed up by a solid knowledge of what fashion is and how it behaves.

References

[1]Nystrom, *Economics of Fashion*, pp. 3–7, and *Fashion Merchandising*, pp. 33–34.
[2]Nystrom, *Economics of Fashion*, p. 7.
[3]Laver, *Taste and Fashion*, p. 202.
[4]Young, *Recurring Cycles of Fashion*, p. 92.
[5]Veblen, *Theory of the Leisure Class*, pp. 106–108.
[6]*Ibid.*, p. 108.

Merchandising Vocabulary

Define or briefly explain the following terms:

Fashion	Taste
Style	Fad
High fashion	Detail
Mass fashion	Silhouette
Classic	Texture
Apparel	Color
Design	Harmony

Merchandising Review

1. What two familiar misconceptions are usually associated with fashion?
2. Distinguish between (a) style and fashion, and (b) style and design.
3. Why has there been such a marked acceleration in the rate of apparel fashion change during the past 100 years?
4. Is it possible to force an unwanted fashion upon the consumer public? Defend your answer.
5. One authority has stated that "fashion mirrors the times." Briefly explain the meaning of this statement and be prepared to agree and support, or disagree and refute, this claim.
6. What are the four components of all fashion? Briefly explain their interrelationship.
7. Name the five "plastic elements" of art. Discuss the importance of each in relation to apparel design.
8. Why is harmony considered the most important of all principles of design?

Merchandising Digest

The following statements have been quoted from the text. Discuss the significance of each, citing specific examples to illustrate its application to the merchandising of fashions.

1. "Acceptance means that a fashion must be considered appropriate to the occasion and purpose for which it is worn."
2. "Color is a key factor in apparel selection for both sexes."
3. "In today's society, many fashions exist side by side. . . ."

2

ENVIRONMENTAL INFLUENCES ON FASHION DEMAND

Just as fashion touches so many facets of living, so in turn does the environment in which that living takes place influence fashion. *Environment* is the sum of the conditions that surround and influence a person. Fashion develops better in some environments than in others. Among societies that are static and ingrown, the demand for fashion is slight and its opportunities to thrive are minimal, but fashion flourishes in societies that enjoy considerable physical, economic, and social mobility.

There are three prime areas of environmental factors that affect fashion demand: economic, social, and psychological. In general, the major environmental influences on fashion demand are:

□ Economic development, for the more economically advanced a country is, the greater its interest in fashion
□ The sociological characteristics of class structure, its mobility, and the size of its middle class
□ The psychological attitudes of the period

Economic Factors

A high level of economic development is essential to the growth of fashion demand since it supplies both the means of production and the enhanced purchasing power requisite to growth. This principle is clearly demonstrated by comparing the dress of people in economically advanced countries like the United States with the prevailing dress in less developed nations.

Quentin Bell, in *On Human Finery*,[1] underscored the relationship between economic progress and fashion by showing that economically backward countries retained their national costumes long after more economically advanced nations had discarded theirs. England, which led the Western world into the industrial revolution, was the first country of the Western world to abandon traditional national dress. Bell points out that Greece, Russia, Spain, and Persia (now Iran), which had little in common with one another except laggard economic development, retained a national costume at a time when countries with more progressive economies, such as Germany, Belgium, Denmark, and Japan, were abandoning theirs.

In the twentieth century, Russia provides a dramatic example of how a country moving swiftly to economic development also moves ahead in fashion. In the first few decades following the 1917 revolution, clothing was drab and utilitarian. By the mid-1950s, however, the Soviet economy had advanced to the point where it was able to place greater emphasis on the production of consumer goods, and the influence of fashion, particularly in clothing, increased. Today, Russian consumers have a fairly wide choice of apparel, and are able to accept or reject a style, to create or discard a fashion.

In China, however, economic development still lags behind that of the Western world. Most of the country's economy is still directed toward the production of industrial goods. Such consumer goods as are available are only the minimum required for food, shelter, and protection. Cloth-

Table 2-1. Total Money Income of Families and Unrelated Individuals, 1950–1965

Median Incomes	1950	1955	1960	1965
Families	$3,319	$4,421	$5,620	$6,882
Unrelated individuals	$1,045	$1,316	$1,720	$2,110
Distribution: families and unrelated individuals with incomes of:				
Under $4,000	68.3%	50.7%	39.6%	33.4%
$4,000 to $9,999	28.9	44.0	48.3	46.0
$10,000 and over	2.8	5.3	12.0	20.5
	100.0%	100.0%	100.0%	100.0%

Source: U. S. Bureau of the Census.

ing and fabrics are rationed, and both men and women dress in almost identical quilted pants and jackets in gray or navy. With little or no choice available, there is little or no fashion. People simply wear what is protective, inexpensive, and practical.[2]

Consumer Income

The economic scene in the United States is in sharp contrast with that of China. Consumers living in the highly developed economy of the United States have their choice of an increasingly wide variety of goods.

The rise in consumer income and the speed with which it has climbed in this country are directly related to the gross national product (GNP), which is the market value of the nation's total output of goods and services in any calendar year. With the GNP now more than 20 times greater than it was at the beginning of the twentieth century, important changes have taken place in personal, disposable, and discretionary incomes in the United States. (See Tables 2-1, 2-2.)

Personal Income That part of a nation's income which reaches the individual consumer's hands is called *personal income*. Per capita personal income in the United States in 1915 was approximately $400. In 1965, it was $2,724, or seven times greater.

Table 2-2. Median Income, Families and Unrelated Individuals, by Age and Sex, 1968

	Families		Unrelated Individuals	
Ages	Male Head	Female Head	Male	Female
14 to 24	$ 6,556	$2,607	$3,141	$2,422
25 to 34	$ 9,120	$3,267	$6,485	$5,107
35 to 44	$10,591	$4,484	$6,161	$4,065
45 to 54	$10,937	$5,756	$5,903	$3,508
55 to 64	$ 9,175	$5,892	$4,784	$3,113
65 and over	$ 4,564	$4,756	$1,916	$1,670
Total	$ 9,096	$4,477	$4,086	$2,239

Source: U. S. Bureau of the Census.

Disposable Income The amount a person has left to spend or save after paying taxes is called _disposable personal income_. It is roughly equivalent to what an employee calls "take-home pay" and provides an approximation of the purchasing power of each consumer during any given year. (See Table 2-3.)

Table 2-3.   Per Capita Disposable Income in 1958 Dollars, Selected Years, 1930 to 1965

Year	1958 Dollars
1930	1,128
1935	1,035
1940	1,259
1945	1,642
1950	1,646
1955	1,795
1960	1,883
1965	2,214

Source: _Long-Term Economic Growth, 1860–1965_, U. S. Department of Commerce, p. 172.

Discretionary Income The money that an individual or family has left after buying such necessities as food, clothing, shelter, and basic transportation is called _discretionary income_. The distinction between "necessities" and "luxuries" is, of course, a subjective one. Even when incomes are identical, there is variation from one household to another as to what may be considered necessities, and thus the amount of money available for "discretionary" spending also varies.

For example, two families of equal size and income live in the same apartment house, but in one family there are two children of the same sex while the other family has a boy and a girl. The first family probably would find a single bedroom sufficient for the children, while the second family might consider a bedroom for each child a necessity. The first family could economize on clothing by handing the older child's clothing down to the younger, while the second family has to buy two sets of clothing. Thus, with the same income and the same number of people to share it, the first family has more discretionary

income than the second because the first family has fewer "necessary" expenses.

In 1959, a team of researchers writing for _Fortune_ magazine concluded that any family income in excess of $4,000 could be considered discretionary income. Using this figure as a basis, they estimated that there was $135 billion of discretionary income in the United States in 1959, and that this figure would increase to approximately $255 billion in 1970.[3]

More recently, the federal government developed a different yardstick for measuring discretionary income, in the course of attempts to measure the extent of poverty in this country. According to its study, a household is considered poor, and therefore without discretionary income, if its total income is less than three times the cost of a minimum nutritionally sound food plan designed by the Department of Agriculture. On the basis of this study, 16 percent of all United States households in 1966, as compared with 22 percent in 1959, were classified as poor, that is, there was a 6-percentage-point rise in the number of households that had a measure of discretionary income.

Consumers in the United States are known to have more discretionary income each year, which means they have more money to spend on the basis of choice rather than need. Choice in spending is essential to fashion demand.

Purchasing Power of the Dollar It is no secret, however, that the purchasing power of the dollar has been declining over the years. Comparisons of past and present income in terms of dollars alone, therefore, can be misleading. Economists meet this problem by relating dollars of income in any given year to the buying power of a dollar in a selected prior base period.

Even on that basis, except for a setback during the depression years of the 1930s, there has been a steady advance in the United States in the consumer's purchasing power, which, in turn, has been conducive to an increase in fashion demand.

Population

The majority of the population of the United States has some sort of discretionary income and thus is able to influence the course of fashion.

There are two other factors relating to population, however, that have an important bearing on the extent of fashion demand.

The first important population factor is the size of the total population and the rate of its growth. The size of the population relates to the extent of fashion demand, while the rate of its growth suggests what tomorrow's market may be.

The second important factor is the age-mix of the population, and its projection into the future, which determines some of the characteristics of the fashion demand and suggests what they may be like in the future.

Size of Population In 1915, the United States had a population of about 100 million people. Fifty years later, the population had almost doubled. Estimates for the year 2015, or 100 years after the 100-million mark was reached, range from a conservative 324 million to an overwhelming 482 million. The population is growing, and growing at an increasingly faster rate. So long as the econ-omy remains stable and the trends in consumer income continue, this means an ever-increasing number of consumers with an ever-increasing amount of money to spend on fashion.

Age-Mix Not all age groups are equally enthusiastic consumers of fashion. Moreover, the rate of growth is not the same for all age groups within the population, nor is it identical for both sexes. These variations in the age-mix of both today and tomorrow are important clues to fashion demand, for each age group has its own fashion interests. (See Table 2-4.)

Especially important is the large and growing population in the 15-to-24 age group, which is the one most responsive to change and most eager for the new. It is also an age group, particularly among its younger members, with minimum restrictions imposed on its spending because of family responsibilities or on its choice of styles because of figure problems. New fashions thrive among these youthful customers, and their grow-

Table 2-4.   Estimates and Projections of the Population of the United States, 1960, 1970, 1980, 1990

Population in Thousands

	1960	1970	1980	1990
Males				
Under 14 years	28,519	30,009	29,193	34,728
15 to 24 years	12,375	18,405	21,230	18,846
25 to 44 years	23,197	23,898	31,133	39,736
45 to 64 years	17,703	20,009	20,471	21,306
65 years and older	7,537	8,335	9,507	10,903
Total	89,331	100,656	111,534	125,519
Females				
Under 14 years	27,581	28,877	27,980	33,263
15 to 24 years	12,208	17,958	20,646	18,244
25 to 44 years	23,937	24,378	31,241	39,577
45 to 64 years	18,503	21,807	22,709	23,263
65 years and older	9,121	11,249	13,557	16,102
Total	91,350	104,269	116,133	130,449

Source: U. S. Bureau of the Census.

ing number probably means increasingly accelerated fashion change.

Senior citizens, or the over-65 group, represent another growing and increasingly influential age group. Longer life expectancy and increased retirement income place the senior citizen in an increasingly important position to affect fashion. Although not as large and powerful a group as the younger customers, the senior citizens' ideas about fashion warrant careful consideration by designers and marketers alike.

Sociological Factors

To understand fashion, it is necessary to understand the sociological background against which fashion trends develop, live, and die. Fashion itself is a social phenomenon that reflects what Cecil Beaton called "the same continuum of change that rides through any given age."[4] Changes in fashion, he emphasized, "correspond with the subtle and often hidden network of forces that operate on society. . . . In this sense, fashion is a symbol."[5]

Thus changes in the social patterns of the times cause changes in the attitudes of the consumer, and these changes in attitude in turn cause changes in fashion.

Leisure Time

The average citizen in the United States today has far more leisure time than his counterpart a half-century ago. In addition to paid holidays, paid vacations, and early retirement, the length of the workweek has been steadily shrinking, and apparently will continue to do so in the foreseeable future.

At the turn of the century, workers put in from 10 to 15 hours a day, 6 days a week, and the average yearly earnings in industry were $673 for men and $361 for women. By 1969, factory workers were averaging $130 weekly for 40 hours of work 5 days a week.

Shortening the workweek has given people much more time for recreation, travel, self-improvement, or even a second job. Increased leisure has initiated many changes in values, in standards of living, and in scope of activities.

Whole new markets have opened up as a result of these changes. New and diverse activities, resulting from the availability of more leisure time, have led to a demand for larger and more varied wardrobes.

Demand for Casual Wear In fashion, the impact of greater leisure time is most clearly indicated by the growth of interest in sportswear or casual clothes. Sportswear has become an important part of that larger and more varied wardrobe.

Sports clothes were on the fashion scene even in the early 1900s, although the clothes that women wore then for tennis or golf were quite similar to ordinary streetwear later. By the 1920s many people had leisure time for active sports or to loll in the sun, and the tradition of floor-length skirts had been abandoned. Appropriate sportswear fashions flourished. Although not everyone had the leisure to play tennis or watch the matches, enough people saw photographs of Suzanne Lenglen, then an outstanding star of the courts, for her free-swinging skirts to become a popular sportswear fashion. The 1920s also gave birth to stockings in suntan shades and to apparel that left some skin exposed to tanning.

Today's casual apparel did not reach its full acceptance until the 1950s, when the great trek to the suburbs was in full swing. Casual wear bloomed in the suburbs, but rapidly spread to the cities. It became commonplace, rather than shocking, to see a woman wearing slacks on city streets.

The outlook for the future is for even more leisure. Pressure now exists for the 4-day, 32-hour workweek. The extra day of leisure, it is predicted, will create both the time to engage in additional activities and the need for goods and services appropriate to such activities. It is also anticipated that many more people will take on a second job, thereby adding to their discretionary income.

Retirement Leisure Leisure of a somewhat different type is enjoyed by a special segment of the population. This is the leisure of the retirees, whose numbers are increasing rapidly. Because of medical advances, pensions, and intelligent planning for retirement, those who have retired

Increasing participation in active sports of all kinds has caused tremendous growth in the design and production of women's sportswear.

from full-time jobs now have both the life expectancy and the means to afford a wide range of interests and activities. Instead of spending their last years quietly at home, many modern retirees are healthy enough and interested enough to take up second or even third careers, to involve themselves in charitable and civic affairs, to travel, to buy new homes, or to take up new studies.

These people introduce a new element into the impact leisure time is having on fashion demand. They want apparel that both suits their ages and figures and is appropriate for their new interests and activities.

Ethnic Groups

One of the major sociological changes in recent years is the change of status of nonwhite groups. Blacks and other non-Caucasians, including Mexican-Americans, American Indians, Orientals, and Puerto Ricans, account for approxi-

mately one-eighth of the country's population today, according to figures from the Bureau of the Census, and projections indicate that that figure will have increased to one-sixth by the year 2000.

Until the late 1950s, more than half the population of these groups had incomes below the poverty mark, a much larger percentage than that found in the white group. Their purchases were dictated by need, not choice; their interest in and influence on fashion were almost nil. They dressed as Caucasians did, and tried to achieve the look of the dominant, successful white group.

By the end of the 1960s, however, new laws and dedicated work on the part of many groups and individuals had brought more education, better jobs, and a new pride to these groups. In addition, they were beginning to have more money to spend.

Fashion reflected the change, particularly among the black group. Afro hairstyles were

widely adopted among black men and women; black self-awareness was expressed in men's clothes patterned on native African dress, and women's clothes were either made of or inspired by African fabrics. New cosmetics for blacks appeared on the market, designed to emphasize rather than camouflage the beauty of dark coloring.

Some of the fashion ideas even began to cross the color line, for a number of whites found that the traditional African styles, fabrics, and patterns had a captivating color and freshness to them—an interesting reversal of the situation that prevailed when for many years white culture alone set the fashion.

The Changing Status of Women

The status, interests, and activities of women in the United States have changed profoundly since the beginning of the twentieth century. These changes have had their effect not only on fashion but on the entire field of marketing. In some ways, it could be said that women have gained some of the goals that the minority groups are now in the process of gaining.

It is almost impossible for a modern woman, accustomed to making her own decisions, managing her own money, and deciding what fashions she is going to accept, to put herself in the place of a woman at the turn of the century. In those days, she could not vote, or serve on a jury, or earn a living in other than a very few kinds of occupations. Her husband or father controlled the purse strings, and she dressed to please him and reflect his status.

Jobs and Money Today, many more women than ever before are working in almost every kind of job imaginable. Because these women spend a large part of each day away from the home, their interest in fashion has been changed. A woman at work, particularly in a white-collar occupation, is susceptible to fashion influences. She meets people. She sees and is seen. She is able to shop, with cash or charge plate, during her lunch hour and on her way home. The incentive, the oppor-

The status of women has changed radically, and career opportunities are now almost unlimited.

tunity, and the means to respond to the appeal of fashion are all present.

In addition, women today have money of their own, earned or unearned, and the freedom to spend it. In 1965, approximately three women in every five, among those 14 years old and older, had incomes of their own. With the power to earn and to spend, it is now usually her acceptance or rejection of offered styles, not that of the male head of the house, that influences the course of feminine fashion.

Education American women today are often better educated than their mothers and grand-mothers, a factor that has definite repercussions on fashion. With an education superior to that of her elders, it is natural that a young woman should turn to her contemporaries, rather than to her mother or grandmother, for advice and approval. Thus the fashions she accepts in clothes, in homemaking, or in child rearing will be those acceptable to her own age group, even if they have little in common with those accepta-ble to the older generation.

Social Freedom Most marked, perhaps, of all the differences in the status of women since the early 1900s is the degree of social freedom enjoyed. The young woman of today feels free to apply for a job, to date without a chaperon, and to go into a restaurant, theater, or other public place un-escorted. She earns and saves money for un-chaperoned travel. If she can afford it, she main-tains an apartment of her own or shares one with other girls. Frequently she owns a car.

Short skirts, like those that prevailed in the 1920s, the early 1940s, and again in the 1960s, are commonly interpreted as a reflection of that fem-inine freedom. So, too, is the simplicity of the styles that prevailed in these periods: chemises, sacks, tents, shifts, and other variations of loose-hanging dresses.

Conjecture and proof, however, do not always go hand in hand on this point. One can theorize that stiff, unyielding corsets went out with a stiff, unyielding moral code—or that they were re-placed, with no special significance, by more flexible materials that could mold the figure without discomfort. One can theorize that the

miniskirts and pantsuits seen even in elegant restaurants during the 1960s were expressions of woman's freedom—or that these same garments became fashionable because of their suitability for hopping in and out of the indispensable auto-mobile.

On one point, however, the relationship be-tween fashion and woman's "place" seems clear and firm: With ever greater freedom of action, women eagerly accept fashions that grant them freedom of movement. Crinolines, hobble skirts, and corsets of the "iron maiden" variety are clearly not compatible with the on-the-go life of the modern woman.

Social Mobility

There are classes within almost all societies, and individuals choose either to stand out from or conform to their actual or aspired-to class. Quentin Bell sees the mainspring of fashion in the process "whereby members of one class imi-tate those of another, who, in their turn, are driven to ever new expedients of fashionable change."[6]

Bell considers the history of fashion inex-plicable without the existence of social classes. He is not alone in his thinking. Other sociologists relate fashion change to changes in social mo-bility and to the effort to associate with a higher class by imitation.

Social Fluidity in the United States The United States is sometimes considered a classless society, but this description is valid only in that there are no hereditary ranks, royalty, or untouchables. Within the same family, one member may climb, while another may slip.

There are classes in the United States, but the most obvious of them are based largely on occu-pation, income, education, or avocation. The effect of class distinction upon dress is sometimes marked and sometimes subtle. The so-called café society, for instance, is known for introducing and adopting the newest fashion styles, but these styles often are next seen, in much less expensive versions, in the fashion-conscious segments of the lower and lower-middle classes—not in the tra-ditionally more conservative middle-middle and upper-middle-class groups.

Fashion helps some people cross class lines, particularly in such pursuits as sports. Ski enthusiasts illustrate this point. There are active ski fashions and après-ski clothes within the reach of every income, and when once donned, only the choice of a ski area is likely to distinguish one class group from another. Concentration is on the sport itself and the social life surrounding it. The right clothes and a pair of skis are the only entrance card needed.

Each individual really belongs to several classes simultaneously, based on his background, his occupation, his income, his place of residence, his hobbies, and so on. Often he indicates his class membership by the fashions he adopts: the casual weekend clothes of the suburbanite, the restrained weekday style of the banking fraternity, the quick adoption of an incoming style that seems to be a mark of these connected with the garment industry and with some of the professional creative jobs.

Middle-Class Growth Most fashion authorities emphasize the causal relationship between the growth and strength of the middle class and the growth and strength of fashion demand. It is the middle class that has the highest physical, social, and financial mobility. It is the middle class that, by weight of numbers, has the majority vote in fashion. Members of the middle class tend to be followers, not leaders, of fashion, but the strength of their following pumps money into the fashion industry, and the persistence of their following often spurs the fashion leaders to seek still newer and more different fashions of their own.

The United States has such a middle class, both with fashion interest and the money to indulge it. The size of that middle class is very large, and its size, as a proportion of the total population, is growing, thanks to the determination of this country to bring all of its population up to a reasonable standard of living. That growth means a widespread increase in consumer buying power, which in turn generates increased fashion demand.

Physical Mobility

Physical mobility, like social mobility, encourages the demand for and response to fashion. One effect of travel is what may be termed cross-pollenization of cultures. After seeing how other people live, the traveler brings home a desire to adopt or adapt some of what he has observed and make it a part of his home environment.

Thus Marco Polo brought gunpowder, silks, and spices from the Orient, introducing new products to medieval Europe. Much later, travelers brought touches of Asian and African fashions to Western dress and home furnishings and later still Latin American and pre-Columbian influences were introduced into North America, thereby dramatically changing fashion's direction and emphasis in this country.

In the United States, people enjoy physical mobility of several kinds. There is life on wheels, for example, which is so much a part of the daily routine for so many people. Both the breadwinner going to work, often in a different city, and the housewife driving to a shopping center are exposed to a broad range of influences during their daily trips. Among these influences is the opportunity to observe the fashions of others and the fashion offerings of retail distributors.

A second form of physical mobility popular among Americans is vacation travel, which takes people on anything from a trip to a nearby lake to a trip around the world. Each trip not only exposes the travelers to many different kinds of fashion influences, but the trip itself demands special kinds of fashions. Those who live out of suitcases for a while, whether for a few days or a few months, want clothes that are easy to pack, wrinkle-resistant, suitable for a variety of occasions, and easy to keep in order.

A third form of physical mobility is the change of residence, which, like travel, exposes the individual to new contacts, new environments, and new fashion influences. According to annual statistics of the Bureau of the Census, one family in five moves in the course of any given year. This has been the statistical pattern since 1948, when the first such study was made. Among those who move, one in every three goes to a different county within the same state and one in every six or seven to a different state. These people bring some of their old fashion ideas to their new residences, and adopt or reject some of the new fashions they find in the new localities.

Communications

In these days of almost instant communication, it is hard to believe that less than two centuries ago, news traveled so slowly that a major battle was fought in a war that had already ended. That was the War of 1812, ended by a peace treaty which had been signed many weeks before the Battle of New Orleans. Nowadays when news breaks, radio and television networks measure in seconds, not months, the time it takes to get that news on the air, and thus to a vast section of the population.

When communication was slower, fashion change was necessarily slower. Word of "what they were wearing" took a long time traveling from one part of the country to another, and fashion trends moved at as leisurely a pace as the news. Today there is not only infinitely faster communication, but there are immense quantities and many varieties of it.

The Print Media Advertisements have taken over by far the largest part of general newspapers and magazines, and many of those advertisements are fashion influences. The Sunday papers are almost too heavy to get across the threshold, not because of the news they carry but because of the amount of advertising they contain. Fashion also has its place in the news columns of those papers and magazines, in the form of a column or section that concentrates on descriptions of new styles and notes about who has been seen wearing what. Even the general news often has some fashion impact when that news is illustrated by photographs and those photographs often show what well-known people are wearing.

There are specialized publications, too, that give even more space to coverage of fashion news. Women's magazines, men's magazines, and magazines for teens of both sexes all put a strong emphasis on fashion coverage. Then, too, there are magazines that contain nothing but fashion information.

Even more specialized are the publications within the trade itself. *Women's Wear Daily* is a newspaper that not only blueprints fashion trends for designers and retailers months before the normal selling season of the merchandise but also reports on what consumers are currently buying and wearing. *Men's Wear* is another trade newspaper, and many of the other individual segments of the garment industry are served by their own regular publications.

The Broadcast Media Television has become an important medium for transmitting fashion information, for the dress of personalities on network shows has a demonstrated fashion impact. A notable example is Johnny Carson, who was credited by the menswear industry with almost single-handedly launching the Nehru look as a late 1960s fashion for men. The clothes of actors and actresses, of notables and other people seen in commercials and on news programs, also have impact. Fashion information is also transmitted through fashion shows and the ads of producers and retailers.

Radio still does its share, too, because it is an excellent medium for a local merchant to tell a local audience about a special sale.

Store Display Even retailing itself is communicating fashion information to the customer more quickly and more vividly than ever before. Two major developments are responsible for this: the proliferation of branches among department and specialty stores, and the trend toward open selling and open storefronts.

The first of these developments has brought the store, and therefore the immediate source of fashion merchandise, physically closer to the customer. If a woman lives in a suburb, she does not have to take a day from her busy schedule for a trip into the city to examine the new fashions available for herself, her family, and her home. Those fashions are on display and on sale in branches almost at her doorstep.

The second development brings the merchandise physically closer to the customer, both inside and outside the store. Before World War II, much of the merchandise a store carried was hidden in cabinets or stockrooms out of sight of the selling area, and customers saw only what was featured in displays. Today open racks and self-selection fixtures put the merchandise right in front of the customer, even if she is merely passing through a department on her way elsewhere. Some of the modern storefronts do the same thing, with windows that go from wall to wall and from floor to ceiling with no backdrop. Just walking past such a store is almost like being right inside.

Psychological Factors

In selecting fashion goods, buying decisions are often influenced by psychological factors. The customer's decision may be indirectly concerned with the product's performance but directly concerned with the psychological satisfaction related to its ownership and use, as well as the social prestige attached to owning the product. For example, the fragrance of an inexpensive perfume may be pleasant, but the scent of the more expensive one gives the purchaser the feeling of luxury, just as the white rug on a woman's living room floor proclaims her freedom from the labor of keeping it clean.

Perhaps the most basic psychological factors involved in fashion demand, however, are those that are primary characteristics of human behavior: boredom, curiosity, rebellion against convention, a need for self-assertion, and a drive for companionship.[7]

Boredom

It is a human tendency to become bored with fashions too long in use, and boredom leads to restlessness. Garments that have been worn throughout a season have tired both the eye and the sense of touch of the wearer. The comments of any woman toward the end of a season illustrate that: "I can't wait to get out of these wools." "I'm tired of that heavy coat." "My clothes simply seem stale."

Such boredom and its resulting restlessness are particularly noticeable in the case of strong colors, dramatic accessories, and outstanding designs. The color, the style, the design begin to grate on both the eyes and the nerves of the wearer. That is why classics, the styles that last and last in popularity, are seldom extreme; their appeal is pleasant and satisfying but muted and undemanding.

Boredom sets in particularly quickly among people who have a concentrated interest in fashion and fashion-dominated products, whether these are clothes, home furnishings, or other articles. As soon as a product loses the first luster and excitement of newness, as soon as something newer appears on the market, these people become bored with what they have and restless to have something new and different.

When boredom and restlessness are felt, people seek change. In fashion, the desire for change expresses itself in a demand for something new and satisfyingly different from what one already has. Boredom and restlessness, therefore, feed fashion demand.

Curiosity

Curiosity is akin to boredom in that it creates restlessness and encourages changes merely for the sake of change. Many people like to experiment. They want to know what is around the next corner, what oil and water really will do when poured together, and what a dress would look like if the line were changed this way, if stitching were added there, and if the hem were shortened or lengthened a bit. Curiosity and the need to experiment permeate fashion.

Hector Escobosa, former head of the fashionable specialty store I. Magnin's, once described fashion as a "constantly evolving tide, seldom capricious, and generally orderly in its constant evolution." He said that fashion "feeds on new designs, and new designs are created by a dynamic compulsion that keeps creators constantly experimenting, striving for something newer, more exciting, more beautiful."[8]

Curiosity, the desire for new sensations and that spirit of adventure that leads to experimenting, is a psychological motive that sometimes comes into conflict with generally accepted ideas of what is beautiful and harmonious. Thus the desire to break away from what has been customary and to try something new in order to appease one's curiosity sometimes encourage acceptance of fashion styles that are not in accordance with currently acknowledged principles of art. If the new becomes accepted, then it becomes true fashion. If it flames and then dies away, its only fashion significance is as a fad.

Individuals with highly developed senses of curiosity often find more satisfaction than most other people in launching new fashions. These are the women who are quick to experiment with new lipstick and nail polish colors, with new cosmetics techniques, with new fragrances, as well as with new styles and new color combinations in apparel.

There is some streak of curiosity in everyone. Some may respond less dramatically than others to the proddings of curiosity, but the factor is there, and it keeps fashion demand alive.

Rebellion Against Convention

One of the most important forces contributing to fashion change and thus influencing fashion demand is a characteristic common among young people—a rebellion against convention. This is more than boredom or curiosity; this is a positive rejection of what exists and a seeking for something new.

Generally, young people from 15 to 25 are the most rebellious, the group that finds adjustment to custom most difficult. One manifestation of the rebellion of youth is the rejection of the fashions of one's parents, and the clothing styles popular among the 15- to 25-year-olds are often radically different from those worn by older groups.

After the age of 25, people tend to settle down, to accept the normal responsibilities of family and career, and to make whatever compromises with custom may be necessary. And as the years go on, the generation that once rebelled finds itself supporting convention against the rebellion of a new, upcoming generation.

When this rebellion is particularly strong, as it was in the 1920s and again in the 1960s, it can strongly affect fashion. In such times, youth sets the fashion, and those fashions are often adopted by consumers of all ages.

Usually the youth-determined fashions are freer, less restricting, more casual, often more daring than those they supplant. Examples are the short skirts of the 1920s and the pantsuits of the 1960s, both fashions initiated by the young. Occasionally, however, youth rebels by bringing more formal styles into popularity for a short time. The elegant Edwardian look sported by some young men during the 1960s is an example.

A possible factor in the timing of important youth movements may be the age-mix proportion of the population and its purchasing power. In the 1960s, for example, when fashion emphasized young ideas and the youthful look, a large percentage of the population and purchasing power in the United States was concentrated among adults under 25. During the depression years of the 1930s, on the other hand, when fashions reflected a more mature outlook, people under 25 constituted a smaller proportion of the population or the buying power.

Acceptance by the majority, remember, is an important part of the definition of fashion. Strength of numbers increases the impact of a youth fashion. The money to express such a fashion provides the means to give it even greater impact.

Self-Assertion

The need to be different is the human desire that gives fashion demand one of its strongest thrusts. It is the need for self-assertion, for recognition. Often it is the need to overcome feelings of inferiority or of disappointment. And often these needs can be satisfied through clothes. The woman who considers herself to be well and fashionably dressed has a kind of armor that gives her protection and self-assurance. The woman aware that her dress is dated is at a psychological disadvantage.

Change in dress often helps to create an illusion of change in personality, a way to overcome feelings of inferiority or of disappointment. The homemaker or office worker who changes into an after-five dress lays aside her everyday personality and, Cinderella-like, is transformed in her own eyes into a more glamorous individual. Similarly, the factory worker who doffs his overalls and dons a white collar or a smart sport shirt on the weekend then considers himself on a par with the executives who set his weekday tasks for him.

Women are believed to have more need for self-assertion, this individuality that fashion provides, than men are. A highly successful marketer of cosmetics credited his spectacular rise to his recognition of this element in the feminine character. "We don't sell cosmetics," he said, "we sell hope." And the need for hope, he explained, grows out of woman's perennial need for assurance, for recognition. Cosmetics, as this producer advertises them, provide that assurance.

Companionship

The desire for companionship is fundamental in man. The instinct for survival of the species drives him to seek a mate, who is one kind of companion, and his gregarious nature encourages him also to seek other companions. Fashion plays its part in all of his seekings for companionship.

Fashion certainly plays a part when man wants to attract woman or woman wants to attract man. Women then dress to please and interest a man, and men dress to impress and interest a woman. Both carefully choose fashions that emphasize what they consider their best points and play down what they consider their faults. The care and concentration with which a woman dresses to go to meet the man of her choice, or a man dresses to go to meet the woman of his choice, are proof of this.

Companionship, however, has broader meanings. In its broader sense, it implies the formation of groups, each of which requires conformity of its members in dress as in other respects. College campuses are a good example, for each campus has its own approved mode of dress for students, determined by the undergraduate idols. Within the framework of college dress, which is generally quite informal, one campus may favor slacks, another shorts, and a third sweaters and skirts.

In the business world, companionship often expresses itself by the acceptance within a particular field of work of a particular style of dress. In the late 1950s and the very early 1960s, the gray flannel suit was so much the accepted style for young executives in advertising and related fields that the phrase "gray flannel suit" identified the young man on his way up in one of these fields.

In the mid-1960s, however, nonconformity became an important distinguishing mark for creative people, both in advertising and in other fields, and the art directors and copy chiefs of advertising agencies seemed to vie with each other in wearing unusual and colorful working costumes.

Flamboyant or subdued, the mode of dress can be a bid for companionship, and can also be the symbol of acceptance within a particular group of companions.

The Individual

The economic, sociological, and psychological factors that influence fashion demand are many. "Fashion promises many things to many people," says economist Dr. Rachel Dardis. "It can be and is used to attract others, to indicate success, both social and economic, to indicate leadership, and to identify with a particular social group. . . ."[9]

Even though the overall factors influencing fashion demand can be identified, and the trend of their probable influence predicted quite accurately, exactly what is behind a single individual purchase of a fashion product can still be perplexing, sometimes even to the customer herself. As market researcher Louis Cheskin says,

> When a woman buys a dress because it is in the latest fashion, she is expressing a wish to belong to "the group." . . . If she chooses a color that she loves, but does not know why, she is acting as an individual, as a unique and distinctive character, independent of group identification. . . .[10]

That customers individually retain unique and distinctive characters, and they do, is one of the reasons why fashion merchandising is so alive, so fascinating.

References

[1]Bell, *On Human Finery*, p. 72.
[2]Hobbs, *I Saw Red China*, p. 66.
[3]Parker and Mayer, "The Decade of the Discretionary Dollar," *Fortune*, June, 1959, pp. 136–138.
[4]Beaton, *The Glass of Fashion*, p. 335.
[5]*Ibid.*, pp. 379–381.
[6]Bell, op. cit., p. 72.
[7]Nystrom, *Economics of Fashion*, pp. 66–81.
[8]Escobosa, "Heartbeat of Retailing," *Readings in Modern Retailing*, p. 390.
[9]Dardis, "The Power of Fashion," pp. 16–17.
[10]Cheskin, *Why People Buy*, p. 158.

Merchandising Vocabulary

Define or briefly explain the following terms:

Environment
Gross national product
Personal income
Disposable income
Discretionary income

Merchandising Review

1. What three environmental factors primarily affect the rate of fashion demand and growth in any society?
2. How does a higher level of education affect fashion interest and demand?
3. What is social mobility? How does the degree of social mobility in any culture affect fashion demand? Illustrate your answer with examples.
4. Why is it difficult to classify modern American society? Upon what factors are social classes in the United States based?
5. What effect does the increased physical mobility of a population have upon its demand for and response to fashion? Illustrate your answer with examples.
6. How have improved means and methods of communication affected fashion interest and the rate of fashion change?
7. Name and briefly discuss the five psychological motives that influence fashion interest and change.

Merchandising Digest

1. Discuss and give examples of how such population factors as size and age composition affect fashion interest and demand.
2. Changes in the social pattern of the times cause changes in the attitudes of the consumer, and these in turn cause changes in fashion. Discuss how (a) increased leisure time, (b) the movement to suburbia, and (c) increased employment of women outside the home have brought about changes in fashion demand.
3. "Each individual belongs to several classes simultaneously." Discuss how a college student belongs to several classes by virtue of his activities, and how he indicates his class membership by the fashions he adopts.

3

Historical Development of Fashions

When a woman touches up her lipstick, puts on her coat, and picks up her gloves, she is paying tribute to fashion trends that reach far back into the history of man. Her lipstick has its origin in the skin decorations used by the earliest caveman whose artifacts have so far been found. That primitive man left drawings on the rock walls of his cave showing that he was fond of painting decorations on both his face and body. The woman's coat is the latest version of the original mantle or cape developed during the Upper Paleolithic period, when the last Ice Age was beginning to thaw and when the animal skins worn by men began to be fashioned into different types of garments. The woman's gloves are not so different from a handsome pair of linen gloves found in the tomb of the Egyptian king Tutankhamen, buried more than 3,000 years ago.

Both fashion and the consumer's reaction to it have their roots far back in the childhood of mankind. To know fashion, it is important to examine those roots and explore why people put on clothes in the first place, and to look at what clothes they have worn, and why, throughout fashion's long history.

Why People Wear Clothes

The reasons why people may have first put on clothes and why they continue to wear them often seem contradictory, capricious, and confusing. In the cold northern regions of the world, men put on the warm skins of animals, but tribes living along the hot, humid line of the equator put on

very similar skins. Pants for men and skirts for women became the customary dress for the Western world well over a thousand years ago, but in the Orient, except in those areas where Western fashion has made a recent impact, men are apt to wear the skirts and women often wear the pants. In Europe and the Americas, women's clothes have for centuries covered most of the body but left the face bare—but in India, until recently, it was much more important for a woman to keep her face covered, and if caught without a veil, a woman would flip her dress up to cover her face.

Psychologists, sociologists, anthropologists, and historians all have given study and thought to dress. In general, they offer three basic reasons why people wear clothes. These reasons, in order of the probable strength of their influence, are decoration, protection, and modesty.

Each reason has exerted its influence in the past and continues to do so in the present. Each reason is as applicable in the most primitive areas of the world as it is in the most civilized ones. Each is logical within the form of just about every variety of culture, regardless of the differences of those cultures. Each plays some important part in what anyone and everyone is wearing, right now, today, in any part of the world.

Decoration

Decoration appears to have preceded dress. Before he wore clothing, early man decorated himself by painting, tattooing, haircutting, scarification, mutilation, deformation, and the addition of external objects to his face and body. The caveman's painting of his face and body was an example of early decoration, and in his cave were found bone necklaces, bracelets, and leg ornaments, and even a primitive version of what must have been a hairpin.

Thomas Carlyle, the British philosopher-historian, saw a spiritual need in primitive man's urge to decorate himself.[1] From the viewpoint of anthropologists and psychologists, however, self-decoration has little to do with spiritual satisfaction. Social scientists consider it instead a form of self-advertisement. Early man advertised his hunting prowess, for instance, by displaying the horns, teeth, skins, or scalps of his kill, animal or human. Removing them from a fallen foe's body and adding them to his own body was a simple way of announcing the conquest. The trophies became a symbol of the hunter's rank, his prestige.

Decoration also served other purposes in the primitive world: to attract the opposite sex, to inspire terror in an enemy, to indicate occupation or locality of dwelling place, to display wealth, or to boast of physical prowess or skill—all forms of advertising one fact or another about one's self.

Modern Decoration Modern forms of decoration can be directly or indirectly traced to primitive decorative forms. Makeup, hair dye, and jewelry of various types come most readily to mind.

Modern woman might be startled to realize that her diamond ring is a modern version of the gold arm ring worn by ancient English rulers or of the wampum belt worn by American Indians. The handbag she carries is similar to the arrow quiver of the medieval archer, and earlier still, can be traced back to the pouch worn by primitive man to carry weapons, game, and various personal possessions. Exaggerated hairstyles and ornate head coverings are modern versions of the tribal or clan chief's mark of authority, his headdress. The decorative brooch is the direct descendant of the pins used by the Greek women to hold together their unsewn garments.

Modern forms of decoration, however, do not distort the body in the direct, bone-through-nose tradition of the primitives. Some scientists believe this is because civilized man has learned to accept his body as it is and has no need to distort it—but

perhaps it may be that contemporary man is merely more clever at deceiving the eye of the beholder without permanently changing the body. Instead of surgically lengthening the eyes, as the ancient Egyptians did, modern woman achieves the same effect with eye makeup. Instead of permanently elongating her neck by

Even the most modern forms of jewelry and makeup can be traced back to antiquity.

31

wearing heavy rings around it, or narrowing her waist by cinching it with tight stays, modern woman chooses her outerwear, jewelry, makeup, and hairstyle to create the illusion of having those features that fashion may require at the moment.

In addition, fashion changes more rapidly today, and accessories can be changed far more easily than can deliberately created physical distortions. Women who have pierced their ears have found this to be so, for many feel they must wear some sort of earrings at all times to avoid a "punctured look," even when most casually dressed or even when long hairstyles cover the ears. And in the Orient, there are still a few elderly women left who had their feet bound as children, when tiny feet were fashionable for the better classes of women, and who have had to totter through life on those distorted feet.

Shape and Line Effects Specific forms of decoration create specific impressions, whether the decoration is makeup, jewelry, or details and trimming on apparel. There are six major forms of decoration used to create a specific effect: vertical, dimensional, directional, circular, local, and sartorial.

Vertical line is used to accentuate upright posture and apparent height. Marie Antoinette's towering headdress or a modern woman's high heels are obvious examples. The decorative details of men's Ivy League clothes gave their wearers the appearance of height and adolescent slenderness by using vertical stripes, narrow ties, narrow coat lapels, and tapered trouser legs. A man of average build not only looked slim in these clothes, but most men looked younger than they were, an important point during the popularity of the look in the early 1950s, when many young men were aware that military service during World War II and the Korean conflict had delayed the start of their careers. The fashion also had a firm grip on the advertising profession, where there was strong emphasis on hiring, training, and promoting youth.

Dimensional shape helps to increase apparent size. For generations men have used shoulder padding and wide lapels to give themselves a muscular look. Women have used crinolines, trains, and padding in various ways and at various times in history to achieve more imposing figures.

Women's fondness for billowing skirts, extended shoulders, and other figure enlargers has been variously interpreted. Some psychologists consider it an expression of the will to dominate; others view it as a declaration that the wearers are exempt from toil, thus a sign of a man's ability to maintain his womenfolk in conspicuous leisure. James Laver regards the crinoline as typical of the marked difference between feminine and masculine dress in eras when the male is in the ascendancy.[2] Conversely, the era of equal rights for the sexes encouraged similarity of dress, to the point that by the late 1960s stores in large cities were specializing in identical garments and accessories for men and women: slacks, jackets, and pullovers for both, headbands and necklaces for both, shoulder bags for both.

Directional form emphasizes movements of the body. Forms classified as vertical may become directional when the body is in motion. Flowing skirts, plumes, scarves, sashes, ribbons, and long loose hair are examples of the directional form, for they slip into movement as soon as the wearer does.

Circular shape draws attention to the round contours of the body, especially the limbs. Belts and bracelets, Elizabethan neck ruffs, and hoops are examples. A modern woman's wristwatch, small and mounted on a bracelet, becomes a circular ornament that makes her arm look round and smooth. A man's wristwatch, large, angular, and mounted on a strap, has a quite different effect.

Local form draws attention to a particular part of the body, rather than to the body as a whole. Rings, combs, pins, and clasps all direct attention to one particular part of the body or away from others. The senorita who tucks a jeweled comb in her hair to call attention to its rich luster, and the bulky woman who wears a decorative pin near her shoulder to direct attention away from her waistline, are both using similar tactics.

Sartorial form embellishes existing garments. Embroidery on blouses, sequins on an evening gown, and jeweled links in a man's shirt cuffs are used for the same end: to add an extra touch of splendor to the garment.

Protection

Among the animals, only man has no natural bodily protection against the elements, no fur, feathers or scales, no thick hide. Yet man has lived, since his most primitive times, in some of the harshest climates of the earth. One of the ways man has protected himself in those climates has been with clothing.

Clothing is believed to have originated as man moved away from the equator and needed protection from the colder climates. It is easy to see the protective value of the layers of animal skins that man added as the temperature dropped. Yet those groups who remained in the tropics also wore clothing, perhaps as a protection from insect bites and thorns.

In time, however, clothing began to have more protective value than merely insulating the body against natural discomforts. It also began to provide protection against danger from enemies and from hazards that man's environment created. It even played an important part, and still does, as protection against imaginary dangers.

Defense Against Real Enemies Armor was first designed to protect man from the claws and teeth of the animals he hunted, and then it was refined to protect him from the arrows and spears of his fellowmen. Today's soldiers no longer wear the cumbersome armor of the medieval age, but helmets to protect the head and camouflaged uniforms are still issued to the military.

Armor has its civilian counterparts in today's football uniform, the riveter's goggles, and the motorcyclist's crash helmet, each an item of clothing intended to protect a man involved in a dangerous occupation or avocation. And when a hazardous activity like sports-car racing or space-walking is in the news, apparel fashions are likely to reflect that fact in some way. Sports-car racing became popular in the 1950s and 1960s, and racing gloves used by participants in that sport became the design inspiration for women's gloves. Space travel hit the headlines, and jumpsuits resembling the astronauts' spacesuits became popular.

Defense Against Imaginary Dangers Primitive man had many weapons for combating imaginary dangers, and clothing and its decoration were among them. The medals, crosses, stars, lucky pieces, charm bracelets, and similar decorative articles that modern men and women wear as ornaments are directly related to the amulets that were used by frightened jungle dwellers to ward off evil spirits.

That clothes in the past have meant more than mere body protection is evidenced by such examples as that of a primitive tribe's chief putting on all his clothes to perform tribal ceremonies but removing them, to keep them safe, if he had to walk in the rain. Such sacramental use of clothing was often intended to draw the holy spirits to a person and yet protect that person from their potent power. The robes worn today by many of the clergy when performing religious ceremonies can be traced to that ancient fashion.

Man often depends upon clothing for protection against an unfriendly world. The recluse may seek refuge from what he considers a hostile world by donning layer upon layer of clothing. A woman may cope with an unfamiliar social event by boosting her confidence with a new dress or hat. Each, in his own way, is protecting himself with clothing against a possible loss of self-assurance, against possible outside strange or unfriendly feelings.

People draw their clothes about themselves in an unfriendly or strange atmosphere and loosen or remove some of them in the secure surroundings of the home. The Mohammedan woman who veils herself from all men but her husband is dramatizing, to an extreme, the tendency all humans have to dress more carefully and formally for the street than for relaxing at home with family and friends.

Shield From Temptation Man sometimes has used clothing as protection against moral temptations and dangers. The veil of the Mohammedan woman is one example. Another is religious dress, which has tended to be severe, enveloping and hiding any suggestion of the figure beneath the costume. Even among the laity, dress has been used for moral protection. Whether the long skirts and the high collars prescribed for Puritan and Quaker women were intended to encourage demureness or ward off the eyes of men is not

known, but the one conclusion that seems plain is that the promulgators of such dress regulations expected clothing to be a shield and a barrier against moral temptation.

Modesty

In some cultures, nakedness is natural and accepted. In others, it is so much the reverse that nudists and sunbathers are obliged to fence themselves in, away from public gaze. In eras like the nineteenth century, when prudishness and social snobbery prevailed, clothes covered the entire body, and the slightest exposure was permissible only among friends and equals. In the freer air of the twentieth century, however, women expose large portions of their bodies with no fear of social punishment.

What is considered modest at one time and in one society is not necessarily so in another. It is the current concept of modesty at any particular time that is important in fashion styling.

Modesty has been described by Flügel as a negative impulse, one directed against the primitive tendency to display either the body itself or the clothing worn on it.[3] Some psychologists say that people basically do not wish to be modest but compromise by being only as expressive as fear of censure allows them to be. Fashion solves the paradox for them by sanctioning the exposure of various areas of the body at different times.

The extent to which modesty inhibits tendencies toward display, either of the body or of worldly goods, is determined not only by one's upbringing and surroundings but also by the conscious or unconscious desire to exhibit physical assets and to conceal liabilities.

Very short skirts, for example, are welcomed by women with pretty legs, but not by others. One psychologist, Knight Dunlap, suggests that it is "no mere chance that increased exposure of the leg has been accompanied by increased use of cosmetics on the face."[4] In this way, women with what they consider unattractive legs can draw attention away from them and to the areas in which they feel they are better equipped to

*Protection is a basic function of clothes—
but protective features can become fashions.*

compete. Dunlap, by the way, made his observation in 1928, when skirts were knee-high and both hair and eye cosmetics were lavishly used. Forty years later, skirts were again high, and hair and eye cosmetics were again heavily used.

Both the amount and the specific areas of the body that modesty allows to be exposed change with fashion. When one area is bared, another is covered. Long skirts were teamed with exposed cleavage in the courts of Louis XV of France and Elizabeth of England. In more recent times, short skirts have been juxtaposed with high necklines and sleeves; strapless or one-shoulder gowns have usually been floor length. When the mini and microminiskirts were most fashionable, in the late 1960s, they were often topped with turtlenecks.

The shift of emphasis to different parts of the body and the constant change in the idea of what constitutes modesty are all part of the movement of fashion, suggesting what styles will be most acceptable to both today's and tomorrow's consumers.

Stability Versus Change

Some fashions have resisted change, remaining immovable long past what might be considered a normal life span, while others have circled the globe with lightning speed. Men's jackets have had the fashion of buttoning on the right for centuries, while what is considered the fashionable color for women's dresses barely endures for a season. The robes worn at a college graduation have remained unchanged for many generations, while the kinds of trousers and dresses worn under those robes change every few years.

Certain economic and sociological factors operating within a culture encourage stability in apparel and discourage change. Laver noted this once when he wrote that there is nothing that can make a style permanent, other than poverty. Other economic and sociological factors tend to discourage stability in apparel and encourage change. Psychological factors exert little influence

What to expose and what to cover up depends upon the current concept of modesty.

on the apparel styling identified with any given culture or period, since such factors mainly affect the individual himself, rather than the population as a whole. Every apparel style, either historic or contemporary, reflects to some degree the interplay of these factors. Many contemporary styles, however, still retain one or more details of design that have remained impervious to fashion change. A man's jacket is an example of mixed influences: stability and change. It may have been buttoned on the right for centuries, but its exact age can be dated almost to the year by the width of the lapels.

Cultural Conditions Favoring Stability

Many forms of dress are fixed by *custom,* or the established manners, usages, and practices of a group of people or an entire society. Customs have their origins in the past and are transmitted from one generation to the next by precept and example. Retention of customs leads to stability in dress.

The very word "fashion" implies the opposite of custom. Fashion signifies change and the discarding of once-accepted styles, either to express individuality or to conform to the new standards and practices of one's contemporaries. Customs differ from fashions, therefore, in that the former are relatively permanent types of social behavior.

Stability of Tradition In custom-bound cultures, such as feudal societies, changes in styles are slow, since the sanctity of tradition or the weight of law outweighs the importance of individual expression. Feudal Japan affords an extreme example: The clothes for every class were regulated. A farmer with property of less than a specified value was forbidden stockings, and the women of his family were forbidden leather sandals. He was required to wear sandals of bamboo, and the women of his household were required to wear either straw sandals or wooden clogs with cotton thongs.[5]

Feudal Europe was almost as meticulous as feudal Japan in prescribing dress regulations. Women of the Middle Ages wore veils and trains of lengths specified according to their ranks. A queen wore a 17-yard train; a king's daughter, 10

yards; other princesses, 7 yards; mere duchesses, 4 yards.[6] The New World at times was also as explicit in its restrictions. According to a 1634 edict, any woman of the Massachusetts colony who wore sleeves with more than one slash was liable to be fined unless her family's estate was large enough to exempt it from the restrictions.[7]

Fixed dress, however, had its advantages. The competitive element and the expense of rapid change were eliminated; the choice of costume was easier; any lack of taste was concealed; the clothing trade was stabilized. In addition, the upper social classes, which were the ones favored by custom, had reason to cling to the habits of the past, since those habits protected their status.

Along with these advantages, however, the regulated groups had to accept limited self-expression and difficulty in adapting to changing needs. The nobility of earlier days appreciated the protection custom gave them, but not the way it limited them—and the women were often the ones who circumvented custom if it happened to interfere with what they wanted to wear.

Stability of Physical Isolation Physical isolation also favors stability of dress style. It shuts the individual off from contact with new ideas. Eskimos living north of the Arctic Circle and Indian tribesmen deep in the Amazon jungles are not among the best customers of metropolitan fashion merchandise, nor are they likely to be deeply influenced by what the young crowd wears in London or Paris.

In the early days of mail-order business, the farmer was so remote from the rest of the world that the merchandise offered to him was utilitarian rather than fashionable. He not only was isolated by the distance between him and the nearest fashion center but also by the absence of the speedy transportation and communication that make such distances unimportant today. By the time his family had received the catalog, pored over it, made their selections, sent in the order, and received the goods, probably months had passed. Today, the very same mail-order companies offer both rural and urban America styles designed by leading couturiers, illustrated in seasonal rather than yearly catalogs, and available for delivery within days.

Custom in Modern Dress Much of today's apparel, however ephemeral its fashion, retains some of the influence of custom. A classic example is the placement of buttons on the right for men, so that the weapon arm remained available while dressing and undressing, and on the left for women, who naturally tend to hold babies on that side and more conveniently use the right hand for buttons. The stitching on the backs of gloves, another example, dates back to the time when sizes were adjusted by lacing at these points.

Some whole dress styles remain essentially the same because of custom. Clerical and academic robes are centuries old, and the habits of women in religious orders were unchanged for an equally long period of time until a radical fashion revolution modernized many of them in the 1960s.

The problem is that change, while often enticing, is also often disturbing or exhausting. Change requires readjustments, and most people dread it as much as they want it. Without an important reason, or without some outside force to provide the impulse, many people will let well enough alone. After all, it really makes no difference on which side a man buttons his coat—or will some fashion designer think differently tomorrow?

Conditions Encouraging Fashion Change

"Fashion is custom in the guise of departure from custom," says Sapir.[8] He considers fashion a solution of the conflict between man's revolt against adherence to custom and his reluctance to appear lacking in good taste.

Cultural factors, or the conditions of society favoring fashion change and the willingness to oppose the power of custom, include:

▫ Education, which leads to questioning the established order

▫ Wars and disasters, which demand change as the price of survival

▫ Technological progress, which introduces new methods, new materials, and new standards of living into a society

Education Learning, which encourages freedom of expression and opens new vistas for the mind,

contributes to the acceptance of new fashions. Freedom of expression may manifest itself in fashion by a readiness to adopt new styles and a rejection of those associated with the former generation. Thus the campus look is usually quite different from the look that prevails among adults in their forties and fifties. In the early 1960s, college girls wore straight, free-swinging hair, while their mothers clung to carefully coifed styles, with each tendril lacquered firmly in place. College men wore full hairstyles, beards, and long sideburns, while their fathers were still adhering to crew cuts or closely brushed styles. A generation earlier, when those same parents were in college, the girls wore sweaters, skirts, and saddle oxfords, while their mothers appeared in public only in dresses and high-heeled shoes. Similarly, college men of that era wore mix-match sports jackets and slacks, narrow lapels, and tapered trousers, while their fathers, seldom seen in sports clothes except on the golf course, wore suit jackets with wide lapels and trousers fairly full at the bottom.

Exposure to art, literature, philosophy, and other studies has a lifelong effect upon an individual's response to fashion. Higher levels of taste, varied interests, more self-confidence, and a greater earning power are usually associated with better education. All enhance the ability to accept and enjoy new styles.

Wars and Disasters Wars and widespread disasters shake people's lives and focus their attention on ideas, events, and places that may be utterly new to them. Because of the changes in their lives, people develop a need for fashions that are compatible with their altered attitudes and environments.

This process is most obvious in changes that took place in this century on the United States social scene, and thus in women's activities and fashions, as a result of each of the two world wars. World War I brought women into the business world in significant numbers, whetted their appetites for independence and suffrage, and gave them reason to welcome styles that were less restrictive of physical movement. World War II drew women into such traditionally masculine jobs as riveting, for which they had previously not been considered strong enough; it put them into war plants on night shifts; it even brought women other than nurses into the military services for the first time in the country's history. All these changes encouraged and gave rise to greater freedom in dress.

The depression of the 1930s, however, was a different kind of disaster with a different effect on fashions. Because jobs were scarce, considerably fewer were available for women. Women went back into the home, and adopted more feminine clothes. And because money was also scarce during the depression, wardrobes became skimpier, and often a single style was made to serve a large number of social occasions.

Technological Progress New materials, new methods of production, and new modes of transportation are among the fruits of technological progress that create a need for and the increased availability of new fashions.

Both the new synthetic materials and the new ways of treating traditional fabrics which have resulted from technological progress have made possible many fashions that could not have been introduced in the past. Bright colors were more readily accepted when they became resistant to fading from sun, rain, or laundry soaps. Pleats were more popular when they were treated so that they retained their crease through many washings. Bulky fashions met lessened resistance when the bulk was achieved without weight. High boots became possible for indoor wear when there was supple, easily cleaned vinyl from which to manufacture them.

Technological progress also has given impetus to fashion by developing new methods of production that have resulted in shorter hours of labor and increased buying power for many people. Thus they have the time to enjoy a wider range of recreational, cultural, and entertainment activities, and the means to purchase appropriate fashions for each.

The influence of developments in transportation on apparel fashions demonstrated itself when the earliest automobiles created a need for dusters, veils, and gauntlets. This influence is still apparent today when modern sports cars and motorcycles encourage the wearing of slacks and short or divided skirts. Air travel, which makes any part of the world and any climate accessible in only a matter of hours, sets up a demand for travel and vacation clothes far more varied and versatile than those needed when a vacation meant a trip to a nearby beach or lake.

Fashion History in the Western World

Even in a field so much concerned as fashion is with what is current, a backward look is essential in evaluating present trends and anticipating those of the future. Fashion merchandisers study the past, not because they expect history literally to repeat itself, but because only in this way can they gain needed insight into the movement of fashion.

No fashion can be divorced from the environment in which it flourished. Fashion and the extent of fashion change reflect the culture in which they exist. From the perspective of the present, it is relatively easy to look back and make a good guess about the social, economic, and psychological influences that have shaped fashions in the past. Having done that, designers, manufacturers, and retailers of apparel can recognize the counterparts of some of these influences on the present scene, assess their probable impact, and prepare for whatever changes would appear to be in prospect for the future.

Prehistoric Through Roman Times: 8000 B.C.–A.D. 500

Man probably put on decorative paint and jewelry first, but clothes no doubt came very shortly thereafter. The first clothes known were animal skins, left over after the all-important meat had been torn from them. At first, these skins were simply slung over the body, but fairly soon they began to be worked into simple garments. Bone needles, as well as buttonlike toggles, have been found among the remains of men who lived in the late Paleolithic period.

Neolithic man used wool and flax fibers to weave cloth, and then dyed this cloth. By this time, certain basic garments were taking form: the tunic that developed into a covering for the upper body, the skirt that gradually divided into trousers, and a mantle or cape that became the coat.

While the methods of making clothes and the materials used for them developed gradually during succeeding centuries, the basic garments that had been developed by primitive man remained surprisingly stable in their styling for a long period of time. The Egyptians made strong use of the tunic, worn in a full-length version by women and, with the addition of a loincloth, in a variety of lengths by men. The Greeks were also fond of the tunic style, sometimes adding a kind of stole draped over one shoulder.

The Roman's toga was a popular version of the tunic, but it was the Romans who finally brought trousers into the civilized Western world. Trousers were being worn by the barbaric inland tribes of Europe, in particular by the Teutons. After the Romans conquered the Teutonic tribes, many Roman soldiers returned home wearing tight trousers under their military kilts. Later on, in the fifth century, when the tide turned and the Teutons became the victors, trousers for men became commonplace in Europe.

The Middle Ages:
Fifth Through Fifteenth Centuries

Little change in apparel styling took place during the early part of the Middle Ages. Europe was in a kind of cultural deep freeze, and its static fashions reflected the absence of new ideas and new influences. Men wore trousers as the normal form of dress, and most women wore a long, rather shapeless version of the tunic.

Then came the Crusades, beginning in 1096 and continuing for two centuries, drawing European nobility into the important cultural areas around the Mediterranean. The Byzantine Empire and the various Arabian sultanates were urban civilizations with trade contacts throughout the world. The ships that took European men and supplies to the wars brought back silks, damasks, tapestries and perfumes, and the returning soldiers brought back new ideas and a taste for luxury.

Fashion began to reflect these changes. Both men's and women's apparel became more form-fitting to display the figure. Elegant overgarments were used. Shoes developed long points and skirts developed long trains. For the first time, all Europe began to demand elegance in clothing.

The Renaissance:
Fourteenth Through Sixteenth Centuries

Fashion as it is known today probably began to thrive during the Renaissance, a period that overlapped the end of the Middle Ages. During this time, new horizons opened in philosophy, art, science, and all facets of life. Change became welcome.

Italian cities were first to reflect such change. Fashions arose there for patterned fabrics woven with threads of silver and gold, for shorter women's gowns and men's tunics, for squared necklines, for lacings that were both practical and decorative. The general fashion look became shorter and wider.

By the beginning of the sixteenth century, the shortened, widened look had reached great extremes in the hands of the Swiss-German costumers. By the middle of that century, Spain had taken the fashion lead, turning the Germanic collar frill into a large stiff ruff, and introducing the corset and knitted stockings.

The English and French adopted versions of the Spanish styles. Paintings of Queen Elizabeth I show her in full, richly brocaded gowns and stiff, high ruffs. Elizabeth is said to have had more fashion influence on the English-speaking world than any other monarch, couturier, or fashion leader, before or since her time. As the Virgin Queen grew older, the court painters began to turn out smooth, stylized, masklike portraits rather than accurately depicting the aging lines of her face, and Elizabeth herself used an increasing amount of cosmetics to hide the effects of time. Ladies of rank followed her lead, with cosmetics made from everything from roses and cherries to turpentine and hog lard.

The Seventeenth Century

Louis XIV, who ruled France from 1643 to 1715, maintained a brilliant court that helped to make Paris both the artistic and fashion center of the Western world. The relationship between the grandeur of the king and the health of his country's fashion industries was not coincidental. By

Louis XIV (1638–1715)

Marie Antoinette (1755–1793)

making Paris the center of fashion for Europe, Louis and his successors ensured an export market that could surmount even the most rigid trade barriers erected by other nations. These monarchs bolstered their personal revenue, strengthened control over a recently centralized France, and secured foreign exchange by having the government take over much of the production of textiles and other related products.

Essentially, France was in the garment business, and it was a very successful business. That success was further stimulated by the widespread distribution of fashion prints, executed by engravers, which showed what was being worn by the French ladies at court.

Fashions for both sexes during the seventeenth century were elegant to an extreme, with lavish use of velvets and satins, gold trim, high-heeled satin shoes, abundant ribbons and lace, and curled wigs.

The seventeenth century, which saw the first permanent English settlement in this country, saw fashion in England itself begin to be divided by politics and religion. The Reformation was taking hold, and men were taking sides. Those who were Puritan in both religion and politics put on somber clothes and cut their hair short, which earned them the nickname of "Roundheads," while those who supported the royalist cause chose the elegant styles and long hair then fashionable in France, partly because the French throne strongly supported the exiled English king.

When Charles II was restored to the English throne, during the second half of the century, there was also a return to elegance in fashion for those in power in England. While the reformers continued to wear their somber clothes, the country's leaders preferred luxury in fashion, and France was their fashion mentor.

The Eighteenth Century

During the Regency period, 1715 to 1730, a more simple elegance with extensive use of softer colors was introduced in France, and therefore throughout Europe. Soon, however, the rococo style of extravagant, elegant structural ornamentation became fashionable. The questionable taste of the rococo period, from 1730 to 1770, was reflected in skirts that were absurdly wide and in gowns ornamented with gathered lace and ribbons, artificial flowers, embroidery. Men's clothing, too, took on width, and had heavy gold and silver embroidery. Curled white wigs, cosmetics, and perfumes were used by both sexes.

By the middle of the eighteenth century, the English, already influenced by the beginnings of the Industrial Revolution, began to find the French styles for men unsuitable for their new way of life. More practical and simpler styles gained acceptance, and England stepped into a role that it was to fill for many years, that of fashion leader in men's apparel. Even before the French Revolution in the 1780s, some of the simplicity England had introduced into men's styles appeared also in women's clothes. Even Parisian ladies adopted the practical, graceful costume à l'anglaise.

French fashion leadership nevertheless remained strong, reaching its climax with the emphasis given to fashion by Marie Antoinette. Her chief milliner and dressmaker, Rose Bertin, was head of the Paris Guild of Milliners, established in 1776, and a forerunner of today's great couturiers. Like them, Rose Bertin was looked to for fashion advice, not only by members of the French court but by customers from other parts of the world. Since the women from other areas were unable to come to Mlle. Bertin's salon to choose and buy, she sent them fashion dolls clothed in her newest models, from which they made their selections.

Fashion in France was largely reserved for royalty and nobility until the French Revolution, when fine clothes fell as much from favor as did the aristocracy. France thus lost its kings, its fashion leadership, and even its fashion industries for a time.

In this country during the eighteenth century, the settlers were mainly influenced by English fashions, and by the limitations of pioneer existence. Those who could afford it, and most of them lived in the cities, wore the latest English garb, but in the frontier areas, the emphasis was on utility and protection. In general, Americans tended to wear heavier, more practical clothes at work than did their European counterparts, thus strengthening the trend toward simpler styling in the apparel for both sexes.

At the close of the eighteenth century, there was a renewed interest in Greco-Roman ideas, resulting from the midcentury unearthing of Pompeii and Herculaneum, the two Roman cities that had been buried under volcanic ash and lava some 1,700 years before. As archeologists dug and shoveled and swept and chipped away the volcanic debris, they uncovered a way of life that had been cut off by disaster in an instant and held by nature in that very instant for many centuries. The remarkably fresh signs of the way of life of the ancient Romans intrigued the world, and fashions reflected this interest.

The fashion manifestations of this interest in England took the form of simple, free-hanging dresses belted just below the breasts. Flat slippers replaced high heels. This costume, a close duplication of classic Greek and Roman dress, heralded the beginning of neoclassicism in apparel as well as art, architecture, furniture, and political and social thinking.

The French immediately took to the classic ideas, adding their own touches through the brief Directoire period, from 1795 to 1804. Obsessed with the desire to imitate the look and mannerisms of classic antiquity, they modified the English costume by removing the long sleeves and using light and flimsy fabrics—so thin, in fact, that a woman's dress could be pulled through a ring. "The last years of the century were witness to an almost unparalleled era of scantily clad women," said Michelle Murphy, in *Two Centuries of French Fashion,* "the more daring of whom donned their garments wet to enhance the illusion of classic marble statuary."[9]

Authorities vary in dating the beginnings of modern fashion. Brenninkmeyer cites the fourteenth-century division of Paris merchant tailors into the "tailleurs" for men and the "couturiers" for women. Laver says fashion really began in the fifteenth century when people discovered that clothes could be used as a compromise between exhibitionism and modesty. Sapir ascribes the acceleration in fashion to the desire for innovation encouraged by the Renaissance.

Fashions in the colonies were simpler than those at court.

Nystrom, however, places the beginning of modern fashion in the latter part of the eighteenth century. By that time, the Industrial Revolution was underway in England, the American Revolution had taken place, and the French Revolution was in the making. Change was touching the political, social, and economic values of the Western world. Wealth was being accumulated by the industrially talented rather than by the traditional nobility; standards of living were rising; urbanization was increasing; the idea of public education had been reintroduced; travel and communications were improving.[10] The tempo of change, in fashions as in life, was accelerating.

The Nineteenth Century

As Europe surged with social and economic turmoil in the early years of the nineteenth century, and as America began to add its influence to the fashion scene, fashion styles continued to record the temper of the times. The century started with the last glimpses of that unexpected reincarnation of Roman times, and it ended with Amelia Bloomer's efforts to make trousers an accepted garment for women.

The Early Nineteenth Century The crowning of Napoleon in 1804 inaugurated the Empire period in France, characterized by modified versions of classic effects. Heavy satins and silks replaced the flimsy materials. Sleeves were short and puffed, and the skirt developed a back-fullness. As the Empire period neared its end, the skirt rose to the ankle in a silhouette that had little to do with the classic model. This was a period of confused art forms.

After 1820, in an attempt to discard Empire influence, designers reverted to the rococo styles. A more natural waistline evolved; skirts lengthened and widened; renewed interest in the sleeve eventually led to the huge leg-of-mutton style.

Mid- and Late Nineteenth Century In 1852, Louis Napoleon established the French Second Empire,

The early and mid-nineteenth century saw both the narrow empire style and the wide crinoline.

and he and his Empress Eugénie made Paris once more the magnet for the fashion and social leaders of Europe. The French fashion industry again boomed. New fashion attention turned from sleeves to skirts, which, supported by the newly invented crinoline, reached fantastic widths. The crinoline was a horsehair underskirt introduced by Charles Frederick Worth, an Englishman turned Frenchman, who is called the father of the modern French couture. The crinoline was lighter and easier to manage than the many petticoats and paddings that gave skirts width in earlier days. It was considered responsible, however, for many fatal accidents, including a holocaust in Santiago, Chile, where more than 2,000 women, all clad in crinolines, perished in a church fire, primarily because their skirts clogged the exits and also were very flammable.

The Franco-Prussian War of 1870 dimmed the brilliance of Parisian social life for a time, but did not lessen the city's importance as a center of the fashion industries. Leadership, however, shifted from royalty to actresses and to models employed by important couture houses, an interesting forerunner of the kind of leadership fashion has today in many countries of the world.

By midcentury, however, revolutions had occurred in many European countries, and economic changes were coming rapidly. The republican form of government was gaining popularity, and royalty and clergy exercised less influence.

Industrialism was spreading, and a new class, whose power was based on wealth rather than birth, was influencing the social and political patterns of life. Labor became a large class with a sense of its own identity, leading to the formation of trade unions; attempts to control the course of politics were initiated; socialism came into being. In America, Thoreau sought the simple life at Walden Pond, and idealistic attempts at communal living got underway at Brookdale Farm and in the Oneida community. New religions came into existence, and the movements for feminine freedom and for education of the masses developed—and paradoxically, there was the fashion of appearing to be in poor health, particularly popular among women, who took to their beds and "declined" whenever they were thwarted.

In apparel, the turmoil of the period reflected itself in grotesque, uninspired styles, corseted and tightly laced, with skirts that again touched the ground. Inspiration and distinction were lacking. The prestigious British throne was occupied by Queen Victoria, whose sentimental attitudes and decorous dress, as well as her fondness for over-filled rooms, did little to inspire fashion. Elegance began to disappear, and the general appearance of women's clothes became modest, bulky, and covered up.

In apparel and home furnishings, industry was making fumbling progress toward mass production. The skilled craftsman was becoming passé, but industry had not yet learned the art of using machines to produce well-made, attractive merchandise.

In the United States the second half of the nineteenth century was distinguished by a period of invention, travel, increasing wealth, and improved communications. Railroads and steamships made transcontinental and transatlantic

Back fullness reached its extreme in the late nineteenth century with the bustle.

Empress Eugénie (1826–1920)

Gibson Girl

travel faster and safer. The telegraph and the telephone helped speed news on its way, and fashion publications helped to carry the word, too. *Godey's Lady's Book,* first published in Philadelphia in 1839, was already well circulated. The abolition movement, the Civil War, and the development of the West kept America in a constant state of flux.

During the early part of this period the United States was responsible for two significant developments that had marked effects on the fashion industry. The sewing machine was invented, making commercial production much faster and less expensive. The paper dress pattern appeared (6 million of them were sold in 1871), greatly facilitating the home sewing of fashions.

In general, during the last part of the nineteenth century, the dissemination of fashion news became progressively faster, easier, and less expensive. The fashion plate, which had come into being, showed what the designers thought was, or would become, the mode. Issued in large numbers, these plates became a medium for spreading the fashion word even before those fashions were worn by the fashion leaders of the day.

Still more evidence of the changes that were taking place: Women were entering the business world; typewriters had been invented, and women were becoming adept typists. Clerical work, done by hand, also employed woman-power; President Lincoln's Secretary of the Treasury had 1,500 women on his clerical staff in 1861. Apparel factories, having acquired the new sewing machines, used women to operate them. Women were also replacing men as teachers, and were taking up nursing careers, additional signs of sociological change.

Nevertheless, women remained dependent on men, and their fashions tended to reflect this fact. Attempts at dress reform, such as Mrs. Amelia Bloomer's effort to popularize the shorter skirt and pantalettes, had little effect on fashion. Crinolines gradually died, but skirt fullness remained. Skirt lines were narrow, but reached extremes in back-fullness with the aid of the bustle. Trains were worn. Lacings were tight. If, as Laver maintains, masculine and feminine fashions diverge sharply when the male is in the

ascendancy, and the distinctions fade when he is not, then the late nineteenth century was truly a period of male ascendancy.

The Twentieth Century

At the beginning of the twentieth century Europe and America were still in the horse-and-buggy era, still under the decorous shadow of Victoria Regina. It was still a world in which the working-man had limited opportunities and limited pay, and the working woman had even less pay and more restrictions.

Before the century had run two-thirds of its course, however, changes occurred on a scale and at a rate without parallel in recorded history. Scientific developments came fast, and in some fields more barriers were broken in a single decade than in centuries before. Two major world conflicts caused empires to crumble, brought new countries and new forms of government into being, and radically changed manners and morals.

The changes, turmoil, and progress of this century were reflected in a dramatic speedup of fashion. From 1910 to 1960, the silhouette of women's apparel ran the gamut of possible variations from wasp waist to no waistline, from full bosoms to flat bosoms, from exaggerated hips to hipless contours.

Before World War I At the beginning of the twentieth century, skirts were long and, for a time, so tight that they were called hobble skirts, since hobbling was about all a woman could do in them. Lace was used in abundance, and the small waist and the large bosom became fashionable.

Yet it was really nightwear that made fashion news during this period. Until the 1900s, the nightclothes of both men and women were versions of the tunic, the men's version a long night-shirt and the woman's version a nightgown. Pajamas now appeared, and rapidly became popular first with men and then gradually were adopted by some women.

The 1920s and 1930s During this period, the broadened range of feminine activities, from bicycle riding to driving automobiles, demanded greater freedom of movement, and hemlines began to climb shortly after World War I. By the mid-1920s, skirts were up to knee-length, corsets were ignored, breasts were flattened, hair was bobbed, and hats were often of the cloche type. Women had rebelled in earnest. Even knickers and some forms of divided skirts were beginning to make brief, daring appearances on the streets and in high school classrooms.

The long and bitter depression period of the 1930s, however, with fewer job opportunities for women and generally lower standards of living for everyone, seemed to encourage a more feminine silhouette. The bosom gradually became noticeable again, as did the waistline. Skirts lengthened a bit, but were neither so tight nor so cumbersome as to impede activity.

Men's clothes also relaxed somewhat. Sports trousers came into common usage, and soft collars replaced the high, stiff linen variety.

World War II   With the outbreak of the Second World War, restrictions upon consumer fabric use and production facilities slowed fashion development in this country and cut it off completely from Paris. The United States became the fashion center temporarily, and American designers began to demonstrate creativity within imposed limits. There were some contradictions: Shoulder lines became square and military, skirts were short and straight, yet the breasts were prominent and the hair was often worn long and free. It was as though women wore austere, military lines as a gesture of unity with their men at war, but also chose fashions that asserted their femininity.

Men's fashions, of course, were almost non-existent. Nearly every man who might play a role in fashion was in uniform, and during the war period, uniforms were required to be worn on leave as well as on duty.

After World War II   Dior's New Look of 1947 was a revolutionary reaction to wartime clothing restraints, with its long and full skirts, narrow waists, and full hips. It also represented an overdue fashion change from the straight or tubular silhouette, a cyclical development that had been interrupted by almost a decade of worldwide conflict. The bell silhouette was not to complete

The restrictive hobble skirt of 1910 gave way to the freer styles of the 1920s and 1930s.

In the 1960s hem length rose and fell as evidenced by the mini, micro-mini, maxi, and midi.

its regular cycle period, however. After moving briefly to the more feminine "baby doll" version in the mid-1950s, the bell silhouette gradually gave way to the tubular silhouette in a variety of versions from the "sack" to the shift.

Throughout the 1950s, however, skirts gradually grew shorter. Women were driving cars, participating in an increasing number of activities, and holding down a wide variety of jobs. Apparel fashions changed to accommodate the many-faceted roles of women.

Men's fashions began to take on a similarity to women's. Women had put on pants, and men began to use more feminine kinds of decoration, fancier fabrics, and more elegant styles. Hairstyles became similar, too, and men reached back to an earlier age for styles of long hair, long sideburns, mustaches, and beards.

Politics and money and youth often determined the fashion leaders of the 1950s and 1960s. Jacqueline Kennedy had all of them working for her. She was the most important feminine influence during the 1960s as First Lady and as widow of the assassinated President, and until after her marriage to Aristotle Onassis. The Beatles stood for both youth and success, and they helped to popularize some of the male Mod styles of the late 1950s and the early 1960s.

One strange offshoot in the 1960s was the further deterioration, among young people, of the deliberately ultracasual hippie group fashions into consciously dirty and ragged styles of dungarees and unkempt hair.

Whether in a white silk miniskirt or in a pair of dirty, ragged dungarees, however, people have kept pace with the social, economic, and psychological changes in their world by the fashions they have adopted. Women's dress, as well as men's, reflects the more nearly equal roles of the sexes at present. Extremes, eagerly accepted and widely copied among young people, accent the restlessness of the age. The extent to which many older people adopt the young styles reflects the demise of authoritarian attitudes and the philosophy that elders are always right.

Today's fashions reflect the world around them. Tomorrow's fashions will be equally faithful interpreters of whatever is to come.

References

[1]Carlyle, *Sartor Resartus*, p. 36.
[2]Laver, *Dress*, p. 46.
[3]Flügel, *The Psychology of Clothes*, p. 54.
[4]Dunlap, "The Development and Function of Clothing," p. 64.
[5]K. Young, *Social Psychology*, pp. 311–312.
[6]*Ibid.*, p. 312.
[7]Murray, *Four Centuries of Dress in America*, p. 27.
[8]Sapir, "Fashion," p. 140.
[9]Murphy, *Two Centuries of French Fashion*, Introduction.
[10]Nystrom, *Economics of Fashion*, p. 226.

Merchandising Vocabulary

Define or briefly explain the following terms:

Modesty   Custom   Fashion dolls   Crinoline

Merchandising Review

1. What are the three basic reasons offered by social scientists as to why we wear clothes? Which of these basic reasons is believed to have preceded the others in point of time?
2. What were some of the purposes served by decoration in the primitive world? Give specific examples of decorative articles which serve the same purpose in modern cultures.
3. Discuss the evolution of clothing as a protective device.
4. Distinguish between custom and fashion. Cite examples of present-day dress that is influenced more by custom than fashion.
5. What conditions tend to favor the retention of custom in dress?
6. What factors tend to favor fashion change in dress?
7. Why is it important for students of fashion merchandising to know something about fashion history?
8. What were the conditions or factors that could be considered responsible for the uninspired, grotesque styles of the mid- and late-nineteenth century?
9. Who was Rose Bertin? What was her contribution to the world of fashion?
10. Discuss significant developments in the last half of the nineteenth century that influenced fashion apparel.
11. Discuss the significant developments in the first half of the twentieth century that influenced apparel fashions.

Merchandising Digest

1. "Specific forms of decoration create specific impressions." Identify these forms, the impression each attempts to create, and at least one example of how apparel may be used to achieve the desired impression.
2. "What is considered modest at one time and in one society is not necessarily so in another." Discuss this statement from the text, and its implications for a fashion merchant.
3. Discuss the effect of the changing status of women during the past century on (a) women's apparel, and (b) men's apparel.

4

THE MOVEMENT
of FASHION

Fashion is constantly in motion. Its movements may be rapid and obvious or slow and barely discernible, depending upon the yeastiness of the social, political, and economic environment. The movements, however, have both meaning and definite direction. From designer to consumer, everyone concerned with fashion is preoccupied with interpreting those movements and estimating their speed and direction.

The retailer who provides selections for his customers faces this problem. So does the producer who has to choose textures, colors, and lines. And so, too, does the woman on a limited budget who carefully inquires about what "they" are wearing before investing in a winter coat.

Recurring Fashions

Styles reoccur in fashion acceptance. Occasionally an entire "look" is reborn, as in the 1960s, when the prevailing straight lines and short skirts strikingly resembled the 1920s fashions. Also in the late 1960s and early 1970s, nostalgic interest developed in Edwardian styles and those of the 1930s. The Edwardian influence was seen in elegant clothes and full heads of hair and sideburns for men. The 1930s influence of fluid, clinging lines in women's clothes, fluffy curls, and bright lipstick gained impetus from the success of the motion picture *Bonnie and Clyde,* which was about a notorious gang of bank robbers of that period.

Sometimes a single costume component or a minor detail that earlier exhausted its welcome and shrank from sight stages a comeback. At other times, a single article of clothing, like the sandals of the ancient Greeks, returns to popularity.

Just as astronomers, after countless observations, learned to predict the appearance of comets, scientific observers of fashion, on a much more limited scale, have attempted to measure the tempo and extent of fashion changes in the hope of finding a predictable rhythm to such change.

Rhythmic Changes in Silhouette

The first significant effort to apply scientific procedure to the study of style changes in women's apparel is credited to A. L. Kroeber, who reported his findings in a 1919 issue of *The American Anthropologist.* Kroeber, then a professor of anthropology at the University of California, had sought to discover patterns of change, if any, by measuring various dimensions of fashion figures at different times in history.[1]

As a basis for his measurements Kroeber used fashion illustrations in three publications: *Petit Courrier des Dames,* from 1844 to 1868; *Harper's Bazaar,* from 1868 to 1918; and a single 1919 issue of *Vogue.* From the two former journals, he selected ten fashion illustrations from each year on a random basis. He measured these illustrations at the skirt hem, at a higher point of the skirt, across the waist, and across the neckline at shoulder height. Length measurements extended from the mouth to the low point of the neckline, the waist, the skirt hem, and the toe. The measure from mouth to toe was considered body length, and all other measurements were converted into percentages of that figure.

When the relationships were compared, observations of 75 years of fashion illustration revealed that:

- Similar skirt length recurred every 35 years.
- Similar skirt width recurred at the rate of once every 100 years.
- Neckline width followed the same course as hem width, recurring at the rate of once every 100 years.
- Neckline length rose in a third of the time required for its descent.
- Diameter of the waist fluctuated irregularly.

According to Kroeber's findings, each silhouette measurement changed at its own pace. Skirt widths and lengths had symmetrical rhythms of change, but length change was three times faster than width change.

In a later study of the period from 1605 to 1936, Professor Kroeber, with a collaborator, Jane Richardson, using somewhat similar measurements, found women's skirts alternating from broad to narrow and from long to short with some regularity, completing the full cycle in about a century. They also concluded that between the extremes of styling, a basic type or ideal costume had emerged in recent centuries. This costume, which they called compromise styling, had a full, relatively long skirt, a rather sharply constricted waist, and an ample, deep neckline.

Basic Skirt Silhouettes

An essential component of any item of apparel is its silhouette. The silhouette is what one sees from a distance, before details and decoration are visible, and therefore is largely responsible for the first impression.

Mrs. Agnes Brooks Young, in *Recurring Cycles of Fashion*,[2] undertook a study of skirt silhouettes and their variations in connection with her primary interest in theatrical costumes. From data

The three basic silhouettes: bell-shaped, bustle or back-fullness, and straight or tubular.

she collected on a 177-year period, from 1760 to 1937, Mrs. Young concluded that, despite widely held opinions to the contrary, there were actually only three basic silhouettes: the straight or tubular, the bell-shaped or bouffant, and the bustle or back-fullness. Moreover, her data indicated that these three basic silhouettes followed each other in regular sequence and recurred in fashion acceptance approximately once every 100 years. She found that back-fullness prevailed from late in 1760 through 1795. For the next 34 years, the tubular silhouette held sway, but from 1830 to 1867 the bell-shaped skirt was fashionable. In 1868, back-fullness again became popular and remained so for 32 years, followed by the dominance of the tubular silhouette from 1900 through 1937.

Each of the silhouettes, with all its variations, had dominated the fashion scene for a period of approximately 35 years, and having reached an excess in styling declined in popularity, yielding place to the next and opposite silhouette in regular sequence.

Although the studies of Young and of Richardson and Kroeber varied in depth and scope, both concluded that women's skirts (which determine the silhouette) alternated from broad to narrow with some regularity, requiring about a century to complete the full cycle.

Breaks in the Cycle

Analysis of the sequence of fashions may not enable one to predict infallibly what is to come, however. Fashion history abounds with illustrations of how political and social progress, extensive trade and commerce between countries, and economic well-being cause new fashions to rise and flourish. On the other hand, widespread economic depression, wars, and other disasters and upheavals cause breaks in the natural, cyclical development of apparel fashions.

Evidence of such breaks in fashion cycles are most dramatically shown in skirt silhouettes. For example, the straight or tubular silhouette was the prevailing fashion from the very beginning of the twentieth century. In the early 1930s, however, when, according to Young's research, the bell silhouette should have been asserting itself, the United States, like most of the world, was in the depths of a crushing depression. For a period of nearly ten years after the stock market crash of 1929, a third of this country's labor force was unemployed and living in desperate want. Against such a background, fashion slowed its pace, as it does in economically underdeveloped countries.

Then World War II, which began in Europe in the last years of the 1930s, spread throughout the greater part of the world in the early 1940s and interrupted all types of fashion development, chiefly through restrictions on consumer use of fabrics. Material shortages continued for a year or more after the war ended in 1945. Had the course of history been more serene, the bell shape might have dominated the fashions of the 1940s instead of for only a brief period from 1947 to the mid-1950s.

The social upheavals in the United States during the 1960s speeded up fashion change again. The rebellious aspects of the times were reflected in hippie dress, typified by long hair, dungarees, and bare feet, while the more mature groups showed their restlessness by their interest in longer skirts and belted-in waistlines, harbingers of a return to the bell silhouette, whose normal cycle had been cut short a decade earlier. Cyclical change in fashion is interrupted or obscured when society itself is in turmoil, and long-range predictions are difficult when the atmosphere is troubled.

The Cycling of Fashion

The term *fashion cycle* refers to the rise, mass popularization, and decline in popular acceptance of a style. This process can be visually represented by a curve similar to the bell curve of a frequency distribution. Some authorities find an excellent parallel to the fashion cycle in the waves of the surf: first a slow swell, then a crest, and finally a swift fall. Meanwhile a new swell in the background is already on its way toward a crest.

Literally, a cycle is a circle, and the term "fashion cycle" conveys the impression that styles go out of fashion and return with relentless regularity. Styles do come back and fashions do recur, but never exactly as they were in the past.

The silhouettes of the 1920s and the 1960s were similar, for instance, and the effect of boyishness and freedom of movement was the same. In both eras, fashion meant short skirts, straight lines, dangling earrings, and long beads. But in the 1920s girls wore cloche hats, whereas in the 1960s they usually went bareheaded. The girl of the 1920s often introduced a flounce into her skirt, starting below the hip; the girl of the 1960s obtained skirt fullness with an A-line, a gradual flare that began at or above the waist.

Stages of the Fashion Cycle

Fashion cycles are best understood by concentrating on the evolution of a style and learning to recognize each stage of its development. There is an orderliness about this development that permits it to be traced and even predicted, on a short-range basis at least, with considerable accuracy. This forward movement of a fashion cycle passes through five phases:

▫ Introduction
▫ Rise
▫ Culmination
▫ Decline
▫ Obsolescence

These phases parallel, to some extent, the timetable suggested by Laver. A style that Laver would term in its "shameless" or "outré" period would be in the introductory and rising phases of its cycle. It is thought to be "smart" when it achieves its culmination. As the fashion goes into decline and obsolescence, it passes through the "dowdy," "hideous," and "ridiculous" stages as identified by Laver.

Introduction   When a producer offers a new style, color, or texture for customer approval, a new fashion is said to be introduced. The new style may be a squared-toe shoe when points prevail, for instance, or a full skirt when most are straight, or white and black in the midst of a color orgy.

New designs generally are introduced in higher-priced merchandise because of the limited sales prospects facing a yet untried style. Mass production and its resultant savings are not possible at this stage; therefore, production costs are high. Allowance must also be made for the risks entailed. There is always some possibility of failure when a producer or seller is experimenting with a new style; therefore, prices must be high enough on those styles that are sold to cover losses on those that are not. Furthermore, people who are quick to embrace the new often patronize only the more expensive stores. They would be unlikely to seek new items in a bargain-basement atmosphere.

Rise   The acceptance of either the original design or its adaptations by an increasing number of customers is referred to as the *rise*. Prices in this phase are lower than at the introductory phase because production is now on a larger scale. In this phase, there are also adaptations or exact copies of an original style, made of less expensive materials, and employing less meticulous workmanship.

For example, a wealthy woman may pay over $1,000 for an "original" dress from a Paris couture house. The style she chooses is made to her measurements, often from fabric unavailable elsewhere, and stitched throughout by hand. Meantime, an American ready-to-wear house may produce *line-for-line copies* of the same style, using less expensive materials, machine stitching, and standard size measurements. The copy may sell for $200 to $300, or even below $100.

Finally, *adaptations* appear. These are designs that reflect the dominant features of the style that inspired them but make no pretense of being exact copies. A broad or narrow shoulder, a full or slim skirt or sleeve, a cinched or eased waist, a bright or subdued color, a smooth or rough texture—any or all of the new features of the original and its copies may be used.

Culmination   That period when a fashion is at the height of its popularity and use is known as the *culmination* of its cycle. The fashion then is in such demand that it can be mass produced, mass distributed, and sold at prices within the reach of a majority of the public. This phase may be long or brief, depending upon how rapidly saturation is reached. The tan trench coat that men wore in the 1920s and the miniskirts that became a uniform for young women during the 1960s are examples of such a culmination. In this phase, just about everyone who wants the style owns one or more versions of it.

Decline The decrease in consumer demand, because of boredom resulting from widespread use of a fashion, is referred to as the *decline*. As stated by one fashion authority, all fashion ends in excess. The reverse of this statement is also true: excess ends all fashions.

When a fashion's decline sets in, consumers may still be wearing it, but they are no longer willing to buy it at regular prices. They are now experimenting with other styles that are still in the earlier phases of their cycles. Stores that lead the fashion parade abandon the style; more traditional stores mark down their existing stock to make room for newer goods; bargain stores still offer it, but at prices well below those that prevailed during the style's culmination phase. Production of the particular style has stopped or is coming to a halt.

There is no predictable timetable for a fashion cycle, since each fashion proceeds at its own speed. One element of timing can always be counted upon, however: the decline is fast, and the drop to obsolescence is much steeper than the rise to culmination.

Obsolescence When revulsion has set in and a style can no longer be sold at any price, the fashion is in its *obsolescence* phase. In merchandising parlance, "you can't give it away."

Length of Cycles

The cycle of innovation, acceptance, and obsolescence applies to all new ideas, including inventions and innovations for the home. Conveniences like refrigerators and automobiles tend to have longer acceptance or culmination phases than do articles that are dependent mainly on taste, such as apparel.

Little study has been made of the time required for fashion cycles to run their course, but experience indicates that the time span between cycles is steadily decreasing. Among the reasons for this speedup are fast-changing environmental factors and the intensified competition among producers and merchants for the consumer's dollar.

Consumers are constantly exposed to a multiplicity of potential fashions. Many of these win enough acceptance for a discernible cycle to get underway. With a new fashion pressing at the heels of each existing one, it is small wonder that the time required today for a fashion to complete its cycle is noticeably shorter than that required a few decades ago.

This acceleration should not be confused with the rapid demise of styles rejected from the start. In the first case, that of the speedy cycle, the fashion lives at a fast pace and exhaustion sets in early. In the second case, there is no life; the fashion is stillborn.

Broken Fashion Cycles

It sometimes happens that the ordinary progress of a fashion cycle is broken abruptly by some outside influence, such as a change in the weather suitable for seasonal goods. Although no formal studies have been made of this phenomenon, fashion producers and merchants hold that the cycle tends to pick up where it left off, once conditions return to normal, or once the season that was cut short reopens the following year.

Examples of this phenomenon constantly occur in fashion merchandising. For example, if long-haired furs finish strong at the end of one winter season, they are likely to come in strong at the beginning of the next winter season. If prints, plain colors, or plaids are popular at the end of one summer season, they usually start off particularly popular the following summer season. If a color builds up an unusual demand during a winter season, and stores cannot get enough of it, the unfulfilled demand usually will carry over to the next winter season and may even set up a demand for lighter versions of the same color during the intervening seasons.

Women's boots, as an element of the outdoor-indoor costume, offer an excellent example of a cycle broken by weather. Boots were at their introductory phase in 1957. Each summer after that their progress was halted; each winter it resumed, gaining in importance. Popularity continued into the early 1970s, when either boots or the "boot look" (achieved by matched shoes and hosiery) were used for indoor and outdoor wear with longer skirts.

Long-Run and Short-Run Fashions

The length of time it takes for individual fashions to complete their cycles varies widely. The terms *long-run* and *short-run* are used to describe fashions that either take more seasons or fewer seasons to complete their full cycles than what might be considered their average life expectancy.

Some fashions tend to rise in popular acceptance more slowly than do others, thereby elongating their fashion life. Some stay in popular demand much longer than do others. The decline in popular demand for some fashions may be slower than for others. Silhouettes, colors and textures, accessories, classics and fads—all vary widely in the length of time each takes to complete a full demand cycle because of their specific and individual characteristics.

Silhouettes Because they change slowly and gradually, as a result of changes in styling details, silhouettes are considered long-run fashions. As previously noted, silhouettes have been found to change completely approximately every 35 years. Actually, however, this change is not abrupt: silhouettes evolve from one to another through a series of changes in detail from one selling season to another. So subtle are some of these changes that last year's garment may not look out of fashion. As a result of a series of almost imperceptible changes over a period of four or five years, however, older apparel may begin to look badly proportioned and out of fashion.

As a general rule, the more detailed an item of apparel, the sooner it becomes dated. It is interesting to note that many foreign and domestic high-fashion designers express pride in the fact that some of their styles remain fashionably correct sometimes as long as 10 or 15 years.

Colors and Textures More superficial elements of fashion, such as colors and textures, are generally considered short-run fashions, mainly because their popularity is often restricted to a single season. In recent years, however, their life-spans have tended to lengthen.

In the late 1950s, for example, white, which formerly had been considered solely a summer color, was introduced as a fashionable color for winter holiday apparel. In 1962, *Harper's Bazaar* helped to popularize white as a year-round apparel color. Later it also became popular as a background color for prints and plaids. A possible explanation for this may be traced to technological developments in fibers and fabrics that have made it considerably less of a chore than it used to be to keep white garments fresh and sparkling. Black, formerly a winter staple, was displaced from the fashion scene in the early 1960s, yielding to brighter colors. It did not stage a fashion comeback until 1967.

Textures, too, have become less seasonally oriented than they used to be. Here again, due to technological advances in fiber and fabric treatments, various textures may continue in popularity without respect to seasonal changes in climate. Cotton, linen, and synthetics may be worn the year around, may be smooth or nubby, crisp or soft, sheer or opaque. Wool may be rough or smooth, crisp or soft, heavy or tissue weight. Synthetics may have the appearance and texture of cottons, wools, silks, linens.

Accessories Scarves, shoes, handbags, belts, cosmetics, costume jewelry, millinery, and gloves are accessories to apparel and tend to have short-run or seasonal cycles. They are worn—or not worn—to complete and carry out the effect created by apparel. At the culmination of the straight or tubular silhouette in the early 1960s, for example, belts were conspicuously absent from the fashion picture. Not until the winter of 1966–1967, when figure-skimming garments and the waistline began to return to fashion, was there any interest in this accessory. By the end of its first winter season, the belt fashion was well past its introductory phase and into the rise of its cycle. Belts in a wide variety of materials and styles were used increasingly on dresses and coats.

The size and shape of scarf fashions tend to change seasonally with currently popular styling in apparel. The increasingly shorter skirts and geometric styling of the earlier 1960s called for small, square scarves. With the introduction of longer skirts and closer-to-the-body styling in apparel, scarf fashions became longer and rectangular, sometimes to be worn as a sash. The maxicoat gave rise to the nine-foot scarf for the ultimate in the long, lean look.

The trend toward nude apparel fashions in the 1960s was reflected in hatlessness, in cutouts in gloves, sportswear, and dresses, in natural makeup, and in natural hairstyles.

Classics At the long end of the time scale are classics, those fashions with cycles that seem permanently arrested at the culmination stage. Classics are usually practical and universally appealing. Among classics are such items as a woman's slip-on pump, neutral shades in women's hosiery, and certain lengths in women's gloves. Additional classics, dating back to the early 1900s but still on the fashion scene, are the shirtwaist dress, the wristwatch, and low shoes.

Classics change, but only superficially. Material, texture, detail, and even silhouette may vary, but the style itself continues in fashion. A woman's slip-on pump may be made of any leather, fabric, or plastic; it may have a blunt or a pointed toe, high or low heel; it may be made in a single color or a combination of colors. Although it changes superficially to relate to current fashions, it remains a slip-on pump—not an oxford, a Mary Jane, a T-strap, or a high-button shoe. Similarly, a shirtwaist dress, whatever its fabric, color, sleeve length, and skirt fullness, remains a shirtwaist—and a direct descendant of the Gibson Girl fashion.

Fads The shortest of short-run fashions are called fads. Their rise is spectacular, and their decline even more so. Occasionally, however, fads fool the experts. Some of them start, as usual, among a limited group, but instead of rapidly reaching saturation and dying abruptly, they spread to general public acceptance and become full-fledged fashions.

Two interesting modern examples of fads that later became fashions are the chemise and the wig. The chemise made its bow in the late 1950s, skyrocketing among younger wearers of inexpen-

sive dresses, and then fizzled out. Later it returned as the shift and became the important dress fashion of the 1960s. The wig began as high fashion early in the 1960s. Costing at least $300, it was strictly a fad that only the wealthy could afford. As less expensive methods of making and selling wigs were devised, they became fun fads for many ages and income brackets. As their practical aspects revealed themselves, they became a true fashion among active women.

Consumer Buying and the Fashion Cycle

Each fashion has both a consumer buying cycle and a consumer use cycle. (See Graph 4-1.) Use continues after buying, and thus the use cycle declines later and less steeply than the one for buying. Consumer buying is often halted prematurely because producers and sellers no longer wish to risk making and stocking a fashion they believe will soon decline in popularity. Instead, they concentrate their resources on new fashions with better prospects of longevity. This procedure is familiar to anyone who has tried to buy summer clothes in late August or ski wear in March.

The consumer buying cycle curve rises directly with the rise of the consumer use cycle, but when the fashion reaches its peak, consumer buying declines more rapidly than consumer use. Just as different segments of society respond to and tire of a fashion at different times, so different groups continue to wear fashions for varying lengths of time after they have ceased buying them. While each class of customer is using and enjoying a fashion, the producer and merchant serving that group are quietly abandoning the style and seeking something newer. Their efforts in this direction are most profitable when they anticipate, rather than follow, the trend of consumer demand.

Factors Influencing Fashion Movement

The fashion cycle has been compared to a force of nature because, in Laver's words, "nothing seems to be able to turn it back until it has spent itself, until it has provoked a reaction by its very excess."[3] Nevertheless, there are factors that can

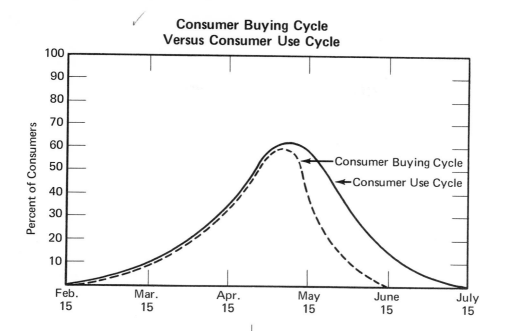

Consumer Buying Cycle Versus Consumer Use Cycle

(graph: Percent of Consumers plotted against dates from Feb. 15 to July 15, showing "Consumer Buying Cycle" and "Consumer Use Cycle")

accelerate or retard the movement of fashion, just as wind can spread a forest fire and rain can slow or halt it.

Accelerating Factors

The influences that exert an accelerating effect on fashion cycles are widespread buying power, increased leisure, more education, increased social mobility, technological advances, sales promotion, and the need for seasonal changes.

Widespread Buying Power More widely diffused discretionary income means there are more people with the financial means to respond to fashion. The more consumers who flock to a new fashion, the sooner it will reach its culmination; the more widespread the financial ability of consumers to turn to a yet newer fashion, the sooner the current fashion will plunge into obsolescence.

Leisure Long hours of work and little leisure permitted scant attention to fashion in the past. More leisure time usually means more time to buy and enjoy fashion of many kinds. In the last 20 years, sharp decreases in working hours and in-

creases in paid vacations have encouraged more use of at-home wear, casual clothes, sports apparel, travel clothes, and different types of ordinary business dress. The increased purchases of these types of clothes give impetus to the cycles of these fashions.

Education The increasingly higher level of education in the United States helps to speed up the fashion cycle in two ways: first, there are more people whose horizons have been broadened to include new interests and new wants; and second, there are more people equipped by education to earn the money needed to satisfy those wants. These interests and wants, accompanied by the means to obtain them, provide a significant push toward the adoption of new fashions.

Social Mobility In a society with few artificial social barriers, the woman with discretionary income can spend it as she chooses. No law or barrier of custom forces any woman of means to refrain from buying the newest and most prestigious styles in dresses, hats, or shoes, thus giving impetus to a fashion cycle in its earliest phases. Conversely, nothing forces a woman of ample means to buy new or even recent styles. If her interest in fashion is not keen, she may build her wardrobe around fashions that are at, or even beyond, the culmination phase of the cycle, thus probably lengthening the life of the cycle.

Technological Advances News, including fashion news, races with lightning speed around the world today. Improved production techniques speed up the manufacturing process. Fast transportation overland, by sea, and by air brings finished goods promptly to retail stores. Little or no time is lost between the moment when the consumer is psychologically and financially ready to add her forward push to the fashion cycle and the time when the goods are available for her to purchase. The development of new fibers, finishes, and materials also speeds up cycles. Many of these not only add utility but also reduce the prices of fashion goods, enabling people of more limited means to buy. The combination of durability and low price encourages those purchases, pushing fashion along in its cycle.

Sales Promotion Publicity and promotion by producers and retailers cannot force acceptance of a new fashion or revitalize a dying or dead one. They have, however, repeatedly accelerated the progress of an acceptable fashion. The publicity given miniskirts early in their cycle is an example. Even as late as 1965, most women were protesting that they would not be seen in above-the-knee skirts. Meantime, thigh-high hems were shown in fashion magazines, on television, in store displays, and in public places by those who had adopted the fashion in its early phases. By 1968, the eyes of even the most conservative woman had grown accustomed to skirt brevity, and it was hard to find a woman whose knees did not show. Without the exposure of publicity and promotion, the fashion cycle for miniskirts might have taken considerably longer to reach its culmination.

Seasonality The consumer demands fashion change in direct response to the changing calendar, varying the weight and look of her garment according to seasonal patterns. Psychological need is as important as a physical need, and sometimes even more so, in this respect, for even in regions where the swing in temperature from summer to winter is very marked, the need for new clothes with the change of seasons is actually less real today than it was generations ago, before central heating and air conditioning. Nevertheless, the need for change exists, and that need continues to spur fashion demand, pushing it along its fashion cycle. This is particularly true in relation to travel and vacation needs, when the consumer travels from one climate to another in a matter of hours, thus setting up a demand for apparel appropriate for each of the diverse climates.

Retarding Factors

Factors that retard the development of fashion cycles by discouraging people from adopting incoming styles or that encourage hanging onto styles that might logically be considered on the decline include habit and custom, religion, sumptuary laws, the nature of the merchandise, and reductions in consumer buying power.

Habit and Custom By slowing acceptance of new styles and prolonging the life-spans of those already accepted, habit and custom exert a braking effect on fashion movement. The restraining hand of habit is at work slowing the adoption of new skirt lengths, silhouettes, necklines, or colors whenever a shopper unconsciously selects styles that do not differ perceptibly from those she already owns. It is easy for an individual to let habit take over. Some consumers are more susceptible to this tendency than others; among these, loyalty to an established style is not so much a matter of fashion judgment as it is a natural attraction toward something that has become familiar.

Custom slows progress in the fashion cycle by permitting vestiges of past fashions, status symbols, taboos, or special needs to continue past their utility in modern dress. Custom is responsible for such details as buttons on the sleeves of men's suits, vents in their jackets, and the sharp creases down the front of their trousers. Custom usually requires a degree of formality in dress for religious services. The trend toward similarity of dress for men and women in this country has permitted women to wear trousers but custom still forbids men to wear skirts.

Religion Religious leaders have historically championed custom and demonstrated their sanction of the old in ceremonial apparel. They have tended to associate fashion with temptation, and have urged their followers to turn their backs on both. Religion today exerts much less of a retarding influence on fashion than at any time in history. Examples of this may be found in the modernization of women's dress among many religious orders and the fact that women no longer consider a hat obligatory when at church.

Sumptuary Laws The law is one of the few forces that can slow or halt a fashion cycle by command. Height of headdress, length of train, width of sleeve, value and weight of material, and color of dress have all been restricted at times to specific classes by law. Such laws were aimed at keeping each class in its place in a rigidly stratified society.[4]

Other laws attempted to keep a society's collective mind on a high level by condemning frippery, as the Puritans did. New England Puritans were prohibited from wearing laces of any kind, slashed sleeves, ruffs, or beavers and punishment was prompt and harsh for anyone found guilty of taking liberties with rules for dress. And while New Jersey was still a British colony, a law was passed stating that all women, regardless of age, rank, profession, or degree, who seduced or betrayed into matrimony any of His Majesty's subjects by virtue of scents, cosmetics, artificial teeth, false hair, or high-heeled shoes would incur the same punishment as that meted out for witchcraft or like offenses.

Local ordinances, however, have a way of falling into limbo if they conflict with a fashion cycle that is gathering strength. In New York during the 1930s, fines were imposed if men or women appeared on the streets in tennis shorts, or if the shoulder straps of bathing suits were not in place. What was considered indecent exposure then is commonplace today: shorts for streetwear and strapless bathing suits.

Nature of the Merchandise The nature of the merchandise concerned is sometimes a factor in slowing the rate at which a fashion cycle moves. Silhouettes change more slowly than do colors, textures, and details. Apparel moves in slower cycles than accessories. Men's fashion cycles are slower than women's.

Reductions in Buying Power Just as increasing spending power can speed up a fashion cycle, so can any decrease in spending power, as a result of economic depression, high taxes and interest rates, inflation, strikes, or a high percentage of unemployment, retard the forward movement of fashion cycles. Similarly, any increase in the number of socially deprived consumers slows down the cycles of fashion. The poor are bystanders in matters of fashion, and bystanders do not keep cycles moving.

Playing the Apparel Fashion Game

According to Madge Garland, a well-known English fashion authority, "Every woman is born with a built-in hobby: the adornment of her person. The tricks she can play with it, the shapes she can make of it, the different portions she displays at various times, the coverings she uses or discards . . ."[5] all add up to fashion.

Many authorities on clothing read a clear message into this alternate exposure and covering of various parts of the body: sex. Flügel sees sexual attraction as the dominant motive for wearing clothes. Laver suggests that those portions of the body which it is no longer fashionable to expose are "sterilized" and no longer sexually attractive, whereas those which are newly exposed are *erogenous*, or sexually stimulating. He sees fashion pursuing the ever-shifting erogenous zone, but never quite catching up with it. "If you really catch up," he warns, "you are immediately arrested for indecent exposure. If you almost catch up, you are celebrated as a leader of fashion."[6] Had he seen the topless bathing suit and the bikini at the time he wrote the above, he undoubtedly would have cited them as examples: the topless bathing suit was ahead of the fashion, and considered indecent; the bikini was in fashion, and considered smart.

Pieces of the Game

The pieces with which the fashion game is played are the various portions of a woman's body. Historically, as each part of the anatomy has reached a saturation point of interest, it has

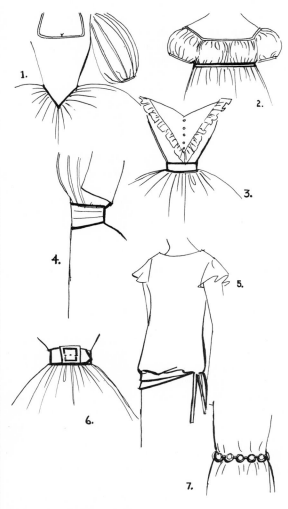

Nearly 400 years of waistlines: 1. 1600, 2. 1815, 3. 1850, 4. 1880, 5. 1925, 6. 1954, 7. 1965.

withdrawn from the fashion spotlight in favor of some other portion.

In the Middle Ages, asceticism was in fashion for a time, and a woman's dress was designed to play down, rather than emphasize, her femininity. The Renaissance, however, a period of greater freedom, highlighted the bosom, and to glorify woman's child-bearing function, the abdominal region was also made conspicuous. If the ladies in some paintings of that day seem pregnant, the effect was intentional and intended as a compliment.

By the eighteenth century, however, the abdomen had lost its appeal. Although the bosom continued to get emphasis, the abdomen was flattened, and heels were raised to facilitate upright carriage. The Empire period also stressed the bosom with a high waistline, but the entire body itself was emphasized with sheer and scanty dresses.

During the nineteenth century, fashion interest shifted to the hips, and thus skirts billowed. Later, the posterior was accented with bustles and trains.

By the twentieth century, emphasis switched from the trunk to the limbs, via short skirts and sleeveless or tight-sleeved dresses. Flügel interpreted this accent on the limbs, together with an underdeveloped torso, as an idealization of youth. He foresaw continued emphasis on youth and boyishness, attributable to women's undiminished participation in varied activities, the steady march of democracy, and increasing sexual freedom.[7]

The Waist As far back as 3000 B.C., women used corsets in some form to diminish their waist measurements. Accentuation of the waist has taken various forms: cinching, padding above and below, and baring the area, as in modern halter tops and bikinis.

The Shoulders Baring one or both of the shoulders in evening wear and on the beach is considered so commonplace these days that it is hard to imagine the furor caused by the strapless gown of the 1930s. Madge Garland points out that Victorians exposed shoulders "shamelessly" and Edwardians "covered them hypocritically with wisps of chiffon."[8] In recent decades, strapless brassieres, half-slips, and dresses lined with their own slips have made it possible for women to expose as much of their shoulders as they choose.

The Bosom   The ancient Minoans exposed their breasts, as did the Renaissance ladies. In more recent times, most women have called attention to the bosom with padding and deep cleavage rather than outright nudity. When padded bras added inches to the measurements of young women, clinging sweaters and plunging necklines heightened the desired effect. Popular movie actresses posed for publicity photographs that advertised their dimensions and increased the popularity of the high-bosomed look. As the decade of the 1960s drew to a close, the "no-bra" brassiere fashion had many adherents among the young, while some of the more daring wore "see-through" apparel, with or without upper body undergarments.

The Hips   A desire for boyish slimness today has replaced the popularity of prominent hips. Yet even at times when "secretary spread" was viewed as the ultimate disaster, there were efforts to increase apparent hip size. In 1947 Dior reportedly padded the hips of his models to make their waists appear smaller. Balenciaga's full skirts and cinched waists in 1954 achieved the same effect. But eventually the unfitted styles triumphed. Whenever the major trend favors the slim, youthful look, hips have small claim to fashion importance.

The Neckline   Early in the twentieth century, the V neck was a daring innovation; women were still accustomed to collars that rose to the ears. As the years went on, the V went deeper, at one time plunging to the waist. In recent years necklines for daytime wear have shown infinite variety. Scoop necks and sunbacks are worn alongside primly buttoned shirtwaists. Standaway collars are used on coats, while turtleneck dresses and sweaters are featured for both indoor and outdoor apparel.

The Feet and Legs   For thousands of years, fashion kept the feet and legs well hidden; only in the twentieth century did ankles appear. Once exposed, however, women's legs began to steal the fashion scene. Skirts rose, and by the 1920s knees were exposed. Then down came the skirt lengths (but never to the extent of earlier centuries) until the 1960s, when they reversed and moved up to midthigh.

The Figure as a Whole   According to Garland, the fashions of the 1950s and 1960s showed off the entire figure: "The modern girl manages at the same time to bare her shoulders, accentuate her bust, pull in her waist, and show her legs to above the knees. It is a triumph of personal publicity over the taboos of the past and the previous limitations of fashion."[9]

This "triumph of personal publicity" in the late 1960s called attention to feet clad only in sandals or low-heeled shoes, to legs sheathed in textured, fishnet, or decorated hose, and to skirts stopping at mid-thigh. It ignored the waist much of the time but accentuated it in sportswear with bikinis and hip-huggers. Sleeveless dresses, natural-line bras, wide but high cowled collars, drop earrings, and dyed hair dramatically cut and arranged gave the eye much to observe. Areas that were normally covered made their bid for attention, too, with cutouts in dresses and gloves. Unlike previous fashion eras, which favored only certain parts of the body, more recent styles have celebrated the whole body.

Rules of the Game

The game of emphasizing different parts of the feminine anatomy at different times has its rules. The first and fundamental rule is that fashion does not flit. Its attention lights on one area of the body and stays with that area, intensifying concentration upon it until every last possibility for excitement has been exhausted.

Laver explains fashion's anatomical emphasis in terms of the sexuality of the body. "Fashion really began," he says, "with the discovery in the fifteenth century that clothes could be used as a compromise between exhibitionism and modesty."[10] Exposure of any part of the feminine body focuses erotic attention on that part. The aim of fashion thus has been to emphasize various portions of the body in sequence. When one

Fifty years of fashions of skirt length fashions, 1915–1965.

part of the body has been overemphasized, it loses its power to excite, and fashion concentration shifts to another area.

This shift occurs, however, only after fashion has gone as far as it can in emphasizing that one area of the body before changing its focus. Crinolines and hoops reached impossible diameters before skirts subsided in width. Tight lacing grew tighter until health was endangered before the practice was abandoned.

The excesses reached in exposing one part of the body prepare the way for its retreat from the fashion scene. A staleness develops; the overemphasized area becomes sterile, or unable to excite, and a new erogenous zone is found. Thus the excesses of the hoops, crinolines, and bustles of the nineteenth century paved the way for the brief, simple skirts of the twentieth century. The enforced skimpiness of skirts in the World War II period prepared women to enjoy not only Dior's New Look of 1947 but also the bouffant skirts that followed it in the 1950s. The teased and towering hairstyles of the early 1960s prepared the way for the simple, long or closecut styles of the later years of the decade. And the clean, crew-cut look of young men in the 1950s set the stage for the masculine manes and mops that dominated the 1960s. Similarly, the microminis of the 1960s signaled that hemlines in the years immediately following would fall if not to the length of the short-lived maxi then at least to a point somewhere between the two extremes.

Garland has suggested a second rule for this fashion merry-go-round: only certain parts of the body can be exposed at any given time.[11] Recent fashions provide ample illustrations: turtlenecks on sleeveless dresses or sweaters, miniskirted dresses with high necklines and long sleeves, strapless evening gowns that reach the floor.

In emphasizing select parts of the body, and sometimes the figure as a whole, fashion abides by a third rule: the cycle is always forward, never reversible. As Robinson has said, "A fashion can never retreat gradually and in good order. Like a dictator it must always expand its aggressions or collapse. Old fashions never fade away; they die suddenly and arbitrarily."[12] This is as true of the pieces of the fashion game as it is of fashion itself.

Predicting the Movement of Fashion

The tastes and fashion preferences of the public follow certain well-defined channels. Everyone who hopes to make or sell fashion goods at a profit is constantly using whatever means he can to identify these channels and direct his own efforts along the indicated courses.

Fashions move constantly, but at varying individual speeds, toward culmination and inevitably toward decline. Predicting which among current fashions will enjoy pronounced consumer demand in the future requires the forecaster to distinguish what the current fashions are, to estimate how widespread they are, and to determine the phase they have currently reached in their cycle. With information on these three points, the projection of current trends, a prime requisite in successful fashion merchandising, becomes possible.

A fashion trend is the direction in which fashion is moving. If the manufacturer or merchant correctly recognizes that direction, and determines whether it is toward or away from maximum acceptance, then he is able to decide whether to concentrate on the fashion, or to bide his time, or to abandon it.

For example, a recognized fashion may be for sleeveless daytime dresses. At the introductory and rising stages, the retailer will stock and promote a progressively larger proportion of sleeveless designs in his dresses. When it seems to him that his customers are reaching a point of saturation with bared arms, he will begin introducing sleeves into his stock in progressively larger numbers. If he has correctly anticipated the timing of the downturn with respect to customer demand, he will have few of the sleeveless styles on hand when decline in demand occurs. His customers may still be wearing the sleeveless styles they have, but they will not be buying them, at least at regular prices, and the retailer will have abandoned the fashion, foreseeing its rapid descent into obsolescence.

Collecting the Data

The ways in which the merchant determines the strength and direction of fashion trends among

A minidress worn with a maxicoat was one late 1960s answer to the confusion about skirt lengths.

his customers have little to do with intuition or clairvoyance. Good, solid facts about customer acceptance are behind most merchandising decisions, instead of that rather vague talent often called "fashion sense."

In quest of pertinent facts, merchants and manufacturers keep a watchful eye on their own sales records to see not just how many units of a given style they are selling but rather what proportion the sales of an individual style bear to the total sales of similar merchandise. "The customer always decides what and when," advised Alfred H. Daniels, then president of Burdine's in Miami. "Happily her past history and pattern give plenty of clues to the future. . . . Throw out the Ouija board, and buy yourself instead a good five-year book or diary."[13] Today, considering the number of sales many stores try to keep track of, he might have added that time on an electronic computer, or even the computer equipment itself, might be a worthwhile investment.

Observations of what is being generally worn are made to augment what the merchant can learn from his own sales and from what others tell him of their sales experience. Actual counts may be made of women at, say, the opening of the opera, to ascertain who and how many wear a new style. These women are often the elite, the fashion leaders, and what they choose to wear may signify the beginning of a new fashion trend. When pantsuits were new, in the winter of 1966–1967, *Women's Wear Daily* frequently reported how many pantsuits were seen at each of the more elegant New York restaurants.

The fashion merchant's dependence upon observation rather than intuition is by no means new. As far back as 1928, Nystrom pointed out: "Changes in fashions may be checked and their trends determined by the simple process of making successive periodic counts of the same styles, among the same classes of people, comparing the result from one period to another, and taking note of the change."[14]

Fashion trends move faster and in a more complex pattern today than they did in the late 1920s, but counts and estimates, properly made, still constitute an invaluable yardstick for measuring the progress of a fashion. However, enough observations must be made so that there is an adequate base for arriving at conclusions. Two swallows do not a summer make, and two swallowtail coats do not make a trend.

Since fashion is a complex phenomenon involving many elements, fashion observations are most helpful if they are made in terms of each of the various characteristics of the style: silhouette, color, hemline, and so on. Thus, in a given season, successive observations may show bright colors predominating, but brown on the rise and black making a tentative entry upon the scene. A concurrent series of counts might each time show fewer women wearing the jewel neckline and more wearing turtlenecks and ring collars.

In addition, counts and estimates should take into consideration the characteristics of the customers as well as the characteristics of a style. The strength and direction of a trend varies in different age and income groups, in groups with different interests, in groups in different areas. What young suburbanites wear to a club luncheon is not necessarily what urbanites wear to a fashionable restaurant. Successful fashion forecasting requires that the merchant first needs to pinpoint what his particular target group of customers are wearing in order to determine what they are likely to wear tomorrow.

Early in a season, or early in the life of a trend, frequent checks are needed. As the surge of demand develops, its course becomes more obvious, and day-to-day guidance is less urgently needed. When the crest is near, frequent checks again are required, for an error in anticipating the time of the downturn can leave the merchant either with large stocks of unwanted goods after the tide has turned or with insufficient assortments when the demand is still strong.

Modern methods of handling such data are a boon to the fashion merchant. Both automatic and electronic systems speed up the collection of information, increase the amount of data that can be evaluated properly, and make it possible to get reports more quickly. Some stores have systems that enable them to feed each day's sales data into the computer at the end of the day, and have a full report, complete with analyses, comparisons, and projections, ready for the buyer and the merchandise manager the next morning.

The typical merchant does not depend solely upon his own observations, however. He consults sources of information about the buying and use habits of consumers other than his own. In his attempt to predict the course of fashion trends, he looks at both the local picture and the total picture, his own sales experience and that of others, and bases his decisions on both his own judgment and that of others. In fashion forecasting the wise fashion merchant draws information from every available source in his effort to evaluate the data he has gathered.

Interpreting Trends

To interpret the data he has collected and organized, the fashion forecaster, whether he is a merchant, a producer, or a designer, must put his knowledge of fashion and fashion principles to work. He not only examines the figures themselves and the pattern they show, but he also takes into consideration certain factors which, like those mentioned earlier in this chapter, serve to accelerate or retard a fashion cycle among his target group of customers. These factors include current events, the appearance of prophetic styles, sales promotion efforts, and the current canons of taste.

Current Events Items in the news can influence customers and affect their response to fashion. For example, the emergence of new nations in Africa in the 1960s, combined with the publicity then being given the civil-rights movement in this country, awakened an interest among many customer groups in prints with African motifs, in safari jackets, and, among blacks of both sexes, in Afro hairstyles. The publicity given to a popular musical group, the Beatles, as another example, encouraged young men throughout the 1960s to let their hair grow to what was then considered daring lengths, and to comb it forward over their foreheads.

Prophetic Styles Good fashion forecasters keep a sharp watch for what they call *prophetic fashions,* particularly interesting new styles that are in the introductory phase. Taken up enthusiastically by the socially prominent, or by the flamboyant young, they may gather momentum very rapidly. Or they may prove to be nonstarters. Whatever their future course, the behavior of these very new ideas provides some indications of interest to qualified observers. The shorn hair of actress Mia Farrow and the Sassoon haircuts of debutantes and actresses in 1966 presaged a strengthening trend toward neat, close hairstyles for women. And, indeed, a year later gamine cuts were well entrenched as fashion hairstyles.

Sales Promotion Efforts Along with the records of past sales, the fashion forecaster gives thought also to the kind and amount of promotion that helped stimulate interest in prophetic styles, as well as the kind and amount of additional sales promotion he can look forward to. A fiber producer's powerful advertising and publicity efforts may have helped fan a feeble flame of interest in colored hose or bulky sweaters into a discernible glow last year. The forecaster's problem is to estimate how far the trend might have developed on its own, how much momentum remains from last year's push to carry it forward this year, and how much promotional support can be looked for in the future. The promotional effort that the forecaster's own organization plans to expend is only one part of the story; outside efforts, sometimes industry-wide, also must be considered in forecasting fashions.

Canons of Taste In judging the impact of new styles, the forecaster relates them to the currently accepted canons of taste and utility. In an era of excessive thrift, one does not expect disposable paper dresses to be received as eagerly as they were in 1966 and 1967. Nor, in an era of uninhibited exposure of much of the body, would one expect to sell many long johns to the young women. In an era of clear, vibrant color, pastels and misty tones often seem to have few advocates. When pastels have their day, bold colors seem crude and inappropriate.

Fashions that are in accord with the currently "accepted canons of art, custom, modesty, and utility," says Nystrom, "are most easily accepted, go furthest, and last longest."[15]

References

[1]Kroeber, "On the Principles of Order in Civilization as Exemplified by Changes in Fashion," pp. 235–263.
[2]A. B. Young, *Recurring Cycles of Fashion*, p. 92.
[3]Laver, *Taste and Fashion*, p. 52.
[4]Binder, *Muffs and Morals*, pp. 162–164.
[5]Garland, *Fashion*, p. 11.
[6]Laver, *op. cit.*, p. 201.
[7]Flügel, *The Psychology of Clothes*, p. 163.
[8]Garland, op. cit., p. 18.
[9]*Ibid.*, p. 20.
[10]Laver, op. cit., p. 200.
[11]Garland, op. cit., p. 11.
[12]Robinson, "Fashion Theory and Product Design," p. 128.
[13]*Buyer's Manual*, p. 197.
[14]Nystrom, *Fashion Merchandising*, p. 84.
[15]*Ibid.*

Merchandising Vocabulary

Define or briefly explain the following terms:

Fashion cycle
Line-for-line copies
Adaptations
Broken fashion cycle
Long-run fashion

Short-run fashion
Erogenous zones
Fashion trend
Prophetic fashions

Merchandising Review

1. Discuss the findings of Richardson and Kroeber with regard to women's dress silhouettes over a period of 330 years.
2. According to Agnes Brooke Young, what are the three basic skirt silhouettes, in what order do they reoccur in fashion, and how often does each reoccur?
3. Name and discuss the five phases through which a fashion passes in its life cycle.
4. What can cause a broken fashion cycle? What happens when the cycle is resumed?
5. What is the difference between the consumer buying cycle and the consumer use cycle?
6. What are considered to be the ''pieces'' in the apparel fashion game?
7. What three basic rules govern the playing of the fashion game?
8. What are the steps one must take in forecasting fashion?
9. What resources does a fashion merchant have for collecting data from which to forecast fashions?

Merchandising Digest

1. From your examination of currently popular women's apparel styles, which silhouette will next become fashionable? Defend your answer. Why do you think the tubular silhouette remained in fashion so long in the twentieth century?
2. Discuss the various factors that tend to accelerate the forward movement of fashion, indicating at least one reason why each factor has an accelerating effect.
3. Discuss the factors that tend to retard the development of fashion cycles by discouraging the adoption of newly introduced styles. Give at least one reason why each factor exerts a braking influence on fashion.

5

Fashion Leaders and Followers

Earlier chapters explained how styles that become fashions are mirrors of the times in which they flourish. Today even women of modest means can wear clothes of practically the same design as those worn by women of wealth. Increased, more evenly distributed discretionary income now enables most women to purchase goods on the basis of their fashion appeal. Improved technology makes mass production and mass distribution of fashion goods economically possible and highly profitable. Speedier communications, better education, and a thriving middle class encourage women to want and to accept the new more readily than did their grandmothers. Finally, the leisure to enjoy fashion, to become bored with prevailing styles, and to seek the refreshment of new ones today prevails among the majority of women in the United States.

These factors have caused fashion to move at breakneck speed in the second half of the twentieth century. As one watches the quick march of new fashions, a few questions arise:

Who starts fashions? Where do they begin? Who sponsors them? Who influences consumers so that a style gains wide acceptance? The answers involve the designer, the manufacturer, the retailer, and, most important of all, the consumer.

Birth of a Fashion

Neither designers nor manufacturers make a fashion or create fashion change. They simply spread before the public their interpretations of current consumer ideas and attitudes. They influence fashion in one important way, however: they provide consumers with an unending series of new styles in greater variety than they can realistically hope to sell in quantity in any given season, and thus enable the consumer to choose those styles that best express her individual way of life. It has been estimated that at least one-third of the new designs introduced by the fashion industries each season fail to become fashions.

Designers and manufacturers are by no means infallible in the choice of designs they believe will win consumer acceptance. There are times when their interpretations may be more extreme than consumers are willing to accept. At other times they may introduce new designs too early, before the public is quite ready to accept them. For example, one manufacturer of women's sportswear put a powerful national promotion behind extremely short miniskirts in the mid-1960s at a time when only very young women in major cities were wearing them. His efforts were a year or so too early; they earned the company much publicity but little business.

There are also times when manufacturers and their designers make the mistake of thinking that all women will go along with a commonly accepted trend. They fail to allow for pockets of resistance in certain areas of the country. As late as the spring of 1967, for example, when chic women of all ages in cities like New York, Chicago, and San Francisco had taken to wearing skirts well above the knee, some stores in the South complained that they could not sell skirts any shorter than an inch or two above the knee. Moreover, these stores had trouble convincing

A designer has to study many styling features and trends to determine what tomorrow's customer will want.

manufacturers that there was actually a market for skirts extending to the knee.

The Designer's Role

A *designer* creates styles and thereby gives concrete expression to fashion ideas. In the United States, the designer is only rarely a manufacturer or the head of a fashion-producing firm. In Europe, however, the chief designer is generally the head of a fashion house, and the firm bears his name. In the United States, a designer may create new and original styles or may adapt and incorporate into his designs those styling features that have proved successful elsewhere. In Europe, to be known as a designer, one must create strictly original designs.

In this country the division of responsibilities is such that a designer is not usually required to carry his ideas beyond the stage of a careful sketch accompanied by colors and materials in which the design is to be executed. Purchasing, production, promotion, and distribution are done by the manufacturer by whom the designer is employed, or to whom the designer, if operating on a free-lance basis, sells his sketches. A manu-

facturing firm may have one or many designers in its employ or may simply buy designs from free-lancers. A designer may be the single creative person in a manufacturing firm or one of a large creative staff.

Occasionally a designer and producer maintain such excellent rapport that they work together for many years; more often, however, American designers tend to transfer frequently from one firm to another. Manufacturers hire, fire, or cherish designers according to how well each understands the other, and how well sales go.

Insight and Intuition A designer grasps a fashion idea and embodies it in new styles. Even the most creative designers, however, are frank to disclaim any power to force acceptance of their styles. Few have said so more effectively than did Paul Poiret, one of the twentieth century's great Parisian couturiers, who once told an American audience:

> I know you think me a king of fashion. . . .
> It is a reception which cannot but flatter me
> and of which I cannot complain. All the
> same, I must undeceive you with regard to

the powers of a king of fashion. We are not capricious despots such as wake up one fine day, decide upon a change in habits, abolish a neckline, or puff out a sleeve. We are neither arbiters nor dictators. Rather we are to be thought of as the blindly obedient servants of woman, who for her part is always enamoured of change and athirst for novelty. It is our role, and our duty, to be on the watch for the moment at which she becomes bored with what she is wearing, that we may suggest at the right instant something else which will meet her taste and needs. It is therefore with a pair of antennae and not a rod of iron that I come before you, and not as a master that I speak, but as a slave . . . who must divine your innermost thoughts.[1]

Insight and intuition, then, play a large part in a designer's success. He must constantly produce novelty and variety to refresh the tastes of consumers. When one fashion is reaching that excess that marks its approaching demise, the designer must have new candidates ready and waiting for the public's favor.

On occasion a style or design takes such firm hold on the consumer's affections that it continues to be popular for many seasons. Designers then give it apparent freshness each season by using new details or new materials. Thus, in 1966 and 1967, when the miniskirt and the tubular silhouette were so widely accepted as to have become almost a uniform, designers added variety and a new look to existing fashions through the use of paper as a dress material or by using large amounts of such trimmings as beads, braid, sequins, or feathers.

Sources of Design Inspiration Even while a fashion is at its height, the restless minds of creative designers are seeking inspiration for new fashions to succeed it. For example, when the miniskirt was at its peak of popularity, several designers turned to the past for new styling ideas. Many, inspired by the motion picture *Doctor Zhivago,* adapted styles of Czarist Russia: ankle-length or midcalf skirts, flaring out from fairly well-defined waists, and trimmed with fur at neck, hem, and cuff. Even though above-the-knee

skirts continued to dominate the fashion scene, maxi and midi lengths began to have limited acceptance, particularly among younger customers. The maxi showed elements of being a fad, but the midi was the forerunner of what would fascinate designers in the next few years and what fashion leaders were going to find new and exciting.

Other designers found inspiration in far places or in such events as the Olympic Games, world fairs, and the widespread dissemination of the works of famous artists. Adele Simpson's introduction of African safari jackets exemplified such sources of inspiration, and so did Yves St. Laurent's burst of enthusiasm for Mondrian-like effects at a time when art circles were showing tremendous interest in Mondrian's work. Both influences were felt in the mid-1960s while the short, straight silhouette was at the height of its popularity; both were concerned with external details; neither was an attempt to argue with the public about the matter of silhouette or skirt length.

Adele Simpson's ideas were triggered by a trip to Africa and gained prompt acceptance because the emerging nations of that continent were front-page news then. African ideas struck a responsive chord in the public's imagination. Similarly, St. Laurent's outlined blocks of color could have been acceptable only to a public already receptive to strong colors and sharp lines.

A designer's reactions to what he sees and feels do not, in themselves, launch a new trend. They simply act as the catalyst that helps him crystallize in new styles the very ideas that the public itself is trying to clarify and express.

Compromise Styling Designers are aware that, as Robinson says, "No single style or design, no matter how brilliantly it is conceived, can claim any independent fashion significance at all, nor can it possess more than a fugitive lease on life."[2] Consumers constantly compare new designs with the old ones they seek to replace.

Designers and manufacturers also know that when a fashion has reached its extreme, there is a swift return to a form of compromise in styling. Richardson and Kroeber documented this tendency in their observations of women's fashions from 1605 to 1936. They noted that a compromise form of styling tended to exist between extremes in styles. They identified this compromise as a fashion with skirts both full and long, with a moderately constricted waist near the point where nature meant it to be, and with an ample decolletage.

Two good examples of compromise styling may be found in recent fashion history. Each followed a period of short, straight lines. Each accented the natural waistline, not by constricting it but by having a full skirt flaring from the waist to midcalf length. The first of these was Dior's New Look in 1947, which so dramatically routed the narrow, short skirts of World War II. The second was the fuller skirt that ended at midcalf, known as the midi, that began gradually making a place for itself in 1967. In *Harper's Bazaar* of September, 1967, three midi styles were shown: a Chester Weinberg skirt, an Oscar de la Renta coat, and an Antonelli coatdress. There were only three, among scores of illustrations, but they were harbingers, or prophetic styles. By 1968, the harsh straight lines that had previously held sway were yielding to curves; waistlines were beginning to be defined; hemlines were likely to be anywhere from midthigh to midcalf. By the spring of 1970, the midi had demonstrated enough fashion importance to be well represented in, if not dominate, the collections of the most trend-setting designers throughout the fashion world.

The Manufacturer's Role

Manufacturers would agree with Robinson that "every market into which the consumer's fashion sense has insinuated itself is, by that very token, subject to [the] common, compelling need for unceasing change in the styling of its goods."[3]

Even in such prosaic items as paper napkins, the need for change has produced rainbows of pastels on grocery shelves, augmented by brilliant deep shades and whites with dainty prints. Similarly, in basics such as bedsheets or even in

Dr. Zhivago, *world travel, and safari attire all inspired new styles during the 1960s.*

babies' panties and receiving blankets, the once traditional white has yielded to a variety of colors, stripes, and prints. There is scarcely an industry serving the consumer today in which the manufacturer's success does not depend in part upon his ability to attune his styling to fashion demand.

In the field of women's apparel, manufacturers are historically committed to producing several new lines a year. A *line* is an assortment of new designs, some actually new in every sense of the word and others merely adaptations of currently popular styles. Hopefully, a few of the numbers in a given line will prove "hot," so precisely in step with demand that their sales will be profitably large.

Like the designer, the manufacturer does not direct the course of fashion. He follows it. He does affect the speed with which fashions develop, however, according to his skill in selecting from the styles suggested by his designers those he will produce. If he is an expert in this field, his judgment about what to produce and what to reject will coincide fairly closely with what consumers are likely to accept or reject. Such a producer gives impetus to fashion change by the promptness with which he offers new styles that have the potential to win consumer acceptance. He can also help existing fashions to run their full course by continuing to produce styles that express these fashions as long as there is consumer interest in them.

On the other hand, producers who are less adept at anticipating customer demand can hold back the course of fashion by failing to recognize and present acceptable new styles promptly. Producers can also blunt the edge of the customer's fashion appetite by continuing to produce styles which no longer interest her. Conversely, they can cut off the life of a continuing fashion by ignoring the still active demand for it.

Occasionally a producer's styles may be too advanced for the fashion tastes of his customers. Such a producer neither accelerates nor retards fashion; his goods simply do not get wide distribution and have little or no impact upon the public.

For the most part, the fashion industries are made up of manufacturers whose ability to anticipate the public's response to styles is excellent. Those who do badly in this respect, even for a single season, usually reap small sales and large losses—and unless they are unusually well financed, find themselves out of business. In the fashion business, the survival of the fittest means the survival of those who give the most able assistance in the birth and growth of the fashions that customers want.

The Retailer's Role

Retailers are in much the same position as producers. They do not create fashion, but they can encourage or retard its progress by the degree of accuracy with which they gauge their customers' interests and preferences. A retailer's function is to anticipate the demands of his customers and to seek out in the market those styles that are most likely to win acceptance among his clientele.

Occasionally, retailers are so intuitive or creative that they are a step ahead of their suppliers in anticipating the styles their customers will accept. Such retailers accelerate the introduction and progress of new fashions by inducing manufacturers to prepare styles that answer the latent demand the retailers sense.

Normally, however, the retailer simply selects from what is offered by the producers. If he does a good job, he picks what his customers want and has it in his store when his customers are ready to buy it. On the other hand, he can hold back a good incoming fashion by failing to stock styles that his customers would buy if given the opportunity. Conversely, he can make the mistake of exposing new styles prematurely—that is, before his customers are ready to accept them. No amount of retail effort can make customers buy styles in which they have lost interest or in which they have not yet developed interest, and stocking such merchandise simply means losses to the retailer.

The more accurately the retailer understands his customers' fashion preferences, and the more accurately he reflects that understanding in the assortments he purchases, stocks, shows, and promotes, the more successful his operation and the more important his fashion role within his community.

Theories of Fashion Adoption

Fashions are accepted by the few before they are accepted by the many. Isolating and identifying those few, and keeping track of their preferences, is an important step in anticipating which styles are most likely to succeed as fashions and how widely and by whom each will be accepted.

Three theories have been advanced to explain the "social contagion" of fashion adoption. These are the "trickle-down" theory, the "trickle-across" or mass-market theory, and the "bottom-up" theory. Each attempts to explain the course a fashion travels or is likely to travel, and each has its own claim to validity in reference to particular fashions or social environments.

Trickle-Down Theory

The oldest and most widely held of the three theories of fashion adoption is the trickle-down theory, which maintains that in order to win a fashion place, a style must first be adopted by people at the top of the social pyramid, after which it gradually wins acceptance at progressively lower social levels. By the time the lowest levels have embraced it, the fashion is no longer new or wanted by those on the heights. According to this theory, a style's acceptance by the masses automatically disqualifies it as a fashion among the elite.

Social Hierarchy The trickle-down theory assumes a social hierarchy in which the lower classes seek identification with the ranks above them, while those at the pinnacle seek disassociation from their social inferiors. The theory suggests that fashions are accepted by the lower classes only if, and after, they are accepted by the upper classes, and that the upper classes will reject a fashion once it has trickled down below their own social level.

Early economists, such as Roe in 1834 and Foley and Veblen at the turn of the century, were among the first to observe this type of social behavior and its effect upon fashion. In 1903 a French sociologist, Gabriel Tarde, compared the spread of fashion to a social water tower from which a continuous fall of imitation could descend.[4] The German sociologist Georg Simmel, one of the first of his discipline to give serious study to fashion, wrote in 1904:

> Social forms, apparel, aesthetic judgment, the whole style of human expression, are constantly being transformed by fashion in [a way that] . . . affects only the upper classes. Just as soon as the lower classes begin to copy their styles, thereby crossing the line of demarcation the upper classes have drawn and destroying their coherence, the upper classes turn away from this style and adopt a new one. . . . The same process is at work as between the different sets within the upper classes, although it is not always visible here.[5]

Acceptability of the Theory The trickle-down theory is still widely held. Among its proponents are such authorities as Barber, Robinson, Laver, Sapir, and Flügel. Flügel, in fact, suggests that sumptuary laws owe their origin to the reluctance of the higher classes to abandon the sartorial distinctiveness that to them represents an indication of superiority.[6]

To some extent, the economic facts of life support the theory that fashion trickles down from one social stratum to another. To design, produce, and sell new styles, a business must operate on profit margins wide enough to cover the costs of experimentation. Originality in dress remains a luxury that only women with ample funds can afford. Some fashions, therefore, appear first on the socially elite. If the style becomes popular, the manufacturers mass-produce it and many customers can afford copies—and the elite seeks something that is newer.

Flaws in the Theory In recent years, largely because of increasing democratization of both life and fashion, several cracks have appeared in the structure of this theory. The trickle-down theory makes most sense when a society resembles a pyramid, with leaders, people of wealth and position, at the apex and followers at successive widening levels below. The social structure today, however, is more like a group of rolling hills than it is like a pyramid. There are many groups, many elites, and many directions other than straight down in which fashion can and does travel.

This changed pattern of fashion acceptance is also a result of the speed with which fashion news now travels, so that all levels are right up to date on fashion innovations. Moreover, accelerated mass production and mass distribution of fashion goods have broadened acceptance of styles by making them available more cheaply and more quickly than ever before.

For these reasons, mass producers today are less likely to wait cautiously for approval from the wealthy. As soon as significant signs of an interesting new style appear, they are ready to offer adaptations or even copies to the public.

Trickle-Across Theory

The trickle-across theory, one of the newer explanations for style adoption, holds that fashions move horizontally within groups on similar social levels rather than vertically from one level to another. Chief exponent of this theory is Dr. Charles W. King, whose research on the adoption of millinery fashions was presented at the 1963 and 1964 conferences of the American Marketing Association.

King points out that the modern social environment, including mass communication and the combined strategies of manufacturers and retailers, impedes most vertical flow. He notes that there is almost no lag between the adoption of a fashion by one social level or another, citing the way Paris fashions are now bought and copied for mass distribution sometimes even before they have been exposed to the elite markets. Trade buyers at the couturier openings ship the models they have purchased home by air and get copies into retail stores often before the custom client, whose garments are made up for her by hand by the same couturiers, has had a chance to wear her new clothes.

The incidence of this horizontal flow also has been observed by some modern supporters of the trickle-down theory. Robinson, for example, recognizes horizontal movement within a particular social stratum when he says that any given group or cluster of groups forming a class takes its cues from those contiguous with it. He claims fashions therefore radiate from a center.[7]

Support for the Theory   King outlines four basic arguments in support of his trickle-across or mass-market theory of fashion adoption:

▫ The industry's manufacturing and merchandising strategies almost guarantee simultaneous adoption of fashions by consumers across socioeconomic groups.

▫ Theoretically, consumers have the freedom to select from a wide range of contemporary and classic styles each season.

▫ Innovators and influential leaders direct the adoption of fashions within each social stratum.

▫ The transmission of information and influence travels across, or horizontally, within social strata, rather than vertically from one level to another.[8]

King defines a fashion *innovator* as a person who is quicker than her associates to try out a new fashion. A fashion *influential* is a person whose advice is sought by her associates; her adoption of a fashion gives it prestige among the group. The two roles may or may not be played by the same individual within a specific group.

Implications for Merchandising   The theory of horizontal fashion movement has great significance for merchandising. It points out the fallacy of assuming that there is but one fashion public, whose tastes are guided only by those on the higher rungs of the social ladder. This hypothesis recognizes that what the wealthy, distinguished woman is wearing today is not necessarily what the suburban wife, college student, or office worker will wear tomorrow or will wait until tomorrow to accept. It admits that there are separate markets in fashion goods as in any other type of merchandise.

The retailer who applies the trickle-across theory will watch his own customers closely rather than be guided solely by what more exclusive stores in his city and elsewhere may be selling. He will seek to identify the groups into which his own customers can be divided in terms of income, age, education, or stage of life. Among his customers, he will look for the innovators and their style choices as well as for the influentials and their selections. What these types wear usually gains widespread acceptance within the group.

The news that socially prominent women are wearing pantsuits in exclusive New York restaurants will have less significance for such a retailer in a small midwestern city than the observation that the leader of the country club set in his own community is abandoning bright colors for black on formal occasions. If the latter is a fashion influential in the community, her dress is the more important weathervane for him.

Industry Practice King draws a distinction between the spread of a fashion within the industry itself and its adoption by consumers. A vertical flow definitely operates within the industry, he concedes: "Exclusive and famous designers are watched closely and emulated by lesser designers. Major manufacturers are studied and copied by smaller and less expert competitors. Design piracy is a well-established competitive strategy."[9] And, as any reader of *Women's Wear Daily* can testify, there is no hotter news in the industry than information about what the top designers and the top producers are showing.

King points out, moreover, that the innovation process in the industry represents a "great filtering system." From an almost infinite number of possibilities, manufacturers select a finite number of styles. From these, trade buyers select a smaller sampling. Finally, consumers adopt a sampling of retail selections and endorse them as accepted fashions.

This process, King maintains, is quite different from the consumer reaction outlined by Simmel and other exponents of the trickle-down theory. The difference lies in the absence of that element once known as "aping one's betters." Today the mass market does not await the approval of the class market before it adopts a fashion as its own.

Bottom-Up Theory

The third theory to explain the process of fashion adoption is relatively new. The bottom-up theory of fashion dissemination holds that the young, especially those of low-income families, are freer than any other social group to adopt new styles because they have no tradition or social position

to hold them back. Similarly, the young from very rich families can take up new styles because their social position is so secure that it is not easily shaken by unusual dress. From below and above, then, a new fashion can close in on the middle class.

The bottom-up theory is set forth in a *Study of Young People,* issued in 1966 by Doyle Dane Bernbach, the New York advertising agency, and is based on research conducted by Dr. Charles W. Slack.

As long as a style remains "encapsulated within a single class," according to the report, it has little universality. As soon as it cuts across class boundaries, "it forms a generalization which the middle class cannot resist." When both lower and upper classes adopt a new fashion, whether it is a lipstick color, a dance, a hairstyle, or a style of dress, the middle class is surrounded by a pincer-like movement and cannot escape.

In the 1960s, the fashion of beads for both men and women started at the bottom, was picked up by upper classes, and then infiltrated the middle classes. The overalls and denim jackets of the Freedom Riders, who were either members or representatives of the lower class, moved from the lower to the upper strata of the social structure. Fashions like long, straight hair for young women, heavy eye makeup, miniskirts, and a variety of apparel styles commonly associated with such economically deprived groups as the American Indian follow the same pattern: a bottom-class start, an upper-class adoption, and then a closing in on the middle class. Beatniks and debutantes embraced these fashions first; office girls, high school girls, and young matrons followed.

Gap-Bridgers During the process of development, a style's acceptance is given such impetus by certain individuals who adopt it that it sometimes seems as if they had originated it. The Doyle Dane Bernbach study calls these individuals "gap-bridgers," because they provide a link between the upper and lower classes, appearing class-free to the middle class. Gap-bridgers are often entertainment stars or other celebrities.

The new fashions encouraged by the gap-bridgers are often hybrids, according to this re-

port, because they combine two or more existing elements that have not been associated before, as the Beatles combined African rhythms and English folk music in their songs.

The gap-bridger spans the gulf between himself and his public by providing a personality with which a wide range of people can readily associate. The report uses Superman, the comic-strip hero, as an example of an idol, with Clark Kent, the mild-mannered reporter, who is Superman's everyday self, as the link with the ordinary man. Superman is the man one yearns to be, while Kent is the man with whom the audience can easily identify. In the same way, the admirer can only dream of being a Beatle, but the gap between him and his idol narrows when he wears the same style of shirt or adopts the same hairstyle as one of the Beatles.

As an example of a fashion now in the process of being changed in accordance with this theory, the Doyle Dane Bernbach report mentions long hair for males. Aside from each generation's desire to look different from its forebears, other factors that the report emphasizes are that:

▫ Long hair was a distinctive style that has been out of fashion for many years but was popular in the past.

▫ The fashion fit the pincer-movement model, having both lower-class and upper-class strength.

▫ Celebrities adopted it, thus bridging the gap.

▫ The fashion was in tune with the general mood of romanticism, a revival that flourished in the 1960s.

Fashion Leaders and Fashion Followers

Each of the three theories of fashion adoption recognizes the existence of leaders and followers in fashion acceptance. The trickle-down theory casts persons of social, political, and economic eminence in the role of leaders. The trickle-across theory recognizes individuals whose personal

The garb of the cyclist, the cowboy, and the "teddy boy" were widely adopted by men of all social levels in the late 1960s.

prestige makes them leaders within their own circles, whether or not they are known elsewhere. The bottom-up theory points to a need for a person who is acceptable as a model to the large middle class to bridge the gaps between that class and the lower-class and upper-class innovators.

Fashion Leaders

The theories of fashion adoption stress that the fashion leader is not the creator of the fashion, nor does merely wearing the fashion make a person a fashion leader. As Quentin Bell explains: "The leader of fashion does not come into existence until the fashion is itself created . . . a king or person of great eminence may indeed lead the fashion, but he leads only in the general direction which it has already adopted."[10] In effect, if a parade is forming, a fashion leader may head it and even quicken its pace. He cannot, however, simply by marching down the street, conjure up a procession, nor can he, by snapping his fingers, reverse an existing procession.

Innovators and Influentials Famous people are not necessarily fashion leaders, even if they do influence an individual style. Their influence, in such cases, usually affects only one striking style, one attribute, one set of circumstances. The true fashion leader is a person constantly seeking distinction and therefore likely to launch a succession of fashions rather than just one. A person like Beau Brummel, who made a career of dressing fashionably, or the Duchess of Windsor, whose wardrobe has been front-page fashion news for decades, influences fashion on a much broader scale.

What makes a person a fashion leader? Flügel explains: "Inasmuch as we are artistically minded and dare to assert our own individuality by being different, we are leaders of fashion."[11] King, however, makes it clear that more than just daring to be different is required. In his analysis, a person eager for the new is merely an innovator or early buyer. To be a leader, one must be influential, sought after for advice within a coterie. The influential person, says King, sets the appropriate dress for a specific occasion in her particular circle. Within that circle, an innovator pre-sents current offerings and is the earliest visual communicator of a new style.[12]

Society Leaders Leaders of whatever group is considered society, from old names to new money, are prime candidates for positions of fashion leadership. The glamour and publicity that surround them cause the ordinary citizen to notice what they wear, or even daydream that some of their luster will rub off on her if she copies their dress.

Royalty in the past has played a major role in introducing and encouraging new fashions. Among the eighteenth- and nineteenth-century royal families of Europe, Marie Antoinette and Empress Eugénie were undoubtedly the outstanding fashion leaders. As democracies replaced monarchies, members of the wealthy and internationally known sets stepped into the spotlight and thus into fashion leadership. Lists of best-dressed women today rarely include queens or princesses; instead, the names are those of wives and daughters of prominent industrialists and political figures, with occasionally a stage, screen, or television personality.

Whenever such women attend a ball, a dinner party, or even a quiet lunch at a smart restaurant, the press reports details of what they wear. So far as fashion is concerned, these women are not just in the news; they *are* the news. Should they go skiing and buy sweaters in a local shop, the purchase is publicized. When they view designers' collections, newspapers announce their selections, if the information can possibly be extracted from those concerned.

Consciously or subconsciously, the public is influenced by what these society leaders wear. If in no other way, the average woman is affected because so many manufacturers and retailers of fashion take their cue from these elite. Right or wrong, people in the fashion business count on the fashion sense of these leaders. They also rely on the exposure given society leaders' clothes in news media to encourage women of ordinary means to adopt similar styles.

People in the News It is not always necessary for people to be socially prominent or wealthy to influence fashion. Fashion is affected by people

whose names appear on the front pages of newspapers, whether or not they appear on the society pages as well.

Stars of stage and screen, by their great exposure to the public, have also influenced fashion but to a greater extent in earlier days. Greta Garbo and Marlene Dietrich, in the 1930s, stimulated the then daring new fashion for slacks. In the 1960s, actresses Marilyn Monroe and Jayne Mansfield encouraged styles that featured a large bosom and a plunging neckline.

An innovator, as previously explained, may be an influential as well. Movie stars at one time were both. In the days before television, motion pictures were the one wide-reaching visual medium of entertainment. What the stars wore, how they combed their hair, how they walked and talked, even the furniture on the sets staged for their acting, became models that were widely copied by the general public. Present-day movie actresses and television figures aspiring to stardom try, through uniqueness of feature, dress, and manner, to increase their impact on the public. Once at the pinnacle, they are widely copied. But, like fashion itself, a star seldom rules alone or for long. The next generation of starlets is already on its way, pushing hard to reach the top.

Over the past few decades, movie stars at various times have popularized certain styles associated with them, such as Clara Bow's pouting lips, Greta Garbo's slouch hat, and Veronica Lake's habit of letting her hair fall over one eye. Each actress, thanks to her personal style and elaborate publicity buildup, gave exposure to a new fashion, thus being an innovator, and inspired other women to follow, thus being an influential leader.

Athletes from time to time have had a powerful impact on fashion. In the 1920s American tennis star Helen Wills sported a visored sunshade, and the French champion of the courts, Suzanne Lenglen, wore a free-swinging pleated skirt. Although each simply dressed in what was most comfortable for her, American women, after watching the international matches, promptly made their apparel the fashion.

Hair styles made popular by Irene Castle, Veronica Lake, Mamie Eisenhower, Jacqueline Kennedy, Joan Baez, and Miriam Makeba.

In the same manner, television personality Johnny Carson's early adoption of the turtleneck in place of formal shirt and tie gave that style wide exposure and considerable impetus. Joan Baez, folk singer and civil-rights crusader, in frequent live and television appearances, prompted many young women to copy her long, straight, and free-swinging hairstyle.

An example of how the clothes worn by women in the public eye influence those later purchased by less well-known women was provided early in the 1960s when three women, each prominent in a different field, were photographed about the same time, all in full-length leopard coats. They were Queen Elizabeth II of England, Mrs. John F. Kennedy, and actress Elizabeth Taylor. Immediately a fashion was firmly launched. With simultaneous sponsorship in such varied groups, spotted furs caught on and spread rapidly. Those who could afford leopard coats bought them; others bought fabric dyed to resemble leopard. Spotted-fur accessories and trims were much in evidence. Even fabrics for garments completely unrelated to outerwear took on a leopard look; lingerie, nightwear, neckwear, and home furnishings also were sold in fabrics printed with leopard spots.

An interesting reversal of the spotted-fur fashion took place in the late 1960s, when a conservation movement, aimed at protecting various animal species in danger of extinction, was backed by an increasingly large group of socially prominent women. These women pledged neither to buy nor to wear any garments made of the skins of the threatened animals—which included at least one species of leopard. Despite the considerable publicity given this conservation movement, spotted furs and fabrics printed to resemble spotted furs continued in popularity. In fact, interest remained so high that shoes printed to resemble spotted furs were available in some lines for spring, 1970.

History provides many examples of fashions associated with prominent individuals, even though these individuals were not otherwise considered fashion leaders. Hungarian patriot Louis Kossuth's visit to America in 1851 is said to have resulted in men's adoption of velour hats, then the style worn by the Hungarian nationalists

of the day. Nearly a century later, General Dwight D. Eisenhower, commanding the Allied forces in Europe during World War II, adopted the short jacket that has been known ever since as the Eisenhower jacket.

A person's prominence, however, is not in itself enough to launch a fashion. The fashion itself must be acceptable, in addition to its association with a distinguished name. For example, General Douglas MacArthur was as prominent a World War II figure as General Eisenhower, yet his sartorial trademark, the way he draped his uniform hat, never resulted in a MacArthur fashion.

Many a fashion in dress or hairstyle is so closely associated with a famous person that the style and the individual remain indelibly linked in the public's mind for decades. Examples include President John F. Kennedy's tousled hairstyle (older generations might connect it with the famous photographs of Charles A. Lindbergh after he had made the first solo nonstop flight across the Atlantic); Coco Chanel's fondness for pearls and multiple chains of beads; Shirley Temple's curls. And although a certain motion picture comedy actor has not played the part of a little tramp for many years, the silly mustache he wore in that familiar role continues to be known universally as a Charlie Chaplin mustache.

Fashion Followers

While some women relish the excitement and risk of fashion leadership, others prefer to be followers. Followers are in the majority within any group or cluster of groups. Without leaders, fashion might stagnate, since there would be no one to effect change. But without followers the fashion industry certainly would collapse.

Mass production and distribution can be profitable only when merchandise is accepted by many consumers. By observing fashion leaders, manufacturers and retailers can predict fairly well what customers' preferences will be in the future. This element of predictability in fashion demand has helped make possible the vast ready-to-wear business in this country. It is also encouraging the trend toward production of ready-to-wear in Paris and other foreign fashion centers.

Fashion leaders may be stimulating and exciting customers for the fashion industries to serve, but fashion followers are the bread and butter of these industries. Almost 90 percent of the dresses produced for ready-to-wear in the United States each year are made to retail at under $25 each. At that price level, there is little room for fashion experimentation. These dresses, and some in higher-priced lines, are for the followers rather than the innovators.

Reasons for Following Fashion Theories as to why women follow rather than lead in fashion are plentiful. Among the explanations are feelings of inferiority, admiration of others, lack of interest, and ambivalence about the new.

Inferiority. Flügel writes, "Inasmuch as we feel our own inferiority and the need for conformity to the standards set by others, we are followers of fashion."[13] For example, high school boys and girls are at a notably insecure stage of life and therefore are more susceptible than any other age group to the appeal of fads. A woman about to face a difficult interview or attend her first meeting with a new group carefully selects new clothes and reveals her insecurity by asking anxiously, "How do I look?" Often an inner feeling of inadequacy can be hidden by wearing a style that others have already proved to be appropriate and acceptable.

Admiration. Flügel also maintains that it is a fundamental human trait to imitate those who are admired or envied, and that the natural and symbolic way to do this is to copy their clothes. An outstanding illustration of his theory was provided in recent years by Mrs. John F. Kennedy. When her husband became President, her clothes and hairstyles were copied instantly among many different groups throughout this country. On a much smaller stage, the young girl who copies the hairstyle of her older sister or favorite aunt demonstrates the same principle; so do college students who model their appearance after that of campus notables.

Lack of Interest. Sapir suggests that many people are insensitive to fashion and follow it only because "they realize that not to fall in with it would be to declare themselves members of a past generation, or dull people who cannot keep up

with their neighbors."[14] Their response to fashion, he says, is a sullen surrender, not by any means an eager following of the Pied Piper.

Ambivalence. Another theory holds that many people are ambivalent in their attitude toward the new; they both want it and fear it. For most women, it is easier to choose that which is already familiar. Such individuals need time and the pioneering efforts of the innovators and influentials among them before they are ready to accept a new fashion.

Varying Rates of Response Individuals vary in the speed with which they respond to a new idea, especially when fashion change is radical and dramatic. Shortly after the introduction of the "New Look" of 1947, Cobliner observed the stages through which Hunter College students passed before accepting the new fashion, and reported his findings in the *Journal of Social Psychology.* First came flat rejection, then admiration and even envy of those who had adopted the style. Finally those who had resisted began to rationalize the style as being more feminine and luxurious. Once having accepted the new style, these girls experienced feelings of "belonging," of security, and of added glamour.[15]

Some fashion followers apparently just need time to adjust to new ideas. Merchants exploit this point when they buy a few "window pieces" of styles too advanced for their own clientele, then expose these new styles in windows and fashion shows and allow customers time to get used to them.

Such conflict was observed in the fashion cycle of women's pantsuits during the 1960s. Norman Norell had introduced a culotte suit in his 1960 collection and a suit with long pants in 1964. Dior had shown a pants-skirt in 1962. Yet, as late as July, 1964, *Women's Wear Daily* reported reservations about pants among members of the Paris fashion industry. A Dior spokesman was quoted as saying that pants were for around the house but not for every day. A St. Laurent spokesman said, "Absolutely not here. Pants aren't anything great." Yet by 1966, pantsuits were featured in the *New York Times* in an article appropriately titled, "Now Everyone Wears the Pants," and by 1968, Eugenia Sheppard, in her syndicated column, was writing, "Anything but pantsuits is square." By that time there were pants for daytime, evening, or at-home wear, and for all shapes and ages. Shock, resistance, and reservations had finally given way to enthusiastic acceptance.

Fashion as an Expression of Individuality

A remarkable feature of today's mass-produced fashions is that, although styles in dresses, coats, handbags, shoes, and other garments may be made by the hundreds or thousands, one rarely sees two women dressed exactly alike. Dress may meet identical dress and hat may meet identical hat on occasion, but the same apparel will be worn with distinctive touches imparted by each wearer. Within the framework of fashion conformity, each person remains individual. Social scientists see in this situation a paradox, an endless conflict between the desire to conform and the desire to remain apart.

Even before the world reached its present impersonal age of numbers—social security, ZIP Code, bank account, automobile registration, time clock, and the like—sociologists and psychologists, as well as fashion authorities, had witnessed the individual's refusal to merge entirely into the mass. Purchasers of fashion apparel in the United States usually go along with general fashion styles rather than risk seeming out of step with the times. However, they continue to assert their individuality in such touches as the way they combine colors and textures, the way they wear costume jewelry, and the way they wear their hair and makeup.

In the late 1960s, one might have seen several miniskirted girls all wearing versions of the same dress, yet each quite individual in appearance. One might wear textured hose, multicolored shoes, and a hat of the same fabric as the dress. The next might wear plain hose, colorful tall boots, and a brimmed hat. Another might have a chain belt low on the hips and be wearing open sandals. Each would have declared herself young and modern by her choice of dress. Each would have asserted her uniqueness by the distinguishing touches added to her costume.

Fashion editor Jessica Daves sums up the miracle of modern ready-to-wear fashion by saying that it offers "the possibility for some women to create a design for themselves . . . to choose the color and shape in clothes that will present them as they would like to see themselves."[16]

The same possibility for carving individuality out of conformity is present today in men's fashions. In the late 1960s, shirts with turtlenecks were widely worn, but they were given individuality by choice of color, texture, and accessories. Some men wore medallions; others had beads; some left the garment unadorned. Similarly, although the fashion for fuller and longer hair was adopted quite generally among young men, each interpreted the fashion to suit his own personality: bushy sideburns, stringy goatee, back hair below the collar, complete "bird-nest" freedom from comb or scissors, or just a modest bang combed forward over the forehead.

The element of nonconformity was seen also in fads among the young, who varied their wardrobes of current fashions with attention-getting styles from flea markets and attics: ancient military uniforms, Victorian dresses, American Indian fringed leather jackets, and bulky raccoon coats, for instance. It was as if, by donning clothes completely out of tune with the times, the individual asserted himself and acquired distinction from others of his own generation for the moment. However, as others joined this protest, the line between individuality and conformity faded.

The Paradox of Conformity and Individuality

For decades, experts have sought to explain why people seek both conformity and individuality in fashion. Simmel suggests that two opposing social tendencies are at war: the need for union and the need for isolation. The individual, he reasons, derives satisfaction from knowing that the way in which he expresses a fashion represents something special. At the same time, he gains support from seeing that others favor the same style.[17]

Flügel interprets the paradox in terms of a person's feelings of superiority and inferiority. The individual wants to be like his fellows "insofar as he regards them as superior, but unlike them, in the sense of being more 'fashionable' insofar as he thinks they are below him."[18]

Sapir ties the conflict to a revolt against custom and a desire to break away from slavish acceptance of fashion. Slight changes from the established form of dress and behavior "seem for the moment to give victory to the individual, while the fact that one's fellows revolt in the same direction gives one a feeling of adventurous safety."[19] He also ties the assertion of individuality to the need to affirm oneself in a functionally powerful society in which the individual has ceased to be a measure of the society itself.

An illustration is the off-duty dress of people required to wear uniforms of one kind or another during working hours. A dramatic example was provided by the returning veterans of World War II. On resumption of civilian life they demanded more colorful, less formal, and more individual clothes than they had ever worn before. White-collar workers wore pink or purple shirts; even colored undershirts had a brief day of popularity in the reaction against regimentation.

A similar instance is provided by the shift dress of the 1960s. For several years, practically every dress in every woman's wardrobe was a sheath; yet the sheath never became a monotonous uniform. Some were shiny, sequined, and cut low at the neck for evening parties; some were in brilliant colors; some had industrial zippers down the front or chain belts low on the hip. Women added their own individual touches in the way they accessorized their dresses: with short or long necklaces, with matching sweaters, coats, and jackets, with shoe styles that got flatter as the skirts grew shorter, or with demure or wildly fanciful earrings. Some shifts were printed in fur patterns, some were actually made out of fur; some added shock value with cutouts in unexpected areas. Some bagged at the waistline and tapered at the hemline; some had the merest hint of a waist indentation and the faintest of flares at the hem. All were shifts, yet each had touches of individuality provided by the designer, the wearer, or both.

Retailers know that although some women like to lead and some like to follow in fashion, all women buy fashion to look pretty and glamorous, to be "in," or to belong. To belong, they follow fashion; to be glamorous, they find ways to individualize it.

Fashion and Self-Expression

In the late 1960s, great stress was placed on fashion individuality. The period was one of affluence, in which the fastest-growing segment of the feminine population in the United States was from 16 or 18 to 30 years of age, the years in which most women could indulge in fashion adventure.

In the slang of the time, there was a great emphasis upon "doing your own thing," or expressing one's personality, rejecting authority, and refusing to be cast into a mold. Instead of adopting any one look, a young woman sought to create her own effect through various components. If the combination of harem pants and long woolen coat or embroidered velvet blouse and black culottes represented the wearer's personality, it was acceptable.

Forward-looking designers of the time recognized this desire for self-expression. One designer declared that basics should be made available, but that the customer should combine them as she saw fit. Another advised women to wear pants or skirts, long or short, according to how they felt rather than according to the occasion. Other designers stressed the fact that young people, eager to sponsor the cause of the world's disadvantaged, did so by adopting the dress of the American Indians, Africans, or Hindus, for example.

Once having tasted such fashion freedom, young people would never conform again, according to one fashion expert, yet the young experimenters had this in common despite individual differences in their dress: a deep-rooted desire to dress differently from the older generations with whom they lived and associated.

For most people, particularly those who lack the time, funds, and vital flair for combining different components into a strictly personal look, the tendency continued to be to accept a fashion or effect as a whole. A touch of novelty in accessories, color, line, or texture, within the framework of prevailing fashion, was enough to satisfy the feeling of individuality that the average consumer craved.

The rules of fashion merchandising as expounded by Nystrom years ago thus continued to prove themselves valid both in theory and in practice.

References

[1]Quoted in Bell, *On Human Finery,* pp. 48–49.
[2]D. E. Robinson, "Fashion Theory and Product Design," p. 127.
[3]*Ibid.,* p. 29.
[4]Gabriel Tarde, *The Laws of Imitation,* Henry Holt and Company, New York, 1903, p. 221.
[5]Simmel, "Fashion," p. 140.
[6]Flügel, *The Psychology of Clothes,* p. 139.
[7]D. E. Robinson, "Economics of Fashion Demand," p. 383.
[8]King, "Fashion Adoption," pp. 122–123.
[9]*Ibid.,* pp. 114–115.
[10]Bell, op. cit., p. 46.
[11]Flügel, op. cit., p. 140.
[12]King, op. cit., p. 124.
[13]Flügel, op. cit., p. 140.
[14]Sapir, "Fashion," p. 140.
[15]Cobliner, "Feminine Fashion as an Aspect of Group Psychology," p. 287.
[16]Daves, *Ready-Made Miracle,* pp. 231–232.
[17]Simmel, op. cit., pp. 137, 140.
[18]Flügel, op. cit., p. 140.
[19]Sapir, op. cit., p. 140.

Merchandising Vocabulary

Define or briefly explain the following terms:

Designer

Line

Fashion innovator

Fashion influential

Gap-bridgers

Merchandising Review

1. Distinguish between the responsibilities of an American designer and those of a European designer.
2. Discuss the role of the manufacturer of women's apparel in relation to fashion change.
3. What is the role of the retailer in relation to fashion change?
4. Describe the "trickle-down" theory of fashion adoption.
5. What is meant by the "trickle-across" theory of fashion adoption? How relevant is it to the dissemination of contemporary fashions?
6. Discuss the more recent theory relating to fashion adoption.
7. What makes a person a fashion leader?
8. Why are most women fashion followers rather than fashion leaders?
9. Discuss the paradox of fashion individuality and fashion conformity.

Merchandising Digest

1. "Neither designers nor manufacturers make a fashion or create fashion change." Discuss this statement and its implications for merchandising of fashion goods.
2. Discuss the significance for merchandising of the trickle-across theory of fashion adoption.
3. "People in the public eye are prime candidates for positions of fashion leadership." Discuss this statement, giving examples of specific types of public figures who exerted fashion leadership and/or the fashions they popularized.

PART 2 ___
MARKETERS
of

FASHION

6

The Materials of Fashion: Textile Fibers and Fabrics

Fashions and the materials from which they are made are inseparable. When a designer works out his ideas, he thinks not only in terms of silhouettes and shapes but also in terms of materials best suited for each silhouette and shape, like the crisp assertion of a taffeta, for instance, or the soft cling of a crepe. Materials are vital to the manufacturer, too, for their choice is a major operating decision and their cost a major investment. The retailer must also carefully consider the materials from which apparel fashions are made because they play a significant role in influencing customers' buying decisions.

More fashion garments and accessories are made of textiles than of any other kind of material. Fashion textiles are the product of a network of primary industries, each with a somewhat different organization and a somewhat different method of operation. An industry that picks its raw fiber from plants in a field, for instance, is organized differently from one that creates its fiber in a test tube—similarly, the industries that produce fibers naturally operate differently from the industry that turns fibers into fabrics.

A basic knowledge of each of these industries is important to those engaged in the merchandising of fashion. Such knowledge not only explains the origin and background of the fabrics themselves, but also shows just how, and how quickly, each industry can be expected to respond to fashion trends in apparel. Such knowledge also makes it possible to evaluate the fashion guidance provided by these industries to apparel producers, retailers, and consumers.

Changes in the textile industries have been rapid and important, particularly in recent years. Not only have there been radical new methods of producing fibers, but important advances have also been made in methods of making and finishing fabrics. All have contributed to an increasing variety of fashion goods and greater excitement in the world of fashion.

The Textile Fiber Industries

A *fiber* is a hairlike unit of raw material from which textile fabric is made. The fibers that are spun into yarn and woven or knitted into fabric influence fashion by determining the possibilities ultimately available in the color, weight, texture, and other qualities of the finished garment.

Fibers are divided into two main categories: natural and man-made. *Natural fibers are derived from plant or animal sources. Man-made fibers,* or *synthetic fibers,* are developed in chemical laboratories.

Considering the wide variety available today, it is difficult to imagine the narrow selection of fibers offered to manufacturers and consumers a century ago. At that time, for instance, it was impossible to produce winter clothing in clear, light colors. Of the fibers then available, wool was the only one with built-in warmth, but because of the naturally creamy color of all wool fibers, plus the limited knowledge of dyeing techniques, woolen fabrics usually were available only in dark colors. In the same way, fashions that required a woman's figure to be subtly controlled by her undergarments would not have been possible even 50 years ago, because such synthetics as spandex had not yet been developed.

History and Development

The fiber industries are of vastly different ages and backgrounds. The natural fiber industries are so old that even Neolithic man is believed to have gathered flax to make yarn for fabrics. The man-made fiber industries, on the other hand, are so young that the oldest among them, rayon, has not yet rounded out its first century. Thus natural fibers have had a very long history of extremely slow development, which has speeded up only in recent years, while man-made or synthetic fibers have had a very short history of amazingly rapid development.

The Natural Fibers Industries The principal natural fibers used in the production of textile fabrics include *cotton,* a vegetable fiber from the cotton boll of the cotton plant; *wool,* an animal fiber from the hair of sheep; *silk,* an animal fiber from the cocoons spun by silkworms; and *linen,* a vegetable fiber from the woody stalk of the flax plant.

Cotton. Cotton, the most extensively used of the natural fibers, thrives in various sections of the United States, one of the world's major cotton producers. It is also grown in the Soviet Union, Brazil, China, Egypt, India, Hawaii, Japan, Mexico, Peru, and the West Indies, and is one of the world's major money crops.

The use of cotton as a fiber has been traced as far back as 3000 B.C. A Hindu song of around 450 B.C. describes in very explicit detail how women of that time picked the cotton bolls and then carded and spun the lint into yarn. A surprising amount of the world's cotton crop is still picked by hand, even in this country, and those Hindu women of more than 2,000 years ago would find much that was familiar today in the sight of a field of cotton being harvested in many parts of the South.

Cotton fibers are of various lengths, depending upon the plant strain and the climate in which it is grown. The longest and finest fibers are used for sheer cotton fabric; shorter fibers go into coarser goods; the very short fibers, called *linters,* that remain on the seed are used mainly in the manufacture of rayon and for such nonfashion products as paper and absorbent cotton.

Wool. Wool for use in apparel comes from Australia, New Zealand, England, Scotland, South Africa, Uruguay, and the United States—those areas that have good grazing conditions for sheep. In colder climates, sheep are likely to have coarser coats more suitable for carpet wool than for apparel.

Early man domesticated sheep and goats for their hair. There are cuneiform records going back to 4200 B.C. that mention weavers, dyers, and wool merchants, and the wool industry has continued since that time as one of the most powerful in the textile field. In England, for example, wool had no rival until the eighteenth century, when cotton became important.

The first United States woolen mill was established in Massachusetts in the late 1600s. Today, the states that count wool-bearing sheep important as farm income include Utah, Nevada, and Colorado. The majority of the woolen mills, however, have remained on the Atlantic coast, about half of them in the Northeast and the other half in the Southeast. In 1965, the United States produced approximately 115 million pounds of wool and imported another 225 million pounds, while exporting only a little over a half million pounds.

Silk. The diet and climate preferences of the silkworm have made Japan, Italy, and China the world's principal producers of silk fiber. The industry began in China, considerably more than 4,000 years ago. Even then silk was considered such an important fiber for fashion fabrics that the Chinese guarded its production with a decree of death for anyone who told the secret to the unauthorized. The silkworm and its culture, called *sericulture,* came west during the late Middle Ages, and France, Italy, and Spain became the important silk centers in Europe. Cortez tried to bring the silkworm to the Americas in the sixteenth century, but failed, and that failure has been repeated on several other occasions. Various sericultural experiments have been tried, over and over again, but none has yet proved successful. All of the 6 million pounds of silk fiber used annually by United States mills is imported.

Silk is the only natural fiber created in a continuous filament, rather than in short fibers that have to be spun together. The cocoons spun by the silkworm yield filaments that are from 800 to 1,300 yards in length.

Silk has always been considered a luxury fiber. In the Middle Ages and during the Renaissance, the sumptuary laws of many countries restricted the use of silk to royalty and members of the elite classes. Even today, silk is used mainly in dressy apparel and usually in higher-priced designs.

Silk used to be a thriving textile business but is no longer. World War II abruptly cut off silk fiber supplies, and by the time the war had ended, the market for silk fabrics made in this country had all but vanished. Those man-made fibers most directly competitive with silk had made an important place for themselves by combining strength, sheerness, and washability. Cotton and wool had developed new versatility, especially when combined with man-made fibers. Silk fabrics produced in countries where labor is now cheap fill the small demand for this material at prices lower than domestic suppliers can profitably meet. Today, silk fabrics represent a minute part, less than one-thousandth, of the United States fiber consumption, just as silk represents an infinitesimal part of a fashion market it once dominated, women's hosiery.

Linen. Linen fiber for fashion fabrics comes principally from the flax plants of Ireland and Belgium. Other producers include Egypt, France, Germany, Holland, Italy, Poland, and the Soviet Union, the latter being the world's chief producer of flax fiber. In the United States, the flax plant is grown mainly for the oil yielded by its seeds.

Flax may have been cultivated by man first for its food value, but it was soon used for its fiber as well. It probably was first grown in the Mediterranean area. Materials made of flax fibers have been found in Stone Age ruins in Switzerland; the ancient Egyptians used linen for wrapping mummies. Eventually, flax cultivation spread throughout Europe, into Asia, and across the Atlantic to the Americas. Flax was a popular fiber crop during the colonial period in this country,

but dwindled rapidly in importance after the invention of the cotton gin in 1792, which made cotton a cheaper fiber to produce. The United States, therefore, imports most of its flax fiber for apparel purposes, and uses about 8 million pounds a year in its mills.

The Man-Made Fiber Industries Like the medieval alchemists who sought to transform base metal into gold, European chemists of the eighteenth and nineteenth centuries sought to create artificial silk. Unlike the alchemists' dream, this dream came true. After a number of contributions by various scientists, the French Count Hilaire de Chardonnet started commercial production in the world's first artificial silk plant in 1891. The first such plant in the United States was established at Marcus Hook, Pennsylvania, in 1910.

At first, the new fiber was called "artificial silk" or "art silk." By 1924, however, the National Retail Dry Goods Association (now the National Retail Merchants Association) recognized that the new fiber needed an identity of its own. The Association coined the word "rayon," and registered it internationally. Man-made fibers had come of age; they could now be given names of their own and be accepted on their own merits. The earliest man-made fibers, rayon and acetate, are the *cellulose fibers,* for they use as their base such natural cellulose products as wood pulp or cotton linters. Nylon, the first of the truly synthetic fibers and the first of the *polymers,* appeared in 1938. It was followed in the years after World War II by other polymers such as the polyesters (Dacron was a leader), the acrylics (Orlon was the first big one), and spandex, an elasticlike fiber. Polymers are so named because they are made by a chemical process called "polymerization," a way of combining simple chemicals into a complex group or fiber with definite characteristics of its own.

Synthetic fibers start out as thick liquids. Then fibers of varying lengths are produced by forcing the liquid through the tiny holes of a mechanical device known as a *spinnerette,* in much the same way that spaghetti is made out of dough.

In the last few decades, chemists have become very important in the field of fashion fibers. In 1965, world production of rayon and acetate fibers was over 3 million tons, and over 2 million tons of various other kinds of synthetic fibers were also produced. Of these, the United States produced about 750,000 tons of rayon and acetate fiber, and about a million tons of other kinds of synthetic fibers.

Table 6-1.   Natural and Man-Made Fibers: Mill Consumption

Pounds Consumed Per Capita, Selected Years, 1930 to 1965

	Cotton	Wool	Rayon and Acetate	Other Man-Made	Flax	Silk
1930	21.26	2.14	0.97	—	0.13	0.65
1935	21.66	3.28	2.15	—	0.10	0.57
1940	29.97	3.09	3.74	0.03	0.09	0.36
1945	32.28	4.61	5.68	0.36	0.05	0.01
1950	30.87	4.18	9.06	0.95	0.07	0.07
1955	26.51	2.50	8.80	2.71	0.05	0.07
1960	23.20	2.30	5.99	4.41	0.03	0.04
1965	23.01	1.99	8.19	10.44	0.04	0.03

Source: U.S. Department of Agriculture.

Organization of the Industries

Because of the vast differences in the origin and characteristics of the various fibers, the fiber industries do not have uniform patterns of organization or operation. Although there may be similarity within groups, the practices of the natural fibers industry differ markedly from those of the man-made fibers industry. It is the difference, again, between something obtained from plants and animals and something created in a laboratory.

In spite of the differences, however, the goal of both groups is the same: to produce as efficiently as possible the fibers favored by consumers and thus needed by the textile fabric field.

Cotton and wool, the major natural fibers, are produced where climate and terrain are favorable. The primary producers of these fibers tend to be many in number and small in size.

There are four major areas of cotton production in the United States. In the Southeast, a considerable quantity of cotton is grown in the Carolinas, in Georgia, and in Alabama, but few farms have even as many as 20 acres under cultivation. In the Mississippi Delta land, particularly in Arkansas, Mississippi, and Louisiana, cotton is an important crop, and many farms are larger than 100 acres. In the Southwest, in areas of Texas and Oklahoma, cotton is a valuable crop, and the land under cultivation by each farmer is apt to be more than 100 acres. In the newest cotton-growing region, New Mexico, Arizona, and particularly California, there are both big farms and high yields per acre.

Much of the wool produced in this country comes from the Utah, Nevada, and Colorado ranges of relatively small ranchers.

Nearly all the natural fiber producers sell their product in local markets, either to mill representatives or, far more likely, to wholesalers. Wholesalers then do their bargaining at the central markets. The important central markets in this country for cotton are in Memphis, New Orleans, Dallas, and Houston, with New York and Chicago also handling a number of transactions although without having the physical goods on hand. Boston is the major central market for wool in the United States, and also handles the import transactions so important to the wool industry.

A man-made fiber can be produced wherever a chemical company erects a plant, which is apt to be where the supplies of raw chemicals, power, and manpower are readily available. Thus there are plants up and down the Atlantic coast, with an increasing emphasis on the Southern states, where labor and other expenses are still somewhat lower than in the North. There is also an increasing number of plants along the West Coast, and concentrations in the interior of the country wherever there are good sources of raw materials or efficient railroads and waterways to facilitate easy shipping of those materials.

These plants, in contrast to the farms and ranches of the natural fiber producers, are huge in size. In addition, sometimes the producing company serves as its own market, not only making the fiber but also weaving or knitting it into fabrics.

Operation of the Industries

The many small producers of the natural fiber industries tend to compete with each other only in the sense that each strives to produce the maximum yield from his resources. Each tries to cultivate those characteristics in his product that will command the best prices in the market. The cotton farmer tries to grow more cotton, of a better quality, on each acre. The sheep farmer tries to develop a hardy herd that will produce large quantities of quality wool per clipping.

Beyond this point, chemistry must take over so that the natural product can be modified to give it the desired attributes. A noteworthy example is *mercerizing*, a process by which cotton yarn is made stronger, more lustrous, and more receptive to certain dyes.

Producers of natural fibers have increased their research activities in recent years in attempts to develop, individually and through group efforts, various methods of imparting additional desirable characteristics to their fibers or to the yarns and textile fabrics made from these fibers. While some man-made fibers offer dimensional stability, for instance, wool and cotton can also offer the same characteristic when woven into cloth if the fabric is preshrunk. Similarly, wash-and-wear and crease-resistant properties, formerly found only in fabrics made from certain man-made fibers, can now be offered in fabrics made of cotton, wool, and linen.

Historically, producers of natural fibers have shown little interest in the various stages through which their products go in the process of being transformed into consumer products. The producers of man-made fibers, on the other hand, are interested in all the stages through which their products will go: yarn, fabric, garments, retail distribution, and ultimate use by the consumer.

Limited quantities of a new or modified man-made fiber are usually first produced in a pilot plant on an experimental basis. If research indicates that both industry and the consumer will accept the new product, additional plant capacity is devoted to it, new applications of the fiber are explored, and new industries are consulted and encouraged to use it.

While this procedure is going on in one chemical company, there is always the possibility that another company may be working along similar lines to develop a competitive fiber. The company that is first to develop a new fiber has no assurance that it will have the field to itself for long. For example, there are many brands of such man-made fibers as nylon, rayon, and acetate already on the market, and quite a roster of companies producing various acrylics, polyesters, and other man-made fibers.

One reason why each important man-made fiber is produced by several chemical companies at almost the same time is that these fibers are engineered to provide whatever characteristics are currently in demand by industry and the consumer. Popular demand for a particular attribute, such as locked-in color, warmth without weight, or imperviousness to wrinkles, sets the same problem before the research laboratories of all fiber producers at the same time. Many of them come up with similar answers.

Merchandising Activities

No matter how familiar fashion fabric and apparel producers and consumers may be with the inherent qualities of each fiber, there is always the need to disseminate information about the newest modifications and their application to fashion merchandise. To do this, producers of both natural and man-made fibers make extensive use of advertising and publicity and market research, and extend various customer services to manufacturers, retailers, and consumers.

Usually the producers of man-made fibers undertake these activities on behalf of their own individual brands and companies. The producers of natural fibers, on the other hand, carry on related activities through trade associations, each representing a particular natural fiber, such as the National Cotton Council, the Wool Bureau, the International Silk Association, and the Irish Linen Guild.

Advertising and Publicity. Producers of man-made fibers maintain a continuous flow of competitive advertising and publicity directed toward both the trade and the consumer. Among the trade media used are such publications as *Women's Wear Daily, Men's Wear,* and *Daily News Record.* Among the consumer media used

Labels often are used to identify a fiber or fabric, describe its qualities, and give recognition to its producer.

are mass-circulation magazines, publications aimed at special segments of the public, newspapers, radio, and television. There is a growing trend among giant man-made fiber producers to use television spectaculars to publicize their brand names and get their fashion messages across to more consumers.

Although natural fibers are not advertised as aggressively as are man-made fibers, strong efforts are made to meet the growing competition of man-made fibers. All advertising of this kind, however, is still being done on behalf of an individual fiber rather than on behalf of an individual producer.

Fiber sources also provide garment producers and retailers with various aids that facilitate mention of their fibers in the advertising of consumer goods. This procedure adds to the impact of the recognition already achieved by the producer's name, trademark, slogan, or logotype. For example, the Wool Bureau encourages the use of its ball-of-yarn logotype in producer and retailer advertising of all-wool merchandise, as well as in displays of such goods.

To help spread the textile fiber fashion story, producers and trade associations continually provide the press with newsworthy information, background material, and photographs for editorial features, to facilitate mention of fashion and fiber in the media. Some of this publicity effort is accomplished by direct contact with the press; some of it is done by supplying garment producers and retailers with glossy photographs and other materials to enhance the effect of their own efforts. A familiar example of fashion publicity on behalf of a natural fiber is the National Cotton Council's annual Maid of Cotton program, the selection of a beauty queen to make appearances all over the country in a fashionable cotton wardrobe made up of designs supplied by famous designers. An example of fashion publicity on behalf of a man-made fiber was furnished when Du Pont introduced Qiana, a new form of nylon, in 1968. First members of the Paris couture were encouraged to present dresses in fabrics made entirely of this fiber, and then intensive trade advertising stressed the use by outstanding United States and European designers of fabrics made from Qiana.

Another form of fiber advertising and publicity is the development of seasonal fashion presentations for use by retail stores. Publicity kits and programs specially prepared for local markets are developed. The objective is to support promotions during peak retail selling periods. Producers may also supply fashion experts to commentate fashion shows, to participate in television "talk" programs, or to address local consumer groups and retail sales personnel. Films about fibers and fabrics also may be utilized to further dramatize the fiber story.

An important phase of the promotional effort is the advertising undertaken by fiber producers in cooperation with fabric and garment manufacturers and retailers. Such shared advertising benefits the fiber in two ways. First, the consumer begins to associate the fiber name with other names already familiar to her, from the name of the fiber source to the name of the retail store selling the garment. This is particularly important when a fiber is man-made and still new. Second, fabric and garment producers, as well as retailers, are encouraged to use and promote the fiber because of the fringe benefit they receive in the form of subsidized local or national advertising.

Market Research Major producers of man-made fibers are constantly engaged in exploring new markets for their fibers. Exhaustive research into the fashion and other markets into which a fiber may penetrate is undertaken by their analysts. Technicians evaluate possible difficulties that may be encountered by fabric or garment producers in using the new or modified fiber and develop methods of dealing with such difficulties. Projections are made of fiber and fabric consumption in specific markets, and studies of consumer reaction to new fabrics, apparel design, and other product features are undertaken. The analysts then offer advice to fabric and garment producers with the expectation that their fibers will win acceptance in new and emerging product areas.

Market research in natural fibers, like advertising and publicity in their behalf, is largely the responsibility of the various natural fiber trade associations, since the small independent producers who make up the industries are not financially equipped to handle such projects. The marketability of natural fibers requires less research, however, since these products are already familiar to producers and consumers and have the prestige of thousands of years of acceptance behind them. Yarn and fabric producers take great pride in their traditional skill in the selection and combining of natural fibers in order to achieve the effects they wish. It is an old saying in the wool industry that the styling of a fabric begins with the selection of the fiber.

Customer Services All the major producers of man-made fibers and many of the smaller firms offer a number of services to direct and secondary users of their products. Producers of natural fibers, working through their associations, also offer many such services. These include:

□ Technical advice to yarn and textile mills, as well as to garment producers.

□ Assistance to textile and garment producers and retailers in locating sources of supply.

□ "Libraries" of fabrics that can be examined by manufacturers, retailers, and the fashion press, with information supplied about where to buy these fabrics, what to pay for them, and what delivery to expect.

□ Fashion advice and information to the textile industry, retailers, and the public.

□ Fashion exhibits for manufacturers and retailers, which, in some instances, are also open to the public.

□ Extensive literature for manufacturers, retailers, educators, and consumers about fiber properties, use, and care.

□ Fashion experts and clothing and textile home economists to address groups of manufacturers, retailers, or consumers, staging appropriate fashion shows and demonstrations.

□ Educational films and audiovisual aids for use by the trade, schools, and consumer groups.

□ Assistance to retail stores in staging promotions of garments in which one or more of the promoted fibers are used. Such assistance may include finding sources of supply; staging fashion shows; developing customized retail-oriented

Courtesy Celanese

Many fiber producers maintain libraries of fabrics containing their fibers.

promotional programs for department and specialty stores, resident buying offices, chain and mail-order outlets; supplying speakers and retail merchandising representatives to interested groups; providing publicity releases and suggested advertising copy; cooperating with retail stores in the cost of local advertising; advising on store displays; and conducting consumer demonstrations and sales training meetings in stores.

□ Textile processing experts to help solve fabric production problems; similarly qualified experts to help solve problems in the production of apparel and accessories.

Marketing Trends

Because of increased competition among fibers and the constant stream of new fibers and new treatments of existing fibers, producers are accelerating their efforts to maintain close contact with users of their merchandise at all stages of production from basic research in the fiber itself to final sale of the end product to the ultimate consumer.

Most of the giant producers of man-made fibers maintain marketing and merchandising divisions staffed by experts in the production and marketing of the yarns, fabrics, fashion goods, and other products in which their fibers may be used. Many such companies have retailing experts in their merchandising divisions to help plan and launch promotions to the consumer. Their fashion and public relations experts work hand-in-hand with merchandising and marketing executives of the direct and secondary users of their products, as the occasions may require.

The natural fiber producers do some research and product testing, and provide fashion guidance through their trade associations, but on a relatively small scale compared to what some of the individual man-made fiber producers do.

Product Research and Development Both natural and man-made fiber producers are constantly seeking improvements in their products and new applications for them. The research facilities of the giant chemical companies develop new fibers, evaluate them, and engineer both existing and new fibers to meet the fashion and performance demands of their expanding and varied markets. Producers of natural fibers, through their industry associations, develop and evaluate mechanical and chemical means of imparting to their fibers, or to the yarns and fabrics made of these fibers, such qualities as dimensional stability, crease retention, wrinkle resistance, luster or matte finish, washability, and any other characteristics that improve their acceptance.

The producers of man-made fibers are particularly active in instructing the fabric industry in the manipulation of new yarns, in developing optimum blends and constructions, in improving dyeing and finishing techniques, and in evaluating customer reaction to the fabrics made from their fibers. Technical bulletins on the proper methods of processing their fibers are issued to the trade and are supplemented by the availability of expert advice on specific problems relating to yarn, fabric, or garment production.

Research into fabric styling and development is also undertaken by most major producers of man-made fibers. Working with fabric producers, these companies develop experimental constructions and sample weavings and knittings well in advance of each new season. They also make available to their fabric customers the services of fabric construction specialists, stylists, print consultants, color experts, and fashion and market experts.

Like consumers of fashion, some textile and apparel companies are eager to try whatever is new, while others are reluctant to do so. Producers of man-made fibers are ready to assist innovative and influential producers each time a new fiber development is launched, and the experience gained is then later made available to those who prefer to follow.

Performance Testing and Licensing Consumer products in which textile fibers are incorporated are required by federal law (the Textile Fibers Products Identification Act of 1960) to bear labels specifying their fiber content by generic name and percentage of each that is used. The brand name or trademark of any of the fibers contained may also be stated, although this is not required by law. Some of these brand names and trademarks, however, have been given exposure to consumers over the years at considerable expense to the producer, and the producer is naturally concerned that these branded fibers should be handled by fabric manufacturers in ways that will enhance and not endanger the brand's acceptance by the consumer.

There are three ways in which producers may sell fibers to fabric manufacturers:

◻ As unbranded products, with no restrictions placed on their end use and no implied or required standards of performance claimed.

◻ As branded or trademarked fibers, with assurance to the consumer that the quality of the fiber has been controlled by its producer but not necessarily with assurance as to either implied or required standards of performance in the end product.

◻ Under a licensing agreement, whereby the use of the fiber trademark concerned is permitted only to those manufacturers whose fabrics or other end products pass tests set up by the fiber producer for their specific uses or applications.

Licensing programs set up by different fiber producers and by processors of yarn vary considerably in scope. The more comprehensive programs entail extensive end-use testing to back up the licensing, exercise considerable control over fabric products that have been licensed, and offer technical services wherever needed to help correct situations in which a given fabric fails to pass a qualifying test. Trademarks used under such licensing agreements are referred to as *licensed trademarks*.

Licensing programs may involve wear tests as well as laboratory tests. They also may specify blend levels, such as when a required minimum percentage of the designated fiber must be contained in the yarn to qualify the product for licensing. Checking products periodically through retail shopping is not unusual.

Fashion Guidance In the face of growing competition, producers of both natural and man-made fibers are looking to the fashion-rightness of their products as a major tool in meeting and beating competition. Forecasting conditions in the

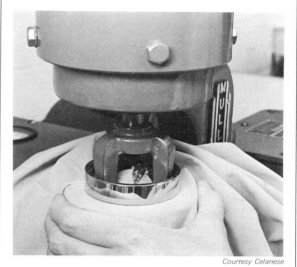

Courtesy Celanese

Fiber producers use machines like this to test the bursting strength of a fabric.

1970s, Louis Laun, president of Celanese Fibers Marketing Company, said: "The war of the fashion cycle will be a faster, tougher war as the world's population gets younger, changes its mind more quickly, and demands more in the way of comfort, wearability, and ease of care in clothing."[1]

The chemical companies that produce man-made fibers had little contact with fashion until their fiber production efforts plunged them into the middle of it. Leaders among them promptly set up departments to study and report on fashion trends and consumer preferences. Today most man-made fiber producers offer a wide range of fashion services to apparel manufacturers and retailers. Their stylists cover market openings around the world and provide fashion reports and forecasts based on these openings; they maintain close liaison with manufacturers in the production of fashion apparel; and they assist producers in getting new fashion ideas off the ground well in advance of each new season.

Producers of natural fibers, because of their long-standing consumer acceptance, heterogeneous nature, and lack of control over end-product applications, were somewhat slower to harness fashion to enhance the marketability of their products. In the period since the close of World War II, however, with help supplied by their trade associations, natural fiber producers made great strides toward improving their products through a scientific approach to production, through development of new treatments for fibers and fabrics, and through an increasingly close liaison not only with the fashion industries but also with the fashion consumer as well.

The Textile Fabric Industry

Between the fiber and the apparel fashion lies the fabric, the basic material out of which the garment or accessory is made. *Textile fabric* is cloth made from fibers by one of the following methods: weaving, knitting, braiding, felting, crocheting, knotting, laminating, or bonding. Sometimes one particular method may be in fashion, such as laminating. At other times, there may be a trend in favor of a combination of methods, such as the bonding together of two layers of fabric. In general, however, most textile fabrics are either woven or knitted.

The textile fabric producers form a single industry, not a network of industries such as the fiber producers do. Within that industry, however, there are patterns of both similarity and difference, depending on the fiber involved, the job being done, and the product required. There are also, throughout the industry, the signs of the impact of technological changes, ranging from increased diversification of products to more expert anticipation of fashion trends.

History and Development

The production of most fabrics begins with the production of yarn. *Yarn* is a continuous thread formed by spinning or twisting fibers together. The earliest step toward mechanization in the textile fabric industry was in the production of yarn, when the spinning wheel was introduced into Europe from India around the sixth century. Spinning remained a slow, tedious process and a home occupation for centuries thereafter, until the British, in the eighteenth century, worked out mechanical ways of spinning cotton fibers into yarn. By 1779, Hargreaves, Arkwright, and Crompton each had made a contribution toward the modern factory production of yarn.

Next came mechanization of the loom, the tool that weaves the yarn into cloth. When the British worked out machine methods of spinning fibers into yarns, they were confronted with an output of yarn much larger than hand-operated looms could handle. The first power loom was invented by an English clergyman, Dr. Edward Cartwright, and patented in 1785. It used water as a source of energy.

The same sequence of mechanization was true on this side of the Atlantic. In 1790, Samuel Slater established a yarn mill in Pawtucket, Rhode Island. A present-day giant in the textile field, J. P. Stevens and Company, is descended from Slater's famous mill. Fabric production remained both a hand operation and a home industry, however, totally inadequate to meet the demand for apparel fabrics, until a New Englander, Francis Cabot Lowell, on a trip to England, visited a textile factory and memorized the detailed specifications of its power-operated machinery. In 1814 Lowell built the first successful power loom and the first textile fabric mill in the United States.

The demands of a rapidly growing country provided an eager market for the output of United States textile mills, and as a result the young industry flourished. Automation and mechanization techniques, developed both here and abroad, have advanced the production procedure to a point where it is now possible for a single operator to oversee as many as 100 weaving machines if the fabric is plain.

Organization of the Industry

As in the fiber industries, no one organizational or operational pattern prevails throughout the textile industry. In the following discussions, reference will be made to "woolen mills" and "cotton mills," but these terms should not be taken literally today. A woolen mill may use other fibers in addition to wool, and cotton mills may use other fibers in addition to cotton. The general pattern of operation, however, was set up long before man-made fibers came on the scene and long before it was customary to combine different fibers into one fabric. Many of the mills that

Table 6-2. Number, Type, and Location of Textile Plants in the United States in 1968

Region	Spinning	Weaving	Knitting	Finishing	Synthetics	Total*
New England	240	303	124	353	14	1,014
Middle Atlantic	190	371	941	563	22	2,215
East North-Central	33	39	82	87	8	246
West North-Central	10	9	22	22	2	55
South Atlantic	705	553	725	710	53	2,042
East South-Central	100	75	123	134	12	303
West South-Central	28	26	18	23	2	71
Mountain	2	6	9	4	0	21
Pacific	17	27	67	63	1	181
						6,148

*Columns do not necessarily add to total figures. Some plants perform more than one operation and are listed in more than one column.
Source: Textile Industries Magazine.

started with wool or cotton and now have added man-made fibers to their list still retain today a mode of operation characteristic of their original pattern.

The textile fabric industry in the United States is composed of approximately 7,000 mills employing nearly a million workers. Some of these mills produce yarn; some weave or knit cloth for apparel and other purposes; some do finishing. All are part of an industry that, in the late 1960s, delivered more than $20 billion worth of goods annually. Even this rate of production, however, has proven insufficient to satisfy this country's vast appetite for textile products, for in those years, almost a billion dollars' worth of textile products were imported, and less than half that amount exported.

Textile mills are widely dispersed throughout the country, partly as a result of the industry's tendency to seek areas where labor and land costs are low and partly because there has been little advantage in concentrating production in any one area through the construction of giant mills or complexes. (See Table 6-2.) A small mill can operate about as efficiently as a large one, since textile machinery has a long useful life and its output can be increased by working two or three shifts. There used to be some concentration of textile mills in the New England states, but in

recent years the southeastern part of the country offers less expensive labor and land. When silk was widely used in garments, there was a definite concentration of silk mills around New York City, the market in which the fabrics were sold, but silk mills have all but vanished from the current scene.

The market centers for textile fabrics are not at the mills but in the fashion capital of the country, New York City. There, on the doorstep of the garment industry, every mill of importance has a salesroom. A fabric buyer or designer for a garment maker, or a retail store apparel buyer or fashion coordinator, seeking firsthand information on what the fabric market offers, only has to walk a block or two to obtain all the information he wants.

Operation of the Industry

A woolen or worsted mill sorts and selects the fibers to be used, spins them into yarn, then weaves or knits them and finishes the fabric. Finishing may include dyeing, napping, and pressing, or treating the fabric to ensure such attributes as nonshrinkage and permanent press. Fashion influences decisions at every step of the way.

For certain effects, yarns may be dyed before being woven or knitted (yarn dyed); for others, fabrics are knitted or woven first and then dyed (vat dyed); in some instances, either the warp or the weft (filling) yarns alone are dyed before weaving, and then the completed fabric is dyed to get a cross-dyed effect. These and many other aspects of fabric production must be considered by the fabric fashion stylist.

Cotton follows a completely different pattern of operation from wool, for cotton passes through many hands in the process of being changed from fiber to finished fabric. Many elements of the styling of cotton cloth can be introduced long after the fibers have been spun into yarn and the fabric has been woven or knitted. A single, basic cotton fabric can present many different faces to the fashion public, depending on how it has been dyed, printed, glazed, or otherwise treated after leaving the loom.

Some cotton mills produce only the yarn. Others weave fabric from purchased yarn but do not carry the process beyond the gray or unfinished state. There are also plants that bleach, dye, preshrink, print, or in other ways impart desired characteristics to fabrics produced by other mills. In the process of being transformed from raw fiber to finished fabric, cotton may travel back and forth to different areas of the country and may change ownership several times. The plants that handle the various stages may or may not be under common ownership, and they may or may not be geographically close.

Many mills no longer limit themselves to working with yarns made of a single fiber. Fibers may be used alone or in conjunction with other fibers, as demand dictates. Any of the various types of mills described above may combine a natural fiber with another natural fiber, or more commonly, a natural fiber with a man-made fiber, to achieve a desired effect. Examination of the fiber content labels on garments will show how ubiquitous the man-made fibers are, and how rayon, in particular, is combined with almost any other fiber to achieve a specific effect.

The *converter* was a dominant figure in the textile fabrics industry before World War II, particularly in the cotton industry. A textile converter, often well capitalized but owning no looms or mills, bought fabrics in the gray and contracted to have them finished (dyed, bleached, printed, or subjected to other treatments) in plants specializing in each operation. He was his own selling agent.

Through close contact with the apparel trades, the converter usually knew, almost from day to day, what colors, textures, and types of fabrics would be in demand. He spared the mills the expense and risk of having to style their lines down to the last detail, or even having to study the fashion market. The mills concentrated on production.

During World War II, conditions made this separation of functions unprofitable. Mills acquired finishing plants; finishers purchased mills; sales agents who had once functioned on commission for textile producers also became part of the new combinations that were forming. The industry became *vertically integrated*.

With vertical integration, the textile fabric industry is inclined to commit itself far in advance to weaves, colors, and finishes. It is necessarily extremely well informed about fashion and alert to incoming trends. Most mills are necessarily inhospitable to the idea of producing short, experimental runs for individual designers. Large-scale operations do not readily "turn on a dime," a feat often required in the fashion business.

The converter, however, is by no means a creature of the past. As an independent operator or as a division of a giant textile corporation, the converter continues to take commonplace, basic fabrics and give them characteristics that make them readily salable to the fashion industries.

Merchandising Activities

It is said that fabric precedes the fashion. This means that a dress designer, for example, cannot create a garment unless he finds cloth that will drape the way he wants it to and will have the colors and textures to give the desired form to his design.

Since the textile fabric industry must work several seasons ahead of consumer demand, it must be early in recognizing the direction that fashion is taking. Long before the average customer realizes that she wants dark velvets, for example, retailers, apparel manufacturers, and the textile industry must see and act upon such a trend. If the textile producers miss the advance signals, retailers and apparel producers can be frustrated in their efforts to serve the fashion consumer.

Advertising and Publicity Fabric manufacturers advertise lavishly, featuring the brand names of their products and frequently the names of specific apparel manufacturers who use their goods. Either with the cooperation of fiber sources or on their own, fabric houses sponsor radio and television programs, run full-color advertisements in a wide variety of mass-circulation magazines and newspapers, cooperate in the cost of brand advertising run by retail stores, and generally make consumers aware of styles that are considered fashionable and of the names of retail stores where they may be purchased.

Fabric producers compete among themselves for the business of apparel producers, for recognition among retail store buyers, and for acceptance by consumers of products made of their goods. They publicize brand names, stage seasonal fashion shows in market areas for retailers and the fashion press, and provide hang tags for the use of garment manufacturers. These tags may bear not only the brand name of the fabric but also instructions relating to its care. Many fabric firms also make educational materials available to schools, consumer groups, and retail sales personnel, and supply information to the consumer and trade press, as a means of publicizing fashion news, fabric developments, and products.

Market Research Fabric producers, like fiber producers, now devote attention to exploring the market potential of their products and anticipating the needs of their customers. Success in the fashion industry depends on supplying the consumer with what she wants, and fashion causes swift changes. Anticipation of such changes requires closeness to the market and a scientific study of trends.

Many of the large fabric producers maintain separate product and market research divisions. The experts work closely with both the trade and consumer markets in studying fabric performance characteristics; many provide garment manufacturers with sample runs of new fabrics for experimental purposes. The market researchers conduct consumer studies relating to the demand for or acceptance of finishes, blends, and other desired characteristics. Such studies also help fabric and garment producers to determine what customers will want in the future, where and when they will want it, and in what quantities.

Customer Services Today's well-integrated and diversified textile companies speak with great fashion authority. They employ staffs of fashion experts who attend market openings around the world and work with designers to create fabrics in those weights, textures, colors, and patterns that consumers will want. And they do this two or three seasons before garments made of those fabrics will appear in stores.

The large textile companies also employ merchandising and marketing staffs whose expertise on fashion trends is available to apparel manufacturers, retailers, the fashion press, and frequently to the consumers. Fashion staffs attend foreign and domestic market openings; issue seasonal fashion forecasts; provide traveling representatives who conduct in-store sales training programs and address consumer groups; stage fashion shows for the trade and press; help retail stores arrange fashion shows and storewide promotions featuring their products; and assist buyers in locating resources for merchandise made from their fabrics. These fashion merchandising experts not only carry the company's fashion message to trade customers but also reach retailers and consumers as well.

Marketing Trends

The major trends in textile fabric marketing include a continuation of the trend toward giantism, more diversification of products, increased product research and development, and the acquisition of foreign production facilities.

Giantism The trend toward mergers and giantism continues. Firms that have integrated vertically have been expanding horizontally as well. _Horizontal integration means absorbing other companies that function at the same level of production: yarn production, fabric production, or fabric finishing, as the case may be._ As a result, the textile industry is composed of fewer but infinitely larger firms than ever before. The largest of these, Burlington Industries, passed the billion-dollar mark in sales early in the 1960s. Its more than 30 divisions operate plants in 15 states, 8 foreign countries, and Puerto Rico.

Diversification of Products Today, the textile industry, in addition to producing fabrics for the apparel and accessories industries, also produces some finished consumer goods, notably hosiery. For example, both Burlington and Stevens knit, package, and promote women's hosiery under their own brand names.

The specialization that once divided the industry into separate segments, each producing fabrics from a single fiber, has all but faded. To meet the needs of the consumer it is often necessary to blend two or more fibers together into a yarn or to combine a warp yarn of one fiber with a weft yarn of another fiber. Mills are learning to adjust their operations to any new and acceptable fiber or combination of fibers fashion demands.

Two of the largest firms in the field illustrate how the industry is moving toward greater diversification of product. Burlington, originally a rayon mill specializing in bedspreads, now owns woolen mills, cotton mills, hosiery mills, and converting operations, providing fabrics for a wide variety of consumer and industrial uses. Under the J. P. Stevens banner are cotton and woolen mills, women's wear and menswear fabrics, knit and woven goods, yarn sales, and women's hosiery. Stevens uses several natural fibers and virtually every man-made fiber available in this country.

Product Research and Development Textile producers constantly engage in technological research. They work closely with fiber, chemical, and machinery manufacturers in developing new ideas and techniques. Their experiments extend to finishes, sizing, yarn treatments, new dyes and dyeing techniques, as well as physical evaluations of fibers, yarns, fabrics, and garments. Only through such experimentation with fibers and techniques can producers develop the fabrics the consumer wants and finds acceptable.

The textile industry is more concerned at present with modernizing plant and equipment than with expansion of capacity. In the past, many textile firms relied heavily upon the producers of man-made fibers for product research. Today, however, competition from imported fabrics spurs efforts to improve domestic plants and products. Nonprofit organizations within the industry are engaged in research for the whole textile field, including, for example, such projects as standardizing terminology for electronic data processing to make exchange of information more readily available. From the research of individual companies have come such major developments as durable-press fabrics, soil-release finish, and laminated fabrics.

Among the larger textile companies, as well as the textile fiber divisions of the giant chemical firms, testing laboratores are quite common. These are concerned with both quality control of present products and investigation of new products, new materials, new equipment, and new techniques.

Other Trends Despite the trend toward giantism, many fabric mills are independently owned and medium to small in size. Their owners look to fiber resources and trade associations for guidance in the styling, merchandising, and marketing of their products. The chemical companies that produce man-made fibers can, because of their size, provide valuable technological and fashion advisory services otherwise unavailable to the small mill operator.

Another trend among fabric producers, particularly the giants, is toward acquisition or establishment of mills abroad. Such foreign-based mills are usually located close to fiber sources. To this convenience are added the facilities, fashion knowledge, and technical skill of their United States owners. By producing some of their goods abroad, manufacturers defend themselves in this country against the competition of foreign-made fabrics and also put themselves in a more favorable position to sell to countries whose tariff walls keep out goods made in the United States.

Reference

[1]*Women's Wear Daily*, March 29, 1968, pp. 1, 20.

Merchandising Vocabulary

Define or briefly explain the following terms:

Fibers	Spinnerette	Yarn
Natural fiber	Mercerizing	Gray goods
Man-made or synthetic fiber	Fabric library	Textile converter
Cotton linters	Licensed trademark	Vertical integration
Cellulose fiber	Textile fabrics	Horizontal integration

Merchandising Review

1. Name the four natural apparel textile fibers. What is the source of each and from what countries are each obtained?
2. Compare or contrast natural and man-made fibers on the basis of the following: (a) size of organization producing them; (b) capital investment required; (c) location of production facilities; (d) predictable supply; (e) uniformity of product.
3. Discuss the steps or procedures involved in introducing a new or newly modified man-made fiber.
4. How do fiber producers generally advertise and publicize their products?
5. List the various customer services offered by most producers of man-made fibers to direct and secondary users of their products.
6. Discuss the three ways in which fiber producers market their wares and the influence they exert on the use of their names or brand names in end-use products.
7. What are the provisions of the Textile Fibers Product Identification Act? Why is it important to the consumer?
8. Discuss the development of the textile industry in the United States.
9. What is the function of a textile converter? What are the advantages to: (a) a fabric mill and (b) the apparel trade of dealing with a converter?

Merchandising Digest

1. "Fiber producers are accelerating their efforts to maintain close contact with users of their merchandise. They are doing this at all stages of production from basic research to final sale of the end product to its ultimate consumer." Discuss some of the ways in which fiber producers attempt to maintain a closer contact with users of their products.
2. Discuss and give examples of the various types of merchandising activities engaged in by producers of fashion textiles in the United States.
3. Discuss current trends in textile marketing. Include (a) giantism; (b) diversification of products; (c) product research and development; (d) foreign expansion.

7

The Materials of Fashion: Leather and Fur

Man used leather and fur for clothing purposes thousands of years before he developed textiles, and they still play an important part in the fashion picture. Leather is particularly important in some of the fashion accessory fields, such as shoes, handbags, and gloves, and is also regaining strength as an apparel material. Fur is primarily an apparel material, used either as the basic material of the garment or as trim on the garment.

In contrast to the methods used for producing textiles, the processing of leather and fur appears primitive and slow. Thus the response of the leather and fur industries to fashion demand is necessarily slow, and fashion trends have to be spotted particularly early. Yet changes are taking place in the industries, largely in improved production methods and techniques, and these changes are giving designers a wider range of products to work with. In addition, these changes may be indicators of the course that fashion may take in the future, not only in leather and fur but also in textiles.

The Leather Industry

The process of transforming animal skins into leather is known as *tanning*. It is the oldest craft known to man. Primitive man not only killed animals for food, but he also devised ways to treat their skins to use them for body covering and a host of other purposes. Modern man slaughters animals that are raised for their milk, meat, or wool, and converts their skins to leather, or he may kill animals for the sole purpose of transforming their skins into leather, as in the case of alligators and snakes.

Civilized man has more precise and varied treatments to apply to animal skins than did his forebears, and therefore he produces more varieties of leather. Today leather may be thick or thin, flexible or rigid, clear or grained, according to need and fashion.

History and Development

The use of leather for apparel and other purposes was commonplace on the North American continent long before the first European settlers arrived. The earliest known tanners in what is now the United States were Indians, who made clothing, moccasins, and tents from deerskins. Although they lacked the knowledge to produce leathers of today's variety and quality, they developed tanning techniques that met their own needs.

The first tannery in the American colonies was established in 1623 in Plymouth by Experience Miller, an Englishman. Peter Minuit, Governor of New Amsterdam, invented the first machinery used for tanning in the colonies, a horse-driven stone mill to grind the oak bark used in converting animal skins into leather.

Mechanization of the industry took a long step forward in 1809 when Samuel Parker invented a machine that split heavy steer hides 25 times faster than was possible by hand. Split hides produce lighter, more supple leather, desirable in shoes, boots, and other apparel.

Yet mechanization, which developed at about the same rate on both sides of the Atlantic, has not appreciably reduced the time required for the actual tanning process. Hides and skins require prolonged exposure to a series of treatments before they become leather. To produce kid leather, for example, requires six weeks from the time the skins are put into work at the plant, in addition to the time required to purchase the skins, ship them to the tannery, receive and inspect them, and start them on their way through the tanning process. However, mechanization has reduced much of the heavy manual labor previously required to stir soaking hides and skins, and to dehair and flesh them. In addition to splitting hides, there are also machines now that emboss patterns and perform other processes formerly done by hand.

Chemistry has made a great contribution to tanning methods by providing new tanning agents that reduce the time required to transform hides and skins into leather and that achieve greater variety of qualities in leather. Modern instruments control solutions for temperature and other factors to assure uniformity of product.

Organization and Operation

What was once a household industry, and still is one in some of the less-developed areas of the world, has today become big business in the United States. Nearly 30,000 production workers are employed in this country's tanneries, turning out nearly a billion dollars' worth of leathers a year for widely divergent uses.

The tanning processes which are the heart of this industry are basically the same as those followed for thousands of years. Although the grease and brains of an animal are no longer used to treat its pelt, tanners still soak pelts to soften them, remove any flesh or hair that may adhere to them, and treat them to retard putrefaction. As recently as a century or two ago tanners still relied principally on such natural materials as hemlock bark to modify leather, but today there is a vast range of chemical and natural agents at their disposal: chrome salts, alum, and oils, for example. As a result, the variety of colors, textures, and finishes available to the fashion industries today is infinitely greater than it was even 50 years ago. So is the variety of animals whose skins are used.

Organization The leather industry in this country is divided into three major types of companies: regular tanneries, converters, and contract tanneries. *Regular tanneries* are those companies that purchase and process hides and skins and sell the finished leather. *Converters* buy hides and skins, farm out the processing to contract tanneries, and sell the finished product. *Contract tanneries* process hides and skins to specifications of converters and are not involved in the sale of the finished product. About half the firms in the industry are regular tanneries. The other half is comprised of about three times as many contractors as converters.

The leather industry is necessarily characterized by specialization because the methods and materials employed vary according to the nature of hides or skins being treated and the product for which each is intended. Tanners of calfskin do not normally tan kidskins; tanners of glove leathers do not normally produce sole leather.

Specialization, however, does not mean that the industry is composed only of small firms. The A. C. Lawrence Leather Company, which works only with calfskin, sheepskin, and cowhide, is the world's largest tanning firm and produces as many as 750 different types and colors of leather in a single year. Allied Kid Company, the world's largest goatskin tanner, employs about 2,000 artisans to sort, select, and process skins at its plant in Wilmington, Delaware.

Most United States tanneries are located in New England, the Middle Atlantic states, and the east North-Central states. In these regions also cluster the industry's major customers, such as shoe and glove manufacturers. Like textile and fabric producers, however, most leather firms maintain sales offices or representatives in New York City for the convenience of their customers.

Sources of Leather Supply Leather was originally a by-product of man's need to kill for food. For instance, men killed deer for food and used the skins for moccasins and jackets. Today leather is still largely a by-product of the milk-, meat-, or wool-producing industries. As a result, leather is lower in cost than it would be if animals were raised for their skins alone.

Although the majority of all leather comes from the cow and calf, fashion uses the hides and skins of many other animals from all parts of the world. Kid and goatskins come from Europe, Asia, Africa, and South America; kangaroo skins come from Australia; capeskin comes from a special breed of sheep raised near Capetown, South Africa; pigskin comes from the peccary, a wild hog native to Mexico and South America; alligator comes from Mexico, South America, and the United States; buffalo comes from Asia and eastern Europe.

The variety of leathers used in making gloves alone illustrates how worldwide are their sources:

▫ *Cabretta* from South American sheep

▫ *Calfskin* from young calves of the United States and elsewhere

▫ *Goatskin* from South America, South Africa, India, Spain

▫ *Kidskin* from Europe

▫ *Pigskin* from Central and South America, Mexico

▫ *Buckskin* from deer and elk in South and Central America, China, Mexico

▫ *Mocha* from Asian and African sheep

In the United States in a recent year, imports of hides and skins exceeded $60 million, but exports were double that amount.[1] The great bulk of the tanneries in the United States supply of raw materials for leather, however, comes from the domestic meat-packing industries.

Leather Processing The leather trade divides animal skins into three classes according to weight. Animal skins that weigh 15 pounds or less when shipped to the tannery are referred to as *skins*. Calves, goats, pigs, sheep, deer, and alligators are among the animals producing skins. Animal skins weighing from 15 to 25 pounds, such as those from young horses and cattle, are referred to as *kips*. Animal skins weighing over 25 pounds each, such as those from cows, oxen, buffalo, and horses, are referred to as *hides*.

The process by which skins, kips, and hides become leather is a lengthy one, and this length

of time is one of the many reasons why the leather industry has to work well in advance of demand. Three to six months are usually required for the tanning of hides. The time is shorter for kips and skins, but the processes are more numerous, requiring more extensive equipment and more highly skilled labor.

In all cases, when the heavily salted skin of an animal arrives at a tannery, it is first soaked for several days in clear water, and then from four to six days in a lime solution.

Hides are then passed through a hair-removing machine. Afterward they are fleshed (rid of fat and blood vessels) with sharp knives, a process done partly by machine and partly by hand. Then they pass through a series of vats, each containing a progressively stronger solution of tannic acid, constantly agitated for uniform tanning. After two to three weeks of this treatment, hides are piled in other vats of tannic acid to soak for two to six months more. Finally they are washed, swabbed with oil, and hung to dry. The skins are then ready for whatever finishing operations are required: dyeing, splitting, shaving, brushing, or embossing, for example.

Preparation for tanning skins and kips begins with painting the flesh side with a pasty solution of slaked lime or a similar substance, which works through from the flesh side and loosens the roots of the hair in two or three hours. The hair is then removed by hand or machine, according to the kind of skin being processed. This step is followed by soaking in lime vats from six days to four weeks, again according to the type of skin. At the end of this time, the skins are swollen, slippery, and rubbery. They are then fleshed and bated (washed and soaked) in a special formula that restores the original texture and consistency. Further washing, pickling, and degreasing operations follow before tanning.

Tanning of skins and kips may be done with minerals, oils, or alum, rather than with the vegetable acid used for heavier leathers. In chrome tannage, skins are churned for several hours in a solution of chrome salts and then soaked overnight in a soda solution. After tanning, skins are oiled, dried, staked (softened by passing a dull knife back and forth by hand or machine), and dyed. Oil tannage, used for such skins as buckskin and chamois, produces a velvety, extremely flexible leather. Alum tannage is used in the United States for skins like mocha, and in Europe for kid and lambskin.

Merchandising Activities

Because tanning is such a slow process, leather producers cannot merely stay abreast of fashion, they must keep ahead of it—and as a result they are among the best and most experienced forecasters in the fashion business. They have to be, especially those who work with the skins or hides of foreign animals. Months before other fashion industries have to commit themselves on matters of color and texture, leather producers have already made their decisions and have started the search for precisely the right dyes and treatments to produce what they expect fashion will want. The time consumed in transforming skins and kips and hides to leather requires the tanneries to project fashion demand several seasons into the future.

Fashion Information Services Having made their assessments of fashion trends very early, leather tanners, like fiber and fabric producers, share their conclusions with their customers. Individually or through industry associations, tanners retain fashion experts to disseminate this information and advise manufacturers, editors, and retailers on future fashion trends in leather.

A typical activity of leather producers is the preparation of fashion booklets for distribution to manufacturers, retailers, the press, and other interested persons. Such booklets are sometimes available a year before the consumer is likely to wear or use the leather products described. Contents would include comments on the general fashion trend; the leather colors and textures suitable for classics, boutique merchandise, and promotional use; swatches of important textures and looks in leather.

Another typical activity, either of individual producers or of industry associations, is the assignment of a fashion expert to work with retailers, manufacturers, and the press to help them crystallize their fashion thinking. This service might take the form of individual conferences, of membership on a committee of producers or retailers, of making fashion presentations to industry, retail, or consumer groups, and similar undertakings.

Yet with all this activity, plus spending three-quarters of 1 percent of each year's sales for advertising, individual tanners are not known by name to the public. A fashion editor describing a leather garment, glove, or shoe is not likely to mention the leather source. Nor is the leather producer likely to be named in retail store advertising or in the advertising placed by the manufacturers of the finished products. As a result, the consumer who may possibly recall names of several fabric and fiber producers would probably have a hard time naming even one tanner.

Trade Associations Tanners have long understood the virtues of working together to promote their products. For decades their industry has supported associations whose function has been to disseminate technical and fashion information to producers, consumers, and the press. Some associations, like the Calf Tanners Association, strive to promote a particular kind of leather, whereas others, such as the Tanners Council, function on an industry-wide basis, working to promote all kinds of leather.

Formerly such associations were primarily concerned with serving those segments of the market that were already customers. Today the major effort is to broaden the market for all types of leathers. Markets that once exclusively used leather, such as the shoe industry, are now shared with other products, making it necessary for the industry to defend its frontiers. Markets which traditionally never used leather, such as dresses, skirts, and coats, now are being actively cultivated by the leather industry.

At the retail level, the leather industry's associations are a valuable source of information in fashion planning and selection. They are also an important source of fashion and technical information for salespeople. For the customer, promotional efforts of the industry associations are reflected in fashion and technical material made available to schools, distributed with merchandise purchased in retail stores, and publicized through the fashion press.

2

1

3

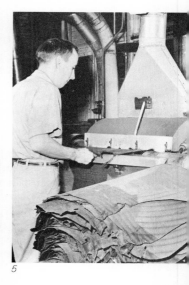

5

4

7

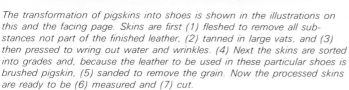

6

The transformation of pigskins into shoes is shown in the illustrations on this and the facing page. Skins are first (1) fleshed to remove all substances not part of the finished leather, (2) tanned in large vats, and (3) then pressed to wring out water and wrinkles. (4) Next the skins are sorted into grades and, because the leather to be used in these particular shoes is brushed pigskin, (5) sanded to remove the grain. Now the processed skins are ready to be (6) measured and (7) cut.

8

Skilled operators stitch the cut sections of the shoe into (8) quarters and (9) uppers and (10) then mold the leather to the last. Next the shoes are (11) soled, (12) heeled, and (13) laid out on an assembly line to be collected into pairs. (14) Finally, the finished shoes are inspected to assure quality control.

9

10

13

11

12

14

Marketing Trends

Until just a few decades ago, the leather industry concerned itself primarily with meeting the needs of relatively few segments of the fashion industries, such as shoes, gloves, belts, handbags, and small leathergoods. Apparel use was restricted largely to a few items of outerwear, such as jackets and coats that were stiff, bulky, and primarily functional in appeal.

Recently, tanning improvements have combined with fashion to make possible leather dresses, skirts, and boots that can be worn indoors as well as outdoors. Chemistry has broadened the leather industry's markets by making new colors and pliable garments possible. On the other hand, chemistry has taken away part of the market by producing synthetic competitors for large segments of the fields that leather formerly dominated. Much of the industry's future may depend upon what chemistry, as well as fashion, has in store for it.

Competitive Materials Because it is a natural product, leather comes in varied shapes and sizes, depending on the size of the animal from which it was obtained. Cutting must be planned in terms of the dimensions and irregularities of the hide or skin. The process is often one of piece-by-piece cutting, which is more costly, time-consuming, and wasteful of materials than working with fabric or plastic sheeting of standardized widths and lengths.

Leatherlike plastics therefore represent competition with leather, as do woven or knitted fabrics. Price often determines which material a producer or consumer will choose, but price is not the only determining factor. Fashion also plays a part, as does the material's appropriateness for the use intended.

Product Research and Development Leather retains and expands its markets by adapting its products to fashion's changing requirements. Before World War II, relatively few colors and types of leather were available in any one season, and each usually had a fashion life of several years. Today, a major tannery may turn out hundreds of leather colors and types each season, mean-

while preparing to produce more new colors and textures for the next season.

To protect and expand their markets, leather producers constantly broaden their range of colors, weights, and textures and introduce improvements that will make their output more acceptable where it now has either limited use or no use at all.

Leather has the weight of tradition behind it; mankind for centuries has regarded fine leather as a symbol of luxury. But today leather shares its hold on the fashion field with other and newer materials. Producers are attempting to meet the competition not only of other leathers but also of other materials through product research and development. Leathers that can be powdered and then reconstituted in the form of sheets of standardized widths and lengths, like textile fabrics, are already in prospect.

Mergers and Affiliations Mergers, consolidations, and affiliations, prevalent in the textile industry during and immediately following World War II, have also taken place in the leather industry. In 1870 there were 4,500 tanneries in operation in the United States; today there are only a few hundred. Additional mergers and a continuing trend toward fewer and larger plants may be possible, but other dramatic changes are unlikely.

Vertical integration, which made possible giantism in the textile industry, has gone about as far as it can go in the leather industry. For years, some of the country's largest tanneries have been subsidiaries of meat packers. Other tanneries have integrated with their main sources of supply. Producers of kid, alligator, kangaroo, or goat leathers, of course, are not candidates for such consolidation, since their raw materials come from abroad.

The Fur Industry

The wearing of fur as a symbol of wealth and prestige dates back to earliest recorded history. High-ranking Chinese are known to have worn furs 3,500 years ago. Greeks and Romans also dramatized rank by fur trim on their clothing. In medieval Europe, fur was a prime status symbol:

Italian cardinals wore ermine as a symbol of purity; English nobles wore it as a symbol of power. By the sixteenth century, Europe's demand for luxury furs was far greater than that continent could supply. Pressure to find new sources played an important role in encouraging exploration and trade and greatly influenced the early development of the North American continent.

The fur industry, even today, is a craft industry, involving small firms and highly skilled workers. Advances in technology have touched it, producing new colors and less expensive furs, but technology has had much less impact on it than on the other industries producing fashion materials.

History and Development

Fur trappers and traders were among the earliest explorers of the North American continent. Their work laid the foundation for much of the colonies' foreign trade, and some of this continent's largest cities were originally founded by trappers.

The English and Dutch organized companies to deal with the Indians for furs, which were often swapped for colored beads and cheap alcohol. Trading posts that were set up to handle the Indians' catch were the first centers of colonization in various parts of what is now the United States. Major cities like Chicago, Detroit, St. Paul, Spokane, and St. Louis grew from such beginnings. In Canada, the French were just as eager to buy furs; as early as 1580 they had 150 ships engaged in transporting furs obtained from the North American Indians.

The colonists themselves and, later, their descendants, used fur for apparel and other purposes. Daniel Boone's coonskin cap and the pioneer's bearskin rug are examples of how to make do with a "luxury" when the necessity is not readily available. For the most part, however, the young country used furs for export purposes, to buy from more developed countries those articles it could not yet produce for itself.

The history of the fur business in the United States is one of growth rather than change. Fur traders still send their agents wherever desirable animals live. There they buy directly from trappers or local merchants to whom trappers may have sold their catches.

Fur trading today is an international venture. Important fur-bearing animals native to the United States include mink and muskrat, fox, beaver, chinchilla, and raccoon, some of which are exported to other countries. This country's chief fur imports are mink and Persian lamb. In a typical year, the value of furs imported by the United States is about three times that of its exports.

A fairly recent development in the fur industry is *fur farming, or the raising and breeding of fur-bearing animals under controlled conditions.* This began in 1880 with silver-fox fur farming on Prince Edward Island, off the eastern coast of Canada. Chinchilla, Persian lamb, fox, and nutria farms, as well as mink ranches, have grown rapidly throughout the United States during the past 50 years. By careful breeding, strains most likely to win fashion and financial success have been evolved. Some of the most beautiful and exotic colors in fur pelts today are the result of breeding to develop colors and markings that meet the changing demands of fashion.

Organization and Operation

Since the fur industry in the United States is basically a craft industry, it is made up primarily of small shops that are usually independently owned and operated. Because of the nature of its raw materials, the fur industry will probably always remain a craft industry, and because of skills and judgments required in working with pelts, the production of fur garments lends itself to neither mass-production methods nor large-scale operation.

Obtaining the Pelts   The first step in the production of fur merchandise is to obtain the necessary pelts. Trappers are the major source of supply of wild-animal pelts, which must be taken only at the coldest season of the year to be of prime quality. The trapper sells pelts to nearby country stores or directly to itinerant buyers. In some areas, collectors or receiving houses accept furs for resale on consignment from trappers or local merchants. When a fur merchant has gathered enough pelts, he may export them or send them to an auction house. Private sale or sales through a broker may also take place.

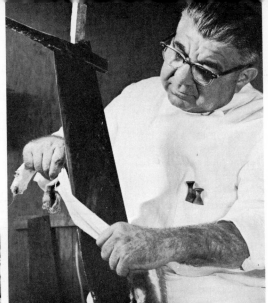

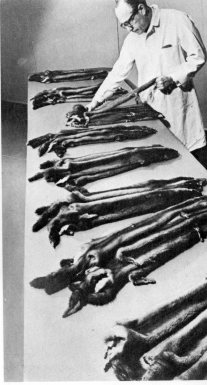

Pelts from all over the world (1) arrive at the manufacturer where they are (2) "fleshed" to remove excess material; (3) dyed, or "striped" to emphasize their natural beauty; and (4) graded to color, size, and hair length to obtain maximum uniformity. (5) The designer then creates cloth mockups to indicate how the garment is to be cut and tailored. (6) The pelts are "let out" by skilled cutters and (7) sewn into long strips which are wetted and (8) tacked to a board in the exact shape required by the pattern. (9) Finally the individual sections are sewn together to create a finished garment, (10) which is then rigorously inspected.

Courtesy Fur Information and Fashion Council

5

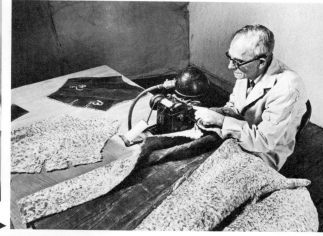

◄ 6

9 ►

7

8

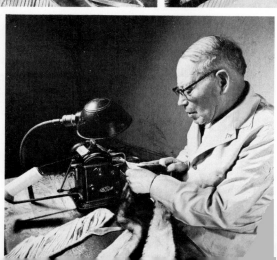

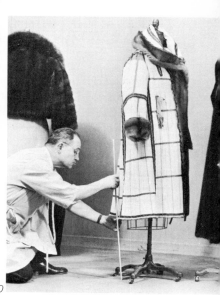

10

Animals on fur farms are carefully bred to develop the finest strains in both color and texture. Fur farmers usually sell their pelts directly to auction houses.

At auctions, fur buyers and manufacturers bid for the pelts, which are sold in bundles. Those who plan to make garments seek matched bundles of skins similar in color and quality which will form a garment of uniform beauty.

The auction trail is an international one that attracts United States fur buyers to England, Scandinavia, and Russia, as well as to various fur market centers in the United States itself and Canada. European fur buyers visit New York, Greensboro, Seattle, Minneapolis, and cities in Canada to obtain pelts of animals native to North America. Except for London, each auction center handles primarily the pelts of its own country. (See Table 7-1.)

Fur Dressing and Dyeing Preparing a fur for use is a process involving hard-won skills, carefully guarded formulas, and expert judgment. No two animals are quite alike, and neither are any two pelts. A pelt, moreover, varies in color and quality of hair from one section of the body to another. The transformation of fur pelts into garments resists machine methods and requires the attention of a trained eye and hand at every step in production.

Fur garment manufacturers contract with dressers and dyers to dye and finish the fur pelts they have purchased. Pelts are softened by both soaking and mechanical means and then dried. Then the flesher, a highly skilled craftsman, removes with a blade any unwanted substances from the inner surface of the skin. For less expensive furs, this process may be performed by roller-type machines. At this point, the pelts are treated with tanning solutions, the formulas of which sometimes are family secrets that have been handed down for generations. Oil removed in the cleansing process is replaced, and the furs are then subjected to various finishing processes which give them qualities required by fashion and the end use for which they are intended. Popular processes include dyeing, plucking, and shearing. Each process requires skill, experience, and often a secret formula or method.

Table 7-1. United States Foreign Trade in Furs

U.S. Buys	From
Mink	Canada, Denmark, Sweden, Norway, Finland, Poland, East Germany, Japan, Netherlands, United Kingdom, and 25 other countries
Persian Lamb and Caracul	Afghanistan, Republic of South Africa, U.S.S.R., and 11 other countries
Rabbit	France, Australia, Belgium, West Germany, and 19 other countries
Squirrel	U.S.S.R. and 5 other countries
Marten	Canada, Czechoslovakia, West Germany, France, and 16 other countries
Ocelot	Brazil, Bolivia, Colombia, Mexico, Peru, and 14 other countries
Sable	U.S.S.R. and Canada
Otter	Brazil, Colombia, Bolivia, and 17 other countries

U.S. Sells	To
Muskrat	United Kingdom, West Germany, Sweden, Canada, Italy
Raccoon	Canada, West Germany, and 10 other countries
Mink	United Kingdom, Canada, Switzerland, West Germany, France, Italy, Belgium, Australia, and 18 other countries
Skunk	France, West Germany, and 3 other countries
Opossum	West Germany, United Kingdom, France, and 10 other countries

U.S. Re-Exports*	To
Persian and Other Lamb	West Germany, Canada, United Kingdom, Belgium, Italy, and 9 other countries
Mink	Canada, France, Italy, and 8 other countries

*Foreign merchandise, i.e., imported merchandise which has not been changed in condition in the United States, including merchandise withdrawn from bonded storage warehouses for exportation.
Source: U.S. Department of Commerce, BDSA, Fur Facts and Figures, A Survey of the United States Fur Industry, 1966, p. 20.

Since fur dressing and dyeing are essentially a series of handcraft operations, its workers are highly skilled and highly paid. This segment of the industry is made up of small firms, some 2,000 of them in New York City alone.

Garment Manufacturing Fur garment manufacturing is also a handcraft industry. After the basic processing which all fur pelts undergo, a series of further steps are required to transform the pelts into finished garments. Each step requires a trained craftsman:

- Designing
- Making a canvas pattern
- Cutting the skins to conform to the designer's sketch, to exhibit the fur to its best advantage, and to minimize waste
- Sewing the cut skins together
- Nailing the wet skins to a board so that they dry in a permanently set shape
- Sewing the garment sections together
- Lining and finishing
- Inspection

Almost every one of the above steps is done by hand, with consideration for each pelt's peculiarities and the differences in color and hair quality in the various parts of each skin. This is in sharp contrast to the mass-production methods of those apparel makers who simply cut and sew fabrics.

For some of the more luxurious furs, the cutting operation may be extremely complex in order to *let out* short skins to a length adequate for garment purposes. Letting out mink, for example, involves cutting each skin down the center of the dark vertical stripe running lengthwise on the skin. Each half-skin is then cut at an angle into diagonal strips one-eighth to three-sixteenths of an inch wide, after which each tiny strip is resewn at an angle to the strip above and below it in order to make the skin longer and narrower. The other half-skin is resewn in like manner. The two halves are then joined, resulting in a longer, slimmer pelt, which is more beautiful than the original. Ten miles of thread may sometimes be needed to join the let-out strips for a single coat. The nailing process may require as many as 1,200 nails. Less expensive furs may get simpler treatment, but even that requires skilled craftsmen.

The fur garment manufacturing industry is made up of many small shops. In 1967, a census of manufacturers showed that there were approximately 900 shops, employing 6,500 workers, and doing an annual wholesale business of about $250 million. This is an output considerably less than that of a single good-sized textile fabric firm. Over two-thirds of these fur garment manufacturing shops employed fewer than 4 workers; only 34 factories had 25 or more employees; 228 employed an average of 13 workers.

Retail Distribution of Fur Garments The prevalence of hand craftsmanship in fur processing is reflected in the high ratio of custom-made to factory-produced garments in the retailing of fur apparel. Yet there is a certain element of bigness in the business because of two fairly common methods of fur retailing: leased departments and consignment selling.

A *leased department* is one ostensibly operated by the store under whose roof it functions but which is actually run by an outsider who pays a percentage of his receipts to the store as rent. *Consignment selling* is that in which the manufacturer places merchandise in a retail store for resale but permits any unsold portion, together with payment for those garments that have been sold, to be returned to the wholesale source by a specified date. Both operations permit the retail store to offer its customers a large selection without tying up vast quantities of capital in inventory.

In a leased department, the operator, or lessee, rather than the store, owns the stock. The lessee may also run departments in other stores, and he can, if necessary, move garments and skins from one location to another. The lessee, a retailer of a special kind, is usually well capitalized and has expert knowledge of both furs and retailing. In consignment selling, the garment producer, in effect, lends stock to a store. If not sold, the furs are returned to the producer for possible sale elsewhere. Producers who sell furs on consignment usually maintain large enough inventories so that they can afford to consign stock to retailers who prefer to operate their fur departments on this basis.

The line between manufacturing and retailing is less clear in furs than in other industries. A retail fur merchant may maintain an assortment of finished garments to show or sell to customers who buy off the rack, but he will also have a supply of skins and a fur workroom so that he can make up custom garments as well.

Merchandising Activities

In contrast to other industries, the fur industry, because it is made up almost entirely of small firms, relies to a considerable extent upon group efforts rather than those of individual entrepreneurs for its merchandising and promotional activities. In some instances, the labor unions, as well as fur traders, dressers, and garment producers, work together to encourage the public's acceptance of a specific fur or of furs in general. To some extent, the industry's merchandising activities are regulated by federal laws that specify how fur products must be labeled and advertised.

Trade Associations The fur industry relies mainly on the efforts of its trade associations to impress upon the customer the fashion and luxury values of its product. Trade associations also assist retailers in promoting fur to the public. The Fur Information and Industry Council does this for the industry as a whole. Individual types of furs are promoted by such specialized associations as the Mutation Mink Breeders Association, known as Emba (a name coined from the group's initials). Associations of both types disseminate publicity and produce educational booklets for retailers, schools, and the general public.

Labeling To capitalize on the consumer's interest in whatever furs are currently fashionable, the industry finds ways to treat one type of fur so that it resembles another, more desirable or more expensive one. This is a harmless way to let a woman on a modest budget look like a fashion leader—provided there is no deception in the sale.

To prevent deception, the Federal Trade Commission, through the Fur Products Labeling Act of 1952, has promulgated rules for the labeling of articles made of fur.

The law requires that the following be stated, both on a label attached to the merchandise and in all advertising of fur products: the English name of the animal; the country of origin; and the type of processing, including dyeing, to which the pelts may have been subjected. If paws or tails have been used, or if parts from used garments have been incorporated, this also must be clearly indicated on both the label and in all advertising. Thus the consumer who buys a Persian lamb coat made from the most desirable sections of the pelts and the customer whose coat is made of paws alone both know exactly what they are buying—and the woman who bought a "Hudson seal" generations ago would be told today that she is purchasing dyed muskrat.

The customer may convince herself that her inexpensive fur or her fabric "fake" fur coat looks just like what wealthier women are wearing, but federal laws will not permit merchant or producer to deceive her with misleading or false labeling.

Marketing Trends

Demand for furs is generally related to a country's economic conditions. During the depression of the 1930s, the output of fur dressing and dyeing plants dropped to half of its 1929 high of over $40 million. In the period immediately following World War II, when the public had much unspent money in its pocket because so little consumer merchandise was then available, output reached an all-time peak of $53 million, a level the industry has not been able to maintain since, despite increasing prosperity. With the resurgence of fashion interest in fur, however, producers expect a rise in total sales.

Expanded Markets Fashion demand in recent decades has brought "little" furs and "fun" furs into play. In the "little" category are stoles and scarves and jackets, which can be worn at any time of the year, not necessarily for warmth. In the "fun" category are skins that may not have the luxury status of mink, sable, or chinchilla,

How Many Men Like This are Left?

Not many. For how long can we count on this patient,

guild-hall type of craftsmanship? We wish we knew.

We are lucky enough to still have a handful of

the greatest of these artisans . . . men we respect, who have been

with us for decades, and will be, we hope, for years to come.

These are the men who make your Bergdorf fur coat:

who let out the skin, who shape the pelt,

who cherish the fur at Bergdorf's—

where they sit on the seventh floor, overlooking the

Park, with a north light uninterrupted from here to Canada.

These are the men who let a proud house sleep easy,

for be it a small jacket or a full-length sable, we know

that each skin has been given every attention

that the most exigent (that's us) could ask.

When your coat is finished and lined with tiny dot-sized stitches

they like to see it. Then they are content:

smiling, proud, pleased with themselves. "Beautiful."

These men are dear to us and warmly valued,

for they represent what remains of a great tradition.

We happen to believe in tradition at Bergdorf's.

ON THE PLAZA • NEW YORK
BERGDORF GOODMAN
5TH AVE., 57 TO 58TH STREETS

Retailers often stress tradition and craftsmanship in promoting furs.

but that have novelty of style or treatment to recommend them. They are not in the major fashion investment category, as a coat of more conventional fur would be. Fun furs are usually young and bold in styling, and not necessarily for outdoor wear; a vest of mole dyed in brilliant colors, for example, might be in the fun category, as would an evening skirt of monkey fur.

Both the little fur and the fun fur fashions have the virtue of keeping interest in furs alive throughout the year, and also of attracting a class of customer whose circumstances may put a full-length mink coat forever out of reach. The outlay required for a little fur or a fun fur is not too much for a young person's purse or for a woman in comfortable but not lavish circumstances.

During recent years, too, there has been a noticeable trend toward greater use of fur as trimming on coats, suits, and dresses, as linings for men's and women's cloth coats and rainwear, and as headwear for both men and women. The popularity of fur hats helped sagging sales of the millinery industry as well as those of the fur trade.

Product Research and Development To harness fashion's pulling power, the fur industry constantly strives to achieve new looks and effects with furs. Experiments lead to new and better ways of preparing the pelts. Shearing, for instance, makes some normally heavy furs lighter in weight and more supple; new dyes transform dull, unattractive colors into more interesting shades. At the same time, mink ranchers, in their search for new colors, are constantly endeavoring to develop new strains. Mutation mink hues today range from blue-black to white, the newest and rarest colors being the most expensive.

It seems unlikely, however, that methods of operation within the fur industry will change radically in the foreseeable future. Thorough knowledge of both fur and fashion is required of all concerned, from trappers and breeders to the salespeople who guide the customer's selection. It is a business composed of experts, each highly skilled in his own narrow area and keenly aware of what goes on both before and after a skin passes through his hands. Mechanization may continue to make some tasks less arduous; chemical or electronic controls may take some of the guesswork and risk out of some phases of fur treatment; but nothing the machine age can produce is likely to replace the trained judgment required at each step in the making of a fur garment.

Reference

[1]U.S. Department of Commerce, Office of Business Economics, *Survey of Current Business,* July, 1968, S-30.

Merchandising Vocabulary

Define or briefly explain the following terms:

Tanning
Skins
Kips
Hides
Fur farming
Letting-out

Merchandising Review

1. Name and describe the three major types of operations into which the United States leather industry is divided.
2. Discuss how mechanization and chemistry have aided the tanning process.
3. Why is the leather industry so highly specialized?
4. Why is product research and development so important today in the leather industry?
5. What is meant by "fur farming"? Discuss its importance to the fur industry today.
6. Differentiate between "leased department" and "consignment selling" as these terms apply in the retail merchandising of fur garments.
7. What are the provisions of the Fur Labeling Act of 1952? How does this Act protect the consumer?
8. Describe the *letting-out* operation sometimes used in the construction of fur garments. What purpose does it serve? How does this process affect the price of the garment?
9. Distinguish between "little" furs and "fun" furs. Cite examples of specific furs that might be used in each of these two categories.

Merchandising Digest

1. "Leather producers cannot merely stay abreast of fashion; they must keep ahead of it." Discuss this statement from the text and its implications for leather merchandising.
2. Discuss the major merchandising activities engaged in by the leather industry.
3. "To harness fashion's pulling power, the fur industry constantly strives to achieve new looks and effects with furs." Discuss this statement from the text, citing specific examples of the increased variety of furs in use and the apparel and accessory purposes for which furs are now being used. Indicate the types of fur that lend themselves to such purposes.

8

MANUFACTURERS of FASHION APPAREL

In production of ready-to-wear apparel fashions, the United States leads the world. Its apparel industry has no peer in size, in efficient production methods, in workers' pay, or in ability to provide attractive fashions quickly and economically to women in every walk of life.

Apparel manufacturing is today a major industry in the United States. The industry employs nearly 1.4 million persons, or one out of every 14 of all those employed in manufacturing in this country. The combined wages and salaries of these people exceed $6.5 billion a year. The total annual output of the industry exceeds $13 billion at wholesale values.

Yet the ready-to-wear industry is relatively young; it was little more than an infant at the turn of the century. The industry has quickly gained flexibility and grown rapidly in size during the few decades of its life. Whereas once Paris was the sole source of fashion inspiration, today the industry gathers its design ideas from the four corners of the world. Whereas once a rigid pattern of seasonal openings and shipping dates prevailed, today the industry is adjusting its timing to meet the public's demand for something new at all times of the year. Whereas once fashion and marketing decisions were based largely on guesswork, today market research and computerized operations prevail.

Ready-to-wear is a fast-moving, complex industry in which patterns of operation, as well as styling and timing, must constantly adjust to the changing tastes and preferences of its consumers. Only those who interpret and satisfy those changing tastes and preferences succeed.

History of the Industry

The first clothing made on a commercial scale in the United States was produced for men who had no women to sew for them—the sailors of whaling ships that put into New Bedford for outfitting. About 1830, production of rough clothes of poor quality began in that city, but demand soon became so great that dealers in other port towns entered the men's ready-to-wear field. Brooks Brothers, stronghold of male conservative elegance, traces back to just such beginnings.

Progress thereafter was rapid with the gold rush and the Civil War stepping up demand for ready-made apparel for men. The sewing machine, invented by Elias Howe in 1846 and later improved by Isaac Singer (who substituted a foot treadle for the handwheel with which it had formerly been operated), helped to speed up production. So, too, did the introduction in 1876 of knives that could cut through several thicknesses of cloth.

Fit improved when the need for Civil War uniforms led to the development of standard size measurements. Prestige attached itself to "store clothes" only gradually, however. Several financial crises near the turn of the nineteenth century caused men who had formerly worn only custom-made apparel to patronize ready-to-wear shops, thus endowing ready-made clothes with some degree of social acceptability.

While men were moving toward ready-to-wear, women continued to make most of their own clothing at home, although some ready-to-wear, mostly cloaks and mantles, was factory-produced.

Working conditions in the garment factories of the early 1900s were crowded, uncomfortable, often unsafe—and hours were long.

By the turn of the century, however, many women's suits, skirts, and blouses were being made in factories, but it was not until the end of World War I that a manufacturer produced factory-made dresses by sewing blouses and skirts together. David Crystal produced the first dresses sold through retail stores. By that time, the women's clothing industry, which is the heart of the fashion business today, had passed the one-billion-dollar mark in product value. By 1967, dresses alone accounted for more than this figure, and the factory value of all shipments made by the women's outerwear industries totaled $6.3 billion.

Labor Unions and Industry Development

An important element in the growth of the ready-to-wear fashion industries in this country was that labor of the right type was available at the right time and in the right place. In the late nineteenth and early twentieth centuries, millions of Europeans sought refuge in the United States. All of them were desperately eager to find a means of earning a living in their new home. Unfamiliar with the country and its language, great numbers of them lived in neighborhoods where others from their land had already settled, often in the same city where they had debarked. Usually that city was New York, where the women's apparel trade had its roots.

Working conditions in the apparel trades at the turn of the century were appalling. Hours were long and pay was small. Factories bore no resemblance to some of the light, cheerful, sanitary plants seen today. Workers, in their efforts to combat these conditions by unionizing, were handicapped by their own poverty and ignorance, by the language barriers among them, by the seasonality of the apparel business, and by the continuing influx of new immigrants even more desperate than themselves to secure work.

Not until 1909 and 1910 did successful strikes among the shirtwaist workers and cloak makers pave the way for the present era of collective bargaining in the women's garment trades. Characteristic of today's methods is the use of joint employer-union committees to set prices for piecework on individual garments, depending on the elements of work involved in each style.

Today, the International Ladies' Garment Workers' Union (ILGWU), the major union in the women's apparel trade, has developed into more than a collective bargaining agency. This union has contributed funds for promoting New York as an industry fashion center and has helped develop schools to train technical workers, designers, and other skilled employees needed in the industry. In addition, ILGWU has subsidized housing and vacation resorts and provided other benefits to make it easier and more pleasant for employees to remain in the city and in the garment industry.

Having come to grips with labor problems early in its career, the women's apparel industry has enjoyed many decades of growth uninterrupted by strikes and lockouts. Management's relations with its employees and the attitude of ILGWU toward the industry have been held up time and time again as outstanding examples of the benefits gained from constructive labor-management cooperation.

Organization of the Industry

The apparel industry is unusual among other major manufacturing industries in the United States in that it is dominated by small firms. There are a few giants, but their output is relatively modest in comparison to the output of giants in other industries.

Producers of women's apparel have developed a pattern of operation capable of rapid response to the changing demands of fashion. Manufacturers can contract or expand their facilities almost at a moment's notice, depending on how well their styles are accepted. New talents can enter the industry with minimum capital and sometimes skyrocket to a size that places them in the ranks of the few giants.

The fashion apparel industry consists of three types of producers: manufacturers, jobbers, and contractors. A *manufacturer* is one who performs all the operations in producing a garment. A *jobber* handles the designing, the planning, the purchasing, the cutting, the selling, and the shipping, but does not handle the actual sewing. The *contractor* is the one whose sole function is to supply sewing services to the industry.

Most contractors are located in the metropolitan New York City area, the traditional center of the garment business. In some branches of the garment trade, however, notably intimate apparel, sewing may be farmed out to contractors as far away as Puerto Rico and Japan.

In recent years some manufacturers have set up sewing plants of their own far from New York City. In upstate New York, in Alabama, or in any area where women with sewing skills are available for employment, small plants have been erected. Training, supervision, and planning requirements of such plants are minimal compared with those of a main plant. Producers already scraping the bottom of the barrel for labor at their headquarters location find this a practical and more economical way to expand their sewing operations.

Many of these producers are small organizations. The dress business alone had 4,577 firms whose output reached $2.4 billion in 1963, a year when, in contrast, the radio and television receiving set production industry had an output of almost the identical value with only 322 firms. In 1963, the 50 largest dress producers accounted for only 23 percent of the industry's total output. By way of contrast, the 50 largest companies in the shoe industry that year produced 57 percent of the total output; in soaps, 93 percent; in aircraft, 99 percent.

Publicly owned giants in the fashion industries do exist, however. One of the largest is Jonathan Logan, which in the early 1960s was first in the industry to pass the $100 million mark in sales. Other large publicly owned producers include Bobbie Brooks, Russ Togs, and, at the upper end of the price and fashion scale, Originala.

But despite the presence of giants, it is possible for a small firm to set up shop and remain in the apparel business with only a modest investment and without the full range of talents and facilities required to process garments from original conception to ultimate distribution. A designer can function as a one-man custom business until he attracts a manufacturer with the capital and productive capacity to bring his work to the attention of a larger clientele. A manufacturer with limited capital but wide marketing and production sophistication can use free-lance designers, farming out his sewing to contractors, thus stretching his capital. A contractor needs no knowledge of fashion, design, or markets; if he can rent space, buy sewing machines, and hire operators, he is in business.

Operational Patterns Within the Industry

The operating procedures that have developed in the fashion apparel industry are outgrowths of two major characteristics of the industry itself: the fact that it is made up predominantly of small firms, and the seasonality of its output. These factors are reflected in the existence of highly specialized firms and in the custom of producing a new *line,* or assortment of styles, for each selling season of the year.

Contract Operation

Contractors specialize in just one phase of the production of a garment: its sewing. Contractors developed early in the life of the fashion industry, with the beginning of mass-production techniques. Contractors serve those producers who have little or no sewing capability of their own as well as those whose current business exceeds their own sewing capacity.

If a contractor is used, cut pieces of the garment are turned over to him by the jobber or, in some cases, by the manufacturer. For an agreed price per garment, the article is sewn, inspected, pressed, and returned for shipment to retail store purchasers. The price charged by the contractor is largely determined by the union which, in collaboration with management, sets the piece rates to be paid for labor.

In the mass production of ready-to-wear a single sewing machine operator rarely makes a complete garment. Each operator in a group sews only a certain section of the garment, such as a sleeve or its hem. This division of labor, called *section work,* makes it unnecessary for an operator to switch from one highly specialized machine to another or to make adjustments on the machine. Any change or adjustment in equipment takes time, and time costs money. In the fashion trade, time lost in making such changes also causes delays in getting a style to the consumer. Delays in production could mean the loss of timeliness and sales appeal before an article reaches its market.

A contractor may arrange to work exclusively with one or more jobbers or manufacturers, reserving the right to work for others whenever his facilities are not fully employed. Such agreements are necessarily reciprocal; if a contractor agrees to give preference to a particular jobber's work, the jobber gives preference to that contractor in placing his sewing orders.

The major advantage of the contractor system is that it provides greater speed and flexibility than would be possible when the entire production is under one roof. It has the disadvantages common to most types of assembly-line production: no individual has full responsibility for the finished product on which he works, and so quality of workmanship and inspection may tend to be uneven.

Specialization by Product

The typical fashion apparel firm specializes in a narrow segment of the overall field, such as misses' cocktail dresses within a specified price range, or sportswear for juniors within a narrow price range. Normally, a house making junior-size dresses, for instance, does not produce half-size dresses for women, nor does a coat house produce dresses. So well entrenched is specialization within the industry that when a firm known in one field is acquired by a firm that produces other types, sizes, or price lines, the acquired firm usually continues to operate under its old name as a wholly owned subsidiary of the parent firm.

Although fashion trends that influence styling in several branches of the fashion apparel busi-

Apparel manufacturing today is mechanized, specialized, and efficient as in this Hawaiian factory.

ness may be the same, the expression given to them is necessarily different in each size and price range. In each segment of the industry, there are designers who have channeled their creative abilities into solving the fashion problems of that particular consumer that the firm visualizes as its market. Sales staffs of each firm are familiar with appropriate retail outlets; purchasing agents, production experts, and other key executives are also familiar with the general nature of the firm's market and its requirements.

Theoretically, nothing prevents a producer from changing or enlarging the field in which he has chosen to specialize. Practically, however, such change is difficult. Designers accustomed to higher-priced lines do not adjust easily to achieving their desired effects on a more economical basis; production staffs used to scrimping on fabrics, stitching, and bindings do not readily adjust to the more lavish use of such materials in

higher-priced merchandise. Sources of supply are different, as are retail outlets. Normally, a variety of size and price ranges exists only among the giants of the industry, who set up separate divisions for each of the many types, prices, and size ranges produced under the corporate umbrella.

Creating a Line

At least two months before consumers are expected to buy their apparel for a specific season, retail buyers are in the wholesale markets, viewing the lines of manufacturers and making their selections. From 2 to 18 months before that time, manufacturers begin wrestling with the problems of creating seasonal lines to be shown to store buyers.

Long before a line begins to take shape, the designer charged with creating it has reviewed all available information on trends, materials, and previous fashion successes and failures, in order to form some idea of what the coming season's line should include. Each design he suggests is either sketched or developed in muslin. The design is then considered both on its own merits and for its suitability to the line as a whole. Many designs may be discarded at this point.

Those designs that seem most likely to succeed are then made up by a *sample hand,* a designer's assistant who is an all-round seamstress. She translates each sketch into a finished garment. Various executives of the firm (sales, purchasing, and production heads, cost experts, and others) then examine the samples. At this point, several designs may fall by the wayside while others may go back for modification.

Producing a Line

After a design has survived these preliminary challenges, a patternmaker makes a production pattern for it in whatever garment size the firm uses for its samples. From this pattern, one or more samples are cut and sewn. If the sample is of acceptable fit and timeliness, its production costs are carefully figured, a wholesale price is determined, the design is given a style number, and it becomes part of the manufacturer's line.

After buyers have viewed a line and placed their orders, it is usually found that some numbers have failed to evoke adequate response to warrant production. These are then dropped, possibly to be revived in a future season when they may prove more acceptable.

For every style that is to be produced, the original pattern is graded or "sloped" to adjust it to each of the various sizes in which the number will be made. Next, the pieces of the pattern in all its sizes are laid out on a long paper, or *marker,* that corresponds in width to the width of the fabric to be used. The marker becomes the pattern's cutting guide.

Cutting of mass-produced garments, except those that require matching, such as plaids and stripes, is done by machine through many thicknesses of material. The individual pieces are then collected in bundles according to size and passed along to the sewing operators, either in the same plant or in a contractor's shop. After sewing, finishing, pressing, and inspection, the finished garments are ready for shipment.

Courtesy Kamehameha Garment Company, Ltd.

Each piece of a pattern is laid out on a marker, which is used as a guide for cutting through layers of material.

As the season progresses, retailers reorder popular numbers, and manufacturers may recut them. For profits and speed, producers concentrate only on the "hottest" or best-selling numbers in their lines and drop any others for which there have been only scattered reorders. The customer who wonders why a retailer cannot special-order a winter coat or dress for her in January does not realize that by that time of year the factories have completed their winter season's production and are working on spring and summer lines.

Centers of Fashion Inspiration

Fashions are not created by industry and pushed upon an unwilling public. Fashions are the industry's interpretation of what it expects consumers to want at a future period, based upon all available evidence at its disposal.

Some individuals within the industry, both in the United States and abroad, are so sensitive to even the slightest hint of change in demand that they seem to be shaping fashion's course. Such individuals are the industry's innovators and influentials, inspiring those who are less intuitive and less quick to discern early signs of trends.

These trailblazers, so far as the Western world is concerned, used to be concentrated in Paris. Paris is still a vital fashion center, but other centers throughout the world have become increasingly influential in the fashion field, particularly since World War II.

Paris, the Fashion Center

For centuries Paris has been considered the fountainhead of new apparel fashions. Ever since the seventeenth century, designers of talent have flocked to that city. Working conditions there are ideal for the creative person: a labor force of superbly trained seamstresses is available; producers of buttons, ribbons, and other fashion components abound there; the availability of a financial backer, such as a French fabric house, is possible for new designing talent; and French laws provide protection from style piracy.

Paris, moreover, has been for centuries considered the world's leading art center as well as a magnet for the wealthy and for socially and politically prominent people from all parts of the world.

Paris Couture The leading French fashion apparel producers are known as members of the *haute couture*. The French term, which literally means "fine sewing," is applied only to those high fashion houses whose designers create exclusive and trend-setting styles. In ordinary custom dressmaking, the customer either directs the styling of her garments or has them designed to her specifications. When a private customer buys from a couture house, she selects an original model that has already been designed and has it made up to her own measurements.

The proprietor or designer of a couture house is known as a *couturier* (male) or a *couturière* (female). Most of the couture houses are known by the names of the designers who head them— Chanel, St. Laurent, Givenchy, Ungaro, and many others. Some houses continue to use the name of the designer even after his death, as in the case of the House of Dior.

Chambre Syndicale For a designer's firm to qualify as a couture house, certain explicit requirements have to be met. In Paris, these requirements have been codified and are rigidly enforced by a trade association known as the Chambre Syndicale de la Couture Parisienne. The Chambre Syndicale requires that members must present styles that are the original works of their own designers; none may be purchased from free-lance designers. All work, except for such specialized work as embroidery, must be done only in the firm's own house. Piece rates and production bonuses are forbidden; all garments must be custom-made by hand. Each house, moreover, agrees to show on live models a collection of at least 50 numbers twice a year at a time and period fixed by the Chambre Syndicale.

The Chambre Syndicale also has regulations governing the sale of designs by its member firms. A retailer or manufacturer who purchases an original model has the right to copy it only in his own country and then only in apparel materials; the cutting of paper patterns is forbidden, since this presumably implies mass reproduction. Manufacturers are usually required to sign an agreement that they will neither hire, lend, nor sell a model to a colleague. Anyone breaking such agreement is subject to a lawsuit and is barred thereafter from attending the collections.

Membership in the Chambre Syndicale is by invitation only and is restricted to those houses that agree to abide by its rules governing copying, shipping dates, issuing of press cards, and so on. No regulatory body with all the powers of the Chambre Syndicale exists in any other country or fashion center.

Viewing Couture Collections Some of the wealthiest and most prominent women in the world patronize the Paris couture houses. What they wear becomes fashion news and influences what other women consider acceptable. Although couture methods of handwork and custom fitting are the antithesis of American mass-production methods, couture collections are a showcase and testing ground for new styles, lines, colors, and looks. When the major Paris couture houses show their new collections, therefore, retailers, manufacturers, and fashion editors from all over the world flock to the scene.

The welcome accorded to the fashion press varies from house to house, and sometimes from season to season. Trade visitors, however, are always welcome, but at a price. To view a couturier's collection, each manufacturer or retailer pays a "caution," or fee; the private clientele and the press do not. Each house sets its own fee. Some charge a flat sum; others require a guarantee that the manufacturer or retailer will purchase one or more numbers from the collection. Fees for retailers are usually lower than those for manufacturers. According to a 1967 listing of cautions for the Paris collection, the most common requirement for retailers was the purchase of one or two numbers. In other cases, they paid fees ranging from $400 to $1,145 for a single admittance. Manufacturers were required to buy one or two numbers or *toiles* (fabric patterns), or to pay fees ranging from $400 to $2,000.[1]

Copies and Adaptations In addition to buying original couture models for resale to their customers, a few of the more prestigious United States retail stores that operate custom workrooms buy models which they then reproduce seam for seam, usually in the same materials as the original. These *seam-for-seam copies* are made up to the special measurements of individual customers, exactly as might have been done in the couture house where the style originated.

Other stores that do not have custom workrooms or the clientele to support such facilities may purchase originals abroad and bring them back to be copied by domestic producers for sale as ready-to-wear. These *line-for-line copies*, although frequently made up in the same fabric as the original, cost only a fraction of the price of the original because they are made in quantity to standard measurements by machine methods instead of being made to individual measurements entirely by hand. Line-for-line copies of couture originals are featured prominently by such mass merchandising giants as Ohrbach's in New York City, as well as by a few fine specialty and department stores.

Volume retailers, such as chain and mail-order organizations, also attend showings of couture collections and buy original models. These models, however, are more likely to be used for inspiration rather than for exact copying purposes. Their *adaptations* incorporate all the important features of the original but adjust these features to the less sophisticated tastes of the clientele to whom they will be sold. Lower-cost machine methods of production ensure that the adaptations can be sold at low prices.

Manufacturers also buy models for copying or adaptation, particularly the latter. Sometimes they reproduce styles in their entirety, but more frequently they buy a model and then adapt some interesting new feature of it, such as a sleeve, neckline, or seam treatment, for use in their own lines.

The impact of the couture on American fashions is not limited to the impact of purchased styles. The overall impression gained from the collections affects the thinking of producers, retailers, and private individuals alike. What buyers reject is as important, in its way, as what they purchase, for both show the direction of current trends in fashion.

ON TUESDAY FROM 9 TO 9 ST. LAURENT AND BALENCIAGA, GIVENCHY AND CARDIN, UNGARO, VALENTINO, MONSIEUR X, DE BARENTZEN AND FABIANI, PERTEGAZ AND PATOU WILL ALL GO ON SALE AT **OHRBACH'S**

Stay for the fabulous fashion show at 5:45. See great copies, all in the original imported fabrics. Fashions on sale this Thursday at 10 AM at Bergen Mall, Paramus, New Jersey. This Friday at 10 AM at Westbury, Long Island.

New York: 34th St. Monday, Tuesday, Thursday, Friday till 9.

This mass merchandiser features line-for-line copies often in original fabrics.

Paris Ready-to-Wear In recent years, members of the Paris couture have been increasingly attracted to the field of ready-to-wear. Rising costs make custom operations decreasingly profitable. In addition, women, even those of enormous wealth and leisure, become impatient with the fittings and delays associated with custom-made, hand-produced garments. Their figures, moreover, are generally so well cared for that most of them can be fitted easily with ready-to-wear clothes from the rack.

Some French couture designers offer ready-to-wear collections, either in boutiques under their own roofs or in special shops elsewhere. These clothes are usually made in factories, rather than in the designer's house, but they bear the designer's world-famous label.

Some members of the haute couture have still another interest in ready-to-wear. They accept from large American retailers, such as chain and mail-order houses, commissions to design exclusive groups of garments for these firms. Production and sales take place in the United States, but the designer's name carries the glamour of foreign fashion. The couturier himself may even, on occasion, make personal appearances in various United States cities to promote his creations.

Other Foreign Fashion Centers

Although Paris has traditionally been considered the foremost foreign source of fashion inspiration, it is not currently the only one. Designers in Spain, Italy, and England hold twice-a-year showings in the best haute couture tradition for private customers, as well as for visiting retailers, manufacturers, and the press. These showings are timed to come just before or after those in Paris, so that visitors can cover all the major foreign centers in a single trip.

> Paris still supplies the spirit, the mood, the essence, but Paris is no longer the only fashion fountainhead. . . . Besides Paris, we have Italy (for superb knits and exciting sportswear), and such exotic, faraway places as Thailand (for Siamese colors, textured silks), India (for handwoven silks, exquisite saris), Japan (for obi sashes, kimono sleeves, subtle and mysterious print designs), and Hong Kong (for Chinese brocades, tribute

> silks, frog fastenings). We also have countries like West Germany, Scotland, Spain, all contributing to the eternal process of trial and error, developing ideas with the hope that the customers will like them. . . .[2]

In Italy, buyers visit the major markets in Rome, Milan, and Florence for sportswear, knits, and leather goods. In Spain, they find elegant gowns. They go to the British Isles and Austria for original sweater designs. In London, long a leader primarily in men's fashions, they find a group of lively young designers who have added "Carnaby Street" and "mod" to the fashion vocabulary. If a single designer can claim credit for catching the mood of the young and expressing it in all its miniskirted freedom during the 1960s, that designer is Mary Quant of London.

Domestic Fashion Centers

Not all fashion inspiration originates abroad. Until recently, however, so great has been the prestige of Paris that many United States designers had to gain experience and recognition there before they could expect recognition in their own country. Nevertheless, even before World War II temporarily eliminated Paris as a fashion center, designers in this country had begun to fill needs that Paris neither understood nor could design for.

Prominent among American fashion creators of yesterday was the late Claire McCardell. Ignoring Paris, she made clothes for women in this country, introducing easy lines that made the most of their figures and also permitted freedom of movement. Among the casual clothes that this world-famous designer created before World War II are types that have remained popular throughout the years: shirtwaist dresses, for example, and skirts with unpressed pleats.

Other design trends indigenous to the United States came from California where Adrian, in the 1930s and 1940s, created clothes for motion picture stars. Adrian's designs popularized such effects as the squared-off shoulder that remained in favor through the 1940s.

Designers working in this country have no protection from design piracy, much as many of them would welcome such protective laws. The regu-

The heart of New York's garment center is
Seventh Avenue, bustling with garment carts.

The New York Fashion Center New York City is not only the fashion apparel production center from which goods are shipped to stores throughout the country, but it is also the sales headquarters for manufacturers whose design and production facilities may be located in any of the 50 states. The heart of the garment district is "SA," or Seventh Avenue, specifically that section of it bounded by 33d Street on the south and by 42d Street on the north.

The crowding, the high cost of space and labor, and other factors make New York a more difficult place to work in, in many respects, than any other area in which fashion producers have developed businesses. So many segments of the industry are in the city, however, that its importance as a center for retail purchasing will undoubtedly continue for many years to come. A merchant and his buyers have only limited time to spend away from their stores. If they can do all their purchasing in a single sector of one city, this is a great advantage. A producer can operate far from New York City's immense sources of supply, skilled labor, and fashion inspiration. But to grow, he has to show his wares where retailers come to buy. In the fashion industries, that place is usually New York's Seventh Avenue.

The California Market California designers, in many cases, have been more alert than those in the East to sense certain trends in the American way of life, particularly the current trend toward more casual living. In the 1930s, when sportswear was beginning to find a place in most women's wardrobes, it was being produced almost entirely by California firms. Major fashion retailers throughout the country sent their buyers to check the California offerings and purchase merchandise that would satisfy their customers' demand for casual apparel.

Ever since those earlier days, the California market has continued to grow in fashion importance until today it is second only to New York as a fashion market center. A huge new California Mart in Los Angeles houses the permanent showrooms of hundreds of firms producing fashion apparel and accessories throughout the United States. This important market also supports an active trade association, known as the California

lations that shelter the French couture would violate antitrust laws here. Nevertheless, even without such protection and without the glamour of a centuries-old reputation such as the Paris couture enjoys, United States designers flourish. Most of them produce factory-made ready-to-wear for sale through retail stores rather than directly to a custom clientele. Their method of operation and their interpretations of fashion appear to be in close harmony with what women in this country want.

Among those in the front rank of design talent in the United States today are Bill Blass, Norman Norell, Pauline Trigère, Adele Simpson, Donald Brooks, Teal Traina, Geoffrey Beene, Herbert Kasper, and George Halley. In California, such talented designers as James Galanos and Rudi Gernreich are well established. The list of first-rate American designers is long and grows longer each season.

Fashion Creators, that sponsors a semiannual Press Week, patterned somewhat after the New York Press Week showing.

Although the California market is perhaps best known for women's swimwear and other types of active sportswear, it has also become an important market for a wide variety of men's, women's, and children's leisure wear, and for more formal categories of women's apparel.

Other Regional Centers Other cities in this country have become centers for the design and production of specialized fashion apparel and, in many cases, have built large merchandise marts to house the permanent showrooms of firms with production facilities in the surrounding area. Dallas, for example, is an increasingly important center for misses' and women's sportswear fashions. St. Louis boasts a number of producers of junior apparel. Miami produces a wide variety of resort wear. New England has apparel producers in the Greater Boston area and intimate apparel producers in Connecticut.

Almost any part of the country can give birth to fashion production attuned to its regional needs. Wherever producers develop fresh, interesting ideas, fashion retailers from other areas soon patronize them and give their styles exposure throughout the country.

Paris, France, has the history, the tradition, and remains the queen of fashion centers—but smart fashion merchandisers do not discount the possibility that Paris, Texas, may contribute something to a fashion trend tomorrow. Fashion now is truly a worldwide business, in creation as well as consumption.

Merchandising Activities

Most fashion producers sell directly to retail stores rather than through jobbers and other intermediaries. The pace of fashion in all but a few staple items is much too fast to allow time for the selling, reselling, or warehousing activities of jobbers or wholesale distributors.

Fashion producers aim their sales promotion efforts at both retailers and consumers. Such efforts take the form of advertising, publicity, and a number of promotional aids designed as customer services for the retailers who buy their products.

Advertising

Today much retail advertising of fashion merchandise carries the name of its producer. As late as the 1930s, however, nearly all retailers refused to allow any tags or labels but their own on the fashion goods they offered for sale. First the depression and then merchandise shortages during World War II helped reverse such attitudes, however. Today, merchants capitalize on brand-name national advertising by leaving labels attached, featuring brand names in their own advertising and displays, and sometimes even setting up special sections for individual brands within their stores.

The apparel industry spends less than one percent of its annual sales on advertising, but the exposure given to its brands is impressive. Some exposure is achieved through paid newspaper and magazine advertising placed by producers themselves, and some results from ads placed in cooperation with fiber and fabric sources.

An important source of exposure is cooperative advertising with retail stores. Advertising that appears in the retailer's name but is paid for entirely or in part by the producer whose goods are featured is called cooperative advertising. This method presents certain advantages to the producer: the retailer's expertise in advertising is made available, and the retailer's intention to adequately stock and display the featured merchandise is virtually assured, since the store pays part of the cost of the ad.

An inexpensive form of advertising used effectively by fashion apparel producers is *trade advertising*. A publication such as *Women's Wear Daily* that features mainly trade news and goes only to readers in a particular industry or business is known as a *trade publication*. This type of print medium has limited circulation and correspondingly low advertising rates. Although the general public does not usually see trade advertising, it is an excellent medium for reaching the retail merchant. Manufacturers use it to announce developments in their lines, and to acquaint retailers with their products. Apparel producers sometimes share ad costs with fiber or fabric producers, thus getting greater mileage from their advertising funds.

Publicity

Whether he spends money on advertising or not, an apparel producer has many opportunities at his disposal to familiarize the public with his brand name through publicity. In order to obtain maximum publicity, a producer sometimes hires a public relations person or firm. Photographs of some of his best-selling numbers are distributed to newspapers and magazines. He may court the attention of fashion editors, society leaders, and television personalities in an attempt to attract the public's eye to his merchandise and name.

In addition to their individual efforts to secure publicity, the major New York couture houses have formed two trade associations, each of which arranges for semiannual showings of the collections of member firms to fashion editors of newspapers and other publications published throughout the 50 states, during a week designated as Press Week. These associations are the New York Couture Business Council and the American Designers Group. The New York Press Week originated during World War II as a substitute for the Paris collections which, of course, were nonexistent during the war years.

Early Press Weeks exhibited merchandise lines that ran the entire gamut of price levels, from lowest to highest. Gradually, however, lower-priced merchandise was eliminated until in recent years New York Press Weeks now feature almost exclusively the lines of higher-priced producers.

As previously noted, semiannual Press Week showings are also now held in Los Angeles under the sponsorship of the California Fashion Creators, a trade association of West Coast, Southwestern, and Hawaiian fashion producers. Unlike their New York counterparts, California Press Weeks feature fashion apparel and accessories for a wide variety of occasions and in a wide variety of price ranges.

These semiannual Press Weeks of the New York and California trade associations attract the attention of the country's newspapers and magazine editors and help publicize the latest trends on the domestic fashion scene.

Promotional Aids

To assist retailers and to speed the sale of their merchandise, many apparel manufacturers provide a variety of promotional aids. The range is vast, and a single firm's offerings may include any or all of the following:

- Display ideas
- Display and stock fixtures
- Advertising suggestions
- Plans for departmental layout and fixturing
- Reorder forms and assistance in checking stock and placing reorders
- Educational booklets for salespeople and customers
- Talks to salespeople by producers' representatives
- Assistance from producers' fashion experts in training salespeople, staging fashion shows, addressing customers
- Mailing pieces for stores to send to customers
- Special promotions and tie-in opportunities

Typical of what can be achieved by close cooperation between producers and retailers is the experience, a few years ago, of a sportswear producer who offered assistance to any store that would stage a travel promotion using the firm's merchandise. A major airline joined in the effort; its stewardesses were available to show customers how to pack and to advise them on clothing needs in various vacation spots served by that airline. The producer's fashion experts planned minimum wardrobes to meet maximum travel demands. The producer, the store, and the airline all contributed to the promotion, and each profited by the interest generated.

Marketing Trends

Some marketing trends that are currently affecting the fashion industries have already been discussed, such as the growth of giant firms and the decentralization of production facilities. Although both of these trends exert some influence on apparel production, their effects are not as pronounced on this segment of the industry as they are on some of the other segments.

Other significant marketing trends include a marked de-emphasis on strictly seasonal lines, increased diversification of product, the licensing of brand names to producers in the United States and abroad, the cultivation of foreign markets, and the use of foreign production facilities for merchandise designed by American producers and intended for sale in the American market.

De-Emphasis on Seasonal Lines

Decades ago, retail buyers came to the wholesale markets early in July to buy fall garments for late August and early September delivery. To ship orders promptly, producers often had to work their people overtime and pay high overtime wages. Since pay scales in the garment trade are high and the workweek is short, overtime rates, usually time and a half, can jeopardize much or all of a manufacturer's profit for the season.

Today, manufacturers show their lines earlier and earlier in order to give themselves more time to produce the more successful numbers from showings and to have seasonal merchandise in the stores when fashion innovators are eager to buy. In some branches of the industry, capsule lines of only a few prophetic styles are shown in April and May and delivered to stores in time for early fall selling and testing. More complete lines, incorporating popular features noted in the capsule showings, are shown a month or so later.

Stores find that customers are less rigid in their shopping habits than they were a generation or two ago. Today's customer tends to do her shopping several times a season, instead of going on just a single seasonal shopping spree. Furthermore, she expects to find new merchandise each time she comes into a store. More customers are also taking vacations throughout the year instead of only during the summer months, thus creating a continuing need for apparel appropriate for a variety of climates and activities.

Seasonal distinctions thus are becoming blurred. The day may come when apparel producers will offer new numbers every month instead of presenting new lines only at seasonal intervals. Experimentation has begun in this di-rection, but as yet it has not become the prevailing practice in the industry.

Diversification of Product

The trend after World War II toward diversification of products throughout the industrial world also has affected the production of fashion apparel. When a firm approaches the limits of its growth in a particular field, it frequently seeks expansion by diversifying. This may be done by acquiring other companies, setting up additional divisions, or simply producing additional items related to the main products.

Impetus toward diversification has often come from fashion itself, which stresses the importance of related wardrobe elements. Many foundation producers now have lingerie divisions, and lingerie houses, in turn, have foundation divisions. A producer of dresses and separates that have a particular "look" may add accessories, even shoes, to his original line. The Villager, for example, began producing classic shirts for women in 1957; within 10 years the firm had purchased firms producing dresses, shorts, slacks, hosiery, coats, shoes, lingerie, and handbags. All were components of the classic look typified by the shirts produced in the company's original line. Where diversification results from fashion's emphasis on coordination, the producer gains, because he can sell to many departments of a store or persuade stores to establish special shops or sections for the sale of his expanded line. Advertising and publicity efforts by both the producer and the retail store become more effective, since many kinds of merchandise now share the cost and benefits. For the consumer, such diversification is usually a convenience. She mixes and matches components of her wardrobe with increased confidence when they are all from the same source and are related to each other in taste and style.

Not all diversification comes from a trend toward coordination, however. Some women's wear producers have ventured into men's lines; some men's firms have tried their hands at women's apparel. There is sometimes fashion logic in such diversification, but at other times the scope is widened simply for broader investment and profit opportunities.

Neither is diversification always limited to bringing related fashion products together. A giant in the fashion field, Genesco, had its origins in the men's shoe business. Its present holdings include both manufacturing (toiletries, dresses, shoes, lingerie, and sportswear) and retailing (a small specialty shop, a large specialty shop with many branches, a chain store organization, and a chain of women's shoe and accessories stores).

Licensing

Diversification does not always require the use of one's own capital; neither does expansion. Some companies in the fashion field expand and diversify by *licensing,* or permitting other firms to produce and market merchandise in the name of the licensor, exacting a percentage of sales as their payment. A familiar example is Fruit of the Loom, a brand name licensed to producers of a wide variety of products.

Licensing is often a route to foreign markets for United States producers. Rather than cope with tariff barriers and compete with lower-priced labor abroad, some of this country's fashion firms license their names to foreign producers. An example in reverse is provided by the House of Dior, a French firm which licenses the use of its name on fashion goods of many kinds, including jewelry, furs, hair products, perfumes, shoes, and stockings, that are produced and sold in the United States.

Foreign Trade

Some branches of the fashion industries in this country have already developed a substantial market abroad. Notable among them are the moderate-priced brassiere firms. Other branches, such as better sportswear, did not discover their export possibilities until the late 1960s. Commenting on this belated awareness of a European market, the editors of *Women's Wear Daily* once enumerated these reasons why United States sportswear should succeed abroad:

First is the rise of a large European middle class. Then there is the increased acceptance of ready-to-wear on the European continent. There is also increased prestige in a "Made in America" label abroad. Finally, American expertise regarding fit, coordination, and merchandising, as well

as the individuality of certain United States fabrics and fashions, are being recognized abroad.

The garment industry, explained the newspaper, has only recently begun to realize that it has come of age and has much to teach the rest of the world about fashion and fashion production. The newspaper blamed this country's rather modest and belated cultivation of foreign markets on "the American fashion inferiority complex."[3]

Foreign Production

Producers in the United States sometimes combine their technical proficiency and understanding of the domestic market with foreign facilities and low-priced foreign labor in order to secure merchandise abroad for sale in the domestic market. In spite of the additional transportation costs involved, many products can be sold at home more cheaply than if they had been made here. Considerable quantities of gray goods, for example, are shipped to Japan for printing and finishing in such forms as Hawaiian prints. The fabric is then returned to this country for production into apparel. Some knit goods, blouses, and men's suits are produced in Hong Kong in styles and materials specified by United States producers.

When a finished article is produced for an American firm in a foreign country, the firm often stations some of its own executives there to direct and supervise the operation. In other instances, a firm may buy or build plants in a foreign country and install a native supervisory staff trained by the owning firm's personnel.

The incentives for United States producers to extend their production activities abroad are many. An important one is that the finished product will usually cost less than if it had been made domestically. At the same time, styling, quality, size measurements, and other features of the goods meet requirements of domestic consumers which often is not true of foreign-made goods. Exclusivity of product is another bonus for the entrepreneur, since it is possible to have fabrics made up especially for him in colors and designs of his choice. However, there are certain disadvantages to foreign production that must be taken into consideration, such as governmental import quotas and the possibility of siphoning off

Sail for the fortunate islands in clothes meant for bright sun and shimmering sands. Tailored with the proper respect for cut and fit and seaming that one expects of John Meyer. In great colors including coral, aqua, tobacco and gold mist. At stores that understand today.

Double-buckle Suit $36
Piped Skimmer $25

Straight-leg Slacks $14
Safari Shirt $10
Tab-over-tab Culotte $17

Mao-collar Dress $23
Loop-pocket Dress $23

Cottons on the beach:
Puff-sleeve Baby Dress $16
Boy-leg Bathing Suit $16

All prices are about.

Some manufacturers diversify through the addition of fashion-coordinated products to their original line.

work that might be done at home by the industry's present and potential workers. Exactly how far a firm can and should go in internationalizing its business, particularly from a production point of view, remains a moot point and deserves careful consideration.

Increased Market Research

Many fashion firms still plan their lines and project their sales almost by instinct. The larger and more profitable ones, however, have gone far beyond depending on intuition alone. They use modern market research methods, including consumer surveys and computerized sales records. These result in scientific forecasts of the nature and intensity of trends in demand that, if heeded, improve the firms' abilities to act swiftly when change is indicated.

A typical computerized operation permits a fashion firm's production management to know from day to day exactly what styles have been ordered and in what quantities, what has been shipped, what raw materials remain in inventory, and what finished goods are on hand. Long before the need becomes urgent, purchasing executives are alerted to reorder successful fabrics and the production department is alerted to schedule further cuttings of successful style numbers. The design department, already planning for the next season, can observe the acceptance or rejection of individual styles and be guided accordingly.

The sales staff, with regional or countrywide figures on sales, often broken down by fabric, color, and type of garment, as well as by style number, is in a position to advise retail stores authoritatively about what to select and when to feature it.

Some individual retailers and producers are experimenting with daily transmittal of sales information from a store's computer to the factory's computer. Such a procedure enables the producer to keep track of the extent of acceptance of each style number in his line just as easily and quickly as if he were on the selling floor.

The fashion apparel industry also carries on research through its associations and unions. For example, when coat sales lagged in 1963 and 1964, an elaborate study was made of customer and store attitudes by the National Board of the Coat and Suit Industry. Members of the fashion industries also utilize findings of research conducted by their suppliers: the fiber, fabric, leather, and fur producers.

In any field as creative as fashion there is always need for intuition, but intuition no longer must function unaided. Computers provide almost instant information on that most vital point: what consumers are actually buying. Other modern research techniques provide such essential information as the prices people are willing to pay, what they have and what they need in their wardrobes, and where they prefer to buy.

References

[1]*Women's Wear Daily*, June 2, 1967, p. 33.
[2]Escobosa, "Heartbeat of Retailing," *Readings in Modern Retailing*, p. 391.
[3]*Women's Wear Daily*, June 24, 1966.

Merchandising Vocabulary

Define or briefly explain the following terms:

Apparel manufacturer	Haute couture	Toile
Apparel jobber	Couturier	Line-for-line copy
Apparel contractor	Couturière	Adaptations
Section work	Chambre Syndicale de	Cooperative advertising
Sample hand	la Couture Parisienne	Trade publications
Marker	Caution	

Merchandising Review

1. Name three important circumstances that served to encourage the development of mass production of apparel in the United States during the nineteenth century.
2. Discuss the effect of extensive immigration on the development of the apparel industry in the United States.
3. What are the specific operations involved in the production of apparel?
4. Name and describe the function of each of the three types of apparel producers found in the United States today.
5. Describe how a garment contractor operates.
6. What is meant by a "line"? Discuss the steps an apparel producer takes in creating a line.
7. What are the requirements a couture house must meet in order to qualify for membership in the Chambre Syndicale de la Couture Parisienne?
8. Where is the major United States apparel center located? What ensures its continued importance as a center for retail purchasing?
9. What is meant by the term "regional apparel markets"? Where are the most important of these located? In what type of apparel does each specialize?

Merchandising Digest

1. "For centuries, Paris has been considered the fountainhead of new apparel fashions." Discuss this statement from the text, pointing out the circumstances that have made this position possible.
2. "In recent years, members of the couture, especially in Paris, have been increasingly attracted to the field of ready-to-wear." Discuss this statement, pointing out reasons for this new development and specific fields in which couture designers have become active.
3. Discuss any three marketing trends now appearing in the production of apparel fashions, showing how the consumer is benefited in each case.

9

MANUFACTURERS OF FASHION ACCESSORIES

Fashion is not just a dress or a coat; it is a total look. To achieve a look, the consumer needs various accessories: gloves, hosiery, jewelry, belt, handbag, neckwear, cosmetics, shoes, intimate apparel. Some of these accessories are always in demand, always a part of the fashion picture. Others have their periods of glory and then eclipse, depending upon what current fashion decrees for the total effect.

When the waistline is fashion's focal point, for instance, belts have their day, as do intimate apparel items that make the waist smaller. Short skirts that expose long lengths of leg encourage decorative hosiery but require shoes that are flat and simple. When longer, fuller skirts with plenty of movement are in style, hosiery becomes less important and shoes acquire higher heels and more feminine looks.

Fashion influences the design and purchase of accessories. For example, in the late 1960s the current fashion look was one of maximum exposure—skirts were short, dresses and bathing suits featured cutouts, and the prevailing silhouette was one of geometric lines. The glove associated with sports-car racing, with cutouts on the back, provided a glove style that capitalized both on the popularity of this sport and the fashion look of the time.

Apparel and accessories today cannot have fashion existence apart from each other. Producers and retailers of garments need an intimate knowledge of accessories in order to advise customers on how each garment can be most effectively complemented with accessories to achieve the desired total look. Conversely, accessories are produced and sold with an eye to how well they complement currently fashionable garments.

Today, the customer expects apparel salespeople and store displays to suggest appropriate accessories; she also expects accessory departments to relate their merchandise to the apparel with which it will be worn. In addition, the fashion consumer is paying increased attention to one-stop shopping: the opportunity to purchase both fashion apparel and fashion accessories in a single shop or department of a large store, where everything with a given look or feeling has been brought together, even though the retailer may have had to comb a dozen different markets to obtain the components.

Thus, although each fashion accessory is produced by separate segments of the fashion industry, all are coordinated with each other and related to current apparel trends. Fashion today emphasizes the total look, and accessories are an important part of that look.

Intimate Apparel

Over the centuries, fashion has made some unrealistic demands of the female figure. Ever since the time of the Cretan civilization thousands of years before Christ, women have endured tight lacing, unyielding stays, bulky padding, layers of petticoats, and an assortment of other discomforts to achieve whatever look was fashionable at the time.

The fashion silhouette regularly goes through cycles of change; the human figure has to be coaxed to change with it. Women, moreover, do not come in uniform shapes and sizes. Whatever silhouette is dominant at a given time is wearable readily only by a minority of women; the majority have to amplify or constrict their figures to wear the current fashion.

Until the late 1950s, foundations (formerly called corsets) and lingerie depended for their acceptance solely upon the manner in which they made it possible for women to look well in fashionable outer garments. By 1960 intimate apparel had developed fashion interest of its own. Women had begun to accept the idea that everything worn, from the skin out, should reflect the same lines and colors. Each seasonally important garment color was related to an appropriate color in slips, panties, bras, and girdles, to achieve a fashion look or carry out a fashion theme. Before the end of the 1960s, undergarments had run the spectrum of color, reflecting the wild color spree in which outer fashions had indulged at that time, and had also echoed such fads as leopard prints, pop art, and vivid florals.

History, Development, and Organization

The present close fashion relationship between foundation garments and lingerie has brought the two industries together and has encouraged mergers among firms that formerly specialized in one or the other of these two branches of intimate apparel. Foundation producers have bought up lingerie firms; lingerie firms have added lightweight foundations to their lines.

The Foundations Industry The retail value of foundation garments produced in the United States exceeds $1 billion a year. The industry employs some 40,000 workers in more than 350 factories, two-thirds of which are in the New York City area. California, with less than 10 percent of the plants, produces a fresh, interesting portion of the industry's merchandise.

Factory production of corsets began in the United States just after the Civil War, when Warner Brothers opened its first plant in Bridgeport, Connecticut. At this time, the bell-shaped silhouette was at the height of its popularity. Both the crinoline and its successors, the bustle-back and the "Gibson Girl" look, required the figure

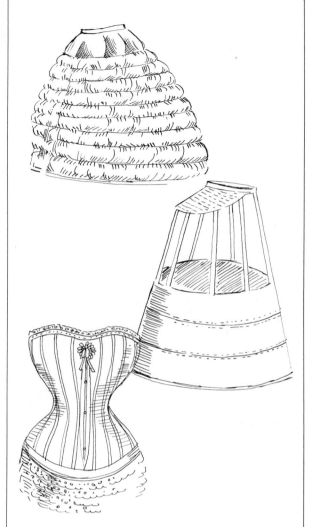

Oldtime crinolines and corsets created the desired silhouette—but often rather painfully.

to be tightly girdled. To achieve the tiny waists that the fashions demanded, women used foundations of sturdy, unyielding cotton reinforced with whalebone or steel "bones." Front or back lacings permitted varying degrees of constriction to achieve proper fit.

The corset industry, producing what are now referred to in the trade as "iron maidens," flour-

Lingerie has become part of the total "look," and knowledgeable producers coordinate it with the current fashion image.

ished. Because the customer usually needed advice, fittings, and alterations to wear these inflexible garments, stores employed skilled fitters or corsetières, and the industry went to great lengths to help train them.

The foundation industry suffered a setback in the 1920s, when the fashion was for straight, loose styles in outerwear. These required little corseting but did demand flattening of the bosom. Bandage-like bras were worn to minimize the bust, while girdles controlled any conspicuous bulges below the waistline.

In the 1930s, the silhouette again became feminine and softly curved. Women coaxed their figures into the appropriate lines with two new types of foundations more comfortable than anything available before: the two-way stretch girdle and the cup-type brassiere. These innovations heralded a trend toward foundations that molded the figure gently but permitted freedom of movement. They also reflected the fashion for easy fit in outerwear, with definite but not exaggerated curves.

Since that era, the foundation industry has produced garments increasingly comfortable and easy to fit. Except for the rare person with a problem figure, a woman today can readily purchase and wear a foundation garment that will adapt her contours to whatever is currently fashionable.

The Lingerie Industry The lingerie industry's annual output has a retail value of $1.6 billion a year and employs more than 75,000 people in over 1,000 plants. More than half of these factories are in New York state, with a fourth in contiguous states.

Originally lingerie, like other apparel, was made in the home. Factory production developed slowly and did not reach proportions that justified considering it a separate industry until 1935. Before that, reports of the Census of Manufacturers included lingerie output and sales data with those of women's apparel.

Mass-production methods in the lingerie industry are very similar to those for apparel. A third of the plants producing lingerie are those of contractors, who provide sewing services for firms that design and distribute the merchandise.

Until the 1930s, most mass-produced lingerie was purely functional, with little variety in style or seasonal change. Cotton was the principal fabric, but wool was also used in extremely cold climates. Silk appeared only in luxury lingerie. Laundry methods of that day involved the boiling, scrubbing, and wringing of clothes, and so discouraged the use of any fabrics that were too delicate to survive such harsh treatment. In the 1930s, rayon began to be used extensively in women's lingerie, and remained a basic fabric material throughout the 1940s. During all of this time, lingerie was considered a staple item; it was relatively untouched by fashion and was produced in limited styles and colors.

The introduction of easy-care man-made textile fibers in the 1950s revolutionized the industry, and lingerie stepped into the fashion spotlight.

Previously, only the largest lingerie companies had sent fashion experts to the Paris openings to report on the lines and colors featured in new apparel styles. As fashion interest began to center around a total look or fashion theme, women began to develop a feeling for color and design harmony in everything they wore. Consequently, the lingerie industry became increasingly aware of the need to keep in close touch with the total fashion picture.

Creative lingerie firms today employ top designing talent, sometimes recruiting them from the apparel field. Styling in all three of the industry's categories—daywear, sleepwear, and at-home or loungewear—closely follows that of apparel. For example, when silver touches were important in evening and after-five apparel, silvery gowns and negligees were shown in the more expensive lingerie lines. When color-mad prints predominated in apparel, wildly patterned slips and panties were featured.

Market Centers

Like nearly all other fashion-influenced industries, the intimate apparel industries have their principal market center in New York City, and major firms of both industries maintain permanent showrooms there.

The industries' trade associations schedule and publicize market weeks in January and June. The dates for showing both foundations and lingerie are coordinated for the convenience of store buyers, since many of them buy both types of merchandise, planning purchases and promotions for both simultaneously. If stores employ separate buyers for these departments, such buyers often work closely with one another in the market, coordinating their purchases and promotional plans.

Merchandising Activities

The merchandising activities of the intimate apparel firms have changed drastically since the close of World War II. Brand names have always been important in these two industries, and much of their merchandising activity has been directed toward the promotion of branded lines.

The major intimate apparel firms advertise widely in both consumer and trade publications.

Ads in consumer publications often mention the names of retail stores that stock the featured merchandise. In addition, many firms offer cooperative advertising arrangements to their retail store customers. Merchants use such cooperative allowances to stretch their own advertising budgets and to tie in at the local level with national advertising of the brands they carry.

Historically, the foundation industry has supplied many services to its retail store customers. Producers have helped train retail salespeople, and have offered retail store buyers assistance in planning assortments and controlling stocks.

By comparison, the lingerie industry was slow in offering services to retail accounts. Because lingerie presented no major fitting problems, producers saw little reason to interest themselves in the retail merchandising of their products. They simply held semiannual showings of their lines and left sales promotion techniques to retailers.

When fashion replaced function as the key factor in intimate apparel, the whole pattern of cooperation with retail stores changed. Lingerie-foundation producers began offering fashion and merchandising advisory assistance and services to the stores. Today manufacturers help stores to stage shows using live models to demonstrate how outerwear and underwear relate to one another. Lingerie houses now assist stores with the layout of retail departments, techniques of display, advertising, and other procedures that help sell merchandise.

Both industries cover the major United States and European fashion markets today, and provide seasonal color and style charts to stores, together with suggestions for relating intimate apparel styles and colors to those of outerwear. The larger firms assist in planning and controlling retail assortments and in staging retail sales promotion events, often in cooperation with a textile fiber or fabric producer.

Marketing Trends

Marketing trends in the intimate apparel industries are similar to those of other fashion-related industries, but of a somewhat more recent origin. The trend toward mergers in other industries during and immediately following World War II did not develop in the intimate apparel industries until the late 1950s. At that time customers began demanding color-coordinated foundation garments. Many small firms that made either brassieres or girdles saw an advantage in joining with one another to produce matched colors. In time, many such collaborating firms merged their ownership and operations in order to meet the competition of larger firms.

Foundation firms also explored the outerwear field. Although efforts to launch outerwear-type bras for sports occasions failed, the introduction of figure control features in bathing suits succeeded. As a result, foundation firms merged with swimsuit makers or set up their own swimsuit divisions.

As enthusiasm for coordinated foundations and lingerie grew, many foundation producers either merged with lingerie companies or set up their own lingerie divisions. Lingerie producers followed the same pattern in relation to foundation firms. More recently, lingerie and foundation producers have merged with textile mills or apparel producers, or have become divisions of industrial conglomerates.

Fashion continues to be the major competitive tool in the marketing of intimate apparel. Vast quantities of intimate apparel, nevertheless, are still sold on the basis of function, in slowly changing styles that involve minimum risk for producer and retailer and minimum price to the consumer. But in the medium to upper price brackets, fashion, rather than intrinsic value, is the motivating element. Keeping in step with fashion has multiplied the industries' problems but has also enlarged their opportunities to sell more goods at higher prices while at the same time giving greater satisfaction to the consumer.

Hosiery

Until the twentieth century was well underway, women's legs were concealed under floor-length skirts, and women's hosiery served a functional rather than a fashion purpose. As skirts moved higher, during and after World War I, women for the first time in over a century became interested in the appearance of their legs.

The success of the hosiery industry as a fashion business is very recent, and has been the result both of product improvements to meet customer demand and of new products and styles to complement apparel fashions.

History and Development

The experience of the hosiery industry from the 1940s through the 1960s provides an excellent example of what happens when fashion either smiles or frowns on an accessory.

Until late in the 1930s, women wore full-fashioned (seamed) silk or rayon stockings, first in black and then mainly in flesh tones. With the introduction of nylon in 1938, limited quantities of hosiery made from this new fiber were sold, and because of their novelty, easier care, and durability, the new hose were eagerly accepted by those who could afford them.

The entry of the United States into World War II restricted nylon to war purposes and made silk unavailable. The only fibers left for women's hosiery were cotton and some rayons of unstable quality, which most women found unattractive. As a solution, many women applied cosmetics to their legs as a substitute for the stockings they could not or would not buy. As the war years went on, however, people became accustomed to the bareleg look, and more and more women went without stockings, either using foot socks inside their shoes for comfort or ignoring hosiery entirely.

When the war ended, limited supplies of nylon fiber were made available to the hosiery industry. By queuing up in retail stores, women were able to buy informally rationed quantities of the leg coverings they had once considered indispensable. Postwar nylon hose, however, failed to charm. Deniers were fairly heavy, fit was not always satisfactory, and colors tended to streak. In protest, women went barelegged again, and the hosiery industry experienced a leveling-off of sales.

As a result, mills and yarn producers, along with nylon fiber sources, turned their attention to the development of sheerer deniers, more elastic yarns, seamless hosiery, and wider color ranges. In 1948, for instance, Du Pont tried launching a powerful advertising campaign on the theme of color-cued hosiery, but response was minimal, as it usually is when attempts are made to launch a fashion with sales promotion rather than on the basis of consumer demand.

Aside from a growing demand for seamless hosiery, which was part of the consumer's acceptance of the bareleg look, product innovations in the industry failed to achieve continuing success. In the 1950s one mill introduced a special treatment for nylon hosiery for which greater comfort and wearing power were claimed; others introduced stretch and no-run stockings; still others tried cotton soles as a comfort feature in nylon hosiery. Consumer interest, however, was only sporadic.

Finally, fashion entered the picture and demonstrated its tremendous power to influence sales. The "total look" and the miniskirt fashions of the 1960s threw the spotlight on legs, and stockings became popular at last. Colors, textures, weights, and new fibers in immense variety were created, shown, and sold. In the single year from 1965 to 1966, sales in pairs of stockings increased 15 percent. By contrast, during the entire decade from 1950 to 1960, sales had increased only 10 percent.

Organization and Operation

In the United States, the hosiery industry annually produces more than 200 billion pairs of socks and stockings for men, women, and children. Half of this output is in women's hosiery. In terms of value, the women's share is somewhat more than half of the total output, with an estimated retail value in excess of $1 billion a year.

The more than 400 plants engaged in the knitting, dyeing, and finishing of women's hosiery employ approximately 50,000 workers. The stronghold of the industry is North Carolina, where 170 plants employ 60 percent of the industry's production workers and ship 60 percent of the industry's total output. Most of the remaining plants are located in the Southern states or in Pennsylvania; none are west of the Mississippi River.

Most hosiery mills perform all the steps necessary to the production of finished hosiery, although some smaller mills may perform the knitting operation only, contracting out the finishing processes.

"Boarding" is the heat-setting process through which stockings acquire their permanent shape, after which they are matched into pairs.

Full-fashioned hosiery is flat-knit to size and length specifications on high-speed machines that shape the stocking as it is knitted. The outer edges are then stitched together on special sewing machines, after which the stocking is dyed. Each stocking acquires permanent shape through a heat-setting process called "boarding." Then stockings are carefully matched into pairs, their welts stamped with a brand name or other appropriate information, and the pairs packaged.

Seamless hosiery is circular-knit, rather than flat-knit, on special machines that shape the stocking during the knitting process. Subsequent steps are dyeing, boarding, pairing, stamping, and packaging, as for full-fashioned hosiery.

Most hosiery producers manufacture both branded and unbranded hosiery in the same mill, employing the same manufacturing procedures for all goods. Some small mills manufacture unbranded goods only, selling their output to brand manufacturers, to owners of private brands, or to retail stores for special price promotions.

Although hosiery is produced far from New York City, it is not necessary for buyers to visit mills in order to see the various lines and discuss fashion trends. Larger mills maintain permanent showrooms and sales staffs in New York City, where semiannual seasonal lines of new colors, textures, and other developments are shown. Smaller mills frequently employ the services of selling agents who maintain offices in New York City for closer contact with the retail and fashion markets.

Merchandising Activities

Traditionally, the women's hosiery industry concentrated its merchandising activities almost exclusively on the promotion and sale of nationally advertised brands. In recent years, however, the industry has become involved in merchandising products for private labeling and for sale in vending machines and other types of self-service operations.

National Brands Major hosiery producers aggressively advertise their brand lines on a national basis and sell them to a wide variety of retail stores across the country. They also usually supply advertising, display, and fashion assistance to help promote retail sales.

At least four well-known brands spend over $1 million a year each for national advertising. At the local levels, they help their retail accounts through cooperative advertising, often supplying them with advertising copy. Further assistance provides designs and displays for coordinating hosiery shades with currently important apparel colors. In addition, they offer inventory control help by inserting a punched card in each box of hosiery; when the contents have been sold, the salesperson is supposed to set the card aside for use in reordering from the producer.

Until recently, branded lines dominated the retail distribution of women's hosiery. Some producers were highly selective of their outlets; others attempted to maintain tight control over prices at which their merchandise could be sold; still others attempted to dictate the amount of stock a retailer should carry.

Today, many of these practices have been discontinued. Control of retail selling prices, once permitted, now is likely to bring action against a producer by the Federal Trade Commission. As a result of increased production and the concomitant need for increased sales, selectivity in retail distribution has largely been eliminated. Customer demand has replaced producer ultimatum as a basis for determining the amount of inventory a store should carry.

Private Brands Chain organizations, groups of retail stores, and, more recently, individual stores have developed their own private brands in competition with nationally advertised brands of hosiery.

If a retailer wishes to sell his own brand, he contracts with a mill to produce hosiery according to his specifications. The finished products are in the colors, sizes, and constructions the merchant wants, and their welts are stamped with his own brand name. The merchant may also design and supply the packaging for his private hosiery brand.

The retailer realizes many advantages by having his own brand of hosiery. To begin with, his cost is usually less, since the price he pays does not include the cost of national brand advertising and promotion. In addition, he can be more selective of colors and constructions and he can build assortments around those specific characteristics most requested by his own customers. Usually he can offer hosiery at lower prices than those of comparable branded goods. Finally, the merchant can develop stronger customer loyalty by offering a product that is unobtainable elsewhere.

Jobbing Individually packaged hosiery lends itself well to merchandising through rack jobbers. A *rack jobber* is one who maintains stocks of convenience goods in supermarkets, drugstores, automatic vending machines, and similar outlets for the casual shopper. Such jobbers usually buy unbranded goods from hosiery mills. They tend to concentrate on staple constructions and shades, using plastic packaging imprinted with such information as size, construction, and sometimes retail price.

Although an increasing amount of basic hosiery is sold through supermarkets, drugstores, and vending machines, the customer interested in fashion turns to established hosiery departments, where display and personal selling techniques encourage her to try more adventurous shades and textures. It is when she buys these fashion-inspired styles that the hosiery industry prospers. At fashion's urging, the consumer buys more pairs and spends more per pair than when she buys on the basis of need alone.

Marketing Trends

As in many other divisions of the fashion industry, there has been a blurring of seasonal lines in hosiery and a growing need to launch new developments whenever fashion, rather than the traditional calendar of market dates, requires them. Retailers are eager to present appropriate hosiery at times that coincide with the introduction of new apparel styles. They apply pressure on the industry for earlier showings so that seasonal merchandise can be shipped soon enough to make coordinated presentation of apparel and hosiery possible.

Once a year, however, the calendar takes precedence over fashion. The vast demand for stockings as Christmas gifts warrants special procedures. Many manufacturers devise special packaging or include free extras, such as hosiery cases with each box, to encourage the purchase of stockings as Christmas gifts.

The trend toward mergers and diversification has brought many formerly independent hosiery producers under the banners of textile industry giants. It has given these small producers the advantage of the fashion research and promotion facilities of these huge companies. Some independent companies have either merged with other small mills or formed voluntary associations in order to compete more effectively with the industry's giants.

Examples of the hosiery industry's product developments include the introduction of stretch hosiery, which opened up whole new markets at a time when sleek, smooth fit was an important element of the bareleg look; textured hosiery, at a time when legs had a strong fashion interest of their own; and pantyhose, in the era of short skirts. These have led to an upturn in the sales of women's hosiery departments that far exceeded the most optimistic dreams of merchants a decade earlier.

Shoes

For centuries, fashion paid little attention to women's shoes. Their purpose was purely functional. Shoes were both high and heavy, worn solely as a protection against uneven terrain, bad weather, or other hazards. It was considered immodest to expose the feminine ankle, so usually only the tip of a lady's shoe could be seen below her long skirts.

Ever since the 1920s, however, women's ankles have been plainly visible, and shoes have taken on both fashion importance and variety. They have run the fashion gamut from sensible to silly styles, from pointed to squared toes, from high to flat heels, and from mere shells to thigh-high boots. In these few decades, women's shoes have developed into a major fashion accessory.

Shoes showed little fashion versatility, however, until after World War II. Up until then, almost the only material used was leather, and the leather industry, in the first half of this century, was principally absorbed in the needs of men's footwear. The women's shoe industry relied on calf, kid, suede, and an occasional reptile. Shoe colors were mainly black, brown, and white, with some beige and navy, and shoe styling was conservative. A single pair of all-purpose shoes often met the needs of an entire season's wardrobe.

Then fashion invaded the women's shoe industry. Leather manufacturers developed softer, more flexible leathers. New plastic and fabric materials were used to give shoes far more interesting and comfortable characteristics than was previously possible. New and varied textures and an ever-increasing range of colors produced styles that could keep pace with changes in apparel.

Organization and Operation

Footwear production is a major industry in the United States. The public spends over $6 billion annually for shoes, boots, slippers, and related articles. Women's shoes alone are produced at a rate approaching 300 million pairs a year, more than the combined annual output of men's, children's, and infants' shoes.

The major centers of production are the Great Lakes region, the St. Louis area, and New England, where the industry had its origin. The westward movement of the industry began when it recognized the importance of the Middle West as a source of hide supplies and cheaper labor.

One of the chief uses of leather traditionally has been in the manufacturing of shoes. In the beginning, shoes were made by hand. The Industrial Revolution brought mechanization to shoe manufacturing, and today's mass-production, assembly-line methods are the result.

As many as 200 to 300 operations may be performed by highly skilled workmen in the making of an expensive, high-quality shoe. For each type and size of shoe in a producer's line, there must be a *last,* or wooden form in the shape of a foot, over which the shoes are built. The variety of lasts, the quality of materials, and the number and type of manufacturing operations required determine the quality and price of the finished shoe.

The range of sizes a shoe manufacturer must produce is enormous. The normal range of women's shoe sizes involves 103 width and length combinations—and this does not include sizes shorter than "4," longer than "11," or wider than "D." Even if a manufacturer limits his production to only the best-selling length and width combinations, his inventory, production problems, and investment are enormous compared to those of a dress manufacturer who makes a style in only five or six standard sizes. Under such conditions, it is not surprising that giants flourish in the industry. One-fourth of the total shoe output in the United States is produced by only four manufacturers.

Opportunity for smaller producers does exist in the shoe industry, however. Unlike manufacturers in most other industries, the shoe producer does not have to invest in machinery if he does not want to. Instead he can lease his equipment, thus keeping the major portion of his capital available for materials and merchandising activities. Nor does he any longer have to produce his own lasts, since other firms now perform this function. Neither does he have to make every part

Through the years women have worn a wide variety of shoe styles.

of the shoe in his own plant; specialists produce many of the standard components, particularly heels.

As it is for other fashion industries, New York City is the major market center for shoes. Most producers maintain permanent showrooms for their lines in New York, regardless of where their manufacturing facilities may be located. Twice a year, seasonal lines are shown to store buyers and the fashion press. Capsule shoe showings are held in other cities too. for the benefit of local merchants, but virtually every maker in the industry participates in the New York showings.

Merchandising Activities

The shoe industry has an active national trade association, known as the National Shoe Manufacturers' Association. Together with the National Shoe Retailers' Association, it disseminates technical, statistical, and fashion trend information on shoes, sometimes winning extensive publicity for footwear. In addition, the leather industry and its associations operate as sources of fashion information for buyers and other retail store executives.

Brand names are important in the shoe industry, and manufacturers advertise extensively in national consumer and fashion publications. The industry spends about $12 million annually for national magazine advertising, of which half is spent on women's shoes.

In contrast with most other fashion industries, many of the larger shoe manufacturers operate retail chain organizations of their own, frequently augmenting stocks of shoes with related accessories like hosiery and handbags. One such retail operation, I. Miller Shoes, has further diversified its retail assortments to include boutique apparel and accessories, such as dresses, coats, belts, and scarves.

Some shoe manufacturers are also involved in the retail field through the operation of leased departments in department and specialty stores. Because of the tremendous amount of capital required to stock a shoe department, as well as the expertise needed to fit and sell shoes, many stores lease these sections to manufacturers or other companies specializing in this area. Surveys made by the National Retail Merchants Association have repeatedly shown that women's shoe departments are among those most commonly leased by its member department stores. A 1964 study by that organization found that 70 percent of the reporting stores had at least one shoe department operated by a lessee.

Marketing Trends

Mergers have been fairly common for several years in the shoe industry. Small producers making a specialized type of shoe have merged with other small firms making other types. Manufacturers of men's shoes have merged with manufacturers of women's shoes. Shoe machinery manufacturers have acquired shoe producers. A recent trend is toward the merging of shoe producers with apparel producers. In some instances such mergers are merely financial, in the interests of diversification; in others, the purpose is to make available to retailers and consumers shoes that complete the "look" of the apparel itself.

Shoe manufacturers continuously devote time, effort, and money to market research and product development. In the process, they experiment with new materials and methods of production in order to enlarge their market potential. Some of the largest companies have established separate merchandising and marketing divisions as a means of searching out new markets and offering additional services to their customers.

Greater emphasis on fashion continues to be the major marketing trend among shoe producers. Designers and other key personnel regularly attend European apparel openings, not only to gather information on trends in apparel but also to observe the styling of European shoe manufacturers, many of whom design special models for the French and Italian couture.

More and more, fashion influences both the styling and color of footwear. For example, when fashion in the 1960s emphasized the total look, shoes were important in achieving the desired effect. Short skirts and geometric lines in apparel required shoes with low heels and broad toes. Longer, fuller skirts and apparel that followed the contour of the body more closely required shoes with higher heels and more pointed toes. When color was rampant in apparel, shoes were shown in lively colors and color combinations to match, blend, or contrast with apparel. With pantsuits, chunky shoe shapes were worn. Shoes and apparel depend upon one another for the total, coordinated look the consumer demands.

Cosmetics

The history of cosmetics is quite as long as the history of fashion itself. Among primitive males, paint was often used to frighten off enemies, deceive avenging ghosts, or advertise rank. Among women, modern and primitive, paints and other cosmetics have been used to enhance attractiveness as well as to conform to current fashions.

The trend in cosmetics is directly related to the overall fashion trend. Some authorities believe that the heavily made-up look is apt to be matched with the exposed and skimpy apparel look. For example, in the 1920s and the 1960s, women wore short skirts and used makeup with a bold hand. The 1930s, on the other hand, introduced soft lines in apparel and a natural look in makeup—and as the 1960s closed and a look reminiscent of the 1930s was coming in, the miniskirt was beginning its retreat, and makeup was acquiring a translucent, natural effect.

Organization and Operation

Cosmetics is a multibillion-dollar industry, dominated by giant producers of well-advertised lines but also including many smaller firms. Also part of the industry are the so-called "private label" houses, which produce merchandise to the specifications and under the labels of chain organizations, national brands, or small independent entrepreneurs. Many of the major producers maintain foreign as well as domestic plants.

The cosmetics and toilet goods industry has enjoyed rapid growth and shows every sign of continuing to remain among the pacesetters of American industry. This is a characteristically "defensive" industry, having the ability to defend itself against economic downturns that cause consumers to curtail their purchases of durable goods. For a few dollars, a woman who has financial, social, or other worries can obtain the cosmetic wherewithal to face the world with confidence.

Cosmetics include products used by both men and women. As defined by the Federal Trade Commission, cosmetics include articles other than soap that are intended to be rubbed, poured, sprinkled, or sprayed on the person for purposes of cleansing, beautifying, promoting attractiveness, or altering the appearance. For such products, the public spends nearly $5 billion a year, plus almost another $4 billion for beauty and barber shop services.

Chemistry, not magic, is the basis of all cosmetic products. Major ingredients of cosmetics at any price level are such things as fats, oils, waxes, talc, alcohol, glycerine, borax, coloring matter, and perfumes. The industry is restrained from using potentially harmful ingredients and from making exaggerated claims about the efficacy of its products by federal law: the Food, Drug, and Cosmetic Act of 1939.

Merchandising Activities

Brand competition is tremendously keen in the cosmetics and toiletries industry, whether consumer sales take place in retail stores or in the home. To popularize and sell its brands, the industry spends enormous amounts on advertising. In 1967 its outlay for television alone was $400 million; another $100 million was spent on magazine advertising. Few industries spend more on advertising than does cosmetics.

Toiletries and some cosmetics that bear nationally advertised brand names are often sold through stores of many kinds, including neighborhood drugstores and supermarkets. The more fashion-oriented cosmetics lines, however, are distributed on a more selective basis, since skilled personal selling is required to explain their use to consumers. In large retail stores, much of the selling is done by trained cosmeticians, known as *demonstrators,* each of whom advises customers in the selection and use of products within a specific brand line. A demonstrator is usually trained by the producer of the line she represents, and manages its stocks and counter displays. The manufacturer of the line concerned usually contributes toward her salary by making an allowance for this purpose to the store.

In smaller stores, where the volume of business done in any one brand is not large, cosmetics counters are generally staffed with salespeople who are knowledgeable about cosmetics but not specialized in any one line and who sell any or all of the brands carried by the store. Manufacturers may or may not contribute toward the salary of such salespeople, but in most cases assist in their training by providing leaflets, samples, color charts, and other appropriate aids.

Most major cosmetics producers employ traveling representatives who are available to their larger retailer accounts as consultants. These representatives usually spend a few days to a week in each store, advising customers, conducting clinics, promoting the sale of new products in the line, and generally assisting in the training and retraining of store personnel responsible for selling the brand line.

Marketing Trends

Competition in the cosmetics industry is extremely keen. Product obsolescence is rapid, and new products or ideas must constantly be introduced.

By harnessing the influence of fashion, the industry has multiplied its potential market many times over and gives every evidence of continuing in this trend. For example, with current interest focused on youth, whole new markets are being developed among mature consumers who seek a more youthful appearance. Another market which has developed as a result of the youth market is a growing demand for skin care and treatment products by adolescents who formerly were not regarded as important cosmetics consumers. Similarly, expanding use of color in apparel has increased the demand for facial and nail cosmetics in a wide range of colors cued to wardrobe colors.

Cosmetics manufacturers have also capitalized on the fashion potential of famous designer names in promoting the sale of their products, principally fragrances. Chanel, Balmain, Lanvin, and Schiaparelli are among the famous French designers long associated with perfumes and colognes. Other well-known designers, such as Dior, Givenchy, St. Laurent, Valentino, Adele Simpson, and Norell, have entered the fragrance field more recently, mainly through licensing arrangements with manufacturers.

By far the most significant current trend in the marketing of cosmetics is the development of whole new lines of men's cosmetics, toiletries, and fragrances. Whereas once the male market was extremely small and restricted to a few toiletries products, today practically every brand-line producer of women's cosmetics has developed, or is in the process of developing, complete lines of cosmetics, toiletries, and fragrances for men. Retail sales of men's colognes alone amounted to more than $60 million in 1968.[1] This burgeoning market represents extensive new business volume for manufacturers and stores alike. Widespread installations of complete men's cosmetics boutiques in department stores are considered by many to be a distinct possibility in the near future.

After years of steady growth, several of the major cosmetics firms are beginning to embark upon ambitious diversification programs. Some are broadening their markets by acquiring foreign firms and facilities, or through licensing agreements. Others have diversified by acquiring pharmaceutical firms. Still others have moved into the fashion apparel field by acquiring European boutiques or even by obtaining financial control of major Paris couture houses.

Jewelry

Since early days, jewelry has served as a response to the love of beauty, as a status symbol, as a form of currency, and as a medium for religious expression. Men as well as women have worn necklaces, bracelets, and other decorative ornaments throughout history. The "love beads" and medallions worn by some young men in the 1960s were no great departure from the protective amulets that men in ancient Rome wore as necklaces; Tibetan Buddhists wore court necklaces derived from Lamaist rosaries; and Renaissance portraits frequently show men wearing heavy gold necklaces.

Organization and Operation

Modern methods of making jewelry may be less arduous than those of earlier times, but essentially they are much the same. Modern jewelry makers melt and shape metal, cut or carve gems, and string beads and shells. Jewelry designers still use enamel, ceramics, and many other materials to express creative ideas.

The jewelry industry in the United States is subdivided into two separate groups, mainly on the basis of intrinsic value or quality of product. One group is referred to as *fine jewelry,* and the other is termed *costume jewelry* or *fashion jewelry.*

Fine Jewelry The counterpart of apparel's haute couture is fine jewelry. Only precious metals—gold and all members of the platinum family (palladium, rhodium, and iridium)—are used in the making of fine jewelry. Silver, although classified as a precious metal, is much less expensive, does not hold stones successfully, tarnishes easily, and is therefore not widely used for fine jewelry. Precious metals in their pure state are too soft to be used alone, and therefore are combined with one or more other metals to produce an *alloy* of the necessary hardness.

Stones in fine jewelry are known as *gemstones* to distinguish them from those that are less attractive and can be used only in industry. Gemstones are natural stones classified as either *precious* or *semiprecious. Precious stones* includes the diamond, emerald, ruby, sapphire, and real or oriental pearl. *Semiprecious stones* include the amethyst, garnet, opal, jade, cultured pearl, and other natural stones that are less rare and costly than precious stones. In recent years, chemists have succeeded in creating synthetic rubies and sapphires. There are also synthetic diamonds, but none has yet been pronounced suitable for jewelry use.

The fine jewelry industry is essentially a handcraft industry. The *lapidary,* or stonecutter, is a craftsman who transforms dull-looking stones into gems of beauty by cutting or carving them according to their size, nature, and the type of setting to be used. Workers in precious metals create unusual and beautiful shapes, often to the specifications of individual customers.

Good jewelry is timeless—this necklace bridges a 3,500-year gap between wearers.

Among the creative fine jewelry houses, as among the haute couture apparel houses, one usually finds design, production, and retail sales all taking place under one roof and one management. Many fine jewelry firms sell only the merchandise they manufacture, much of which is custom designed. Others supplement their original designs with merchandise purchased from other manufacturers. Because of the nature of the materials used, the originality of designs, and the superb workmanship, fine jewelry is usually high to moderate in price, although some fairly inexpensive bracelets, earrings, and rings may be found among fine jewelry assortments.

Costume or Fashion Jewelry Costume, or fashion, jewelry may be compared to mass-produced apparel. Materials used in the manufacture of costume jewelry are plastics, wood, glass, brass, or other base metals (such as aluminum, copper, tin, lead, and chromium), some of which may be coated with more costly metals like gold, rhodium, or silver. Stones and simulated pearls used in costume jewelry are made from clay, glass, or plastic, and while attractive and interesting in surface appearance, have none of the properties of natural stones.

Costume jewelry is frequently subdivided into four classifications: tailored (made entirely of metal); stone set (in which imitation or simulated stones are combined with metal); pearls (simulated); and novelties (enamels, wood, and so on).

Most of the large, popularly priced costume jewelry houses employ stylists who design seasonal lines or adapt styles from higher-priced lines. The majority of this jewelry is produced in New England and the Middle Atlantic states, with Providence, Rhode Island, as the center of the costume jewelry industry. Concentrated mass-production facilities there turn out jewelry to the specifications of individual jewelry firms much the same as apparel contractors work with apparel manufacturers and jobbers. Mass-manufacturing methods prevail. In contrast to the hand shaping of metal used in fine jewelry, the metal used in costume jewelry is usually cast by first melting it and then pouring it into molds to harden; then designs are applied by painting on colored enamel or etching the metal by machine.

Although most costume jewelry sold in retail stores today is mass-produced, there are some exceptions. Individuals with creative talent may set up small retail or wholesale operations catering to customers primarily interested in unusual styling. Some entrepreneurs who started from such small beginnings have become large-scale producers. Others prefer to remain small, working mainly in one medium, such as copper or ceramics. The smaller companies serve only a limited clientele and often design jewelry items to the specific requirements of their customers.

Marketing Centers

New York City is the principal market center for both fine and costume jewelry. Major firms maintain permanent showrooms there as a convenience to store buyers and also to keep in close contact with developments in other segments of the fashion industry.

Seasonal showings, held semiannually, are sponsored by the industry's trade association, the Jewelry Industry Council. Buyers of both fine and costume jewelry attend these showings to preview fashion trends for the coming season, to keep abreast of developments in the industry, and to buy for their seasonal needs.

Merchandising Activities

Fine jewelry firms traditionally have concentrated their merchandising activities on providing retailers with adequate assortments of a wide range of fairly staple items, such as diamond rings and watches. They depend more on a multiplicity of customer services, prestige, and highly discreet forms of advertising than do costume jewelry retailers.

The larger costume jewelry firms offer seasonal lines so broad that they can easily adapt to whatever trend fashion may be taking. Because they contract the production of their merchandise, emphasis can swiftly be switched from less popular items to production of those in greater demand. The larger firms also market much of their merchandise under brand names and advertise widely in national consumer publications.

Some of the larger costume jewelry firms offer advertising assistance in the form of advertising mats or cooperative advertising allowances. Some help to plan and maintain retail store assortments. Some supply display fixtures. Some offer fashion guidance and traveling representatives to help train retail salespeople and to serve customers on the retail selling floor.

Leased jewelry departments are fairly common in the merchandising of fine jewelry. A large amount of capital is required to provide adequate assortments, and specialized knowledge is needed to sell this merchandise. Therefore, large-scale operators, who in many cases are also manufacturers, provide retail stores with stock, trained personnel, and advertising, returning a percentage of sales as rent to the host store.

Marketing Trends

Greater emphasis on fashion is the major trend in both branches of the jewelry industry today. More individual styling is necessary to keep abreast of the current emphasis on personal expression in dress as well as to attract younger customers.

Some firms are broadening their lines. Such firms as Cartier and Tiffany, for example, traditionally have been synonymous with superb service, custom designing, fine workmanship, creative genius, and high prices. Today, however, both these firms, as well as many other fine jewelry merchants, have broadened their appeal to include lower-income groups by offering costume jewelry of original design and excellent quality at modest prices. Some firms have further broadened their assortments to include high-quality china and giftware.

Some of the larger costume jewelry manufacturers, especially in the men's field, have begun to adopt a "big business" attitude toward diversification of product, although this is not yet a general industry practice. Speidel (watchbands) has had excellent response to men's colognes; Swank is offering colognes, sunglasses, travel accessories, and all types of men's gifts. Whether other firms follow their lead remains to be seen.

Gloves

Historically, gloves have served many purposes besides the obvious one of protection and warmth. At one time, an English knight going into battle carried his lady's glove on his sleeve as a good luck charm. In the exchange of property, the giving of a glove once symbolized good faith in the transaction. Gloves have also been used to denote rank or status; prior to the sixteenth century, for instance, only men of the clergy or of noble rank wore gloves.

The use of gloves as an important costume accessory dates back hundreds of years. During her reign, Queen Elizabeth I of England is credited with having set the fashion of elaborately jeweled and embroidered gloves for women. Today, although gloves may not be as widely worn as they formerly were, except for warmth, they are still considered an indispensable accessory item for the well-dressed man or woman.

Women wear gloves today primarily as a costume accessory. Therefore, to be in fashion, gloves must closely relate to current apparel fashions in styling, detail, and color. For example, fashions in glove lengths are largely determined by the fashionable length of sleeves, particularly coat and suit sleeves, and fashionable apparel trimmings also find their counterparts in glove ornamentation. Just as there are classic styles in apparel, so, too, there are classic styles in gloves: the untrimmed white wrist-length glove, for wear on dress occasions, and the "suit" glove, which extends a few inches beyond the wrist, for more general wear.

Organization and Operation

In the early days of the twentieth century, fashion interest focused on the well-gloved hand, and the glove business flourished in the United States. The glove material most favored by fashion at that time was leather. Today, however, knit and woven fabric gloves dominate the field. For dress and casual wear, three pairs of fabric gloves are produced annually to each pair of leather gloves.

Leather Glove Production Production of leather gloves originated in Europe hundreds of years ago as a highly specialized craft. Today, United States factories producing leather gloves are still essentially craft-oriented, and for that reason are relatively small compared to most other factories producing fashion accessories.

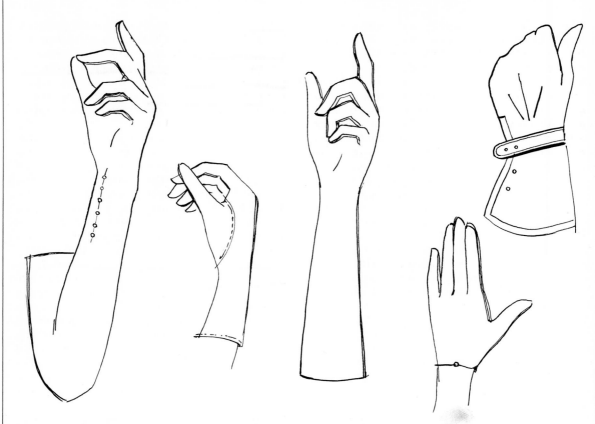

The five basic glove lengths are (from left to right) the opera, four-button or suit, eight-button, shorty, and gauntlet.

Most of the manufacturing operations are hand-guided or, in some cases, done completely by hand. As a result, factories have remained small, few machines are necessary, and comparatively few workmen are employed in any one factory. Moreover, producers tend to specialize, performing just one manufacturing operation, such as cutting or stitching, farming out the other operations to nearby plants, each of which performs its own specialty. Since the major producers are still mainly located in the Gloversville, New York, area, such production arrangements generally are satisfactory.

The price and quality of leather gloves are determined mainly by the grade of leather used, the amount of handwork involved in their pro-

duction, and the type of stitching used to close their seams.

Fabric Glove Production   In contrast to the methods employed in the production of leather gloves, much of the production of fabric gloves is mechanized. The most favored and most durable glove fabric used today is a double-woven fabric. Although double-woven fabrics made of cotton or nylon yarns are the most popular, it is possible to use almost any fiber in producing this particular type of fabric. Regular knit gloves are made of woolen, acrylic, or cotton string yarns.

Prior to the 1960s, almost all fabric gloves were manufactured in half-inch sizes. As a result of market research and product development undertaken by fiber and fabric firms, specially treated yarns can now give stretch properties to fabric gloves. Fitting problems thus have been somewhat simplified, and the number of sizes required to fit customers has been substantially reduced. This development, in turn, permits manufacturers and retailers to respond to fashion change with minimum risk, since their investment in a style is smaller than it would be with many separate sizes.

As in the case of leather gloves, the price and quality of fabric gloves are largely determined by the type of material used, the amount of handwork involved in producing the gloves, and the type of stitching used to close the seams.

Today, although fabric gloves are produced in various parts of the country, Gloversville remains the major production center for fabric as well as leather gloves, with a few plants producing both types.

Market Centers

The major market center for both leather and fabric gloves is in New York City. Many glove firms maintain permanent showrooms, where they show seasonal lines to store and resident office buyers. The typical glove firm offers a very wide and versatile assortment of both domestic and imported gloves in a rather wide range of prices.

Merchandising Activities

The merchandising activities of the women's glove industry, as a whole, have tended to lag behind those of many other fashion accessories industries, and compared with the dollars spent on consumer advertising by other segments of the fashion industry, outlays for glove advertising are modest. Only a few large producers with nationally distributed brand lines have actively promoted their products or offered even limited merchandising services to their retail store customers. In recent years, however, because of stagnating sales and competition from imports, particularly of leather gloves, many glove producers have begun to think more seriously about merchandising techniques.

A few firms that are owned by conglomerate organizations frequently have their products advertised under the parent company's common brand name. The larger independent firms advertise their brand names from time to time in fashion and other national consumer publications, but neither consistently or aggressively. A few producers offer their customers some form of cooperative advertising arrangement, while others have newspaper mats available for stores that want to tie in with national brand-name advertising.

Although most of the larger producers of women's gloves employ fashion stylists, few make their services available to their retail store accounts except on rare occasions. Sales training aids are limited mainly to color charts. This lack of merchandising activity may be partly responsible for the consumer's general lack of interest in gloves.

For years the glove industry has maintained a trade association known as the National Association of Glove Manufacturers, with headquarters in Gloversville. This association's activities, however, have concentrated mainly on tariff questions and federal agency regulations and rulings rather than on publicizing the industry and its product. In the late 1960s, however, eleven major glove producers, all members of the national association, organized a Glove Fashion Council, which survived only into the summer of 1970. Major objectives of the organization were to maintain close liaison with the apparel industry, provide more comprehensive fashion reports to glove manufacturers, set up retail sales training programs and fashion press briefings, and formulate fashion publicity campaigns.

Marketing Trends

Sales of domestically produced leather gloves have suffered considerably in recent years from the competition of cheaper imports. To meet this challenge, the industry is trying to improve manufacturing procedures in order to reduce production costs. In addition, improved materials, resulting from product research and development in the leather industry, are expected to increase the market potential of domestically produced leather gloves. For example, many leather gloves today are washable by hand and come in a widening range of fashion colors.

In recent years, some of the larger glove producers have begun to acquire foreign factories, either through direct purchase or by acquisition of controlling interests. Through such acquisition, they hope to produce gloves that meet the fashion and wear requirements of United States customers, provide the merchandise at lower prices because of lower labor costs, and to some extent overcome the problems connected with direct import of foreign merchandise.

Handbags

Among fashion accessories, the one that provides the greatest comfort to women and the greatest source of amusement to men is undoubtedly the handbag. Enormous tote or tiny clutch, it holds the various items women want to carry with them but do not have the pockets to accommodate.

Purses to hold money have been in use ever since coins, as a medium of exchange, were first used. The modern handbag, however, developed from the *reticule*, a small drawstring bag introduced in the late eighteenth century when close-fitting dress fashions provided little or no room for pockets. Although skirts have ballooned and subsided many times since, the custom for a woman to carry a receptacle and leave the pockets empty has endured.

The modern handbag is much more than a carryall, however. It is an essential addition to the well-dressed woman's attire, harmonizing with, dramatizing, or contrasting with the rest of her outfit.

Organization and Operation

The handbag industry is quite small compared to some of the other fashion industries. The total industry output is about $250 million at factory prices, or less than $500 million at retail.

Firms producing women's handbags are also quite small. Fewer than half employ as many as 20 people each. Manufacturing is concentrated in New York City, where more than two-thirds of the industry's factories produce nearly two-thirds of the annual handbag output.

Leather, once the most important handbag material, has lost much of its eminence, except for the finer quality handbags in calfskin, goatskin, alligator, and lizard. Some heavy-duty tote bags are still made of leather, but today that material represents only a small percentage of the handbag industry's output. Plastic handbags outnumber leather ones by about five to one. Handbags are also made of fabric, metal, straw, beads, string, and whatever other material lends itself readily to the demands of current fashion.

Fashion and personal taste decree whether a handbag should blend or contrast with the costume color. Shapes may be long or short, pouch or swagger, draped or boxy, but in general they are designed to harmonize with the currently popular apparel silhouette. Textures may be rough or smooth, dull or shiny, according to the current fashion look and the individual's interpretation of that look.

Materials required for the 20 to 40 different parts of a handbag are usually cut by dies or by hand, much as shoe parts are cut. The various parts of the bag are then machine-stitched together. Liners, fillers, and stay materials are glued into the bags and, as a final process, the necessary fasteners are attached. In most cases, the frame is the most important and costly part of the handbag.

The handbag market center is New York City, close to the major garment industries. Permanent showrooms are maintained where seasonal lines may be viewed at least twice a year.

Merchandising Activities

Brand names are of comparatively little importance in the handbag industry. Fashion is the keynote. Industry sales rise or fall according to how successfully individual producers have anticipated trends and succeeded in preparing to meet fashion demand.

Furthermore, few producers are large enough to advertise on a significant scale or engage in much cooperative advertising with retail stores. Even those who do advertise tend to emphasize dependable quality rather than fashion importance. The customer's impression of what is fashionable in handbags is gained primarily from the assortments offered in retail departments, in store displays, and in "total look" newspaper advertising and fashion publication advertising.

Popular handbag styles include the tote, pouch, box, clutch, and over-the-shoulder.

Marketing Trends

The handbag industry devotes little concerted effort to improving marketing techniques. There is a trade association, the National Authority for the Ladies' Handbag Industry, but it is not a fashion spokesman for the industry. Manufacturers prefer working as individuals in determining and interpreting fashion trends rather than pooling technical and fashion information and market research.

Some of the larger manufacturers of handbags have recently diversified their product lines to include luggage, as well as personal leather goods such as wallets and key cases. Through advertising and promotion of new colors, textures, patterns, and shapes in these related lines, attention indirectly underscores the fashion importance of the handbag as a fashion accessory.

Millinery

The wearing of millinery for decorative effect as well as warmth and protection can be traced back through history for some thousands of years. Throughout the years, hairstyles, available materials, manufacturing skills, and the spirit of the times all have influenced women's millinery fashions. Historically, millinery has been an important segment of the fashion industry. Rose Bertin got her start in fashion's hall of fame as chief milliner, as well as dressmaker, to Queen Marie Antoinette of France.

Hats once were worn proudly, as symbols of freedom. In ancient Rome, freed slaves wore crimson caps to indicate their new status. The liberty cap worn at the time of the French Revolution also symbolized freedom of a kind. In the modern world, special kinds of hats symbolize

professional status or rank. The cap of the graduate nurse, the academic mortarboard, the chef's
hat, and the headgear worn by some members
of the clergy all denote rank in their particular
fields. For others, going hatless has become
something of a symbol of freedom. Today women
of all ages and positions in life display attractive
coiffeurs on many occasions where hats would
once have been de rigueur.

The widespread feminine rejection of hats is
a phenomenon of the past few years. During this
time, the millinery industry in the United States
has researched, publicized, and campaigned in an
extensive effort to reverse the trend, but to little
avail. Self-criticism by the industry, criticisms of
retail promotions and those of fashion editors,
and publicity photographs of prominent women
in attractive hats have accomplished little. Furthermore, fashions in hairstyles during recent
years have also served to diminish interest in
millinery. A woman who has just spent a considerable sum of money to have her hair styled and
set is understandably loath to cover it or muss
it by donning a hat.

Organization and Operation

The millinery industry is largely a handcraft industry comprised mainly of small firms. Seven
of every ten plants employ fewer than 20 persons
each. The 20 largest firms in the industry produce
only a fifth of the annual output, which, in the
1960s, was little more than $100 million at factory
value.

Nearly all suppliers to the industry, such as
producers of ribbons, flowers, feathers, and so on,
are concentrated in the New York City area. Less
than 5 percent of the approximately 700 millinery
factories in the United States are located outside
the Middle Atlantic region.

The industry has a small proportion of important original designers, most of whom create
millinery for an exclusive custom trade as well
as for resale through stores in the upper price
brackets. Among the producers of inexpensive
millinery, copying, rather than design skill, is the
accepted pattern of operation. In some instances,
cheap copies of a currently "hot" number may
represent the entire line a firm offers.

New York City is the principal market center
for millinery. Major producers of expensive millinery maintain showrooms, and often workrooms,
in the city. Producers of inexpensive millinery
and suppliers to the industry also have their
showrooms there.

Merchandising Activities

Because profitable millinery retailing requires a
constant stream of new styles, retailers frequently
lease their millinery operations to operators who
virtually live in the market. Relatively few retail
millinery departments are store-owned.

Millinery lessees, or syndicates, as they are
known, maintain large staffs who daily canvass
the market in all price ranges. These syndicates
also offer substantial assistance to small producers in the form of fashion and design advice,
information about sources of trimming supplies,
and so on. The typical millinery syndicate keeps
an extremely close eye on fashion trends, has
expert fashion analysts on its staff, and issues
bulletins to its client stores, not only on millinery
but on the entire fashion picture.

The millinery industry has an active association, the National Millinery Institute, which
works hard to promote interest in hats. Its efforts
range from coaxing prominent women to permit
the use of photographs that show them wearing
hats to exhorting producers and merchants to
stock millinery in sizes for women whose heads
are larger or smaller than average.

Marketing Trends

Accelerated interest in fur head coverings during
recent years has improved and extended the
market potential of millinery. Exploitation of this
interest takes such forms as devising methods for
creating quality fur hats at lower prices, using
new and unusual furs for millinery, and introducing more creative designing.

Fashion trends, however, offer the industry its
brightest hope. The return of the "small head"
look in hairstyling makes the wearing of hats
more comfortable, and the return of longer skirts
makes the hat once more essential to the well-
dressed look. In addition, the emphasis on individuality in fashion encourages women to wear
hats, described by *Harper's Bazaar* once as the
"accessory of fantasy and personality."

Reference

[1]*U.S. Industrial Outlook,* Business and Defense Services Administration, U.S. Department of Commerce, Washington, 1969, p. 137.

Merchandising Vocabulary

Define or briefly explain the following terms:

Full-fashion hosiery	Fine jewelry	Semiprecious stones
Boarding	Alloy	Lapidary
Rack jobber	Gemstones	Costume jewelry
Last	Precious stones	Reticule
Cosmetics		

Merchandising Review

1. Name the two major industries comprising the intimate apparel industry. What are the separate types of garments produced in each?
2. Describe the major merchandising activities engaged in by present-day producers of intimate apparel.
3. Into what three major areas are the merchandising activities of the hosiery industry divided?
4. Why have shoes become an important fashion accessory during the past two decades?
5. How do shoe manufacturers distribute and promote their products?
6. Discuss the merchandising activities most commonly engaged in by cosmetics producers.
7. Name the two categories of merchandise into which the United States jewelry industry is subdivided. What are the distinguishing characteristics of each of these categories?
8. What are some of the services provided by large costume jewelry firms to their retail outlets?
9. Discuss the glove industry in the United States today. In terms of materials and method of manufacture, what three major types of gloves does it produce?
10. What is the primary purpose of a handbag? Why is it considered an important fashion accessory?
11. Discuss the relationship between cosmetics and hairstyles and trends in fashion apparel, illustrating how cosmetics are used to complement the apparel.
12. What is a millinery syndicate? Describe its operation.

Merchandising Digest

1. "Fashion today emphasizes the total look, and accessories are an important part of that look." Discuss this statement from the text and its implications for the retail merchandising of apparel accessories.
2. Discuss how changing fashions and technology have influenced women's hosiery.
3. Discuss the historical significance of headwear. What factors do you think are largely responsible for the fashion of going hatless?

10

RETAIL DISTRIBUTORS of FASHIONS

The moment of truth in the fashion business comes when the consumer inspects the assortment of merchandise offered by a retail distributor. Success in the fashion business is achieved when that consumer decides to make a purchase. Unless that decision is made, all the creative and productive efforts it took to put that merchandise in front of the consumer were useless. Unless the consumer buys, fashion design and production are merely exercises in futility.

The various techniques employed in the retail distribution of fashion merchandise are determined by the interests and standards of living favored by the target customers of each retail firm. Changes in distribution patterns follow closely in the wake of changes in customer demand. This is why some fine department and specialty stores that once concentrated on offering high-priced merchandise to an elite group of consumers now have expanded their fashion assortments to include moderate price lines and erected branch stores in middle-class suburbs. Chains that once catered solely to practical customers with limited incomes are now upgrading both their fashion assortments and their upper price limits.

Adhering rigidly to time-honored ways of doing business in today's highly competitive economy spells doom for retail distributors of fashion apparel. Flexibility is the key to their success and growth. As the customer changes, so must retailers' methods of serving that customer change if they wish to do business.

History and Development of Fashion Retailing

Fashion retailing is the business of buying fashion apparel and accessories and reselling them to the ultimate consumer. It had its beginnings in the outdoor bazaars of the Orient and marketplaces of the Mediterranean, where people came together to buy, sell, and barter goods of all kinds. Some of these early tradesmen were weavers, potters, goldsmiths, and other kinds of artisans who produced the goods they offered to customers; others obtained their stock from traders who had brought the merchandise from distant countries by ship or caravan. Still another kind of early retailer deliberately sought out his clientele: this was the peddler, who carried his wares either on his back or on pack animals and followed routes that often took him away from his home area for a year or more at a time.

Out of these early beginnings came today's elaborate network of retail distributors. Today, there are nearly 2 million retail establishments in the United States alone: stores, mail-order houses, and firms that sell their products from door to door. Of these, at least one distributor in ten devotes a major part of its efforts to the selling of feminine apparel and accessories. In addition, many retail firms who specialize in the distribution of other types of merchandise also handle limited varieties of fashion merchandise: food stores that sell hosiery, for example, and drugstores that sell cosmetics.

From Marketplace to Store

As civilizations spread out from mild climates into less temperate zones, artisans and retailers moved indoors. Although food continued to be sold in outdoor marketplaces, clothing, accessories, and allied crafts were offered in stores and shops, which provided not only protection of the goods from inclement weather but also better storage facilities.

During the Middle Ages, craft guilds came into existence. Master craftsmen were responsible for the training of a number of apprentices. Each master craftsman lived and worked in his own home, which was usually located on a street or in an area crowded with others belonging to the same guild. Customers seeking a particular kind of product would tour the streets occupied by the merchants and craftsmen specializing in that product. The modern descendant of the guild shop is considered to be the specialty store, whose staff is expected to offer the same fashion expertise and knowledge of a specific type of merchandise that medieval shoppers expected of guild craftsmen.

Department and variety stores are considered to be the modern descendants of those early retailers who bought rather than produced goods for resale, as well as of the bazaars and marketplaces in which such goods were sold, because each offers many kinds of merchandise at one location. Other descendants are those gradually vanishing forms of outdoor excitement: the market days in small European towns, when farmers and craftsmen alike display their goods for sale in the central market square. In a sense, suburban shopping centers, with their cluster of various kinds of retail shops, are also contemporary versions of the bazaar and marketplaces of earlier times.

Development of Retailing in the United States

Among the first explorers of the North American continent were traders who set up trading posts to collect furs, bartering food, liquor, and jewelry with trappers and Indians for the prime pelts which they sold in European markets. Many of these early trading posts later developed into some of the larger cities on the continent, such as New York, Chicago, Detroit, and St. Louis.

Towns that soon developed along the eastern coast of the North American continent had shops and stores much like those of European towns, but along the frontier and in sparsely settled farming areas, different forms of retailing developed. The general store, which carried a wide variety of consumer goods and took goods as well as cash in payment, became an important retail distribution center in those early days. The peddler also played an important role, going from town to town and from farm to farm with his limited assortments of otherwise unavailable merchandise. Later, mail service became more reliable, and a third method of rural retail distribution developed: mail-order selling.

The General Store Many of the earliest general stores in America developed from fur trading posts. In the beginning, their stocks consisted solely of utilitarian items; fashion merchandise was not carried. As more farmers and ranchers settled along the frontier, however, the women in those pioneer families became customers for rudimentary fashion goods, and stores added sewing notions and bolts of fabric. Since money was a scarce commodity on the frontier, bartering remained the main way of doing business.

As the frontier pushed westward, and as larger communities and the beginnings of prosperity followed, there were more fashion consumers of relative wealth to be served, and the stores increased their stocks of fashion merchandise accordingly. Some of the wealthier sent away to stores on the East Coast for their fashion purchases; others patronized specialty shops that had sprung up as the frontier towns grew in size. In the rural areas, the country general store continued to thrive until the 1920s, when easier and faster ways of transportation and communication brought more sophisticated resources for fashion goods within the reach of rural customers. Even then, however, the farmer's wife was still likely to buy her fabrics and her clothes from the same general store to which her husband sold his crops, from which he borrowed money in lean years, and from which he bought farm tools, household needs, and clothes for himself and his family.

The peddler was a welcome sight to yesterday's housewife, for he brought the essentials of a general store to her doorstep.

Even in their heyday, however, country general stores were never in close touch with fashion trends. Many proprietors never went to the New York markets at all, but instead bought their goods from traveling salesmen or from wholesale houses that flourished at such halfway metropolitan points as Baltimore for the South, and Chicago for the Midwest.

As the population expanded, many of the barter-type general stores switched to a cash-only basis, thus becoming strictly retailers of merchandise, rather than bankers and dealers in farm crops. Some of today's largest general merchandise and department store regional chains grew from just such "cash store" beginnings. Macy's is an example.

The Peddler The typical peddler who went from house to house along the country roads of America was often a Yankee and his pack held an assortment of such tools and materials of fashion as needles, pins, threads, combs, and ribbons and laces. In addition to supplying the utilitarian needs of the rural housewife, the ped-

dler also served as a source of fashion information for the consumer and as a source of customer preference information for the producer. But a peddler's route invariably was a long and slow one, and sometimes it was a whole year before he returned to market centers to replenish his wares and to report what he had gleaned from his customers.

Although now extinct, the peddler has left his mark on this country's retailing in several ways. For example, the notions department in modern retail establishments supposedly got its name from the phrase "Yankee notions," a term used to describe the clever and useful gadgets the itinerant peddler carried in his pack.

The contemporary descendant of the early peddler is the door-to-door salesman. Door-to-door is still an effective way to sell some fashion products, particularly if the salesperson is a woman trained to offer fashion advice. Foundation garments and silk stockings once were sold rather extensively door-to-door. Today, however, cosmetics dominate the field, so far as fashion products are concerned.

Direct descendants of some of the early peddlers today operate department stores that are among the largest in the country. For instance, Adam Gimbel set down his peddler's pack and opened a retail store in Vincennes, Indiana, in 1842. The Gimbel organization, which includes the Saks Fifth Avenue stores, is still owned by his family.

Mail-Order Sellers As mail service became faster and more reliable, a new form of retailing developed for those who had the cash but were not close to urban centers: mail-order selling. Montgomery Ward, founded in 1872, was first in the field. Mail-order catalogs brought descriptions of low-priced apparel and home furnishings right into the rural home, permitting women to make their selections at leisure and place their orders conveniently.

Compared to the assortment offered by a city store of that period, early mail-order catalogs had little variety or fashion excitement. Their styles were basic; there was no attempt to anticipate developing fashion trends. Compared to what the country general store had to offer, however, the pages of the mail-order catalog opened up a whole new world of fashion to the rural customer at prices she could afford.

With the advent of the automobile, mail-order companies found themselves competing with city stores rather than country stores for the business of the rural customer. As a result, the larger mail-order houses began to open retail stores of their own in the 1920s. In the 1930s, catalog centers were opened, to which customers came and either wrote up their own orders or were helped by salespeople in making their selections of merchandise not in the store's stock. Today, a customer can shop at any of the major mail-order companies in person, by mail, or by telephone.

Since the end of World War II, mail-order catalogs have become increasingly fashion-oriented. Farm families, with more money and more education than ever before, have become sophisticated, fashion-wise shoppers. City dwellers, always known for their fashion-consciousness, have discovered that mail-order catalogs offer an easy way to shop. Styling of catalog merchandise, particularly of apparel, has become more sophis-

ticated. Recently, several large catalog houses have commissioned famous European couturiers to design small groups of apparel exclusively for them.

Today, each major mail-order house, such as Sears, Roebuck and Company, Montgomery Ward, and The J. C. Penney Company, sends a trained fashion observer to couture openings. This expert reports back to the company's apparel and accessories buyers. Outstanding fashion trends, and garments illustrating these trends, are presented to the firm's buyers, who in turn may arrange to have garments that incorporate trends believed to be significant made up and included in the firm's catalog assortments. Catalog apparel styles, albeit less extreme and less sophisticated than those included in the stocks of most urban specialty stores, are very much in step with current fashion trends.

Modern Types of Retail Fashion Distributors

Retailers exist to serve their customers. As their customers change, so, too, must they change. Successful retailing of fashion, like fashion itself, depends upon customer acceptance. No one has ever been able to force a fashion upon the public or withhold one that the public demanded. And no distributor of fashion, not even the greatest and most prestigious, can survive for long if he does not, in the late Marshall Field's words, "Give the lady what she wants!"

Retailers have developed various forms of organization and methods of operation to give that lady what she wants. There are retailers who stock many different types of merchandise and retailers who specialize in limited types of merchandise. There are retailers who offer a variety of services and retailers who offer only a few. There are retailers who serve those willing to spend large sums of money casually for their fashions and retailers who concentrate on customers who watch every cent carefully. There are also retailers who own no retail outlets of their own but operate departments in the stores of others.

Some of these types of retail establishments that strive to meet the current fashion needs of

Courtesy Gladding's, Providence, R.I.

Gladding's, which dates back to the 1700s, is a contender for the title of the country's oldest department store.

customers have been on the scene for a long time. Others represent new forms of retailing that developed in the early and middle years of this century in response to customer demand.

The Department Store

The department store gets its name from the fact that it seeks to present many different kinds of merchandise, each in a separate area or department of its own, all under one roof. A department store is defined by the Bureau of the Census as one that employs 25 or more people and sells general lines of merchandise in each of three categories: home furnishings; household linens and dry goods; and apparel and accessories for the entire family.

Department store managements add a few other requirements to the federal government description, not the least of which is that the store accepts its share of community responsibility and makes itself something more than just a place to shop.[1] If a department store can stage a fashion show for a local charity, or lend its space for an art show or club meeting, or participate in community affairs in some other way, it will usually offer to do so without waiting to be asked. Such community service not only generates goodwill but also, by creating an awareness of the store and its merchandise, increases the flow of fashion information among consumers quite apart from, and in addition to, whatever the store does specifically to publicize and sell its merchandise.

Organizational Structure Department store organization does not lend itself to the clear lines of authority that one often finds in other businesses—and therein lies one of the strengths of this form of retailing. Its management recognizes that retailing is a "people business," and that insistence upon a tightly structured organization can inhibit the kind of creative, intuitive thinking needed to understand consumers. Rigid organization also can interfere with quick adjustment to changes in consumer demand.

A department store in the 1960s might have had an organization chart of anywhere from two to six functional *pyramids,* or lines of authority, each headed by an executive responsible to the president of the company. The organizational structure found in most medium-sized department stores today consists of the following four pyramids:

▫ Finance and control, including credit, accounts payable, and inventory control

▫ Merchandising, including buying, selling, and merchandise training of salespeople

▫ Operations, including management of the store building and personnel

▫ Sales promotion, including public relations, advertising, and display

Smaller firms may combine two or more of these areas of responsibility under one executive, according to the time and talent available. Some firms consider merchandising and sales promotion inseparable functions and therefore combine them. Many large organizations add a fifth pyramid for personnel, instead of including it as a subfunction of operations. Multiunit organizations often add a sixth pyramid for branch store management.

Overlapping authority and responsibility occur frequently in the department store field. For example, salespeople are trained by operations executives in ringing up sales, handling delivery requests and charges, and the like, but they are given merchandise and fashion information by the buyers and by the fashion coordinator.

Where there are several branches, the overlapping can become even more complex. In an effort to adapt the merchandise of each individual branch to the fashion character of the community it serves, branch-owning department stores have developed relationships within their organizational structure that defy charting. For example, a branch store department manager may be assigned to supervise assortments and selling activities, as well as to report customer reaction to store buyers. In performing these functions, he works with, but not over or under, each of several buyers. The resulting relationship between a buyer and such a department manager is neither line (authority) nor staff (advisory) but is a little of both. (See the chart on page 166.)

Merchandising Policies The department store was a pioneer in offering customer charge and return privileges. This willingness to accept merchandise returns was one of the foundation stones on which the late John Wanamaker built his business. His first store, opened in Philadelphia in 1876 in an old freight station, was a men's clothing store. A year later he had added such departments as ladies' goods, household linens, upholstery, and shoes, making a total of 16 departments in all. Wanamaker advertised that any article that did not fit well, did not please "the folks at home," or for any other reason was unsatisfactory could be returned for cash refund within ten days.

Linked naturally to the cash refund policy was a system of marking the retail price clearly on the merchandise instead of indicating its cost in code and haggling the price between customer and salesclerk. Although Wanamaker is often credited with being the father of the one-price, no-haggling system that now prevails in retailing, other pioneer merchants, such as Marshall Field and Adam Gimbel, are known to have initiated such a system in their stores at almost the same time.

The department store's policy in relation to fashion merchandise is initially to spread a broad, shallow assortment before the customer, and then to narrow and deepen the investment behind those styles, colors, and prices to which customers show a good response. As the terms are used in fashion merchandising, a *broad assortment* is one encompassing many styles. A *narrow*

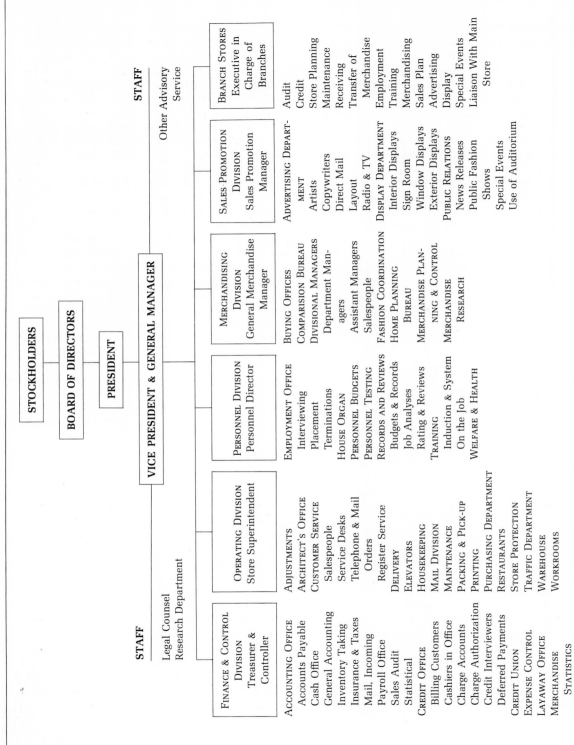

STOCKHOLDERS

BOARD OF DIRECTORS

PRESIDENT

VICE PRESIDENT & GENERAL MANAGER

STAFF

Legal Counsel
Research Department

STAFF

Other Advisory
Service

FINANCE & CONTROL DIVISION
Treasurer & Controller

ACCOUNTING OFFICE
Accounts Payable
Cash Office
General Accounting
Inventory Taking
Insurance & Taxes
Mail, Incoming
Payroll Office
Sales Audit
Statistical
CREDIT OFFICE
Billing Customers
Cashiers in Office
Charge Accounts
Charge Authorization
Credit Interviewers
Deferred Payments
CREDIT UNION
EXPENSE CONTROL
LAYAWAY OFFICE
MERCHANDISE
STATISTICS

OPERATING DIVISION
Store Superintendent

ADJUSTMENTS
ARCHITECT'S OFFICE
CUSTOMER SERVICE
Salespeople
Service Desks
Telephone & Mail
Orders
Register Service
DELIVERY
ELEVATORS
HOUSEKEEPING
MAIL DIVISION
MAINTENANCE
PACKING & PICK-UP
PRINTING
PURCHASING DEPARTMENT
RESTAURANTS
STORE PROTECTION
TRAFFIC DEPARTMENT
WAREHOUSE
WORKROOMS

PERSONNEL DIVISION
Personnel Director

EMPLOYMENT OFFICE
Interviewing
Placement
Terminations
HOUSE ORGAN
PERSONNEL BUDGETS
PERSONNEL TESTING
RECORDS AND REVIEWS
Budgets & Records
Job Analyses
Rating & Reviews
TRAINING
Induction & System
On the Job
WELFARE & HEALTH

MERCHANDISING DIVISION
General Merchandise Manager

BUYING OFFICES
COMPARISION BUREAU
DIVISIONAL MANAGERS
Department Managers
Assistant Managers
Salespeople
FASHION COORDINATION
HOME PLANNING
BUREAU
MERCHANDISE PLANNING & CONTROL
MERCHANDISE
RESEARCH

SALES PROMOTION DIVISION
Sales Promotion Manager

ADVERTISING DEPARTMENT
Artists
Copywriters
Direct Mail
Layout
Radio & TV
DISPLAY DEPARTMENT
Interior Displays
Sign Room
Window Displays
Exterior Displays
PUBLIC RELATIONS
News Releases
Public Fashion
Shows
Special Events
Use of Auditorium

BRANCH STORES
Executive in Charge of Branches

Audit
Credit
Store Planning
Maintenance
Receiving
Transfer of
Merchandise
Employment
Training
Merchandising
Sales Plan
Advertising
Display
Special Events
Liaison With Main
Store

A typical organization chart for a large department store.

Courtesy NRMA

assortment concentrates on relatively few styles. The term *deep* is applied to an assortment that includes a comprehensive range of colors and sizes in each style, while the term *shallow* means an assortment that contains only a few sizes and colors in each style.

Not only is the merchandise physically grouped into separate departments by type, such as notions, sportswear, or cosmetics, but the typical department store has special sections or departments keyed to the interests of each important customer group it serves: budget departments; moderate-priced misses, junior, and women's departments; "better" or higher-priced apparel departments; sometimes couture departments; teen shops; maternity shops; bridal salons; special boutiques for those with extreme tastes; career girl shops; and many others.

Modern department stores may offer a variety of selling services within a single store, depending upon the nature and sometimes the price level of the merchandise involved. In higher-priced apparel departments, a salon type of selling service often prevails. In this type of service, merchandise other than that used for display purposes is kept out of sight and the salesperson brings out styles for the individual customer's inspection. Self-selection is the type of selling service most commonly employed by department stores today, however. In this form of selling service, merchandise is arranged on open racks, counters, or shelves, for the customer's inspection. Salespeople are available to assist customers by providing information about the merchandise and by completing the sales transaction once a customer has reached a buying decision. A few department stores employ self-service with check-out counters for certain types of merchandise that readily lend themselves to this type of selling service, such as nationally advertised and prepackaged goods of relatively low unit cost.

Nationally advertised brands usually play an important role in a department store's fashion stocks and are prominently featured in its display and advertising. To avoid looking too much like competing stores that feature the same brands, department stores may seek items that will be "confined," or exclusive with them in their own communities. Within the framework of the anti-trust laws, this is difficult to do unless a buyer is alert enough to discover some small new resource that other stores have not yet found. An alternative is to buy from a larger resource some styles that were made up experimentally but not put into the regular line.

The very size of the department store's fashion operation is frequently one of its major problems. Buyers, especially those who are merchandising departments in several branches in addition to the parent store, necessarily concentrate their purchases with resources who are able to deliver large quantities of merchandise. They tend to buy only those styles about which they feel sufficiently secure to place substantial orders. The buyer who needs a minimum of 48 pieces of a style has a different merchandising problem from the buyer who needs only 6 or 12 pieces.

Branch stores usually depend upon main store buyers to merchandise their fashion stocks. This has one important advantage: if a customer finds a dress she likes in one branch but the store does not have the size or color she wants, a telephone call to the main store will determine whether any of the other branches have the dress in both the right size and the right color. If so, the salesperson can arrange to have it delivered to the customer's home on the next regular delivery. A small specialty shop, competing with the branch of a department store, can call upon no such reserve, and special ordering of a desired color or size from the manufacturer usually involves too long a delay for most shoppers.

The Specialty Store

According to the Bureau of the Census, a specialty store is one that carries limited lines of apparel, accessories, or home furnishings. A shoe store, a jewelry store, or one handling women's apparel and accessories—these are classified as specialty stores. In the trade, however, retailers use "specialty store" to describe any apparel and/or accessories store that exhibits a degree of fashion awareness, even if it carries goods for both sexes.

Specialty stores are widely varied in size and type. They range from the tiny Mom-and-Pop store, run by the proprietor with few or no hired assistants, to huge departmentalized institutions

Neiman-Marcus, in Dallas, is a large and luxurious departmentalized specialty store, whose image is projected through its decor.

that resemble department stores. Some are single-unit stores; some are units of chains; some are suburban branches of central city stores.

The great majority of specialty stores are individually owned, have no branches, and are not units of chains. The composite sales of these single-unit stores, however, represent less than half the total volume done by all specialty stores. The larger share of business is done by multiunit specialty stores or those that are units of local, regional, or national chains. Peck and Peck, for example, is a specialty store chain with units throughout the country.

Organizational Structure The organizational structure of a specialty store tends to vary with its size. Since the majority are fairly small and the range of merchandise carried is somewhat narrow, their organizational structure tends to be simple, with only two or three functional pyramids or lines of authority. In these cases, the merchandising and sales promotion functions are frequently performed by a single executive.

In the smallest operations, the store owner is likely to participate personally in all facets of running the business, assisted by one or two lower-echelon executives.

In larger specialty stores, the organizational pattern is similar to that of a department store of equivalent size. While the medium-sized stores have a three- or four-pyramid organizational structure, the larger stores include a fifth pyramid for personnel, and the largest, multiunit firms usually add a sixth pyramid for branch store liaison and management.

Merchandising Policies The specialty store generally concentrates on pleasing a specific, carefully profiled kind of customer, instead of trying to serve a broad range of customers, as department stores do. The customer selected by the specialty store as its target may be high-fashion or budget-minded, fashion innovator or follower, teen-ager or senior citizen, to give just a few examples.

The usual merchandising approach of the specialty store is to have broad and shallow assortments within the framework of what its target customer may be expected to accept. Accessories are usually carefully related to apparel, and fashion coordination is stressed in display, promotion, and selling techniques. Many of the better-known specialty stores carry only current and high fashions, in moderate- to high-price lines, and function so effectively in these areas that consumers tend to think of "specialty store" in terms of slightly higher prices and newer fashions than in the department store.

Self-selection selling is used in specialty stores where it is appropriate, but there is likely to be more emphasis on personal selling than in department stores. In the medium- to higher-priced stores, emphasis is placed on remembering what each individual customer has purchased and what her friends have purchased. The accent is on individuality so that a customer may avoid the risk of seeing her dress on another woman. When such stores select merchandise from nationally advertised lines, they usually avoid the *Fords* (styles that are copied at a variety of price lines). Because they can often buy only a few units of a given style, specialty stores can and do make greater use of small resources than can department stores.

Fashion leadership and exclusive styling are the foundations on which many of the country's successful specialty stores have been built. The proprietor, often right on the selling floor and in daily contact with customers and salespeople, is extremely well equipped to recognize fashion preferences among his customers and know the right moment to introduce new trends to his clientele.

Like department stores, multiunit specialty stores generally merchandise their branches from the main store. They enjoy the same advantages over local competition that department store branches do: a skilled fashion merchandiser who directs the operation from the parent store and a large stock from which to draw wanted colors and sizes.

The Chain Organization

Chains are groups of stores, centrally owned, each handling very similar goods, that are merchandised from a central headquarters. Large national chains with a great many units may group these units under the merchandising direction of various regional headquarters which, in turn, function under the direction of the national merchandising staff. A chain store unit frequently differs from a department store branch in that in the former there may be less effort made to adapt the fashion emphasis to the specific community served than there is in the latter.

Chains that deal in fashion merchandise may be national, regional, or local. They may be general merchandise chains, with only a portion of their assortments devoted to fashion goods, or they may be specialty chains, devoted exclusively to a narrow range of fashion apparel and/or accessories.

Some of the general merchandise chains that today distribute impressive quantities of fashion merchandise started originally as mail-order firms: Sears, Roebuck and Company and Montgomery Ward, for instance. Conversely, The J. C. Penney Company, which began as a chain operation, now has a thriving mail-order catalog business.

Organizational Structure Large chains often develop extremely elaborate management patterns. A specialist is in charge of each detail of the operation, such as real estate, packaging, finance, warehousing, or quality control. Whereas a department store might leave the acceptability of a manufacturer's seaming or size measurements up to the buyer concerned, a chain might have a quality-control department devoted to formulating requirements for various garments and assisting manufacturers in complying with such requirements, all this quite apart from the efforts of the chain's buyers.

Central buying prevails among chain organizations. The larger chains usually have elaborate systems of supervision and reporting, so that their buyers are kept informed at all times of what is selling and what remains in stock at each of their many units. In addition to stock and sales information received from the individual units, buyers also may be guided by reports from fashion and economic experts on the headquarters staff.

Smaller chains are necessarily simpler in their organizational structure. They have fewer experts and more general executives at the management level.

Accurate control of inventories and sales is essential to chain operation. The "system," or method of reporting used, is looked on by a chain, large or small, as the vital artery that carries its lifeblood. Without rapid accurate sales and inventory reporting, a fashion chain can flounder. For this reason electronic systems to handle their tremendous flow of merchandising data are now commonplace among chains.

Merchandising Policies Although there are a few conspicuous exceptions, most chains are concerned with offering practical quality at moderate prices. They make little effort to assert fashion leadership, placing emphasis instead on consistent value and promotional pricing. Selling service is usually of the self-selection type, with clerks available to answer questions and to ring up sales. Private labeling is used to a large extent. With its own brand names and goods manufactured to its own specifications, each chain has merchandise not readily comparable with the offerings of competing stores. Display is used to indicate what the assortments contain, rather than to highlight fashion features and coordination possibilities of the merchandise.

Chains that specialize in popular-priced apparel and accessories generally function at a fast and furious pace, since the stock they carry has usually reached the peak of its fashion cycle. Central buying and merchandising and minimum efforts to individualize the assortments in their various units are characteristics of many such chains.

Some of the largest national chains, however, give the individual store manager considerable freedom in merchandise selection. In such cases, buying is done centrally, and the headquarters merchandising staff prepares both a list of merchandise available and a suggested model stock plan for each of its unit stores. Some chains then give a store manager the authority to adjust the stock assortment at his discretion, tailoring merchandise offerings more precisely to the needs of the community served. This gives the individual unit of the chain a certain amount of merchandising flexibility, without forfeiting the advantages inherent in centralized buying.

The Discount Store

The discount store is impossible to define. For example, "mass merchandiser," a term often used in connection with this type of store, could apply equally well to many large department stores. In general, discount operations emphasize bargain prices, large volume, and minimum customer service.

Until the 1950s, the term "discounter" applied only to dealers in durable goods. In out-of-the-way locations and with no advertising, discounters sold household appliances and housewares on a low-price, cash-and-carry basis. Their prices were below the manufacturers' list prices, a procedure that was considered illegal in those days, although the laws have since been changed.

Merchandising Policies During the 1950s, discounters began adding soft goods to their durable goods offerings. At first, these efforts met with only mediocre success, since most discounters lacked experience in this field. Recognizing the volume potential in soft goods, many discounters turned over the merchandising of their soft goods and fashion departments to leased operators, who

Today chain variety stores are emphasizing fashion apparel, as this Honolulu unit of Woolworth's shows.

had more expertise along this line. Today, a large majority of such discount store departments are operated by lessees.

The discounter is necessarily an opportunist in merchandising. In order to take advantage of opportune buys wherever they may turn up, discount store buyers usually have ample authority to act quickly and decisively. Because of this, and also because of the tremendous quantities of merchandise their stores can use, discount store buyers have become important factors in their various markets.

While some discount stores operate with no regard for fashion, value, taste, or anything but low price, others maintain a consistent level of taste and offer styles that are still in the early fashion stages of their fashion cycles. Ohrbach's for example, buys from foreign couture collec-

tions and invites the socially elite to semiannual first showings of its line-for-line copies.

Although nationally advertised fashion brands are usually not available to most discounters, some producers make up secondary lines under different labels for discount distribution. On occasion, items from major producers' lines appear in discount stores, usually, however, with the brand labels removed.

In discount store selling, frills are eliminated. Merchandise is stocked on racks or tables for the customer to help herself. Self-service prevails. Employees are present only to direct customers and straighten the stock. The customer makes her own selections and then takes them to a cashier's desk where sales are rung up.

Transactions are usually made for cash, although some discount stores today accept checks,

Chapter 10
Retail Distributors of Fashions

Courtesy Two Guys

Self-service racks and display tables are featured by discount stores.

bank credit cards, or offer credit plans of their own. Refund policies are generally liberal: money back if the goods are returned unworn in a specified number of days. Delivery service, if available, is usually restricted to bulky items and often involves an extra charge. Paperwork is kept to a minimum: the price tag, stamped at the time of sale by the cash register, does duty as a sales slip, and refunds are usually made in cash, eliminating credit slips and extensive recordkeeping.

In recent years, discount retailers have improved their merchandising techniques, upgrading their services, their locations, and their efforts to attract customers. Discount stores now advertise widely, provide free parking in the suburbs, and have convenient city locations. In fact, Korvette's, one of the oldest and best-known discount operations, with two prime locations in New York City and dozens of stores in other

major cities throughout the country, refers to itself as a "promotional department store."

Creative merchandiser or scavenger of producer overstocks, the discount store serves an important fashion function in selling enormous quantities of fashion goods. Whether these styles are at the exciting beginning or dismal end of their fashion cycles, their production and sale help to keep the fashion industry humming.

The Variety Store

Variety stores once referred to themselves as "limited price variety stores," to underscore the fact that they carried a wide range of merchandise in a limited number of low price lines. Some literally were 5-and-10-cent stores, with all merchandise priced at either a nickel or a dime. Others sold goods priced up to a dollar. Fashion merchandise was represented only by such utilitarian articles as socks and underwear, ribbons and buttons, simple hair and dress ornaments. Chain operations dominated the field.

In the 1930s, the larger variety chains began broadening their assortments and extending their price ranges. They grew into what are now known as "general merchandise stores," a term applied rather loosely by retailers to stores that primarily carry limited lines of apparel and accessories for men, women, and children, as well as limited assortments of home furnishings.

Merchandising Policies In this process of evolution, variety stores have vastly upgraded their appearance, service, and assortments. Their original stores had bare wooden floors, no fitting rooms, and few, if any, customer services. All sales were cash-and-carry. Apparel and accessories were of the most utilitarian type, with little or no fashion appeal. Modern units of such chains as the F. W. Woolworth Company or J. J. Newberry, by contrast, are well lighted, air-conditioned, carpeted or surfaced with resilient floor coverings, and equipped with fitting rooms. Fixtures are modern, well-designed, and supplemented by attractive fashion displays. Customer services, such as charge privileges and delivery, have been added. Their fashion assortments, while remaining low in price, have been broadened to include dresses, coats, shoes, sweaters, slacks, and intimate apparel for the entire family.

Self-service, as a selling technique, generally prevails in variety stores, although some limited personal selling may be provided. Well-labeled merchandise is packaged, binned, or hung for the customer's inspection. Assortments are fairly broad and generally basic. Fashion assortments are usually limited to styles that are well into the culmination phase of their fashion cycles. Displays remain largely functional, but an effort is made to bring out important fashion points of the merchandise.

Because the fashions that are featured have already proven successful before making an appearance in these stores, and also because of their low pricing policies, variety stores make their major appeal to the lower-income customer who wants to be fashionably dressed.

The Leased Department

The leased department is a special form of retailing. It is a department in a retail store ostensibly operated by the store but actually run by an outside organization. The lessee owns the department's stock, merchandises and staffs the department, pays for its advertising, abides by the store's policies, and pays the store a percentage of sales as rent. Essentially, the operator of a leased department is an expert in some merchandise or service that a retail store finds unprofitable to handle directly.

Lessees in the fashion field include service as well as merchandise departments. Services commonly leased include the beauty salon, shoe repair, and jewelry repair. Merchandise departments commonly leased include millinery, shoes, fine jewelry, and furs. There are also some leased departments that handle women's apparel, but these are more likely to be found in discount stores than in department or specialty stores, and they usually concentrate on lower-priced goods.

Department stores, large and small, make extensive use of leased departments, as do chain and discount organizations. Specialty stores tend to restrict leased operations to services, preferring to handle the merchandising of goods themselves.

The operator of a leased department may be a local person, functioning in a single store, or a giant organization, doing business in hundreds of stores across the country. In the case of the larger operators, traveling supervisors regularly visit their various locations, to confer with both the store management and the department manager, to help them cope with problems that may arise, and to plan for future growth.

Merchandising Policies   The fashion merchandising policies of a leased department are dictated by the terms of its lease and must conform to those of the store in which it operates. Assortments and services must be on a level with those of all the other departments, so that the customer has no indication that the department is not store owned and operated.

Some of the larger leased department organizations are immensely flexible in their approach to individual store policies and can function on almost any level of fashion and service that may be required. Others limit themselves to narrow fields, such as popular-priced shoes, and seek connections only with stores whose merchandise and service policies are compatible with their own.

Leased department operators are in a unique position with respect to the fashion industries. They are usually in daily contact with their markets and are sometimes established in a wide variety of stores. They can give impetus to incoming styles or clear producers' stocks of declining styles, according to the merchandising policies of their host stores. The successful, long-established operators sometimes know their industries better than do the producers themselves. Such operators are equipped to give fashion guidance to their sources of supply as well as to the store they serve.

The Franchised Store

Relatively new, but growing, in the fashion field is the franchised store. This is an independently owned store that sells branded lines of merchandise or services supplied by a franchiser. The franchiser helps the retailer design his store and plan his stock. All merchandise is purchased from the franchiser, who in some cases may also be a manufacturer. In addition to his profit on the sale of the merchandise to the retailer, the franchiser usually collects a percentage of sales as compensation for the use of the franchise brand name.

The merchandise assortments handled by fashion franchise stores are usually narrow in range and low to medium in price. In addition to whatever advertising is done by the franchiser on a national basis, franchise stores advertise locally under the guidance of the franchiser. By the public, a franchise store is often believed to be a unit of a specialty store chain, and in reality it operates in much the same way, except that there is a proprietor, rather than a hired manager, in charge.

Merchandising Activities of Retail Fashion Distributors

The fashion retailer must constantly observe and analyze his customers while remaining alert to developments in the wholesale markets and to activities on the competitive scene. The essential activities of retail fashion merchandising, outlined originally by Dr. Paul Nystrom,[2] include:

◻ Analyzing what prospective customers will want

◻ Planning how to act upon estimates of customer demand

◻ Selecting and buying the goods

◻ Promoting the sale of the goods purchased in anticipation of demand

◻ Solving the problems of competition

The kind of organization required to handle these merchandising activities is illustrated in the chart on page 166, which shows the typical merchandising structure of a large department store or large departmentalized specialty store.

In large stores a general merchandise manager heads the merchandising division. At the next lower level are divisional merchandise managers, who are responsible for broad groupings of related departments, such as ready-to-wear or home furnishings, and who report to the general merchandise manager. Reporting to the divisional merchandise managers are the buyers, who are responsible for the actual selection of goods and the management of the departments in which these goods are sold. Reporting to the buyers are their assistants, a head-of-stock, and departmental salespeople.

Staff Aids

In handling its continual cycle of buying and selling activities, the merchandising division of a large retail store has a variety of staff aids upon whom to call for information and advice. Some of these are part of the store organization; others may be outside experts. There are six major staff aids.

The Fashion Bureau A fashion bureau may consist of an individual or a whole department whose job is to collect and assess information on fashion trends from all available sources, both within and outside the store, and to make such information available to the merchandising, advertising, and display executives. A well-organized fashion bureau also recommends ways to coordinate the purchases and presentations of the various store departments, directs fashion shows, and assists in employee fashion training. The store executive who heads this activity is generally known as a "fashion coordinator."

The Comparison Bureau Acting as the eyes and ears of the merchandising division, the comparison bureau's job is to keep track of what the competition is doing. Some stores rely on their buyers and merchandise managers to do this job, but others prefer setting up a separate comparison bureau, believing that its staff can perform the work more extensively and more objectively than merchandising executives are able to do. Comparison bureau employees are encouraged to examine and compare both merchandise and services from the point of view of the customer rather than the merchandising professional.

Comparison shoppers go into other stores, note the response to offerings there, observe how prices, assortments, and services compare with those of their own store, and then report their findings back to the home store for appropriate action. These shoppers sometimes purchase new items not yet carried in their own store, or items that appear comparable in quality but lower in

Larger retailers have testing bureaus similar to this quality control department where Hanes Hosiery checks its products at all stages of manufacture.

price than the offerings of their own store. These items are brought back to the home store for study by appropriate buyers and merchandise managers.

The Unit-Control Bureau Unit-control systems, discussed in detail in Chapter 13, keep track of sales and stock, giving buyers and merchandise managers up-to-date information about buying trends and inventory positions. Smaller stores often include unit control as one of the jobs within the jurisdiction of the buyer, but larger stores usually centralize these operations, and the unit-control bureau provides regular reports to the buyers and merchandise managers.

The Testing Bureau Among the largest stores, such as Macy's, and some of the large chains, such

as The J. C. Penney Company, special testing laboratories are maintained by the organization to examine prospective or in-stock merchandise from the standpoint of its performance in use. This work may be done routinely, as a quality control of all goods purchased by the company's buyers, or it may be done at the request of a buyer who is considering a new type of merchandise or a new resource. The cost of the necessary equipment and staff makes a testing bureau too expensive for stores of modest size. Smaller stores use commercial testing laboratories when the need arises.

The Research Department Research departments serve every area of store operation. Their work for the merchandising division may include such assignments as analyzing traffic patterns within a department in preparation for improving the layout, analyzing operating figures in search of ways to improve profit, or analyzing the local trading area to see whether the store's share of its market is rising or dwindling. Collecting and analyzing information takes time that merchandisers do not always have available. A research department has the time, the detachment, and the experience needed for providing operating executives with the information they need to make decisions whether those decisions involve customers, merchandise, or merchandising methods.

The Resident Buying Office Most stores retain the services of a buying office in the New York market. The primary function of a resident buying office is to provide merchandising assistance to its member stores. Some of these offices also provide central merchandising facilities for their client stores. How these offices are organized and how their activities dovetail with those of store buyers and merchandise managers are matters covered in detail in later chapters.

Trends in Retail Fashion Distribution

A major trend in fashion distribution is movement toward bigness: in size of organization, in number of units, in breadth of assortments. This trend affects department stores, specialty stores, chain organizations, discount organizations, and other forms of retailing. There is also a trend toward expanding assortments and improving their quality, as fashion customers become more knowledgeable and are both willing and able to spend more on fashions.

Mergers

Both department and specialty stores in their early history were primarily independent and family owned. In the 1930s, a trend toward bigness and mergers began, when Federated Department Stores, Allied Stores, and other ownership groups were formed. At that time, the Macy interests owned several stores, each in a different city, as did the Gimbel family and May Depart-

Another trend is toward central distribution systems. Here merchandise from various suppliers is received in boxes and on hangers at a fashion distribution center of a major chain.

At the center, garments are stored on automated overhead racks awaiting ticketing and distribution to units of the chain.

ment Stores. The trend has not only continued but accelerated, and by the end of the 1960s, only a few of the country's larger stores were still individually owned.

Mergers in the retail field normally are carried out in the financial arena, through exchange of stock or purchase of controlling interests. The store or chain itself remains apparently unchanged in the public eye. For example, there is nothing about the operation of the S. Klein discount stores to indicate that they are under the same ownership as the McCrory national variety chain. Most customers are unaware that the Bonwit Teller stores are among those owned by the many-faceted Genesco Corporation. The Bullock stores in southern California are among

those owned by Federated Department Stores. Lord & Taylor, New York, and Goldwater's, Phoenix, are both owned by Associated Dry Goods Corporation. Although operating under their original owners' names, Kaufman's in Pittsburgh and G. Fox in Hartford are both owned by May Department Stores.

At another level, there is a growing trend among smaller stores to affiliate loosely with one another on a voluntary basis for purposes of information exchange and group purchasing. Each store retains its own identity, and each owner retains complete control of his store. No financial joining is involved. However, the heads of stores that are affiliated in this manner get together regularly to compare methods and results, and feel such meetings result in better and more profitable storekeeping for all concerned. Affiliations of this type are often organized and guided by an accounting firm or by a management consultant firm that specializes in the retail field.

Branch Expansion

Both department and specialty stores have vastly increased their volume and their buying power in fashion markets by opening branches. During the 1930s, big city stores, such as B. Altman & Company, Best & Company, and Lord & Taylor in New York, began to open suburban branches. The trend toward branch openings intensified after World War II. Branches became larger and more numerous, contributing an increasingly larger share of total sales volume.

Until recent years, branches were located principally in suburbs of the cities in which the parent stores are located. The trend today, however, is toward opening branches far from the trading area of the parent store. Lord & Taylor, for instance, currently has branches in Pennsylvania, Massachusetts, Maryland, Connecticut, and New Jersey, with additional branches in other states in the planning stage. Saks Fifth Avenue has units as far as 3,000 miles away from the parent store.

Both branching and merging have not only increased the stores' volume, but they also have increased the stores' fashion impact. A store that individually is not large enough to afford a fashion specialist can enjoy this benefit as a branch of a large organization or a member of an ownership group. In the same way, a single retailer with faith in a fashion trend may not be able to muster enough buying power on his own to encourage a manufacturer to experiment, but as a member of a group of stores, he often can.

The trend in branch store operation today is toward ever larger branches, established at ever greater distances from the parent stores, with branches being given increasing merchandising and operational autonomy.

Expanded Assortments

Fashion retailers of all kinds show a trend toward expanding their assortments and casting aside self-imposed restrictions as to the price lines and types of merchandise they can sell. Such shifting, changing, and expanding is not simply the merchant's way of attracting more business. It is his answer to customer demand.

Relatively little buying power for fashion goods is now concentrated in the hands of those few women with unlimited wealth and leisure. The girls with jobs and the housewives with children to raise and homes to manage are now also important fashionwise customers. Their time is limited, and they have no inclination to run from store to store to assemble the components of their wardrobes; they demand a faster and more convenient way of shopping. Nor do they have any inclination to assemble unrelated pieces of a costume; they want coordinated merchandise. This is a demand that merchants are trying to meet with their expanded assortments.

Trading Up

People in the fashion business like to point out that today's fashion customer is amenable to *trading up,* a term meaning buying in higher price lines than those she has formerly been accustomed to. The reasons, as discussed in Chapter 2, are related to such factors as:

- More discretionary income
- Greater diffusion of that discretionary income
- More activity for women outside the home
- Better education for women

The trend toward trading up is reflected in the fashion assortments of most progressive stores and in increased emphasis on personal selling. Trading up is a slow and gradual process, because the customer will accept just so much of an increase at a time. It is the customer, not the merchant or the manufacturer, who sets the rate for trading up.

References

[1]Beatrice Judelle, "The Changing Customer, 1910–1960," *Stores*, November, 1960, p. 24.
[2]Nystrom, *Fashion Merchandising*, pp. 10–12.

✈ Merchandising Vocabulary

Define or briefly explain the following terms:

Fashion retailing	Variety store	Fashion bureau
Department store	General merchandise stores	Comparison bureau
Specialty store	Leased departments	Testing bureau
Mom-and-Pop store	Franchised store	Trading up
Chain organization		

Merchandising Review

1. In relation to fashion assortments, what is meant by the terms broad, narrow, deep, and shallow?
2. Describe briefly any three of the major forms of fashion retailing.
3. What is meant by a *pyramid* in department store organization? Name those most commonly found in larger stores.
4. Under what conditions should fashion stocks be (a) broad and shallow; (b) narrow and deep?
5. What advantages does a department store branch have over other stores in attracting and serving the fashion customer?
6. What advantages does a specialty shop have in meeting its local fashion competition?
7. What are some of the major sources of strength that chain stores enjoy in distributing fashion merchandise?
8. What are some of the major attractions of the discount store to the fashion customer?
9. To which forms of retailing would you turn for fashion merchandise in the early, culmination, and declining stages of its cycle?
10. In which stores would you expect to find (a) nationally advertised brands in strong representation; (b) private brands primarily; (c) opportune buys of national and unbranded goods?
11. What staff aids are likely to be available to the fashion merchandising division of a large store? Name three and describe the function of each.

Merchandising Digest

1. Discuss any two major trends in fashion distribution and show how they reflect changes in the consumer's way of life.
2. Discuss the following statement and its implications for the fashion retailer and fashion producer: "The moment of truth in the fashion business comes when the consumer inspects the assortment of merchandise offered by a retail distributor."
3. Discuss the following statement from the text: "Changes in distribution patterns follow closely in the wake of changes in customer demand."

PART 3 _____
Retail
Merchandising
of

FASHION

11

Interpreting Customer Demand

Successful fashion retailing is a result of the careful and continuing study of consumer demand. Against the background of fashion and its movement, each merchant studies customer demand as it relates to the particular segment of the population that he seeks to serve. Only if a retailer is prompt to recognize and act upon changes in demand can he expect to assemble an assortment of merchandise that will meet with the approval of his clientele.

It is the customer, not the merchant or the producer, who decides which styles shall become fashions. It is the customer whose preferences determine what goods should be included in a retailer's assortment, in what quantities, at what time, and at what prices. By accepting or rejecting what is available to her, the customer indicates to the retailer not only the nature of her present wants but also the direction her preferences are likely to take in the future.

The Marketing Concept

Until the twentieth century, producers in the United States paid little attention to consumer preferences. The country was growing rapidly, and supplies of manufactured goods were not yet equal to the demand. Customers had little alternative but to accept whatever merchandise was offered.

During the first three decades of the twentieth century, however, mass-production techniques were developed. Ample supplies of goods in increasing variety became available, and producers found that they had both excess productive capacity and increased competition. As a result, a change in the attitudes of management began to develop, in the fashion industry as well as in industry in general. Marketing efforts at all levels became more customer-oriented.

Producers and retailers alike have become increasingly aware that the success of their operations depends upon their ability to produce and make available to regular and prospective customers those specific products that these customers want, in the quantities, at the time, and at the prices that these customers want them. This marketing philosophy, one that is consumer-oriented rather than producer-oriented, has come to be known as the *marketing concept*.

Before the marketing concept became widely accepted, producers, and often retailers, had operated on the assumption that promotional efforts alone could get the consumer to buy anything they wanted him to buy. Producers and retailers also believed that if they agreed on what was to be the fashion, the consumer had no choice but to accept it. As a result of such thinking, some promotions failed because the products concerned were not in line with customer demand, while other promotions succeeded because they were in behalf of products customers wanted and would have bought even without promotion.

Recent fashion history provides many illustrations of promotions that proved futile because they sought to launch unwanted fashions, as well as many illustrations of fashions that gained popularity virtually without promotion, simply because women wanted them.

A classic example of the failure of promotion was the premature and unsuccessful introduction of the sack dress in the 1950s. In the 1960s there was an example of the reverse situation, when there was an unfilled demand for pantyhose long before the hosiery industry produced and promoted this item. When skirts began to rise, women wanted an easy, ungartered look. After a period of experimentation, pantyhose became widely accepted.

It has taken the business world a long time to reach the conclusion that has been candidly expressed by two authorities: "In the main, the residual profit or yield on promotional effort tends to vary with the acceptability of the thing promoted."[1] The marketing concept puts its emphasis on the consumer's needs and interests, not on the producer's or retailer's promotional efforts, as the major determinant of the success or failure of fashion goods.

The Changing Customer

The many changes that have taken place in life since the early days of the twentieth century have affected the behavior of the American woman as a fashion customer. She has a higher standard of living and more discretionary income than her forebears. She is also more likely to be employed outside the home than her counterpart of a generation or two ago. She is better educated, enjoys a wider variety of interests, travels more, and enjoys more social mobility. She also has better taste.

And she continues to change.

It is the fashion merchant's function to recognize these changes in his customers and to provide goods and services in accordance with the resulting changes in customer demand. Such changes may require, for instance, the addition of new categories of clothing such as ski wear or "his-and-hers" outfits. They may require the addition of new higher price lines, or the introduction of luggage in patterns and colors related to apparel fashions. Whatever changes occur in a customer's interests or her ability to buy, the merchant must make corresponding changes in his assortments.

Among the changes most difficult for merchants to recognize are those that occur as a result of changes in customer taste. Since taste is a very

The customer is the boss; she rejected the sack quickly, but accepted a modified version a few years later.

personal thing, a good merchant does not let his own taste dominate his assortments. He makes every effort to recognize and yield to the tastes of his customers.

Adapting to the tastes of others is not always easy, especially when that taste differs radically from one's own. How far a retailer should go in changing his assortment to meet a new trend depends upon his customers. When the fashion for hard colors and lines was at its height in the mid-1960s, such designers as Balenciaga and Mme. Grès resisted the trend and continued to produce garments with the grace and elegance that had always characterized their creations. Throughout the period when skirts rose to midthigh, Chanel refused to conform, and all her skirts remained one inch below the knee. Each of these great houses retained its following among women whose tastes remained more conservative.

Some merchants, in that period of crude colors and harsh lines, edited the styles, eliminating from their assortments those that they considered in poor taste. Among their relatively conservative customers, this was acceptable. Other retailers, regardless of personal preferences, accepted even the most garish of the then popular fashions, because they knew their customers' tastes ran in that direction. Thus each fashion merchant accepts change only to the degree that he expects his customers to accept it.

Elements of Customer Demand

In determining the potential demand among a store's customers for fashion merchandise, the retailer must consider a number of factors. The merchandise itself must be analyzed in terms of the various style elements that may either contribute to or militate against its acceptance. The merchandise must be studied in the light of customer buying motives, particularly those psychological motives involved in making fashion purchases. The store's own image, its regional location, and the season of the year must also be taken into consideration.

It is not enough for a merchant to know about general fashion trends and general consumer demand trends alone. The merchant must study the particular merchandise in terms of its particular appeal to his store's customers. Fashion merchandise selected for sale in any store must meet the fashion demands of its customers in styling, timing, and pricing.

Style Selection Factors

It is easier to evaluate a piece of fashion merchandise if each of the elements that combine to make it acceptable or otherwise is separately considered. Listed below are the major *selection factors* that significantly influence the customer's choice of most fashion goods:[2]

□ Silhouette: tubular, bell, or back-fullness; the degree to which the garment under consideration is moderate or extreme in this respect

□ Decoration or trim: presence or absence of buttons, bows, piping, ruffles, and so on

□ Materials or fabric: degree of thickness, weight, or opacity; components; durability

□ Surface interest: the roughness or smoothness of the material

□ Color: the actual color or colors; the intensity thereof

□ Workmanship: construction, stitching, shaping, finishing

□ Size: the designated size; the accuracy of fit

□ Sensory factors: odor, as in leather or perfume; sound, as in the crackle of taffeta; or such negative elements as the unpleasant smell of some leather substitutes and the squeak of poorly made shoes

□ Ease and cost of maintenance: wash-and-wear, permanent press as economy features; the expense of caring for and storing furs as an element of their cost

□ Brand: confidence in a name associated with satisfactory experience; lack of confidence in one that has poor associations or none; status, or lack of it, associated with brand name

□ Utility: the warmth of a coat, the support supplied by a sturdy shoe, the capaciousness of a handbag, the hangers and ties inside a suitcase that keep clothes in order

□ Price: the exchange value that the consumer places upon all the above attributes and any others that may be given consideration when making a purchase.

Thus the merchant has to start his determination of whether or not a fashion item should be stocked by examining a number of facets about the item itself. He has to look at its styling and detail, at the way it is put together, at its practicality, and gauge whether it might appeal to his customers at the price he would charge for it.

Buying Motivation

In order to gauge an item's appeal to the customer, the fashion merchant has to understand customer buying motivation: why people buy *what* they buy. One of the early marketing authorities to study buying motivation was Dr. Melvin T. Copeland. He divided consumer buying motives into two classes: "rational," or those based on appeal to reason, and "emotional," or those originating in instinct and emotion, representing impulse or unreasoned promptings to buy.[3] Rational motives were thought to include such factors as durability, dependability, comfort, economy of operation (as in wash-and-wear materials), and price. Emotional motives were thought to include such factors as imitation, emulation, quest for status, prestige, appeal to the opposite sex, pride of appearance, the desire for distinctiveness, ambition, and fear of offending.

With the development of market research and the findings of experimental psychology, it became obvious that buying motives are neither so simple nor so readily categorized. Every individual has his own complex personality which controls his motivations.

Jon G. Udell, director of the Bureau of Business Research and Services, University of Wisconsin, worked out a theory that buying motives encompass both conscious and unconscious reasons and thus should be classified not merely as "rational" or "emotional" but along a bar scale of motives.[4] Udell's bar scale runs from "operational," which is the satisfaction to be derived from the physical performance of a product, to "psychological," which is the satisfaction to be derived from the

consumer's social and psychological interpretation of the product and its performance.

Every purchase is made for a variety of reasons that can best be measured along a bar scale of motives

When selecting fashion goods, utility is seldom of as much concern to the customer as the psychological satisfactions to be derived from ownership and use of the product, as already discussed in Chapter 2. Yet fashion buying decisions are not always clear-cut. An operational element may very well be present, too. A typical example would be the reasons why women bought boots in the 1960s.

Early in that decade, most such purchases were made on the basis of operational motivation. Then shoe boots were worn in place of shoes and used primarily to keep feet and ankles dry and warm. They were both more attractive and more convenient than the traditional galoshes. As the 1960s progressed, shoe boot styles improved, and more and more women adopted them for their fashion rather than for their utilitarian values. Boots became available in a variety of heel heights appropriate for a variety of occasions, in a wide range of colors to match or complement a widening range of costume colors, and in lengths for wear with all types of apparel from pantsuits to miniskirts. By the end of the decade, the array of boots available still did their initial job of keeping feet and legs warm and dry, but their increased fashion importance and the resultant psychological satisfactions derived from their use was underscored by the fact that they were designed for wear indoors as well as outdoors.

Patronage Motives

The fashion merchant, eager to collect an assortment that will please his present customers and possibly draw additional customers, has to consider *patronage motives*: the reasons that induce customers to patronize one store rather than another, or why people buy where they do.

Distance is one such reason. For convenience items, such as underwear and inexpensive hosiery, women often patronize the nearest store, even if it happens to be a supermarket or drugstore with only a small selection of basic styles. For fairly routine fashion purchases, such as moderately priced blouses, slacks, and sweaters, customers are willing to travel farther, if necessary; suburban women can be counted on to travel several miles to a shopping center where they can find a good selection. For important fashion purchases, such as furs, fine jewelry, or formal dresses, women may travel many miles. Women who live in the suburbs may go considerable distances to patronize stores in high fashion shopping centers or in the nearest large city. Women who live in small urban areas frequently make their fashion purchases in the major stores of nearby large urban areas.

As far as fashion merchandise is concerned, a customer's reasons for choosing one store in preference to another are likely to be based on the store's fashion reputation, the assortments it offers, its price ranges, and its merchandising policies. Other prime considerations are the services offered (credit, adjustments, delivery, parking) and the attitude of the salespeople. Finally, the customer includes the location, size, and layout of the store in making her patronage decision.

Each successful fashion store has to offer fashion merchandise that reflects all the facets of the fashion image that store wants to show to its customers, for customers mainly base their patronage on that image.

Regional Variations in Demand

Variations in the way of life, in the composition of the population, and in climate bring about variations in the demand for fashion goods in different parts of the United States.

Women in the Western states are quicker than most to take up the new, especially if it is casual and informal. In fact, those who live along either of the two coastlines are less conservative than those who live in between. Women in the smaller cities of the Midwest and of the South are often slow in adopting extreme styles.

Sometimes regional preferences in apparel come about as reflections of the racial stocks from which the population is drawn. In the Great Lakes region, for example, many residents are descendants of German and Scandinavian immigrants. Blue-eyed and fair-skinned, they are partial to the color blue, whether it is in or out of fashion.

Sometimes climate is responsible for variations in demand. San Francisco, for example, is famous as a "suit city," whether or not suits are fashionable elsewhere, and also as a city whose women never store their furs. The city's climate makes a removable jacket comfortable for daytime wear, and chilly evenings make the warmth of a fur stole welcome even in summer.

Differences Between City and Suburban Demand

Fashion demand in the suburbs is usually different from that in central cities, and often there are differences among the various suburbs of a single central city. Department stores find that, although their branch customers may be in the same income brackets and have essentially the same taste level as their city customers, their apparel preferences differ. Living is more casual in the suburbs than in the city.

When department stores first branched out vigorously into suburbia, generalizations about branch stores and their customers were made freely: "The branch customer doesn't buy dressy clothes; she buys in lower price lines; she shops closer to the time of need." As the stores studied their branch customers more carefully, however, they found that the suburban woman does buy dressy clothes, and does buy clothes in price lines as high as those patronized by her city counterpart. If the branch stores lack the classifications or price lines the customer seeks, or if their stocks are too meager to present an adequate selection, she simply does not buy at the branch; instead, she buys downtown or in some other suburban store that has better assortments.

In order to channel some of the better dress, fur, and dressy coat business into the suburbs and take advantage of customer demand, some stores occasionally bring large quantities of such merchandise into a branch for a special fashion presentation. At such times, the customer can see and select from a plentiful assortment. Later, any excess stock may be transferred to another branch or back to the main store.

The lesson in consumer demand that department stores learned about their branch store customers was that women prefer to make their important fashion purchases from plentiful assortments.

Seasonal Variations in Demand

In areas where the change of seasons is strongly marked, the demand for warmer or cooler clothes follows the traditional calendar. In regions like Southern California or Hawaii, however, there is practically no seasonal climatic change and little reason for seasonal variations in the weight or character of garments offered for sale. Some of the northern parts of the country have short springs and summers, and most of their fashion demand is for cold-weather clothes. In the South, the reverse is true; there is only a short winter season and little demand for warm clothes, and so fashion interest concentrates mainly on styles, materials, and colors that provide summer comfort.

More than weather is involved in selling seasons, however. There are also selling seasons linked to holidays and certain times of the year when customers have come to expect special sales.

Holidays and Special Occasions An obvious example of the fashion demand patterns determined by the calendar is the need for new clothes for children and young adults when schools open each fall. Stores recognize this natural peak of demand by preparing appropriate assortments, setting up special departments if necessary, and running special promotions for back-to-school clothing. Thus, on a hot day in late August, stores are often filled with mothers outfitting their school-age children with warm dresses, suits, sweaters, and coats.

Holidays such as Easter, Christmas, and the New Year create a demand for clothes to wear for social events. In June merchants peak their assortments of wedding gowns and trousseau

merchandise, as they do in such other favorite bridal months as September and December.

Vacations are another seasonal spur to fashion demand. Although winter vacations are increasingly popular, summer remains the favored time for the annual visit to the shore or for a trip abroad. Stores try to time their offerings of travel clothes to conform to the vacation habits and resultant fashion demands of the communities they serve.

Special Sales Events Some of the exigencies of storekeeping have trained consumers to expect and patronize special preseason or postseason sales that have little relation to the normal pattern of demand but that have become traditional bargain-hunting periods. The merchant's need to clear out odds and ends of old stock before bringing in new season styles has established a traditional pattern of semiannual sales in many merchandise categories, from bed sheets to boots, and in such fashion items as lingerie, hosiery, and shoes. Even elegant shops whose policies are firmly against off-price offerings find it necessary to stage semiannual clearances.

Another example of artificially timed demand is the August preseason sale of winter coats and furs. The history of this sale goes back to the 1920s and earlier, when coat factories had long layoffs between seasons, followed by periods of desperate rush and expensive overtime work. In order to reduce the need for overtime work and provide their workers with more regular employment, manufacturers made concessions in price to retailers who ordered and accepted delivery in advance of the normal delivery time. The retailers, in turn, offered winter garments to their customers at prices below normal if they bought them in August. In those days before air conditioning, a considerable price inducement was necessary to bring women into stores and get them to try on winter coats in midsummer heat. Customers came and made their selections, however, and the August advance coat sale became a tradition.

A Leveling of Seasonal Demand The element of seasonality in the demand for fashion goods that are designed specifically for hot or cold weather has been diminishing in importance in recent years. With good heating and air-conditioning systems, consumer demand for fashion merchandise tends increasingly to ignore the outdoor climate. In areas where summers are hot, air conditioning makes an indoor sweater desirable occasionally. Where winters are cold, central heating can make heavy indoor clothing oppressive. Styles and materials that bridge the seasons are becoming steadily more important.

Another factor that upsets the traditional impact of the calendar upon fashion demand is the ease and speed of travel. Consumers can take a brief vacation, even a weekend trip, and reach a climate radically different from the one at home. A customer who lives in a mild climate may turn to the stores she regularly patronizes in search of warm clothing for a ski weekend—and the customer who lives in a cold climate, planning a quick trip south, may descend upon her favorite store in midwinter with cool, lightweight clothes in mind.

The fashion merchant has to provide what his customers want, regardless of the calendar, the buying patterns of past generations, or the operating patterns of the garment-producing industry. The timing and nature of consumer demand change constantly and put the merchant under pressure to get the type of merchandise the customers want when they want it from the producers with whom he deals.

Aids in Determining Customer Preferences

Fashion merchants often seem gifted with second sight in anticipating accurately what their customers will want. Actually, the fashion sense of an able merchant is simply the fruit of hard work: checking his own store's past experience, determining consumer demand through every available outside source, and using representative customers as sounding boards. In today's fashion merchandising, instinct and intuition are no match for facts and conscientious research.

Although most stores base their fashion merchandise selections on some sort of systematic research, such research is particularly important in the larger store. In a small specialty store, the owner, who is usually his own merchandise manager, can collect customer preference information by glancing at the sales records, talking to his customers, and listening to his resources. In larger stores, determining customer preferences is a more complex job of research, for the number of customers served may be in the hundreds of thousands instead of just in the hundreds, and the number of fashion items offered and resources involved may be multiplied proportionately. Smaller stores may need only pencil and paper to do a good customer research job from their sales and stock records, but larger stores often use electronic data processing systems to collect and analyze such consumer demand information on a continuing basis.

Information From Store Customers

Any store that has been in business for more than a season has in its records of sales a treasury of information about its customers' responses to previous merchandise offerings. This information, properly interpreted, shows what customers have bought, what they have wanted to buy, and what has not interested them. It also indicates what fashion trends may be developing and what trends may be passing their peak.

It is assumed, of course, that the store or department being studied has a clearly defined target group of customers. These are not necessarily the same individuals month after month or year after year, but they are people of similar incomes and taste levels and with similar degrees of daring or timidity about incoming fashions. If a store's customers are too heterogeneous a group, or if a store has been shifting its sights, aiming first at one and then at another type of target customer, its past history will not be a reliable basis on which to build future plans.

Past Sales Records It can be assumed that those items which sold at the fastest rates in the past had the strongest natural appeal to customers. If fast sellers have some features in common, such as color, price, detail, or texture, these features can be an important indication of the nature of customer demand. For example, if the unadorned round neckline usually described as a "jewel neckline" is a feature of nearly all best-selling blouses, in several prices, in several colors, it can be assumed that the jewel neckline is gaining in demand over other types. On the other hand, if beige blouses are the best sellers, regardless of neckline, then it is color that is influencing the customers and beige the color that is most important in the tide of demand.

Pretesting New styles are first bought in wide variety but in small amounts. Customer reaction and sales are then observed. Styles that sell promptly presumably are those with strong natural appeal to the store's customers; they are reordered, and the others are dropped.

There are many other ways to pretest new styles, including staging fashion shows early in the season and observing customer reactions and noting purchases, showing vendors' lines to salespeople and inviting their comments, and preseason sales, such as the August coat sales, that indicate which styles have the most popularity.

The *trunk show* is also a form of pretesting. A producer sends a store a sample of every style in his line, and the store exhibits these samples to customers at scheduled, announced showings. The women who attend see every style the producer has available, not just those styles the merchant has already chosen to stock. If a customer sees a style she wants that is not carried by the store, she can order it. The merchant, meantime, has a chance to see how his selections from the producer's line compare with what interests his customers, so that he can tailor his assortments to his customers' wants.

Markdowns Downward revisions in the selling prices of merchandise are *markdowns*. Good retail practice requires that all markdowns be entered on a store record, and a reason given in each case. Since markdowns are often used to clear out slow-moving stock, an analysis of the styles that had to be reduced often shows what merchandise features failed to attract sufficient customers, thus indicating how the merchant should readjust his assortments in the future. For example, a line of particularly vividly colored vinyl jackets may do well in a high-priced version

in a special boutique and in a low-priced version in the budget department, but a moderate-priced version offered in the regular sportswear department may be such a slow seller that most of the stock ends up on the markdown rack. A logical assumption, then, is that the extreme in sports jackets, properly priced, is acceptable to the top and bottom strata of the store's customers, but the group in the middle, who are traditionally conservative, are not interested in this type of merchandise.

Want Slips When a customer requests something that is not in stock, salespeople report the situation on forms known as *want slips*. (See Form 11-1.) These can be particularly interesting as a means of studying customer demand, for they are one of the few indications a store has of what customers would buy if the store had it available. Study of these unfilled customer wants helps a merchant correct possible errors in filling demand for particular sizes, prices, colors, or types of items. A dress department, for instance, might stock only quite conservative styles in sizes 18 and 20—but want slips might show that customers wearing these sizes would like to find more lively and youthful styles from which to choose.

Advertising Results Stores try to determine the amount of business that is transacted as a direct result of advertising. This is often hard to determine, unless a customer arrives at the store with ad in hand or mentions the ad to a salesperson. However, if an ad promotes a particular line or item, increases in sales immediately after the ad appears are usually attributed to the promotion. The response to the advertising of a specific style is usually an indication of the degree of customer interest in the style, particularly if several styles receive equal advertising emphasis but show considerable differences in arousing customer interest.

In a departmentalized store, the buyer for one department sometimes can obtain valuable guidance from the results of advertising done by related departments in addition to the results of his own ads.

MERCHANDISE WANT SLIP

Department No. _42_

Date _8/17/-_

Name _Sara Davies_

The following Requested Merchandise is not in Stock:

Description (Item, Color, Size, Price)	No. of Calls	Buyer's Remarks
1 pc. sheath, brown, 10, $29.98	2	On order

The following Stock is getting low:

Mfr., Style, Color, Price	Pieces On Hand	
Aiken, 6912, red, $19.98	3	Discontinued

SUGGEST A SUBSTITUTE

Form 11-1

Returns, Complaints, Adjustments When a store accepts a return from a customer or makes an adjustment on goods that failed to give satisfaction, all the details about the transaction are recorded. These records are warnings for store buyers, telling them which goods have not been found acceptable by customers and why. For example, if customers return laminated fabrics because they separated in cleaning, then the buyer should consider finding a more reliable source for laminated fabrics. In addition, the buyer would have to accept the fact that a certain degree of prejudice would have developed against laminates, thereby influencing customer demand, and additional promotion, stressing the reliability of the new fabrics, might be needed.

Customer Surveys Many customers are quite willing to tell a retailer what they like and what they do not like about his store, what interests them in the merchandise assortment and what does not interest them. Such surveys can be quite informal, and yet provide a clear indication of trends. The buyer or store owner, chatting with customers on the selling floor and observing expressions and listening to remarks made by the customers, learns a good deal about the nature of customer demand and how the store's assortment is viewed by the customer. Formal surveys can be made by mail or personal interview to determine, for example, what price lines are favored, what types of merchandise are wanted by regular or potential customers, and what services are expected.

Salespeople Because of their constant, direct contact with customers, salespeople usually can provide valuable information about what customers want. In larger stores, salespeople are really the stores' only links with their customers, for store buyers seldom can spend much time on the selling floor. Salespeople can report whether customers bought certain styles eagerly or reluctantly, and whether they asked for any particular items that were not immediately available. Sometimes the information gathered from salespeople is the first indication a store may have of a change in a trend; at other times, what the salespeople report will reinforce and amplify what a merchant may already have suspected from his own observations and from store records.

Outside Sources of Customer Demand Information

Merchants also look beyond their own doors for indications of consumer demand. What they learn from outside sources may confirm what they deduce from their own experience—or it may indicate points they have missed, or perhaps misinterpreted. A typical case would be that of styles or items a store has not yet stocked but which are enjoying good demand in other stores.

There are many specific sources to which a merchant turns for information, including his competitors and his suppliers. To an alert retailer, however, everything he sees and hears around him has fashion significance. What people wear to the theater and restaurants; what the local personalities are wearing; what the national celebrities are wearing—there are many guides that help a fashion merchant determine what the customer demand in his own store may be.

Competitors Merchants and their buyers regularly study the advertising of other stores. They visit the selling floors of competing stores to see what is stocked, what is featured in displays, and what seems to be selling. They compare the assortments and the values offered by competitors with their own. If they find a weak spot in their own merchandising, they mend it promptly. On the other hand, if they find a price line, an item, a style in which they are enjoying good customer acceptance but which the competition appears to be neglecting or handling poorly, they put more inventory and more promotion behind their own strong item and make it even stronger.

Resident Buying Office The resident buying office that provides a store with representation in the New York market also continually provides it with current information on the general trend of consumer demand. The means used include market bulletins, reports on new items, fashion forecasts, and lists of styles and items that are best-sellers in other client stores. During periods when store buyers are in the market to view producers' lines, the resident buying offices hold clinics, or meetings, at which buyers from their various client stores can discuss fashion, merchandise, and merchandising. Separate clinics are held for buyers specializing in each category of merchandise, so that the discussions can be fully detailed; there are also group meetings for heads of stores and for merchandise managers.

In addition, individual store managers and their buyers may consult the market representatives of the buying office about markets, fashions, and retail experience. At the resident buying office, buyers from many noncompeting stores meet informally, and frequently compare notes on consumer demand.

Manufacturers and Their Salesmen The producers with whom a store deals can contribute information about the reasons why they sponsor certain styles and trends. Their lines have been planned to meet anticipated consumer demand and tested against the reactions and sales experience of many retail buyers. A well-prepared salesman usually is ready with the fashion story and the consumer response story, as well as the product story, of the merchandise he is offering.

Some of the most accurate information about consumer demand comes from producers. Today, major producers in each branch of the fashion business are large enough to utilize modern electronic equipment in collecting and analyzing information about sales trends quickly. Such a producer thus is in the position to tell a merchant what styles are selling at what rate in each part of the country. He can give advice about the styles that might prove to be best for the store and the time when they should be offered. He can also give details about ways other stores have presented similar merchandise and what the results have been.

Research Studies Individual manufacturers, industry associations, publications, and government agencies occasionally make research studies in which consumers are polled about what they want to buy, where and when they prefer to buy, and their reasons for buying or not buying. The purposes for which surveys are undertaken are varied, but each contributes some useful information about customer buying patterns.

Typical of such studies is one made in the mid-1960s by the National Board of the Coat and Suit Industry. Women shopping in coat departments were questioned about what they wished to buy, what they had bought, and their reasons for not buying. A major finding was that many women had not seen the colors they wanted in department store stocks.

Another typical survey was made by a foundation and lingerie producer to ascertain ages, heights, weights, and dress sizes of customers, as well as to gather information about the kinds of

SUMMER'S STATUS T-TOPS

#Bardot

#5159

#5139

WE HAVE SAMPLED THESE TOPS TO
SOME OF YOU, AS WE BELIEVE IN
IN THE LOOK, THE PRICE, THE
COLORS...

WATCH THEM, SO YOU MAY
REORDER IMMEDIATELY!

IMPORTED FROM FRANCE, THESE
TOPS HAVE A WONDERFUL INTERNATIONAL
FASHION FLAVOR...WHICH GROWS MORE
IMPORTANT EACH SEASON, WITH THE
GROWING POPULARITY OF INTERNATIONAL
FASHION EXCHANGE!!

#Bardot $2.75 each
Short sleeved T-shirt with fashion-
right pocket; contrast braid trim.

#5139 $2.75 each
Short sleeved T-shirt with single
pocket; contrast stripe trim.

#5159 $7.00 each
High turtle neck, long slim sleeves,
all-over rib stitch.

ALL STYLES: Sizes XS-S-M-L-XL
100% Cotton...Sanforized
Black, White, Turquoise, Orange,
Navy, Dark Brown, Powder Blue

Resource: FashionRep's
Delivery: 30 days receipt of order

FOB: Los Angeles...Terms: Net

Buying offices provide their member stores with regular bulletins about current market trends.

foundations, lingerie, and sleepwear they preferred.

A popular form of survey made regularly by some consumer magazines and sporadically by others is undertaken to determine how many of each of a list of items their readers buy per year and what they pay for each.

Newspapers, Magazines, Trade Publications
Fashion merchants obtain insights into consumer demand from publications, both those that are intended for the general public and those dedicated to readers within some sector of the fashion business.

Fashion news is reported in almost all consumer newspapers and magazines. The merchant keeps track of this news, and also of any fashion advertising in such publications, so that he will know what influences may be creating or discouraging fashion product demand among his customers. Magazines that give special emphasis to fashion, such as *Vogue* and *Harper's Bazaar,* or to fashions for specific groups of consumers, such as *Seventeen, Ingenue,* or *Mademoiselle,* go to considerable effort to keep the fashion merchant informed about the merchandise featured in their pages. They also provide him with their assessments of fashion trends among the particular segments of the public that they serve, and with information about how best to reach and influence their readers. Consumer magazines spend enormous amounts on research in order to know their readers better, and they are usually more than willing to share the results of these studies with fashion merchants.

Trade publications are expert in assessing fashion and market developments. Some of these publications are aimed primarily at the retailer, telling him what merchandise is new and good, and how stores are promoting it successfully. Examples are *Intimate Apparel, Handbags and Accessories, Jewelers' Circular-Keystone,* and *Boot and Shoe Recorder.* Others, like *Women's Wear Daily,* address themselves to all branches of an industry, from the retailer to the sources of the primary materials used in manufacturing the products concerned. From both the horizontal (primarily retail) and vertical (entire industry) types of trade publications, the fashion merchant

gets a highly professional assessment of consumer demand and the influences that are being exerted upon it.

Reporting Services There are services to which a merchant can subscribe to keep him abreast of what other stores are doing. For example, *Retail News Bureau* reports on the advertising that has been done by New York stores. *Retail Memo,* provided by the American Newspaper Publishers Association, offers capsule news of particular interest to retailers each week.

Fashion Consultants Independent fashion consultants sell their expertise to merchants to supplement that of a firm's own executives. The usual pattern of operation is to issue bulletins that report on fashion trends, indications of consumer demand, retail activities, and related subjects. Oldest in the field is the Tobé service, founded in 1927 by the late Tobé Coller Davis. A similar service, Beryl Tucker Young Trends, specializes in children's fashions. Another well-known fashion consultant is Estelle Hamburger, an outstanding authority on fashion promotion.

Consumer Advisory Boards

A third source of useful information for retailers is supplied by the consumer advisory boards organized by individual stores from among specific types of customers or potential customers in the community. These boards give the retailer a consumer's-eye view of store policies, services, assortments, and fashions. In addition, they assure a flow of favorable publicity among the circles in which the board members move and also in news media, if the board members or their activities are considered newsworthy.

College Boards Perhaps the oldest and most firmly entrenched of consumer committees is the college advisory board. There is hardly a department or specialty store large enough to set up a college shop that does not have such a board. A college board is made up of at least one upperclassman chosen from each college that is important to residents of the area. Before the selling season begins, these young women (and occasionally young men) serve as advisers to the store

RETAIL NEWS BUREAU
'A *Confidential* Reporting Service'

ITEM (S)—

SWEATER & PANTS
MISSES SIZES
$10.00 & $23.00

RESPONSE*			
FAIR	GOOD	STRONG	SELLOUT
	X		

DM	**RESOURCE**

HAYMAKER
498 7TH AVE.
N. Y. C.

REPORT NO. JS-IM07029-6

STORE BERGDORF GOODMAN

PAPER TIMES 7/16

AD. SIZE FULL PAGE

WEATHER FAIR

*Shopped 3 Times

BERGDORF GOODMAN
FIFTH AVE., 57 to 58th Sts., N.Y., N.Y. 10019
ON THE PLAZA

Polo Partners

A good classic match. Haymaker makes it the
best teamed play for any sporty day. Game
colors are wicker, ivy or ensign blue. Sweater
shirt's acrylic knit, 34 to 40, **$10**. Knit pants
are wool, 8 to 16 **$23**.

DETAILS: CLASSIC MATCH...........

STYLE #1971R: ACRYLIC KNIT LONGSLEEVE, PLACKET FRONT PULL-OVER
SWEATER. WICKER, IVY OR ENSIGN BLUE. SIZES 34-40.$10.00

STYLE #1364R: WOOL KNIT PANTS. WICKER, IVY OR ENSIGN BLUE. SIZES
8-16. $23.00

ADVERTISED MERCHANDISE WAS DISPLAYED ON WALL SHELVES IN THE TOWN &
COUNTRY DEPARTMENT, THIRD FLOOR. RESPONSE TO THE AD IS RATED VERY
GOOD.

Errors subject to correction

● MERCHANDISE REPORT OF **RETAIL NEWS BUREAU**, 232 MADISON AVE., NEW YORK N. Y. 10016 ●

Copyright **1970** An Independent Agency Reporting the News of Retailing—Promptly, Accurately, Completely. MU 6-7134

*Subscribing to an independent reporting service can give a retailer a steady flow
of pertinent information on consumer demand.*

College boards keep retailers in close touch with what is being worn on different college campuses.

buyer in building an assortment. In the August and September selling rush, they serve both as salespeople and as advisers to college-bound customers. They may also informally model apparel.

Teen Boards Teen or high school boards are often set up for girls and occasionally for boys. Activities of these boards differ from those of college boards in several respects. Actual sales work usually is not involved; activities are year-round, since the high schools are located in the store's trading area. Teen boards, unlike those for college students, often engage in activities beyond fashion merchandising alone. For example, working through their teen boards, stores may sponsor such projects as charm schools, dressing dolls for deprived children, club meetings, window decorating contests, record-playing sessions, and the preparation of fashion columns for school newspapers. Some stores have similar activities for preteens, but usually on a more restricted scale.

Accustoming girls of these younger age groups to visit a store regularly lays the foundation for making fashion customers of them in their college, career, and married years. And the store, having "watched them grow up," is better able to anticipate their wants and to encourage them to comment freely to management if the assortments or services are lacking in some respect.

Career Girls Although many stores have special shops and special promotions for career girls, relatively few have clubs or boards for this segment of their customers. More commonly, they reach career women through special programs and fashion shows. On these occasions, the merchants observe their reactions to the merchandise, invite orders, and encourage comments.

One store that does have a career girl activity runs a club for them with meetings devoted to informative programs emphasizing fashion. One club member is chosen by lot every second week to select and accessorize several stock garments she considers ideal for the working girl. Her selections are then featured in the store's boutique for career women.

Club Women Women who belong to civic organizations constitute members of another fairly common customer advisory board. The prototype is the Consumer Advisory Board, organized by Gertz Department Store, Jamaica, New York, in 1940.[5] Presidents of local chapters of women's clubs meet with the store president at a luncheon once a month during their terms of office. They counsel him on desired improvements in store assortments or operation, and he arranges informative programs on subjects they request. If the topic of hosiery is selected, for instance, a hosiery buyer might speak on the fashion, quality, and wear features to consider when purchasing stockings. The subjects on which the board members request programs, as well as their comments on store assortments and services, provide invaluable guidance on the nature of current consumer demand.

References

[1]Wingate and Friedlander, *The Management of Retail Buying*, p. 91.
[2]Based on Wingate and Friedlander, op. cit., p. 92.
[3]Copeland, *Principles of Merchandising*, pp. 155–167.
[4]Udell, *A New Approach to Consumer Motivation*, pp. 8–9.
[5]*Stores*, July-August, 1965, p. 150.

Merchandising Vocabulary

Define or briefly explain the following terms:

Marketing concept	Patronage motives
Selection factors	Trunk show
Buying motives	Markdowns
Operational motivation	Want slip
Psychological motivation	

Merchandising Review

1. Contrast the characteristics of the typical customer of the mid-twentieth century with those of her forebears.
2. Name and describe any five elements or selection factors that have an important influence on the purchase of fashion merchandise.
3. Do you think price is a major selection factor in the purchase of fashion goods? Defend your answer.
4. What are some fashion goods purchased primarily from psychological motives?
5. Name at least five reasons why customers patronize one store rather than another.
6. What factors are primarily responsible for (a) regional variations in demand; (b) seasonal variations in demand?
7. From what sources in the merchant's own store may he obtain information on customer demand?
8. From what sources outside his store may a merchant obtain information on customer demand?
9. What is the primary purpose of a consumer advisory board? What types of consumer boards are most commonly found today in retail stores?

Merchandising Digest

1. Discuss the development of the *marketing concept,* indicating the factors responsible for its development and its implications for producers and retailers of fashion goods.
2. "In the main, the residual profit or yield on promotional effort tends to vary with the acceptability of the thing promoted." Discuss this quotation, citing examples of the styles that have failed to achieve fashion status despite heavy promotional efforts.
3. "The element of seasonality in demand for fashion goods has been diminishing in importance." Discuss this trend, giving reasons for its development and examples of specific fashion items which are experiencing a seasonal and more year-round demand.

12

Budgeting the Fashion
Merchandise Dollar

The need for scientific financial management in retailing is a phenomenon of the twentieth century. In earlier times, a merchant's inventory was composed mainly of staple items with a smattering of apparel fabrics and sewing notions. Most apparel and accessories were made in the home. With few fashion goods at stake, most merchants could order goods twice a year, buying enough each time to cover their needs for a six-month period. Often such purchases arrived as single shipments and were sold off gradually as the season progressed. Plans and budgets of how much should be spent and for what types of merchandise were often in a merchant's head rather than on paper.

Today, budgeting for a fashion department or store is an increasingly complex task. The risks involved in acquiring and maintaining a fashion inventory are great as well as varied. As fashions change, so must retail assortments change if customer demand is to be met. Stocks must be peaked to coincide with the peak in customer demand. Extended delivery dates may require a retailer to commit capital for purchases far in advance of the time when the merchandise will actually be available for sale. In addition, branch store expansion, modernization of facilities, high taxes and interest rates, rising operating costs, and customer demand for expanded assortments require huge additional capital investment.

Today, there can be nothing hit-or-miss about the way a store invests its money in fashion goods. Sound financial planning and control, together with sound assortment planning, are essential to a profitable operation.

Approaches to Financial Management

Modern financial management in retailing requires advance planning of both the amounts of money needed to finance a store's purchases and the amounts of revenue expected from sales. Only by planning in advance can management provide for the financial needs of the business.

Scientific retail financial planning involves:

□ The closest possible estimate of the sales potential of the store as a whole and of its various merchandise or selling subdivisions

□ The planning and control of stocks in terms of dollars, so that the inventory investment will be large enough but no larger than that required to produce the sales that are planned

□ Calculation of a markup percentage on purchases sufficiently high to cover not only the costs of such purchases but also all costs involved in running the business with an adequate margin of profit

□ Establishment of systems for record keeping and reporting that will provide management with timely information on how well plans and budgets are being implemented

The Goals of Financial Planning

The major goals of scientific financial management in retail merchandising are:

□ To have an inventory that is neither too large nor too small for anticipated customer demand

□ To time the store or departmental purchases so that the merchandise is available for sale neither too early nor too late for customer demand

□ To keep purchases in line with the store's ability to pay for them

□ To have funds available for new goods when they may be needed

The Tools of Financial Management

The merchant uses two principal tools in his financial planning: the dollar merchandise plan and the open-to-buy.

The *dollar merchandise plan or budget* is a projection, in dollars, of the sales goals of a department, a classification, or an entire store for each month of a six-month period. It indicates the rate at which money should be used for purchases in order to maintain the desired relationship between sales and inventories.

The dollar merchandise plan is similar in purpose to a personal budget. It shows the merchant the income expected and the expenditures anticipated during a particular period, just as a personal budget balances expected income against proposed expenses for a given time. In the same way that a person has to check what he actually receives and spends against his budget, so must the merchant check his actual merchandising results against those projected in his plan. If the results are below those planned, he makes every effort to improve his merchandising techniques so that the planned figures will be achieved. If conditions differ from those that existed or were anticipated at the time the plan was drawn up, he revises his original estimates.

The *open-to-buy* is a calculation, made at frequent intervals throughout a given period, of the amount of merchandise that can be received into stock during any particular period without exceeding the planned closing stock level at the end of the period. Open-to-buy may be calculated either in units of merchandise or in dollars. A detailed discussion of open-to-buy will be found in Chapter 14 and in Appendix 2.

The dollar merchandise plan looks to the future; it is drawn up to serve as a guide for a selling period that has not yet begun. The open-to-buy is concerned with the present; it is a control device to keep stocks in line with actual sales.

Use of Retail Figures

The majority of department stores and departmentalized specialty stores operate under the retail method of inventory evaluation. In this system, all records of transactions affecting the inventory of a store, department, or classification—such as sales, purchases, markdowns, transfers, and charge-backs—are recorded at their retail values. Stores on the older "cost" system of inventory evaluation (usually very small stores) keep their records of purchases and inventory on the basis of the actual cost of the merchandise.

Stores operating under the retail system plan their merchandise budgets and assortments entirely on the basis of retail values. Since the majority of departmentalized stores use the retail system of accounting, all values referred to in subsequent discussions of merchandise planning are retail values, unless otherwise indicated.

The Dollar Merchandise Plan

As already defined, the merchandise plan or budget is a careful integration of a sales program and the stock needed to achieve those planned sales during a specific period of time.

In a small store, where the owner is in constant touch with all operations, a formal merchandise plan may be unnecessary. However, even in a small store with limited capital resources, some preplanning of purchases and other elements of the merchandising operation is necessary.

In large retail organizations an elaborate plan or budget is essential. The very size of the establishment requires the distribution of merchandising responsibilities among many individuals. The merchandising plan provides a guide for each of these individuals in their efforts to secure desired sales and profit results. In addition, a carefully prepared merchandise plan furnishes a yardstick against which store management can measure the performance of those executives charged with the responsibilities of the merchandising operation.[1]

Organization of the Plan

In a small organization, the planned figures ordinarily are those for the store as a whole. In larger stores, separate budgets are first developed for each department or classification. Later these separate budgets are incorporated into a master plan at the divisional level, store level, or both.

The merchandise plan, whether for a single department or for a store as a whole, should be prepared in a form such that its significance becomes clear and its information plain to all who work with it. The format of the plan varies considerably from store to store, both in scope and amount of detail. The ideal is to present the plan in the simplest form possible and in terminology familiar to everyone who will be using it.

The period covered by a merchandise budget may vary from one month to a year, but the usual planning period is six months. The spring season, February through July, is usually planned in one budget and the fall season, August through January, in another. In most cases the seasonal plan is later broken down into monthly or, in some cases, weekly subdivisions.

Merchandise plans are drawn up several months in advance of the period to which they refer. The length of time varies from store to store, but plans are necessarily completed and approved before actual buying for the season begins.

Buyers usually play an active part in preparing their departmental budgets. The store's accounting department supplies information on the previous year's sales, stocks, and other operating figures. The merchandise manager outlines the store's goals for the department in the period for which planning is to be done. Armed with this information, each buyer then uses his own specialized knowledge to develop the initial merchandising plan for his department.

In larger stores, after the merchandising plans have been approved by the merchandising division, they are then sent to the controller. He, in turn, reviews them and, together with the general merchandise manager, makes any adjustments that may be necessary from the storewide point of view. Finally, the departmental or divisional plans are combined into the store's master plan.

Departmentalized stores with many branches usually make separate merchandise plans for each department in each of their branches, in cooperation with the departmental buyers and respective branch store managers. Branch merchandising plans are then incorporated into the total store's departmental and master plans. Stores with only a few branches generally combine merchandising plans for their branch operations with those of each of the parent departments.

A good merchandise budget is both specific and flexible. Since the plan is an attempt to forecast conditions and develop strategies far in advance of the period covered, the plan is not presumed to be a completely authoritative projection. As the season unfolds, therefore, the figures in the budget should be reviewed, both in relation to actual results achieved and in the light of the more accurate information that has become available concerning the balance of the season.

Elements of the Plan

Merchandise plans vary considerably from store to store, both in scope and detail. The basic elements planned in a typical merchandise budget are sales, stocks, markdowns, and purchases. In addition, the merchandise plan may include other important seasonal goal figures, such as initial markon or gross margin, estimated stock shortages, cash discounts, stock turnover, and workroom costs. Also considered are those operating expenses that are closely related to sales, such as selling salaries, advertising and delivery expenses, administrative salaries, and other costs of doing business.

The merchandise planning form (Form 12-1) is a composite based on many forms currently in use.

Preparing the Basic Dollar Merchandise Plan

The preparation of a dollar merchandise plan requires the projection, month by month, of the sales that a store or department expects to achieve; the projection of the stocks needed to make these sales possible; the estimation of the probable amount of retail price reductions that will be made; and a calculation of the purchases which should be made in each month if stocks are to be maintained at the desired level.

These projections, estimations, and calculations are not produced by guesswork or hopeful thinking. They are based on facts and experience, the

SIX MONTH MERCHANDISING PLAN

Department Name _____ Department No. _____

	PLAN (This Year)	ACTUAL (Last Year)
Workroom cost		
Cash discount		
Season stock turnover		
Shortage reserve		
Operating expenses		
Operating profit		

SPRING 19—		FEB.	MAR.	APR.	MAY	JUNE	JULY	SEASON TOTAL
FALL 19—		AUG.	SEP.	OCT.	NOV.	DEC.	JAN.	
SALES	Last Year							
	Plan							
	Percent of Increase							
	Revised							
	Actual							
RETAIL STOCK (BOM)	Last Year							
	Plan							
	Revised							
	Actual							
MARKDOWNS	Last Year							
	Plan (dollars)							
	Plan (percent)							
	Revised							
	Actual							
RETAIL PURCHASES	Last Year							
	Plan							
	Revised							
	Actual							
PERCENT OF INITIAL MARKON	Last Year							
	Plan							
	Revised							
	Actual							

Comments

Merchandise Manager _____   Buyer _____

Controller _____

Form 12-1

facts of past results and the experience of skilled store executives that enables them to make logical assumptions.

Planning Sales

The first step in the preparation of a merchandise plan is to make a realistic estimate of prospective sales, based upon external factors, internal factors, and general fashion trends that are likely to influence the volume of sales. Finally sales goals are established for each month of the season being planned.

External Factors   External factors—those outside of the store or its control—include employment prospects, general economic conditions, population changes, and the competitive situation. The opening of a new plant in the area, for example, increases spending power in the community. Conversely, the possibility of strikes or shutdowns among local employers means a potential loss of spending power in the trading area.

Optimism regarding the future encourages consumer spending; threats of new taxes, higher interest rates, or declines in economic activity tend to discourage spending.

Sales prospects are affected by the growth or lack of growth in the area's population, by changes in the proportion of high-income to low-income families, by changes in the age composition of the population. A new housing development for young families, for example, provides a potential boost in sales in children's, juniors', young women's, and young men's departments. A high-rise apartment, appealing to older couples, may favor departments selling higher-priced, more conservative clothes and home furnishings.

The effect of new or expanded stores and shopping centers in the trading area is analyzed, and consideration is given to the possibility that stores in other communities, within easy traveling distance, may be gaining or losing power to draw off some of the local retail business. On the other hand, if any local competitors have closed up shop, or if new highways or parking facilities have made it easier for customers to get to the store, there is reason to anticipate sales growth.

Internal Factors Internal factors—those within the store or its control—include physical changes within the store that either enhance or diminish the sales prospects of individual departments, such as the opening of new branches, the general trend in store sales, and the number and extent of promotions the store's management expects to undertake during the season being planned.

Physical changes within a store can affect the sales prospects of various departments within the store. For example, if new escalators are being installed with landings at the entrance to Department X, sales of that department presumably will benefit. On the other hand, if Department Y had to be moved to a less prominent location or perhaps had its floor space reduced because of the alteration, Department Y's sales may suffer. Not only do relocation, expansion, or contraction of a department's selling space affect sales, but so do the acquisition or elimination of display fixtures, a change of decor, and any change in the proximity to departments carrying related merchandise.

If a new branch is to be opened within the planning period, the additional anticipated sales in that branch should be taken into account. The fact that there may be a shift in the location of sales with a possible diminution of the main store sales as a result of the transfer of some patronage from there to the new branch should not be overlooked in the planning procedures.

If the store as a whole is enjoying expanded sales, each department within the store usually profits from the increased customer traffic. The reverse is true if the store as a whole is losing ground.

A department's sales are affected by the amount of promotion the store plans in its behalf. Its sales opportunities are enhanced if the store as a whole plans increased promotional effort, since this usually will bring increased customer traffic. Such efforts may be general, intended simply to bring more people into the store, or may be aimed at specific groups, such as career girls, young mothers, or teen-agers. In the latter case, only those departments in which the merchandise has particular appeal to the group being courted can expect significant sales benefit.

Fashion Trends Fashion trends are frequently the most important factor influencing sales. These usually affect the fates of several departments at one time, pushing up the sales potential of some and depressing the sales prospects of others. For example, if the trend is toward dressier apparel, dress departments can budget optimistically, but departments selling sportswear and other casual attire will plan more cautiously. Similarly, fashion trends in outerwear also affect the sales planning of other fashion departments. For example, a trend toward fitted waistlines undoubtedly will increase the sales potential of the belt department as well as that of the foundation department. A trend toward shorter skirts places more emphasis on legs, thereby increasing the sales potential of hosiery departments.

Establishing Sales Goals Retailers usually express their sales goals in dollars and as percentages of increase or decrease in actual sales compared to the corresponding period of the previous year. The percentage of change, however, is not necessarily the same for each month of the season. Each month's sales goals are separately set within the framework of the seasonal plan, after careful consideration has been given to the previous years' sales for the same month, to that percentage which each month has normally contributed to total annual sales, and to the other factors influencing the sales potential.

Since the pattern of consumer demand also varies both seasonally and monthly, this fact must also be taken into account when planning monthly sales goals. If there were no such variations, each month would contribute an equal number of dollars to the year's total sales volume. A glance at Table 12-1 will show this to be far from the case. In planning sales, the merchant allows for the fact that not only do the number of business days vary from month to month but that there are some months of the year in which the customers buy more freely than in others.

Monthly sales volume, as a percentage of the total year's sales, also varies from department to department because of the seasonality of the merchandise that each handles and the curve of consumer demand for that merchandise. For example, toy departments and often fur departments do the bulk of their annual business in a relatively few months of the year.

The pattern of monthly sales volume in many fashion departments is affected by Easter and by its variation in date from year to year. Table 12-1 illustrates this point. Compare the March and April shares of the year's business in 1964, when Easter was early (March 29), with those for 1965, when Easter was late (April 18).

Holidays and other special days, such as Valentine's Day, Mother's Day, and Father's Day, give rise to variations in demand. The extent to which each influences monthly sales planning depends upon the nature of the merchandise and the extent of the department's promotional plans.

In estimating the sales potential for each month the buyer or store manager also considers any special circumstances that may have affected sales the previous year but that can be ignored in this year's planning. For example, some sales may have been lost in the previous year because of delivery delays. If no delivery problems are anticipated this year, sales may be appreciably better because of this one factor alone. Similarly factors affecting sales in previous years, such as unseasonable weather, special promotions held in competing stores, and special attractions that drew customers to one's own store, should be taken into account.

Most buyers keep some kind of personal notebook in which they list special conditions that have affected sales, such as weather, their own advertising and that of their competitors, and changing market conditions. Notes are also written on the back of the planning or budget form that supplies the first step in planning a new budget when it is pulled out of the files at a later date.

Another familiar device is the "Beat Last Year" book, in which comparative daily sales are recorded for as many as five successive years. Notes like "rain," "parade," and "half-page ad" (noting the item advertised) remind the buyer of the story behind sales figures for each day.

In the case of a new store, a new branch, or a new department within an established store, past sales records are not available as a guide. Research, formal or informal, combined with careful judgment, must take the place of experience. Market studies, consultations with other merchants or other buyers, and discussions with bankers and vendors are all helpful in arriving at sales goals for the new enterprise.

Form 12-2 indicates how the seasonal merchandise plan looks when seasonal and monthly sales goals have been set.

Table 12-1. Percentage of Year's Sales Made in Each Month of Year, 1964 and 1965

Misses' Apparel and Accessories (Total)
Departments of Department Stores

	1964*	1965**
January	5.9%	5.8%
February	6.0	5.6
March	8.7	7.5
April	7.8	9.0
May	8.1	8.0
June	7.0	7.0
July	6.2	6.3
August	7.5	7.4
September	8.8	8.7
October	9.4	9.3
November	9.4	9.8
December	15.2	15.6
	100.0%	100.0%

* Easter, March 29.
** Easter, April 18.
Source: Board of Governors, Federal Reserve System.

Department Name _Misses' Dresses_ Department No. _42-11_

SIX MONTH MERCHANDISING PLAN

	PLAN (This Year)	ACTUAL (Last Year)
Workroom cost	1.0 %	1.0 %
Cash discount	4.4 %	4.3 %
Season stock turnover	2.7	2.6
Shortage reserve	1.5 %	1.6 %
Operating expenses	31.0 %	31.5 %
Operating profit	9.1 %	7.8 %

SPRING 19—		FEB.	MAR.	APR.	MAY	JUNE	JULY	SEASON
~~FALL 19=~~		AUG.	SEP.	OCT.	NOV.	DEC.	JAN.	TOTAL
SALES	Last Year	1,210	1,830	1,420	1,450	1,620	1,080	8,610
	Plan	1,250	1,450	1,850	1,450	1,700	1,200	8,900
	Percent of Increase	3.3	−20.8	30.3	0	4.9	11.1	3.4
	Revised							
	Actual							
	Last Year	3,450	4,250	3,500	3,040	3,400	2,900	2,100 *

Form 12-2

Planning Stock

The next step in dollar merchandise planning is to estimate the amount of stock that will be needed to support the planned monthly sales. Such planning and control of stocks, in terms of dollar investment, constitute an essential part of the merchandise plan or budget.

The objective in planning a beginning-of-the-month inventory is to provide an assortment of sufficient depth and breadth that customers will be able to find the range of styles and prices that they want. At the same time, limits are set on the size of the inventory investment to discourage buyers from purchasing more than they can realistically expect to sell and to avoid tying up in inventory more dollars than needed to produce the planned sales.

Considerations in Stock Planning Since sales during any month can only be realized if the stock from which such sales are to be made is first provided, it is considered good practice to plan stocks for the beginning of each month rather than for the end of the month. In any event the planned beginning-of-the-month (BOM) stock is identical with the end-of-the-month (EOM) stock for the preceding month. Only such rare events or catastrophes as fire or extensive theft that have occurred after the close of business on the last day of the month would affect this balance.

Two major considerations influence the fashion merchant as he plans his BOM stocks. First, he must have an adequate opening assortment on hand, in sufficient quantity, to meet anticipated customer demand until he can secure stock replacements for goods sold. The best dollar stock plans for fashion departments are those built up from unit assortment plans, or model stocks, in which minimum quantities of each item needed are detailed by classifications, price lines, types, colors, and sizes. (Assortment and model stock planning are discussed in detail in Chapter 13.)

The merchant's second consideration is to plan his BOM stocks in relation to anticipated sales so that a desired seasonal stock turnover may be realized, markdowns minimized, and a steady flow of new, fresh merchandise assured throughout the month.

The same external, internal, and fashion factors that influence the planning of monthly sales also influence the planning of monthly stocks, and must be evaluated accordingly.

Variations in Monthly Stock Goals   In planning monthly stock goals, stocks should be brought to a peak just prior to the time when sales are expected to reach their peak. By peaking stocks before consumer demand reaches its crest, merchants are able to present maximum assortments and to avoid being out of needed styles, sizes, and colors when the public is in the mood to buy.

Similarly, beginning-of-the-month stock plans are reduced as a selling season approaches its close and demand decreases. Other factors help the merchant to reduce his inventory as the season ends: unsold seasonal goods are marked down; new goods that may be brought into stock are usually manufacturers' closeouts, which are purchased and resold at prices lower than earlier in the season.

Stock-Sales Relationships   Over the years, department stores and departmentalized specialty stores have learned to guide their stock planning by using past relationships between the dollar amount of stock on hand at the beginning of a calendar month and the amount of sales planned for that month. This relationship is called the *stock-sales ratio*, which is defined as the number of months that would be required to dispose of a beginning-of-the-month inventory at the rate at which sales are made in (or planned for) that month. The formula used for calculating this relationship is:

$$\text{stock-sales ratio} = \frac{\$ \text{ BOM stock}}{\$ \text{ sales for month}}$$

Applying this formula to the February planned sales and stock figures appearing on Form 12-3:

$$\text{stock-sales ratio} = \frac{\$3,500}{\$1,250}$$

$$= 2.8$$

Table 12-2.   Stock-Sales Ratio

Department Stores With Total Annual Volumes of Over $1 Million, 1967

	Jewelry (fine and costume)	Coats and Suits	Men's Furnishings
February*	4.8	2.9	6.7
March	3.5	1.9	5.7
April	4.5	2.7	6.3
May	3.3	3.1	6.2
June	4.1	4.9	3.8
July	5.5	4.6	6.0
August	4.0	3.4	5.6
September	3.8	3.0	5.1
October	4.6	2.9	5.6
November	3.5	2.9	3.6
December	1.6	2.2	1.5
January	7.1	2.7	6.3

*Department stores generally operate on a fiscal year that runs from February 1 to January 31 of the following calendar year.

Source: *Departmental Merchandising and Operating Results of 1967,* Controllers' Congress, National Retail Merchants Association, New York, 1968, p. 11.

The stock-sales ratio is an important tool in stock planning in that it directly relates sales to stock requirements. Appropriate stock-sales ratios may be derived from a store's own experience or from typical experience compiled by such trade associations as the National Retail Merchants Association, or from combinations of the two. Ratios will vary, of necessity, from month to month, from department to department, from one type of retail operation to another, and from one type of merchandise to another. They depend primarily upon the cycle of demand and the merchandising policies of the individual store. Once a sales goal has been set, the stock needed at the beginning of any month can be determined as follows:

$ BOM stock = $ planned sales $\times$ stock-sales ratio

Using the figures from Table 12-2 as an illustration of the application of this formula, assume that a merchant plans February sales at $2,000 in each of three departments: Coats and Suits, Jewelry, and Men's Furnishings. Applying the February stock-sales ratios listed in this table, the amount of stock at retail value that he should have on hand February 1 in each of these departments is found to be:

Jewelry $2,000 \times 4.8 = \$ 9,600$
Coats and Suits $2,000 \times 2.9 = \$ 5,800$
Men's Furnishings $2,000 \times 6.7 = \$13,400$

Stock Turnover Unlike the stock-sales ratio, which is used in planning beginning-of-the-month stocks, *stock turnover* refers to the number of times that an average stock of merchandise (inventory) has been turned into sales during a given period. The formula for determining the rate of stock turnover during any given period is:

$$\text{stock turnover} = \frac{\$ \text{ net sales}}{\$ \text{ average inventory}}$$

For example, using Form 12-3, we can find that the planned average stock for the spring season is $3,257, by adding all six beginning-of-the-month stocks to the end-of-season stock and dividing that sum by seven, the number of inventory figures used. Dividing the season's total planned sales of $8,900 by the average stock of $3,257, a stock turnover rate of 2.7 is found for the six-month period.

On a storewide basis the typical stock turnover figure for department stores is somewhat better than three turns a year. In 1967, for example, the average stock turnover for all stores was 3.48. In women's apparel departments, however, turnover was well above that figure: 7.1 in budget dresses, 4.8 in the main floor blouse bar, 6.0 in millinery.[2]

The rate at which stock is turned into sales directly affects retail profit objectives since no income is realized until merchandise on hand is sold. A direct attempt to achieve a desired rate of

					PLAN (This Year)		ACTUAL (Last Year)
Department Name *Misses' Dresses* Department No. 42-11							
SIX MONTH MERCHANDISING PLAN	Workroom cost				1.0 %		1.0 %
	Cash discount				4.4 %		4.3 %
	Season stock turnover				2.7		2.6
	Shortage reserve				1.5 %		1.6 %
	Operating expenses				31.0 %		31.5 %
	Operating profit				9.1 %		7.8 %

		FEB. AUG.	MAR. SEP.	APR. OCT.	MAY NOV.	JUNE DEC.	JULY JAN.	SEASON TOTAL
SPRING 19— / ~~FALL 19~~								
SALES	Last Year	1,210	1,830	1,420	1,450	1,620	1,080	8,610
	Plan	1,250	1,450	1,850	1,450	1,700	1,200	8,900
	Percent of Increase	3.3	-20.8	30.3	0	4.9	11.1	3.4
	Revised							
	Actual							
RETAIL STOCK (BOM)	Last Year	3,450	4,250	3,500	3,040	3,400	2,900	2,100 *
	Plan	3,500	3,800	4,300	3,600	3,000	2,500	2,100 *
	Revised							
	Actual							
	Last Year	110	160	220	150	210	200	1,050

Form 12-3

206

stock turnover is made by limiting beginning-of-the-month stock to a predetermined stock-sales ratio. (Stock turnover as a measure of buyer efficiency is discussed further in Chapter 14.)

Planning Markdowns

Having planned monthly sales and beginning-of-the-month inventories, the fashion merchant is now almost ready to calculate the amount of stock he should purchase throughout each month in order to achieve his planned sales and stock goals. Before he does this, however, he may decide to estimate the dollar value of markdowns it will be necessary for him to take each month because markdowns reduce the retail value of the inventory just as sales do.

As defined in Chapter 11, a markdown is a reduction in the retail price of a single item or group of items. It represents the dollar difference between the previously recorded price of merchandise and the price to which the merchandise is being reduced.

Not all stores, however, take markdowns into consideration when planning seasonal budgets. Some elect not to plan markdowns on the premise that this procedure encourages buyers and department managers to take reductions even if they are not necessary. Other stores that omit markdowns from their seasonal budget plans prefer to regard the dollar value of markdowns actually taken as a reserve or hedge against a possible decline in actual sales from those that were planned. However, the standard procedure among large stores is to recognize the inevitability of a certain amount of markdowns, particularly in fashion goods, and to include markdowns in their merchandise plans.

Purpose of Markdowns Wise fashion merchants use merchandise markdowns to speed the sale of slow-moving, damaged, and out-of-season goods, in order to make room for new merchandise. Markdowns are also used as a means of meeting price competition and for adjusting retail prices to declining market values. Markdowns are most useful if regarded as a tool rather than as a curse. They help to release capital that would otherwise be tied up in stock and make funds available for reinvestment in more salable merchandise.

Because of rapidly changing consumer demand, markdowns are generally larger and of greater importance in departments devoted to fashion goods than in departments in which the merchandise is more staple, such as blankets or lawn furniture. By using markdowns judiciously to clear out seasonal goods promptly, fashion merchants avoid the very considerable risks involved in carrying the goods beyond their normal selling period.

Markdown Terminology In retailing, the term *markdown* refers to the dollar amount of difference between the previous price and the reduced price to which merchandise is marked. To express the relationship between accumulated markdowns and net sales for a given period, a markdown percentage figure is used. *Markdown percentage* may be defined as the dollar value of the net retail markdowns taken during a given period, divided by the dollar value of net sales for that period. For example, Form 12-4 shows that February markdowns are planned at $110, and February sales at $1,250. Expressed as a formula, markdown percentage is:

$$\text{markdown \%} = \frac{\$ \text{ markdown}}{\$ \text{ net sales}}$$
$$= \frac{\$110}{\$1,250}$$
$$= 8.8\%$$

Retailers use the term *retail reductions* for all reductions that occur in the retail value of the inventory, including merchandise markdowns, discounts allowed to employees and other special customers, and stock shortages. Merchandise markdowns, however, constitute the major part of retail reductions and vary considerably from month to month, particularly with respect to fashion goods. These are the markdowns that are usually planned when seasonal budgets are drawn up. Estimates of special discounts may be included with merchandise markdowns or shown separately when planning the seasonal budget. Provisions for reductions caused by stock shortages are usually made by setting up special monthly reserves for such contingencies.

SIX MONTH MERCHANDISING PLAN	Department Name _Misses' Dresses_ Department No. _42-11_		PLAN (This Year)	ACTUAL (Last Year)
	Workroom cost		1.0 %	1.0 %
	Cash discount		4.4 %	4.3 %
	Season stock turnover		2.7	2.6
	Shortage reserve		1.5 %	1.6 %
	Operating expenses		31.0 %	31.5 %
	Operating profit		9.1 %	7.8 %

SPRING 19—		FEB.	MAR.	APR.	MAY	JUNE	JULY	SEASON TOTAL
FALL 19=		AUG.	SEP.	OCT.	NOV.	DEC.	JAN.	
SALES	Last Year	1,210	1,830	1,420	1,450	1,620	1,080	8,610
	Plan	1,250	1,450	1,850	1,450	1,700	1,200	8,900
	Percent of Increase	3.3	-20.8	30.3	0	4.9	11.1	3.4
	Revised							
	Actual							
RETAIL STOCK (BOM)	Last Year	3,450	4,250	3,500	3,040	3,400	2,900	2,100*
	Plan	3,500	3,800	4,300	3,600	3,000	2,500	2,100*
	Revised							
	Actual							
MARKDOWNS	Last Year	110	160	220	150	210	200	1,050
	Plan (dollars)	110	160	150	200	200	200	1,020
	Plan (percent)	8.8	11.0	8.1	13.8	11.8	16.7	11.5
	Revised							
	Actual							
	Last Year	2,120	1,240	1,180	1,960	1,330	480	8,310

Form 12-4

Only merchandise markdowns and special discounts are included in the monthly and seasonal figures found in Form 12-4. Reductions caused by stock shortages appear separately as a percentage of the total season's planned sales and are found in the upper right-hand corner of this form.

Factors in Planning Markdowns A certain percentage of any retail store's stock will always have to be marked down before it can be sold. Some stock may have to be marked down more than once. Since markdowns result in lowered *gross profit* (the difference between the cost of the merchandise and the price at which it is finally sold), they must be planned and controlled.

Markdowns are usually planned as a percentage of each season's planned sales. They may then be allotted to individual months, according to the merchant's estimates of when and to what extent monthly markdowns are going to be needed to move the goods. In establishing the markdown estimates, the experience of previous seasons and of other stores is considered, together with the general business outlook for the period ahead.

The chief factors to be considered in establishing seasonal markdown goals are:

▫ The past experience of the store or department
▫ Trends in wholesale prices (markdowns tend to increase during periods of falling wholesale

prices and decrease when wholesale prices are rising)

□ Comparative figures of similar stores

□ Amount of old stock on hand at the beginning of a new season

□ Changes in merchandising policies and methods that may have occurred since the previous year or that are about to occur

In allocating the season's markdown estimate to individual months, the merchant considers not only dates throughout the season when changes in customer demand are expected to occur, but also store policy in taking markdowns. Large stores tend to take markdowns while there is still sufficient customer demand to move the goods quickly at minimum price reductions. Small stores tend to postpone the taking of markdowns, preferring to clear their stocks only at the end of a major selling season.

Planning Purchases   *end – beg.*

Having entered monthly sales, beginning-of-the-month stocks, and monthly markdown goals on the planning form, the merchant is now ready to calculate the value of the purchases that can be made each month if stocks and sales are to be kept in balance. *Planned purchases* comprise the amount of merchandise that can be brought into stock during a given period without exceeding the planned end-of-the-month inventory.

In most large stores, purchases are planned on a monthly basis. However, some smaller fashion merchants, particularly those who make infrequent market trips, budget their purchases on a seasonal or market-trip basis. Planned purchases are derived from planned sales, stocks, and, when applicable, markdowns by simple arithmetical computation.

The calculation of monthly purchases begins with the month's planned closing inventory (the next month's BOM figure). To this amount is added an amount equivalent to the sales that are planned for the month, which represents the stock needed to replace what is expected to be sold. If markdowns are planned, their amount is also added because markdowns decrease the value of the inventory just as sales do. The amount of inventory already in stock at the beginning of the month is then subtracted from this total. The remainder represents the planned purchase figure for the month.

The formula for calculating planned purchases, therefore, is as follows:

planned purchases = planned ending stock + planned sales + planned markdowns − BOM stock

Applying this formula to the February figures given in Form 12-5:

planned purchases = $3,800 + $1,250 + $110 − $3,500
= $1,660

Although most stores plan their purchases at retail value, as was done here, some smaller stores still use cost value. If desired, the equivalent cost value of retail purchases can be calculated easily by multiplying the retail value of the planned purchases by the cost complement of the planned markon percentage for the period. (The cost complement is 100 percent minus the retail markon percent.) For example, if the February markon is planned at 44 percent and February retail purchases are planned at $1,660, the cost value of the $1,660 figure may be determined as follows:

$ cost = $ retail value × (100% − retail markon %)
= $1,660 × 56%
= $929.60

Supplemental Elements in Dollar Merchandise Planning

Many retailers, particularly large department stores and departmentalized specialty stores, expand their budgeting procedures beyond the four basic elements discussed above. They frequently include in the dollar merchandise plan any of several additional elements that directly affect the profit of the operation. Important among these elements are estimates of markon or gross margin, stock shortages reserve, cash discounts earned, turnover, operating expenses, and profit.

In some cases, only seasonal goal figures include these elements. In other cases, both seasonal and monthly dollar and percentage-to-sales

Department Name *Misses' Dresses*			Department No.		*42-11*		

SIX MONTH MERCHANDISING PLAN		**PLAN (This Year)**	**ACTUAL (Last Year)**
	Workroom cost	1.0 %	1.0 %
	Cash discount	4.4 %	4.3 %
	Season stock turnover	2.7	2.6
	Shortage reserve	1.5 %	1.6 %
	Operating expenses	31.0 %	31.5 %
	Operating profit	9.1 %	7.8 %

SPRING 19—		FEB.	MAR.	APR.	MAY	JUNE	JULY	SEASON TOTAL
FALL 19=		AUG.	SEP.	OCT.	NOV.	DEC.	JAN.	
SALES	Last Year	1,210	1,830	1,420	1,450	1,620	1,080	8,610
	Plan	1,250	1,450	1,850	1,450	1,700	1,200	8,900
	Percent of Increase	3.3	-20.8	30.3	0	4.9	11.1	3.4
	Revised							
	Actual							
RETAIL STOCK (BOM)	Last Year	3,450	4,250	3,500	3,040	3,400	2,900	2,100 *
	Plan	3,500	3,800	4,300.	3,600	3,000	2,500	2,100 *
	Revised							
	Actual							
MARKDOWNS	Last Year	110	160	220	150	210	200	1,050
	Plan (dollars)	110	160	150	200	200	200	1,020
	Plan (percent)	8.8	11.0	8.1	13.8	11.8	16.7	11.5
	Revised							
	Actual							
RETAIL PURCHASES	Last Year	2,120	1,240	1,180	1,960	1,330	480	8,310
	Plan	1,660	2,110	1,300	1,050	1,400	1,000	8,520
	Revised							
	Actual							

Form 12-5   *end - beg*

figures are worked out. Goal figures of each of these supplementary elements of the dollar merchandise plan, together with the figures representing the previous year's actual performance, are usually supplied by the store's controller or fiscal division. Such goal figures reflect the financial objectives of the store, as determined by top management, and are rarely left to the discretion of departmental planners.

Guidelines in budgeting these additional elements of the dollar merchandise plan are the store's own experience, figures available from the National Retail Merchants Association, and frequently figures supplied by the store's resident buying office.

Not on test

Markon

Markon is the difference between the cost and the retail price of merchandise. *Markon* is a term that has largely replaced "markup" among large retail stores as a designation of the difference between cost and selling prices. Most stores express markon as a percentage of retail value, thus:

$$\text{retail markon \%} = \frac{\$ \text{ retail} - \$ \text{ cost}}{\$ \text{ retail}}$$

Some smaller stores and most manufacturers, however, calculate markon percentages on the basis of cost, or:

$$\text{cost markon \%} = \frac{\$ \text{ retail} - \$ \text{ cost}}{\$ \text{ cost}}$$

Even though a fashion merchant uses the retail system of accounting and employs the first formula given here in his own calculations, he needs to be familiar with the second formula as well, since it may be used in discussions with suppliers and other retailers.

The difference between the delivered cost of merchandise and the retail price placed on it when it is first brought into stock is called the *initial markon*. When the initial dollar markon on either a single purchase or the total purchases over a given period is divided by the total dollar retail value of those purchases, the resulting figure is known as the *initial markon percentage*.

Retail stores plan initial markon percentage in order to ensure that the income derived from sales will be adequate to cover all expenses incurred in the operation of the business and also will yield a reasonable profit. In addition, this income must be sufficient to cover anticipated reductions in the retail value of the inventory, such as markdowns, stock shortages, and discounts allowed to customers and employees.

Discussion of the calculation by which management arrives at an initial markon figure is presented in Appendix 2. Only the formula used in determining the amount of markon needed is presented here:

$$\text{Initial markon \%} = \frac{\begin{array}{l}\text{profit} + \text{expenses} + \text{markdowns} \\ + \text{ stock shortages} \\ + \text{ discounts allowed} \\ + \text{ workroom costs} \\ - \text{ cash discounts earned}\end{array}}{\begin{array}{l}\text{net sales} + \text{markdowns} \\ + \text{ stock shortages} \\ + \text{ discounts allowed}\end{array}}$$

The following examples use the percentage figures and the dollar figures from Form 12-6 to illustrate this procedure. All percentages are based on estimates of planned net sales:

$$\text{Initial markon \%} = \frac{\begin{array}{l}9.1\% + 31.0\% \\ + 11.5\% + 1.5\% + 0\% \\ 1.0\% - 4.4\%\end{array}}{\begin{array}{l}100\% \text{ (net sales} + \\ 11.5\% + 1.5\%\end{array}}$$

$$= \frac{49.7\%}{113\%}$$

$$= 44\%$$

or:

$$\text{Initial markon \%} = \frac{\begin{array}{l}\$810 + \$2,759 + \$1,020 \\ + \$134 + \$89 - \$392\end{array}}{\$8,900 + \$1,020 + \$134}$$

$$= \frac{\$4,420}{\$10,054}$$

$$= 44\%$$

Thus it can be seen that the buyer for Department 42-11 will be required to secure a 44 percent initial markon on purchases during the spring season in order to realize an operating profit of 9.1 percent. Some of these purchases may yield a higher or lower percentage than that planned, but the buyer's aim throughout the season is to keep the average markon as close as possible to the planned 44 percent figure.

Gross Margin

Instead of initial markon percentage, or sometimes in addition to it, some stores plan gross margin of profit. *Gross margin* represents the dollar difference between net sales for a period and the net cost of merchandise sold during that period. Procedures for arriving at gross margin are demonstrated in Appendix 2. Although gross margin is essentially a seasonal goal figure, many stores establish monthly goals as a means of evaluating progress toward the projected seasonal goal. *Gross margin percentage* is calculated by dividing the dollars of gross margin by the net sales for the period.

Cash Discounts

Cash discounts are the percentages or premiums allowed by manufacturers off the invoiced price

SIX MONTH MERCHANDISING PLAN

Department Name *Misses' Dresses* Department No. 42-11

	PLAN (This Year)	ACTUAL (Last Year)
Workroom cost	1.0 %	1.0 %
Cash discount	4.4 %	4.3 %
Season stock turnover	2.7	2.6
Shortage reserve	1.5 %	1.6 %
Operating expenses	31.0 %	31.5 %
Operating profit	9.1 %	7.8 %

SPRING 19— FALL 19=		FEB. AUG.	MAR. SEP.	APR. OCT.	MAY NOV.	JUNE DEC.	JULY JAN.	SEASON TOTAL
SALES	Last Year	1,210	1,830	1,420	1,450	1,620	1,080	8,610
	Plan	1,250	1,450	1,850	1,450	1,700	1,200	8,900
	Percent of Increase	3.3	−20.8	30.3	0	4.9	11.1	3.4
	Revised							
	Actual							
RETAIL STOCK (BOM)	Last Year	3,450	4,250	3,500	3,040	3,400	2,900	2,100 *
	Plan	3,500	3,800	4,300	3,600	3,000	2,500	2,100 *
	Revised							
	Actual							
MARKDOWNS	Last Year	110	160	220	150	210	200	1,050
	Plan (dollars)	110	160	150	200	200	200	1,020
	Plan (percent)	8.8	11.0	8.1	13.8	11.8	16.7	11.5
	Revised							
	Actual							
RETAIL PURCHASES	Last Year	2,120	1,240	1,180	1,960	1,330	480	8,310
	Plan	1,660	2,110	1,300	1,050	1,400	1,000	8,520
	Revised							
	Actual							
PERCENT OF INITIAL MARKON	Last Year	43.6	44.0	43.8	43.9	43.8	43.6	43.8
	Plan	44.0	44.0	44.0	44.0	44.0	44.0	44.0
	Revised							
	Actual							

Comments

Represents end-of-season stock

Merchandise Manager *T. J. Evans*   Buyer *Jane Dean*

Controller

Form 12-6

212

of their merchandise if payment is made within a certain specified period of time. Such discounts are given to encourage the prompt payment of invoices.

Cash discounts are an important source of profit for a store or department, and for that reason are included in most dollar merchandise budgets as a percentage of net sales, as a percentage of purchases, or both. Cash discounts earned increase gross margin, if discounted invoices covering purchases made during the period are recorded at their net cost. They also serve to increase gross margin if purchases are recorded at their invoiced prices and the total of all cash discounts earned during the period is subtracted from the gross cost of the merchandise sold. They serve to increase net profit if considered as "other income," instead of as a reduction in the cost of merchandise, and as such are added to operating profit. (See Appendix 2.)

The buyer or department manager, however, has no control over the taking of cash discounts. Decisions regarding the payment of invoices which determine whether or not a cash discount is earned rest entirely with the store management.

Dating As a term used in conjunction with cash discounts, *dating* refers to the period of time allowed by a vendor for the taking of cash discounts.

Terms The amount of discount allowed and the length of time during which it is allowed are the *terms* of the purchase. These vary widely from industry to industry. Among fashion industries, "10 EOM" dating usually applies. This means that the cash discount may be taken if the invoice is paid within ten days following the last day of the month in which the invoice is dated. The percentage of cash discount allowed, however, varies widely from one fashion industry to another. For example, in the apparel industry, the usual terms are "8/10 EOM" (8 percent cash discount allowed if the invoice is paid within 10 days after the end of the month in which it is dated); in the handbag industry, 3/10 EOM; in the millinery industry, 7/10 EOM; and in the glove industry, 6/10 EOM.

Anticipation An extra discount granted by some manufacturers for the prepayment of their invoices before the end of the cash discount period is called *anticipation*. Traditionally, anticipation has reflected the current bank interest rates, and has usually been figured at the rate of 6 percent a year (360 days) or .5 percent a month (30 days). As bank interest rates change, however, so do the average anticipation rates.

Anticipation is taken on the net amount of an invoice and in addition to any other discounts that might apply. It is not a part of the original purchase transaction covered by the invoice, but a tender of prepayment made by the purchaser, provided the seller accepts the arrangement. Department stores traditionally have made profitable use of their capital by taking anticipation whenever possible.

Stock Shortages and Overages

Stock shortages or overages represent the difference between the book inventory (the value indicated by the store's accounting records) and the physical inventory (the actual value determined by taking a physical count). When the book inventory is greater, there is said to be a *stock shortage*. When the physical inventory is greater, this is said to be a *stock overage*. Stock shortages are experienced with consistent regularity by retail stores. Stock overages occur very seldom.

As discussed earlier, stock shortages are classified for accounting purposes as retail reductions, together with markdowns and special discounts to customers. Since they can be determined only when a complete physical inventory is taken, which is usually only once or twice a year, most stores set up monthly reserves for such shortages. This means that a certain percentage of sales is reserved to offset the anticipated difference between book inventory and the actual physical inventory.

Shortage reserve percentages are usually based upon past experience. The percentage is determined at the beginning of a season or year, and does not change from month to month. Actual differences between the value of the book inventory and the value of the physical inventory, as determined from an actual count, are compared to the accumulated shortage reserve when the physical inventory is taken. If the actual shortage is less than the reserve, gross margin is increased by the amount of the difference. If the actual shortage is greater than the reserve, gross margin is thereby reduced by an equivalent amount.

Since stock shortages decrease a department's profit and are essentially the responsibility and problem of the buyer, many stores include seasonal shortage reserve figures in their dollar merchandise plans.

Operating Expenses

There are two kinds of expenses that are incurred in the operation of a selling department: direct and indirect.

Direct expenses are those that occur as a direct result of the operation of a specific department and that would cease if the department itself ceased to exist. Examples of such direct expenses are salespeople's salaries, buyers' compensation, expenses incurred in connection with buying trips, advertising costs, and delivery charges.

Indirect expenses are those that do not directly result from the operation of a department, but are shared by all departments of the store, such as compensation of top management executives, rent, utilities, maintenance, supplies, receiving, and marking expenses.

Many stores that include operating expenses as an element of the dollar merchandise budget make it a practice to plan advertising expenses and selling salaries separately as seasonal or monthly percentages of planned sales, since these expenses are intimately related to the actual production of sales. On Form 12-6, however, all operating expenses are grouped together and shown merely as 31 percent of planned sales for the season, with no attempt to budget specific types of operating expenses or to plan them by months. The six month plan in most stores does not include a budget for indirect expenses.

As discussed earlier, departmental operating expenses must be taken into account when calculating the initial markon percentage if a profit is to result. Thus, in a sense, they are budgeted, and provision is made for covering them.

References

[1]Barker, Anderson, and Butterworth, *Principles of Retailing,* p. 338.
[2]*Departmental Merchandising and Operating Results of 1967,* p. 317 and 320.

Merchandising Vocabulary

Define or briefly explain the following terms:

Dollar merchandising plan	Markon
Open-to-buy	Initial markon
Stock-sales ratio	Gross margin
Stock turnover	Cash discount
Markdown percentage	Anticipation
Retail reductions	Stock shortage
Gross profit	Stock overage
Planned purchases	Direct expenses

Merchandising Review

1. What major objectives do retail stores hope to accomplish through the application of sound financial planning techniques?
2. What are the fashion merchant's two principal planning tools for achieving these major objectives? Describe the function of each.
3. Why has it become more essential for fashion merchants to utilize scientific approaches to financial planning today than was formerly the case?
4. Discuss the responsibilities of each of the following store executives with regard to drawing up dollar merchandising plans: (a) the buyer; (b) the merchandise manager; (c) the store controller.
5. Why is it essential that any merchandising plan be flexible and subject to periodic review and adjustment?
6. What are considered to be the essential elements in any dollar merchandising plan? What other elements are sometimes planned by some stores?
7. What specific conditions should be considered in estimating the future sales potential of a department or a store?
8. Why do fashion trends frequently have a more important bearing on a department's sales potential than do business conditions? Give examples to illustrate your answer.
9. What factors should be considered in setting maximum and minimum levels for beginning-of-the-month stocks?
10. Differentiate between the two types of stock-sales relationships that are considered in dollar merchandising planning.
11. Why do most stores consider markdowns an essential element of the dollar merchandising plan, particularly in fashion departments?
12. Why should purchases be planned in advance of a selling season? What is the formula for determining planned purchases?
13. Why is initial markon on purchases considered by many merchants an important element of the dollar merchandising plan? How is it determined?
14. Why do many stores take stock shortages into consideration when developing dollar merchandise plans?
15. Discuss the differences between direct and indirect operating expenses.

13

BUDGETING THE FASHION
MERCHANDISE ASSORTMENT

A well-balanced merchandise assortment is perhaps the most potent tool any retailer can use to attract and hold customers. Such factors as location, layout, facilities, services, and promotional effort are also important, but the cornerstone of the customer-winning structure is the merchandise assortment. If people are to continue to patronize a store, the merchandise itself must at all times be what they want.

Retailers for many decades have described good assortments as those containing the right merchandise, at the right time, in the right place, in the right quantities, and at prices that customers are both willing and able to pay.[1]

Each merchant strives to build assortments to conform with what is considered right by the particular customers he wishes to serve. He studies their merchandise preferences and lays down guidelines for himself and his buyers to follow in developing and maintaining assortments. These guidelines cover such matters as degree of fashion leadership, price ranges, quality standards, depth and breadth of assortments, emphasis to be placed on exclusivity, attitude toward standardized and branded merchandise, and the extent to which basic assortments should be maintained.

Assortment Planning

The objectives of assortment planning, discussed in detail below, are similar to those of financial planning. To achieve these objectives, successful merchants give careful consideration to the store's merchandising policies as they relate to the characteristics of merchandise offerings; to external, internal, and fashion factors affecting their businesses; to their own past experience; and to all other sources of information concerning what customers can be expected to want in the period for which planning is being undertaken.

□ To guide the merchant in buying and assembling in inventory those styles, sizes, colors, and price lines that will accurately reflect anticipated customer demand during a given period

□ To time the delivery of purchases to the store so that each individual component of the inventory is available for sale neither too early nor too late for customer demand

□ To keep purchases in line with the store's ability to stock, display, promote, and pay for those purchases

□ To keep enough funds always available for the purchase of new or additional goods when and as they may be needed

□ To relate anticipated demand for each type of fashion goods to the demand for all other types in the inventory so that similar fashion influences and price levels will be reflected throughout the entire assortment

"Top-Down" Versus "Built-Up" Assortment Planning

Like the dollar budget, the assortment plan begins with a review of past experience and a consideration of future prospects. The dollar budget, however, is concerned only with how much money the customer spent last year and how much she may be expected to spend in the up-coming season. The assortment plan is concerned with the specifics of what she bought last year and what she may be expected to buy in the season for which plans are being made.

The majority of stores first develop a seasonal dollar merchandise budget, based on anticipated sales, optimum stock levels, markdowns, and purchases, as described in the preceding chapter. It then becomes the responsibility of the buyer to allocate these budgeted funds in such a way that his purchases will provide a merchandise assortment that is at all times balanced to cus-tomer demand. This method of budgeting is often referred to as *top-down planning*.

In a growing number of retail stores, however, merchandise assortment planning precedes financial planning, particularly in fashion de-partments. Under this method, which is known as *built-up planning*, sales, beginning-of-the-month stocks, and purchases are planned in units by classification, price lines, and any other sig-nificant category. Then the unit plan is converted into a dollar plan, by multiplying the number of units planned in each classification by their ap-propriate retail prices and then adding all classi-fication subtotals to obtain a departmental total.

Table 13-1 illustrates how a casual dress de-partment, with two major classifications, might construct its sales plan for February using this method. First, the number of unit sales antici-pated at each price line within each classification are determined. Next, the retail value of the unit sales planned at each price line within each clas-sification is computed. Finally, both the units and their dollar equivalents are totaled to produce the overall departmental planned sales for February.

In planning the stock needed at the beginning of each month or season, stock-sales ratios are applied to the unit sales planned at each price line within each classification, and totals are derived in both units and dollars, as in sales planning. Finally, planned purchases in both units and dollars are calculated for each price

Table 13-1. Unit Sales Plan

Dept.: #40

Name: *Casual Dresses*

Season: *Spring 1970*

Month: *February*

Class	Price Line	Description	Planned Sales Units	Planned Sales Dollars
12301	$ 9	Dresses, misses'	30	$ 270
12302	12	Dresses, misses'	36	432
12303	15	Dresses, misses'	40	600
12304	20	Dresses, misses'	38	760
12305	25	Dresses, misses'	15	375
12306	30	Dresses, misses'	12	360
12300		Total, Dresses, Misses'	171	$2,797
12801	$ 9	Dresses, juniors	25	$ 225
12802	12	Dresses, juniors	32	384
12803	15	Dresses, juniors	36	540
12804	20	Dresses, juniors	30	600
12805	25	Dresses, juniors	18	450
12806	30	Dresses, juniors	10	300
12800		Total, Dresses, Juniors	151	$2,499
		Total, Casual Dresses	322	$5,296

Table 13-2. Foundation for Assortment Planning

Review of College Shop Sales for Previous Year

	Shop A		Shop B	
	Units	Dollars	Units	Dollars
Skirts at $10 each	30	$ 300	35	$ 350
Skirts at $15 each	50	750	40	600
Total skirts	80	$1,050	75	$ 950
Sweaters at $18 each	30	$ 540	25	$ 450
Sweaters at $25 each	40	1,000	70	1,750
Total sweaters	70	$1,540	95	$2,200
Slacks at $12 each	50	$ 600	30	$ 360
Slacks at $20 each	60	1,200	80	1,600
Total slacks	110	$1,800	110	$1,960
Car coats at $30 each	50	$1,500	18	$ 540
Car coats at $40 each	9	360	15	600
Total car coats	59	$1,860	33	$1,140
Grand Total	319	$6,250	313	$6,250

line in each classification, and for the department as a whole, using the procedure described in the explanation of dollar purchase planning in Chapter 12.

Variations in Assortment Planning

Assortments carried in similar departments will vary from store to store, depending upon the merchandising policies of each store and the preferences of its target group of customers. For example, consider two merchants planning assortments for college shops that had identical sales of $6,250 in skirts, sweaters, slacks, and car coats the previous year. Table 13-2 shows two of the many ways in which that $6,250 could have been distributed among the four categories, assuming for simplicity's sake that there were only two price lines in each category.

Shop A's customers showed considerable interest in car coats last year; shop B's customers had little interest in these garments but bought sweaters lavishly. Shop A's customers showed a fairly strong interest in lower-priced goods; shop

B's customers had a pronounced interest in higher-priced lines.

If the merchants of these two shops look to the future with equal optimism, they might draw up dollar merchandise budgets of equal size. Their assortments, however, will be different. Each will build his assortment on the basis of prior years' experience and, as has been shown, each one's customers exhibited a different pattern of demand. It is as if each were setting out to buy a home in the same price range but with different specifications.

Factors in Planning Assortments

In planning his assortment to reflect customer preferences, each merchant considers the same factors that he weighs in drawing up his dollar merchandise budget. These factors affect not only how much customers may be expected to spend but also how they will distribute their purchases.

External Factors   General and local economic conditions have a marked effect on a merchant's

planning of his fashion assortments. If he antici-
pates greater affluence in his trading area or a
larger proportion of affluent customers than previously served, he will plan an assortment that
includes more high-priced goods than before, as
well as a larger proportion of new and relatively
untried fashions and probably a more generous
representation of strictly "fun" apparel.

If, on the other hand, his community has
suffered financial setbacks, or the unemployment
rate is increasing, or taxes and interest rates are
escalating, then he will plan an assortment in
which the more expensive goods involve minimum fashion risk and in which styles are versatile
enough to make a limited wardrobe adequate for
many varied occasions.

The local competitive situation is also taken
into account, since changes in that area may have
a direct bearing on the components of a fashion
assortment. If, for example, a low-priced hosiery
shop has recently opened near a quality department or specialty store and is making an aggressive bid for business, the hosiery merchant in the
larger establishment may decide to play down the
utility items in his stock and strengthen his assortments of the finer quality and newer styles
in hosiery.

Internal Factors Internal factors also affect the
assortment plans for any or all parts of a store's
inventory. An enlarged or refurbished selling
floor may be able to accommodate a larger and
broader assortment than was previously possible.
Relocating related departments so that they are
next to each other may encourage each to carry
larger assortments in matching colors and patterns.

The opening of new branch stores directly
affects the planning of fashion assortments, for
the merchandise preferences of new customers
to be served must be recognized and provided
for.

The extent and type of promotional activities
the store intends to engage in during the period
for which fashion assortments are being planned
also has a direct bearing on the components of
those assortments. For example, if the store intends to increase its use of television presentations during that period, departmental fash-

ion assortments should carry generous quantities
of the merchandise to be featured. If a store's
management has decided to embark on an advertising campaign stressing the values to be found
in its merchandise offerings, then value must be
of prime consideration when planning each departmental assortment.

Fashion Factors Fashion trends, of course, exert
a powerful influence on assortment planning.
Fashion makes the difference between what was
the right assortment yesterday and what will be
the right assortment tomorrow. This is true both
of apparel and of accessories assortments. Whatever the trend, fashion rarely affects one department in the apparel or accessories groups without
influencing the assortments required in all the
others.

The degree to which a store's customers show
a marked preference for fashions in the introductory, rise, culmination, or decline phases of these
cycles becomes a prime factor in unit assortment
planning. While most women choose their apparel and accessories from more than one of these
phases of a fashion cycle, they tend to favor
merchandise in one phase more than that in the
others. Fashion assortments must be planned
with these customer preferences in mind.

Sources of Information for Planning

In collecting facts to guide assortment planning,
the merchant's primary source is his own records
of what he bought, sold, and marked down in
corresponding past seasons. He also seeks information from other store buyers, from his suppliers, and from his resident buying office about
what other customers, similar to his own, purchased last year and what they may be expected
to purchase this year.

All indications of consumer preferences in the
past are weighed against what the merchant can
learn about future fashion trends, on the general
as well as on the local scene. He compares notes
with buyers of related departments within his
own store. He analyzes what he reads about
fashion trends in trade and fashion publications.
He notes what is featured in consumer publications and what is being planned for future editorial coverage. If his store serves customers who

want to be first with the newest styles, he may visit couture houses in this country and abroad for indications of incoming trends in demand.

✓ **Model Stock Planning**

To maintain the delicate balance between expected demand and the receipt of new merchandise into the fashion assortment requires careful planning. Practical assortment planning begins with a *model stock,* which is a unit assortment plan, within dollar budgetary limits, with its components distributed in such a manner as to best satisfy customer demand at a specific time.

In preparing a model stock, three preliminary steps need to be taken:

1. A decision must be made as to the selection factors involved, such as classifications, types, prices, colors, sizes, and any others that are important in the customer's buying decision.
2. A determination must be made of the important dates within the six-month season for which model stocks should be constructed. These dates are mainly determined by the special selling periods occurring within the major season, such as Easter, Father's Day, and so on.
3. Sales for the months immediately preceding and following the date for which a model stock is intended should be planned in units, and the total translated into dollars as a check against the dollar departmental classification plan.[2]

The actual planning of a model stock involves deciding on the optimum quantities to have on hand on a specific date in each of the major selection categories, such as price lines, types, colors, sizes, and so on. Needed quantities are determined by applying to the sales planned for the following period appropriate stock-sales ratios based on past demand and present indicators of future demands.

Successive model stock plans may be made for each of the months in a seasonal merchandise plan or they may be set up for specific selling periods occurring within the six-month season. For example, one model stock may be planned for March 15, if Easter falls late in March or early in April; another for May 1, for the summer selling season; and a third for July 1, as a target date for reducing the assortment as the summer season draws to a close.

Model stocks must be planned well in advance. This involves estimating sales by the various selection factors long before the season actually starts, and placing orders on the basis of such estimates early enough to ensure delivery at the proper time. Not only are delivery periods growing longer but there is a growing trend among fashion producers to dispense with strictly seasonal lines and the recutting of best-selling styles throughout a season in favor of a continuous introduction of new styles throughout the traditional selling season.

Herein lies the reason why a basic stock plan is used for staple merchandise and a model stock plan is preferred for fashion merchandise. A *basic stock plan* specifies the minimum and maximum units of specific style numbers that should be on hand at all times throughout a season or a year. The rate of sale of staple merchandise is relatively constant; styles may be reordered; delivery periods are relatively short. A model stock plan, on the other hand, indicates the quantities of merchandise that should be on hand on any specific date by broad, general characteristics, such as type, size, and price line, rather than by style number. As model stock replacements are required, merchandise having similar characteristics or selection factors to that which was sold is sought in order to bring the stock up to plan. Today's fashion customer wants to see a constant flow of new merchandise in the stores and departments she patronizes.

Table 13-3 is an example of a March 15 model stock plan for a junior coat department in a year when Easter falls very late in March.

Other stores, other departments, other seasons may require a model with an entirely different distribution of prices and styles, and with different proportions devoted to basic, current, high fashion, and novelty merchandise. A May 1 model stock for this junior coat department would also be entirely different, since at that time stocks should be peaked for the summer selling period. It would again be different on July 1, as the summer selling season draws to a close and

Table 13-3. Model Stock Plan

	No. of Units	Total Retail
One very basic style to retail at $30; one color; no less than one coat in each of five sizes (7-15)	5	$ 150
A second basic style to retail at $40; three coats, all in different colors, in each of five sizes (7-15)	15	600
Two current new styles to retail at $40; two colors in each of five sizes (5-13)	20	800
Two current new styles to retail at $50; two colors in each of five sizes (7-15)	20	1,000
Two current new styles to retail at $60; two colors in each of five sizes (5-13)	20	1,200
High fashion styles, assorted, to retail at $75; assorted colors; two in each of five sizes (7-15)	10	750
Novelty styles to retail at $50; assorted colors; one coat in each of five sizes (7-15)	5	250
Total model stock, March 15	95	$4,750

spring-summer merchandise must be cleared out to make room and to release funds for fall-winter coats in this category.

Unit Planning and Control

Since fashion is not static, one season's model is seldom useful for the next season without adjustment. At the beginning of each season, fashion buyers and merchants rework their models. They add some items and eliminate others, amplify the assortment in some types and selling prices and reduce it in others. For information to guide the building of a model, the buyer turns to his unit control records. These show what was bought and the rate at which it was sold in previous seasons.

Unit control is the term applied by retailers to systems that record the number of pieces or units of merchandise bought, sold, in stock, and on order. Systems developed for this purpose vary widely from store to store and from one type of merchandise to another. They also vary widely in the amount of detail encompassed and the methods by which figures are collected and reported. Those used for fast-changing fashion merchandise are necessarily designed to alert the merchant to the slightest faltering or acceleration of demand for a style, color, or other element of customer preference. Systems used for more staple, slow-changing goods may reveal only the broad outlines of demand and yet be quite adequate for their purpose.

Types of Information Recorded

Whatever the system used, or whatever the type of merchandise, unit controls are devised to show:

▫ Net sales in number of units

▫ Stock on hand and on order in number of units

▫ Further breakdown of general sales and stock figures into such relevant categories as cost and retail prices, style numbers, sizes, colors, vendors, and merchandise classifications, all shown in terms of number of units

The breakdown of sales and stock figures involves deciding which aspects of the merchandise provide the merchant with the most useful clues to the exact nature of customer demand. One must accommodate as many of these clues in the system as cost and facilities will permit. In inexpensive women's blouses, for example, it may be important to record unit sales and stock figures by size, price lines, broad style categories, and color. In more expensive dresses, it may be desirable to record separate figures for each style number. In men's shirts, the size, style, color, fabric, and price line may be required.

Deciding how much information about a specific category of merchandise should be collected for unit control purposes is a difficult matter. Each merchant or buyer seeks to develop a system that provides him with the facts he needs and yet is not burdened with nonessential details. The operation of the system should be fast enough to give the merchant meaningful help in keeping assortments constantly geared to the pattern of customer demand at a reasonable cost.

The forms used for recording unit control data vary widely, and those shown in this chapter are typical rather than standard. Each store or department must have the forms that meet its own needs, even if this requires examining several forms used by others and then drawing up one's own. In actual retail practice one sees many variations of forms serving the many purposes of unit control. Those offered here have been drawn up to help the student visualize the procedures involved.

Types of Systems

The two major types of unit control are those that record purchases and sales as they occur, thus maintaining a perpetual inventory record, and those that depend upon periodic counts of the stock as a basis for calculating whatever sales have occurred between counts. Within each type, many variations exist.

Perpetual Inventory Control A *perpetual inventory system* is a unit control system in which orders, receipts, and sales are recorded as they occur and stock on hand is subsequently computed from such records. Controls of this type are particularly applicable to men's suits, fine jewelry, women's and children's ready-to-wear, and other merchandise of relatively high unit price. Perpetual controls are also used for other types of merchandise in which the degree of acceptance of individual style must be closely watched. Although the cost of maintaining perpetual inventory controls is substantial compared to that of simpler systems, it is not high in relation to its value to the merchant who wants and uses the detailed information provided.

A perpetual inventory record begins when an order is placed. Separate records are kept for each style or for groups of styles that are treated as a single category. On this record, notation is made of the number of pieces ordered and such identifying information as style number, vendor, classification, cost, and retail prices.

When the goods are received, the number of pieces on order is appropriately reduced, and an entry is made to show the exact number of pieces received into stock. Sales are recorded as they take place, and the number of units remaining in stock is thereby reduced. Returns to vendors, which decrease the stock on hand, are also recorded, as are returns from customers, which increase the stock on hand.

In such systems, entries are made of the dates and amounts of orders, receipts, sales, and other stock changes. Tally marks are generally used for size and color distribution, with one mark representing a single unit of merchandise.

In manually maintained perpetual inventory systems, and especially those that record sales and stock by size and color, a common practice is to tally merchandise on order in pencil. When goods are received, the individual pencil tallies are inked over. As each unit is sold, an appropriate tally mark is crossed off. Customer returns, which represent additions to stock, are re-tallied in red. Red crossmarks are used to indicate returns to vendors, which represent reductions in stock on hand. The number of units sold and those remaining in stock are thus easily identifiable.

Form 13-1 shows how a perpetual inventory record of an individual style might look after the buyer has received into stock 72 pieces of one style. The goods were ordered on August 15, and at that time tally marks were made in pencil, by color and size, of each item ordered. When the merchandise was received on September 5, the "on order" entry was circled to indicate that it had been received in full, and an entry was made to this effect in the "received" block. Penciled tallies of the sizes and colors ordered were then inked over to indicate that the exact number of pieces had been received.

Form 13-2 shows how the inventory card for the same style number might look after the style had been on sale for two weeks. Sales had been recorded daily, noting size, color distribution, and total number of units sold each day. Sales by week were also recorded. In this case, the buyer

DAILY SALES

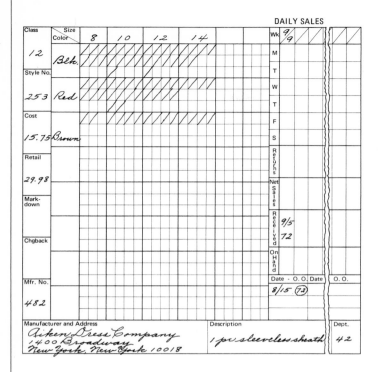

Form 13-1: The buyer placed an order for 72 units of a sheath, in sizes 8 through 14, in three different colors. When the order was placed, this perpetual inventory card was prepared, with full details about composition of the order, the vendor, classification and style number information, cost price, and the retail price at which the units are to be sold. This is the way the card looked right after the order was received into stock. The receipt date has been added, the "on order" number circled to show that the order has been received in full, and the original pencilled tally marks have been inked in.

Form 13-2: Two weeks later this is how the inventory card might look. Sales by size and color have been entered daily by cross-hatching of the tally marks, appropriately noting any returns that have been made. Daily and weekly unit sales have also been entered so that stock on hand can be readily computed. The result is a detailed day-by-day record of how this style is selling by size and color.

DAILY SALES

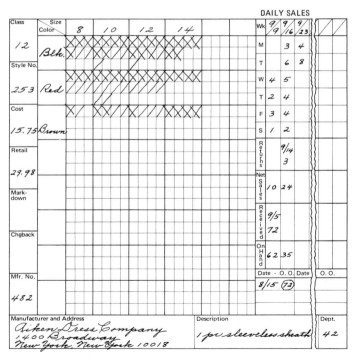

223

could see that he underestimated the demand for larger sizes and for black. If he reorders, he will note the date and number of pieces in the "O.O." (On Order) section of the card, again making appropriate pencil tally marks to indicate the colors and sizes ordered.

Status summaries of sales and inventory investment may be calculated at any given time from the perpetual inventory records, sometimes with the previous year's figures also presented for comparison purposes. These are usually issued weekly or monthly, and they may be either manually or electronically prepared. Forms 13-3 and 13-4 are data processed rather than manually prepared. Price lines, rather than specific style numbers, are analyzed, together with classification subtotals and the department totals.

Whatever the exact method, the perpetual inventory system enables the merchant to compare the total number of units sold of each style or group of styles from day to day and week to week, as well as to know the total number of units sold thus far in the season. The importance of this knowledge becomes apparent if one considers the example of two styles, each of which has had sales of 60 pieces during a ten-week period. If weekly sales figures are available, a situation like the one in Table 13-4 becomes obvious: one style is dwindling in acceptance while the other is growing in popularity. Without such weekly figures, this important difference can be missed.

Table 13-4. Sales of Two Separate Styles

| | Units Sold | |
	Style A	Style B
Week #1	10	2
Week #2	10	2
Week #3	10	2
Week #4	8	3
Week #5	7	5
Week #6	6	7
Week #7	3	8
Week #8	2	8
Week #9	2	10
Week #10	2	13
Total, 10 Weeks	60	60

Periodic Stock Control A unit control system in which stock is counted and recorded at regular intervals and sales for the intervening period are computed is a *periodic stock count control*. Such a system is best suited to the control of relatively staple types of merchandise, such as children's socks, women's tailored slips, some cosmetics, handbags, hosiery, notions, and other fast-moving items that are relatively low in price and stable in demand. Cost of operation is less than for a perpetual inventory system.

In periodic stock control, sales are not recorded as they occur but are calculated from inventory changes occurring between one count and the next. The information yielded is neither as accurate nor as detailed as that provided by perpetual inventory systems. It is sufficient, however, to indicate trends and to show when replenishments are needed.

In such a system, the stock is counted at regular intervals, the length of the interval depending upon demand and supply factors, and the amount on hand is noted. Also noted are any amounts received into stock since the last count was taken. Sales are calculated as follows:

sales = stock at last count + merchandise receipts since last count − stock at present count

This type of system permits the merchant to analyze the rate of sale of specific items during successive periods, to see if sales are holding steady, gaining, or falling off. The same system can also be used in categories served by perpetual inventory systems as a check on rate of sale. For example, instead of counting the number of pieces of each individual style, the merchant may periodically count the number of cocktail dresses, theater coats, or garments of some other general type in stock. Such figures give him a broad view of demand, one that he might miss by focusing attention only on the details of experience with each of many individual styles in each category.

The common procedure for periodic counts is to divide the stock into sections and specify the dates on which specific counts are to be made. Responsibility for making these counts is distributed among the various salespeople and assistants. By dividing the work in this way, no one person or no one day is overburdened.

SALES REPORT

WEEK JAN. 24-31, 19—

REPORT #1

CODE	PRICE RANGE	DEPT.—CASUAL DRESSES	WEEK		MONTH TO DATE	
			UNITS	$	UNITS	$
700	8.98	DRESSES-MISSY	17	153.00	61	549.00
702	10.98	DRESSES-MISSY	20	220.00	40	440.00
704	13.98	DRESSES-MISSY	25	350.00	56	784.00
706	19.98	DRESSES-MISSY	20	400.00	78	1,560.00
707	26.98	DRESSES-MISSY	8	216.00	34	918.00
708	36.98	DRESSES-MISSY	4	148.00	17	629.00
		TOTAL MISSY	94	1,487.00	286	4,880.00
710	8.98	DRESSES-JUNIOR	22	198.00	76	684.00
712	10.98	DRESSES-JUNIOR	27	297.00	95	1,045.00
714	13.98	DRESSES-JUNIOR	21	294.00	81	1,134.00
716	19.98	DRESSES-JUNIOR	10	200.00	42	840.00
		TOTAL JUNIOR	80	989.00	294	3,703.00
		TOTAL CASUAL DRESSES	174	2,476.00	580	8,583.00

Both forms Courtesy NRMA

Form 13-3

SALES AND INVENTORY REPORT

MONTH ENDING JAN. 31, 19—

REPORT #2

CODE	PRICE RANGE	DEPT.—CASUAL DRESSES	E.O.M. BALANCE 1/1/—	PURCHASES $	SALES $	MARK UP/ DOWNS $	MARK UP/ DOWNS % TO SALES	E.O.M. BALANCE 1/31/—	PURCHASES TO DATE	SALES TO DATE	MARK UP/ DOWNS TO DATE
700	8.98	DRESSES-MISSY	742.00	608.00	549.00	30.00	5.4	771.00	3,120.00	2,760.00	146.00
702	10.98	DRESSES-MISSY	616.00	480.00	440.00	35.00	8.0	621.00	2,390.00	2,307.00	175.00
704	13.98	DRESSES-MISSY	1,320.00	925.00	784.00	49.00	6.3	1,412.00	4,625.00	3,820.00	250.00
706	19.98	DRESSES-MISSY	3,214.00	1,726.00	1,560.00	179.00	11.5	3,201.00	8,630.00	7,800.00	898.00
707	26.98	DRESSES-MISSY	2,087.00	1,100.00	918.00	149.00	16.2	2,120.00	5,420.00	4,582.00	750.00
708	36.98	DRESSES-MISSY	1,485.00	610.00	629.00	57.00	9.00	1,409.00	3,080.00	3,050.00	294.00
		TOTAL MISSY	9,464.00	5,449.00	4,880.00	499.00	10.2	9,534.00	27,265.00	24,319.00	2,513.00
710	8.98	DRESSES-JUNIOR	700.00	520.00	684.00	42.00	6.1	494.00	2,600.00	3,542.00	210.00
712	10.98	DRESSES-JUNIOR	1,493.00	1,100.00	1,045.00	84.00	8.0	1,464.00	5,625.00	5,225.00	418.00
714	13.98	DRESSES-JUNIOR	1,970.00	1,320.00	1,134.00	130.00	11.4	2,026.00	6,700.00	5,570.00	647.00
716	19.98	DRESSES-JUNIOR	2,143.00	1,008.00	840.00	60.00	8.1	2,251.00	5,030.00	4,100.00	301.00
		TOTAL JUNIOR	6,306.00	3,948.00	3,703.00	316.00	8.5	6,235.00	19,955.00	18,437.00	1,576.00
		TOTAL CASUAL DRESSES	15,770.00	9,397.00	8,583.00	815.00		15,769.00	47,220.00	42,756.00	4,089.00

Form 13-4

225

								Coverage	
Class	Style	Cost	Unit Retail	Description	Color	Min. Pack		Min.	Max.
268	140	14.50 dz.	$2.00	Stretch glove	White	1 dz.		12	36
268	140	14.50 dz.	$2.00	Stretch glove	Blue	1 dz.		12	24
268	140	14.50 dz.	$2.00	Stretch glove	Red	1 dz.		12	24

Department No. 15

Vendor Ricci Glove Company
Gloversville, New York

Ship via Lee Transport

Manufacturer No. 123

Terms 2/10/E.O.M.

Form 13-5 (left-hand page)

The most convenient way to keep such records is in a loose-leaf notebook with a pair of facing pages assigned to each group of items. (See Form 13-5.) On the left-hand page are listed style numbers, classification, description, vendor's name and address, cost and retail prices, minimum packing for each item, and other details needed for writing up an order. Also noted are the minimum and maximum quantities of each item that should be in stock.

The basic or model stock of an item usually serves as the basis for determining the minimum quantity that should always be in stock. In determining the maximum desirable quantity of each style, the merchant first projects the sales that are expected to be made between one count and the next. Next he estimates the delivery period—the average time required for a reorder to be shipped and received into stock. He also must allow a *cushion* or *reserve* for unexpected delays either in the placing of reorders or in their delivery. He then calculates his reorder as follows:

$$\text{maximum quantity} = \text{estimated weekly rate of sale} \\ \times \text{(delivery + cushion periods)} \\ + \text{minimum stock quantity}$$

For example, in Form 13-5, the weekly rate of sale of style 140, white, is found to be 6. In this case the delivery period is two weeks. If the cushion is set at two weeks and the minimum quantity of stock at 12, then:

$$\text{maximum quantity} = 6 \ (2 + 2) + 12 \\ = 36$$

Stock counts are reviewed immediately after they are taken, and each item that is at or near its minimum is reordered at once. At all times the quantity of an item on hand and on order should approximate the maximum quantities established for it if stocks are to be maintained in direct relation to demand.

The minimum packing for each item is a factor to consider in reordering. An item may be retailed individually but purchased by the half-dozen, the dozen, or the gross. Makers may ship quantities as small as the half-dozen or the dozen, but the cost of ordering and paying shipping charges on such small orders may make it wiser to order in lots of three or six dozen.

Classification, style number, description, color, cost and retail prices, minimum packing, and minimum and maximum stock units needed—all these points are noted on the left-hand page of this type of control form. The information is a guide for the merchant and for any assistant to whom the task of preparing reorders of fairly staple goods may be delegated.

Department _15._

Manufacturer No. _123_

Class	Style	Date 9/7				Date 9/21				Date 10/5			
		O.H.	O.O. 9/10	Rec. 9/20	Sold	O.H.	O.O. 9/23	Rec. 10/2	Sold	O.H.	O.O. 10/7	Rec. 10/17	Sold
268	White 140	20	(12)	12	10	22	(12)	12	12	22	(12)	12	
268	Blue 140	20			8	12	(12)	12	4	20			
268	Red 140	30			10	20			8	12	(12)	12	

Form 13-5 (right-hand page)

On the right-hand page, entries are made of the quantities on hand and on order on the dates assigned for counts, and of merchandise receipts since the last count. Finally, sales are calculated for the period since the last count. The right-hand page is often punched in both margins so that it can be turned and used on the second side. This page carries only the briefest identification of the items, often only a page number, since all necessary details are on the facing page.

The right-hand page is usually columnar with blocks of columns assigned to each reorder count and with space above each block for the date on which the count was made. The columns are usually headed:

OH   (amounts on hand when count was made)
OO   (any order placed since last count was made)
REC   (merchandise received since last count was made)
SOLD   (sales made between counts, a figure calculated by adding receipts to previous count and then subtracting present count)

Reserve Requisition Control For fast-moving, low-priced items, particularly those that are packaged, *reserve requisition control* is often used. This is a form of periodic stock count control in which the stock on the selling floor is considered sold and only the reserve stock is counted. A reasonable amount of stock is kept on the selling floor, but the main supply is in a remote reserve stockroom. As the forward (selling floor) stock runs low, more is requisitioned from the reserve.

Under this system, sales can be calculated by adding up the requisitions and by considering as sold everything that has reached the selling floor. Periodic counts of stock can be made, but only the reserve stock is counted.

Whether the system is run by requisition checking or by counting the stock in reserve, either method facilitates counting and recording of fast-moving merchandise. It is much faster, for example, to count one carton of 144 pairs of hosiery in the reserve stock than to make a count on the selling floor of 48 separate boxes, each containing three pairs. And it is much easier to record requisitions for 36 pairs of one style and 24 pairs of another than to record possibly 30 individual sales transactions involving the same 60 pairs.

Visual Control What merchants call "eyeball control" or *visual control* is another form of periodic stock count control. It involves the assigning of a rack or bin to each style, size, or classification, and a periodic check to see if any one of these bins or racks looks too empty or too full.

Berry's

Fifth Avenue at 56th Street
New York, New York

STORE NAME	DEPT. NO.	ORDER NO.
Berry's	42	M 184925

BILLING, PACKING, AND SHIPPING REQUIREMENTS
1. INVOICE MUST BE ENCLOSED WITH SHIPMENT, AND CARTON CONTAINING INVOICE MUST BE SO MARKED ON THE OUTSIDE
2. MERCHANDISE FOR TWO OR MORE DEPARTMENTS, SHIPPED AT THE SAME TIME, MUST BE BILLED AND PACKED SEPARATELY, AND INVOICES AND CARTONS PLAINLY MARKED FOR THE SEPARATE DEPARTMENTS. HOWEVER, ALL SUCH SHIPMENTS MUST BE COMBINED UNDER ONE BILL OF LADING.
3. DEPARTMENT, ORDER NUMBER AND WEIGHT MUST BE SHOWN ON THE INDIVIDUAL CONTAINERS.
4. ALL GARMENT PACKAGES MUST CONTAIN COLOR AND SIZE LISTS BY STYLE NUMBER

NAME _Aiken Dress Company_
ADDRESS _1400 Broadway_
CITY AND STATE _New York, New York 10018_

TERMS _8/10 EOM_

WITH ANTICIPATION FOR PREPAYMENT

DATE OF ORDER	DUE DATE AT STORE	CANCEL BY	HOUSE NUMBER
8/15/-	9/10/-	9/10 Will be cancelled or shipment returned at vendor's expense.	482

SHIP TO: _Main Store_
Fifth Avenue at 56th Street
New York, New York

STYLE NUMBER	CODE OR CLASS	DIS. LETTER	DESCRIPTION	8	10	12	14	TOTAL QUANTITY	UNIT COST	TOTAL COST	UNIT RETAIL
253	12		1 pc sleeveless sheath								
			Black	6	9	9	6	30	15 75	1,134.00	
			Red	6	10	8	4	28			
			Brown	2	4	4	4	14			
								72			

SIZES

ROUTING INSTRUCTIONS

FOLLOW OUR ROUTING - WE CHARGE BACK ANY EXCESS TRANSPORTATION COSTS TO YOU.
☐ F.O.B. STORE NAMED OR WAREHOUSE
☐ 1 TO 20 LBS. - PARCEL POST DIRECT TO STORE - DO NOT INSURE
☐ 21 TO 50 LBS. - REA EXPRESS DIRECT TO STORE - MINIMUM VALUE (SPECIFY COMMODITY TARIFF ON WAYBILL)

OVER 50 LBS. (TRUCK ROUTING) _IOU Service_

SPECIAL ROUTING INSTRUCTIONS _Hanger Service_

VALUATION EXCEPTION: NO DECLARATION OF VALUE IS TO BE MADE BY THE VENDOR EXCEPT ON FURS AND JEWELRY, IN WHICH CASE ACTUAL VALUE UP TO $1000 SHOULD BE DECLARED.

FORM 312 REV. 12-63

This order subject to conditions of purchase appearing on the reverse side and is a contract only when confirmed by merchandise office signature.

GRAND TOTAL COST	1,134.00
GRAND TOTAL RETAIL	
% MARK UP	

Jane Dean DEPT. MGR.
T. J. Evans DIV. MDSE. MGR.

Form 13-6

The merchant makes an on-the-spot judgment about action to be taken as he checks the bins and racks.

Fashion merchandise does not lend itself usually to visual control. The only exception is a very small operation in which the proprietor's memory represents the record. One other exception might be the boutique or specialty shop catering to customers who want one-of-a-kind items or the newest and most exotic styles.

The Mechanics of Unit Control

Unit control involves setting up procedures for collecting data on additions to or subtractions from the stock, from the time an order is placed with a vendor through the time the item is sold to a customer. The principal sources of such information include purchase orders, receiving records, sales records, merchandise transfers, returns and cancellations, and price changes. How each is used in a unit control system is described.

Purchase Orders When a purchase order is placed, the store owner or buyer retains one or more carbons for reference and for making appropriate entries in the unit control records. (See Form 13-6.) The amount of information entered in the records depends upon the type of system used. In general, however, the purchase order is the source of such important control information as:

▫ Date of order

▫ Department number

▫ Classification of merchandise ordered

▫ Vendor's name and address

▫ Number and description of styles ordered

▫ Cost and retail prices of each style

▫ Quantities ordered

▫ Details of color and size, if any

Multi-unit stores, such as department or specialty stores with several branches, usually prepare order forms with separate sets of columns for each unit for which the merchandise is bought. In this way, a single order can cover purchases made in behalf of as many locations as are to be served. All but the last two items on the list above are descriptive of the order as a whole. In the columns assigned to each individual unit, however, quantities and applicable details of color and size are specified for each location. The more units to be served, the wider the form becomes. With such a form, however, the buyer can see as he places an order whether or not he has planned a balanced assortment of styles, sizes, and colors for each unit. When the goods are received at the store, the order specifies how the buyer wants the goods to be distributed among the various branches.

Receiving Records Good retail practice requires that a record be made of each piece of merchandise received by a store. (See Form 13-7.) A copy of this record is turned over to the unit control clerk, who updates the "On Order" entry with another entry indicating the number of pieces received and the date on which they were received. If the total order is received, some systems merely circle the "On Order" entry to indicate its receipt.

The many purposes served by receiving records can be observed by examining Form 13-7. The form shown is in two parts: one above and one below the horizontal dotted line. In the upper right-hand corner of both parts is a number, one of a consecutive series, that is assigned to an incoming shipment and that is used for all future identification of that particular shipment.

The left-hand section of the upper part of the receiving form provides space for information that will be needed by the accounting department in processing the invoice for payment, including the buyer's approval or exceptions. The right-hand corner of this upper part has space for recording the number of cartons or packages comprising the shipment, the name of the carrier, and the date of its delivery to the store. When this upper part of the receiving form is attached to an invoice, it becomes an *apron,* a form designed for information and signatures required by the accounting department before it enters an invoice on the store's books.

The bottom part of the receiving form provides space for itemizing the merchandise received and indicating how many of each size and color have been counted. (Some printed forms have two or three printed size scales. The receiving clerk cancels those that do not apply; if necessary, he cancels all three and writes in an appropriate scale.) From this information, the order can be checked, and the work of making out price tickets and affixing them to the merchandise can proceed. When this lower section, or a carbon of it, is passed to the unit control clerk, it supplies the details needed to keep the style cards up to date.

Sales Records In perpetual control systems, the unit control clerk receives for every sale either a sales check or a price ticket stub identifying the article sold. This information is then manually recorded on the appropriate style sheet. (In periodic control systems, sales figures are not recorded as they occur. Instead, the sales for a specific period are calculated as the difference between one inventory count and the next.)

Some of the new electronic systems eliminate the manual recording of sales. When a salesper-

RECEIVING RECORD

No. 16181

Received From *Aiken Dress Company*

Address *1400 Broadway* City *New York, New York 10018*

Date Received *9/5/—*

Department	Order No.	Transportation Charges		Buyers Approval or Remarks	Received Via
		Total Paid	Charge Shipper		
42	*M 58957*	*14.40*		*Jane Dean*	*I O U Service*

Due Date	Terms	Invoice Passed	Discount		Amt. of Invoice	Retail Value	Pkg's.	Pieces	Cartons
9/10	*8/10 EOM*	*9/10/—*	*8/10 EOM*	*$90.72*	*$1,134*	*$2,158.56*		*72 (hangers)*	

ATTACH INVOICE HERE

- -

Received From *Aiken Dress Company*

No. 16181

Mfg. No.	Unit Cost	Color	Description	Size						Quantity		Class	Unit Price
				8	10	12	14			Amt.	Unit		
482	*15.75*	*Blk.*	*Style 253*	6	9	9	6			*30*	*ea*	*12*	*29.98*
482	*15.75*	*Red*	*Style 253*	6	10	8	4			*28*	*ea*	*12*	*29.98*
482	*15.75*	*Bro.*	*Style 253*	2	4	4	4			*14*	*ea*	*12*	*29.98*

Order Checked	Mdse. Checked	Price Tickets	Mdse. Marked	Cost Extension	Retail Extension	Merchandise Received	
						Stock Room	Department
H L C.	*F. B. J.*	*n d C.*	*m n d*	*$1,134.00*	*$2,158.56*	*a g C*	

Form 13-7

son rings up a transaction on one of the newer cash registers, a tape showing price, style number, and other control information is produced that can be fed directly into a computer. The computer, having previously been fed "On Order" and "Received" information, automatically adjusts the inventory figures.

Merchandise Transfers Departmentalized stores frequently transfer merchandise from one department to another and from one store or branch to another unit. Special forms are used to report such transactions. Transfers are equivalent to sales for the department or location releasing the goods and equivalent to purchases for the one receiving them. Form 13-8 illustrates a report of the movement of merchandise between the various locations in a branch-owning store. An ap-

No. E 54165

BRANCH STORE TRANSFER

From *Main* To *Westchester*

Dept. *42* Date *September 7, 19—*

Style	Description	Qty.	Retail Unit	Retail Extension
253	*1 pc sheath*	*12*	*29 98*	*359 76*
	8 10 12 14			
	Black 1 1 1 1			
	Red 1 1 1 1			
	Brown 1 1 1 1			

Written by *Janet Bauer*

Checked by *Paula Anders* Container *38*

Form 13-8

propriate entry for all such merchandise transfers is made on the unit control record and, in some cases, depending on the store's accounting system, also on the firm's books to indicate changes in the value of inventories of both the issuing and the receiving locations.

Returns and Cancellations When merchandise is returned by a store to a vendor, a form known as a *charge-back* is issued. (See Form 13–9.) A charge-back is the equivalent of a store's bill covering the merchandise returned to its vendor.

Copies of these forms go to the unit control clerk, so that stock totals of individual styles may be appropriately decreased. Should a customer make a return to the store, a *credit slip* is issued. A copy of this credit form goes to the unit control clerk, who adds the returned article to the record of the total currently in stock.

All returns are carefully recorded on the forms used in perpetual inventory control. If periodic stock count is the control method used, however, small adjustments like these are usually ignored. Only a charge-back of major proportions, such

Form 13-9

as the return of an entire shipment, is likely to be entered.

Form 13-10 illustrates a typical *order cancellation*. Whether or not a special form is used for cancellation of an order, a covering entry must be made promptly on the control forms so that whoever studies the controls will not mistakenly think that an additional supply of merchandise is still on order.

Price Changes Unit control records indicate the retail prices at which articles are placed in stock as well as any price changes that may occur thereafter. In most stores, a special form is required for reporting all changes in retail prices. (See Form 13-11.) Copies of these forms are routed to the unit control clerk as well as to the inventory control office.

Advantages of Unit Control

In evaluating unit control, a truer picture is gained if it is realized that the word "control" is somewhat of a misnomer. A better term would be "unit records," since the systems merely record and report but do not exert control. Traditional trade terms are not readily changed, however.

The striking virtue of unit control is that these records make it possible for a buyer to refer to a detailed picture of sales and inventory while sitting at his desk or working in the market. The records are usually maintained in terms of style numbers, and the data on each style card or periodic stock count record can be compiled into reports that show department-wide sales by price line, vendor, size, color, or whatever other feature is relevant. Thus a buyer can go into the market armed with such facts as: most of Vendor A's

---

No. 18101

To *Aiken Dress Company*
1400 Broadway
New York, New York 10018

Berry's

CANCELLATION

Date *September 7, 19—*
Dept. No. *42*

We regret we are obliged to cancel the items listed below from our order number *M-58963* placed *8/16/—* for delivery *by 9/15/—*

Reason *Failure to ship merchandise by cancellation date*

STYLE NO.	DESCRIPTION	QUANTITY	COST	EXTENSION
409	2 pc. pleated shirt, long sleeve	24	14.75	354.00

Signed *Jane Dean* _____ Buyer
Approved *T. J. Evans* _____ Merchandise Manager

Form 13-10

232

(X) TO SHOW TYPE

X	MARK-DOWN
	CANCELLATION OF MARK-DOWN
	ADDITIONAL MARK-UP

PRICE CHANGE

DEPT. NO. 42

B 29001

DATE August 10, 19—

ISSUE SEPARATE SHEETS FOR MARK-DOWN CANCELLATION, MARK-UP, STOLEN, AND SALVAGE ITEMS.

SHOW REASON BY LETTER		ORIGINAL MARK-DOWN NUMBER	CLASS	ITEM DESCRIPTION VENDOR — STYLE	QUANTITY	SEA. LET.	VERIFIED QUANTITY	OLD RETAIL	NEW RETAIL	DIFFERENCE	AMOUNT
A. PROMOTIONAL PURCHASE REMAINDERS	E	—	17	Cotton lace, 385, No. 1120	4	M	4	25 00	18 00	7 00	28 00
	F	—	12	Sleeveless print, 482 No. 491	3	M	3	23 00	15 00	8 00	24 00
B. SLOW MOVING OR INACTIVE STOCK											
C. SPECIAL SALES FROM STOCK											
D. PRICE ADJUSTMENTS											
E. BROKEN ASSORTMENTS AND REMNANTS											
F. SHOPWORN, SOILED OR DAMAGED											
G. ALLOWANCE TO CUSTOMER											
H. STOLEN											
J. SALVAGE											

DO NOT ENTER ANY PRICE CHANGES BELOW THIS LINE

DEPT. MGR'S SIGNATURE	DATE	MDSE. V. P. OR MGR'S SIGNATURE	DATE	MARKER'S SIGNATURE	DATE		TOTAL	52 00
Jane Dean	8/10	T. J. Evans	8/10	Ann Hogan	8/12			

Form 13-11

numbers had to be reordered, while most of Vendor B's had to be marked down before they could be sold; fewer size 16s were sold this season than in the previous one; or the department sold as many $20 units this year as last.

Facts, rather than memory, provide a dependable guide to the nature of consumer demand, even in the immediate past. And facts make it possible for a merchant to keep track of all the varied ramifications of consumer demand in an operation of vast size or widely dispersed units.

Properly used, unit control systems also contain a built-in reminder element that encourages action when conditions require it. Periodic stock counts and periodic reports of sales by price line or other factors serve also as reminders to the merchant to check the assortment for completeness and balance against the current indications of consumer demand.

Assortment planning, like the dollar merchandise budget, is necessarily subject to change if conditions show that the original guidelines need adjustment. Unit control records and reports provide the means of checking a plan against actuality at intervals.

Disadvantages of Unit Control

Unit control systems, however, are not always properly run or properly used, and there are some jobs the systems cannot do.

In working with unit controls, carelessness anywhere along the line can result in inaccurate and therefore misleading figures. This is true even with electronically figured data, since the computer digests only the information fed into it. If it is fed wrong stock counts and incomplete or inaccurate sales reports, it will turn out inaccurate reports.

Manual systems are slow, and the clerks handling them may be so far behind in their work that their reports are of little use by the time the buyers receive them. Electronic systems, on the other hand, are sometimes unwisely planned to give so much detail and give it so frequently that the merchant is drowned in data and unable to digest all that is put before him.

Unit control involves substantial costs, particularly when used for fast-paced fashion merchandise. But cost is a relative factor. In general, a merchant weighs the cost of maintaining unit controls against the benefits to be derived from them. If a store provides its buyers with good unit control data that they do not use, it has a costly system indeed. On the other hand, if a buyer is deprived of unit control information and must plan an assortment by guesswork, the store is practicing a costly economy.

There is one very important indication of consumer demand that unit control systems cannot reveal: what items, colors, or sizes customers wanted to buy but could not because they were not present in the assortment. Up to a point, the control records do show unfilled demand, in that they show that a number enjoyed brisk sales, then was out of stock for a week or two, and when restocked resumed its brisk sales. They do not show the requests made by customers for merchandise that never was a part of the assortment. The only ways buyers can find out about these unfilled wants of customers is through want slips, customer surveys, or competitive shopping, all discussed in Chapter 11.

Classification Merchandising

"A *classification* is an assortment of items, all of which are reasonably substitutable for each other to the customer when she is buying for a specific end-use." This is the definition of the National Retail Merchants Association, the group that standardized classification merchandising categories, thus increasing this system's usefulness as a highly sophisticated retail tool. Merchandising by classification is used by retail management to balance assortments against demand; to balance promotional efforts, selling space, and sales help against sales and demand; and to evaluate buyer performance.

The objectives of classification merchandising are:

□ To identify trends in demand

□ To provide a common language for the exchange of information

□ To provide control in relating stocks to sales, with resulting better turnover, fewer markdowns, and increased sales

□ To make possible supplier preticketing and cooperation in inventory replenishment[3]

History and Development

The forerunners of classifications were *dissections*. A dissection was any portion of a departmental inventory for which a buyer kept separate records, usually of sales and usually set up in terms of markets patronized. Just before a market trip the buyer would arm himself with last-minute sales and stock information for each dissection. Thus the dress buyer, for instance, might come to market prepared with separate sales figures for silks, woolens, and cottons, and a current inventory evaluation for each. If a few individual vendors were highlighted in a buyer's scheme of things, each vendor's line might constitute a separate dissection.

The methods used for collecting data were crude but adequate for the purpose at that time. Vendors and markets were generally specialized; coat manufacturers did not make dresses, and neckwear sources did not make blouses. A buyer could total up his purchases at retail from the various vendors within a dissection, subtract the stock on hand of that dissection, and have a dissection sales figure for the season. Another method was to require salespeople, at the end of each day, to total their sales slips by dissection. This was not yet the age of the many-branched stores, nor was it a period when salespeople could command a substantial enough rate of pay so that the extra clerical work was costly.

Since World War II, however, more sophisticated, consumer-oriented procedures for collecting merchandise data have become necessary as a result of such developments as these:

□ Consumer wants have become increasingly diverse, and a vast, rapidly changing variety of goods is produced to satisfy those wants.

□ Customers tend to buy from want rather than need. Many customers have adequate wardrobes and, if they cannot find what they want, there is no reason for them to compromise and buy something not fully acceptable. Pleasing the customer, therefore, requires great accuracy in analyzing and meeting demand.

□ Because department and specialty stores have more branches and employ more part-time sales help than they did in the past, buyers no longer have much time for direct contact with customers or the salespeople who serve them, or even with the stock on the selling floor. Records have become indispensable to keep buyers abreast of what their customers are buying or not buying.

□ Similar merchandise is being produced in many markets as manufacturers diversify their output. Similar merchandise is also being carried in more than one department of the store, even if the store is only of moderate size.

Under these circumstances, the dissection has proved too crude a tool to provide an accurate picture of fashion demand and how it is being met. Departmental figures, too, are unable to yield information that is precise enough to constitute a useful guide to fashion demand, for such figures embrace many subdivisions and the ups and downs of the individual components are concealed. Vendor records are also inadequate, since they too may include diverse types of merchandise. Unit controls offer more detail, but they are often slow and the detail they offer is so concerned with individual style numbers that trends do not stand out sharply and quickly.

In contrast, the classification system is geared for today's merchandising scene. It is consumer-oriented, for it classifies merchandise in terms of consumer end-use. It is also store buyer-oriented, for it groups merchandise into the categories buyers want to watch for trends in demand. A classification would comprise, for example, dressy coats or casual hosiery. It would not consist of Vendor X's line, style number 123, or a specific material or price line. From the customer's point of view, one dressy coat is a reasonable substitute for another, regardless of vendor. In the same way, one pair of casual hose may substitute for another—but not for a pair of sheer stockings from the same maker. Classifications have subdivisions within them, but the

objective in setting them up is to keep even these finer breakdowns broad and uncluttered by detail so that trends in demand stand out clearly.

While the theory of classification merchandising was bolstered by the gradual change in the marketing concept, the adoption of this system of inventory control by stores has been made considerably easier because of the advances in recordkeeping equipment. The major time and expense costs lie in setting up the system. Once the system has been set up and the equipment programmed to handle it, it becomes very close to automatic. Electronic data processing equipment, for instance, can capture the necessary sales information right at the point of sale, automatically accumulating and analyzing that information, and feeding out reports tailored to merchandise management needs.

Procedures

In using classifications to plan and control a fashion assortment, the merchant usually works with both unit and dollar figures. A 1960 study made in large department stores showed that 65 percent of those employing classification data used both types of information; 26 percent used unit data only; 9 percent worked with dollar figures alone.[4]

Standard classifications divide department store merchandise into four levels of merchandise breakdowns. These four levels are:

1. *Merchandise Groups:* Major group, first-level break, analogous to divisions of a store. Example: Adult female apparel.
2. *Demand Centers:* Family group, second-level break within each merchandise group, analogous to departments in the store. Example: Women's and misses' dressy coats within adult female apparel group.
3. *Classes* or *Classifications:* Third-level break, related to groups or assortments of items that are related for end-use purposes within a demand center. Example: Coat ensembles within the women's and misses' dressy coat demand center.
4. *Categories* or *Subclassifications:* Fourth-level break, items that are interchangeable from the customer's point of view. This level is not standardized but provides a basis for the store's own

internal merchandising and control in greater detail. Example: Brocade coat ensembles within the coat ensemble class.[5]

The appropriate classification number of each item is printed on its price ticket. As each item is sold, the salesperson assigns the sale to its proper classification by making an extra notation on the sales check or by striking a special key on the cash register.

Dollar merchandise budgets and open-to-buy figures are calculated by classification rather than by department in some stores, and are calculated by classification in addition to departmental figures in others. Assortment planning is done by classification and by price line or other subdivisions within each classification.

Thus a buyer of coats might develop merchandise budgets separately for women's and misses' dressy coats and for women's and misses' casual coats. Within the dressy coat demand center, the buyer might further break down his budget into classes, such as lightweight, trimmed winterweight, untrimmed winterweight, and coat ensembles. For each of these classes, the budget might again be broken down into fabric content, texture, price lines, bright colors versus dark colors, or whatever additional broad divisions were relevant to that season. The casual coat budget would be similarly divided. As the season progressed, purchases, sales, and inventory records would be maintained for the designated classifications and subclassifications. If, in the course of a season, any classification or subclassification showed sales that differed markedly from expectations, the buyer would have reason to investigate.

Evaluation of the Classification Method

Adoption of the classification method of inventory control entails certain advantages and disadvantages for the fashion merchant. Advantages are that it makes consumer-oriented data available; it indicates the broad outlines of demand; it makes exchange of data with other stores possible; and it permits the retailer to use price tickets applied by the resource. A few of these advantages, however, have related disadvantages, which have to be taken into account.

Consumer-Oriented Data   That classifications organize data in terms of consumer end-use is an advantage to the fashion merchant. The figures are consumer-oriented and thus are clear indicators of customer demand. Yet setting up a classification system and living with it involve a change from the merchant's traditional habit of thinking in terms of departments, markets, and resources, and that change may be hard to make.

Absence of Confusing Detail   The absence of detail makes the collection of classification data faster and less costly than more traditional systems. The corresponding disadvantage is that to investigate a problem or opportunity that has been highlighted by classification data, the merchant must turn for details to other sources, such as unit controls or discussions with salespeople.

For example, assume that the casual hosiery classification shows marked sales increases. For the buyer to find out just which styles and colors are enjoying the sharpest increases, he must study his unit control records, check his actual stock, discuss the condition with salespeople, or do all three. Only then might he discover, for example, that browns in all patterns and cable-stitch styles in all colors were responsible for the upsurge in sales.

To continue with this example, assume that another hosiery buyer does not have classification data but simply organizes his unit controls by brand and price. He would see an upsurge in sales, but he could not readily pinpoint it as a demand for casuals. Many of his brands and price lines would include both casual and dressy stockings. All brands and price lines could conceivably show increases. Only when this buyer analyzed his vendor-oriented data, style by style, would he see the development that was quickly obvious to the first buyer: a great demand for casual hosiery.

Exchange of Data   Until 1967, classification categories were not standardized, and merchants had no way of comparing their figures with those of other stores with whom they exchanged such information. In 1967, however, the National Retail Merchants Association published *Standard Classifications,* and established the basis needed for exchange of data. This standardization guide also laid the groundwork for exchange of classification data between retailers and producers, an exchange that is becoming increasingly popular.

In most cases, a resource assigns classification numbers to his merchandise, sometimes setting up subclassifications of particular interest to the stores with which he deals. As store buyers place their orders for merchandise, those orders are analyzed by classification for the first indications of trend patterns. As sales occur in the stores, the retailers feed back the retail sales data to the resource, giving the resource an accurate picture of customer preferences from a number of stores almost as soon as the sales are made. The resource is then able to feed back general trend information to the individual stores, as well as to adjust design and production plans to meet the upcoming changes in customer demand.

In the case of staple stocks, the tie-in can be even closer between store and resource. An automatic reorder system for basics can be set up by the store and linked to the resource by computer, so that sales data are fed directly to the resource and the resource is authorized to ship replacement stock whenever the sales data indicate that the stock has diminished to a specified level.

Preticketing and Other Advantages For stores that make extensive use of classification data, there are still more benefits:

□ Industry preticketing, a rising tide that began in fairly staple goods, is now reaching fashion merchandise. Its development is closely tied to the spread of classification controls. Instead of each store marking and punching the sales tickets for its goods, the manufacturers from whom the articles are purchased do this work on a large scale, with obvious economy. (See Form 13-12a.) The more uniform the classifications used among stores, the more producers will supply the service.

□ The system enables the store's entire assortment to be reviewed readily to check for merchandise duplications or omissions. A classification is sometimes carried in several departments of a store, each duplicating the others' assortments to some extent, and all ignoring some areas in which demand is light but should be met. A classifica-

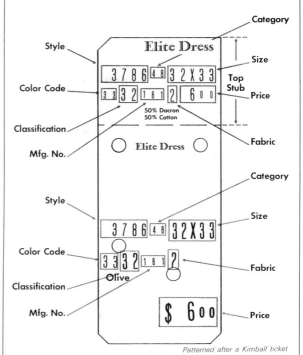

Form 13-12A: Resources can print and punch unit control data on price tickets for stores, using industry-adopted numerical codes.

tion system pinpoints such a situation promptly so that it can be corrected.

□ Areas of both good performance and poor performance can be seen promptly by management and then acted upon. Because departmental figures include the results of handling many kinds of merchandise, they do not give as clear a picture of trends, profits, and deficiencies.

Assortment Planning and Control in Multi-Unit Stores

Multi-unit stores are of two types, each with different problems in and different methods of assortment planning and control. These types are (1) branch-operating department and specialty stores and (2) chain organizations. Although the two types of stores traditionally have had almost opposing methods of organizational responsibility for buying and selling, both are gradually

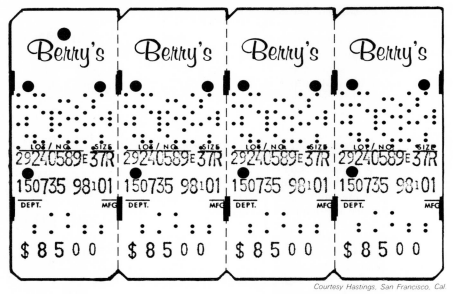

Courtesy Hastings, San Francisco, Cal.

Form 13-12B: Garment price tickets, print-punched by store, has four identical stubs. First is to report sales; second, for any returns; other, for resale and re-return.

modifying those methods. They are still very different types of organization, but not as different as they once were.

Branch-Owning Department and Specialty Stores

The planning and control systems used by branch-owning department and specialty stores are essentially those described above. Merchandising is done by the parent organization; the branches concentrate their efforts on selling. Buyers at the parent store plan the assortments, making adjustments to differences in the pattern of demand among the various branches. If the branches are large, or distant, or numerous, there is usually separate merchandise budgeting, separate assortment planning, and separate unit controls for each branch. Records are centralized so that the buyers have ready access to them at their offices.

Recordkeeping and reporting forms and procedures are much the same as for a single store, although an additional line or column is added for each branch and for the total of the entire group of stores. Variations in consumer demand among the branches are studied closely, and assortments are planned accordingly.

For example, one branch may be at the shore and enjoy a continuing, strong demand for beach and boating wear from early spring well into the fall. Another branch may be in a suburb where fairly formal social activities, centering around home and country clubs, continue throughout the summer, and there the demand may be for dressier clothes rather than for fashions designed for active sports. In a third location, customers may have fallen into the habit of buying casual clothes at the branch and formal or better ready-to-wear at the main store. All such factors have to be taken into consideration when assortments are planned for a parent store and its branches.

If a retail store has only a single branch, management does very little formal planning of the branch's assortment, as branch and main store stocks are considered as one. Only the sketchiest of branch plans and reports are on paper; instead, direct observation is used. A buyer simply selects from a newly received shipment those styles that he thinks most suitable for the branch and has them transferred there. Frequent exchange of information keeps the main store's merchandising staff aware of the branch situation.

In general, therefore, the more numerous a store's branches, or the larger their size, or the greater their distance from the main store, the greater is the need for precise assortment planning for each branch, plus detailed records of branch sales and inventory.

Transfers of Merchandise In almost all branch operations, merchandise is freely transferred, according to need, from one location to another. A number that is out of stock at a branch is replenished from the main store's supply; a customer who cannot get her size or color at one branch is served from the stock of another branch or the main store. A style that fails to win acceptance at one branch is called back to the parent store or tried out at another branch.

The ability of branch-owning stores to transfer merchandise back and forth as needed makes it simpler to satisfy the problem of meeting consumer demand at each location. On the other hand, it does complicate the recordkeeping. This complexity makes it difficult for manual systems to keep track of the necessary data. Electronic systems, on the other hand, allow a buyer to control assortments in many widely separated locations with an absolute minimum of personal contact with the customers, personnel, and inventory at each store.

Trends Among branch-owning department and specialty stores, chiefly those with numerous large branches located at a distance from the parent store, there is a definite trend toward relieving buyers of responsibility for sales supervision in all store locations.

Another trend is to allow individual branches greater autonomy in assortment planning and merchandise decision making. In addition, there

is an increasing use of electronic data processing for control of assortments. Branch-owning stores are adopting an increasing number of the successful operational techniques practiced by chain organizations.

Chain Organizations

Chain store procedure separates buying and selling functions much more sharply. The buying staff is guided in its fashion market work by figures on the total sales and inventory of the chain. This broad indication of consumer fashion demand is refined down to the needs of the individual units of the chain by special staffs at regional distribution centers. At these centers, the staffs seasonally plan a basic fashion assortment for each store in the light of its sales history.

The telephoning and requisitioning that help a branch of a department or specialty store to locate exactly what the customer wants in another branch's inventory have no parallel in chain store merchandising. Chain units periodically report their fashion sales to the distribution center via stubs of price tickets. These periodic sales reports frequently are accompanied by observations of customer preferences. The distribution center supplies replenishments to each unit, not necessarily identical items to those that have been sold but items of the same general type.

The tickets used by large chains are of the print-punch type, with information on color, size, price, vendor, style, and store number printed and also punched for the computer. When these stubs are fed into a computer, which in large chains is about once a week, the distribution center gets a report on what has been sold at each store and what remains in stock. The distributor, working with figures on individual stores and the entire group of stores served by the center, is in a position to note and make adjustments for any variations in demand at individual stores. Personnel in the stores are also encouraged to call attention to trends.

Chain operations do not use unit controls to follow the fates of specific style numbers as do department and specialty stores. For their purposes, broad categories are more workable merchandising guides than individual style numbers.

References

[1] American Marketing Association, "Report of the Definitions Committee," *Journal of Marketing*, October, 1948, p. 21.
[2] Wingate and Friedlander, *The Management of Retail Buying*, p. 190.
[3] NRMA's *Standard Classifications*, pp. 10–30.
[4] Beatrice Judelle, "Classification Merchandising in the Fashion Departments," *Stores*, September, 1965, p. 20.
[5] NRMA's *Standard Classifications*, p. 30.

Merchandising Vocabulary

Define or briefly explain the following terms:

Model stock	Reserve requisition control
Unit control	Charge-back
Perpetual inventory control	Classification
Periodic stock count control	Dissection

Merchandising Review

1. What are the major objectives of assortment planning?
2. To what three factors should a fashion buyer give careful consideration when planning assortments? Briefly discuss how various aspects of each of these factors affect the composition of merchandise assortments.
3. What is the fashion merchant's prime source of information when planning an assortment? What other sources of information also provide him with useful data?
4. Name and describe (a) the two major types of unit control systems; (b) two less frequently used types of unit control systems.
5. For which types of merchandise are each of the above systems best suited?
6. What specific types of information are most commonly recorded in a perpetual inventory control system?
7. From what store forms are each of these types of information obtained?
8. Discuss the relative advantages and disadvantages of maintaining unit control systems.
9. Under the standardized method of classification control, into what four levels or breaks is all merchandise grouped for purposes of analysis? Briefly describe the nature of each of these levels or breaks.
10. Name at least five types of information required on a purchase order form for perpetual inventory control record.

Merchandising Digest

1. "Since World War II, more sophisticated, consumer-oriented procedures for collecting merchandising data have become necessary. . . ." List four reasons why more sophisticated and consumer-oriented procedures for collecting merchandising data have become necessary and cite examples to illustrate each of these reasons.

2. "Multi-unit stores are of two kinds, each with different problems . . . and different methods of assortment planning and control. These types are branch-operating department and specialty stores and chain organizations." Discuss assortment planning and control in these two types of multi-unit stores, comparing and contrasting the problems involved and the planning and control methods employed.

14

MANAGING FASHION ASSORTMENTS

Chapters 11–13 have explained how merchants guide and control their fashion assortments to reflect as accurately as possible the demands of their clientele. This chapter is concerned with the guides and controls used by retailers to ensure that the function of meeting consumer demand will be performed profitably as well as efficiently. Presented here are the procedures used to direct merchandising operations and the yardsticks used by management to evaluate merchandising performance. These measuring devices can be applied to the store as a whole, or to its individual departments, or to the particular area of responsibility of a buyer or merchandise manager.

A department store uses the same procedures and criteria for evaluating the merchandising function in all its departments. Assortments of fashion merchandise, however, are highly volatile, compared with such products as mattresses and bedsprings. The risks and rewards involved in the merchandising of fashion goods and services are correspondingly great. Every retail merchandising executive involved with apparel or accessories therefore has a special need to become thoroughly familiar with the management tools discussed in this chapter.

Inventory Control

Retailers plan their dollar investments in fashion assortments well in advance, as we have seen in Chapter 12. Such an investment is controlled by adjusting purchases to reflect any and all actual variations from planned sales and stocks. The retail value of merchandise on hand is constantly evaluated in the light of customer demand. The value of retail stocks is based on their value to customers rather than on their actual cost price.

The Retail Method of Inventory Evaluation

The method of accounting in which all entries relating to an inventory are reported at their retail values is called the *retail method of inventory evaluation*. This accounting system is used today by all large retail organizations and a growing number of smaller ones, and thus is the most widely used system.

Under this system each selling department or classification represents a separate accounting unit. At the beginning of each accounting period, inventories are recorded at both their cost and retail values. Subsequent purchases throughout the period are also recorded at both cost and retail, and inbound transportation charges are added to the billed cost of purchases as an additional cost of the inventory. Other changes in the value of an inventory, such as sales, markdowns, transfers, returns to vendors, and so on, are recorded at their retail values. The difference between the total cost and the total retail values of all merchandise handled throughout a period is called *cumulative markon*. The cumulative markon percentage is obtained by dividing the difference between the total retail and the total cost of the merchandise handled by the total retail figure.

To determine the retail value of inventory on hand at any time during an accounting period, subtract the retail value of the net sales and the markdowns taken since the beginning of the accounting period from the retail value of the total merchandise handled (the beginning inventory plus net purchases). To obtain the cost value of the inventory on hand, multiply its retail value by the complement of the cumulative markon percentage (100 percent minus the cumulative markon percentage).

This system of accounting enables the retailer to calculate both the cost and retail values of his inventory at any time without resorting to taking a physical inventory.

Normal business accounting procedure evaluates unsold inventory in terms of its cost values, while sales are recorded at their market values. Under such a system of accounting, neither the market value of the inventory on hand nor the profitability of the operation can be determined unless a physical inventory is taken or a series of complicated calculations made. Hence, the retail method of inventory evaluation was devised.

The retail method of accounting involves the following steps:

1. A physical inventory is taken at current retail selling prices by listing and totaling the prices appearing on the price tickets for each item of merchandise comprising the inventory.
2. The markon percentage of the total merchandise handled during a given period is determined.
3. The cost of the aggregate inventory is derived by multiplying its total retail value by the complement of the cumulative markon percentage.

The Book Inventory

Under the retail method of inventory evaluation, it is essential that a perpetual book inventory be maintained for each separate accounting unit for periodic comparison with the results of a physical inventory. The *book inventory* is the value of the inventory as indicated by the store's account books. (See Form 14-1.) The book inventory may or may not agree precisely with the physical inventory on a given date, but every effort is exerted to keep the book figures as accurate as possible. The figures used to compute the book inventory are derived from various store records that report additions to and subtractions from the inventory value, as these changes occur. Responsibility for the initiation and accuracy of these records is solely the buyer's and represents a major portion of his job.

Because entries are made in the book inventory as changes are reported to the accounting department, management can have a current retail evaluation of its inventory investment at any time—monthly, weekly, or whenever wanted, either for the store as a whole or for any accounting subdivision. In stores that use computers, inventory values are adjusted at the instant that related figures are fed into the machine. Reports can be printed out by the system as frequently and in as much detail as desired.

Book Inventory Procedures Each new fiscal year starts with book and physical inventory in perfect agreement because at the beginning of the fiscal year, or sometimes more frequently, as accurate a physical count of stock as possible is taken. If this count differs from the book inventory figure for the close of the previous period, the physical count is accepted as correct and book records are adjusted to conform with it.

Subsequent entries are then made in the book inventory of all transactions affecting the value of the inventory as they occur:

1. Purchases are recorded at both cost and retail, a procedure that requires the merchant or buyer to indicate the retail price of the goods listed on each invoice for shipments received from vendors. Items purchased at a cost of $8 a dozen, for example, might be assigned a retail price of $1 each. The addition of one dozen of this item to the inventory would be entered as a cost value of $8 and a retail value of $12.

To facilitate this bookkeeping procedure, large stores usually require buyers to *pre-retail* their orders; that is, to indicate intended retail prices on all purchase orders. When goods are received, the retail value of each vendor's invoice can be calculated and the goods marked and placed on sale even if the buyer is not available at the time. With the varied demands on a buyer's time, particularly in large stores, it is practically impossible for him to be present when each purchase arrives.
2. Sales are recorded either on cash registers or sales checks. From register tapes or duplicate sales checks, a total sales figure for each department or classification is obtained daily and entered as a credit or decrease in the book inventory.
3. Returns made by customers are recorded on sales credit forms, which are totaled daily and

Store _Westchester_

DEPARTMENTAL INVENTORY LEDGER

Year Ending _January 31, 19—_

| Period Ending | Purchases and Transfers | | | Freight and Express (4) | Add'l Markon (5) | Accumulated | | | Net Sales (9) | Deductions at Retail | | Shortage Reserve (12) | Total (13) | EOM Inventory | | |
	Cost (1)	Retail (2)	Percent (3)			Cost (6)	Retail (7)	Percent (8)		Markdowns Amount (10)	Percent (11)			Cost (14)	Retail (15)	Percent (16)
Beg. Inv.	32,276	52,227	38.2	–	–	–	–	–	–	–	–	–	–	–	–	–
Feb.	6,000	10,000	40.0	37	120	–	–	–	11,500	590	5.1	173	12,263			
YTD	38,276	62,227	38.5	37	120	38,313	62,347	38.5	11,500	590	5.1	173	12,263	30,802	50,084	38.5
Mar.	7,200	12,000	40.0	45	–	7,245	12,000	39.6	13,000	650	5.0	195	13,845			
YTD	45,476	74,227	38.7	82	120	45,558	74,347	38.7	24,500	1,240	5.1	368	26,108	29,571	48,239	38.7
Apr.																
YTD																
Oct.																
YTD																
Nov.																
YTD																
Dec.																
YTD																
Jan.																
Year																

KEY: YTD = Year to Date

Column 1 = Billed Cost of Purchases
Column 2 = Retail Value of Purchases

Column 3 = $\dfrac{\text{Col. 2 – Col. 1}}{\text{Col. 2}}$

Column 6 = Col. 1 + Col. 4

Column 7 = Col. 2 + Col. 5

Column 8 = $\dfrac{\text{Col. 7 – Col. 6}}{\text{Col. 7}}$

Column 9 = Net Audited Sales

Column 10 = From Markdown Book

Column 11 = $\dfrac{\text{Col. 10}}{\text{Col. 9}}$

Column 12 = 1.5% of Col. 9
Column 13 = Col. 9 + Col. 10 + Col. 12
Column 14 = Col. 15 x complement of Col. 8
Column 15 = Col. 7 – Col. 13

Column 16 = $\dfrac{\text{Col. 15 – Col. 14}}{\text{Col. 15}}$

Form 14-1

244

entered in the books as a debit to (or increase in) the retail value of the inventory.

4. When price changes are made on merchandise after it has originally been placed in stock, a record is made on price change forms and forwarded to the accounting department, which then increases or decreases the value of the inventory by an appropriate amount. Price changes may take the following forms:

□ Additional markon, or increases to prices above those at which the goods were marked when first received into stock.

□ Markdowns or reductions in the retail price of goods already priced and in stock.

□ Markdown cancellations, or increases in price to offset all or any part of previously taken markdowns (such cancellations may occur, for instance, after a special sale for which goods from regular stock were briefly reduced).

5. Any transfer of goods from one department or accounting unit to another is recorded as a decrease in the inventory of the issuing department and an increase in that of the receiving department. If there are branch stores, transfers of merchandise from one to another are similarly reported and entered on the inventory records. Each store devises its own forms for reporting such transactions.

6. Merchandise returned to vendors for credit is reported to the accounting department on a charge-back form listing the items and amounts returned. Although the vendor is charged back only at the cost price of the goods, the store's records reflect the retail value of the return as well as its invoice price. Each such transaction reduces both the cost and retail values of the inventory.

Some charge-backs are not concerned with returns but with claims or allowances, as when merchandise is damaged but still salable. In such cases, only the cost price of the adjustment is entered on the books of the store from the charge-back. Any adjustment in retail price is made separately and reported as a markdown on an appropriate form.

7. Sometimes merchandise is loaned by one department to another for displays or may go to the advertising department for sketching and study. In such cases, the borrower signs a loan slip, making himself responsible for the article's return to the issuing department. At inventory time, any outstanding loan slips are accepted as though they were pieces of merchandise and counted in the lending department's total.

Merchandise on Order In addition to the records described above, stores keep careful tally of orders placed but not yet delivered. A running total is maintained of both the entire amounts on order and the amounts scheduled for delivery in each future month. (See Form 14-2.) These "on order" amounts are not recorded in the book inventories but are kept on file and carefully watched, since they represent impending upward changes in the inventory with future obligations to pay. If an order is canceled by either the store or the vendor, the appropriate amount is deducted from the "on order" retail figure for the month in which delivery was originally expected.

For example, the book inventory of a department or classification on the first of June may be precisely as planned. Yet the department may have outstanding orders for June delivery that use up most of June's purchase budget. As a result, the department's open-to-buy on the first of the month will be negligible. The book inventory shows the retail value of the inventory on hand, whereas the "on order" file shows the amounts committed for receipts of merchandise in both the current and future periods.

The Physical Inventory

Errors inevitably creep into records, even those maintained by computers. Sales may be rung up at the wrong prices; price changes and transfers may be made for more or fewer pieces than were actually involved; transactions may be incorrectly identified as to department or classification. Actual shortages also occur through pilferage and shoplifting. With the multiplicity of items and transactions involved, the book inventory is never exactly the same as the true marked retail value of all goods in stock. This is the reason for the physical count that is taken at the beginning of each fiscal year or sometimes more often if a

WEEKLY REPORT OF OUTSTANDING ORDERS

Orders of $50.00 and over must be reported individually. Orders under $50.00 should be reported collectively under "Small Purchases." Report all cancellations in Red.

Department 42-11   Date 3/17   Sheet No. 1

Order No.	Order Date	Vendor	Total Retail	March Cost	March Retail	April Cost	April Retail	May Cost	May Retail
				On Order by Month					
91428	3/4	Aiken Dress Co	450	252	450				
91478	3/11	Supreme Dress Co	1,600			896	1,600		
91464	3/8	Lane Dress Co	1,080	322	540	322	540		
91514	3/15	Casualaire	3,200					1,856	3,200
Total Small Purchases			130	70	130				
Total on Order			22,268	876	1,511	9,361	16,140	2,678	4,617
Open to Buy						(261)	29,700		43,100

BUYER'S SIGNATURE
Janet Dean

MDSE. MANAGER'S SIGNATURE
T. J. Evans

Form 14-2

special situation, such as excessive shortages, warrants it.

Inventory Procedure   The taking of a physical inventory requires a precise cutoff on a given date. Every merchandise shipment received by that date must be counted, marked, and entered in the book inventory. Every sale, every return, and every price change up to that date must also be entered. This assures that the book inventory is updated to the exact time of the physical inventory.

In a physical inventory, every piece of merchandise in stock must be counted. The physical count is best made after store closing hours, so that selling does not confuse the stocktaking. Ideally, the count is made by crews not directly concerned with the merchandise they are checking, but the ideal is not always practical. Salespeople may do the counts for their own sections and try to start counting while customers are still about. The resulting totals may then be less than accurate, especially if a clerk thinks he knows,

and therefore does not check, the contents of cartons or boxes in less accessible stock locations.

Inventory Forms   Sheets on which the counts are entered are usually provided by each store's accounting office. (See Form 14-3.) They require a listing, at the left, of an identifying style number or other description. To the right of the description are columns in which the counter enters the exact number of pieces of each item found in stock, the marked retail price of each, and a breakdown of the quantities by age of merchandise, as marked on the price ticket. Each sheet is identified as to department, classification, or other subdivision.

When the counts have been completed, the forms are returned to the accounting office. There the totals are calculated and compared with the book figures, and any necessary adjustment in the book figures is made.

Stock Shortages and Overages

In the normal course of business, the physical

inventory rarely tallies precisely with the book figures. If the physical inventory falls below the book figure, the discrepancy is called a *stock shortage;* if it is above the book figure, the difference is called a *stock overage.*

Overages are rare and are found most commonly among stores with several branches. One may be charged in error for another's shipment or credited in error with another's sales, thus increasing the book inventory without increasing the actual physical inventory.

Shortages are common. They normally reach from 1 to 2 percent of the year's net sales in department stores. Some departments have higher percentages than others, due mainly to the nature of the merchandise handled and the selling techniques employed. Open selling and self-service tend to increase departmental shortages because they permit greater opportunities for undetected theft. Some departments, such as jewelry and cosmetics, have higher-than-average shortages because their merchandise is more susceptible than others to theft, damage, and spoilage. In some fashion departments, notably those serving teen-agers, shortages may go above 3 percent of net sales.

Stores constantly strive to reduce shortage figures by greater accuracy in taking physical inventory; by exercising more care in recording purchases, price changes, and sales; and by greater watchfulness against theft. It is an old saying in the department store field that although shortages may not be the fault of the buyer in whose department they occur, more buyers have

INVENTORY   No. 16766

Department 41-11   Date January 31. 19 —

Classification No. 12301 Location Stockroom   Fixture No. 1

Style No.	Description	Quantity	Unit (ea., doz., etc.)	Season Letter	Unit Retail Price	Change Plus	Change Minus
1234	Dress	18	ea	H 5	8 98	ok	
789	Dress	13	ea	H 6	8 98	ok	
1401	Dress	9	ea	H 6	8 98	ok	

COUNTED BY A. G. D.   LISTED BY T. B. C.   CHECKED BY E. A. M.

INSTRUCTIONS

1. Only one classification of merchandise to a sheet.
2. If unit is dozen, retail price per unit must also be per dozen. If unit is each, price must be each, etc.

Form 14-3

DEPARTMENTAL PURCHASE JOURNAL

Department No. __42__   Month __Sept. 197–__   Sheet No. __1__

Vendor	Date of Invoice	Receiving or Charge No.	Cost	Retail	Discount	Balance Paid or Due Us
Aiken Dress	9/2/7–	16181	1,134.00	2,158.56	90.72	1,043.28
Aiken Dress	9/19/7–	66375	47.25 Cr.	89.94 Cr.	3.78 Cr.	43.47 Cr.
Elite Dress	9/6/7–	16450	675.00	1,259.58	54.00	621.00

Form 14-4

been fired for shortages than for any other reason. Shortages diminish profits, and a profitable operation is the buyer's responsibility.

The two major causes of shortages and overages are clerical errors and physical merchandise losses. Common clerical errors include:

▫ Failure to record markdowns properly

▫ Mistakes in calculating retail values

▫ Mistakes in charging or crediting departments

▫ Mistakes in recording merchandise transfers

▫ Mistakes in recording returns to vendors

▫ Mistakes in recording the physical inventory

Physical merchandise losses occur through:

▫ Theft by customers and employees

▫ Failure to obtain receipts for merchandise loaned

▫ Breakage and spoilage

▫ Lost or incorrectly marked price tickets

▫ Sales-check errors

▫ Providing samples of yard goods, perfume, etc., for customers

Departmental Purchase Journal

In departmentalized stores, a separate record is maintained for each department or classification of all invoices charged to it, transfers to other stores or departments, and all charge-backs made to vendors covering returns, short shipments, and other claims. This record is called the *purchase journal*. It has the same function as a purchase journal under any other type of accounting system, except that the retail value as well as the cost of each invoice, transfer, or charge-back is recorded, and it refers only to an accounting unit (the department or classification) rather than to the whole store. The wise buyer keeps his own record of such transactions to compare with the monthly or semimonthly report issued by the store's accounting office on which are listed all debits and credits made to the book inventory of each accounting unit. Form 14-4 shows the departmental purchase journal as the store's accounting department might report it, and Form 14-5 shows the record a buyer might keep.

The entries made for each invoice show the vendor's name, the total cost and the total retail of the invoice, the receiving apron number, transportation charges, and discount and anticipation earned. Similar notations are made for all charge-backs to vendors and merchandise transfers to other accounting units.

The purchase journal also gives the buyer the information he needs to compare the dollar amounts of his merchandise receipts against his planned purchase figures. Knowing what he has received and what he has on order, the buyer can decide whether to speed up or slow down the pace of purchasing to conform to the merchandise budget. In addition, the purchase journal enables the buyer to check on the accuracy of the figures for purchases charged to his department.

Since the buyer knows his department's sales figures from daily reports, he can work out his

Department No. __42__   Month __Sept. 197–__   Sheet No. __1__

Vendor	Date of Invoice	Style No.	Quantity	Unit Cost	Unit Retail	Apron No.	Total Cost	Total Retail	Discount	Balance Paid or Due Us
Aiken Dress	9/2/7–	253	72	15.75	29.98	16151	1134.00	2158.56	90.72	1043.28
Elite Dress	9/6/7–	491	36	18.75	34.98	16450	675.00	1259.28	54.00	621.00

Form 14-5

own open-to-buy estimate at any time, using the purchase figures shown in the purchase journal together with his own file of unfilled orders. The figures thus obtained may not be as precise as those provided periodically by his management, but they have the virtue of being immediate and current.

Merchandising Reports

Each fashion buyer in a departmentalized store receives a number of reports from his store's accounting office to guide him in operating his department more profitably. The same reports are also given to top management and, in large stores, to the appropriate divisional merchandise managers as well. Thus the figures are available at both buying levels and management levels for study and for deciding what action should be taken based on what such reports reveal.

Sales Reports

As noted in Chapter 12, sales constitute the basis of all merchandise planning and control. Therefore, actual sales results are studied closely to evaluate their effect upon other elements of the merchandise budget. A number of reports are available to the buyer for this purpose.

Flash Sales Reports Daily reports of sales, by department or classification, or both, are routinely developed from the unaudited sales checks and cash register tapes for the previous day. They compare the day's sales with those of the same selling day of the previous year, and are circulated early the following business day to merchandising executives. These are usually referred to as *flash sales reports*. If a store has branches, the sales of each are usually shown separately from those of the main store, and there is also a grand total for all locations combined.

Periodic Sales Reports Sales reports may be prepared on a daily, weekly, or monthly basis. In larger, branch-owning stores, these recapitulations show both main store and individual branch store sales in units and in dollars, by classification, price line, style number, color, size, and vendor. (See Form 14-6.) In smaller stores, departmental sales may be reported simply in units and dollars by classification.

Weekly reports give the buyer a quick, on-the-spot review of sales at all locations and encourage earlier action than would be possible if sales were reported only monthly. In addition to the weekly sales figures, some reports, particularly those that are obtained from computers, sometimes show cumulative sales for the month or season to date and sales for the corresponding period of the previous year.

"Beat Last Year" Book The simplest form of daily sales record kept by the buyer is the "Beat Last Year" book, which is like a three- or five-year diary. It has a line for each day and a column for each year. Sales figures are entered day by day, and pencil subtotals are inserted to show

SALES REPORT

Department No. __42__ Class __12__ Period __9/9/–__ Page __2__

Price	Style	Mfr.	Color	Size	Main Sales	Main Credits	Total Branch Sales	Total Branch Credits	Branch 2	Branch 3	Branch 4	Total
19.98	654	354	Beige	10	1		1		1			2
			Green	12	1		3		1	1	1	4
			Black	14	2		0					2
19.98	125	523	Brown	14	2		1				1	3
			Green	16	2		2			1	1	4
29.98	253	482	Brown	8	0		1				1	1
			Red	10	0		1		1			1
			Black	12	1		1			1		2
29.98	1010	464	Brown	8	1		2		1	1		3
			Green	12	2		1				1	3
			Black	16	2		0					2
			Total		45		39		12	12	15	84

RECAP

Color	Main 8	Main 10	Main 12	Main 14	Main 16	Main 18	Main Total	Br. 8	Br. 10	Br. 12	Br. 14	Br. 16	Br. 18	Br. Total	Price	Units Main	Units Br.	Total
Black	1	1	3	5	2	2	14		1	1				2	14.98	7	10	17
Green	1	1	4	3	3	3	15	2	4	5	5	1	1	18	19.98	8	12	20
Brown	1		1	2	3	2	9	2	3	3	2	1		11	26.98	10	7	17
Beige		1	1	1			3	1	1	1				3	29.98	14	6	20
Red								1	1	1				3	36.98	6	4	10
Gray		1	2	1			4			1	1			2				
Total	3	4	11	12	8	7	45	6	10	11	8	3	1	39		45	39	84

Form 14-6

sales up to any point in the month. Special conditions affecting sales, such as bad weather, transit strikes, or promotional efforts, are usually noted as well.

Stock and Sales Reports

Sales alone tell only part of the merchandising story. The other part concerns stocks. Therefore retailers have developed reports that are supplied

WEEKLY SALES AND STOCK REPORT

DIV. | STORE NO. | CITY | WEEK ENDED 01/07/– | PAGE 6

CODE	PRICE GROUP	CODE DESCRIPTION / PRICE	SEASON TO DATE SALES PLAN	SEASON TO DATE SALES THIS YEAR	TREND	BEGINNING ON HAND	ADJUSTED PHYSICAL INVENTORY	SALES	RECEIPTS	ADJ PLUS	ADJ MINUS	ENDING ON HAND	INTRANSIT	COVERAGE PERIOD	SALES FOR COVERAGE PERIOD PLAN	BALANCE OF SALES FOR SEASON PLAN
241		DRESS PLASTIC														
	1	3.00 5.00	32	16	50–	15						11	24	9	29	6
	3	6.00 8.00	85	36	58–	13		4				13	36	5	11	1
	5	9.00 11.00	20	9	55–	32						32		8	6	
	7	12.00 999.00		1		1–						1–		8		
	9	4.97												7		
241		TOTAL UNITS	137	62	55–	59		4				55	60		46	7
		TOTAL DOLLARS*	897	408				16				440	324		249	31
242		CASUAL PLASTIC														
	1	3.00 5.00	8	11	38	20						20		9	13	1
	3	6.00 8.00	199	72	64–	24		3				21	24	5	11	2
	5	9.00 11.00	56	25	55–	25		1				24		8	6	
	7	12.00 999.00	49	6	80–	6						6		8	6	
	9	3.97		10		6–						6–		7		
242		TOTAL UNITS	312	124	58–	69		4				65	24		36	3
		TOTAL DOLLARS*	2065	868				29				504	168		255	17
352		FRENCH PURSES														
	2	2.00 3.00	22	3	86–	14		1				14		6	5	1
	3	3.50 UP	6	3	50–	21		2				20		7	5	
	9	.97		7		19		3				17		6		
352		TOTAL UNITS	28	13	69–	54		6				51			10	1
		TOTAL DOLLARS*	87	27					48			133			34	3
		DIVISION TOTAL														
		TOTAL UNITS	1191	536		92		46				94			193	1929
		TOTAL DOLLARS*	4807	2365				198				377			667	7409

*CENTS OMITTED IN DOLLAR FIGURES

Form 14-7

DEPARTMENTAL OPERATING STATEMENT

Department No. 42-11 Month March Year 19—

Line		This Month				Year to Date						Line
		Plan		Actual		Plan		Actual		Last Year		
		$	%	$	%	$	%	$	%	$	%	
1	Gross Sales	38,000	108.0	39,476	108.6	69,120	108.0	71,396	108.2	72,669	108.3	1
2	Customer Returns	3,000	8.0	3,142	8.6	5,120	8.0	5,411	8.2	5,569	8.3	2
3	NET SALES	35,000	-9.3	36,334	3.8	64,000	-4.6	65,985	3.1	67,100	2.1	3
4	Beg. Stock @ Retail	66,500	39.6	65,816	39.6	82,800	—	81,950	39.5	86,520	39.2	4
5	Net Retail Purchases	60,200	40.0	58,960	40.0	76,400	40.0	76,102	40.0	78,559	39.5	5
6	End. Stock @ Retail	86,900	39.9	83,541	39.8	86,900	—	83,541	39.7	89,720	39.3	6
7	Markdowns	4,450	12.7	4,565	12.6	7,660	12.0	7,868	11.9	7,590	11.3	7
8	Employee Discounts	350	1.0	336	.9	640	1.0	658	1.0	669	1.0	8
9	Shortage Reserve	525	1.5	545	1.5	960	1.5	990	1.5	1,141	1.7	9
10	Workroom Costs	350	1.0	340	.9	640	1.0	690	1.0	672	1.0	10
11	Cash Discounts	2,990	8.3	2,830	7.8	3,667	5.7	3,653	5.5	3,707	5.5	11
12	GROSS MARGIN	13,056	37.3	13,446	37.0	22,912	35.8	23,092	35.0	23,322	34.8	12
13	Advertising	1,120	3.2	1,417	3.9	2,048	3.2	2,111	3.2	2,416	3.6	13
14	Special Events	210	.6	291	.8	384	.6	396	.6	537	.8	14
15	Buying Salaries	1,155	3.3	1,200	3.3	2,112	3.3	2,178	3.3	2,214	3.3	15
16	Buyer's Travel	175	.5	218	.6	320	.5	397	.6	402	.6	16
17	Selling Salaries	2,660	7.6	2,834	7.8	4,864	7.6	5,015	7.6	5,299	7.9	17
18	Stk & Cler. Salaries	280	.8	284	.8	512	.8	530	.8	604	.9	18
19	Supplies	70	.2	75	.2	128	.2	135	.2	135	.2	19
20	Delivery	140	.4	185	.5	256	.4	270	.4	268	.4	20
21	Other Direct Expense	1,050	3.0	1,091	3.0	1,920	3.0	1,992	3.0	2,015	3.0	21
22	TOTAL DIRECT EXPENSE	6,860	19.6	7,595	20.9	12,544	19.6	13,014	19.7	13,890	20.7	22
23	DEPT. CONTRIBUTION	6,196	17.7	5,851	16.1	10,368	18.2	10,078	15.3	9,432	14.1	23
24	Indirect Expense	4,095	11.7	4,178	11.5	7,488	11.7	7,536	11.5	7,851	11.7	24
25	TOTAL EXPENSES	10,955	31.3	11,773	32.4	20,032	31.3	20,620	31.2	21,741	32.4	25
26	OPERATING PROFIT	2,107	6.0	1,673	4.6	2,880	4.5	2,492	3.8	1,581	2.4	26

Form 14-8

to buyers weekly, semimonthly, or monthly, showing inventory on hand and on order, actual sales results, planned sales and stocks, and the sales and stocks for the corresponding period of the previous year. In addition to the figures concerning the current period, such reports usually show cumulative figures for the year to date. (See Form 14-7.)

If electronic data processing is available, reports may show not only departmental totals but also classification and subclassification totals. (Form 14-7.) Thus a buyer whose total departmental sales and stocks are about at the level of planned figures may see that some classifications are far enough above or below plan to require corrective action. Similarly, where there are branches, a separate set of figures for each location may reveal a need for action at one or more sites, whereas overall figures for all stores combined may mask such a need.

Departmental Operating Statements

Buyers and their management also receive regular reports on the financial aspects of each department's total merchandising operation. (See Form 14-8.) These reports, referred to as *departmental operating statements,* include actual and planned dollar sales figures for all phases of the merchandising operation: gross sales, returned sales, markdowns, purchases, gross margin of profit, operating expenses, merchandise on order, cash discounts earned, and so on. These are usually issued monthly, but in some large stores, a midmonth flash report is also provided. Figures are usually stated both in dollars and as percentages of net sales.

Gross margin—the difference between net sales and the net cost of sales—is usually considered the key figure on these operating reports. It is an important index of how profitably a department has been operated and a major factor in the evaluation of a buyer's efficiency as a business manager.

Open-to-Buy Reports

For the buyer, the open-to-buy report is a financial tool to keep the inventory investment in line with plans and actual sales. (See Form 14-9.) When a bright new item or trend appears the buyer who wishes to exploit it must move promptly. If he does not have enough open-to-buy, he can either rearrange his plans for other purchases to make room for the new fashion or else ask management for extra purchasing funds while there still is time to act.

From the viewpoint of top management, the open-to-buy report reflects the buyer's competence and character. The overly optimistic buyer tends to buy too heavily and to be chronically overbought, even when his selections are excellent. Another type of buyer who overstocks is the one whose selections tend to fall just short of being right and therefore sell more slowly than planned. Some buyers tend to underbuy, even though they have a gift for anticipating what customers will buy and for presenting it to them temptingly. They may have too little confidence in their own judgment or too much confidence in the ability of resources to deliver additional stock in a rush. Accuracy in planning and skill in merchandising to the plan reveal themselves in a

CODE	PRICE RANGE	E.O.M. INV. 1/31/7 -	FEB. ON ORDER	AVAILABLE FOR SALE	PLANNED SALES	ANTICIPATED MARK DOWNS	PLANNED E.O.M. INV.	OPEN TO RECEIVE FEB.	MAR.	ON ORDER APR.	MAY	JUNE-JULY	OPEN TO BUY MAR-JULY
12301	8.98	771	100	871	500	40	750	419	300	800	1000	100	2885
12302	10.98	621	85	706	425	30	900	649	500	1000	250	0	2625
12304	13.98	1412	210	1622	800	70	1500	748	200	1400	1400	50	3410
12306	19.98	3201	610	3811	1600	120	3000	909	800	800	0	0	4310
12307	26.98	2120	350	2470	1000	80	2500	1110	1000	750	500	0	4820
12308	36.98	1409	300	1709	600	50	1200	141	150	150	100	100	2530
TOTAL MISSY		9534	1655	11189	4925	390	8850	3976	2950	4900	3250	250	20580

OPEN TO BUY REPORT

MONTH ENDING FEB. 29, 197—

Courtesy NRMA

Form 14-9

department that has adequate stocks yet always has some open-to-buy available for unexpected developments.

Evaluating the Merchandising Operation

Management and the individual buyer use many other yardsticks to measure the success of a department's operation and to guide it toward even greater accuracy in meeting consumer fashion demand. Among these are basic stock lists, age-of-stock reports, analyses of markdowns, analyses of customer returns, vendor analyses, stock turnover figures, and others. Each is a way of keeping track of or exploring the significance of some facet of the merchandising operation that affects that operation's overall profitability.

Basic Stock Lists

An item of merchandise is described by fashion merchants as *basic* or *staple* if it enjoys such consistent demand that it should be in stock in a complete range of sizes and colors at best-selling price lines throughout a year or season. A basic may be a specific item or a group of substitutable items, such as women's service weight stockings in neutral shades, nurses' oxfords, or women's white tailored slips.

When a store runs short of an item that enjoys consistent demand, customer goodwill is at stake as well as sales. Stores therefore encourage or require their buyers to list specific items in their departments that are considered basic each season and to set up periodic stock counts or similar ways of making sure there is always an adequate supply of these goods. Many stores require that a list of such items be retained in the merchandise manager's office. The latter may, at unannounced intervals, send someone into a department to check the basic stock and report any listed items that are not on hand or are in low supply. A buyer whose department repeatedly makes poor showings on such checks is subject to criticism.

To ensure adequate stocks of basic merchandise, some stores draw up two separate budgets for each department or classification: one for basics and one for more volatile merchandise. Executives of such stores believe that an over-

stock elsewhere in a department should not deprive the buyer of needed open-to-buy for basics. Other stores have a policy of permitting basics to be reordered regardless of the state of the departmental open-to-buy. Still others leave the entire matter in the buyer's hands, expecting him to reserve part of his budget and enough of his open-to-buy for his basics.

Age-of-Stock Reports

Retail stores usually place a coded season letter on each price ticket. The *season letter* is a code that indicates the month of the year in which the merchandise was received into stock. In fast-moving fashion categories, the season letter may also include a numeral or some other code to indicate the week, in addition to the month, in which the article arrived in stock. Some stores put the complete coded date of receipt on the price ticket of each piece of fashion merchandise.

By flipping through the tickets on a rack of garments, a merchant can quickly see which ones have been in stock too long and should be given attention. In some stores, and for some merchandise, a week is considered a long time; in other cases, a month may not be considered long.

Age-of-stock reports are reports that provide information in summary form of the amount of stock in each of a number of age groups, as indicated by their season letters. Such reports may be prepared by the accounting office from data listed on inventory sheets or from special inventories taken of all or part of a department's stock for age-record purposes. The reports are created by dividing the listing of stock into age groups, totaling each group, and then showing what percentage of the total inventory each age group constitutes. Buyers are required to recheck these reports periodically, indicating what steps have been taken to dispose of old merchandise. (See Form 14-10.) Some stores, particularly those using electronic data processing equipment, run off actual lists of the specific items of merchandise that are too old. These lists are presented to the appropriate buyers for action.

Apparel departments for women and misses typically have very little inventory that is more than six months old. One of the larger chain organizations requires that all women's apparel

PRIOR STOCK

Department No. 4-2-11
Sheet No. 1

Class.	Style No.	Article (List each classification separately)	Season Letter	Inventory Qty Date 1/31/-	Inventory Unit Price	First Month Qty Date 2/28/-	First Month Unit Price	Second Month Qty Date 3/31/-	Second Month Unit Price	Third Month Qty Date 4/30/-	Third Month Unit Price
12301	1234	Dress	RC4	5	8.98	2	6.00	0	—	1	—
	789	Dress	RC5	7	8.98	4	6.00	1	4.00	0	—
	1401	Dress	RC5	3	8.98	3	6.00	1	4.00	0	—
12302	239	Dress	RC4	6	10.98	4	8.00	2	6.00	1	4.00
	141	Dress	RC5	8	10.98	4	8.00	1	6.00	0	—
	984	Dress	RC5	1	10.98	0	—	—	—	—	—
12308	957	Dress	RC3	1	36.98	1	26.00	1	22.00	0	—
	245	Dress	RC4	2	36.98	1	26.00	1	22.00	0	—
	698	Dress	RC5	2	36.98	1	26.00	0	—	1	—
Season			RC3	27	462.40	14	226.00	3	36.00	0	—
Season			RC4	41	923.60	22	468.00	7	66.00	3	28.00
Season			RC5	64	1,578.80	31	740.00	11	118.00	3	44.00
Total				132	2,964.80	67	1,434.00	21	220.00	6	72.00

NOTE: These sheets must be returned to the Merchandise Office on the 5th of each month with all data shown complete.

Form 14-10

remaining in stock 10 weeks after its receipt must be marked down.

Before World War II, it was common for management to record and pursue slow sellers until those items were finally eliminated from stock. With the faster pace of fashion and the higher cost of clerical help since that time, stores now tend to rely instead upon spot checks and unit control records to make sure that buyers locate and act upon stale fashion merchandise.

Markdown Analyses

Downward revisions in retail prices are reported whenever they are made. To facilitate accurate reporting, stores provide forms for this purpose, on which buyers itemize price adjustments in detail and indicate their reasons. Analyses of markdowns and reasons for them yield clues to a buyer's proficiency in keeping within budgetary limits, his accuracy in gauging customer demand, and the quality of his departmental supervision.

Markdown Causes The National Retail Merchants Association recommends using these classifications for causes of markdowns:

- Promotional purchase remainders
- Fabrics or quality
- Style or pattern
- Color
- Sizes
- Quantities (including overstock conditions as well as excessive quantities of specific styles)
- Special sales from stock
- Broken assortments, remnants, shopworn goods
- Price adjustments to meet competition, because of generally falling prices, or to consolidate or eliminate price lines
- Allowances to customers on adjustment claims[1]

Buyer Responsibility for Markdowns Hardest to recognize but most in need of correction are markdowns due to poor timing. These stem from offering merchandise too soon or too late for its season or for that stage of the fashion cycle to which the store's customers are attuned. Such markdowns may be reported under almost any of the headings above, but the discerning eye of an experienced merchandise manager will usually recognize them for what they are and search out the roots of the buyer's problem.

Errors in timing the presentation of merchandise to the consumer are not always solely the fault of the buyer. There are occasions when tardy deliveries or uncertain weather conditions are to blame. Since late deliveries frequently represent potential markdowns, buyers are expected to weigh the advisability of accepting overdue shipments against the possibility of slackening consumer demand.

Delay in taking markdowns or failure to take adequate markdowns, however, is definitely the fault of the buyer. Fashion merchandise deteriorates so rapidly that stores caution their buyers against postponing markdowns or making only timid reductions once they recognize that goods are not readily salable. Yet buyers often engage in wishful thinking; they postpone the inevitable and then have to slash prices drastically in the end. The markdown book records it all, and management finds in that book a vital index to the buyer's competence.

Customer Returns

The extent to which sales are returned in a fashion department is also an important index of the buyer's competence. If a large proportion of the goods sold is brought back for credit, there is something obviously wrong with the assortment, the merchandise, the selling techniques used, or a combination of all three. A persuasive salesperson or a low price may encourage a customer to purchase a dress. If the dress is unflattering, unfashionable, or poorly made, however, the customer is likely to have second thoughts about it after getting it home, and back it goes to the store.

The nature of the merchandise also affects the ratio of returns to sales. In departments devoted to women's and misses' apparel, the rate of returns to gross sales normally exceeds 10 percent. In departments devoted to men's and boys' wear, the rate of returns is well below 10 percent.

Vendor Analyses

A retailer rates his suppliers in terms of how accurately their merchandise meets the needs of his customers. Sometimes there is an affinity between one vendor's designs and the preferences of a store's customers that persists for seasons and years. Sometimes the affinity is fleeting.

To help evaluate his department's resources, a buyer may, with the help of his store's accounting office, maintain records of his dealings with each vendor. Typical forms used for this purpose show vendor name and address, each month's purchases at cost and retail, and the year's or season's total purchases. Charge-backs are listed separately, as are markdowns, if these have been recorded by vendor. A buyer thus can see if a resource has added to the past season's profits or to its problems.

Buyers also consolidate and list the yearly totals for their principal vendors so that they can compare one with another. (See Form 14-11.) They rank them according to amounts purchased, initial markon, percentage of markdowns, or other criteria. The list of principal resources has another function. The management executives of departmentalized stores usually contact at least once a year the few best resources for each of their many departments. Often such contact between the heads of the store and the heads of the manufacturing firm leads to better understanding and to long-range planning that benefits vendor, store, and consumer.

Stock Turnover

The more rapidly its retail stock is sold, the more profitably a store operates. Good turnover is the fruit of careful planning and wise management. Retailers are very conscious of the stock turnover in each of their departments.

As explained in Chapter 12, turnover, or stock turn, is calculated by dividing net sales for a year by the average retail value of the inventory for that year. A common error, however, is to use only season-end or year-end inventories, omitting the intervening months. At the end of a year or season, fashion inventories are at a low point. To base the average only on these lows would be to calculate a deceptively high turnover rate, causing the store to congratulate itself on what actually may have been a poor performance.

Improving Turnover The only sensible way to improve turnover is to examine the details of the assortment, identify the slow-selling classifications or items, and dispose of them through better display, better selling techniques, or as a last resort, markdowns. The buyer should then build up the stocks of fast sellers.

Turnover cannot be improved merely by slashing the buying appropriation, nor can elaborate classification and unit control data do more than lead the merchandising executive to those parts of the stock with the best and the worst turnover. The merchandise itself must be inspected. When the extremely slow-selling numbers are gathered on one rack and the really fast-selling ones on another, the differences between them generally stand out sharply. The buyer can see that his clientele is accepting certain lines, colors, and prices, and rejecting others. Better assortment planning then becomes possible, and better turnover results.

Not all causes of slow turnover are correctable. If imports must be bought and paid for long before they reach the selling floor, or if domestic merchandise in irregular supply must be bought well in advance in order to ensure timely delivery, turnover necessarily suffers. But the deliberate sacrifice of turnover to secure desirable merchandise is by no means an error of the same magnitude as the stifling of turnover through inept management of the fashion assortment.

Importance of Good Turnover In explaining the value of good turnover, more than one merchant has likened fashion merchandise to fresh fish: both deteriorate promptly! A good rate of turnover in fashion merchandise results in:

▢ Minimum loss of sales appeal

▢ Reduced hazard of soilage and damage from handling

▢ Increased open-to-buy and the opportunity to freshen assortments with new goods, especially important when the same customers visit a given store or department frequently

▢ Accelerated interest on the part of salespeople, most of whom become bored with lingering stock

Department No. _4-2-11_   **RESOURCE FILE**

Resource No.	Name/Address	Contact Name / Telephone No.	FOB Point	Terms / Cash Discount	Advertising Allowance
482	Aiken Dress Company 1400 Broadway New York, New York 10018	Joseph Leonard 736-0900	N.Y.C.	8/10 E.O.M.	50/50 to 5% purch.
376	Elite Dress Company 1410 Broadway New York, New York 10018	Harold Raskin 734-9450	N.Y.C.	8/10 E.O.M.	50/50 to 3% purch.
917	After Five Fashions 1385 Broadway New York, New York 10018	Albert Owens 736-1285	N.Y.C.	8/10 E.O.M.	None

Form 14-11 (left side)

□ Increased interest of customers in constantly changing stock

□ Reduced inventory investment (which, in turn, means a reduction in interest on borrowed capital, reduced insurance costs, reduced stock space requirements, and reduced opportunities for pilferage)

Excessively High Turnover Good turnover, however, is not always the highest rate obtainable. While fashion merchandise turns at a higher rate than more staple merchandise, there are disadvantages in an excessively high rate of stock turnover. Too high a rate of stock turn implies inadequate stocks, unbalanced assortments, and loss of goodwill when customers cannot find wanted styles, colors, and sizes. In addition, high handling and billing costs may have been incurred by placing many small orders rather than a few large ones. The added expense detracts from profit.

Other Operational Yardsticks

Other yardsticks applied by retail management to the operation of a department include the number of sales transactions, the average gross sale, and sales per square foot. Each of these sheds light in its own way on one or more aspects of the buyer's competence and the efficiency of the merchandising operation.

Transactions The more transactions a department rings up in a year, the more customers it is assumed to have served. If the number falls off from one year to another, this is a possible indication of failure to attract or sell customers or both. The transaction figure itself is not an index of major importance, but its fluctuations are useful guides when hunting clues to the strengths or weaknesses of a department.

Average Gross Sale On an annual, or sometimes seasonal basis, stores divide the net sales of a department by the number of its sales transactions. The result is the *average gross sale*. A rising average gross sale may indicate rising prices, successful efforts to sell higher-priced qualities, successful efforts to sell more than one item to a customer, or all three. A higher average gross sale, when compared to the previous year's figure, can mean a better merchandising operation or just rising prices. When combined with a rising transaction figure, however, it usually means that a department really is pleasing its customers.

Freight Allowance	Year 19– 70					Year 19–71				
	Merchandise Returns	Net Purchases		Markdowns		Merchandise Returns	Net Purchases		Markdowns	
		C	R	$	%		C	R	$	%
No	$362 (1%)	34,568	59,600	1,195	2.0	$597 (1.7%)	35,392	63,200	1,580	2.5
No	$240 (1.9%)	12,615	21,750	654	3.0	$976 (7%)	13,938	24,890	1,170	4.7
No	$396 (20%)	1,982	3,540	354	10.0	Did not use				

Form 14-11 (right side)

Sales Per Square Foot Stores annually calculate the number of square feet of selling space assigned to a department and divide that number into the department's total net sales for the year. The resulting figure, dollar sales per square foot, is an index to how well the department has paid its "rent" to management. Most misses' and women's apparel departments in department stores have figures well above those of the store as a whole. In 1967, the figure for a store as a whole, exclusive of basement departments, was $73; for women's, misses', and juniors' coats and suits, $96; for women's hosiery, $185; for jewelry, $173; for men's clothing, $101.[2]

In departmentalized stores, management usually is amenable to expanding the selling area of a department or classification that shows exceptionally high sales per square foot. It may condense those departments that make a poor showing in this respect. Suggestions from buyers for rearranging their departments or installing new fixtures are more acceptable to management if there is indication that increased sales per square foot will result.

References

[1]*Buyer's Manual*, pp. 257–259.
[2]*Departmental Merchandising and Operating Results of 1967.*

Merchandising Vocabulary

Define or briefly explain the following terms:

Retail method
  of inventory evaluation
Cumulative markon
Book inventory
Purchase journal
Flash sales report

Departmental operating statement
Basic stock
Season letter
Age-of-stock reports
Average gross sale

Merchandising Review

1. Why is the retail method of inventory control better suited to a merchant's needs than conventional or cost methods of accounting?
2. What are the three major reasons for discrepancies between the book and physical inventories?
3. Name and describe the four types of merchandising reports in common use today among retail stores of all types.
4. Discuss a fashion buyer's responsibility with relation to markdowns.
5. List and give examples of ten major causes of markdowns.
6. What are a retailer's prime considerations in evaluating his suppliers of merchandise?
7. How does a merchant go about improving turnover?
8. How can a fashion merchant improve his department's rate of stock turnover?
9. What benefits result from improving the rate of stock turnover?
10. Discuss the effect upon a department's book inventory of each of the following: (a) purchases; (b) sales; (c) customer returns; (d) returns to vendors; (e) additional markons; (f) markdowns; (g) transfers to other departments.

Merchandising Digest

1. "Hardest to recognize but most in need of correction are markdowns due to poor timing." Discuss reasons why.
2. If a department were converted from personal selling to self-service, what effect would this be likely to have on: (a) its percentage of stock shortage; (b) its operating profit?
3. "Good turnover is not always the highest rate obtainable. While fashion merchandise turns at a higher rate than more staple merchandise, there are disadvantages in an excessively high rate of stock turnover." Discuss the disadvantages of an excessively high rate of stock turnover and its implications for well-balanced assortments.

15

Selecting Fashion Merchandise for Resale

Planning procedures prepare the retail buyer or store owner for one of the biggest jobs in fashion merchandising: the selection of individual styles from among those presented by producers. Up to this point, the buyer's plans have been quantitative, in terms of how many units and dollars should be invested in garments or accessories of given types. Up to this point, too, others at the store may have participated with the buyer in planning efforts by supplying data, expressing opinions, or setting policies and limits on purchases.

When he views a producer's line, the buyer must make qualitative decisions, and he must make them quite on his own. Should he choose this style or that, in this shade or that one? To the uninitiated, successful buyers may seem to exercise an uncanny intuition at this point in selecting precisely what their customers are ready to accept, but the mysterious sense that guides the buyer's decisions is nothing psychic or esoteric, just conscientious information gathering, sound appraisals, and thoughtful planning.

Buying for a fashion department is a fairly continuous process that can take place anywhere from the buyer's desk to the market centers. Reorders of goods previously stocked may be placed at any time by mail, telephone, or telegraph. New items may come to the buyer's attention and be ordered as a result of a visit to the store by a vendor's representative or a visit by the buyer to regional trade shows in locations near the buyer's stores. *Regional trade shows*, sometimes called caravans, bring together briefly the lines of several resources. Held in a central

location, such shows give nearby merchants an opportunity to see a fairly substantial cross section of what the market offers without having to make a trip to a distant fashion center.

By far the most stimulating place to buy, however, is a major fashion market such as New York City. Here the buyer can view many lines, each in its entirety, and can get a comprehensive picture of what an entire branch of the fashion industry has to offer.

The Buying Plan

A merchant or buyer on a trip to the wholesale markets leaves his store prepared to spend a great deal of money. To make sure that this money is not spent haphazardly, and to show that there is need for the trip, most stores require a written buying plan to be drawn up and approved prior to departure. A *buying plan* is a general description of the types and quantities of merchandise a buyer expects to purchase. It also sets a tentative limit on the amount of money to be spent, so that purchases will be kept in line with actual sales and the stock figures in the merchandise budget.

The more enthusiastic a retail buyer is about fashion merchandise, the more he needs the stabilizing influence of a written buying plan. It is a constant reminder to him to avoid going overboard for the first new and exciting goods he encounters, unless his budget and assortment plan permit him to buy freely and still not neglect other sectors of his assortment.

Berry's

BUYING PLAN

Department No. _42-11_   Date _2/14/19—_

Plan to be in market for ___3___ days from ___3/3___ to ___3/5___ . Open to buy for period _$1,362_

Reason for Trip (Special Events, Market Showings, etc.) _Additional Easter merchandise; review summer lines_

Class	Description	Retail Price	(A) Units on Hand 2/24	(B) Units on Order 2/24	(C) Total (A + B)	(D) Planned Unit Sales for Period	(E) Planned Unit Stock as of 3/31	(F) Total Units (D + E)	Sales This Period Last Year	Open to Buy (F − C)	Plan to Buy Units
1230	Dresses	19.98	26	18	44	19	30	49	33	5	9
1230	Dresses	24.98	41	10	51	21	40	61	38	10	15
1230	Dresses	29.98	26	12	38	18	36	54	30	16	15
1230	Dresses	34.98	24	6	30	12	24	36	21	6	10

Jane Dean
DEPARTMENT MANAGER

T. J. Evans
MERCHANDISE MANAGER

Resources to Visit and Comments _Aiken Dress Company — preferred resource_
Darling Dress Company — good reaction last year
Town and Country — sells competitor; Hardy and Wells
Elite Dress Company — good jacket dress resource

New Resources _Check Resident Buying Office for new resources._

Form 15-1

A buying plan makes all the difference between going to market to see what is offered in coats, for example, and going to market to find coats at specific retail price lines, in specific quantities, with specific delivery dates—all in accordance with budget, assortment plan, present inventory, present commitments, and sales potential of the coat department. Until a buyer or store owner actually inspects producers' lines, the buying plan cannot be completely explicit. To be without one, however, invites unplanned assortments, poorly related to consumer demand.

The buying plan is part of the homework that every retailer undertakes before making any major commitment of funds to buy fashion merchandise. Department stores generally do not release travel funds to their buyers until a plan has been made and has been approved by the merchandise manager. Form 15-1 illustrates a simple buying plan prepared by a buyer.

Information Required for a Buying Plan

In addition to identifying data such as department number and name, date of trip, destination, and length of stay, a typical buying plan requires detailed information about a number of other points. They include various estimates in both dollars and units of merchandise, emphasizing the importance of keeping both the merchandise budget and the merchandise assortment plan in mind when preparing the buying plan.

When the buyer has supplied all the information required in a buying plan, the merchandise manager is in a position to evaluate the need for the trip and also to bring his greater experience and judgment to bear upon the tentative decisions that a buying plan represents.

Reason for Trip The purpose of a buying trip may be to attend regular seasonal showings of lines, or to seek out special values for a forthcoming promotion, or to bolster a section of the assortment that is enjoying an unexpected burst of demand. It also may be to investigate a secondary market center, or perhaps to visit foreign fashion centers in quest of unusual items. The reason given for making the trip, as well as some of the other data in the buying plan, also shows

management whether the trip is urgent, routine, or exploratory.

Open-to-Buy Open-to-buy is the amount of merchandise that can be added to the inventory of a department in a given period without exceeding planned stock levels. The formula for calculating open-to-buy is:

$$\text{open-to-buy} = \text{planned sales} + \text{planned closing stock} - \text{present inventory} - \text{goods on order}$$

Open-to-buy can be figured either in dollars or in units of merchandise. Both are usually shown on a buying plan. The dollar figure on the buying plan automatically shows management whether or not the proposed purchases are within the financial limits established in that season's merchandise budget. The unit figure is a check against the season's assortment plan. In some cases, open-to-buy figures are shown for several months into the future; this is especially useful if the buyer intends to make commitments far in advance of the expected receipt or sales of the goods.

Stock on Hand and on Order For each classification of merchandise to be purchased, the plan lists present stock levels and any amounts already on order for delivery during the period for which the buying plan is being made. Usually each price line of stock is entered separately, with the stock on hand and on order calculated both in units and in dollars. Both cost and retail prices per unit are shown, and totals are given in terms of retail dollar value. By comparing these figures with those in the merchandise budget and the assortment plan, management can determine whether or not the intended purchases are within the budgetary limits set for the department or classification and are in line with the assortment plan of the department or classification.

Sales for the Period The buying plan, prepared just before a trip to market, includes the most recent sales estimates and reports available. These are in units and often also dollars. If the buying trip is made before the start of a season, the figures in the plan will be those on the dollar merchandise budget and the merchandise assortment plan. If the selling season has already begun, actual sales figures to date will be included. If the merchandise budget and the assortment plan have been adjusted to meet current conditions, the adjusted figures are used. The important point is that the buying plan includes the most up-to-date sales figures available at the time it is prepared.

Planned Stock at End of Period The planned end-of-period inventory figures, in both dollars and units, are important in planning the buying of fashion goods. Because demand rises rapidly to a peak in fashion goods, and falls off even more sharply after the peak has been passed, it is very important to keep the inventory within the established limits. If a fashion merchant brings in too much stock and has more than planned at the close of a selling period, it is likely that he will have to take heavy markdowns to get rid of that excess stock. If the buyer plans to make purchases for more than a month or two, then the planned stock for the end of the season is entered in the buying plan. If buying is short-term, then only the current month's closing stock estimate may be needed.

Quantities to Be Purchased Based on his judgment of sales potential, availability of merchandise, market conditions, and other factors, the fashion merchant indicates on his buying plan how much of each type of merchandise, in terms of both units and retail dollars, he wants to purchase on this trip in order to maintain an assortment balanced to meet consumer demand. Quantities to be purchased vary with the timing of a market trip, the store's merchandising policies, the type of merchandise, and delivery conditions. At the start of a selling season, perhaps only trial quantities are ordered, while larger quantities may be purchased with more assurance as the season advances. Most stores establish loosely defined percentages of the seasonal open-to-buy that may be purchased early. The experienced buyer saves some part of both his unit and dollar open-to-buy for later in the season, for unexpected opportune purchases, for reorders, and as

a hedge against changing customer demand that would require changes in the assortment.

Additional Data Some plans provide space for the buyer to enter later the amounts of his actual purchases. These entries are usually placed alongside the approved, planned figures. A number of stores require the buyer to submit, at the conclusion of each trip, a detailed reconciliation of all orders placed, by classification and price line, with quantities approved on the original buying plan. Either of these procedures underscores the importance of adhering to planned figures unless there is good reason.

A few store managements require a list of resources the buyer intends to visit. Such a list is usually expected to include the names of one or more resources with which the store has not yet had dealings, but whose potential the buyer will explore. It also includes resources with which the department has already dealt, sometimes for years.

This requirement serves a double purpose. It stimulates the buyer to make realistic plans as to which and how many producers he will try to visit in the time available to him. In addition, it reminds him to inspect the lines of resources that have been proven successful in customer acceptance, and yet it helps him avoid the danger of going only to his regular resources. Just as any business constantly seeks new customers, so an alert store seeks new and gifted resources to add fresh and interesting touches to its assortments.

Some buying plans also include a figure provided by management representing a purchase dollar limitation for the market trip. This amount may be higher than the total of the planned purchases listed, and may actually exceed the open-to-buy, since it may include a provisional allowance for opportune purchases. In a store committed to fashion leadership, this leeway permits the buyer more flexibility, should he find a new trend developing in the market. For buyers dedicated to bargain hunting, this extra money may mean additional opportunities to snap up good buys on the spot without hurting their regular assortments and without having to contact the store for permission to exceed planned figures.

Detailed descriptions of purchases to be made are not necessarily included on buying plans, since the buyer, not knowing precisely what he may find, cannot be more specific than "pleated skirts," "ruffled blouses," or "girls' 7–14 party dresses."

How a Buyer Plans

Before actually drawing up a buying plan, the fashion merchant or buyer reviews his stock in several respects. He checks his basic needs; he studies any overstock conditions; he notes any items that are winning strong acceptance; he takes upcoming sales events into consideration. This overall review is intended to give him a good idea of exactly what his needs are and what he should be looking for in the market.

Model Stocks In most stores, the first consideration is to see that the model stock is provided for. The model stock, remember, is the planned assortment of styles, sizes, colors, and price lines that should be in stock at certain times during the season. No matter how large the stock may grow as the season nears its peak, if some elements of the model are missing, the assortment will be less than complete in the eyes of the customer. Therefore, any replacements that are needed for the model stock go into the buying plan.

Overstock Any section of the assortment that exceeds its planned size requires analysis. The adjustments needed to reduce such overstocked conditions may affect buying plans for categories that otherwise are proceeding according to plan. For example, slow sellers in a higher price line may have to be marked down into a lower price line. In such cases, buying plans for the lower price line may have to be adjusted to take such additions to the existing stock into account. There also may be some common factor among a department's slow sellers which can be regarded as a warning against further purchases of a disappointing price line, color, fabric, detail, line, or other features customers have not favored. Experience in one part of the assortment can mean adjustments in assortment plans throughout the classification or department.

"Hot" Items Items, new or otherwise, that have demonstrated greater customer acceptance than was anticipated receive thoughtful consideration from the buyer. Even though they may not have been prominent in the original assortment plan for the season, it may be necessary to make an important place for them. To do that, buying plans for other items may have to be cut back.

If the "hot" item is one the buyer has heard about but has not yet actually had in stock, he may reserve judgment on its sales potential among his particular customers until he has seen and studied it in the market. Then buying plans for the more predictable and familiar items may be drawn up indicating where cutbacks can be made if the "hot" item is added to the assortment.

Special Events If the buying trip for which the plan is drawn involves preparation for a promotional event, special sale, catalog distribution, or similar activity, the buyer fortifies himself with details on what was offered to and bought by the store's customers on similar occasions in the past. If a buyer is about to purchase children's gloves, for example, for the store's Christmas catalog, it is important to know how many of those sold from the previous year's catalog were knitted or leather, bright colors or neutrals, matched to caps and scarves or sold separately, and how many were sold at each price. Then this information has to be weighed against what appears to be this year's trends in children's gloves.

Importance of Complete Data When the buyer is drawing up a buying plan, he is in the store. All the sources of information on present conditions and past experience, described in Chapters 12 and 13, are available to him. Once in the market, however, he has only the "nutshell" data of the buying plan itself to consult. The more thoroughly he checks while still at the store, the more valuable and informative the capsulized data on the buying plan will be.

Timing of the Market Trip

It is almost impossible to operate a fashion shop or department without at least two market trips a year. When and how often a buyer goes to

FASHION CALENDAR FOR NEW YORK SEASONAL OPENINGS[1]
(Better and High-Priced Apparel Lines)

Month	Back-to-School Minor [2]	Fall Major	Holiday Minor	Resort and Cruise Minor	Spring Major	Summer Major	Transitional Minor
April		Showings					
May	Showings	Showings					
June							
July	Delivery	Delivery					
August	Delivery	Delivery					
September			Showings	Showings			
October				Showings	Showings		
November			Delivery		Showings		
December				Delivery			
January				Delivery		Showings	
February					Delivery		
March							
April						Delivery	
May						Delivery	Showings
June							
July							Delivery

Notes:

1 The trend is to earlier manufacturer's openings to ensure better deliveries.

2 A major season in children's and junior wear.

Key:

Manufacturers Showings

Store Delivery

market are determined by the size of the store, the volatility of fashion in the merchandise concerned, and how far away a store is from the market. A store that wants to build or maintain a strong fashion image may send its buyers to market many times a year, so that they will catch even the faintest whiff of new developments. A retailer who features price above all else may also have his buyers in the market frequently, but on scavenging expeditions for special buys. Plans for a special promotion may require buyers to make an extra market trip in search of unusual values.

Few fashion buyers feel they can function effectively if they do not get to the market for manufacturers' openings. These openings are occasions for exhibiting new styles in their greatest variety and with the maximum of showmanship. To view a series of lines this way is both exciting and educational for the buyer.

The dates of such openings vary from one segment of the fashion business to another, according to the lead time required for production and delivery of goods, the convenience of the market date for buyers, and the seasonality of consumer demand for the goods. Easter, for example, is a time for purchasing new spring clothes, even in climates where winter weather still prevails or where spring has already arrived. In order for the retailer to have ample selections of spring goods in stock by February, manufacturers of apparel show their spring lines as early as the preceding October, and buyers come to market at that time.

The sample fashion calendar above shows the months in which better apparel manufacturers show their new lines, as well as the months in which the merchandise begins to arrive in the stores. The recent trend has been for earlier openings with a longer spread between showings and delivery dates. This allows ample time to get the goods produced and into the stores when the consumer wants to see them. By contrast, spring lines in the 1930s opened in January, and fall lines opened in July. In each case, delivery took eight to ten weeks.

Resident Buying Offices

Most buyers of fashion merchandise, with the possible exception of those from the smallest and most exclusive shops, make resident buying offices their first port of call on a market trip. A *resident buying office* is an organization located in a major market area that provides market information and representation to its client stores. These stores are usually fairly similar in size and class of trade but are located in different towns and cities and do not compete with one another.

Nearly all resident buying offices have their headquarters in New York City; some have branches in other important market centers both in the United States and abroad. Most of the major offices cover the whole range of department store merchandise, from fashion accessories to home furnishings. A number, however, serve only specialty stores. A few restrict themselves to a narrow range of merchandise, such as infants' and children's wear, or even to a single department, such as millinery, which requires constant scouring of the market for new ideas and items.

Types of Resident Buying Offices

There are two major types of resident buying offices—independent offices and store-owned offices. An independent resident buying office actively seeks out noncompeting stores as paying clients, while the store-owned office is entirely owned by the store or stores it represents and works exclusively for them.

Independent Offices The numerically dominant type of resident buying office is the *salaried* or *fee office*, which is independently owned and operated and charges the stores it represents for the work it does for them. Such offices enter into annual contracts with noncompeting stores to provide market services in exchange for an annual stipulated fee or "salary" based upon each individual store's sales volume.

This type of office strives to familiarize itself with each client store's individual operation and needs and to meet those needs with a broad range of services, including development of private brand merchandise, central buying and merchandising of certain categories of fashion merchandise, and group purchasing of store equipment and supplies. Among the oldest and best known offices of this type are the Mutual Buying Syndicate; Kirby, Block and Company; Felix Lilienthal and Company; and McGreevey, Werring and Howell. Also in this category are a number of specialized offices, such as Youth Fashion Guild, which serves only children's shops, and Arthur Holman, which deals only in millinery.

Store-Owned Offices Resident buying offices, owned and operated by the stores they represent, are divided into three groups: private offices, associated or cooperative offices, and syndicate offices.

An office that is owned and operated by a single, out-of-town store and performs market work exclusively for that store is called a *private office*. Such an office is actually a staff bureau of the store, located in the market rather than in the store itself. Because of the investment involved and the high cost of operation, only very high volume department and specialty stores maintain their own private resident buying offices. Some stores maintain a private office within the independent or associated office to which they belong. In this way, a store has access to all of the services of the larger office and yet has in the market its own representative who is on the store's payroll and is directly responsible to the store's management.

A second type of store-owned office is an *associated office,* which is one jointly owned and operated by a group of independent stores. This type of office also is frequently referred to as a *cooperative office.* Membership is by invitation only, and is considerably more expensive than if the store were a client of a salaried office. Stores that belong to an associated office, however, usually are highly homogeneous as to sales volume, store policies, and target groups of customers, and as a result, their relationship is generally an intimate one, extending to an exchange of operating figures and the sharing of merchandising experiences. The operating expenses of an associated office are allocated to each member store on the basis of sales volume and amount of services required. There are relatively few associated resident buying offices. Typical are the Associated Merchandising Corporation, Frederick Atkins, and Specialty Stores Association.

A third type of store-owned resident buying office is generally known as a syndicate office. A *syndicate office* is an office maintained by a parent organization that owns a group of stores. The office performs market services for those stores that are members of the corporate ownership group. Some offices of this type have more authority than their counterparts in salaried or associated offices for the placing of merchandise orders to be delivered to member stores. In others, authorization from store buyers is required, despite the close corporate relationship. Examples of syndicate offices are those maintained by Allied Stores Corporation, Associated Dry Goods Corporation, and May Department Stores.

Organization of the Resident Buying Office

The typical resident buying office is organized along lines similar to those of a merchandising division in a department store. There are market representatives, whose positions parallel those of retail store buyers. There are merchandise managers, who supervise groups of market representatives. There is a fashion coordinator who is responsible for information on the overall fashion picture. All of these specialists are available to store buyers who visit the market, although most of a visiting buyer's needs can be handled by the market representative alone.

Other executives in the typical buying office provide sales promotion ideas and aids, and operate various buying activities for member stores, when requested. In most offices, there also are facilities for exchange of information on their retail operations, purchasing of miscellaneous supplies for store use, and other activities pertaining to retail store operation. These last are supplementary services, performed in addition to the resident buying office's primary function of keeping in close and constant contact with markets and merchandise so as to facilitate the store's merchandising activities.

The Market Representative's Job A *market representative* is a specialist who covers a narrow segment of the total market and makes information obtained about it available to buyers of stores served by the resident office. He "lives" in his market and makes himself an authority on supply, demand, styles, prices, deliveries, and any conditions affecting supply and service to retailers. He visits resources, sees lines, checks into general conditions of supply and demand, verifies trends, seeks new "hot" items, hunts up specific items requested by client stores, and follows up on delivery or other problems referred to him by store buyers.

The early hours of each working day are spent at his desk, reviewing mail from stores, seeing items and lines brought to the office's sample rooms by vendors' salesmen, and being available to any store buyer who may be in the market.

Afternoons are usually spent in the market, tracking down items, reviewing lines in producers' showrooms, and keeping in touch with what is happening in the industries assigned to him for coverage. In the late afternoon, the market representative returns to his desk, often to prepare a special bulletin to the stores on something he feels they should know about immediately. It might be an opportunity for a special buy from a manufacturer who is closing out remainders, for instance, or the discovery of a new and exciting item that buyers should have a chance to consider without waiting for a market trip.

Consulting the Market Representative A buyer visiting the market checks in at once with his store's resident buying office and reviews his buying plan with the appropriate market representative. In the light of current supply and demand situations, fashion developments, and other pertinent factors, the buyer and market representative determine what changes, if any, should be made in the buying plan.

A great deal of market time is saved for the

Courtesy The Broadway-Hale Stores, Inc.

The market representative in a buying office keeps in daily touch with trends in her product specialty.

buyer through such early conferences, since the market representative can direct him toward those resources best able to fill his needs. If the buyer comes to market hoping to locate some item he has not yet seen but has heard about and hopes to find, the market representative will either suggest appropriate resources or advise against hunting for it, depending upon the availability and marketability of the particular item.

Buyer Clinics

During major market weeks, when most buyers are in New York, the resident offices usually arrange a series of meetings or clinics for each group of buyers of certain types of merchandise. These sessions are designed to give the buyers an idea of current fashion and market situations before they start visiting the showrooms of individual producers.

At such meetings, the market representatives and other speakers discuss fashion, supply, retail prices, and market problems. Occasionally a manufacturer comes before such a meeting to present his line, or a new sales promotion program, or an idea for more effective merchandising of his products. In the course of such discussions, a buyer may develop a new perspective in relation to his buying plan that enables him to make adjustments to improve the plan, or he may emerge from the meeting with increased confidence in the advisability of following his plan.

Central Merchandising

With the information that unit controls provide, even a knowledgeable outsider, remote from a store, can gain sufficient insight into the preferences of customers to be able to plan assortments and select merchandise for them. Thus, in such fast-moving fashion categories as inexpensive dresses and budget sportswear, a resident buying office can perform this service for subscriber stores all over the country. The advantage of a central merchandising operation of this type is that the buying office's representatives are in the wholesale markets daily and can make fresh selections or follow up on deliveries of orders constantly. This service is extremely valuable for smaller stores, because they usually cannot afford to send their buyers into the market more than twice a year, which is not often enough to keep a stream of fresh, newsworthy fashions coming into stock.

In such a central merchandising operation, each store provides the buying office with a dollar merchandise budget and an assortment plan, to which it adds general observations about its customers' preferences, such as "no sleeveless dresses" or "our people like wide necklines." Using these guides, the resident buying office orders the garments it considers appropriate for each store. The store reports receipt of merchandise, sales, markdowns, and customer returns, just as if it were reporting to a unit control department under its own roof. The records are kept in the buying office, however, so that the merchandiser in charge of the central buying operation has a finger on the pulse of demand in each store.

Group Purchases

Sometimes the market representative or the store buyer may suggest group action in a buying situation. Through *group purchase,* identical merchandise is bought by several stores at one time from a given resource, so that all participants may share in the advantages of a large-volume purchase. Such a group purchase might involve the development of special merchandise for the exclusive use of member stores, the pooling of purchases in order to obtain financial benefits, or the encouraging of production of a new fashion item that is not yet widely available in the market but is one in which the stores have confidence.

A buying office may organize a group purchase when a manufacturer offers closeout merchandise in a quantity that is too large for one store to handle but might be adequately apportioned among several stores. Another time when group purchasing may be used is when the office prepares a group catalog for such occasions as Christmas or back-to-school. When the catalog is one that can be used by a number of stores, a substantial reduction in printing costs can be realized by all the participating stores. Items selected for such a catalog, however, must be agreed upon by all the buyers, and each must plan to set aside sufficient open-to-buy for the numbers chosen by the group. Thus participation in group purchases may, on occasion, involve adjustments in the planned assortments.

Other Sources of Information in the Market

A good fashion merchant is always hungry for fashion information. Armed with data about his own store's experience and guided by a thoughtfully developed buying plan, the fashion buyer continues accumulating facts and opinions as he pursues his course through the market. His major sources are the experience of other buyers from his home store, fashion periodicals, manufacturers, trade associations and trade shows, and other stores and their buyers.

Experience of Other Home-Store Buyers

In addition to his own department's experience, the department or specialty store buyer also calls upon the experience of other fashion buyers within his own organization. Some retail merchandising executives make a point of having all their fashion buyers confer at the end of each day in the market so that they can pool their experiences and guide each other.

For example, a dress buyer's expression of confidence in a long, unbroken line may reinforce a foundation buyer's confidence in girdles that narrow the hips. At the same time, the interest in lengthening the body line may encourage the accessories buyer to explore resources for long scarfs and necklaces that further narrow and lengthen the figure. Each buyer's evaluation of current fashion trends, as interpreted in his own market, helps the others evaluate what they find in their markets and helps project a more uniform storewide fashion image.

Fashion Periodicals

Consumer magazines, both those that devote themselves primarily to fashion and those for whom fashion is but one of many subjects of its editoral coverage, represent a good source of fashion information for the retail buyer. They are in a position to give him advance information on the fashion trends to be featured editorially in upcoming issues and the specific styles to be used as illustrations of those trends. In addition, the fashion magazines share with the retailer their considerable knowledge of fashion itself and of the particular segment of fashion's consumers to which their pages are addressed.

The editors of these magazines, like fashion buyers, do not rely upon intuition to guide their selection of fashions. They study their readers assiduously, often with the aid of elaborate consumer research projects, observing how their readers live, dress, work, and relax. Like successful fashion merchants, they are in such close rapport with their readers that they can forecast rather accurately the styles that will win acceptance in the months ahead.

Editorial Credits When a fashion magazine editor selects a garment or an accessory item to be

Courtesy Deering Milliken, Inc.

Manufacturers' showrooms often feature displays that show how fashion components fit together.

featured in a forthcoming issue, the usual policy is to invite one or more stores to permit their names to appear with the illustration as retail sources for the merchandise. Such a mention is known as an *editorial credit*. If a store accepts a credit, it is expected to stock the featured item in sufficient quantity to satisfy local demand. A well-chosen credit does not materially affect the buying plan, since the merchandise is considered to be within the framework of what the store's customers would normally accept. Ideally, a credit simply highlights an item the store might have selected anyway on its own merits.

Trend Information Buyers in the market who call at the editorial offices of magazines usually can see photographs or samples of future fashion features for several months ahead. A talk with any of the fashion or merchandising editors will give the buyer information about the trends the various selections exemplify, reasons why these trends are important to the magazine's readers, and suggestions for encouraging members of the magazine's particular public to buy the featured items.

For example, in 1967, when belts were returning to the fashion scene after a long absence, the editors of a magazine for younger women realized that their readers had not been adults long enough to have had personal experience in using belts for fashion and figure effect. The magazine illustrated a variety of belts and ways to wear them, and suggested to retailers that they also make an effort to acquaint younger customers with the belt's possibilities. Such a customer service is easily overlooked by a mature buyer whose personal experience with fashion covers a long sweep of years and trends.

Resource Information Consumer magazines, as a matter of course, provide retailers with lists of those manufacturers who produce the garments and accessories to be shown in future issues. Their service to the retailer often goes beyond this point, however. As a result of having spent many hours in the market, the fashion editor usually can direct a buyer to resources for merchandise he wants—not necessarily something featured in the magazine, and yet within its field.

Fashion News and Insights Whether or not a retailer accepts an editorial credit, buys the editorially featured styles, or seeks suggestions as to resources, he still can profit by visiting the offices of those periodicals whose readers most closely resemble his own customers in tastes and interests. He is almost certain to come away with information and insights that aid his market work. If nothing else, in the case of publications whose impact is strong among his customers, he will know what merchandise and fashion news will be given exposure, and he can plan to reflect similar influences in his assortment, if he chooses to do so.

All this, of course, is in addition to the fashion buyer's required reading of periodicals devoted exclusively to fashion news in both consumer and trade categories. Magazines such as *Vogue, Harper's Bazaar, Esquire,* and *Gentlemen's Quarterly Magazine* provide the buyer with a background on incoming fashions, as do such trade publications as *Women's Wear Daily* and *Men's Wear.* Regardless of the stage of the fashion cycle at which his customers buy, every merchant needs to keep abreast of the newest trends. Only in that way can he evaluate the prospects of whatever fashions he has purchased or is considering purchasing for his own store.

Manufacturers

There is much that a producer of fashion merchandise can give the buyer by way of useful information. If the manufacturer is a major one in his field and has fairly wide distribution, his experience, activities, and marketing plans provide invaluable assistance to the buyer who is in the market to select merchandise.

The Manufacturer's Fashion Thinking A top-ranking producer usually has carefully thought-out reasons behind his decision to make up certain styles, to use certain materials and colors, and to ignore others. He can also indicate which numbers in his line are frankly experimental and possibly prophetic, which ones are new but nevertheless definitely expected to make a secure place for themselves, and which are carry-overs of fashions that are no longer new but remain in demand. Equally important is information explaining why he has perhaps ignored some of the ideas that others in his field have taken up. All this becomes part of the background data a buyer's mind processes in order to arrive at decisions concerning his own assortment.

Retail Experience Manufacturers, without betraying confidences, often can pass along valuable information about what outstanding retailers have bought, how they have arranged their departments, trained their salespeople, and promoted and displayed the merchandise. For example, in a line of fairly classic sportswear, the maker may reveal that one store achieves exceptional turnover and does many times the volume of equivalent stores elsewhere by keeping rigidly to a rule of frequent stock counts and fill-ins. In another instance, the buyer may be told of a spectacular fashion event through which a store successfully promoted higher-priced garments than it had sold previously. By picking up ideas about how other stores have achieved good results with a line, a buyer may be encouraged to purchase and sell more freely than he had previously expected.

Promotion Plans A maker's plans to invest promotional effort in a line, style, or trend have direct bearing upon buying decisions. A buyer must weigh the possible impact of such promotion upon his own store's customers and buy accordingly. For example, a producer may have plans for a series of advertisements in various consumer magazines. If one or more of these publications is influential among the buyer's customers, this fact may cause him to buy more freely of the producer's line than he would otherwise do. On the other hand, if the buyer believes that the producer's promotional program will have little effect upon his store's customers, it will have equally little effect upon the amount he purchases from the firm.

Occasionally, without attempting to relate the manufacturer's advertising directly to its impact on the store's customers, a buyer may find his own confidence in a fashion confirmed by the fact that a manufacturer has such confidence in it that he is planning his season's promotional outlay around it.

Selling Techniques A buyer is likely to purchase radically new merchandise with greater confidence if he can glean workable ideas for its display and sale. Manufacturers often can offer such ideas. For example, when stretch hosiery for women was first introduced in the 1950s, many buyers hesitated to purchase it because it looked quite unimpressive if shown to customers in the usual way: by having the salesperson open a box of folded stockings and thrust her hand into the upper portions of the top stocking. When buyers were told of the successes achieved by stores that displayed the stretch hosiery on leg forms, some of them, confident that they had or could obtain a sufficient supply of such forms, were encouraged to buy more freely.

Regional Variations A resource with national distribution is usually completely familiar with regional variations in timing, color preferences, and other marketing matters. Certain garments, for instance, may be bought earlier and may enjoy a longer season in the South than in the North; certain colors may be perennial favorites in some areas, but may fluctuate in popularity in other areas. A buyer who is new to a store or department can obtain helpful guidance on such points from dependable manufacturers. Records left by the preceding buyer may not show clearly the reasoning that governed timing and assortment choice in the past, but a manufacturer often can clarify the situation in a few words.

Trade Associations and Trade Shows

Associations of manufacturers and of retailers assist the fashion buyer in many ways. The nature and frequency of the assistance available, however, are not uniform throughout the fashion industries. Some associations offer more help to the buyer than others, and each buyer learns to familiarize himself with what assistance is to be had in the industries from which he buys.

Retail Buyers' Groups Associations or clubs for buyers of a single classification of merchandise provide an opportunity for the exchange of opinion with others. At the very least, such an opportunity aids the buyer in clarifying his own ideas about fashion and market conditions. In some

instances, groups of this kind provide a medium through which buyers can transmit to an entire industry their preferences in matters ranging from the dates when lines should be opened to the sizes of stock boxes to be used. Many such associations are subsidized by the industries concerned, or by trade publications, or both.

Trade Shows Retail or manufacturer groups, and sometimes independent entrepreneurs, establish trade shows at which a great many manufacturers in a given industry exhibit their lines under one roof and at the same time. "Under one roof" usually means a hotel, or two or three hotels, in which several floors are set aside for exhibit space. With an absolute minimum of time and travel, the buyer can see almost every line he wants to see, can make comparisons, and can exchange opinions in "corridor talk" with other buyers from all over the country. The impact of seeing so many lines in so short a space of time is great, and a clear-cut impression of what the market offers can be gained readily. This is especially helpful in industries in which small firms predominate. The buyer can look in on dozens of them in one day at such a show, instead of trekking from building to building, up and down elevators, and possibly covering only four or five showrooms in as many hours.

Among the industries in which such shows are regularly staged for retail buyers are shoes, foundation garments, notions, and piece goods.

Fashion Bulletins Many manufacturers' associations publish fashion bulletins for buyers, to alert them to fashion trends and to explain their significance in terms of retail opportunities. Since whatever helps the retailer to sell an industry's products also helps the industry itself, some of these associations retain experts in retail merchandising and promotion to contribute suggestions to buyers about advertising, selling, and display ideas related to current fashions. Especially noteworthy are the bulletins of some of the associations in the raw materials fields, such as fibers, furs, and leathers.

Retail Conventions Retailers' associations regularly hold conventions or meetings for their members. Some of the sessions are devoted to subjects of interest to fashion merchants and buyers, especially in areas that present unusual problems or opportunities. The National Retail Merchants Association, at its annual convention (always held in New York City in early January), devotes sessions to such departments as hosiery, lingerie, dresses, or accessories, whenever fashion developments (or the lack thereof) in the merchandise concerned make these worthwhile. For many years, also, a regular feature of NRMA conventions has been a discussion of the ten outstanding fashion promotions of the previous year and the elements that made them successful.

Other Stores, Other Buyers

The buyer meets with representatives of non-competing stores through his resident buying office. In the market, he finds himself in contact also with a host of other buyers. Informal conversations, even those that are fragmentary, become the medium for exchange of opinions and experience with other retailers.

In addition to such contacts, buyers visiting a market city make a point of looking over the merchandise and displays of the local stores. Chatting with a local buyer about some of the new ideas or new merchandise seen in the department may prove stimulating and profitable to the visiting buyer.

Making the rounds in a large city also provides an opportunity to gauge the progress of a particular fashion. The buyer can observe where it stands in its cycle and how much or how little emphasis is given to it in stores of varying degrees of fashion leadership. If a style is featured by stores whose clienteles purchase at a later stage of the fashion cycle than his own, the buyer has reason to be wary of that style. If stores higher up on the fashion totem pole than his are featuring the style, then that might suggest that it is something his customers will want soon.

Visiting other stores is also a way to check how far the copying-down process may have progressed with styles that interest a buyer. If his is a medium-priced store, for example, he may decide against ordering an otherwise acceptable style because he sees that it has been "knocked off" and is already in basement departments and discount houses.

Working the Market

It has been said that there are as many ways of shopping (or "working") the market as there are buyers. Each buyer develops his own technique or procedure for covering a vast amount of ground and doing it with a minimum of physical strain and a conservation of mental energy. The primary purpose of the trip, the length of the trip, and the number of resources that have to be covered all influence the manner in which each buyer works.

In spite of the differences among buyers, however, certain basic rules apply under any circumstances. They underline the importance of proper preparation before each day's investigations begin and proper concentration while examining each line.

Order of Seeing Lines

Before setting out each morning, the buyer should have a tentative itinerary set up for calls to be made that day. The schedule cannot be too rigid, since delays are bound to occur. Nevertheless, some sort of itinerary helps a buyer to make sure that each day in the market produces its expected quota of calls.

Some buyers, aware of the difficulties of moving about through densely crowded streets, visit lines in what may be called geographical order: one building at a time. With dozens of manufacturers in each skyscraper in Garment Town (an affectionate name for the Seventh Avenue apparel showroom area), the calls in one building alone can be a good day's work for a buyer. On the other hand, the building-by-building technique may fail to produce an overall impression of trends, because each building tends to draw tenants dealing in the same type and price level of goods. To get a general view, several buildings must be visited.

Other buyers, at some cost to their time and feet, ignore geography and each day see lines across the board by type and price, so that they can compare one with another while impressions are fresh.

A third approach is to visit first the buyer's *major resources,* those from which his department has consistently bought a substantial portion of its merchandise needs in past seasons. Under normal circumstances, a buyer can expect to continue to purchase an important share of his needs from these resources, so long as their merchandise continues to meet consumer demand in his store.

Rapport between a buyer and such a resource is usually excellent, and the exchange of ideas and information rapid. The buyer can cover much of his requirements at once and proceed to complete his market tour in a more relaxed frame of mind. Also, when he knows what his major resources are showing, a buyer is in a better position to evaluate the styles he sees later in other showrooms.

Still another approach is by price line, or seeing the higher-priced resources in each class of merchandise first, and then continuing through each group. Although the rule has its exceptions, a buyer usually finds more fashion news, more daring, a surer touch, and more awareness of the fashion reasons favoring particular lines, colors, and textures among the higher-priced makers than among those in the lower brackets. Buyers who prefer this method point out that it gives them a quick overview of fashion trends as a preliminary to the study of all the other lines to be seen on the market trip.

The choice of method is usually the buyer's, unless the store has specific governing rules. In a store that strives for fashion leadership, buyers may be required to see the fashion leaders among their resources first, and then to meet with the store's other fashion buyers to evaluate what they have seen and to decide which fashions or "looks" are right for their store. Only then are they free to go on with the rest of their market work.

Showroom Procedures

The buyer who is conscious of the value of time makes a practice of letting resources know when to expect him at the showroom and what he is looking for especially. This procedure ensures his being greeted by the salesman who handles the store's account or by a showroom salesman who has had time to brief himself on the store's previous purchases. Rapport can thus be established quickly.

In the days when a market trip was an adventure in sharp bargaining, both the salesman and the buyer sought to retain the upper hand in the encounter, one to sell what he most wanted to unload and the other to buy what seemed to be the best values. Today each strives for better understanding of the other's problems, and each knows that what is good for both parties is more desirable than for one to profit at the expense of the other.

Managements urge their buyers to listen to the salesmen's comments and suggestions and to avoid cutting off what can prove a source of useful information. They instruct them, also, to tell the resources about their successes with the line, and to express appreciation of business courtesies extended—if only to prepare for some possible future day when they may have to request a favor or dispensation from the resource. Business, and especially the exchange of information about the fashion business, proceeds best in an atmosphere of mutual respect. And respect is what modern retailers expect their buyers to achieve in the market.

Taking Numbers

Normally buyers do not write up orders when they look at each new season's lines. Instead, they take numbers. *"Taking numbers"* means writing an adequate description of each style the buyer is considering as a possible selection, including number, size range, colors, fabric, price, and any other relevant details. At the end of the trip, the buyer compares numbers for similar merchandise from all resources and weeds out duplications and the less desirable styles.

If this restraint is not exercised, a buyer may order too lavishly from the first few resources he visits, leaving no funds for possibly better numbers seen later. Until an order has been placed, the buyer is free to change his mind. Once he has written up and placed an order, however, he has committed his store to take the merchandise, and a change of mind at that point requires canceling an order without justification, a practice condemned as unfair to the resource.

A buyer in the market examines all available lines and ''takes numbers,'' writing a description of all possible choices; then makes the final decision about what to order after everything has been compared.

In some classifications, such as scarfs, gloves, hosiery, or costume jewelry, the lines a buyer views may be very extensive, and he may find it difficult to write a sufficient description of each number for later recall. For such merchandise, buyers list the most desirable numbers first and those that are least acceptable last. Later, when all lines have been seen, cuts can be made from the bottom up to avoid inadvertently sacrificing any exceptionally good styles.

After eliminating "duds" and developing the best possible list of numbers, some buyers work again with the resident buyer, calling on the market representative's intimate knowledge of the lines for help.

Writing the Order

An *order* is a contract to buy the merchandise specified. To ensure that the contract covers all required points and to avoid committing the store to unacceptable conditions, buyers write up their orders only on the forms provided by their own stores (or, in some instances, on the forms of their resident buying offices) and never on the seller's form. Prevailing practice is to write up orders after leaving the market and to have them countersigned by the merchandise manager or other store official.

The typical order form requires the buyer to specify:

□ Date of order.

□ Resource's name and address, together with shipping point, if different from showroom address (a seller may maintain a sales office in New York City but produce and ship from elsewhere).

□ Shipping instructions, including the date by which the shipment should be completed, the route by which it should be sent, and any special arrangements relating to shipping costs.

□ Terms of payment (how soon after shipment the bill must be paid, and with what discount).

□ Department and/or classification for which the goods are purchased.

□ Address of store unit to which shipment should be made (if store has more than one).

□ Any special directions about packing and shipping (for example, a store with several branches may request each branch's goods to be separately packed and labeled, even though all merchandise is to be received at a central marking location).

□ Details of styles purchased, including number, description, and cost price. Descriptions, depending upon the article, may specify color, fabric, size, or other points. There should be enough information to make it easy for the store's receiving department, as well as the seller's shipping room, to know exactly what the order covers.

□ Retail price (shown only on the store's copies of the order, not on the vendor's copy). The buyer indicates the unit selling price he intends to place on each style number. Thus the retail as well as the cost value of each purchase can be calculated, and the initial markon percentage can be worked out. On copies of the order that are intended for the marking room, the column of cost figures is blacked out, and only the retail prices, needed for making up price tickets, are visible.

□ Any special arrangements concerning the purchase (for example, the seller may agree to contribute a specified amount, on specified conditions, toward the advertising of a purchase; or as is sometimes the case, particularly in placing orders for such merchandise as furs and high-ticket jewelry items, the buyer may have the privilege of returning unsold goods by a specified date).

□ Standard trade practices. Established many years ago by the National Retail Merchants Association, in cooperation with the associations representing the apparel trades, these practices are usually printed on the back of each store's order blank. The provisions spell out the obligations of buyer and seller to one another and define what constitutes fair or unfair practice in relation to an order.

Merchandising Notes

At the time he writes up his order, the buyer also may write up brief notes about the merchandise, his reasons for choosing it, and the overall impression he gained from his market trip. From these notes he later prepares training talks for

A buyer visiting a manufacturer's showroom may be shown one style after another, each plucked from a rack that contains samples of every item the resource is offering.

his salespeople about incoming merchandise and fashion trends. These notes also may serve as memos about the selling points of the goods for the advertising and display departments. If he does this work while the merchandise is fresh in his mind and while his enthusiasm for it is strong, some of the excitement of his market trip will spread to everyone else at the store who will eventually be concerned with its sale.

Testing New Fashions

Astute merchants avoid taking too many chances as to which fashion will be accepted by their customers and which will get only a cool reception. There is an element of Russian roulette in letting oneself be carried away by enthusiasm for a new fashion that has been seen in the market. The same risk is present when a buyer assumes that his own idea of the right color, line, or texture is identical with that of his store's customers. A near-miss in judging the acceptability of a new fashion can be a costly error for a merchant. He risks his fashion reputation in the community, as well as his capital, every time he selects a new style for his stock.

Most merchants greet a new fashion with the *sample-test-reorder* technique. They buy in small quantities in a wide range of possibly acceptable styles to observe customer reaction. Then they reorder in substantial quantity those styles that appear to have won a favorable reception; the rest are quickly marked down and cleared. The customer casts the deciding vote.

For example, suppose that every indication points to a growing popularity of pale, neutral woolen dresses. A buyer may feel very strongly that off-white will be the preferred neutral and that shirtwaist types will be the preferred styles. Instead of buying heavily of off-white shirtwaists alone, however, the buyer will perhaps try white, off-white, and pale beige and will purchase each of these colors in several styles. When the goods arrive at the store, he will observe customer comments as well as sales to determine which colors and styles are best received. He may find that pale beige is as well received as off-white; he therefore should order ample quantities of both colors. He may also find that shirtwaist styles with convertible collars are most acceptable and that cuffed sleeves are evoking better response than push-up sleeves.

At this point, the buyer places large orders for dresses with the acceptable points. These may or may not be the same points that he believed would be successful when he was in the market. His actual experience permits him now to buy with confidence and in quantity.

The testing procedure is not without its difficulties. In offering his customers a wide range of styles at the start of the season, a merchant inevitably stocks certain numbers that will have to be marked down because they are hard to sell. In general, however, the losses thus sustained are far less than they might have been with no trial balloons at all.

A growing difficulty lies in the length of time it takes for a manufacturer to deliver goods, particularly those of a highly seasonal nature. Manufacturers cannot always produce at short notice the numbers that buyers wish to reorder. A retailer whose initial purchases were too cautious may find his racks nearly bare as the season progresses, with no prospect of receiving his reorders until after the peak of demand has passed.

Here is where experience and judgment come into play. A buyer on a market trip has to sound out resources' ability to deliver and the prospects of ample or restricted supplies of merchandise, as well as fashion developments. If he has reason to believe that an eminently salable number will be hard to reorder later, he may forego the test routine and place a substantial order at once. If he has done his market work properly, checking all sources of information available to him, he can reach a wise decision on this point and on others affecting his buying.

Merchandising Vocabulary

Define or briefly explain the following terms:

Buying plan	Trade shows
Resident buying office	Major resource
Market representative	Taking numbers
Group purchase	Order
Editorial credit	Sample-test-reorder

Merchandising Review

1. What factors determine how often buyers go to market? For what reasons, other than viewing seasonal lines, do buyers make market trips?
2. What are the major purposes served by a buying plan?
3. Name at least five valuable sources of fashion information available to the buyer while on a market trip.

4. Name at least five activities engaged in by a market representative.
5. Name and describe the two major types of resident buying offices.
6. In what specific ways can fashion periodicals be a valuable source of information for the retail buyer?
7. What are the four approaches from which a buyer can elect to plan his daily market itinerary?
8. What is meant by "taking numbers"? Why is it advisable when working the market to take numbers rather than to write the order at once?
9. Name at least five types of information required on a typical store order form.
10. Name at least ten types of information that is entered on most buying plans.
11. What important considerations should a buyer take into account when preparing a buying plan?

Merchandising Digest

1. "There is much that a producer of fashion merchandise can give the buyer by way of useful information." Discuss this statement from the text, pointing out the various ways in which a manufacturer can help a buyer make fashion decisions.
2. "Astute merchants avoid playing hunches as to which fashions will be accepted by their customers." Discuss this statement from the text and its implications for the merchandising of fashion goods.
3. "A merchant or buyer on a trip to the wholesale markets leaves his store prepared to spend a great deal of money. To make sure this money is not spent haphazardly, and to show that there is a need for the trip, most stores require a written buying plan to be drawn up and approved prior to departure." Discuss the various ways in which a buying plan can be of inestimable help to a buyer when he is in the market.

16

Promoting Fashions:
Advertising and Display

Fashion merchants have never believed that customers would come to their doors without encouragement or reminders. Everyone in the fashion business, from the designer with a new sketch to the merchant with new numbers in stock, is anxious to talk about, show, and promote the sale of his goods. This active effort is essential to a profitable operation because fashion moves at such a fast pace: no one today can afford to have yesterday's ideas and yesterday's look still in stock.

The methods used by fashion merchants for promoting sales vary widely, since each chooses the approach that complements his own store's merchandise and clientele. A small, exclusive shop may rely entirely on word-of-mouth advertising, supported by an occasional call from the owner to a faithful customer. A large, low-priced emporium may make extensive use of newspapers, throwaways, radio, and television to bring in crowds. The promotion drum may be beaten gently or blatantly, but it must be beaten if fashion goods are to be sold before age withers their style—and their salability.

Sales Promotion
Organization

In stores of medium to large size, there is usually a sales promotion division which is responsible for promoting sales through advertising, display, and publicity undertaken to attract people to the store. In some stores, personal salesmanship is also considered part of this function. *Sales pro-*

motion, therefore, may be defined as the coordination of advertising, display, publicity, and personal salesmanship in order to promote profitable sales.

In stores where there is a relatively modest amount of promotional activity, there is usually a sales promotion manager who is directly involved in managing each and every one of these activities. Where the volume of promotional activity is too large for such an arrangement, there usually will be an advertising manager and a display manager functioning under the sales promotion head, who himself may handle publicity and its close relative, public relations. Very large stores have a publicity manager as well, who supervises special events, the activities of consumer boards, fashion shows, and so on, thus leaving the sales promotion head, often a vice president, free for policy forming and for long-range planning.

The chief executive of the sales promotion division is responsible for preparing storewide seasonal sales promotional plans and budgets. Such plans spell out in general terms the extent to which the various sales promotion techniques will be used to produce the dollar volume of storewide sales planned for the period. In the plans are incorporated such special merchandising events as anniversary sales, community bargain days, and back-to-school promotions, as well as the important day-to-day promotional needs. Each subdivision of the sales promotion division then prepares its own seasonal plan and budget for implementing the master plan within limits imposed by the master budget.

The funds to finance the sales promotion efforts are allocated by the store's management in terms of planned sales. The percentage relationship between the promotional budget and the planned sales varies according to the type of store and the policy it adopts with respect to promotion. For large department and specialty stores, the budget, including the cost of operating the sales promotion division as well as the purchase of advertising space, time, and materials, is likely to be from 3.5 to 4.5 percent of sales.

By far the largest share of the sales promotion division's budget each season is allocated to advertising, and the lion's share of the advertising budget is usually allocated to newspaper space. In spite of the emphasis given to newspaper advertising, however, it is not the only medium used by stores. Rarely does a fashion merchant rely solely on a single sales promotion technique. Instead, most merchants use every available method, and relate their efforts in each area to their activities in all others.

Thus, when a newspaper advertisement is run, good retail practice requires the same merchandise and its selling points to be featured in window and departmental displays. It also requires salespeople to be briefed on what is being featured and why. In addition, when possible, publicity is sought along the same lines. Each part of the total sales promotion effort enhances the effectiveness of the other parts and increases the total impact upon the customer.

Fashion Advertising

The use of paid space or time in any medium—newspapers, shopping news bulletins, magazines, direct mail, radio or television broadcasts, or billboards—is advertising. (See Form 16-1.) All are used by retailers to promote the sale of fashion merchandise to consumers. Trade publications addressed to business or professional people, including those in the fashion industries, are not part of the retailer's promotional program, although they are a major medium for producers to promote sales at earlier stages of production and distribution.

Not all advertising is done for the purpose of achieving direct sales response. Some ads are of the prestige or institutional type and cannot show direct and measurable sales results.

A *prestige* or *institutional advertisement* is one that "sells" the store rather than specific merchandise. It may discuss a new fashion trend; it may point out the store's value as a headquarters for fashion news, for bargains, for clothes for the family; or perhaps it may publicize a community event. Any merchandise mentioned in the ad is incidental. The ad's value to the store is measured in such intangibles as prestige, goodwill, and store image.

A *merchandise* or *promotional advertisement* is one that endeavors to create sales of specific items. Goodwill, store image, and enhancement of the store's fashion prestige are incidental, although they are nevertheless considered when any such ad is planned and prepared.

Retailers have an adage: "Goods well bought are half sold." Half the process of selling fashion to the consumer, they believe, consists of analyzing her wants and offering her assortments that are geared in every possible respect to those wants. The remaining half of the selling effort, which is the business of arousing the consumer's buying impulses, requires just as much careful planning and precise execution as does the earlier half. In sales promotion, as in buying, chance and impulse must defer to planning and preparation.

The Advertising Plan

Since the major part of the money spent by retail stores in promoting the sale of merchandise is used for advertising, the terms "advertising plan," "sales plan," and "sales promotion plan" have come to be used loosely and interchangeably among retailers. To avoid confusion, the term "advertising plan" is used here with reference solely to the planning of ads. The term "sales promotion plan" refers to the total promotional plan, including display and special events as well as advertising.

An *advertising plan* is a forecast for a specified period of time, such as a season, quarter, month, or week, of the advertising that a store intends to employ in order to attract business. In general, such a plan outlines the dates on which advertise-

CANVAS THE CITY,

THE COUNTRY,

THE WORLD—

TOTES

ALWAYS GET THE VOTE!

Canvas is the one.
Our spacious, weightless,
cotton canvas bags
carry not only the vote,
but any number
of town and travel necessities.
Though we don't suggest
you vote on the basis
of good looks alone,
we know you'll flip
for the great colors,
done with zippy
contrasting webbing trims.
Come meet the designer,
Lee Stemer,
who will be here
Monday and Tuesday from 11:00 to 4:00!
Clockwise from top:
Roll: red, navy, black or natural, 17 x 10, 17.00
Shoulder Bag: natural, tan, navy or red, 11½ x 10½, 16.00
Kangaroo Pocket Tote: natural, black, navy, red, .
yellow, Kelly green, pink, brown or beige, 17 x 12½, 11.00
Ring: navy, natural, black, yellow, Kelly green,
pink, red or tan, 11½ x 10, 15.00
Maxi Tote: red, navy, black, natural or tan, 16½ x 13, 18.00
Wait till you meet their running-mates:
handsome belts specially made in the very same
cotton webbing to match the trims!
These for M or L sizes, 6.00 Mail and phone.
Please add .75 for delivery charge outside regular delivery area.
In our Handbags and Belts, First Floor,
they have the unbeatable **Touch**
Fifth Avenue at 56th Street, New York

Berry's

Form 16-1

ments will be used, the departments and items to be advertised, the estimated sales expected to result from such ads, the media to be employed, the amount of space or time to be used in each medium, and the cost thereof. The cost is usually estimated both in dollars and as a percentage of the sales expected to be realized.

The outlay for newspaper space, the most widely used medium among fashion retailers, amounts to more than 2 percent of the typical department store's annual net sales. In individual fashion departments, newspaper space costs vary; they amount to about 3.4 percent of sales in coat departments, 2.7 percent of sales in junior dress departments, and 1.9 percent of sales in handbag departments.[1]

Preparing the Plan   As a store works out its dollar budget and merchandise assortment plan, it also works out the upcoming season's promotional plan, which includes the advertising plan. The time for this procedure is about 60 days before the start of the six-month period covered, if the plan is to cover an entire season.

The overall plan is prepared first. Like the six-month merchandise plan, it is a general guide to the timing and amount of advertising to be done by each department in the store. Exact dates, selection of media, decisions as to size of ads, writing of copy, and other details are worked out later, quite close to publication time.

Both the budget and the schedule of the general plan are prepared with the understanding that unforeseen developments may require sudden adjustments, just like those that merchandise plans sometimes require. An advertisement that produces spectacular sales results may be repeated promptly, even if the original plan did not call for a second run. Conversely, a planned ad may be scrapped if the merchandise to back it up is not in stock or for some other sound reason.

After the general plan has been prepared, the seasonal plan for each selling department in the store is broken down into monthly plans. These are drawn up about a month prior to the month to which they apply, and they specify the item or items to be advertised, the dates on which ads will appear, the size of each ad, and the medium in which it will appear.

Sources of Information for Planning   Like the merchandise plans, the advertising plan is based on past experience, present conditions, and future expectations. Sales promotion departments keep careful records of what they advertised in past seasons, how it was advertised, at what cost, and with what results. The buyer's "Beat Last Year" book has its counterpart in the advertising department's scrapbook. Such a scrapbook contains tear sheets of all advertising previously run. On each ad is noted the dollar cost of the ad and the sales that resulted from it, as reported by the department for which the ad was run. When drawing up an advertising plan for a new season, the planner goes through the scrapbooks for similar periods of previous years and studies both the ads run and their sales results. Each season's plans incorporate as many features as possible of successful advertising used in the past, and avoid the features of advertising that did not produce the desired sales results.

The same factors that buyers and merchandise managers review when preparing their merchandise budget and plan are important in preparing promotional plans. These factors include conditions inside and outside the store; management's goals; indications of promotions planned by resources, publications, and competitors; and any other factors that might affect the store's own plans.

The experience of other retailers is also utilized in planning. In addition to the store's own advertising scrapbook, the sales promotion executive studies the advertising of other stores, particularly that of competitors whose advertising results have been observed and that of friendly noncompeting stores in other communities which are willing to exchange advertising information.

Through such sources as the store's resident buying office, the National Retail Merchants Association, and various trade publications, each retail promotion executive keeps in touch with the promotion experience of other stores. Reports of what is being advertised, shown, and sold in the country's top fashion stores are eagerly studied. So, too, are the advertising pages of consumer fashion magazines. Such reports are often a source of inspiration to the advertising manager. He evaluates them, however, in terms of his own store's target group of customers. He knows that the spectacular results from an ad placed by Saks Fifth Avenue, for example, might not be duplicated in his own store if he placed an identical ad. Yet the approach used by a retail leader may trigger an idea that can be used for his own store.

Finally, advertising staffs constantly need information from the merchandising division in order to develop effective copy and illustrations. They expect buyers and merchandisers to spell out the position taken by the store on specific fashion trends and to indicate noteworthy features of items that have been singled out for mention in ads.

Newspaper Advertising

Newspaper advertising is the promotional mainstay of department stores, large specialty stores, and chain stores. Department stores spend over 2 percent of each sales dollar to purchase such space; apparel specialty stores spend more than 2.5 percent of sales.[2]

Retailers use local newspapers extensively in promoting fashion merchandise because their customers are mainly from within the areas served by such newspapers. Producers, on the other hand, whose fashion goods usually have national or at least regional distribution, favor national magazines for their ads but cooperate with their retail store customers for grassroots coverage.

Among merchants, newspapers are the preferred advertising medium because retailing needs immediate impact and broad local exposure. The time between preparation and insertion of an ad can be quite short, and last-minute contingencies can be handled readily. Compared to a monthly magazine whose ad pages close weeks before publication, the newspaper is virtually instant advertising. A daily paper normally can accept changes almost up to the moment that its presses begin to roll—and this is only a matter of a few hours before the edition is on the streets.

Speed is vital in promoting fashion merchandise. A newspaper ad can be prepared for new and incoming fashion merchandise even before the goods are in stock, provided the resource has made a firm delivery promise. Should there be an unforeseen delay in the availability of the merchandise, the ad can be pulled at the eleventh hour. The importance of this last-minute flexibility is obvious, especially in view of the sample-test-reorder procedure used in connection with new styles.

In a community where several newspapers are published, each attracts a particular readership in terms of income, education, and interests. The retailer advertises in the paper that appeals to the readers who are most similar to his own clientele in fashion and price position. In New York, for example, stores that feature fashions in the early stages of their cycles usually buy space in *The New York Times,* which reaches affluent, city-oriented, fashion-aware customers in the city and its metropolitan area. Stores or departments that offer fashions in the peak and the declining stages of their cycles have less reason to use the *Times,* and therefore rely upon other city or suburban papers. Occasionally an enterprising suburban or small-town store will advertise its newest fashions in a prestigious big-city paper that reaches into its community. Much of the paper's circulation is wasted so far as such a store is concerned, but the use of a city newspaper dramatizes the store's fashion authority in the eyes of city-oriented members of its community.

Preparing the Ad The preparation of a routine ad begins with the buyer. Although the sales promotion division has already reached a tentative decision about when and where the ad will appear and how much space will be used, it is the buyer who initiates a formal *"request for advertising."* (See Form 16-2.) The buyer gives a brief, carefully factual description of the style he has selected, along with such points as price, sizes, colors, and fabric. The description also includes a few words that tell what is important and exciting about the goods from the customer's viewpoint. These words are the keys that the skilled advertising executive needs to write the copy.

For example, the buyer might say: "The small waistline is news, and it is in line with the romantic revival that is occurring. The full skirt and wide sleeves add grace and make the waist look smaller. The print is flowered, very new, a first for us. The manufacturer unconditionally guar-

ADVERTISED MERCHANDISE INFORMATION

Advertising information and the merchandise to be illustrated must be in the Advertising Department two weeks prior to the week in which the ad runs in the newspaper.

Department No.
74

Date Ad Runs
June 1, 19—

Item	Regular Price	Sale Price
Cotton canvas tote bags	Bags $11-18	No
Matching webbing belts	Belts $6	

Paper

New York Sunday Times (7 columns full)

List features in order of importance

1. Spacious, weightless, cotton canvas totes for town or travel.

2. Five featured styles, wide assortment of colors, darks, neutrals, high shades

3. Webbing trim in contrasting colors, belts in cotton webbing matching bag trim

Sizes Roll: 17×10, $7, Kangaroo pocket, 17×12½, $11, Shoulder: 11½×10½, $16, Ring: 11½×10, $15; Maxi: 16½×13, $18.

Colors Roll: red, navy, black, natural; Shoulder: natural, tan, navy, red; Kangaroo and Ring: natural, black, navy, red, kelly green, pink, tan; Maxi: red, navy, black, natural, tan

Art Instructions Sketch woman's torso showing belt, bags cascading down length of page

Additional Comments Designer in N.Y. store on 6/7

Submitted by Dorothy Smith, buyer

Date Received in Advertising Department May 15, 19—

Does manufacturer share cost of ad? Yes Is credit claim attached? Yes

Merchandise at Following Stores:

- ☒ New York
- ☒ Manhasset
- ☒ Westchester
- ☒ Short Hills
- ☒ Philadelphia
- ☒ Wynnewood
- ☒ Jenkintown
- ☒ Chicago
- ☒ Oakbrook
- ☒ Cleveland
- ☒ Boston
- ☒ Troy
- ☒ Palm Beach

Reason for Advertising:

- ☒ New Line
- ☐ Season Opening
- ☐ Sale
- ☐ Special Purchase
- ☐ Staple Stock
- ☐ Clearance

Quantity on Hand Date Ad Runs	Date Merchandise will be in Stock	Total Retail value of Merchandise	Use Trade Mark or Label	Is Manufacturer Paying for Ad?	Extra Delivery Charge?	Telephone Orders?	Mail Orders?	Mail Order Coupon?
250 pcs	5/26 complete	$3,750	Yes ☐ No ☒	Yes ☒ No ☐ 20% of Payment	Yes ☒ No ☐ Amount? 75¢	Yes ☒ No ☐	Yes ☒ No ☐	Yes ☐ No ☒

Form 16-2

SIGN ORDER

Berry's

Copy:
(Print)

Eight days' production time is required in the sign shop after this requisition is received. All orders must be signed by the Advertising Department before execution.

COTTON CANVAS
TOTES
FOR TOWN AND TRAVEL
$11.00 to $18.00

Remarks

Dorothy Smith
Buyer

_____
Advertising Department

Order No.
52385

Department No.
74

Date of Order
May 14, 19 —

Date Needed
May 23, 19 —

Date of Ad
June 1, 19 —

INDICATE QUANTITY			
	2 x 3		
	3½ x 5½		
	5½ x 7	Upright	
		Oblong	*26*
	7 x 11	Upright	
		Oblong	
	11 x 14	Upright	
		Oblong	
	14 x 18		
	22 x 28		

CHECK APPROPRIATE BOXES			
	Promotion		
	Clearance		
	Special Purchase		
	New Line		
	Fashion News		X
	Trade Name Used?	Yes	
		No	X

Form 16-3

antees the fabric (polyester) to be washable and to require little or no ironing." The copywriter might write that the item "looks romantically fragile in the store's own flower print that is easily kept fresh." The fashion artist who sketches the garment may emphasize the small waist, dramatize the swing of the sleeves and skirt, and enhance the romantic mood by giving the model's face a soft hairdo and a dreamy-eyed expression.

Manufacturers sometimes provide glossy photographs or sketches of their garments, suggested copy and layouts, or mats, to assist in the preparation of retail ads. (A *mat*—short for *matrix*— is a paperboard mold on which picture and/or copy are impressed and from which a plate can be made for reproduction of the material on newsprint.) These advertising aids are given by the manufacturers to the buyer, who routes them to his store's advertising department. The decision as to whether or not to use a specific aid rests with the sales promotion division.

When an Ad Breaks At the same time that an ad is to be run, promotion plans may call also for window and department displays. In such cases, the buyer works with the display department to ensure proper presentation of the merchandise in the windows. It is also the buyer's responsibility to order appropriate signs (Form 16-3) from the store's sign shop, and to arrange for departmental displays of the advertised merchandise. Thus, on the day that an ad breaks, customers will find the item or items on view and properly identified.

Some stores mount tear sheets (clippings) of each day's ads on walls in or near elevators, escalators, restrooms, and other areas of heavy customer traffic for additional exposure. Each department usually exhibits its current ads on its own selling floor where browsing customers may see them. Each buyer is responsible for making sure that his salespeople know what is advertised, where it is stocked, and what the selling points are, so that they can talk intelligently to customers about the merchandise.

In stores that do a considerable amount of telephone order business, each day's ads are also posted in the order board area to aid the telephone operators.

Reporting Results Advertising departments generally request, for future guidance, a report from the buyer of the results achieved from each merchandise ad. (See Form 16-4.)

Advertising results of merchandise ads are measured in terms of dollars and unit sales. Buyers are expected to report, usually on a printed form, such points as: how many advertised items were in stock before and 3 days after the ad ran; how many were sold; total sales of department; weather conditions; special display effort; and any other pertinent data that would help evaluate the ad's pulling power.

Buyers and advertising executives learn from such reports which items and approaches produce the most sales among the customers of the store and department concerned. Thus a sound basis for future planning is laid.

Planning in Smaller Stores Planning and reporting are less formal in relatively small stores where there is no advertising specialist to concentrate on promotions. Even in the smallest shop, how-

---

ADVERTISING RESULTS

Department *74-3 Handbags*

Date of Ad *June 1, 19—*

Media *New York Sunday Times*

3 Day Results *13 Stores*

No. of Units Sold *175*

DOLLAR SALES:

Advertised Item *$2,625*

Total Department *$7,824*

Note: *This form must be turned in to Merchandise Manager before noon the 4th day after ad has run. Merchandise Manager will initial and send promptly to Sales Promotion Manager.*

Buyer's Signature *Dorothy Smith*

Merchandise Manager's Initials *T.J.E.*

Form 16-4

ever, good management demands at least a rough guide as to what is to be spent, in which areas, and with what expectations. A record of ad results also needs to be kept so that past experience can guide future decisions. Often all that is needed is a scrapbook of ads that have been run, with marginal notes about costs and results.

The store with no staff advertising expert or agency often finds that many aids in constructing ads are available free or at little cost. Mats, layouts, and copy suggestions are usually offered by manufacturers, publications, and resident buying offices. Part of the work on a market trip involves canvassing the possibilities of obtaining suitable material of this type, so that when the buyer or owner returns to the store he knows not only what merchandise to advertise but also how best to present it in an advertisement.

Smaller stores often use media that larger ones brush aside. The cost of a newspaper ad looms large in the budget of a tiny establishment, so its proprietor also uses less costly media such as direct mail. Considerable use is also made of such resource-provided aids as statement enclosures, display cards, package enclosures, and the "as advertised in" posters supplied by consumer magazines.

Cooperative Advertising

Retail advertising for which the costs are shared by the store and the producer of the merchandise on terms agreed to by both is called *cooperative advertising*. (See Form 16-5.) The practice offers advantages to both parties, but it also presents some problems or opportunities for abuse.

Advantages of Cooperative Advertising Among the advantages to the fashion merchant of cooperative advertising are the following:

□ There is more money available for advertising. "Co-op" money is added to whatever amount the store has budgeted from its own funds for promotion.

□ The added money enhances the impact of the store's advertising in two ways. First, there is an increase in the amount and frequency of the store's ads, and thus of the impact of the store's name upon the public. Second, the additional space purchased with co-op money helps the store to earn a lower cost rate on all its advertising and thus be able to buy more space for its money. Newspapers usually give progressively lower rates as the total linage purchased increases.

□ Cooperation from the producer in other respects is more certain, once he has invested funds of his own in the store's advertising. Prompt deliveries, assistance in training the selling staff, and other services are more likely to be available.

□ In the case of a brand, or line, or item that is new to the area, the producer shares introductory promotion costs with the store and thus shares the initial risk.

From the producer's point of view, the benefits include the following:

□ His money buys more advertising space than if he placed the ad directly. The retailer, as a consistent buyer of space, commands lower rates than a producer could earn with occasional advertising.

□ He gets expert retail advertising help in the preparation of his ad, if the store concerned is medium-sized or larger. Retail copy and art are geared to local interests and are developed to achieve prompt response.

□ The prestige of the store's name reinforces the acceptance an item may enjoy on a regional or national basis—a fact especially valuable to lines or brands being introduced in a new area.

□ The retailer, having invested funds in advertising the merchandise, can be more readily counted upon to carry adequate stocks, build window and departmental displays, and brief the salespeople on the selling points of the goods.

□ In large cities, where the manufacturer's line may be sold also through small neighborhood stores, the impact of a major store's advertising helps the sale of the line in the small, outlying stores as well.

Disadvantages of Cooperative Advertising From the store's point of view, the major drawback in cooperative advertising is that buyers have been

Department *4 1-11*

NOTICE OF PAID ADVERTISING

Manufacturer's Name *Aiken Dress Company*

Attention of *Jack Shapiro*

Manufacturer's Address *1400 Broadway*
New York, New York 10018

Newspaper Date *May 16, 197-* Name *New York Times*

Date _____ Name _____

Describe Merchandise *Banlon dresses, styles 420, 674, 1060*

_____

_____

_____

_____

_____

_____

_____

_____

ADVERTISING AGREEMENT

Manufacturer Agrees to Pay:

☐ 1. Full Charge   4. Your Share as Agreed _____

☐ 2. One-half Charge   5. Up to Amount of _____

☒ 3. *25 %* ___ Charge   6. Other _____

Person with Whom Agreement Made *Jack Shapiro* Date *Feb. 16, 197-*

Special Billing Instructions *Send tear sheet with duplicate of charges.*
Deduct from Aiken Dress Co. account payable

Buyer's Signature *Dorothy Smith*

To Be Filled Out By The Advertising Department

Lineage, Total Ad *600* _____ Rate $ *1.70 line*

Cost, Total Ad $ *1,020* _____ Amount to Be Billed $ *255.00*

Treasurer's Bill No. *A 61729*

Form 16-5

known to "buy" advertising rather than merchandise. Because of pressure from their managements or because of their own eagerness to see their departments promoted, some buyers pass up good fashion merchandise for which there is little or no cooperative money available in order to buy less desirable styles that have advertising funds. This practice not only contributes to the creation of poor assortments but also advertises the existence of such assortments. Wise managements refuse to accept advertising money for goods that are not worthy of promotion with or without contribution from the resource.

From the standpoint of the resource, a major drawback of cooperative advertising is the danger of inadvertently discriminating against some customers in favor of others. Participation in the advertising of a renowned store that uses a big metropolitan daily may be worth much more to a producer than participation in the advertising of a small shop that uses only a local suburban weekly, and yet, under the provisions of the Robinson-Patman Act (a section of the antitrust laws), a producer in such a situation might seem to be granting discriminatory allowances to the larger store. Rather than leave themselves open to charges of making offers for which only large stores can qualify, some apparel firms have simply abandoned cooperative advertising entirely.

Miscellaneous Fashion Media

Fashion retailers use a variety of media other than newspapers to promote sales. Among them are radio, television, direct mail, telephone solicitation, and magazines. The decision as to when and if any of these is to be used in behalf of a specific department's merchandise generally rests with the store's sales promotion manager. Buyers, however, familiarize themselves with the possibilities inherent in each medium, so that they can request those they consider useful. Conversely, in theory, a buyer could conceivably ask to be excused from participating in promotional efforts involving some medium he considers inappropriate to his merchandise. In practice, however, the retail buyer who declines promotional efforts of any kind or in any medium approved by his store is rare or nonexistent.

Radio For certain segments of the population, radio advertising of fashion merchandise supplements or substitutes for newspaper space. The teen-ager's transistor radio and the car radio of the employed adult who drives to work make the medium useful for reaching these groups. Stores that cater to teen-age girls have found that radio is almost indispensable as an advertising medium, since these young customers are exposed to radio far more than to newspapers. Each store, each area, each clientele, presents a different situation. Where radio reaches customers more effectively than newsprint, stores use it. There is no universal rule.

Television Television, and particularly color television, seems an ideal medium for showing fashion merchandise to the consumer. Fashion merchants, however, were slow to use it at first. Costs were high, and production problems were difficult. Lacking the expertise to use the new medium effectively, many retailers tried it and then dropped it as unprofitable. There were exceptions, nevertheless. Burdine's of Miami, for instance, was proficient at television fashion shows by 1963, and was chosen in that year to stage a half-hour musical presentation of cotton fashions in conjunction with the National Cotton Council.[3]

By the late 1960s, several factors had brought major retailers and many small merchants into TV advertising. The cost of prime time had become less expensive in relation to the rising costs of newspaper space; there was an increasing number of firms specializing in producing television shows and commercials for buyers of broadcast time; the pulling power of television was constantly being demonstrated to retailers by the broadcasting systems. Stores in areas served only by weekly newspapers found television a means of reaching their customers more frequently. Stores in large cities found that television enhanced the pulling power of their print advertising and helped them tell the fashion story more effectively. By 1969, several prominent retailers were committed to television,[4] and the use of the medium was sufficiently common among retailers in general for the National Retail Merchants Association and the Television Bureau of Advertising to establish an annual competition for the best television commercials telecast by retailers.

Direct Mail Advertising sent to the individual consumer via mail lends itself readily to fashion promotion purposes. Small stores have used this medium in such simple forms as postcard announcements of sales or postcard illustrations of featured garments. Both large and small stores use the colorfully printed statement enclosures provided by garment and accessories producers to show items in current assortments. Large stores, in fact, are offered so many such inserts that they turn away more than they use.

The effectiveness of the medium is difficult to pinpoint in most stores, since customer response may take the form of a telephone order or a personal visit to the store. Occasionally, stores will advertise an item by direct mail only, to measure the medium's pulling power, but this procedure is not common practice with respect to fashion goods.

Catalogs issued by department and specialty stores at Christmas and for back-to-school goods are familiar indeed. Early preparation and the need to maintain good stocks of catalog items limit this medium to fairly well established fashions for most stores. Conversely, individual stores have used direct mail successfully to introduce new fashions and new fashion seasons. Here direct mail is not used so much to sell specific items as to imbue customers with the excitement of fashion and prompt their visit to the store.

Direct mail is a favorite medium for selling bridal fashions. Invitations to engaged girls urge them to visit the bridal salon for advice on wedding plans and for the selection of clothes for the wedding party.

A special form of direct mail is the personal note from a salesperson or specialty shop owner to an individual customer to inform her of new styles and invite her to visit the store.

The use of a mail-order coupon in newspaper advertising is another way for stores to sell fashion merchandise by mail. In addition, using coupons enables the stores to reach out and expand their circle of charge customers. Persons who wish to buy at home but do not have charge accounts with the store are encouraged to send in an order COD or to enclose a check. Often the coupon has a box to be marked if the customer wishes to open a charge account. Fashion items that lend themselves especially well to such treatment are those which do not require trying on, such as some intimate apparel, classic blouses, hosiery, and dresses for porch and patio wear. The Sunday newspaper is a favorite medium for such coupon advertising. Customers are at home, the store may be closed, but pen, envelope, and postage stamp are almost always at hand.

Telephone Solicitation Department and large specialty stores use the telephone constantly to receive orders from customers, but they are cautious in using it to solicit sales. In most communities, solicitors for everything from carpet cleaning to calisthenics classes have overused the telephone to such an extent that the fashion stores tend to avoid it. Usually the only kind of fashion promotion done by telephone is by a salesperson who calls a customer who knows and relies upon her. The risks of arousing resentment through indiscriminate calls are too great for most fashion retailers.

Magazines Retailers are generally best served by local advertising media, but there are occasions when they seek to augment their fashion prestige by placing ads in consumer magazines with national circulation. Preferred for this purpose are fashion publications, brides' magazines, and sophisticated magazines of general interest. Such advertising is rarely expected to sell the fashion item shown, although sales may well occur. Its purpose is to emphasize that the retailer's fashion message is sufficiently important to be carried in the pages of a publication whose fashion authority is nationally recognized. This is *prestige advertising*, intended to emphasize the store's image: as a place to buy one-of-a-kind jewels, as a salon for devastating evening gowns, as a headquarters for practical travel clothes and accessories, or whatever the case may be.

The merchandise selected for such treatment must be carefully chosen because of the length of time that elapses between the closing date (when all copy and illustrations must be in the hands of a publication) and the date of issue

Courtesy Sears, Roebuck and Company

The telephone order department in any large store is supplied with copies of current ads, so that each operator knows exactly what promotion materials customers have seen. These Sears operators also have complete catalogs.

(when the magazine reaches the newsstands or the mailboxes of its subscribers). Garments or accessories that receive advertising of this kind are often prophetic styles typifying incoming trends or else timeless classics.

The impact of this advertising is that it impresses upon the local consumer that the shop, whether in Atlanta, or Dallas, or Little Rock, is on a par with the country's best in fashion authority and desirable fashion assortments.

Fashion Display

A method of sales promotion widely used by all retailers of fashion is *display,* the impersonal, visual presentation of merchandise.

Unlike advertising, display has the advantage of addressing itself to the customer when she is physically present inside or directly outside the store. It speaks to her when she is in, or almost in, a buying situation, and thus it has an opportunity to prompt her to action. That action is the vital one of asking about and perhaps buying the merchandise displayed. The consumer at whom display is aimed has already made the preliminary moves of leaving her home or place of business and approaching the store. Whether she is consciously on a buying errand, consciously examining what the stores are showing, or whether she is just moving along and idly watching displays, she is already on the retail scene. Effective display can make capital out of that propinquity, arouse a buying impulse, and cause a sale to occur.

Window displays are intended to entice the customer into the store, and interior displays are intended to guide the customer to specific departments and interest her in specific merchandise.

Window Display

To a fashion retailer, a store window is useful for selling merchandise, promoting an idea, or publicizing the store as a place to buy. Its primary function, in one of retailing's puns, is "to make the passer buy." For this purpose it must be arresting and as dramatic as it can afford to be in the context of the store personality and the merchandise involved.

Windows are usually entrusted by merchants to skilled experts on their staffs, or to free-lance display men, in the case of smaller stores. The medium is considered too important for the untrained hand and eye. Direction is provided to the display expert, however, about what to show and the purpose which each window is intended to serve. If the window is intended to draw people into the store, there are ways of checking its effectiveness. Experts in the display field have painstakingly measured results produced by various techniques: what percentage of the passersby looked, or stopped, or went inside the store as a result of different methods of presentation.

But windows, like ads, are not always used for direct selling. They may be used to set the mood of a season, as are some of the merchandise-free windows that great stores install for Christmas. One of the most famous of these was the bank of Fifth Avenue windows that Lord and Taylor, New York, devoted solely to bells for many successive Decembers. Windows that show Santa bringing gifts, or families opening packages on Christmas morning, or glamorously dressed adults on their way to parties are also quite commonly used by large stores at this period of the year. Rather than suggesting specific purchases, these windows remind the customer of gifts and of the store as a source.

Fashion Messages Windows are an excellent medium for conveying a fashion message. They may be used to dramatize a new color, for example, by showing garments and accessories in a particular springtime yellow, or an autumn brown, or a loud print in which a certain color predominates. They can dramatize a new look, or skirt length, or season of the year, or return of a long-absent fashion complement, like the belt or the little black dress.

Because the window should arouse interest and stimulate the customer to refresh her wardrobe, the actual styles selected for display are usually more extreme and in earlier stages of their fashion cycle than much of the assortment inside the store. If the window merchandise is not too different from what already hangs in customers' closets, it cannot do much stimulating. Arresting qualities are essential.

A familiar retail summary of this philosophy is, "Show royal blue; sell navy." The royal blue excites the customer's buying impulses, but once inside the store, she buys her familiar, wearable navy. If navy alone had been in the window, her eye might have glanced off it without receiving the message that it was time to buy some Easter clothes.

How-to-Wear-It Windows Windows are used also to tell customers how to wear or use fashion merchandise. The effective ones answer the shopper's unspoken question about how to wear a new fashion or what to wear with it. A window that shows a manikin dressed in a new costume with hat, gloves, hosiery, shoes, and handbag makes it easier for the customer to visualize herself in the clothes than the window that presents merely one or two components of the current look. An excellent example was afforded by the opaque, patterned hosiery that came firmly into fashion in 1966 and 1967, when miniskirts were reaching their extreme of brevity. Shown merely as hosiery, these stockings elicited little reaction from customers. Shown on manikins dressed in the current short fashions, they motivated women to stop and buy.

A similar technique is used when new colors or combinations are introduced. In one spring season, when pink was a new idea for wear with navy, stores devoted windows to examples of this combination, in subdued as well as dramatic ways, so that a customer, whatever her temperament or place in the fashion parade, could see

Window displays may occasionally concentrate on a seasonal or institutional theme; this Christmas window is both an acknowledgement of the season and an image-aid for the store.

that she could wear and enjoy the new color combination. Such window displays help the customer translate a piece of fashion news into a personal interest in buying.

Direct-Sell Windows Window displays that aggressively try to make a sale also have a function in promoting fashion merchandise. Not all customers are concerned with newness and glamour; most have to consider the hard fact of price as well. For such customers, the discreet price marker in the more elegant windows gives way to poster-sized announcements in the windows

of less expensive stores saying that the dresses are "two for $7" or that any hat in the window is $4. Also for the price-conscious customer are the windows that present a veritable cornucopia of items: many kinds, many classifications, arranged with only the thought in mind of showing as much as possible in a small space. Display men who do windows for neighborhood shops of modest size are experts at such techniques; so are the display staffs of shoe, hosiery, and general merchandise chains.

The fact that windows of this type rarely convey fashion excitement should not in any way belittle their importance in the promotion of fashion merchandise. Vast quantities of apparel and accessories are sold as a result of such windows. These windows are the workhorses of fashion window display, and the merchandise they promote, even though it may be at or past the peak of its cycle, constitutes a substantial share of the total volume of fashion goods sold at retail.

Building a Window Display Large stores assign window display space to their various departments well in advance, thus giving the buyer time to let the display staff know which styles are to be shown and what message the buyer hopes to convey. As in the case of newspaper advertising, the store may require from the buyer a form stating what is to go into each window assigned to his department and what signs are to be used with the merchandise. If related items from other departments are used, the buyer or assistant may take the responsibility of selecting and signing for them and seeing that they are eventually returned to the lending departments. Some stores have display coordinators who take the responsibility of securing related merchandise.

The success of a window display that seeks to convey a fashion message depends to a great extent upon the selection of appropriate related items. Small boutiques, with no professional help in arranging their windows, often create real "stoppers" (and sales makers) by showing a just-right necklace or scarf or other accessories with each dress or suit or coat. At the height of the hatless vogue in the mid-1960s, a millinery syndicate executive observed that boutiques in New York's Greenwich Village were selling many more hats in proportion to their size than even the most aggressive of the uptown stores. His explanation: no dress or coat was ever placed in a boutique window without an appropriate hat. Although customers of the Village shops wore hats no more often than other women, they bought them, thanks to the messages of the windows.

Interior Display

Once a customer has entered a store, the chances of converting her browsing activities into buying impulses can be enhanced by interior displays. These may be true point-of-sale efforts at the spot where the goods are sold, or they may be displays in such places as overhead ledges, corners, platforms, or entrances to departments. Often they repeat a theme expressed in windows and once again drive home the message, whether it be the advent of a new season or the opportunity to buy a bargain. In large stores, general displays are the work of professionals on the display staff.

Within a department, displays of fashion merchandise are usually worked up by the buyer, his assistants, or the salespeople. Ingenuity, knowledge of the merchandise, and proximity to the point of sale make up for the absence of the professional's touch. Departmental displays may be of several kinds.

Vignettes A product or group of products shown in use is a *vignette*. A typical vignette might display a manikin in a nightgown and matching peignoir, wearing slippers of appropriate style and color, and seated in a boudoir chair to complete the suggestion of a woman preparing for bed. Department store buyers are often neglectful of display opportunities of this type because of the legwork involved in assembling the necessary merchandise, but the impact of such a display at the entrance to a department is often enough to draw passing customers to its counters or racks.

Item Displays A single garment or accessory may be featured in an *item display*. The display may be created by putting one piece on a form or T-stand, or by showing several versions of a style: a shoulder bag in several sizes, for instance, or a group of stockings in several colors.

Assortment Displays One of each of the style numbers currently in a section of stock may be shown, identified, and priced in an *assortment display*. Such a display is generally used for basic items and permits the customer to make at least a tentative selection while waiting to be served. A classic example is the usual wall display of white shirts behind a men's furnishings counter. The windows of shoe chains follow the same pattern, and their interior displays of slippers,

Interior displays are usually designed as vignettes, or item displays, or assortment displays—but this one, which dominates the entire store, is simply a lavish floral tribute to spring.

boots, or shoes are also of this type. Scarf departments use assortment display when they fan out their folded stock of each price and type, permitting the customer to see the entire range at a glance.

Self-Selection Racks Although they are not usually thought of as such, self-selection racks are definitely a type of departmental display. In order

to emphasize the breadth of the color assortment, no more than two or three garments of a given color are put together on the rack or T-stand. To feature the mix-match possibilities, as in sportswear separates, all of a pattern or color may be grouped in one area. The first arrangement says, "Choose from our rainbow assortment." The second says, "See how many components we offer in each color." If the rack is merely a hodgepodge, the implication is that the assortment is broken or unplanned, as on a clearance rack. The buyer, within the framework of store policy, decides which message should be conveyed and instructs stock and sales personnel accordingly.

Other Efforts Interior display utilizes many additional small but effective aids: a counter card, extolling the virtues of the goods; a sign atop a rack of clothes, stressing a major selling point; a garment laid open across a lighted, glass-topped counter to emphasize its sheerness and perfection of weave; a sample article attached to a rack of packaged articles to invite the customer's examination. The little things that are done inside the store, as well as the big, dramatic windows, are all part of the effort to promote the sale of fashion merchandise by means of display.

Vendor Aids

Producers of fashion merchandise, from coats to corsets to cosmetics, have shown themselves keenly aware of the selling power of good retail display. Eager to help stores harness this effective tool in behalf of their merchandise, many vendors in the fashion business develop dealer aids, which they supply free or at modest cost to stores. Vendors will also provide speakers and demonstrators at times, to create a live display.

Counter and Window Cards Intended to be used in windows, on counters, or with interior displays of the vendor's merchandise, counter and window cards usually name the brand and recite the selling points of the item or brand. Cards of the "as advertised in" variety bear a mounted reprint of the producer's advertisement in the publication concerned. Smaller retailers generally use these gratefully to supplement their limited display facilities. Large stores are likely to have a policy against the use of such cards, preferring that all announcements be made in their own sign shop and in the store's own style.

Forms and Fixtures To facilitate the display of specific merchandise, resources sometimes provide stores with free or inexpensive forms and fixtures for their merchandise. The equipment often bears the brand name of the fashion producer who supplies it. Familiar examples are the bust and torso forms provided by makers of women's foundation garments and the self-selection racks in which packaged bras, panties, or classic blouses are offered for sale.

The development of good self-selection fixtures is often a process requiring a greater investment in research and design than even a large store is willing or able to make. A vendor, however, whose products are sold through many hundreds of stores, can profitably underwrite such an investment. This is particularly true of producers who have so many retail outlets that their best avenue of expansion is to sell more through each outlet than to scrape the bottom of the barrel hunting for new retail accounts.

The fixtures developed by vendors generally prove to be very effective in displaying the merchandise, highlighting its sales appeal, and providing ample space for an orderly supply of stock on the selling floor. Some of these fixtures are almost boutiques in themselves, notably those developed for branded lines of small leather goods, shirts, and related articles.

The fashion industries, although they are now quite active in this area, by no means pioneered the use of fixtures. That effort was made by such industries as greeting card publishing, notions, and some branches of the houseware field. By the mid-1950s, however, prepackaging and self-selection had entered many branches of the apparel field, and by the winter of 1966–1967, packaging had become so much a way of life that one sportswear producer achieved brilliant success by packaging a dress in a can, purely as a promotional device. The dress, of course, was thoroughly packable, since its fabric was one of the man-made fibers, and the producer's point was simply to profit through innovation.

Windows To have his merchandise featured in the windows of a well-recognized store is a feather in the cap of a fashion producer. Aside from the sales that result from the local exposure, a certain prestige is gained by the producer. If the line has been deemed good enough for windows in such a store, buyers from other stores may ask with increased confidence for window space for the line in their own stores.

Vendors therefore go to trouble and expense to make it easier or more attractive for stores to use their goods in windows. They provide window cards, sometimes devise props and background panels to lend interest to the merchandise, and at times hire experts in retail display to design windows and supply diagrams and sketches from which retail accounts can work.

Demonstrations and Exhibits To help consumers understand the virtues of new materials, producers sometimes provide exhibits or demonstrations on retail selling floors. Experience has proved this approach an excellent one for getting the message across to the consuming public, for it brings out and answers questions that may be on the consumer's mind and promotes the sale of merchandise embodying the new idea.

Speakers and exhibit material supplied by producers have been especially useful to retail stores in explaining new fibers, fabrics, and finishes. When the first man-made fibers were developed for textile use, for example, some producers sent representatives into the stores to explain how their fibers were made and how they should be handled. In the period immediately following World War II, when many new fibers were being produced, one of the major women's magazines garnered prestige by sending speakers and demonstrators into stores to acquaint consumers with the qualities of all the new fibers then on the market.

With the introduction of wash-and-wear clothes in the early 1950s, and of an unusually absorbent nylon in hosiery a decade later, customers saw merchandise being dunked in water to demonstrate its virtues. Stretch fabrics, durable press, and other fabric developments have also inspired store demonstrations organized by producers. So, too, have complexion care treatments, false eyelashes, new types of makeup, hair treatments, and wigs.

Perennial problems, such as the fitting of foundation garments or the selection and packing of travel wardrobes, also prompt producers to develop talks and demonstrations for use in retail stores. The retail selling floor is an auditorium in which many fashion producers are eager for a chance to perform.

References

[1]*Departmental Merchandising and Operating Results of 1967*, pp. 3, 18–19, 22–23.
[2]Ibid., pp. 2–5.
[3]*Stores*, April, 1964, pp. 35–36
[4]Bernard Groger in *Women's Wear Daily*, February 1, 1968, p. 35.

Merchandising Vocabulary

Define or briefly explain the following terms:

Sales promotion
Prestige or institutional
  advertising
Merchandise or promotional
  advertising
Sales promotion plan
Advertising plan

Advertising request
Advertising mat
Cooperative advertising
Display

Merchandising Review

1. What means are most commonly employed by retail stores in promoting the sale of fashion goods?
2. What types of advertising media are commonly employed by retail stores? Which type is most widely used and why?
3. Name at least three sources from which a fashion merchant may obtain helpful information when planning fashion promotions.
4. What are the buyer's major responsibilities in connection with running an ad?
5. What information is usually requested on an advertising results form? What purposes are served by such a report?
6. What are the advantages and disadvantages of cooperative advertising?
7. What is meant by direct-mail advertising? Name three specific forms it may take.
8. Name and briefly describe three types of departmental fashion displays.
9. Identify three types of vendor aids supplied by producers to retail stores either free or at a modest cost. Of what value is each of these to the retail merchant?

Merchandising Digest

1. "Goods well bought are half sold." Discuss this statement and its implications for fashion merchandising.
2. "Windows are an excellent medium for conveying a fashion message." Discuss this statement from the text and its implications for the fashion merchant.
3. Assume you are a retail merchant of women's apparel and accessories. What activities might you undertake in promoting the sale of dresses, for example?

17
Promoting Fashions: Publicity and Personal Selling

Advertising and display by no means exhaust the list of tools available to the fashion merchant in promoting the sale of his merchandise. There are two other tools that play especially important roles: publicity and personal selling.

Publicity, like advertising, reaches out for the consumer's interest as she reads her paper, watches or listens to TV or radio broadcasts, or even as she talks with friends and neighbors. Personal selling, like display, makes contact with her when she is already in a shopping situation, about to make a purchase. Publicity speaks to her, as advertising does, in her capacity as a member of the general public. Personal selling, unlike any other tool of sales promotion, is concerned with her individual wants, questions, and preferences: it puts her in the central role of customer.

Different as each tool is from the other, both publicity and personal selling are potent forces in promoting the sale of fashion merchandise.

Fashion Publicity

The free and voluntary mention of a firm, brand, product, or person, in some form of media is *publicity*. Most publicity appears in print or broadcast media or is transmitted by word of mouth. (The print media are mainly newspapers and magazines, and broadcast media are television and radio.) In promoting the sale of fashion merchandise, publicity helps by making a trend, style, producer, retailer, or other facet of the fashion business better known to the public.

Because publicity is not purchased but is given free by the medium concerned, it is the medium that determines how much time or space is appropriate and what words or pictures are to be used. This is the essential difference between publicity and advertising, for the recipient of publicity does not have the privilege of saying when, where, and how his message will be disseminated, nor can he ensure that it will be disseminated at all. The merchant or producer who is the source of the publicity information merely makes the facts available and suggests, if he wishes, a manner of presentation. He does have the privilege, however, of specifying a release date (a date before which his announcement may not be published), even though he may have placed it in the hands of the news media weeks in advance.

The way in which fashion news is originated by designers, producers, and wearers of fashion merchandise has been discussed in earlier chapters. This chapter is concerned with the efforts of retailers to publicize fashion in general and their own fashion assortments in particular.

Methods of Obtaining Publicity
Retailers usually seek fashion publicity on a fairly dignified level. In calling attention to newsworthy developments within their stores or actually creating news by causing something newsworthy to happen, such as fashion shows or personal appearances of celebrities, stores provide selected media with information of potential interest to their audiences. In turn, these media may then

devote space or time to telling their readers or listeners about such happenings.

In his attempts to gain publicity, a retailer makes news available promptly and, preferably, in advance of the expected event. In addition, he refrains from flooding media with information that is not newsworthy, for to overdo the publicity effort is to invite editors to turn a deaf ear.

Following are several methods of passing fashion news along to print or broadcast media.

Press Releases A retailer may issue press releases before or after newsworthy events such as a visit from a celebrity, the opening of a new department, or the introduction of a new fashion development. A *press release* is a written statement of news that has occurred or is about to occur, specifying the source of the information and the date after which its use is permissible. Press releases may originate with the store or may be provided to the merchant by resources whose products are involved.

Telephone Calls Sometimes the retailer may alert news media to happenings with only a telephone call. If the store is staging a fashion show to raise funds for charity, a call to the editor of the women's page of the local newspaper may bring a photographer and a reporter to the show.

Fashion Consultations Merchants often make their expertise available to the media to encourage accurate and stimulating fashion publicity for their store. A retailer does this by welcoming questions on fashion subjects from the press and answering them as completely as possible, thus encouraging editors to check with him on the accuracy and completeness of fashion news from other sources. The merchant can also achieve some of the same results by being available as a speaker on fashion subjects before school groups and other consumer meetings. In both ways, he helps keep fashion and fashion merchandise in the public eye.

Media Used

Retail merchants look to both print media and broadcast media when seeking fashion publicity. Most retailers find that the publicity given their activities by local newspapers engenders greater consumer interest than any other media they use. Magazine publicity can be of considerable value, but often lacks the newsy quality and local impact of newspaper coverage. Radio and television publicity also can be very useful, but again, the approach may not be as localized as the newspaper—and no one can tear out a mention in radio or on a television show for future reference.

Newspapers As a consistent user of advertising space in local newspapers, a retailer often gets preferential treatment in obtaining publicity. For maximum effect from publicity, the retailer selects the paper that seems most likely to reach the readers who will be interested in the particular publicity message. Which paper appeals to which group of readers is something the retailer already will have learned in the course of selecting media for his advertising.

Newspapers are also generally more receptive to store requests for publicity than are other media because of the frequency of their publication. Fashion editors and women's page editors have daily pages to fill and Sunday features to prepare, and are usually happy to be informed about store events that have local news value.

The local fashion publicity efforts of retail merchants gain strength from such industry efforts as the semiannual Press Week showings in New York and Los Angeles, described in Chapter 8. If the fashion editor or women's page editor of a newspaper has attended either or both events, she has seen the lines of the sponsoring producers well in advance of their presentation to the public by retail stores. She has brought back with her the producers' press releases and photographs of styles the individual producers consider the most prophetic. Such an editor is not only conversant with fashion trends as a result of her Press Week experience, but has also become somewhat personally involved in helping these trends develop on the local scene. With this background and this attitude, she is more receptive than she might otherwise be to the fashion publicity efforts of her local merchants.

Magazines Consumer magazines make a practice of showing fashions editorially and of mentioning one or more stores as sources for purchasing the merchandise. These mentions, discussed in Chapter 15, are known as editorial credits. The decisions to offer an editorial credit to a store rests with the publication. The decision to accept or decline the credit is made by the store, which takes these factors into consideration, among others:

□ The value, in terms of publicity among customers and in the market, of a credit in the periodical concerned. Not every periodical has equal value in the eyes of a given store.

□ The confidence the store places in the style that is to be credited. If the sales potential of a style does not warrant stocking, displaying, and promoting it on its own merits, a store may decline the credit. The store may still carry the style, but simply prefer not to give it the merchandising and promotional emphasis that go along with the acceptance of a credit.

□ The crediting of other stores. Some merchants prefer not to accept a credit if other stores also are mentioned, or if the other stores mentioned are of an appreciably different type from their own.

□ The importance of the resource to the store. A store may use a credit as a means of establishing a relationship with a desirable but as yet unused resource. Conversely, it may decline a credit rather than share editorial mention with a resource not otherwise important to it.

□ The number of concurrent credits the store may have accepted in other publications. Too many credits appearing at approximately the same time can upset the store's own assortment and promotion plans.

Accepted and acted upon, an editorial mention publicizes the store and its fashion merchandise among readers of the magazine who are within its trading area. Properly managed, such credits enhance the prestige of both periodical and retailer among consumers and producers.

Magazine advertising credits may also be available. *Advertising credits* are mentions of a store's name in the advertisement of a producer. Such an ad also might include the names of fiber and fabric sources or other appropriate producers

whose products contributed to the featured item of merchandise. The factors a store considers in accepting or rejecting such a credit are much the same as those considered in the case of editorial credits.

Radio and Television A retailer who is a consistent user of radio and television advertising sometimes enjoys preferential treatment in obtaining broadcast fashion publicity from local stations, just as is the case with newspapers. And just as each newspaper has special appeal to certain groups of readers, so does each radio and television program or station have special appeal to more or less clearly defined groups of listeners.

The retailer becomes familiar with the nature of such specialization through observing the results his own advertising has achieved. He augments what he has learned from his own experience by studying the research material prepared by each broadcast medium to indicate the number and kind of people who tune in to its programs. Then, to achieve maximum benefit from fashion publicity placed with broadcast media, the fashion retailer seeks to obtain mentions from those stations and programs whose listeners he believes will be most responsive to his message.

Sources of Fashion Publicity Material
Fashion publicity material may, and often does, emanate from a wide variety of sources. Chief among such sources is the store's own fashion coordinator or ranking fashion authority. Other sources include fashion shows, visits to stores by fashion designers and producers or their representatives, the efforts of producers themselves, and the efforts of trade associations or the public relations or publicity agents for such associations.

The Fashion Coordinator In any retail organization, much of the fashion publicity obtained is a result of the fashion coordinator's activities. The *fashion coordinator,* usually a woman, is the store's ranking fashion authority. Her duties, which are discussed in detail in the next chapter, include such publicity-generating activities as staging fashion shows, in or out of the store, and arranging clinics or demonstrations at which visiting designers or manufacturers will speak.

She may also represent the store as a speaker on fashion before consumer or business groups in the community, thus becoming news in her own right.

Fashion Shows Whether the retailer's store is a Paris designer's salon or a small shop on Main Street, there is nothing that tells the fashion story to customers quite so clearly and excitingly as a fashion show. The usual presentation employs models, music, and a commentator, making it possible for the audience to see and to hear about fashion. Simpler ways of running shows are possible, of course, and some very effective presentations have been done by commentators who simply hold up each garment in turn as it is being discussed. The glamour treatment, however, is more likely to draw large audiences and win publicity, and this method is the one stores generally use.

Such fashion shows may be held to benefit a local charity or for the store's own purposes. In the former case, admission is charged and the proceeds are turned over to a designated charitable organization. In the latter case, admission is free and may be open either to the general public or only to those who have been invited to come.

Fashion shows may be held on a selling floor or in the restaurant or auditorium within the store, or they may be held outside the store, according to the occasion and the facilities required. Some shows feature the fashions of a single producer; others assemble numbers from many lines. Shows may be general in nature, appealing to a cross section of the store's customers, or planned for specialized audiences, such as teen-agers, college or career women, prospective brides, expectant mothers, or women with distinctive interests in travel, sports, or fashion.

Ways in which retailers assemble audiences for these shows are as varied as the kinds of shows they stage. If the event is on behalf of a charity, the sponsoring organization sells the tickets and usually offers the services of its members as models. If the event is geared to a relatively small, special-interest group, such as brides or expectant mothers, personal invitations may be mailed out. For across-the-board audiences, announcements

Courtesy Mollie Parnis

The formal fashion show is one of the most exciting and dramatic ways to promote fashion.

may be placed in the store's advertising, in its windows or in its elevators, or on radio broadcasts.

Cooperation in the staging of a fashion show may be provided by a consumer publication, a merchandise resource, a fiber or fabric producer, or any other organization with a reason to help the retailer put a fashion message across.

Publicity is achieved by word-of-mouth and by informing the press and broadcast media, through direct contact or through press releases, about what is being done and why it is being done. Occasionally fashion shows are so original in some aspect that the publicity lingers on long after the fashions themselves have gone. Such was the case in the summer of 1967, when a New York department store staged career fashion shows in a nearby park, drawing favorable comment in both consumer and trade press and winning a National Retail Merchants Association award for being one of the "Top Ten" fashion promotions of the year.

Visits From Designers or Vendors A visit from a designer, a vendor, or his representative, can often help a store earn considerable publicity for itself, for the vendor, and for the particular fashion area involved. Some representatives are capable speakers and appear on local television shows or give press interviews on fashion trends. These fashion authorities may address groups of customers or school groups, or act as commentators for store fashion shows, or hold clinics and act as consultants to individual customers.

Occasionally a designer or the representative of an apparel manufacturer presents a trunk show as a means of letting customers see and select from a producer's full line instead of from the necessarily limited number of designs any particular store stocks. (The trunk show's usefulness as a method of pretesting customer preferences was discussed in Chapter 11.) A *trunk show* is a presentation by a designer, producer, or representative, of samples of his line, held at the store. The representative brings a trunk of samples to the store, gives several scheduled showings, and takes special orders from any customers who choose styles, colors, and sizes not in the store's stock.

Advance announcements about trunk shows are made in press releases and ads. During and after the event, word-of-mouth publicity inevitably grows out of the customers' excitement over the special treatment accorded them. Further opportunities for publicity may be created by having models show the garments informally in the tearoom, or by showing the line on models at a breakfast or luncheon show for the benefit of a local charity. Interviews with the visiting vendor may be arranged with print and broadcast media, if the vendor is an authority on some special aspect of fashion or is otherwise newsworthy.

Maximum publicity benefits result from such vendor visits when the buyer or merchant who is handling the visit discusses the possibilities early with his store's publicity staff. The publicity executive needs to know why the visitor is newsworthy and whether or not he is capable of participating productively in press conferences, television interviews, and the like. Arrangements for such supplementary appearances have to be made well in advance, not only with the press but also with the visitor. If a vendor knows, for example, that he will have five or ten minutes on television, he may bring along a special group of unusually photogenic style numbers to show, and possibly even a highly photogenic model.

Fashion Producers The fashion publicity efforts of stores are frequently supplemented by the work of the vendors' own publicity staffs. Sometimes these fashion producers channel their publicity efforts through the stores, by making available suggested press releases and glossy photos of the styles they consider important. Sometimes the manufacturers issue the publicity material directly to the news media.

In their releases, they may spell out their fashion philosophies and indicate how these are reflected in their current lines. It is not unusual for them to call the attention of fashion editors to the names of local stores carrying their lines. On occasion, a producer may circulate reproductions of magazine pages on which appear either his advertising or editorial mention of his styles, at the same time pointing out the local stores that have received advertising or editorial credits.

When such publicity is channeled through the store, the store's fashion coordinator and publicity staff have the opportunity to evaluate it and integrate it with their own efforts. When the producer channels it directly to the news media, however, the store need not be caught unaware. The fashion coordinator, of course, knows what editorial credits and advertising credits have been accepted by the store and can be on the alert for publicity about them that emanates from the producer. The buyer, too, being in intimate touch with his various resources, is in a position to know which among them work directly with news media. If necessary, the buyer can suggest that the vendor route his publicity material to the store, so that the power of the store name can be utilized and the store can coordinate its efforts with those of its resources.

Trade Associations Buyers and merchants who keep in close touch with the industries from which they purchase fashion goods sometimes can coordinate their own store publicity efforts with those of trade associations serving their markets. Such associations frequently release publicity to print and broadcast media on new developments in their particular areas of fashion, and relate these developments to current trends. Some of the fashion industry trade associations have fashion publicists on their staffs or retain the services of public relations firms, such as the one headed by Eleanor Lambert, originator of the New York market's Press Week.

When an industry trade association launches a drive to publicize its fashion message or its merchandise, or both, the buyer or merchant usually receives in the mail suggestions for tying in with such publicity efforts: ideas for press releases, photographs, recommendations for fashion events. If such material is passed along to the store's publicity staff and discussed with them, it often is possible to work out ways to benefit locally from the national publicity efforts of these associations.

Fashion Selling

Effective use of advertising, display, and publicity brings a customer to the store ready to make a fashion purchase. At this point, unless the purchase is routine or the store is of the self-service type, a salesperson steps into the picture.

Modern retail salesmanship is conceived as helping customers to buy. Some authorities define it as "the business of helping people to understand their needs and of showing them how those needs can be satisfied through the purchase of merchandise and service."[1] Retailers have their own succinct definition of good salesmanship: selling goods that won't come back to customers who will.

Fashion selling requires a more sophisticated type of salesmanship than is required by most other consumer goods, since decisions center around taste rather than such more readily measured qualities as durability and utility. Fashion salespeople need all the qualities that are required for selling goods of other types, but in addition they need to be able to respond swiftly and surely to the customer's changing taste. This is essential if they are to show the customer that the goods are attractive, becoming, and appropriate.

Methods of Selling Fashions

Modern retailers have a wide range of selling methods at their command. The choice of the method or methods used is made by the merchant, depending upon the kind of goods to be sold, the degree of fashion leadership the store or department asserts, the price lines of the merchandise, the prevailing shopping habits of the store's customers, and any other relevant factors.

Among the most commonly used methods are personal selling, simplified selling, and mail and telephone selling.

Personal Salesmanship In this method of selling, a salesperson actively assists the customer in choosing articles suited to her individual taste and needs, and seeks to do this in such a way that the customer will return to the store or department for future purchases. The goodwill engendered by pleasing customers and serving their interests, by helping them identify and satisfy their wants, is the foundation upon which fashion stores or departments build their continued patronage.

The most exacting type of personal selling is *salon selling*. It is often used in stores or departments that sell fashions in the introductory or early rise stages of their cycles. In salon selling, no stock is exposed to the customer's view except that which is brought out for her inspection by the salesperson. Close rapport is needed between customer and salesperson if this type of selling is to be successful. An advantage of this method is that, once a mutual understanding has been developed, the customer usually comes back to the store to be served by "her" salesperson, who understands her wants and how to satisfy them.

Since each salesperson is apt to develop a personal following of customers who return to her repeatedly and trust her suggestions, stores may encourage salespeople to maintain card files on their customers, noting style and color preferences, sizes worn, price lines preferred, and other pertinent personal information. Salespeople then use these files to tell customers about new styles that have arrived in stock and about other fashion developments designed to keep alive the customers' interest in both the store and its fashion assortments. Specialty stores in particular encourage salespeople to develop such personal followings. Department stores, on the other hand, tend to discourage this except in their high fashion departments.

Simplified Selling There has been a significant trend among mass distributors of fashion goods to employ simplified, less costly selling methods in preference to highly personalized selling service. The trend has its origins in rising costs of labor and other operating expenses, tremendously increased competition, decreasing store loyalty among customers, and the preference among large segments of the shopping public for methods less formal than salon-type selling.

In *self-selection selling,* merchandise is displayed and arranged so that the customer can make at least a preliminary selection without the aid of a salesperson. Open wall racks, T-stands, display shelves, bins, and tables are among the fixtures most commonly used in self-selection departments. Salespeople are available to answer customers' questions about the merchandise, to check for styles, sizes, and colors not on the selling floor, to assist in the fitting room if required, and to ring up the sale once the customer has made a buying decision. This is the most prevalent fashion selling technique today, and it is found in stores and departments handling all types of fashion merchandise, except those at the uppermost reaches of the price scale where personal selling is more usual.

In a *self-service operation,* the customer not only makes her selection from the goods on display but also brings her purchase to a check-out counter where she makes payment and where her purchase is wrapped. Most self-service operations have stock personnel on the floor to keep the merchandise in order and to check, when requested by customers, for sizes and colors not on display, but there are no sales personnel as such to give the customer fashion information and advice.

Self-service is the selling method most favored by discount operations and others whose low prices require holding services to a minimum. Self-service techniques, however, may be employed by stores of the traditional type in some of their fashion departments, particularly those handling prepackaged, brand-name goods, such as pantyhose, bras, or classic shirts.

Although self-service is usually equated with savings and bargain opportunities, this method of selling fashion is by no means used exclusively for low-priced merchandise, closeouts, and "distress" merchandise. Both medium-priced and high fashion goods have also been sold successfully by this method. Ohrbach's and Alexander's, two discount fashion operations based in New York, make extensive use of self-service. Yet buyers from both these retail organizations regularly visit the European couture showings, as well as accessories and ready-to-wear fashion markets. Both stores have bought couture styles abroad, either for resale as imports or for line-for-line copying. Ohrbach's has been especially successful in attracting women of wealth and distinction (and publicity value) to its showings of imports and domestically produced line-for-line copies. The fashion leaders attend an invitation-only preview of the styles which they may order before the goods go on the open racks.

Self-service racks and counters are used more and more often to sell prepackaged, branded goods.

Mail and Telephone Selling A store can sell fashion products successfully by mail or telephone only when the customers have firm confidence in the store's assortments, its fashion position, and its understanding of customer wants and tastes. Readiness on the part of the store to accept returns is essential; returns are higher than on goods selected by the customer in person. Since customer returns reduce net sales and indirectly reduce profit, mail and telephone selling is usually restricted to merchandise whose markon is large enough to offset the cost of subsequent returns. In addition, such selling is usually restricted to classic styles and to merchandise that does not involve size and fit. Hosiery, some classifications of intimate apparel, and porch and patio frocks are typical of the kinds of fashion goods that may be sold by mail or telephone.

Requirements for Success in Fashion Selling
Customers prefer to buy their fashion merchandise from stores whose decors and assortments reflect their own current fashion and taste levels. They also prefer to buy from salespeople who themselves represent these same fashion and taste levels in appearance, manners, speech, and method of presenting the goods.

Selection of salespeople is an important phase of successful fashion merchandising. Their appearance, their grounding in fashion information, and their approach to their work are of deep concern to the merchant or buyer, for the salesperson is the ultimate link between the store and the customer.

Personal Qualifications There are certain essential attributes that a buyer or merchant seeks in fashion salespeople. Selling is greatly aided when salespeople have developed such personal qualities as:

▫ Attractive appearance, scrupulous cleanliness, businesslike dress, careful grooming

▫ Good manners and good business etiquette

▫ Animation, alertness, promptness in attention to customers

▫ Ability to form a quick estimate of customers and their preferences, as well as a sympathetic appreciation of their problems

▫ Ability to speak well, a pleasing voice, a lively and intelligent expression, clarity of speech, and a knowledge of when to talk and when to listen

▫ Orderliness in thinking, talking, working; accuracy in handling records, reports, and other paperwork

▫ A good memory for faces and names

▫ A friendly, tactful manner and, above all, sincerity[2]

Fashion and Merchandise Knowledge Fashion salespeople need to know not only the fashion points of the merchandise they have been assigned to sell, but also what fashion itself is, how it works, and what the current fashion trends are and which way they are going. Those who sell apparel need to be knowledgeable about the fitting of garments. Whatever the salesperson sells, she should be able to guide customers in selecting related apparel and accessories, in her own and other departments, that will achieve the desired look. Above all, the fashion salesperson needs an appreciation of the fashion values of merchandise, so that she can state its price with confidence.

Success in fashion selling often depends upon the ability of a salesperson to convey to customers those intangibles that make up an essential part of the value of fashion goods. Equally important is the ability to understand and sympathize with the problems of individual customers, and to exercise patience and diplomacy in aiding a faltering customer to overcome objections and obstacles in the path of accepting a style.

It is taken for granted that successful fashion salespeople are thoroughly familiar with the facts about the merchandise they are selling: its quality, materials, workmanship, and so on. A thorough knowledge of the merchandise is basic to any retail selling. Fashion goods, for all the intangibles that go to make up their value, are no exception.

The Individual Approach One of the most important points in selling fashion merchandise is the necessity of individualizing each sale, of avoiding any attempt to handle either the merchandise or the customer in an impersonal or routine way. Probably no other experience in the business world creates so much animosity or ill will as treating someone as just one of the masses rather than as an individual. When that person is a customer, such treatment can mean a lost sale.

In fashion selling, personal taste is an all-important factor in making a buying decision. Success in selling fashion merchandise, therefore, depends upon a salesperson's ability to cater to that personal taste and treat each customer as an individual.

This need to individualize the fashion customer is among the major problems confronting retailers of fashion merchandise today. Mass production and mass merchandising have made low prices possible, but often at the expense of the individualization of services offered to customers. The retailer's problem, for which there appears to be no easy solution, is to continue to give the customer the attention and service fashion goods require, and yet to cope with rising costs of operation and with profit margins that are being narrowed by competition. This is not exclusively a problem of large stores. Even in a tiny shop, the proprietor is hard put to provide individual services to customers and yet find time to perform all the many chores involved in running the business—or else to achieve the profit margin out of which he can pay to have these chores performed by others.

Training of Fashion Salespeople

Good fashion salespeople can be trained through thoughtful, unending efforts. In order to sell any merchandise well, a salesperson must be well acquainted with the goods, their uses, their selling points, and any special care they may need. In order to sell fashion merchandise well, a salesperson also needs to know the fashion picture as a whole and the significance of those elements that directly concern his or her merchandise.

To sell the extreme types of dangling earrings that were offered in 1967, for example, a salesperson needed to understand the 1920s look that was then popular. To sell belts or foundation garments that defined the waist in 1968, she needed to understand the romantic 1930s look that was enjoying a revival. Only when a salesperson understands the total fashion look can she explain to the customer how its various components are related to one another. And only then can she anticipate the coordination problems each new look presents and help her customer solve them, making acceptance of the new easier.

Not all salespeople should be expected to be expert fashion consultants, although such a state of affairs would surely be a happy one for the fashion business, but it should be recognized that there is a weakness among many salespeople about just this kind of information, and this deficiency causes considerable customer dissatisfaction. When salespeople acquire such fashion information, from the buyer, from fashion publications, from employee fashion shows and fashion training bulletins, they are better equipped to act as consultants to their customers. When salespeople radiate assurance and fashion authority, customers buy with more confidence. That is why the late Hector Escabosa, then president of I. Magnin and Company, San Francisco, besought merchants to "pamper, love, and cultivate" fashion salespeople, because "in their effectiveness rests our fate."[3]

Small Stores In small shops, informal training of salespeople goes on in the course of the day-to-day operation of the business. Fashion points of the merchandise are explained to the sales personnel by the buyer or store owner as the goods come into stock. In the relatively small store, that buyer or store owner often is on the selling floor for much of the day and can answer any questions posed by customers.

Frequently, salespeople in small stores are asked to view lines shown by visiting representatives of the store's resources and to express opinions with respect to the salability of the merchandise. They may be encouraged, moreover, to ask questions and to discuss the merchandise with the vendor representative. He, in turn, may be asked by the store owner or buyer to hold meetings with the sales staff to discuss fashion features of the line he represents. Such a presentation may be made to all salespeople in the store, not only those who sell in the department that handles his goods. This is because smaller stores are more likely than large ones to ignore departmental barriers and to train their salespeople to sell in all departments, helping the customer to assemble her entire outfit—apparel, intimate apparel, and accessories—to achieve a desired look.

Large Stores and Chains In large, departmentalized stores, fashion training is more formalized. Seasonal fashion reports, often in the form of illustrated leaflets, are prepared by the store's training department in conjunction with the fashion coordinator. Buyers, and sometimes merchandise managers, hold meetings for salespeople upon their return from market trips, to report on the fashion trends they observed and to describe the merchandise they have purchased. In each department, the buyer or assistant holds weekly meetings, at which the sales staff is told about scheduled advertising for the upcoming week, the fashion points of the merchandise to be featured in these ads, and anything else that will help them do a more informed, fashion-conscious job of selling.

In chain organizations, the fashion coordinator issues to each unit a summary of fashion trends in both ready-to-wear and accessories. This summary is sent into the stores at the start of each season and reports the trends noted at each major market opening. In addition, the central buyers of fashion goods alert the appropriate fashion department managers in the various units of the chain to current fashion developments. The usual medium is a fashion bulletin, which features sketches of items, swatches of the materials in which they come, and detailed descriptions, in-

Courtesy The Broadway-Hale Stores, Inc.

*Buyers often use meetings to keep their
sales staffs up to date on fashion news.*

cluding colors and sizes available. Still another
form of fashion training occurs when new styles
are sent from the central buying office of the
chain into some or all units for testing purposes,
together with pertinent information about fashion
features and selling points.

Employee Fashion Shows   One of the most
effective devices for briefing a fashion sales staff
is the presentation of a fashion show for them.
The employee fashion show may be as formal and
elaborate as one staged for customers, or it may
be casual, using salespeople as models and sub-
stituting give-and-take conversation for prepared
commentary. In some cases, it may consist simply
of fully dressed and accessorized mannequins,
displayed with explanatory signs in employee
lounges or cafeterias. The basic idea, however,
remains the same: to show concretely what lines,
colors, or combinations thereof are expected to
prove acceptable to the store's customers this

season, and to call attention to points of difference between last year's or last season's styles
and those of the new fashion trend.

Employee fashion shows in a large store are
likely to be planned and carried out by the fashion coordinator or any buyer whose fashion sense
and knowledge have the respect of the store staff.
Shows are also often carried out, on a less ambitious scale, by buyers of related departments for
the benefit of their combined sales forces. A
foundations buyer and a lingerie buyer, for example, might use the show technique to explain
coordination in intimate apparel and to prepare
their staffs to sell in either department, if this
should be necessary in order to offer customers
the complete coordination package. Similarly, a
group of accessories buyers might work with a
dress or coat buyer to explain how the current
season's scarfs, belts, or jewelry can be combined
effectively with the prevailing styles and colors
in apparel.

Vendor Aids   Obviously, it is to the interest of
producers of fashion merchandise to do what
they can to maintain a high level of retail salesmanship on behalf of their merchandise. Among
the steps they take to assist stores in this area
are: giving talks, distributing promotional literature, and showing products in use.

Talks to salespeople are usually given by the
sales representatives who call upon buyers. Often
these talks are given in meetings held before the
store opens, but sometimes a vendor may invite
the entire sales staff, the buyer, and other store
executives to dinner and an evening meeting
outside the store. The presentations made at these
latter meetings are often quite elaborate, with
charts, slides, film, or modeling.

Sales literature, in the form of brochures, is
often given to salespeople for study and reference. Typical literature would be the booklet of
a coat manufacturer on a currently important
fabric or leather, a fiber or fabric producer's
leaflet about a new textile development, a foundation maker's explanation of figure types and
how to fit them, or a lingerie or hosiery producer's
size chart.

Manufacturers train people to sell and instruct salespeople in the use and benefits of their

Courtesy The J. L. Hudson Co., Detroit, Mich.

Cosmeticians often have been trained by and are paid by the manufacturers whose products they sell, even though they seem a part of the regular store staff to the average customer.

products. Demonstrators visit stores to attract customers to clinics, to assist in the training of salespeople, or both. The expert corsetière, the hairstylist, and the instructor sent from a fiber or fabric source to explain the use and care of new products are typical visiting demonstrators. Other demonstrators become permanent parts of the store staff. These appear to be in the store's employ but are paid, at least in part, by a producer who trains them to sell and stock his firm's goods. In large stores, cosmeticians and the representatives of some nationally advertised hosiery brands are likely to be permanent demonstrators.

Others Who Train Salespeople Retail selling efforts are also of vital interest to producers who

may be several steps removed from direct contact with the consumer. These include fiber sources, both natural and synthetic; leather and plastic processors; makers of special finishes or treatments for fabrics; associations dedicated to publicizing the merits of fibers, fabrics, leathers, or other fashion materials; and consumer periodicals. From these outside organizations may come a battery of aids for helping to train salespeople: talks and demonstrators, exhibits, leaflets, and film and slide presentations.

Everyone in the fashion business, from the producers of fibers to the makers of finished goods, has a vested interest in improving the quality of retail selling. The reason is plain: if goods move only sluggishly across retail counters,

Buyers provide their sales forces with merchandise information, display techniques, and sales procedures.

the supply lines all the way back from retailer to manufacturer to source of raw material become choked with unsold goods. Often the fashion salesperson seems to be the focus of all eyes in the trade: unless he performs his function well, little is sold to the customer. Nothing happens in the fashion business until something is sold.

In addition to all those who cooperate in the training of retail salespeople at no charge to the merchant, there are also professionals who sell their training services. Some come into stores, hold rallies, give pep talks on the art of selling, and generally try to stimulate people to get out of their ruts. Others offer film presentations to achieve the same ends. Although these services are usually concerned with salesmanship in general, their impact upon fashion salespeople is quite as strong as upon those in other merchandise departments.

The Buyer's Responsibility for Selling

In departmentalized stores, the buyer shares with the store's training department the responsibility for salesmanship in his department. The training staff teaches store systems and procedures to new employees before sending them to the selling floor. Thereafter, unless asked to help, the training department leaves the salespeople in the buyer's hands, intervening only with storewide efforts to increase accuracy, encourage courtesy, discourage unnecessary deliveries, and so on. On-the-job supervision, for example, is generally the responsibility of the buyer in small stores or his assistant in large stores. Although storewide or divisionwide efforts to present current fashion information or teach basic merchandise information may sometimes involve the store's training staff, as a general rule each buyer is responsible for providing his sales force with merchandise information and with selling tips or techniques.

Merchandise Information As the fashion authority for his department, the buyer is the primary source of information on merchandise carried by the department. He is expected to alert his sales force to current and anticipated trends and to indicate how these trends will affect sales prospects. He might, for example, explain how a trend toward skirts with blouses or sweaters but no jackets will benefit the sale of belts.

The buyer is also expected to relay to his sales force information about the quality and value of the department's merchandise. He should detail the specific selling points of an article, emphasizing to his salespeople the features that might make the merchandise more desirable to a customer.

Sometimes the buyer may also have to teach salespeople how to arrange the merchandise in stock: how to fold dresses, how to place dresses on racks, or how to replace shoes in boxes. Or, he may have to point out to his salespeople the most effective way of displaying merchandise to a customer. For example, he might show how a dress can be held against one's body to achieve the best effect, or demonstrate how a customer, invited to hold a scarf near her face before a mirror, can be assured that a color becomes her.

Selling Tips Because of his fashion expertise, the buyer can also provide salespeople with effective selling tips. He may supply data on the use and care of merchandise which his sales force can then pass on to the customer. Or he may coach his salespeople on proper size and fit.

The buyer may also tell his salespeople what related items—even from other departments—to suggest to enhance the customer's enjoyment of her purchase. For instance, he may show how to suggest to a customer that extra belts give variety to a dress or skirt that comes with its own belt. Or, how a coat or dress neckline may seem more flattering if a scarf is suggested for wear with it. By briefing salespeople on such suggestions, the buyer makes it easier for them to close the sale on a major item of apparel or on an important accessory. Moreover, it helps salespeople to impress upon customers the idea that the store is a headquarters for fashion advice.

Training Methods

The salesperson may be the ultimate link between the store and the customer, but it is the buyer's training and supervision that makes that salesperson a strong, productive, profitable link for both store and customer. In order to convey needed information to salespeople, the buyer, or his assistant, employs a variety of techniques.

Departmental Meetings Each week, usually before the store opens, departmental meetings are held to review new or incoming merchandise and upcoming ads, to give pep talks, and to report any departmental problems, changes, or opportunities. Ideally, these are discussion meetings, but often the pressure of time makes them a series of rapid-fire announcements. Some fashion stores, to dispense with formality and avoid the atmosphere of a stereotyped, dull session, use instead a daily five-minute "huddle" just before the opening bell.

Fashion Shows and Reports In addition to what may be done on a storewide basis, the buyer may present fashion shows for his own salespeople to point up his department's merchandise. He may also provide informal market reports, written or oral, telling his salespeople what he has seen and heard in the market.

Bulletin Boards Leaflets, clippings, and other matter related to the department's merchandise may be posted on conveniently located bulletin boards. Commendation for special selling achievements, appropriate announcements, and bits of cartoon humor also find their way to such bulletin boards.

Miscellaneous Other training media may include posted reprints or preprints of ads run by the department and posted or circulated printed material such as trade magazines of resources.

References

[1]O. Preston Robinson, Christine H. Robinson, and George H. Zeiss, *Successful Retail Salesmanship*, 3d ed., Prentice-Hall, Inc., Englewood Cliffs, N.J., 1961, p. 2.
[2]Nystrom, *Fashion Merchandising*, pp. 187–188.
[3]Escabosa, "Heartbeat of Retailing," *Readings in Modern Retailing*, p. 395.

Merchandising Vocabulary

Define or briefly explain the following terms:

Publicity	Personal selling
Press release	Salon selling
Advertising credit	Self-selection
Fashion coordinator	Self-service

Merchandising Review

1. Explain how publicity differs from advertising. What is the major purpose of fashion publicity?
2. Name at least five types of audiences that fashion shows might be designed to reach. How is publicity achieved for such shows?
3. In what ways can a vendor's representatives earn fashion publicity both for the vendor and the store?
4. What factors are considered by a store when deciding whether to accept or reject the offer of an editorial credit?
5. What methods are most commonly employed in passing fashion news along to print or broadcast media?
6. What different types of information should a salesperson have about fashion merchandise in order to sell it well? What methods do stores employ in imparting this information to salespeople?

7. From what outside sources may stores seek help in upgrading and maintaining a high level of retail salesmanship? What type of assistance does each source provide?
8. What means might a buyer employ in conveying to his salespeople needed merchandise and fashion information?
9. Differentiate between the following types of fashion selling techniques: (a) salon selling; (b) self-selection; (c) self-service. Indicate the types of stores or departments in which each prevails or to which it is best suited.
10. What is meant by ''a personal following''? What techniques are employed in maintaining this personal relationship? In what situations may it be most effectively employed?

Merchandising Digest

1. ''The buyer is expected to be the source of all merchandise information and the fashion authority in his department . . . .'' Discuss this statement from the text, pointing out the specific types of information a buyer is responsible for providing to his salespeople.
2. ''Fashion selling requires a more sophisticated type of salesmanship than is required by most other goods.'' Discuss this quotation from the text in the light of qualities required in retail salespeople.

18
Fashion Coordination

Retail fashion coordination demands teamwork of a high order. If the customer is to be able to find compatible apparel and accessories in a store's stock, that store must see to it that the assortments in each of its fashion departments are related to those in all of its other fashion departments. Not only must these assortments be of the "right" type but they also must be presented at the "right" time, the time when customers want to buy. Important to fashion coordination, therefore, is the timing of fashion merchandise offerings to coincide with peak fashion demand.

From merchandise manager to promotion director right down to part-time salespeople, everyone in the store must convey the store's fashion story with the proper emphasis, with perfect timing, and in a way that induces the store's regular and prospective customers to buy.

Fashion coordination begins with the selection of the merchandise and the building of assortments. From there it extends to the training of sales personnel, the effective use of advertising and display, the staging of promotional events, and the garnering of favorable publicity.

The Fashion Coordinator

In all but the smallest stores, responsibility for fashion coordination is usually vested in an executive known as the fashion coordinator. In some stores, the fashion coordinator reports to the top merchandising executive; in others, to the sales promotion director.

The major responsibility of the fashion coordinator is to assist in promoting sales of fashion merchandise throughout the entire store. In this capacity, the fashion coordinator is responsible for analyzing fashion trends, for advising merchandising executives in relation to the buying of coordinated and related fashions, for helping devise the most effective presentation of fashion merchandise to customers, and for building a fashion reputation for the store.

Usually the coordinator is a woman who functions in an advisory capacity, as a staff aide to management (see Chapter 10), who achieves the goals of fashion coordination by being stimulating and persuasive in working with other store executives rather than through any authority she may have to approve or reject their merchandising decisions. She works with nearly everyone in the store, advising on buying, selling, advertising, publicity, and display activities, to coordinate the timing and emphasis of all fashion assortments so as to present a related picture to the store's customers.

Merchandising Responsibilities

The basic merchandising responsibilities of the fashion coordinator (or of any store executive who undertakes the coordination function) are:

□ To evaluate current fashion trends in terms of the store's clientele, image, and merchandising policies

□ To alert management and buyers to incoming fashions, even before they become important to the store, so that appropriate action can be planned well in advance

□ Conversely, to supply early warning about fashions currently important in the store's stocks but which appear likely to wane in customer interest soon

□ To assist buyers, when requested, in selecting for their respective departments merchandise that correctly interprets those fashion trends that are currently important to the store

□ To assist buyers, when requested, in correlating their merchandise with that of other departments of the store

When this job is well done, the store's fashion merchandise is well coordinated, and its customers can select from its various departments apparel and accessories that go well together. Obviously, customers buy more readily under such circumstances, much more readily than when each item under consideration poses a problem of what to wear with it or where to find suitable related items.

Market Work To get the information she needs to carry out her merchandising tasks, a fashion coordinator visits all the major markets—not to buy merchandise for the store but to get a clear picture of the currently popular fashions and to scan the fashion horizon for possible future changes, so that she can advise management and buyers on trends in the overall fashion picture.

Her market work may take her to showrooms not covered by her store's buyers, to fabric, fiber, and leather producers from whom she can obtain opinions about incoming trends. She may be in the market before her store's buyers, or with them, or both. She also regularly visits the offices of fashion and consumer magazines that are important to her store's customers in order to assess their themes in upcoming issues and the value to various departments of her store of the editorial and advertising credits offered to each.

With this broad background of information, the coordinator is in a position to offer meaningful advice to individual buyers about offerings in their markets. Although she may not know any one market as thoroughly as does the buyer who covers it for the store, she will know, for example, what colors will be important in dresses during the forthcoming season, and can relate this information to the hosiery, belt, and scarf buyers so that they have the appropriate shades available in their respective assortments. She may not know which producer has the best accessories, but she will know the ideal sizes and shapes to go with the new dresses and coats for the coming season. She advises, recommends, and informs; the rest is up to the buyers.

Achieving Coordination In order to effect successful coordination among the various fashion departments of a store, top management first must make certain storewide decisions. The degree of fashion leadership for which the store wishes to be known must be determined, as well as the extent of the merchandising and promotional efforts to be given those fashions.

The fashion coordinator consults first with the store's management about what fashions should be promoted, to what extent, and when. Next, she works with store executives responsible for carrying out such decisions, and assists each of them in implementing management's decisions.

For example, if management has decided that the young look is one the store is to sponsor, each buyer will select colors, silhouettes, and prices with that theme in mind. The advertising department may draw its fashion figures more leggy and wide-eyed than before, and the display department may pose its manikins in less sophisticated stances. Fashion shows will be paced at a brisker tempo, built around the youngest, liveliest themes the fashion coordinator can think of.

In another season or in another store, the romantic look may be the one that will subtly affect its assortments, fashion art, displays, store decor, advertising copy, and special events. The services of the fashion coordinator are available to any and all departments in achieving an effective interpretation of whatever promotional theme the store chooses.

Within the framework of the fashion theme the store has chosen to promote, there is often opportunity for a coordinated promotional effort within a single merchandising division. A group of accessories departments, for example, may decide to stage a promotion of its own with no direct tie-in with apparel departmental plans. If neutrals are strong in apparel and touches of bright color are to be introduced by accessories, these latter departments may join in promoting brilliantly colored shoes, handbags, jewelry, scarfs, and blouses, or in featuring accessories in a single bright accent color, such as hot pink or emerald.

The prime objective of the fashion coordinator, whether she suggests ideas or merely assists in carrying them out, is to make sure that the assortments and presentations of each department are in harmony with the overall picture of fashion that the store seeks to present. She also may be called upon to advise buyers on items to feature in their department displays and windows, and on those to be featured in advertisements. She coaches display men, advertising people, and salespeople in how to show and what to say about the merchandise, and acts as liaison between apparel and accessories departments, in furthering the store's efforts to give the consumer a clear, consistent picture of how to achieve the looks currently in fashion.

Fashion Forecasting From what she has seen in the market or learned from other sources, the fashion coordinator draws up detailed seasonal fashion forecasts for the merchandising division of her store. These forecasts cover such points as trends in silhouette, materials, colors, textures—in short, the look or looks that are expected to be accepted by the store's customers in the coming season.

Such a forecast may indicate, for example, that while texture may still be important in hosiery, stocking colors are toning down toward the neutrals. Or it may indicate that the heirloom look in jewelry goes well with certain nostalgic styles in dresses and blouses. The forecast may define whether favored colors in the coming season will be contrasts or monotones, bright or subdued, and whether or not some specific range of colors is featured above others. From such forecasts, knowledgeable buyers are able to proceed with more assurance, promotion executives can begin planning events, and display people can decide upon the materials to look for in their own markets. If, for example, the fashion trend is toward delicate colors and dainty fabrics, the fashion coordinator's forecast alerts the display department to the need for backgrounds that will not be too vividly colorful for the incoming merchandise. The manikins may have to have their faces redone in more natural-looking colors,

and their wigs may have to be replaced with others in softer styles. If they were not forewarned of the changing fashions, the display executives might be unprepared to show the new merchandise at its best.

Forecasts are supplied by the fashion coordinator as often and in as much detail as management specifies. Usually, however, they are made on a six-month basis, just as merchandise plans are. In some cases, such as Easter or back-to-school, forecasts may be made for shorter periods of time. Later, after the buyers have done their market work but before the selling season actually begins, a fashion coordinator may prepare a preview presentation of the upcoming season's fashions as a way to acquaint all sales and promotion employees with the themes the store plans to emphasize in the coming season.

Sales Training Responsibilities

A fashion-educated selling staff is a major asset to any store that sells fashion goods. In each individual selling department, the buyer is the source of all merchandise information—but for the overall fashion picture and for information on combining elements to achieve the currently fashionable look, the fashion coordinator may be called upon for training aid. Working with the store's training director, she may prepare seasonal fashion presentations for the salespeople.

Such presentations may take the form of fashion shows, sketch-and-copy pamphlets, talks illustrated by merchandise from stock, color slides, or any combination of these that is suitable to the store and its facilities. So important is this aspect of fashion coordination and promotion that some large, multiunit stores have a policy each season of preparing a fashion show for all employees, even those only remotely concerned with fashion. Initially, the show is presented to buyers and branch store managers who assemble at the main store for that purpose. Repeat performances then are staged in the main store until all employees concerned—salespeople, display staff, advertising staff, and so on—have attended. Finally, the show "goes on the road" to the store's branches. At each showing, those who attend are given a brochure to help them remember what they have seen. Selling sentences, suitable for the

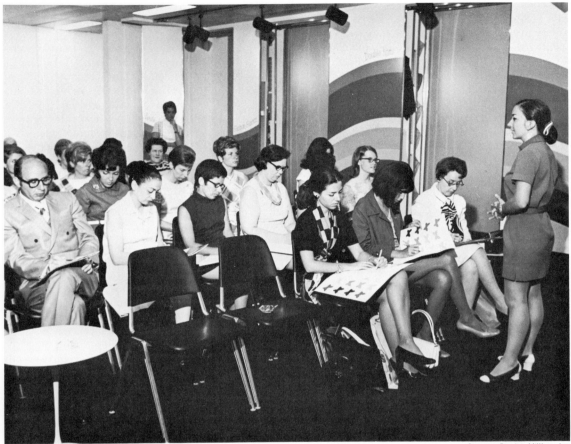

A fashion coordinator not only visits the major markets but also the important fiber and fabric resources, so that she can learn, and be able to describe to her store's buyers, all the facets of the current fashion trends.

salespeople to use in talking to customers, are worked into the show's commentary and are repeated in the booklets.

Sales Promotion Responsibilities

The advertising and display staffs look to the buyers for merchandise information about the specific goods to be featured in ads or windows. For background information on how the featured merchandise relates to the overall fashion picture and what to show with it, they turn to the fashion coordinator.

Although the fashion coordinator may not write a line of advertising copy or sketch a fashion figure, she is expected to see that the copy, figure, featured merchandise, and related items shown are all compatible with one another and in line with the store's fashion story. Similarly, she may never set up a display in a window or department of the store, but she is very likely to be called upon for advice by those who do the displays, about how to put the various elements of the outfit together, down to such fine points as the right spot for a jeweled pin or the right way to drape a scarf on a manikin.

When stores stage promotional events featuring their fashion assortments, the fashion coordinator is very much in the picture. She may suggest the events, play a leading role in them, or simply stand by to see that the details of the fashion story are correctly presented.

Fashion shows for customers may be held in or out of the store, as direct sales builders or as public relations efforts to assist charitable and civic causes. They may be held in branch stores to enhance the fashion images of those stores. They may be formal, using models on a runway, or informal, with models strolling about a restaurant or departmental selling floor. They may even be staged so simply that the commentator merely takes garments from a rack and holds them up while she explains their fashion points to a small, intimate audience. Stage-managing such fashion shows, as well as coordinating the outfits and preparing the commentary, is usually the responsibility of the fashion coordinator.

Many other events also may be used to underline the importance of fashion coordination. There may be talks and discussion meetings for customers of a particular type, such as teen-agers, career women, or expectant mothers. There may be occasions to talk to women's clubs and similar groups outside the store about current fashions and fashion trends that are of special interest to each particular group. In all such cases, the fashion coordinator is usually involved.

The coordinator also works with visiting fashion experts in staging their presentations. For example, a fiber source may send one of its fashion experts to stage a show of garments in which one of its newer fibers is used; a foundation producer may send a representative to select apparel and undergarments from stock and stage a presentation to show how each relates to the other; a garment producer may bring a trunk show; a consumer magazine may stage a fashion presentation on a theme it is currently sponsoring. The store's fashion coordinator, in such instances, makes sure that the presentation is in line with the store's fashion policy, assists in tying in all advertising, display, and personal selling, and secures as much publicity as the particular type of event warrants.

Fashion Coordination in Retail Organizations

The primary objective of all retail fashion coordination is the same, regardless of store size or type: to create and maintain a definite, specific fashion reputation for the store. Achieving this objective involves advice, aid, and assistance in merchandising, sales training, and sales promotion areas, regardless of store size or type.

The manner in which this objective is achieved, however, as well as the personnel, skills, and responsibilities connected with the achievement of such coordination, varies widely by store size and type.

Large Retail Stores

The job of presenting coordinated fashion assortments in large, multiunit retail organizations is an awesome one indeed. Not only must the fashion assortments in the various branches meet the diverse needs of local customers, but also they must reflect the distinctive fashion image of the store organization as a whole. Dozens or even hundreds of fashion departments and their respective buyers must be considered and served; hundreds or even sometimes thousands of employees must be trained.

In order to accomplish this gigantic task, a large store maintains a well-staffed fashion office to assist its coordinator. Members of the fashion staff are often assigned certain specific areas of responsibility. For example, one may be charged with the responsibility for coordinating all special events. Another may be in full charge of all fashion shows. Still another may work with one or more of the store's consumer boards.

The fashion coordinator for a large store usually attends all market openings, both at home and abroad; maintains close contact with local newspaper and national magazine editors; attends charity balls and first nights at the theater and opera, and frequents newly discovered and fashionable resorts and other "in" gathering places, in order to observe at firsthand what fashion leaders are wearing for such occasions. Through these observations, the coordinator seeks advance indication of fashion trends that have or will have meaning for her store's customers. For example, if she sees a number of women wearing evening pajamas with a full, graceful sweep at these events, she reminds appropriate buyers in her store to seek out slacks and jumpsuits with similar leg fullness. If passementerie trim is the outstanding feature of a leading Paris couturier's collection, she can advise her store's ready-to-wear and accessories buyers with assurance to look for items in their markets that feature similar details of design.

The fashion coordinator for a large store is responsible for suggesting suitable seasonal fashion themes to be promoted throughout her store and for coordinating all sales promotional efforts toward this end.

In some of the largest retail organizations, the title of the store's fashion executive is "fashion director." A fashion director may be assisted by a fashion coordinator for women's and children's apparel and accessories departments, another for home furnishings fashions, and still another for men's and boys' fashions.

Medium-Size Stores

The coordination of fashion assortments in medium-size retail organizations does not require as much experience or training as in larger volume firms. Former buyers frequently become fashion coordinators in medium-size stores, as do young and ambitious former assistants to large store fashion coordinators.

In stores of this size, with few branches or none, with fewer fashion buyers, fewer departments, and fewer employees than in mammoth organizations, the fashion coordinator may perform her function with only a small staff or, in some cases, even alone. If the store is at a distance from major fashion markets, she may attend openings in those markets only once a year or even less frequently, relying for her knowledge on the observations of fashion editors, fashion reporting services, her store's buying office, and the observations of her own store buyers after they have completed a market trip.

Fashion coordination in medium-size stores is far less complicated than in larger stores for several reasons:

First, each fashion buyer in a medium-size store is responsible for merchandise in a larger number of classifications than is a buyer in a larger store. Thus the buyer in the medium-size store is already more alert to the coordination aspects of the many classifications for which he buys. For example, one buyer in a medium-size store may be responsible for all intimate apparel, whereas in a larger store that same merchandise may be segmented into several separate departments, such as foundations, sleepwear, daywear, and loungewear, each with its own buyer. One buyer in a medium-size store might be responsible for coats and suits in all size and price ranges, whereas in a larger store such merchandise may be segmented into several departments, each featuring separate size and price ranges and each having its own buyer.

Second, effective training of salespeople is more easily accomplished in medium-size stores than in larger stores because, in the former, buyers are on the selling floor more frequently. Thus they are in a better position to stimulate their sales personnel and, at the same time, provide them with pertinent fashion information about the various kinds of merchandise they have been hired to sell.

Third, coordination among the fashion assortments offered by related departments is easier to achieve in medium-size stores than in their larger counterparts mainly because there are fewer buyers involved. With fewer buyers there are fewer personality conflicts and there is easier exchange of information about what is selling and what is not selling.

Small Stores

Ideally, every store should have a fashion office or a fashion coordinator to assist it in building and maintaining a fashion reputation through better coordinated assortments. There are many small retail firms, however, that either cannot afford to hire a full-time fashion specialist or for other reasons are obliged to achieve coordination without a full-time executive to take charge of this important store function. In such cases, responsibility for fashion coordination may be delegated to one of the store's buyers, or to a merchandise manager, or be assumed by the store's manager or owner himself.

The Buyer as Coordinator The fashion buyer in a relatively small departmentalized store is usually responsible for merchandising a larger number of related classifications than is the buyer for a medium-size or large store. For instance, in a smaller store, one buyer may be responsible for buying all types of merchandise in the accessories group, whereas a medium-size store would have several accessories buyers, and in a large store there would be even more buyers, each highly specialized as to type of merchandise.

The same factors that aid the buyer in the medium-size store in matters of coordination are even more influential for the buyer in the smaller store. The buyer for a group of departments or classifications in a smaller store becomes responsible for coordinating several pieces of the fashion picture as a normal part of his job when planning purchases, promotions, displays, and in the training of his salespeople. In addition, not only is such a buyer in close daily contact with his salespeople, but his salespeople in small stores often sell in more than one department and thus are more aware of coordination than if they were narrowly specialized.

Coordination in the small store is also easier to accomplish because very few buyers are involved. If only a few buyers cover the entire apparel and accessories fields, it is a simple matter to get them together either in the store or in the market to work out a coordinated fashion picture for the store. In the market or at home, it is easy for one buyer to exchange fashion ideas with another over lunch or on a coffee break. In a small organization, simple shoptalk often takes the place of much of the liaison work that a fashion coordinator does in a larger store.

Other coordinating procedures also are simpler in a small store than in a large one. Because the departments are usually physically close, displays of accessorized costumes benefit both apparel and accessories departments: a customer who likes what she sees on display can buy the entire outfit, if she chooses to, right on the spot. Salespeople are more apt to keep one another informed in the same way that their buyers do; they chat about merchandise and fashion during breaks in their workday and while doing their personal shopping. There is also likely to be less regimentation in a smaller store and more feeling of belonging and of personal interest in the store and its merchandise.

The Merchandise Manager as Coordinator It often happens that the head of a fine small specialty shop, or the apparel and accessories merchandise manager of a small department store, takes over many of the functions that a fashion coordinator might normally perform. Sometimes this is done because the store has no budget for a coordinator; sometimes the reason is that fashion is the merchant's first love, and he refuses to be divorced from it.

Many a merchandise manager who has worked his way up from a buying job refuses to lose contact with fashion resources. Like the fashion coordinators of other stores, he visits fiber, fabric, and leather firms, talks to merchandising executives of consumer publications, and visits the key resources of each of his principal fashion departments. Against this background, such executives can readily coordinate the merchandising and promotional efforts of their fashion departments. It is usually also part of the normal routine for such executives to counsel their buyers regarding sales training and other phases of fashion coordination.

The Owner as Coordinator In the very smallest of stores, those run by the owner with perhaps a salesperson or two, the owner is buyer, coordinator, merchandise manager, and sometimes even housekeeper. In such stores, the right hand always knows what the left is doing, and there is little need for liaison activities.

But the demands on the time and energies of the owner are enormous. The solution for many such shop owners is to concentrate on serving only one very narrow group of customers, seeking out and remaining faithful to those few resources whose merchandise has proved to be of exactly the right character for the selected clientele. Or sometimes a tiny store may divorce itself entirely from the coordination problem and specialize in dresses, sportswear, furs, or accessories. Such a store will attempt to key its offerings to the tastes of the community it serves, suggesting in general terms those components of the costume that the customer will have to go elsewhere to buy.

Chain Store Organizations

The fashion coordinator of a national general merchandise or specialty store chain has many of the responsibilities of the large store coordinator, plus others that are unique to chain store operation.

Chain organizations largely restrict their fashion offerings to proven styles, those that have arrived at the culmination stage of their individual cyclical development. Fashion rightness, quality, promotional prices, and private labels are stressed in their advertisements, displays, and other sales promotion efforts. In recent years, major general merchandise chains, such as Sears, Roebuck and Company, Montgomery Ward, and The J. C. Penney Company, have made gigantic strides toward upgrading both the breadth and quality of their fashion assortments. Samples of this upgrading may be found in the exclusive designs of Mary Quant for The J. C. Penney Company and the traveling fashion shows featuring foreign designers and their exclusive designs for Montgomery Ward. Catalogs of these chain organizations also reflect an increased awareness of the power of fashion to move huge quantities of apparel and accessories. This is attested to by the increased number of pages devoted to illustrations of fashion apparel and accessories, as well as by the use of color to further emphasize the fashion features of their assortments.

The fashion coordinator of a chain organization usually attends both domestic and European fashion market openings in order to keep abreast of fashion trends. On occasion she also may visit other foreign markets, particularly those in the Far East, for additional fashion inspiration. On such market trips, she may buy several original models that incorporate certain new details of design she believes should be featured in the fashion assortments offered by her firm in its stores, catalogs, or both. She also may arrange to have internationally famous designers create exclusive models, which, after consultation with the firm's merchandising executives, may be re-produced by domestic manufacturers to the specifications and under the private label of her firm.

After viewing the major collections, the coordinator prepares a detailed market report which goes out to the manager of each store unit in the chain. Such a report serves to keep both store managers and their fashion sales staffs abreast of current trends in fashion apparel and accessories.

The fashion coordinator also carefully evaluates these fashion trends that she has observed and, in close cooperation with her firm's merchandise managers, central and regional fashion buyers, as well as other merchandising executives, attempts to pinpoint customer preferences and determine the best means of achieving coordinated fashion presentations throughout the chain.

The major responsibility of the chain organization fashion coordinator is to expedite mass distribution of fashion goods on the basis of their wide appeal, good taste, quality, and moderate price. This responsibility is in direct contrast to that of the coordinator for a large specialty store, for example, who seeks to build and maintain her firm's reputation for fashion leadership.

An Example of Retail Fashion Coordination

An illustration of how fashion coordination was achieved by one major department store organization is provided in the following summary of a talk given at the annual convention of the National Retail Merchants Association in 1966 by Ardelle Tuma, fashion coordinator for Carson Pirie Scott and Company of Chicago. Miss Tuma was involved in every step of the program outlined below, in management decisions, in advertising and display, and in the buying of the merchandise.

The store's management had decided to take an immediate, direct, and long-term step toward educating the public along fashion lines. It was recognized that the store would have to underwrite a substantial part of the advertising budget for this type of fashion promotion, since its buyers would be loath to spend their departmental advertising dollars on promotions that might not bring immediate sales response.

In order that the ads should have a distinctive look, a fashion artist with a fresh, creative approach was sought and found. The advertising format was planned in advance of market openings, but with enough flexibility so that changes could be made later, if necessary. It was agreed that all ready-to-wear advertising should also feature appropriate accessories selected by the store's fashion office.

Each week during the season-long promotion, the store ran one ready-to-wear ad featuring coordinated apparel and accessories. Each of these ads was followed a day later by an accessories ad that tied in directly with the preceding apparel ad. If one ad presented sweaters and pants, for example, the accessories ad also showed sweaters and pants properly accessorized. The items shown in the two ads each week were not necessarily identical, but they were based on identical themes.

Response to the advertising was excellent, far beyond what the store had expected. The store, however, did not rest its fashion case merely on advertising; windows and first-floor fashion aisles also told a coordinated fashion story. Windows were used to illustrate major fashion ready-to-wear themes, and accessories departments were instructed on what to show to complete those featured themes. During such peak fashion selling periods as Easter, the store devoted a bank of four windows to accessories, in each case giving major impact to a specific fashion look or story. Each window included a fully dressed manikin, showing customers how to achieve a particular fashion look. Inside the store, each accessory department coordinated the merchandise in its own displays with that of the apparel featured in the windows. And, of course, when the customer reached the ready-to-wear floor, she again saw the window theme emphasized there in departmental displays.

In addition, the store also held daily fashion shows in its tearoom. All fashion shows were coordinated and produced by the store's fashion office and reflected the same fashion themes as those featured in advertisements and displays.

Thus, using ads, windows, interior displays, and fashion shows, the store offered a coordinated presentation of fashion which tied ready-to-wear and accessories together in all possible media. With the help of the fashion coordinator all along the line, the merchandising, promotion, and display departments moved together to educate the customer in coordinated fashions and, at the same time, to brighten the store's fashion image.

Boutique and Shop Merchandising

A relatively new approach to fashion merchandising recognizes that it takes more time and fortitude than the average woman can muster to buy apparel and accessories that go well together unless these are assembled and offered for sale in a single spot. If they are not, the customer is obliged to go from store to store, or from department to department within a large store, initiating perhaps a dozen different transactions, each with a different salesperson, in order to complete her fashion shopping.

To simplify the shopper's task, boutiques and shops have sprung up, each of which is dedicated to serving some special type of customer or some special need of the average customer. Here components of a look or costume or special-purpose outfit are assembled in advance, so that coordination is made easy for the customer and so that a single transaction, carried through with the aid of a single, knowledgeable salesperson, is all that is required.

Some of these boutiques and shops are separate enterprises, entire stores devoted to fashion customers of a specific type. Others are set up as separate departments within a department or large specialty store, distinguished from the rest of the store not only by their merchandise but also by their decor and atmosphere.

The Boutique Approach

Boutique is the French word for "shop." In the fashion business, the term has come to be associated with unique merchandise, generally in very new or extreme styles, and with imaginative presentation of goods. Occasionally a style that gets its start in a boutique becomes a popular best seller. When this happens, boutiques usually lose

Boutiques offer coordinated assortments of the very new, the very unusual, or the very specialized, brought together in a separate department within the store or in a store complete within itself.

interest in it, because they are dedicated to newness, exclusivity, and few-of-a-kind designs, rather than to fashions that have already won wide acceptance.

Fashion coordination finds full expression in a boutique, whether it is operated as an independent store or as a special department within a large store. Everything that is shown to the customer in a boutique is in the same trend, and the apparel and accessories offered for sale are so well coordinated that a shopper can outfit herself in a single visit.

Boutiques are not new but they are far more numerous and important in today's affluent, fashion-alert society than they were a generation

or two ago. There have always been some shops in which well-to-do women could find distinctive, well-coordinated clothes and accessories. And in large department and specialty stores in major cities, there have been corners, galleries, or alcoves set off from the general flow of traffic and devoted to merchandise more expensive and of higher fashion appeal than that offered elsewhere in the store.

What is new about today's boutiques is that many of them are dedicated to women whose tastes run to extremes in avant garde or "way out" styles, or are confined to clothes appropriate to a current popular sport. Such boutiques are generally strikingly different from other depart-

The boutique emphasis is on exclusivity and few-of-a-kind designs; even the displays identify the boutique as the place to find something different, often slightly more expensive but also of high fashion appeal.

ments on the selling floors of their stores; even their decor is dramatically keyed to the special interests of the target customer group. Buying for a boutique may be done by one buyer who covers several markets for appropriate merchandise or, as is often the case in departmentalized stores, the responsibility may be shared by buyers for several of the store's regular departments. In the latter case, each participating buyer selects for the boutique such styles as are suitable for it, reserving for his regular department other styles that have wider, less specialized appeal. The salespeople in a boutique are carefully chosen and trained to understand its target customers, its merchandise, and the coordination techniques employed.

The prosperity of a boutique does not depend entirely upon the ability of the merchant to judge correctly the needs and tastes of special groups of customers. Some, although skillfully operated, have a relatively brief life, simply because interest in the special fashions to which they have been devoted is not yet strong enough or has already died down. Boutiques of the "unisex" type could not have prospered in the 1950s, for example, and remained successful only so long as there was interest on the part of a sufficient number of customers in dress-alike clothes for both sexes.

The Shop Approach

Special shops, either independent or as departments within departmentalized stores, have existed for many years and continue to be established in increasing numbers as the means of presenting coordinated apparel and accessories to special groups of customers. For example, teen shops within department stores date back to the 1930s, and those set up as separate enterprises are not much younger. College, maternity, and bridal shops have also been long familiar.

Among fashion merchants, a *shop* differs from a boutique in that it is not dedicated specifically to new and few-of-a-kind styles but rather to the fashion demands of customers whose requirements differ sufficiently from those of the general consumer to make it worth the merchant's while to assemble appropriate merchandise in a separate store or in a designated area of a large store. Typical of such shops are those devoted to coun-

A shop, whether set up within a larger store or as a separate enterprise, has carefully chosen assortments designed to meet the needs of particular groups of customers, such as maternity clothes, or swimwear, or college fashions.

try clothes, maternity clothes, ski or swim wear, career fashions, college clothes, and clothes for young women with couture tastes but ready-to-wear budgets.

In each such shop, the atmosphere, merchandise, selling techniques, and fashion coordination are all geared to the interests of the particular customer to be served. Teen shops, for example, are informal, lively, and often noisy places, with high-decibel renditions of popular recorded music. In department stores, teen shops are usually set aside from regular departments for the dual purpose of providing an area where young customers can feel at ease and of screening more mature customers from the sometimes wearying exuberance and group shopping habits of the young.

As in boutiques, the special shop has its own carefully selected and trained salespeople who are capable of both understanding and assisting the type of customers for whom the shop has been planned. In department and large specialty stores, buying for such a shop is generally done by a single buyer, who covers many markets to gather the apparel and accessories needed. On the other hand, shops featuring merchandise of a seasonal nature, such as ski shops, may present merchandise contributed by buyers of several different departments in the same store. For such shops, the display props that created the special-department atmosphere are removed when the peak of demand has passed; the merchandise is distributed among the departments whose buyers purchased it; and the salespeople are reassigned.

A separate enterprise devoted to special-purpose, highly seasonal apparel and accessories, however, is seldom found, since this would mean a period of almost complete hibernation between one year's selling season and the next. Instead, one is likely to see a ski shop, for example, transformed into a camping or water sports shop as summer approaches. Expertise in sports equipment in general, rather than expertise in dressing customers for a single sport, becomes the lure for shoppers.

The Bridal Shop One of the special shops most frequently encountered in retail stores today is that devoted to the bride. A skilled bridal consultant assists the bride in the selection of her gown and those for the members of her wedding party. Services offered usually include answers to questions on etiquette and dress, and a visit by the bridal consultant to the bride's home just before the wedding to make any necessary last-minute adjustments in her costume. In addition, if the bride wishes to be photographed in her wedding gown before the day of the ceremony, the bridal shop usually can make arrangements for this as well.

The bridal shop in department and large specialty stores is capable of bringing added business to other departments of the store. Because the customer comes into the store for fittings, advice, and reassurance, she tends to purchase much of her trousseau there as well. Moreover, the bridal shop is usually located so that the bride and members of her wedding party, on their way to and from the salon, pass through departments featuring other fashion merchandise and are subjected to the appeal of their displays.

Bridal Gift Registry A related service offered in stores that have home furnishings, as well as apparel and accessories, is the bridal gift registry. Here the bride, again assisted by a skilled consultant, sets down her preferences in furnishings and equipment for her new home. As friends and relatives call at the registry, they are told not only what the bride prefers but also what items so far have been purchased or promised. Each gift shopper who inquires then indicates what he plans to buy, and this information is duly noted on the bride's record card. Thus duplication of gifts is avoided and post-wedding returns and exchanges are minimized.

The bridal shop is a selling department; the bridal gift registry is primarily a service. Both, however, perform an important, though indirect, function in the sale of fashion merchandise throughout the store. Aside from the impact on the bride, both services bring a great many of the bride's friends and relatives into the store. All are exposed to countless displays of coordinated apparel and accessories, both in the store's windows and on its selling floors. Service to the bride

The bridal shop is a traditional feature of many larger stores; it is staffed with
skilled specialists, and in addition to selling bridal wear, often offers many services,
from advice about etiquette to arranging for photographs.

is one way of reaching out for additional customers in approximately the same social and economic level as hers.

For special groups of customers with needs and tastes that differ from those of the average, shops and boutiques simplify the customer's coordination problem and thus encourage her to buy more fashion merchandise.

Merchandising Vocabulary

Define or briefly explain the following terms:

Fashion forecast
Boutique
Shop
Bridal gift registry

Merchandising Review

1. What are the merchandising responsibilities of a store's fashion coordinator?
2. How does the market work of a fashion coordinator differ from that of a buyer?
3. Name at least three possible sources from which a store's fashion coordinator can draw information on fashion trends.
4. Name three store activities, other than buying and merchandising, in which the fashion coordinator's fashion forecast can be put to practical use.
5. Describe the sales training responsibilities of the fashion coordinator for a large store.
6. Name at least six specific responsibilities of a retail store fashion coordinator.
7. What are the fashion coordination responsibilities of a buyer in a small store that has no coordinator?
8. How do the fashion coordinator's responsibilities in a chain or catalog operation differ from those of the fashion coordinator of a specialty shop or department store?
9. How does a boutique differ from other shops or departments that cater to the specialized needs of narrow segments of the public?
10. Name five or more examples of the shop concept commonly found in department stores and large specialty shops today.

Merchandising Digest

Be prepared to discuss the following statements or topics in class or to prepare a written report as assigned by your instructor.

1. "Retail fashion coordination demands teamwork of a high order." Discuss this quotation from the text in the light of its significance in retail merchandising.

2. ''It often happens that the head of a fine specialty shop or the apparel and accessories merchandise manager of a department store takes over many of the functions that a fashion coordinator would normally perform.'' Discuss this statement from the text, indicating why and how a merchant discharges fashion coordination duties.

19

Developing a Fashion Image

Fashion retailing is a highly competitive and fascinating business. One of its most fascinating aspects is the way merchants use a specific interpretation of fashion as a means of attracting customers to their stores. Retailers, of course, have a whole arsenal of other weapons to use for this purpose: price, location, service, hours of business, and credit terms, to name a few. But when they compete with each other by using fashion itself as the attraction, they are matching their respective abilities to understand the consumer's fashion preferences, to find the goods that represent those preferences, and to present those goods to the consumer in well-coordinated assortments.

In competing this way, each fashion merchant tries to project a store image, and a fashion image within that store image, that will attract the customers he wants to serve.

A *store image* is the character or personality that the store presents to the public. In the words of a great fashion merchant, Stanley Marcus, head of Neiman-Marcus in Dallas, an image is "an honest reflection of what the store actually is. It should accurately mirror what the store stands for in service, values, quality, assortments, taste, aggressiveness, and citizenship."[1] A store image, then, is not something that merely has been dreamed up in the minds of its management and held up to the public for admiration. Rather, it is the opinion that the public has of the store as a result of the latter's policies and activities, the sum total of whatever makes one store individual and different from others in the community.

A store's *fashion image* is that aspect of its overall image that reflects the degree of fashion leadership the store exercises and the stage of the fashion cycle that its assortments represent. Merchandising activities play a stellar role in creating a fashion image, but all phases of store operations contribute to the total effect.

The Target Group

The first step in creating a fashion image is to define the store's *target customers,* those people for whom the merchandise, the service, and the whole atmosphere of the store are planned. Only when a store has a clear-cut and definite picture of the customers who constitute its target group can it create a successful fashion image.

A store relates its merchandising, promotion, decor, selling techniques, services, participation in community affairs, and even its housekeeping to that target customer it seeks to serve. Elegant fashion merchandise cannot be offered against a background of dusty displays and untidy fitting rooms, nor do customers expect to find bargain-priced shirts or skirts in departments with ankle-deep carpets and highly attentive salespeople.

One of the clearest illustrations of image development is presented by departments and shops that cater to teen-agers. The merchandise and atmosphere are young. Everything is informal, sometimes to the extent that soft-drink machines are installed in such departments and no one takes exception if some of the customers walk around sipping from cans or paper cups. Salespeople are young, or at least young at heart, and fond of teen-agers. Promotion has a youthful zip and makes liberal use of the slang terms currently popular among the teens.

By way of contrast, consider a department or shop that caters to mature women of wealth and distinction. Its selling floor is spacious, plush, and quiet. Service is attentive and discreet. Garments are brought forth for the customer's inspection, fashion features are pointed out, and selections are sent home on approval if desired. A customer who wishes to try on certain garments is courteously assisted in the fitting room.

In such an atmosphere, the typical teen-age girl might succumb to an attack of shyness or a fit of giggles. On the other hand, a mature customer can be so distracted by the noise and lively confusion of a teen shop or department that she may flee to more subdued surroundings without giving the merchandise itself more than a superficial glance.

Stores serving areas in which the preferences of its potential customers are fairly similar tend to adopt somewhat similar fashion images, but stores with a variety of target groups to choose from have a variety of fashion image possibilities open to them. A sampling of some of the fashion images projected by stores in the New York City area shows how diverse that variety can be.

Macy's considers itself a mass fashion store, selling to almost everyone and presenting styles at almost every stage of their fashion cycles, an appropriately broad target for a store that claims to be the world's largest. Henri Bendel is a specialty store that defines its customer as "the well-to-do, big city customer who wears sizes 2–12, and who is contemporary without being kooky."[2] The units of the Peck & Peck chain concentrate on women who like fairly classic, tailored apparel, and who are not charmed by spectacular extremes. The Lane Bryant stores serve the woman with the fuller figure, whatever her age. Bergdorf-Goodman caters primarily to the woman with ample funds and a keenly developed fashion sense. The stores and catalogs of such chains as Sears, Roebuck & Company or The J. C. Penney Company have as their target groups those customers from low to middle income who, although not necessarily experimenters in fashion, are fashion-conscious and demand good value in the merchandise they buy.

Advertising can help to define and attract the target customer the store wants to serve.

Pull-on pants, very V'd vest, dashingly collared shirt and a scarf to tie up the red, white and blue-ness of it all. Impeccably done in Trevira® polyester knit (because this is the Trevira® Era and we know you're going places!). 8 to 16, 76.00*

*Slightly higher on the West Coast

Peck & Peck presents the traveling quartet. For a certain kind of woman.

Each store or group of stores in these examples has its own character in merchandise, in decor, in promotion, and in display. It would not be difficult, given the descriptions above and a few days in which to inspect these stores and review their assortments and advertising, for someone completely new to the city to identify each by its merchandise, its ads, its windows, and the behavior of its sales staffs. Not only is the merchandise different in each store, but the whole atmosphere of each store is different. Each store has developed the atmosphere most natural and most comfortable to the target group of customers that the store wants to attract.

Elements of Fashion Policy

Once a store has defined its target group or groups of customers, it then builds and maintains the fashion image that will attract those customers through its fashion merchandising policies. A policy is "a settled, clearly defined course of action or method of doing business deemed necessary, expedient, or advantageous. Policies are to business what sailing charts are to a seaman."[3] A *fashion merchandising policy* is a long-range guide for the fashion merchandising staff, spelling out the store's fashion aims, standards of quality, price ranges, attitudes toward competition, and any other elements that may be pertinent.

A fashion merchandising policy constitutes management's instructions to the buying staff, but it is also of concern to the nonmerchandising executives who are responsible for keeping their areas of operation in line with the store's merchandising aims.

For example, if it is a policy to carry goods of superlative quality, the store's wrapping and packing materials would also be of excellent quality, and its adjustment department would be expected to take a liberal attitude toward customer complaints. If the policy, on the other hand, is to have quality that is merely adequate, wrapping and packing may be of minimum quality and the adjustment office may take a tougher line with customers who have complaints. Another example: If there is a policy to emphasize newness,

the advertising department may not be permitted to run ads featuring clearance merchandise, except for discreet twice-a-year announcements. If the policy is to emphasize bargains, however, there may be purchases and promotions of seconds and irregulars, mention of comparative prices in advertising, and general assurances that the store will not be undersold.

Fashion merchandising policies, therefore, are closely intertwined with almost every activity of the store, so that the image presented to the public is consistent throughout.

The Merchandise Assortment

Basic to a store's fashion merchandising policy is a determination of the degree of fashion leadership that its merchandise assortments will show. The composition of its assortments is influenced not only by the type of styles brought into stock but also by the length of time they are permitted to remain in stock.

For example, if the store chooses as its target customers those who want to be first with the newest, store buyers will be instructed to assemble assortments that consist primarily of *prophetic styles,* those that are harbingers of incoming trends. Buyers probably will be required to apply a high initial markon to their merchandise in order to compensate for the risks involved when fashions are at the early experimental stages of their cycles. They will also be allowed quite liberal markdowns, because these are almost inescapable in such an operation. They will be expected to mark down nonstarting styles promptly, and clear out any styles that are copied into lower price lines or that show signs of being already well on the rise in their cycles of demand.

By way of comparison, a store that caters to women who want to be in fashion but not necessarily among the experimenters will offer an assortment made up primarily of securely established styles. Such assortments may contain several versions of any particularly good style, or they may contain mainly classics with a sprinkling of forward-looking styles. Policy may specify that a few pieces may be purchased above the normal price range of the store or department and ahead of the store's normal position with relation to the fashion cycle. This procedure lends prestige to the regular assortment and provides exposure to styles still too new for the clientele but likely to prove acceptable somewhat later. "Getting the eye used to it" is one way to prepare customers for incoming fashions.

A store of this type will not require initial markons as high as those in a store carrying more experimental styles, since risks are not so great at this stage of the fashion cycle. Its policy on markdowns may not be especially liberal, unless the store has a policy of refusing to be undersold and therefore requires its buyers to price everything as low as (or lower than) similar merchandise in competing stores.

Large stores often offer customers a choice in degree of fashion leadership, by having different departments, each of which features styles at a different stage in fashion acceptance. In such a store, each department usually has a different merchandising policy. The elite department may have a policy of immediately clearing any styles that have been copied down or even faintly echoed in the less expensive departments. The medium-priced departments may have a policy of doing the same with any of their styles that closely resemble the stock of the store's basement or budget departments. When an individual style, a total look, a color, or a detail moves into a lower price level, the fashion merchandising policy of these stores usually requires its higher-priced departments to purge their stocks of similar merchandise.

Some stores adopt quite drastic fashion merchandising policies. For example, one department store with a small, extremely high fashion department under its roof refuses to allow that department to reorder any of its styles. Moreover, if more than 6 to 12 pieces of a style are sold, store policy requires that the style be relegated to other departments, for it is considered to have become too commonplace for the individualists who patronize that very special department.

Sales Promotion and Selling Techniques

Sales promotion and selling techniques take their cues from the degree of fashion leadership evident in the merchandise assortments. Each has

to be coordinated with the overall fashion image if the target group of consumers is to be attracted and turned into customers.

Stores that wish to be known for their fashion leadership are among the first to promote the new, stressing it in their advertising and displays. Their ads talk themes, looks, and ideas, such as "city blacks," "the Cossack look," and "midi lengths." Both window and interior displays underline the advertised themes, looks, and ideas, with strong emphasis on fashion coordination. Price is played down, and designers' names are played up.

Stores catering to the vast middle group of customers avoid advertising extremes in styling, although such stores may have a policy of showing a few prestige numbers in their displays. In general, both advertising and displays stress not the newness but the rightness of the styles promoted. Price is given prominence only in proportion to its importance to the particular target customer group.

Stores in the mass merchandising category give strong prominence to price in their advertising. The typical approach is, "For $10, you too can have . . . ." Since the fashion leaders and the middle group have already proved the importance of the fashions concerned, these stores concentrate on promoting their availability at budget prices. Their assortments usually contain quantities of nearly identical merchandise, thus reinforcing the idea that a particular fashion has made its mark.

Selling techniques are keyed to the fashion image the store wants to project in much the same way. In prestige stores, salespeople are coached to speak with authority about fashion, to present new ideas with confidence, and to give full service to the customer. Stores catering to the middle group of customers usually display their merchandise on open racks, but salespeople are present to answer customer questions and assist them in finding the desired styles in the right colors and sizes. Self-selection fixtures dominate the mass merchandisers' selling floors, with store personnel limited primarily to stockclerks and cashiers.

Many experts believe that it is at this point, the point of sale, that a store either succeeds or

RENAISSANCE COLORS . . .

THE NEW ART IN ARNEL®

FOR THE NEW PACE-SETTER

Robert-David Morton puts the rich colors

of the Renaissance together in a tri-tone manner

that adds a whole new dimension to the midi.

It's the sort of thing you must see,

in color, to appreciate . . .

the way Renaissance greens, navy,

purples and red are played together!

Truly a summer sensation in Celanese®

Arnel® triacetate for sizes 6 to 12.

The collection, $115 to $145.

Sutton Place, 3rd Floor, New York and all stores.

Sorry, no mail or phone.

The "total look" ad puts its emphasis on what's new in head-to-toe fashion coordination.

fails in its attempt to establish a particular fashion image—and that the salespeople are the key to that success or failure. Herbert Wittkin, former head of Stern Brothers, New York, explained it this way in a 1964 speech:

> We can spend literally millions of dollars in merchandise investments; we can spend many millions more on display and merchandise presentation and advertising; we can spend unlimited energy and time in trying to influence people to think well of us—only to have it all go down the drain because of a surly sales clerk. . . . Our salespeople talk to our customers and convey a feeling with everything they do—in the way they look—the way they smile—the way they shrug their shoulders—in short, they project our image more forcefully than any other element in the store. If they are warm, friendly, alert, fashionable, efficient people, our customers make the equation that our store is all of those things. If they are brusque, short-tempered, curt, unpleasant, their impact is deadly and frequently permanently damaging . . . .[4]

Other Essential Elements

There are still other important elements to be considered by a store's top management when establishing its fashion merchandising policies. Clear-cut decisions must be made as to the quality of the merchandise it will handle, its pricing policies, and its position relative to the depth and breadth of its assortments, to exclusivity of products, and whether private or national branded goods will be featured. Each of these elements must be in harmony with the overall fashion image the store wishes to create and maintain.

Quality Standards A store sets its quality standards in terms of those of its customers. In the top brackets, durability may be of minor importance, but fineness of material and care in workmanship may be important criteria. Among the middle group of customers, both durability and good fit may be important, the latter because of the high cost of alterations in relation to the price of the garment. At the low end, customers may evaluate each piece of merchandise in terms of the price asked for it, and stores may need no set standard of quality other than that the goods be represented honestly.

Grades Some types of fashion merchandise, such as hosiery and shoes, are graded by the producer either as "perfect" or as "irregulars" or "seconds." Less-than-perfect goods are graded "irregular" if they have defects that may affect appearance (even a color unsatisfactory to the designer) but not wear. "Seconds" are factory rejects that have faults that may affect wear. Depending upon the clientele, store policy may exclude anything except perfect goods or it may permit irregulars and seconds to be offered in special promotions or by basement departments. It is what the customer wants and expects that determines policy, in this as in so many other phases of fashion merchandising. If the customer demands perfect goods, the store gives them to her; if she accepts slight irregularities at concessions in price, the store follows her lead and makes them available when possible.

Prices There are a number of facets to any store's price policy on fashion merchandise. These facets include:

The Selling Price. Store policy usually specifies whether prices should be rounded off or placed at a point a few cents below the even dollar. A store that caters to fashion leaders may use rounded prices: $200 for a dress, for example, is a price that sounds much more luxurious than does $199.95. A store that caters to the budget-conscious customer may insist on prices below the even-dollar mark: 95¢ rather than $1 for a pair of stockings, for example, gives the impression that the store has moved mountains to offer stockings worth $1 for a few cents less.

The Price Range. The highest and lowest selling prices permitted for the merchandise concerned form the price range for the department or store.

The Price Lines. The price points at which balanced assortments are to be offered for the customer's choice are the price lines. In stores that permit similar merchandise to be carried in several departments, each catering to a different level of income, policy may prohibit overlapping of price lines between departments or may allow some overlapping of price lines so long as there is no duplication of merchandise. Again, it is the customer's shopping habits that influence the policy; if such habits clash with established store policy, adjustments in the policy are made to permit the customer to find what she wants where she wants to find it.

Comparative Prices. When merchandise has been marked down, some stores permit, while others forbid, both the old and the new prices to appear together on price tickets and in advertising copy. Comparative prices suggest bargains—which mass merchandisers always find a good drawing point, which the middle group of stores sometimes like to emphasize, and which the high fashion stores seldom use to attract customers.

Depth Versus Breadth Assortments The degree of fashion leadership the store has chosen to project usually determines how deep and how wide its assortments will be. Broad, shallow assortments, presenting a large variety but not a large stock of any one style, are characteristic of stores and departments catering to fashion leaders. Middle-area inventories usually include broad assortments early in the season, when new styles are still being tested for acceptance, but relatively narrow and deep assortments later in the season, once the trend of demand is clear. Mass merchandisers concentrate on narrow, deep assortments of proven popular styles. A few stores that are large enough use both techniques: broad and shallow stocks on the outer fringes of demand and narrow, deep stocks where demand is clearly defined.

Exclusivity "Ours alone" is an important selling point for stores that cater to fashion leaders. Middle-area stores also use exclusives, when available, as a competitive weapon. Exclusive styles may come from several sources: foreign markets; small factories; new, young designers; sometimes large manufacturers who prefer exclusive distribution and sell to only one store in an area. Some stores consider exclusives so important that their buyers are expected to work with producers toward having special styles made up for the store.

Brands A private brand, meeting standards specified by the retailer or his buying office, can be used by a store to dramatize exclusivity, to assure consistent quality, and to create or meet price competition, among many other purposes. A nationally advertised brand, on the other hand, can give store and customer alike a guarantee of quality and fashion correctness, and can offer the store the additional advantage of cooperative advertising or other useful concessions. Stores at the top of the fashion scale are less likely to feature a brand name than to give prominence to a designer's signature. Chain and mail-order companies, on the other hand, consistently feature their own private brands. Nationally advertised brands are the backbone of assortments found in middle-area stores. These same nationally advertised brands are sometimes offered by mass merchandisers, too, but then almost always as the focus of an important promotion, with their prices cut dramatically to enhance the store's image as the place to find bargains.

Changing a Fashion Image

Stores sometimes find it either necessary or advantageous to shift their sights and to aim for a different target group of customers than the one for which their fashion image was originally created. Such a change may be necessary if the character of the community the store serves undergoes a marked change and the store is losing business. Such a change may also be advantageous if the store wants to reach out for additional groups of customers not previously served, or to fill a merchandising need temporarily left unfilled by competing stores, or even to retreat from a merchandising area in which the competition has become too fierce.

The classic case of the necessity to change an image is that of the neighborhood store whose original customers have moved out of the area and have been replaced by people of other income or ethnic groups. If the store is to continue to do business at its old location, it must adjust its fashion image to attract the new potential clientele flowing into the area. If, on the other hand, the store wants to retain its original image, it must move to a different area where it can find

Courtesy Allied Stores Corp.

Brand names, manufacturer or retailer, nationally advertised or private, tell the customer what to expect in dependability, quality, fashion rightness.

enough customers of the original type to support it.

Department stores in the years since World War II have been faced with such problems of adjusting to shifting groups of customers. In many cities, there was a flow of middle-class and well-to-do families out to the suburbs in the 1950s. Department stores have followed them there with branch stores, but had to reconcile themselves to the loss of some of their downtown store demand for medium- to higher-priced goods. In the 1960s, however, there was something of a return flow of well-to-do customers to the city, as well as a general increase in the income and taste levels of almost all types of customers, and the department stores had to readjust their central-city images once again, in atmosphere as well as merchandise, to a level attractive to these customers.

Changing an image, once it has been established, is not easy, and is usually a slow and gradual process. The store has to teach its customers to forget the old familiar face it has turned to them for years and to become accustomed to a new face. Some stores that have changed successfully have taken a decade or more to complete the process. A gradually changing assortment, a gradually changing tempo in promotion, a gradual shift in the quality of selling and other services—all permit a store to replace the customers it has lost or no longer wishes to serve with new customers year by year.

One of the most sweeping image turnabouts in recent years occurred when discounters added fashion apparel to operations that formerly had been concerned only with hard goods. Starting with what might be called a negative image as nonfashion retailers, these merchants used assortments, displays, and advertising in their attempts to get people to consider them as apparel and accessories outlets. Some fumbled and ruined their businesses, but there have been some spectacular successes.

A few of the discounters, originally well entrenched in the fashion field at its lower levels, have successfully moved up the ladder toward the earlier stages of the fashion cycle and toward higher-priced merchandise. Ohrbach's and Alexander's, in New York, are especially noteworthy in this respect. Each made the change by opening a store in an area of the city with greater fashion prestige than the store's original home enjoyed. Ohrbach's abandoned its original location entirely. Alexander's retained its existing stores but gave the new unit impressive lighting, wide aisles, and glittering chandeliers to convey the impression of high-income customers and high fashion. Both stores invited top socialites to special, well-publicized showings of import collections, and turned these special showings into regular seasonal events. No one facet of the operation in either store carried the whole burden of changing its image; merchandising, publicity, promotion, display, and selling techniques all worked together to produce a new image.

Types of Fashion Images

Based on the target group of customers it seeks to win, each store, or department within a store, works to create its own fashion image. This image may be anything from fashion leadership to bargain paradise, from the immensity of a vast building to the intimacy of a tiny boutique.

In general, a fashion image is distinguished by its degree of fashion leadership and by the store organization's size and type of operation.

Degree of Fashion Leadership

Although the degree of fashion leadership a store chooses to assume can be at any point along a graduated scale, stores can be divided generally into three categories: those who project a high fashion image, those who are mass marketers, and those who are in between.

Fashion Leaders   Those merchants who elect to deal in high fashion, who cater to the women who want to be in the forefront of fashion and can afford the price, have a relatively straightforward course in creating a fashion image. The styles must be new and prophetic; every department in the store must be coordinated with every other; and the customer, whether she wants bras, shoes, handbags, or slenderizing treatments, must have her wants understood perfectly. This is easily said, but it involves a superlative job of coordinating the market work, the selections, the emphasis, and the promotion of every component of every new look in fashion that the store chooses to represent. Dresses must relate to coats, and slips must relate to dresses; loungewear must relate to outerwear; all accessories, from bedroom slippers to bath salts, must be in tune with the fashion trend.

Stores that achieve such fashion leadership in their merchandise assortments have such distinctive advertising that their ads can be easily recognized even without the store name. Their promotions are usually around a theme rather than concerned with specific items of merchandise. They speak of looks, ideas, and collections, rather than of individual dresses, shoes, or handbags. When they do advertise a specific item, it is promoted not as an item alone but as a necessary component of a currently acceptable fashion theme. Prices are mentioned almost as an afterthought and never prominently.

Salespeople in such stores are extremely well trained in fashion and coached in how and when to advise customers. If necessary, they are expected to leave the departments to which they have been assigned in order to help a customer assemble her total outfit, from foundation to furs. Alterations to improve the fit of garments are made with meticulous care; returns are accepted no matter what the reason. Physical surroundings are compatible with what the customer is accustomed to in her own home: rich carpets, beautifully upholstered chairs and sofas, expensive draperies, wall treatments, and lighting fixtures.

Public relations activities of such stores are likely to be of the played-down type. The head of the store may give society-page parties to select groups of customers and friends. Fashion shows may be small and intimate, run by a store executive who knows everyone in the audience by name and who probably has a good idea which favorite designer's clothes are in the closet of each one. Publicity on behalf of the store is likely to be in terms of having dressed the bride at a fashionable wedding or of the store owner's personal participation in community projects.

Mass Marketers At the opposite end of the price and fashion scale, the approach toward creating a fashion image is equally direct. The image that mass fashion merchants strive for is one of bargains and of fashions that have already had time to become widely accepted. The customer who represents the target of such a store does not expect service; she is satisfied to wait on herself, try on garments in crowded fitting rooms, and stand in line at a cashier's desk to pay for her purchases. Crowds do not repel her; instead, they imply that the bargains must be especially good to draw so many shoppers. Little or no luxury is evident in the surroundings; expensive carpets, draperies, and furniture give way to the simplest and most functional of furnishings and lighting. The store may be comfortable, but it is not likely to be lavish.

Coordination of an outfit in mass fashion stores is strictly the customer's job. Although the store may have provided related accessories to go with its clothes, it is up to the customer to collect them from the assortments unaided and to put the right pieces of the fashion puzzle together. This task is not difficult, however, since the fashions with which she is concerned are familiar by the time they reach the mass level of price and service. The coordinations have been worked out, tested, and worn about town for some time before the fashion has reached that peak or waning stage at which she buys. Just as it is not difficult to coordinate Early American styles in home furnishings because they are so well known, so can almost any customer coordinate apparel and accessories in fashion trends that are at or past their culmination and are very familiar.

The In-betweens Retailers who lie between these two extremes have the advantage of aiming at the largest area of customers, but they have the problem of marking out the particular segment of that area they plan to serve and then adjusting their merchandising, service, and promotion policies accordingly.

Timing is a major element of their problem. It is not as easy for them to judge the precise stage of the fashion cycle in which their customers are interested as it is for those retailers whose customers are always fashion leaders or those whose customers are always content with fashion in its final stages. Instead, their customers are the ones who are neither first nor last to adopt the new.

They are the customers who looked approvingly at displays of colored foundations for several years before they actually wore anything but white. They are the customers who were outraged at the early miniskirts but, two years later, let their own skirts creep above the knee. To judge the precise moment when such customers are ready to taste the new, and to know how much emphasis to place upon it in assortments, promotion, and personal selling, is a challenge to a retailer's merchandising skill and fashion knowledge.

Another challenge to the in-betweens is devising ways to suggest the appropriate combinations of apparel and accessories to their customers. These customers do not buy with the sure touch of fashion leaders, nor have the fashions they are buying become so familiar that coordination is almost automatic. Since personal selling for these customers cannot be as lavish as for those at the top of the income scale, and since these are women who may not want to be pushed into spending more than they planned, there is a limit to what can be done by the salespeople. Advertising and display usually do an important job here, showing how, for example, the right scarf, necklace, or jeweled pin will set off the neckline of a coat or dress.

These are the stores, too, that face the most plentiful competition, and they function in an area in which one store's merchandise tends to look much like that of another. No matter how carefully the store has assembled and coordinated its fashion merchandise, it cannot depend entirely upon its merchandising skills in building its fashion image.

In their quest for distinction, some stores of this type make a point of managing their stocks to keep them complete at all times. Their image then becomes that of the store that "always has something for me." Some seek distinction by adding a plus to their service; "smiling service," for example, is the philosophy of one small store whose management insists upon friendly greetings, cheerful acceptance of returns, and even pleasantness in efforts to collect overdue bills, as a way of making the store stand out from others with similar merchandise, similar services, and similar appearance.

Service and atmosphere that have no direct connection with fashion also help build a distinctive image for an individual store. Some stores are so meticulous about every detail of service that their customers feel reassured about the care that has been devoted to assembling their fashion assortments. Others lend luster to their names by using distinctive wrappings and boxes that customers are proud to be seen carrying. (The implication is that the smart wrap encloses equally smart merchandise.)

Some stores do things with such éclat that people automatically link their names with fashion excitement. Neiman-Marcus, the well-known Dallas store, indulges in such delightful irrelevancies as offering "his and her" camels in one of their Christmas catalogs. The natural reaction of the public is to assume that a store whose customers can afford such spectacular gifts is a good place to shop—not only for a $5,000 fur coat but for a $5 fashion gift as well.

Size and Type of Organization

Both size and type of organization affect a store's fashion image; they facilitate or complicate the job of creating and maintaining that image.

The Giants Giant retailers have special image considerations because of their size. Some of them sell to such a broad range of the public that they need to segment their image, presenting one face to those customers who are in the lead of the fashion parade and another to the slower-moving groups. They often handle this through special departments or shops, each one establishing an image for a specific group: teens, tall girls, maternity customers, sophisticates, lovers of casual wear, or career or college girls. Their huge size that causes this problem also allows them to solve it through such shop merchandising, whereas smaller stores, with more limited floor space and assortments, cannot set up shops quite so freely.

Large stores often make capital of their bigness. They stage promotions on a spectacular scale. Instead of devoting one or two windows to a new fashion, they devote block-long batteries of windows to an idea. They hire display executives

*Inventive and persistent repetition of a theme often gets the point across; A&S
played up its large assortments with a series of ads repeating in many languages,
this time in Hawaiian, "A&S—it's worth a trip from anywhere!"*

who are highly creative and whose windows and interior displays are remembered for years. They turn their main floors into flower shows, as Macy's in New York City and Hess Brothers in Allentown, Pennsylvania, do each spring. Or they regularly run ads that stress the vastness of their assortments; New York's Abraham and Straus does, using humor to make the point that one should never say something cannot be bought unless one has first tried that store.

Very large stores have special facilities, such as auditoriums, that they lend to civic groups. Often the auditorium is used by the store for a fashion show or demonstration that is expected to draw large crowds. On other occasions, one of its selling floors may be a more appropriate scene for such a show. Informal shows may be staged in a store's restaurant. Finally, given the coverage provided by their many branches, the giant stores can quickly and completely announce their fashion stories through an entire metropolitan area and even beyond the limits of that area.

The Small Independent At the opposite end of the size scale is the small, independently owned shop in which the proprietor is likely to be the entire top management team himself: merchandiser, policy maker, promotion expert, and image brightener. Such stores, even though they may employ several salespeople, cannot afford and may not need the acres of advertising space that large stores use to enhance their image.

Small operations have their own special weapons for image building, based on the personal touch. Salespeople and proprietors know customers by name; they suggest apparel to coordinate with what is already owned; they send personal notes to tell customers when new merchandise of suitable type has arrived. They have coins readily available for parking meters; they gift-wrap beautifully and individually; they provide innumerable friendly, person-to-person small services that cannot be offered practically by large stores. For instance, some small retailers may offer free alterations, adding the niceties of custom-fit to ready-to-wear purchases.

In their merchandising, some small stores even capitalize on their smallness. They buy only a few pieces, or even single pieces, of a style. The customer who purchases a dress or coat from such a store can be certain that she will not meet herself on the street, at the bus stop, or at the club luncheon. She is made to feel like an individual in an image-conscious small store, not like just one more specimen of genus customer.

Chain Organizations Units of apparel chains, general merchandise chains, and mail-order companies often use the weapons of both large and small stores.

Among the large-store techniques used by a general merchandise chain, for instance, might be the establishing of special shops within its stores to feature a particular look, such as country casuals. Or an apparel chain may run a continuing series of newspaper ads of institutional type, such as those run by the specialty store chain, Peck & Peck, about the "special sort of woman" for which its stores and the merchandise assortment they carry are designed.

Other chains find ways to offer some of the personalized service characteristic of small stores. One mail-order company, for example, instructs its telephone operators to give their names to customers so that each customer can be made to feel that there is a "special" operator who knows her and is interested in her. Salespeople may be encouraged to obtain customers' names for notification of special sales or new merchandise. Customer files may be kept to facilitate coordinating future purchases with what is already owned. Although the merchandise in one unit of a chain may not differ markedly from what is offered by another unit of the same organization, nevertheless it is possible for the staff of each unit to develop warm, friendly relations with customers. In this way, each customer feels she is receiving personal attention and advice when making her fashion purchases.

References

[1]*Stores,* January, 1960, p. 17.
[2]Gold, *How to Sell Fashion,* p. 31.
[3]Nystrom, *Fashion Merchandising,* p. 195.
[4]Wittkin, "An Image Is a Multi-Faceted Thing," *Readings in Modern Retailing,* p. 230.

Merchandising Vocabulary

Define or briefly explain the following terms:

Store image	Fashion merchandising policy	Second grade
Fashion image	Prophetic styles	Price range
Target customers	Irregular grade	Price line

Merchandising Review

1. Why is it important to have a clear-cut idea of the store's target group of customers before attempting to define its fashion image?
2. Identify three of the elements that play an important role in creating and enhancing a store's fashion image.
3. What sound reasons might a store have for seeking to change its fashion image?
4. What are some of the things a store can do to achieve a distinctive fashion image if heretofore it has been neither a fashion leader nor a mass merchandiser of the bargain store variety?
5. Describe the merchandise, selling, and promotion services you would expect to find in a store whose image is one of fashion leadership.
6. Describe the merchandise, selling, and promotion services you would expect to find in a store whose image is one of opportune buys and bargains.

7. In addition to the degree to fashion leadership desired, what other elements must be considered in establishing a store's fashion merchandising policy? Identify four such elements, briefly explaining each.
8. What are some of the image-building devices available to an independent store that may be too small to advertise?

Merchandising Digest

1. Discuss the following statement from the text: "Changing an image, once it has been established, is not easy, and usually is a slow and gradual process."
2. Discuss the following statement from the text: "A merchandising policy constitutes management's instructions to the buying staff, but it is also of concern to the nonmerchandising executives. . . ."

Appendix 1
Career Opportunities
in Fashion

Fashion is fun; fashion is excitement; fashion is big business. Fashion is also a seemingly endless parade of career opportunities for those who want them and prepare for them. The fashion field is so vast, however, that the beginner needs a guide to the path that will lead him to his goal in fashion work, whether that goal be merchandise manager or photographer, fashion model or designer, copywriter or boutique owner.

This Appendix offers such a guide. Its brief description of the areas open to those interested in fashion may save the beginner some initial uncertainty and direct him to that part of the fashion field in which he will be most capable and feel most content.

Whichever part that may be, it is sure to be an exacting and stimulating place to work. Some fashion careers are more rewarding than others in terms of money and recognition, but whatever career is chosen, it is certain to develop an awareness of people, to leave no room for boredom, to provide a quantity of hard work, and to give full satisfaction for that work.

Scope of the
Fashion Business

The size and influence of the field of fashion cannot be measured in dollars alone—but, indicatively, out of every dollar of personal consumption expenditures in the United States each year, about 12 cents is used for such direct manifestations of fashion as apparel, accessories, and personal adornment.

Nor can what is included in the fashion field be readily defined. Fashion is a reflection of the consumer's way of life, and it manifests itself in cars as well as clothing, in houses as well as hats, in any commodity or service in which the consumer exercises personal choice.

The "fashion industries" are commonly considered to be those engaged in producing apparel and accessories for women, including girls in their early teens. In this Appendix, as throughout the book, any reference to "fashion industries" means these, unless others are specifically mentioned. The term "fashion business," however, tends to include all industries and services connected with fashion: manufacturing, distribution, advertising, publishing, and consulting—anything encompassing any type of merchandise or service in which fashion's touch has made itself felt.

Some industries go along for years with little regard to customer preference and little customer demand for change. But when preferences develop and demands become diverse, even those industries have to develop an understanding of fashion. To the career seeker, the spreading influence of fashion to industries far distant from feminine apparel and accessories means this: what is learned about fashion in the fashion industries themselves sooner or later has application to almost any other industry serving the consumer.

The person who enters fashion enters a field that is far-flung and many-faceted. Such a field provides freedom: freedom to grow, freedom to change jobs or direction, freedom to move to different cities or even to different countries without having to begin anew in an unrelated type of work.

International Character of American Fashion

The American fashion business is in contact with every part of the world. Raw materials are imported from remote areas—such materials as furs, hides, fibers, to name a few. Manufactured goods, too, including some apparel and accessories, are imported from all over the world. Also imported are ideas and inspiration, not only from the couture houses of Europe but from any part of the world where general news or fashion news is being made. Even outer space is within fashion's territory, as evidenced by jumpsuits and other apparel inspired by astronaut gear.

American goods and ideas are exported. Many American manufacturers allow their lines to be produced abroad under franchise agreements. American fashions are produced in foreign countries to the specifications of American firms. Producers from other countries send their young people to Seventh Avenue and to the fashion industries' technical schools to prepare them for fashion careers, and sometimes the producers themselves seek United States know-how to help them establish or improve their fashion business. In addition, the United States exports its know-how in fashion retailing. Stores from all over the world are members of the National Retail Merchants Association. Foreign delegates attend NRMA conventions as special guests, and the NRMA has sent delegations of American retailers to visit foreign stores.

Within the borders of the United States, fashion activity is everywhere. Seventh Avenue in New York remains the heart of the apparel-producing industries, but there are also creative centers in Los Angeles, Dallas, Miami, and cities of the Middle West. Even in some seemingly unlikely small towns, there are mills and factories that need people to guide their output along current fashion lines. And there are retailers of fashion in every major city, in every suburb, and in every small town.

To the person planning a career in fashion, these facts mean that geography need not fence him in. Almost any location in this country and throughout the world is one in which fashion work of some sort can be found or created.

Facets of Fashion Activity

Not only is fashion work ubiquitous, but its activities are varied enough to interest widely differing kinds of people. Some activities, such as designing, advertising, and display, demand a high degree of creativity and originality. Others, such as fiber and fabric research and development, require a scientific bent. Still others, such as plant management and retailing management, call for business acumen and administrative skills.

Strong feet and outgoing natures are indispensable in retail or wholesale selling, and also in the market work of retail buyers, buying office representatives, magazine editors, and their assistants. Writing, photography, and sketching are much used in the fashion field, and there is demand for those with appropriate skills. Sewing skills, even when they are not coupled with a designer's creativity, can lead to such interesting work as sample making. Teaching ability has its place in personnel work, in supervisory work, and in the schools devoted to fashion training.

Natural endowments, such as a good face and figure, sometimes make a modeling job possible, and through it an entry into other phases of the fashion field. Theatrical training has its place, too, especially in planning more sophisticated fashion shows, such as when a fiber company introduces a new product to retail audiences.

Even such mundane talents as orderly work habits and willingness to please, if coupled with an interest in fashion, can add up to a stimulating assignment as a receptionist, an assistant, or a secretary to an executive in one of the many branches of the fashion industry. Such jobs often offer the opportunity to discover and develop hitherto unrealized abilities.

Careers in Manufacturing

The principal manufacturing industries in the fashion field require fashion-oriented people to guide their production, reinforce their selling efforts, and disseminate fashion information to their customers and to the consuming public. Of course, these industries also require technical experts of many kinds, skilled and unskilled factory labor, and office workers of various types. Our concern in this Appendix, however, is only with those functions in which fashion is an essential element.

These industries include the raw materials producers, the apparel trade, suppliers to the apparel trade, the accessories trades, and the home sewing industry.

Raw Materials Industries

The greatest number and variety of fashion careers in the raw materials field are found among the producers of fiber and fabrics. This is not only a big field but also a field that is very much interested in and keeps close contact with every other phase of the fashion business. There are similar positions, but in smaller number, among other raw materials producers and their industry associations.

Fashion Expert Fiber producers and fabric houses have fashion departments headed by individuals with a variety of titles who attend fashion openings, keep in close touch with sources of fashion information, and disseminate the fashion story throughout the organization. Candidates for such positions usually bring fashion expertise to their jobs and acquire the necessary information about the fiber or fabric products from the company's technical staff.

The fashion department's activities often require personnel with the ability to coordinate apparel and accessories, to stage fashion shows, to work with the press, to assist individual producers and retailers with fashion-related problems or projects, and to set up fashion exhibits for the trade or for the public. These extremely varied demands made upon all who work in such departments constitute an excellent training school, and even at the clerical level the beginner in such a department learns much about fashion and is able to train herself for promotion.

Fabric Designer While it takes technical skills to produce a fiber, it takes both technical and artistic skills to produce a fabric. Fabric companies employ designers who have both technical

knowledge of the processes involved in producing a fabric as well as artistic ability and a sure touch in anticipating fashion trends. The fabric designer, who works far in advance of the apparel trades, needs fashion radar of superlative quality. Some designers concentrate on their own ideas, while others are expected to work out fabric designs for creative clients. In either case, the chief designer for a fabric mill makes fashion decisions that can involve vast investments every time a season's line is prepared.

Fabric Stylist Many fabric companies employ a fabric stylist to revise existing fabric designs or adapt them for specific markets. Some people find this job a career in itself; others use it as a stepping-stone to the job of fabric designer.

Fabric Librarian Most major man-made fiber sources maintain libraries of fabrics that are made from their fibers. These libraries consist of fabric swatches clipped to cards on which detailed descriptions and sources of supply are recorded. The librarian in charge is expected to be a gracious hostess who is capable of discussing fashion and fabric matters with callers and who is ready to refer special requests or problems to the right executives of the company.

Educational Consultant Most of the fiber producers and some of the fabric houses maintain departments to convey technical information about products to people who may not have had the benefit of a technical education. These may be apparel producers, or retailers, or even consumers. Educational departments answer inquiries, prepare exhibits, address groups of retail salespeople or consumers, and stage demonstrations. In addition to a knowledge of both the technology and the fashion influence involved, graciousness is a must in this work, along with an ability to talk to people at any educational and social level.

Industry Consultant Most of the fiber companies and some of the fabric houses assign executives to study the individual industries in which their product is used, including the fashion industries. These men act as a liaison between their firms and the industries in which they specialize. If a company is about to introduce a new fiber, fabric, finish, or treatment, its industry consultants work with the industries, encouraging producers to try the new product and helping them to solve any problems related to its use. The help these consultants give may also extend to the retail level, assisting retailers in launching fashions that employ the new product.

Publicity Executive In both fiber and fabric companies, the publicity staff keeps in touch with technical as well as fashion matters and makes information about company products available to the trade and consumer press. Usually product stories can be tied to fashion information, enhancing their appeal to editors and readers alike.

The publicity executive in charge of the department generally has a thorough understanding of fashion and journalism, along with a pleasing personality and a good memory for names and faces. These attributes are essential in preparing press releases, working with photographers who provide illustrative material for those releases, and working with members of the press who seek help on feature stories or who want background information. Skill in subtle salesmanship is useful in placing unsolicited stories, when an editor has to be convinced of the value and interest of the story to his publication's audience.

In the major fiber-producing companies, there may be a corps of publicity executives, each specializing in one or two closely related industries. One may concentrate on the use of specific fibers in apparel fabrics, for instance, while another may specialize in the use of the company's fibers in rugs and carpeting. In smaller organizations, there may be only one such executive. In any case, there are usually typists, secretaries, and assistants—and a beginner who starts in any such capacity is in an excellent position to learn the art of fashion publicity.

Other Areas Both fiber and fabric industries offer career opportunities in sales, market research, and promotion. These are not always fashion jobs, however, and rarely are they open to beginners. Some experience within the company and some specialized skill in the field are likely to be more important than a knowledge of fashion alone in getting such jobs. Advertising, including its more exciting aspects such as the production of television shows, is often handled by advertising agencies rather than by the company's own advertising department.

Apparel Trades

For creative people, the fashion plum of the apparel trades is the designer's job. But the climb to this top job is often laborious and uncertain, and the footing at the top may be slippery. New talent is always elbowing its way in, and even the most successful couture designers are haunted by the prospect of a season when their ideas do not inspire, do not have customer appeal.

Designing So much of an apparel firm's life depends upon the styling of its line that the designing responsibility is rarely entrusted to a beginner, even a fantastically talented one. There are matters of cost and mass production techniques involved, for example, and unless one is working in a couture house, there is also the business of judging accurately the point in the fashion cycle at which the firm's customers will buy.

For moderate-priced and mass-market producers, the designer's job may be one of adapting rather than creating. Immense skill may be required, nevertheless, to take a daringly original couture idea and modify it so that it appears bright and new but not terrifyingly unfamiliar to a mass-market or middle-income customer.

The beginner, aside from offering designs on a free-lance basis, can seek a number of jobs below the designer level and hope to work up. Several of these jobs are described below.

▫ *Assistant Designer.* As a member of a large designing team, the assistant works under a head designer. Designing talent, indicated by submitted samples, and good technical knowledge are expected so that the assistant can help the designer in every aspect of the work. Also highly desirable is a good disposition and the ability to accept and learn from criticism. In the tensions and frustrations that surround a head designer's job, correc-

An artist, a model, and an ad manager get together to create a fashion-right advertising layout that will capture the customer's interest, explain the important features of the merchandise, and hopefully make the sale.

Courtesy The Broadway-Hale Stores, Inc.

tions and suggestions may not always be made with the utmost tact.

□ *Patternmaker.* From the designer's sketch or sample, a pattern is made from which a sample garment is cut. The sample is tested for fit and appearance, and may require adjustments or even a new pattern. Once acceptable results have been achieved and production of the new style decided upon, the patternmaker "grades" the pattern,

which means he makes up a separate pattern for each of the sizes in which the style will be produced. The need for patience and technical skill is obvious, and these should be coupled with an understanding of sketching, draping, construction, and good workmanship.

□ *Sketcher.* From the designer's rough drawings, working sketches are made for the information of the sample hand and also for illustrations to be used in the showroom book. The showroom book includes smart fashion sketches of the entire line, along with swatches of the materials used for each number illustrated.

□ *Sample Maker.* An all-around seamstress constructs a garment from a sketch or pattern. If it is to be modeled, the sample maker adjusts it to fit the designated model perfectly. The job of a sample maker is a particularly instructive one for future designers, since it provides training in the fundamentals of design, sketching, pattern making, and construction.[1]

Advertising and Publicity An advertising manager, with possibly an assistant or two, usually handles advertising and publicity. Whether or not the firm is large enough to have an advertising agency (and most are not), there may be ads placed in cooperation with retailers or in cooperation with fiber and fabric sources. Publicity, usually a part of the advertising job, involves sending out press releases, interesting consumer publications in some of the firm's new styles, and so on. Promotion kits for retailers are prepared under the direction of the advertising manager, as are statement stuffers and other direct-mail pieces offered for retail use. An aspiring assistant in this job has a distinct advantage if he has had enough retail advertising experience to be able to draw up rough layouts and suggest copy for store use.

Sales Opportunities The salesmen who call upon retail stores should know the fashion points as well as the value points of their merchandise. Nowadays, salesmen are expected to be able to address retail salespeople, if invited to do so, or even to take part in forums and clinics for consumers.

Showroom sales are sometimes handled by a junior salesman who is awaiting the opportunity to cover a territory of his own. At other times, a showroom girl, with good disposition, good feet, and a good memory, is hired. She is expected to greet customers, understand their requirements, show the line, and help them place orders. Good appearance is especially important here, since the showroom girl sometimes has to substitute for a model.

An understanding of retail merchandising, promotion, and fashion coordination is extremely helpful in all sales jobs in the apparel field. When selling to a retailer, it is important to understand his needs, his problems, his method of operation, and what stage of the fashion cycle is of major interest to his customers. With such a background, a salesman can present a line more effectively and, moreover, can collect and develop sound retail merchandising and promotion ideas for his accounts.

Suppliers to the Apparel Trades
Belts, buttons, zippers, and other minor but necessary components of garments are produced and sold by companies that range in size from one-man operations to large national firms whose names are familiar to every woman who has ever changed a button, inserted a new zipper, or done the least bit of home sewing. A great deal of business with apparel producers is done by tiny firms that offer little opportunity to the outsider. Some of the larger producers, however, offer job opportunities in selling to the apparel trades or to retailers, working either for one firm or as a commission representative for several firms.

Fashion trends cause ups and downs for producers in this field, with consequent variations in selling opportunities. When fashion favors the industrial zipper, for example, no amount of salesmanship is likely to create a market for delicate buttons or ruffling; when shifts are in, the most persuasive salesman is balked in his efforts to sell belts. In this field, a knowledge of fashion is important if producers are to know what products to offer and when to resign themselves to temporarily diminished sales prospects.

A salesman calling on the apparel trades should know, in addition to the fashion significance of what he offers, something about garment production, for the mechanics of production play as much a part as fashion does in a line's profitability. A salesman calling on the retail trade usually finds himself selling to the notions department, whose buyer may not be strongly fashion-oriented, and he must be especially skilled in presenting the fashion story of his wares, not only to the buyer but also to the salespeople. A notions department carries such a miscellaneous assortment of goods, from shoe polish to swim caps, that the fashion aspects of some of its assortment are often overlooked in sales training programs: the supplier salesman who can help the department on this point becomes doubly welcome.

Some of the larger producers of such items as buttons and zippers keep close track of fashion's impact on their business. Among these firms it is not unusual to employ a fashion expert who analyzes trends to guide production toward the most salable types, sizes, and colors. The same expert also may have responsibilities in such other areas as publicity and promotion. In a large button firm, for example, the fashion expert may work out new and acceptable ways to use buttons to highlight the current fashion features of garments. She may then publicize these uses to apparel producers, notions departments, and to the press. She also may work out displays that help retailers sell her company's buttons to the over-the-counter customer. Such fashion specialist jobs are few, but they are fascinating for those who like widely varied activities. Entry is through the understudy route or through acquiring sufficient fashion experience in other fields to be hired from the outside as a full-fledged expert or consultant.

Accessories Trades

For the artistic person, the design of accessories is a huge field in which a talented beginner or an experienced free-lancer can find exciting creative opportunities. Many of the firms in the field are small; they depend upon free-lance designers to style their lines and upon their industry trade associations to promote and publicize their products.

A background in apparel fashions is necessary to design accessories that coordinate with the related garments, and a knowledge of production procedures and problems is essential—designing for commercial purposes has to result in a practical as well as a fashionable style.

The larger firms and the large industries in the accessories field offer some positions that combine fashion coordination and publicity functions. Similar jobs also exist in some of the trade associations serving these industries. Those firms

that do national advertising, such as the better-known makers of shoes, handbags, and gloves, have advertising departments that work with agencies and suggest or develop tie-ins for retailers.

Selling jobs require fashion knowledge. The salesman or the showroom girl who can give the retail buyer the fashion background of the merchandise has a natural advantage over the one who knows only quality and workmanship points.

A particularly interesting field of work is among the millinery syndicates, which are so close to their industry that they are almost a part of production. In these syndicates, the fashion staff works closely with both producers and retail stores, not only on millinery trends but on overall fashion trends and fashion coordination as well. Entry to these fashion staffs is usually through the assistant route or from an allied field as an already established expert.

Jobs in the accessories field can lead to other fashion fields, too. One of the country's most successful fashion coordinators, who headed the coordination work at a major buying office for years, got her start as a fashionist for a millinery syndicate. She won the job because she looked better in hats than other aspirants—but she succeeded because she brought to the job an excellent mind and sound training in fashion fundamentals.

Home Sewing Industry

The 40 million girls and women in this country who make clothes for themselves[2] are quite as fashion-conscious as those who buy ready-to-wear—and often more so. Some sew for the pleasure of it; others, to have garments of better quality than they could otherwise afford; still others, because their fashion ideas are a jump ahead of what they can find in the stores.

The industries that serve these home sewers include the sewing machine companies, the notions producers, the pattern companies, and the over-the-counter divisions of fabric companies. All these industries have learned—some of them the hard way—that fashion is a more effective spur to home dressmaking than either economy or figure problems. All the industries use fashionists who can interpret fashion trends in terms of what the home dressmaker wants and what she can accomplish. Designers for the pattern companies are as much in step with fashion as those for apparel producers, but with an emphasis on finding ways to achieve currently important effects without taxing the skills of the average seamstress or demanding too much time in the production of the garment.

The fashion staffs of industries serving the woman who makes her own clothes have to learn the art of making instructions simple and clear. They work with photographers and sketchers to achieve illustrations that will show both how to make the garment and how the finished garment will look. Particularly in the fabric and pattern fields, members of fashion staffs have to be able to stage fashion shows for stores and give talks to consumers describing and illustrating how easily fashion can be created at home.

Working with schools and with schoolgirls is also vitally important, for if this effort is allowed to lapse, the industry may lose a generation of home sewers. Sewing used to be learned at home, but many families have relinquished this training to the schools.

For those with designing ability, pattern companies offer jobs for people to begin as assistants and work up. For those with a flair for fashion coordination, publicity, sales, or a combination thereof, excellent career opportunities are offered by the pattern companies, the sewing machine companies, and some of the larger firms in the sewing notions field. Entry can be as an assistant, or as an established expert with experience gained in a related field.

Careers in Retailing

One unique element of retailing is that there is scarcely a fashion career goal that cannot be reached through a retail organization. Even designing has its chance for expression among the few stores that still have custom workshops and their own designers. For the most part, a retail career demands a keen interest in merchandise, an equally keen interest in people, the sort of business acumen that recognizes the importance of attention to detail as well as long-range planning, energy, and a keen understanding of fashion.

Every phase of retailing demands the ability to deal pleasantly with people: customers, suppliers, and fellow workers alike. One of the earmarks of the successful buyer, merchandiser, or fashion coordinator is the ability to win the cooperation of subordinates as well as superiors. A much-admired and successful department store buyer was fond of saying that she was so fortunate in the cooperation she received from salespeople, publicity director, her fellow buyers, and others who worked with her, that she would not do a thing to complicate their jobs. Her subordinates and her colleagues told the story differently: she was so thoughtful and considerate that there was nothing they would not do to help her.

Merchandising Careers

The starting place for most merchandising careers is in selling. Here one experiences face-to-face encounters with customers and the problem of anticipating what they will want.

From a selling job, the next move may be to head of stock, a position in which one salesperson is more responsible than others for observing the condition of the inventory, reporting "outs," noticing and reporting slow sellers, and advising the buyer on unfilled customer wants. In branch stores, this position is usually handled by a department manager who acts as liaison between salespeople and buyer and may be responsible for two or more related departments. Both the head of stock in a large store and the department manager at a branch may do some of the more routine reordering, subject to the buyer's approval.

The assistant buyer's job is the next step upward. As an understudy to the buyer, the assistant buyer may be called in to view the line of a visiting salesman or, if he is fortunate, taken occasionally to the market on a buying trip. Usually, however, the assistant relieves the buyer of floor supervision, helps to train and supervise salespeople, processes branch questions and requests, or writes up reorders for basic stocks subject to the buyer's approval. The assistant buyer may find himself verifying prices on incoming merchandise, telephoning resources in another city to expedite merchandise on order, posting advertising proofs and dispatching them to the branches, running a meeting with salespeople on new merchandise or fashion or salesmanship, scheduling hours for sales and stock help, among other tasks.

The buyer is virtually in business for himself, in the sense that he has to budget and plan his expenditures, select the actual merchandise for the inventory, and decide what is to be advertised or displayed, and why. The job involves from two to a dozen or more market trips a year. The buyer must have the ability to teach and train subordinates and the ability to work well with advertising, display, personnel, and other divisions of the store.

Usually, the merchandise manager, whether he is a general merchandise manager or a divisional merchandise manager, is either a former buyer or a graduate of a school of retailing or business administration, or both. He has sufficient knowledge of budgetary controls and principles of management to supervise buyers. He coordinates the efforts of a group of departments, with or without the aid of a fashion coordinator, so that the fashion picture each department presents to the public is related in theme, timing, and emphasis to those presented by the others.

The final merchandising career level is top management, which demands, in addition to fashion and merchandising know-how, an understanding of every phase of store operation, from housekeeping to finances. To travel the road from selling up to policy making is not impossible, but neither is it easy—a store may have hundreds or thousands of employees, but it has only a few people on its top management team.

Retailing provides a special way in for those well-qualified beginners who are recruited on college campuses or are selected from among store employees who have demonstrated executive potential. For such people, large stores conduct formalized junior executive training programs. Total store orientation is provided through rotating job assignments in all phases of store operation and through regularly scheduled classes, usually conducted by heads of the various activities of the store. Those who successfully complete the training program qualify for junior

executive positions, and they are assigned according to the talents and abilities they have shown during the training period.

The other way into large department and specialty stores is through their personnel departments, which interview, screen, and train desirable applicants 52 weeks of the year. A personal visit, with a preparatory mail contact if the store is in a distant city, is advisable. First, however, anyone interested in a merchandising career should examine a store's advertising, display, and merchandise before making an application; unless one feels at home in a particular store, it might be wise to look to other retail establishments for employment.

Smaller stores are necessarily less formal in their interviewing, hiring, training, and promotion procedures. Openings are fewer, and advancement may come more slowly than in a larger store. In a small organization, however, there is little chance of being lost to sight, and there is ample opportunity to learn every phase of store operation as part of each day's work.

As a general rule, those who enjoy administrative work and can function well with clearly defined responsibilities are well advised to investigate the larger retail organizations for the start of their careers. Those who enjoy a shirtsleeves atmosphere, who are versatile, and who get pleasure in dealing with challenges of any sort (from digging out after a snowstorm to working up a spectacular fashion display), will probably enjoy the variety of work in a smaller store.

Sales Promotion Careers

The career opportunities in sales promotion include jobs on the advertising staff, the publicity and public relations staff, and the display staff.

Copywriters and artists who begin in retailing usually enjoy a tremendous advantage ever afterward. If they leave the field and go into advertising agencies or go to work for producers, they carry with them an understanding of consumer reaction that can be learned in no better school than the retail store. There is something exciting about a lineup of customers waiting for the store to open, and by their presence telling a copywriter that the ad he wrote for last night's paper was good. Even if the merchandise offered was

Courtesy The Broadway-Hale Stores, Inc.

An interview is almost always a part of getting a job in any company, large or small. It is wise to apply by mail first, show up promptly, and be prepared to produce convincing qualifications for the job being sought.

a real "door buster" special, the size and temper of the waiting crowd tell the copywriter just how effective his words were.

Publicity assignments usually grow out of copywriting jobs, although outsiders are sometimes hired for this work. Involved are such diverse activities as alerting the local press to newsworthy happenings, arranging for television interviews of visiting celebrities, and working up elaborate events—whether in the name of fashion, community, or charity—that will brighten the store image. Writing ability and the ability to

Career Opportunities in Fashion

357

handle contacts are important, but in a large store the ability to keep track of details is even more important. If a department store undertakes to stage a fashion show, the publicity person in charge of the event may be responsible for checking on models, merchandise, invitations, press coverage, runway, musicians, notices inside the store, notification of all store personnel, and so on.

Display executives usually start as assistants, with a willingness to work hard. They advance in position if they demonstrate artistic sense, a knowledge of fashion, the ability to speak in visual terms to the store's customers, and the ability to pick up important selling points from buyers. Because there is a great deal of heavy physical work and after-hours work involved, women do not usually enter this field, although some have become display directors in smaller stores or have done excellent display work in the course of assisting in or running small shops.

Fashion Coordination Careers

Partly merchandising and partly promotion, the fashion coordination job is ideal for people who love fashion, know how to work with others, and are absolutely tireless. The job involves working with a great many people, from resources to staff to customers, and its goals are accomplished through recommendations and advice rather than direct orders. A store's fashion coordinator may have worked her way up through the merchandising or promotion staffs, and she may have come into the store with sufficient outside experience in fashion to meet the store's needs.

The fashion coordinator's evaluation of a fashion trend or any aspect of it must be right, for she is making recommendations to experienced merchandisers, each of whom knows his own particular market better than she can hope to learn it. Each buyer is staking part of his budget on her judgment when he follows her recommendations. Every ad that is written in line with her suggestions and every sales training session that is staged with her help is done on the assumption that she knows how to read fashion's future. A beginner who has a chance to work as an assistant to such a fashion coordinator soon learns that intuition is no match for systematic checking and rechecking. A considered opinion arrived at by one fashion expert alone is not always as safe a base for merchandising and promotion operations as the combined thinking of a store and a market full of expert watchers.

Sales-Supporting Careers

Retail stores have openings in fields not directly related to the buying, selling, and promoting of merchandise. These activities, which may involve more than half the manpower of a store, include personnel, employment and training, accounting, customer services, and adjustments, among many others.

Of the many sales-supporting job opportunities, training is the field in which a fashion background is most likely to be of direct use. Large stores with well-staffed training departments sometimes assign one training executive to each merchandise category to assist buyers in training salespeople. A training executive assigned to a group of fashion departments, for instance, might compile a reference library of basic information on fashion merchandise and also collect and route current information on fashions. She might set up courses to teach salespeople and prospective buyers the basic elements of fashion. She might be called upon to devise contests and quizzes to keep salespeople alert, or to encourage them to sell related items.

A background in fashion aids materially in this work, not only in the apparel and accessories departments but in any others that find themselves becoming part of "the fashion business."

Chain and Mail-Order Careers

Chain and mail-order companies offer careers that are similar to those offered by other stores, with this important exception: buying, merchandising, publicity, and fashion coordination are usually handled by the headquarters staff rather than by the individual store itself.

Career advancement, if one starts in a chain or mail-order unit, is from selling to departmental management, then to store management, then to regional or central management. Those interested in such fields as buying, fashion coordination, promotion, catalog preparation, merchandising,

Many stores and other fashion businesses have interesting jobs not directly related to buying and selling; for instance, a computer programmer or anyone else trained in data processing work can find many opportunities.

and quality control start as assistants in regional or central headquarters and work their way up the management ladder.

Many highly specialized jobs in chain and mail-order companies call for intimate knowledge of the fashion business. For instance, the quality-control department of one chain was called upon by the merchandising division to devise a size range for girls who fell between two size ranges currently offered by the children's market. The chain then made its new size range measurements available to any producers who wished to adopt them, whether or not they were resources of that chain.[3]

Whatever special assets the beginner presents—apparel production techniques, laboratory know-how, copy or art experience, selling, buying, coordination—the chain and the mail-order companies can use them, but not always in the city or region where the applicant lives.

Career Opportunities in Fashion

Resident Buying Office Careers

Fashion careers in resident buying offices center around market work. Market representatives "live" in their markets, see every line that is important (and many that are not), and know supply and delivery conditions as well as they know fashion. Market representatives also learn to work with any number of bosses: their own supervisors, the heads of the subscribing stores, and the buyers in the stores they serve.

Entry into the market representative's job is by the apprentice route. Beginners work as assistants, literally running errands in the market all day. If the smile, the ability to remember, or the arches are weak, the career may never develop. The major job of an assistant is to follow up on details, to check with resources on deliveries and other questions that may arise, and spare the time of the market representative. In the process, the beginner gets to know the markets, the buying office routines, and the needs of the client stores. If the work is done against a background of fashion training, it is more easily mastered and promotion is apt to be more rapid.

Buying office people demonstrate tremendous physical and mental stamina in attending showings, handling mail and telephone calls, and working with visiting buyers. But they have no selling departments to oversee, no branch stores to visit, no Saturday work, and no sales goals to meet. They concentrate on specific markets.

Fashion coordinators in buying offices must function with an especially sure touch. Any errors of judgment on their part can mean wrong advice given to a number of subscribing stores. They tour the major market sources to collect information, check their findings with appropriate market representatives, and consider what fashion publications have to suggest.

A resident buying office fashion coordinator usually has a secretary and an assistant, at least one of whom is trained in fashion or sketching. In either job, a beginner with fashion training can quickly learn a great deal more than she dreamed there was to know about fashion forecasting, markets, and coordination, all of which knowledge she needs if she wants to advance in her field.

Promotion staffs in resident buying offices are fairly small. In offices serving large stores, their function may be little more than reporting on what other stores are doing or what the New York stores are promoting. In offices serving small stores, they may draw up ads for the stores to use and send them out in the form of either rough layouts and copy suggestions or mats. The smaller the stores served by the office, the less likely it is that these stores will have full-fledged advertising departments and the more important it is for the office to supply them with such special assistance.

To find a place on the promotion staff of such an office, it is necessary for an applicant to bring with her retail advertising experience or examples of how she would prepare a retail ad. Sketching and a flair for layout are helpful; writing ability is essential.

It is possible eventually to establish one's own buying office, provided one starts small, with a few client specialty shops and a versatile staff. Specialty shops have fewer departments, and they need fewer—but very capable—market representatives than department stores need. The outlay in capital, office space, and staff is relatively small if one starts with only the fashion departments.

Advertising, Publishing, Consulting, Trade Associations

There is a wide variety of careers in those organizations that service the fashion business, including jobs in advertising agencies, on publications, at consulting firms, and at trade associations. Each area has its own requirements, but there are important jobs in each area in which an understanding of fashion is vital.

Advertising Agencies

Beginners, even those with special skills, often have a hard time entering the agency field. College graduates complain that they go to dozens of agencies and are offered nothing more exciting than a mailroom job—and yet agencies complain that college graduates do not apply for jobs.

A solution to the problem may be to avoid the biggest and best-known agencies and seek a foothold in those of modest or small size. There the pay is likely to be small, the office tiny, and the future problematical, but the opportunities to work and learn are good, and they prepare one to apply, well armed, to a major agency.

Among the careers in advertising agencies are:

Account Executive The man or woman who brings in the business, solicits accounts, acts as liaison between client and agency staff, plans campaigns and calls upon the technical skills of the agency staff to develop them is an "A.E.," or account executive.

Copywriter These creative people call themselves "wordsmiths," but actually they are idea people, capable of originating campaigns. Starting spot: copy cub. Top spot: copy chief.

Artist The artists not only have creative talent and artistic ability but also understand the graphic arts, can specify type faces and sizes, and know the problems of reproducing material in various media. One starts with a skill and learns on the job.

Fashion Coordinator Agencies handling fashion accounts need personnel to guide campaigns, assist in client contacts, and provide the fashion background that other specialized agency executives may lack. Even an agency that does not handle fashion accounts may have a fashion consultant on the staff to make sure that the figures in illustrations and television commercials are wearing apparel, accessories, and hairstyles that are currently acceptable.

Other Possibilities Clerical, secretarial, and various technical jobs abound in large agencies, and can offer the beginner a foothold. For example, the media department is a haven for those who understand statistics, for it measures the worth of a publication's or broadcast station's audience in terms of cost and the client's product. The research department investigates available information to guide the client's marketing and advertising efforts and does some studies on its own. The traffic department follows up on production schedules and makes sure that deadlines for advertising insertions are met.

Essential for any agency job is the ability to work well under pressure. Agency people do not acknowledge the word "impossible" in meeting deadlines.

Consumer Publications

Nearly all consumer publications carry some sort of fashion material, and some consumer publications are devoted exclusively to fashion. Opportunities are immensely varied, both in editorial work and in those behind-the-scenes activities that go into the publishing of a magazine or newspaper.

Editorial When fashion is discussed in a publication, that publication's fashion judgment must be authoritative. Whether the publication is devoted entirely to fashion or whether it simply runs a fashion section, the editor's job is to discover what the reader responds to, locate that fashion in the market, and illustrate examples of it at the right time. The editorial job can be all the more complicated because of pressures from publicity-hungry producers. An editor may cover the entire fashion market or just one segment of it, depending on the size of the publication's staff.

Large fashion staffs generally can absorb a few green assistants. For small pay, these girls do legwork in the market and a thousand other chores. They learn how to select and how to work with models, photographers, and an art department. They learn how to cut down a lengthy prose poem about a new style to a dozen words, if that is all the space allowed for a caption. Fashion know-how and the ability to work against time and with people are vitally important—at times, even more so than writing or sketching skills.

Small fashion staffs, like those on newspapers in small cities, do no market work but depend on press releases that come from the wire (syndicated news) services and from producers and retailers of fashion merchandise. Spending time as a general assistant in such a fashion department, which may also cover society news and garden-club activities, is useful preparation for big-city, big-publication jobs.

Merchandising Behind the scenes, the merchandising editors of national publications and their staffs work to make sure that readers anywhere in the country can buy the merchandise that is featured editorially. They do this by reporting to retailers in advance of publication the details of what is to be run, why it is important, and from what resources it is available. With their formidable knowledge of markets, merchandise, and retailing, these editors are also well equipped to offer retailers practical suggestions about how to merchandise, promote, and display the editorially featured items.

Developing a following among retailers is good sales strategy for a magazine that sells advertising to producers. Therefore, the merchandising staffs are required to be extremely knowledgeable and often quite creative about retailing. Some of them work up promotional package ideas that stores can adopt bodily—even quite large stores with their own capable promotional staffs. A typical "package" for a store begins with a theme that ties in with the magazine. To promote the theme, the publication's staff suggests merchandise and resources for it, as well as suggesting advertising copy for various types of media. If the merchandise lends itself well to fashion shows or displays, the retailer receives scripts, posters, diagrams, and even the offer of an editor's services as a commentator. Many of the awards given by NRMA for outstanding retail fashion promotions are captured each year by just such packages developed by publications.

Merchandising staffs are usually large enough to absorb a beginner. Tirelessness and willingness are essential; so is versatility. The beginner may be combing markets for weeks; then acting as hostess in a temporary showroom where future editorial styles are being shown to store buyers; then drafting copy for a suggested retail ad; then acting as liaison with outside experts hired to work up displays that have been suggested or work out the design of boutiques.

Advertising Sales Selling advertising space is the major source of revenue for a publication. The many aspects of selling accommodate various talents. Those with a gift for salesmanship approach producers and their advertising agencies. People with a flair for research help the salesmen to sell by supplying facts that indicate the ability of the publication to enlist retail cooperation or that measure the buying power of the publication's readers. Those with a flair for persuasive writing may find a place on the advertising promotion staffs, where they work out presentations to help the salesmen conduct meetings with prospective advertisers.

Fashion background, sketching ability, and writing ability are aids to the beginner. Personality and contacts are vital in selling jobs, after one has become familiar enough with the publication to be entrusted with such assignments.

Trade Publications

Vertical publications, such as *Women's Wear Daily,* address all levels of fashion production and distribution from raw materials to retailing. Horizontal types address only producers or only retailers. Most trade publications are narrowly specialized, as in the intimate apparel field or the shoe field, and are published only once a month. All offer opportunities for beginners with an interest in fashion.

Except on *Women's Wear Daily,* which is the giant in the fashion apparel field, an editor spends about three weeks of the month in his market and one week in going to press. His assistant and secretary may be beginners learning how to make market calls, select new products for illustration, and write up what they have learned. *Women's Wear Daily* segments its editorial coverage, with specialists in each field. In this publication some fields are reported daily; others, only once a week.

Trade publications hire beginners who are trained in publication procedures or journalism. Typing is indispensable, as is a durable smile for contacts with the trade and a good memory for names, places, and people. Knowing a particular industry is helpful, and knowing retailing even more so, because there is a regular need for articles for and about retailers. A good deal of rewriting is done from correspondents' reports and publicity releases.

Consulting Services

The most glamorous of the consulting services involved in the fashion field is, of course, the fashion consultant. Of these, the oldest and best known is the Tobé service, founded by the late Tobé Coller Davis. As a young woman, she was hired to advise a retail store on its fashion merchandise by bringing the customer point of view to bear on its selections and promotions. From this start, she developed a syndicated service to which stores all over the country subscribed. With what is now a large staff, the firm covers and interprets fashion news in such a way that buying, merchandising, and coordinating executives can be guided by the views of skilled observers in every important fashion center. Reports, bulletins, clinics, and individual advice are the subscribers' diet.

Some of the other services, like Amos Parrish & Company, combine general advice on store operation with fashion information advice. Others exist primarily to make the skill of an expert in fashion promotion, such as Estelle Hamburger, available to interested stores.

In approaching any enterprise of this kind, the beginner is wise to offer some qualifications in addition to a background in fashion: typing, writing or sketching ability, or some retail experience. Some of the "graduates" of these services have gone on to become fashion coordinators for major retailers, buying offices, or producers. The opportunities to learn are great, if one has the stamina, ambition, and ability to work under pressure.

Some public relations and publicity consultants perform free-lance services in manufacturing and retailing. Writing skills, resourcefulness, and a knowledge of how to handle contacts of many kinds are basic equipment for job applicants to such firms. The beginner can enter as a secretary or copywriter to learn the techniques of getting product publicity and favorable mentions for client firms.

Television

Fashion-oriented specialists are beginning to find exciting careers in television. Many advertising agencies today engage outside companies to create fashion commercials for client producers or retailers.[4] The high cost of television time and production limits its appeal to retailers, but some make good use of television to present fashion. A fashion background alone is not sufficient to provide a beginner with an entry into this field. Some understanding of the technical aspects of the medium is vital.

Trade Associations

One of the more interesting byways in the fashion field is trade association work. Industries, retailers, and professionals of all types form associations and hire executive staffs to do research, publicity, public relations work, handle legislative contacts, run conventions, publish periodicals, run trade shows, or perform any other services members may require. Tiny or large, a trade association affords great variety of work to its staff. Versatility is thus a paramount requirement. An assistant entering trade association work will find a background in the specific field served helpful, but the ability to communicate well is just as important.

The Millinery Institute, EMBA (Mutation Mink Breeders Association), and NRMA (National Retail Merchants Association) are a few of the many trade associations active in fashion or retailing fields. The 1961 Directory of National Associations of Businessmen, a publication of the United States Department of Commerce, lists 2,000 national associations. There are also local chambers of commerce, local and regional industry and merchant groups, and many others. Shopping centers have merchants' associations that employ promotion executives to keep the centers in the public eye. Regional markets, like the New York and Los Angeles fashion markets, sometimes form associations to establish and publicize seasonal market dates.

Jobs in these areas are not always available when sought, but they are usually interesting and secure when found, and they put one in touch with business people at their very best: when they are working together for a common cause.

Owning Your Own Store

A common question from students of fashion is: "How much capital would I need to open a store of my own?" To which one businessman answered, "Enough to stay in business the second year and profit from the first year's mistakes."

Capital is essential, of course, but the prospective store owner also needs a thorough understanding of finance, personnel, general business conditions, store design, fixturing, and the thousand and one other things that concern a merchant. Large stores handle these problems with a corps of specially trained executives or through outside consultants. But the man or woman who starts a fashion shop with little more than drive and a desire to make good has to handle everything alone.

Behind some of the success stories of small stores, it should be pointed out, there is often a brother, or sister, or parent, with the business background that the fashion expert lacks. The one-man success story often turns out to be a family success story, with one member of the group as an expert at figures, another a genius at handling people, and the flag-bearing third person with a real sensitivity to what the public will accept.

To run one's own store, a person must feel equal to any problem that comes along—and in business, they come along frequently. Hiring and firing, placing and canceling ads, finding resources, making merchandise budgets, pricing goods and taking markdowns, paying bills and meeting payrolls, making displays, wrapping the packages, sweeping the sidewalk—they are all part of the owner's responsibility in a small operation.

But suppose the spirit is there and money is available, a basic question then is, "Have we enough money?"

To illustrate how that question can be answered, assume that the amount available is $25,000. From that figure, deduct rent on the contemplated shop premises for at least two months,

to allow time for setting up fixtures and purchasing the initial stock. (If the landlord gives a concession, this allowance need not be made.) Now deduct the cost of the very simplest of fixtures: wall racks, a few tables covered with plain cotton cloth, some T-stands, and whatever other fixtures may be needed to display the goods. Consider the minimum amount it will cost to make the windows an attractive background, even if only with crepe paper. Add to that the cost of making or improvising dressing rooms.

From what is left, deduct personal living expenses for a month or two (until sales begin coming). The figure left is the amount available for investment in merchandise. But wait! First comes the trip to the market. In future seasons, the market may come to the merchant in the person of manufacturers' salesmen, but until the store becomes known and respected, this is not likely to happen.

Suppose that $20,000 remains for merchandise at this point. Assuming a 40 percent markon, initial purchases can represent a maximum of $33,000 of stock at retail. (Remember the cost of incoming transportation!) If we use dresses as an example, and if normal stock turn occurs, that stock will turn five times a year and achieve perhaps $150,000 in net sales after markdowns—that is, if all goes well, and the buying and selling happen exactly as planned, with no misjudgments or impossibly late deliveries. The normal retail profit, after expenses, is about 2 percent of net sales, or $3,000 on net sales of $150,000. But in a small operation, the owner may do at least half the selling, on which he is entitled to at least 7 percent, based on typical selling salary costs, and that could add another $5,200 to the owner's income.

If resources are expected to extend credit, the first action before making any purchases at all is to visit the local bank with a statement of assets drawn up by an accountant. Then a similar statement is submitted to Dun & Bradstreet and to the credit managers of firms from which the potential merchant wishes to buy. Bills must be paid on time, even if that means skipping meals. Once credit is established, buying is easier. Resources gain respect for a new retailer who has demonstrated ability to run a business by paying bills promptly. Bankers may be willing to offer short-term loans to bridge periods of heavy inventory investment. The Small Business Administration may help with funds beyond what bankers can provide, so that the business can expand.

On a much smaller scale, if the commitment to owning a shop is strong, but the capital is weak, it may be possible to set up a boutique. If permitted, boutiques can be set up in one's home. Zoning laws should be checked to be sure this is permitted. Postcards and the telephone can be used to solicit business. By keeping careful note of what each customer buys and offering her items in terms of what will complete her wardrobe, the shop can buy on a tiny scale, for cash, if necessary. Heavy stocks are to be avoided, even if it means special ordering, for heavy stocks mean money tied up in inventory.

Most important ingredient of all: preliminary experience working in a specialty or department store and learning from experts about methods and budgets. Good, solid buying experience makes one an excellent manager. Buyers who start their own stores after a few years of successful experience generally prosper. They have that precious asset: know-how.

References

[1]Brockman, Helen, *The Theory of Fashion Design*, p. 7.
[2]Brenner, *Careers and Opportunities in Fashion*, p. 25.
[3]"The Story of Penney Tweens," *Stores*, March, 1965, p. 28.
[4]Brenner, op. cit., p. 125.

Appendix 2
Merchandising Arithmetic

Merchandising, according to the American Marketing Association, refers to the planning involved in marketing the right merchandise, at the right place, at the right time, in the right quantities, and at the prices customers are willing and able to pay. By definition, then, retail merchandising is a business activity involving the purchase of goods for purposes of resale to ultimate consumers. The goal of merchandising, as well as that of any other type of business activity, is profit, or a reasonable return on invested capital. A basic knowledge of the fundamentals of bookkeeping and competency both in handling and interpreting figure relationships are essential if the merchandising activity is to be carried on successfully.

Every merchant in every store, no matter how large or small, prepares a periodic budget based upon anticipated sales and the inventory that will be required to produce such sales. In addition, he maintains some type of system for recording sales, purchases, markdowns, inventory value, and operating expenses. Periodically, reports or summaries of such bookkeeping records are prepared, not only for tax purposes but also for study and comparison with budgeted figures for the same period.

Although such records are uniformly kept in dollars, many retail merchants also convert their summary dollar figures into percentages, with net sales equaling 100 percent and all other operating figures shown as a percentage of sales. Percentages have a particular relevance in retail merchandising, in that they provide a common language for measuring the results of an operation, for budgeting and control procedures, and for comparing and evaluating one period with another, one department with another, or one store with another. Dollar figures alone are of little value in such comparisons.

Before undertaking a review of merchandising arithmetic, the student should bear in mind that the accounting records maintained today by all but the smallest stores are kept in terms of their retail values, as indicated on each item's price ticket. All other business organizations and some small retail firms keep their accounting records on the basis of cost prices. A detailed explanation of the retail method of inventory evaluation may be found in Chapter 14.

There are two major financial statements that are prepared periodically by every business organization. One is a *balance sheet,* which shows the assets, liabilities, and net worth of a business on a specific date, usually the last day of a calendar or fiscal year. The other is a *profit and loss, income,* or *operating statement,* which is a summary of the income and expense of an operation over a given period of time. The latter type of statement, which is required by income tax regulations to be prepared annually, may also be prepared on a quarterly or semiannual basis.

The balance sheet of most business organizations is designed primarily for the information and use of the firms's top management and its stockholders, and indicates in broad, general terms the financial condition of the firm as a result of its total operation over a specific period of time. The profit and loss, income, or operating statement, on the other hand, relates to actual operating results and is designed to show the profit or loss accruing to the business as a result of four basic factors: namely, sales volume, cost of merchandise sold, expenses incurred in carrying on the business, and miscellaneous sources of income other than those directly related to the business in which the firm is primarily engaged, such as rental income, dividends, and so on.

It is with the profit and loss, income, or operating statement, rather than the balance sheet, that merchandising executives are primarily concerned. Every merchant, as a businessman, should understand the principles underlying profit and loss. The ability to analyze and evaluate profit and loss statements is the basis of successful merchandise management.

The Operating Statement

Although many business firms prepare profit and loss statements only once a year, small retail firms prepare quarterly or semiannual statements, known as operating statements, to provide a closer control over their operations. (Form A-1 is an example of an operating statement in common use today among small stores.) Most medium- and large-volume retail firms, however, prepare monthly operating statements for even closer control. In the case of small stores that are not departmentalized, the operating statement usually covers the merchandising and operating results of the store as a whole. In larger, departmentalized stores, where each department represents a separate accounting unit, monthly operating statements are prepared for each department as well as for the store as a whole. A monthly departmental statement is usually referred to as a *department manager's operating report*. The main objective of this report is to present to the merchandising executive in charge of each department pertinent information on sales, cost of the merchandise sold, operating expenses, and the resulting operating profit or loss for each month.

There is no standardized form used by retailers for making up an operating statement. Some stores limit their report to such monthly dollar figures as gross sales, customer returns, beginning and ending inventories, net purchases, mark-

downs, employee discounts, shortage reserve, workroom costs, cash discounts earned, gross margin, and total operating expenses. (See Form A-1.) Other stores may include on these reports the planned figures as well as actual results so that the department manager or buyer may see how closely he is adhering to his budget. Still other stores show planned figures and actual results, not only for a given month, but also cumulative figures for the year to date.

Large branch-owning retail organizations that are centrally merchandised frequently break down the departmental operating statements into separate columns for planned figures, actual results, year-to-date results, and last year's results for the same period, for the main store as well as for the branch operation. In addition, large stores also tend to show on their operating reports a detailed breakdown of direct expenses, such as advertising, selling salaries, delivery expenses, and so on, as well as indirect expenses, such as the department's share of store management expense, maintenance, insurance, taxes, receiving and marking expense, and so on.

A retail merchant buys products which he hopes to sell at a higher price. Out of the revenue derived from sales, he hopes to recover not only the total cost of the merchandise he has purchased but also all other expenses incurred in the operation of his business, and have a profit left over. In highly simplified form, the relationships that form the basis of any operating statement, no matter how detailed, are: net sales minus total cost of merchandise sold equals gross margin (or gross margin of profit); and gross margin minus operating expenses equals operating profit. For example, referring to Form A-1, we find:

$$\text{Gross margin} = \text{Net sales} - \text{total cost of merchandise sold}$$
$$\text{Operating profit} = \text{Gross margin} - \text{operating expenses}$$

Or

$$\text{Gross margin} = \$100,000 - \$63,000$$
$$= \$37,000$$
$$\text{Operating profit} = \$37,000 - \$28,500$$
$$= \$8,500$$

Operating Statement
For the Period February 1–July 31, 19—

			%
Gross Sales		$110,000	
Less Returns and Allowances		10,000	9.1
Net Sales		$100,000	100.0
Inventory, Feb. 1, 19—	$20,000		
Gross Purchases	$73,000		
Less Returns and Allowances	4,000		
Net Purchases	69,000		
Transportation Charges	1,000		
Total Cost of Merchandise Handled	$90,000		
Inventory, July 31, 19—	25,000		
Gross Cost of Merchandise Sold	$65,000		65.0
Cash Discounts Earned	3,000		3.0
Net Cost of Merchandise Sold	$62,000		62.0
Net Workroom and Alteration Costs	1,000		1.0
Total Cost of Merchandise Sold		63,000	63.0
Gross Margin		$ 37,000	37.0
Operating Expenses:			
Administration	$ 2,500		
Buying	5,000		
Selling	12,000		
Advertising	3,500		
Occupancy	5,000		
Delivery	500		
Total Operating Expense		28,500	28.5
Operating Profit		$ 8,500	8.5

Form A-1

Sales

Every operating statement starts with *gross sales,* from which are deducted customer returns and allowances in order to arrive at *net sales.* In a customer return, the customer is refunded the full purchase price of the merchandise, either in cash or credit. In an allowance, the customer keeps the merchandise but is given some reduction from the marked selling price because of some dissatisfaction with the goods.

For example, if a customer buys a $50 dress, the dress department is credited with a $50 sale. However, if this dress is returned and the customer is given full credit, the department's net sales will be $50 less than its gross sales. Similarly, if the customer discovers, after taking the dress home, that it has an imperfection, but agrees to keep it if given an allowance, then the department's gross sales and its net sales will vary by the amount of the allowance.

Net sales form the most vital section of the entire operating statement, representing the total revenue out of which the retailer pays for purchases and all expenses incurred in the operation of the business. Therefore, net sales are the basis for determining all operating ratios. With net sales set at 100 percent, all other items on the operating statement can be expressed as percentages of those net sales.

Cost of Merchandise Sold

On Form A-1, the total cost of merchandise sold during the period February 1 through July 31 was $63,000. The cost of merchandise sold is determined by taking the cost value of the inventory on hand at the beginning of the period ($20,000) and adding to it the billed cost of net purchases made during the period (gross purchases, minus returns to and allowances made by vendors, or $69,000). Next freight and express charges paid by the merchant on incoming purchases ($1,000) are added. The sum of these figures is the total cost of merchandise handled during the period ($90,000).

At the close of the period, however, there remains a stock of merchandise on hand, the cost of which ($25,000) must be subtracted from the total merchandise handled, leaving a gross cost of merchandise sold amounting to $65,000.

Two other factors that affect the actual cost value of the merchandise sold are cash discounts earned and alteration or workroom costs. Different retail accounting systems handle these factors in different ways.

Some systems disregard them at this point in the operating statement and obtain gross margin by subtracting the gross cost of merchandise sold from the net sales for the period. Under one system, cash discounts earned, which are the amount by which the actual cost of the merchandise is overstated, are added to the operating profit as "other income." Under still another system, the cash discount is subtracted from the billed amount appearing on each invoice, and all purchases are recorded at their net or discounted cost. Alteration or workroom costs, which are expenses incurred in preparing the merchandise for sale, are considered in both cases to be an operating expense.

Most retail accounting systems, however, favor placing cash discounts earned and alteration or workroom costs in the cost-of-merchandise-sold section of the operating statement. In Form A-1, the gross cost of merchandise sold is reduced by the amount of cash discounts earned ($3,000) in order to arrive at the net cost of merchandise sold ($62,000). Net alteration or workroom costs of $1,000 (total costs minus income from alterations paid for by customers) are then added to the net cost figure in order to arrive at the total cost of merchandise sold, or $63,000.

Gross Margin

The difference between the total cost of merchandise sold during a period and the net sales for that period is called *gross margin.* It represents the amount that the merchant has left from net sales revenue, after subtracting all costs of merchandise sold, to cover his operating expenses and profit.

While initial markon, which is not shown in the operating statement, represents the amount by which the original retail price of goods exceeds their billed cost, gross margin represents the amount above their cost that is realized when the goods have actually been sold. One of the major causes of lowered gross margin is markdowns, since they reduce the spread between the actual cost of the goods and the revenue derived from their sale. In the merchandising of fashion goods, where markdowns usually run higher than for more staple goods, their effect on gross margin is significant. For this reason, planned markdown figures must be carefully adhered to, if anticipated gross margin is to be realized.

Gross margin percentage is determined by dividing the dollar amount of gross margin by the dollar amount of net sales. Using Form A-1 as an example:

$$\text{Gross margin \%} = \frac{\$ \text{ gross margin}}{\$ \text{ net sales}}$$

$$= \frac{\$37,000}{\$100,000}$$

$$= 37.0\%$$

Operating Expenses

The expenses of operating a retail business may be classified for analytical purposes in a great many different ways. The Controllers' Congress of the National Retail Merchants Association has established standardized divisions of such expenses, but for purposes of this text, operational expenses are classified as either direct or indirect. *Direct* (or controllable) *expenses* are those that are directly related to the operation of a department and would cease if the department were discontinued, such as salaries of buyer, assistant, and salespeople; advertising; selling supplies; and delivery. *Indirect* (or fixed) *expenses* are those pertaining to the operation of the store as a whole which would continue even if the department were discontinued, such as store maintenance, insurance, salaries of general executives, and taxes. Indirect or fixed expenses of a department are usually prorated on the basis of its percentage contribution to total store sales. (See Chapter 12.)

The percentage relationship of operating expenses to net sales is determined by dividing total dollar expenses by total dollars of net sales. In Form A-1, for example:

$$\text{Operating expenses \%} = \frac{\$ \text{ expenses}}{\$ \text{ net sales}}$$

$$= \frac{\$28,500}{\$100,000}$$

$$= 28.5\%$$

Profit

The difference between gross margin and operating expenses is known as *operating profit.* This is the profit from operations, or trading in merchandise, as distinct from the profit derived from any other source. Operating profit is the figure of interest to the hired buyer or merchandiser who has no control over other investments.

Other income may come from a variety of sources, such as interest earned, dividends received, or carrying charges received on installment accounts. When other income is added to the operating profit, the result is the *net profit before taxes.*

Markon

The basic ingredient of a merchant's profit is markon, a term preferred today instead of the older term "markup." Normally, the selling price of an item should exceed its cost by an amount sufficient to cover operating expenses and still leave the desired profit. To this end, stores usually plan *initial markon,* or the amount above billed cost they plan to mark merchandise when it first arrives in stock, taking into consideration such relevant factors as operating expenses, desired profit, workroom costs, retail reductions (markdowns, employee discounts, and stock shortages), and cash discounts. (See Chapter 12.)

Expressed as a formula, markon equals the retail price minus the cost price:

$$\$ \text{ Markon} = \$ \text{ retail} - \$ \text{ cost}$$

Markon Terminology

It is important that all merchandising students understand the following relationships as they apply to the concept of markon:

□ *Initial* or *original markon* refers to the difference between the delivered cost of merchandise and the original retail value placed on the goods when they were first brought into stock.

□ *Cumulative markon* refers to the difference between the total cost and the total original retail value of all goods handled to date, within a specific period, including the beginning inventory.

□ *Maintained markon* refers to the difference between the delivered cost of merchandise and the price at which it is actually sold. Maintained markon allows for markdowns and stock shortages but not workroom costs or cash discounts earned.

□ *Markon percentage* refers to the percentage relationship between dollar markon and either the cost or retail value of the merchandise. Under the retail method of inventory evaluation, only the markon based on the retail value is used.

Useful Formulas

The concept of markon involves three basic elements: markon itself, cost price, and retail price. Given any two of these elements, the third can always be found. The following formulas may be helpful to the merchandising student in solving problems relating to markon.

Determining Markon Percentage Markon percentage, based on the retail price, can be determined if dollar cost and dollar retail are known. Similarly markon percentage based on cost can be determined if dollar cost and dollar retail are known.

Formulas

$$\text{Retail markon \%} = \frac{\$ \text{ retail} - \$ \text{ cost}}{\$ \text{ retail}}$$

$$\text{Cost markon \%} = \frac{\$ \text{ retail} - \$ \text{ cost}}{\$ \text{ cost}}$$

Problem

If an item of merchandise costs $6 and is retailed at $10, what is (a) the markon percentage on retail, and (b) the markon percentage on cost?

Solutions

(a) $$\text{Retail markon \%} = \frac{\$ \text{ retail} - \$ \text{ cost}}{\$ \text{ retail}}$$

$$= \frac{\$ 4}{\$ 10}$$

$$= 40\%$$

(b) $$\text{Cost markon \%} = \frac{\$ \text{ retail} - \$ \text{ cost}}{\$ \text{ cost}}$$

$$= \frac{\$ 4}{\$ 6}$$

$$= 66\tfrac{2}{3}\%$$

Determining Dollar Cost When dollar retail and retail markon percentage are known, dollar cost can be determined as follows:

Formula

$$\$ \text{ Cost} = \$ \text{ retail} \times (\text{complement of retail markon \%})$$
$$= \$ \text{ retail} \times (100\% - \text{retail markon \%})$$

Problem

If an item retailing at $10 represents a 40 percent markon, what is its cost price?

Solution

$$\$ \text{ Cost} = \$ \text{ retail} \times (100\% - \text{retail markon \%})$$
$$= \$ 10 \times 60\%$$
$$= \$ 6$$

Determining Dollar Retail When dollar cost and retail markon percentage are known, dollar retail can be determined as follows:

Formula

$$\$ \text{ Retail} = \frac{\$ \text{ cost}}{\text{complement of retail markon \%}}$$

$$= \frac{\$ \text{ cost}}{(100\% - \text{retail markon \%})}$$

Problem

If an item costs $6 and a retail markon of 40 percent is desired, what retail price should be placed on it?

Solution

$$\$ \text{ Retail} = \frac{\$ \text{ cost}}{(100\% - \text{retail markon \%})}$$

$$= \frac{\$ 6}{60\%}$$

$$= \$ 10$$

Determining Initial Markon Percentage The initial markon that a store or department places on its goods must be large enough to allow for markdowns, employee discounts, stock shortages, and all operating expenses incurred and provide a reasonable profit.

As shown in the following formula, calculation of this percentage starts with planned net sales for the period. In order to determine the numerator of the equation, operating expenses and retail reductions (markdowns, stock shortages, and discounts to employees and customers) are estimated, and an operating profit goal determined. These figures are then added together to determine the markon necessary to cover the cost of merchandise sold. If cash discounts are considered an offset to the cost of merchandise sold, they are subtracted from the other figures in the numerator because they represent additional income which contributes to profits and does not require a markon to cover. If alteration or workroom costs are considered a cost of the goods sold rather than an operating expense item, they too must be added to the numerator of the equation.

To determine the denominator of this equation, the total of all anticipated retail reductions is then added to planned sales in order to restore such sales to their original retail value.

The final step is to divide the elements of markon by the original retail value of the goods expected to be sold.

Formula

$$\text{Initial markon \%} = \frac{\begin{array}{l}\text{expenses} + \text{retail reductions} \\ + \text{ workroom costs} + \text{profit} \\ - \text{ cash discount}\end{array}}{\text{sales} + \text{retail reductions}}$$

Problem

Calculate the initial markon percentage required when operating expenses are expected to be 31.0 percent of net sales; markdowns and employee discounts, 11.0 percent; stock shortages, 1.5 percent; alteration costs, 1.0 percent; desired operating profit, 4.0 percent; and cash discounts, 4.5 percent.

Solution

$$\begin{aligned}\text{Initial markon \%} &= \frac{\begin{array}{l}31.0\% + 11.0\% + 1.5\% \\ + 1.0\% + 4.0\% - 4.5\%\end{array}}{\begin{array}{l}100\% \text{ (sales)} + 11.0\% \\ + 1.5\%\end{array}} \\[2mm] &= \frac{44\%}{112.5\%} \\[2mm] &= 39.1\%\end{aligned}$$

If cash discounts earned are considered as additional income rather than a reduction in the cost

of goods sold, and alteration costs are considered an operating expense rather than an addition to the cost of goods sold, initial markon percentage is determined as follows:

Formula

$$\text{Initial markon \%} = \frac{\begin{array}{l}\text{expenses} + \text{retail reductions} \\ + \text{ profit}\end{array}}{\text{sales} + \text{retail reductions}}$$

Problem

Calculate initial markon percentage when operating costs are expected to be 32.0 percent of net sales; markdowns and employee discounts, 11.0 percent; stock shortages, 1.5 percent; and the desired operating profit is 4.0 percent of net sales.

Solution

$$\begin{aligned}\text{Initial markon \%} &= \frac{\begin{array}{l}32.0\% + 11.0\% + 1.5\% \\ + 4.0\%\end{array}}{\begin{array}{l}100\% \text{ (sales)} + 11.0\% \\ + 1.5\%\end{array}} \\[2mm] &= \frac{48.5\%}{112.5\%} \\[2mm] &= 43.1\%\end{aligned}$$

Averaging Markon

Although initial markon goals may be planned for a store or department, rarely, if ever, do all items carried, even those in identical retail price lines, yield the same percentage of markon. For example, although the majority of dresses in an assortment priced from $14.95 to $15 may have a billed cost of $8.75, some may have been purchased for $8.25, others may be promotional remainders for which the store paid $9 or $9.25, and still others may have been marked down from higher price lines.

In the same way, within the same dress department, the markon obtained varies from price line to price line. For example, a hypothetical store regularly retails $8.75 cost dresses at about $15, a price yielding an initial markon of 41.7 percent. Those costing $10.75 and priced at $18 yield a 40.3 percent markon, and $11.75 goods retailed at $20 yield a 41.25 percent markon. To complicate matters even more, promotional goods often yield a lower than regular markon. Furthermore, all price lines are not stocked or sold at the same rate.

When initial markon goals have been established for a store or department, the buyer must balance below-goal markons with above-goal markons in order to achieve the planned markon necessary for a profitable operation. The same formulas used for determining item cost, retail, and markon percentage are used in averaging.

Finding Average Cost When average retail and desired markon percent are known, average cost may be determined as follows:

Problem

A handbag buyer plans to buy 100 handbags, to retail at $8 each, for a special sales event. His planned markon for this event is 40 percent. If his first order for this sale is for 20 handbags costing $4 each, (a) what is the total maximum he can afford to pay for the remaining 80 handbags if he is to realize his planned markon percentage? and (b) what will be the average cost of the 80 handbags he still has to purchase?

Solutions

(a) First find total retail:

$100 \times \$8 = \$800$

Then find total cost:

Cost = $ retail $\times$ (100% − M%)
    = $800 $\times$ 60%
    = $480

Subtract purchases to date:

$20 \times \$4$ cost = $80
$480 − $80 = $400

Remainder of $400 equals balance to spend on remaining 80 handbags

(b) Average cost of each of the remaining 80 handbags to be purchased:

$$\frac{\$400}{80} = \$5$$

Finding Average Retail When total cost and desired markon percentage are known, average retail may be determined as follows:

Problem

A sportswear buyer was offered a group of sweaters as a manufacturer's closeout, consisting of the following: 15 slipovers at $3.75 cost; 21 cardigans at $4.75 cost; and 30 decorated sweaters at $5.75 cost. If he buys all 66, what single retail price can he offer them for to get a markon of 40 percent?

Solution

First find total cost:

$15 \times \$3.75 = \$\ \ 56.25$
$21 \times \$4.75 = \$\ \ 99.75$
$30 \times \$5.75 = \$172.50$
Total cost $= \$328.50$

Next find total retail:

Retail = $ cost ÷ (100% − M%)

$$= \frac{\$328.50}{60\%}$$

$$= \$547.50$$

Average retail price:

$$\frac{\$547.50}{66} = \$8.30$$

Finding Average Markon Percentage When total retail and planned markon percentage are known and some purchases have been made, the markon percentage needed on the balance of the purchases may be determined as follows:

Problem

A shoe buyer plans to buy $3,500 worth of shoes at retail for a back-to-school promotion and obtain an average 40 percent markon on his purchases for this event. The first order he places is for 100 pairs of shoes costing $7.50 each, which he plans to retail at $12 each. What markon should the buyer obtain on the balance of his purchases if he is to realize his markon goal of 40 percent?

Solution

Total planned retail = $3,500

Then find total planned cost:

Cost = retail $\times$ (100% − M%)
    = $3,500 $\times$ 60%
    = $2,100

Next subtract purchases to date:

$100 \times \$12\ \ \ = \$1,200$ at retail
$100 \times \$7.50 = \$750$ at cost

Remainder equals balance yet to buy:

$3,500 − $1,200 = $2,300 retail
$2,100 − $ 750 = $1,350 cost

Find markon % on balance yet to buy:

Markon % = $ Markon ÷ $ Retail
= $950 ÷ $2,300
= 41.3%

Discounts and Terms of Sale

Discounts are allowances made by vendors on the billed price of their goods. *Dating,* a term usually found in conjunction with cash discounts, refers to the period of time allowed by a manufacturer for taking cash discounts. *Terms of sale* refer to the combination of allowable discounts and the time allowed for taking such discounts. A buyer buys terms as well as merchandise. Taking advantage of terms of sale can result in extra profit for a department or a store by reducing the cost of purchases.

Most retailers, however, do not figure a cash discount as a reduction in cost of merchandise when determining the selling or retail price of an item. Instead, they regard it as a profit cushion, a hedge against not being able to realize the full markon on all purchases, a cushion against markdowns occasioned by buying errors. This is particularly relevant to departments or stores handling apparel and accessories in the earlier stages of their fashion cycles.

The manufacturer, on the other hand, figures discounts as one of his costs when pricing his products. In allowing the retailer the customary cash discount, the vendor is simply giving back to the retailer the extra charge he has included in his price for that purpose.

Types of Discounts

There are various types of discounts, chief among which are quantity discounts, trade discounts, and cash discounts.

Quantity Discounts In order to encourage larger orders, some manufacturers set up a quantity discount schedule for purchases above certain specified minimum quantities. Such discounts are stated as a percentage off the quoted price and apply in addition to other discount allowances. This practice is more prevalent in hard lines industries than among fashion industries.

Trade Discounts Some industries quote list prices, which are suggested resale prices, that serve as the basis for discount deductions. If a chain of successive discounts is given, each discount is calculated on the net price remaining after deducting the preceding discount. For example, if a cosmetics manufacturer allowed Store X a series of trade discounts amounting to 30 percent, 10 percent, and 5 percent on an invoice for $100 at list prices, the net amount of the invoice would be $59.85, computed as follows:

30% of $100	$ 30.00
Plus 10% of $70	7.00
($100 − $30)	
Plus 5% of $63	3.15
($70 − $7)	
Total discounts	$ 40.15
Invoice at list prices	$100.00
Less discounts	40.15
Net invoice amount	$ 59.85

Cash Discounts A cash discount is a premium allowed off the invoiced price of merchandise if payment is made within a certain specified period of time in advance of its regular due date. For example, if the cosmetics invoice above also carried terms allowing a 2 percent cash discount if the invoice were paid within ten days, the net amount remitted to the manufacturer within this period would be $58.65:

Net invoice	$59.85
Less 2% cash discount	1.20
Net invoice amount less cash discount	$58.65

In effect, cash discounts are interest payments made by the vendor in exchange for the settlement of an obligation in advance of its due date. Cash discounts may appear on the operating statement as a deduction from gross cost of goods sold or as a reduction in the amount of each discounted invoice. In either case they serve to increase the final gross margin. As an addition to operating profit, however, they are regarded as additional income with no effect on gross margin.

Types of Dating

Dating refers to the specific period of time in which a cash discount may be taken. The cash discount and the dating are expressed in two numbers: the first number is the percentage of cash discount allowed, and the second number is the period of time, in days, within which it is effective. For example, terms of 1/10 mean that 1 percent discount may be deducted from the billed cost of an invoice if payment is made within ten days following the date of the invoice. In addition, terms usually indicate the length of time allowed for net payment of the invoice, for example, 1/10 net 30, usually expressed as 1/10, n/30.

Many types of dating practices prevail, although they tend to be standardized within various industries. The most common types are listed below.

Regular or Ordinary Dating The most common form of dating for stores that have a credit rating which allows them to buy on credit is regular or ordinary dating. In this type of dating, two periods of time are stated: the number of days following the invoice date in which a stated discount may be taken, and the number of days from the invoice date that the full amount of the invoice must be paid. For example, 2/10, n/30 means that a 2 percent cash discount may be deducted if the invoice is paid within ten days following its date. The full amount of the invoice under these terms is due within 30 days of its date, or the bill becomes delinquent.

Net Terms No cash discount is allowed in the type of dating called net terms. Net terms consist solely of the number of days following the date of the invoice that its face value is due and payable, or else it becomes delinquent. For example, terms of n/30 mean that the face value of the invoice is due and payable no later than 30 days following the invoice date.

COD "Cash on delivery," or COD, means that payment is required before the goods can be released by the carrier. This type of dating usually applies when a firm's credit has not yet been established.

Extra Dating Just as in regular dating, extra dating is calculated from the date of the invoice, but a specified number of extra days are granted in which the discount may be taken. For example, 8/10–30X means that a cash discount of 8 percent may be taken if payment is made within 10 days plus 30 extra days, or a total of 40 days, from the date of the invoice. Vendors may give retailers extra dating for purchases made in advance of a regular buying period, for larger quantities, or for various other reasons.

Advance or Post Dating Like extra dating, advance or post dating extends an additional period of time for the merchant to avail himself of the cash discount privilege. However, in this instance, the date of the invoice itself is advanced to a date mutually acceptable to both buyer and seller. Advance dating is extended by manufacturers to encourage buyers to receive goods earlier than they ordinarily might choose to have them in stock or earlier than their budgets would normally permit. For example, if shipment of merchandise is made on March 15 against an invoice carrying terms of 2/10 and dated June 1 rather than March 15, a cash discount of 2 percent can be taken if the invoice is paid by June 10.

ROG Dating Sometimes vendors allow stores located at a distance from their shipping point ROG terms, or receipt-of-goods terms, which means that the discount period does not start until the goods are received by the store. The purpose of this arrangement is to permit distant stores time enough to receive and check the merchandise before payment falls due for the taking of a discount. For example, terms of 3/10 ROG means that a cash discount of 3 percent may be taken if the invoice is paid within 10 days after the receipt of the merchandise by the store.

EOM Dating EOM terms, or end-of-month terms, mean that the days for allowing discounts are counted from the end of the month in which the invoice is dated instead of from the actual date of the invoice itself. EOM dating is common throughout the fashion industries. Where EOM terms prevail, merchandise shipped on or after the 25th of one month is considered to have been shipped on the first day of the following month. For example, if the terms of an invoice dated May 27 are 3/10 EOM, a 3 percent cash discount is deductible if the invoice is paid by July 10, because the invoice is treated as if dated June 1.

Anticipation

With the vendor's consent, a store may sometimes pay a bill before the last day for deducting discount, and may then deduct *anticipation* which is interest allowed for prepayment of an invoice. The usual rate is 6 percent a year (computed as 360 days) or .5 percent a month (30 days) for whatever period the invoice is prepaid. Prepayment of an invoice before the expiration of the discount period is considered somewhat similar to loaning money to a vendor, and the payer is considered eligible to receive bank interest rates on loans. Where anticipation is allowed, it is taken in addition to any other discounts that may apply.

Problem

If an invoice for $100, dated July 12 and carrying terms of 2/10–60X, is paid on August 20, (a) by how many days was payment anticipated? and (b) what amount was remitted to the vendor?

Solutions

(a) The discount period is 70 days (10 plus 60), which means that the last date for discount is September 20. Since it is paid on the 39th day from the date of the invoice, however, it is prepaid, or anticipated, by 30 days.

(b) Paying the invoice on August 20, the store is entitled to deduct 2 percent cash discount in addition to .5 percent for 30 days' anticipation:

$$\text{Discount} + \text{anticipation} = 2\% + .5\%$$
$$= \$100 \times 2.5\%$$
$$= \$2.50$$
$$\text{Amount remitted} = \$100 - \$2.50$$
$$= \$97.50$$

Retail Reductions

Under the retail method of inventory evaluation, any difference between the retail value placed on merchandise when it is first received into stock and the price at which it is actually sold must be accounted for in the book inventory. These differences are referred to as retail reductions, since they reduce the total retail value of the inventory. They consist of the following: merchandise markdowns taken to correct various buying errors or failures that may have occurred; discount markdowns resulting from allowances made to employees, the clergy, and other favored groups; and stock shortages resulting from theft, breakage, and careless recordkeeping.

Retail reductions reduce ultimate profit by reducing the spread between the cost price of the merchandise and the price at which merchandise is actually sold. Stock shortages particularly affect profit since not only is initial markon lost but the billed cost of the merchandise as well.

Merchandise Markdowns

Markdowns are reductions in the retail price of a single item or a group of items. A markdown occurs whenever merchandise is reduced, either from its original price or from a previously recorded price. Markdowns are calculated as follows:

$$\$\text{ Markdown} = \text{previous selling price} - \text{new lower price}$$

For example, if a coat is reduced from $60 to $48, the dollar markdown is computed as follows:

$$\text{Markdown} = \$60 - \$48$$
$$= \$12$$

Markdown Percentage The dollar value of markdowns taken, expressed as a percentage of net sales, is the *markdown percentage* and is calculated as follows:

$$\text{Markdown \%} = \frac{\$ \text{ markdowns}}{\$ \text{ sales}}$$

For example, if a dress department had February sales amounting to $1,250 and took markdowns amounting to $110 during the month, its markdown percentage for February amounts to :

$$\text{Markdown \%} = \frac{\$110}{\$1,250}$$
$$= 8.8\%$$

Markdown Cancellation A price rise to or toward a prior retail price is a *markdown cancellation*. For example, if regular stock merchandise is temporarily reduced for a special, limited period of selling and then returned to its original selling price when the special sales event is over, the resulting markup is called a markdown cancellation. A markdown cancellation, however, cannot be used to make the price of any item higher than it originally was. Markdown cancellations are usually permitted only in the accounting period in which the original markdown was taken, and are deducted from gross markdowns to arrive at net markdowns.

Problem

1. If a coat buyer marked down 20 coats from $85 to $58 for a special two-day Columbus Day sale, what was the amount of this markdown?

2. If, at the conclusion of the sale, the buyer found he had five of the marked-down coats left and decided to return these to their original selling price (a) what would be the amount of the markdown cancellation? and (b) what would be the amount of his net markdowns for this sale?

Solutions

1. $ Markdown = no. of units × (previous price − markdown price)
$$= 20 \times (\$85 - \$58)$$
$$= 20 \times \$27$$
$$= \$540$$

2. (a) $ Markdown cancellation = new price − markdown price
$$= 5 \times (\$85 - \$58)$$
$$= 5 \times \$27$$
$$= \$135$$

   (b) Net markdown = $ gross markdowns − $ markdown cancellations
$$= \$540 - \$135$$
$$= \$405$$

Special Discounts

Discounts of varying percentages and for varying purposes are offered by most stores to their employees and their dependents. These are known as *employee discounts*. The dollar and percentage amount of such reductions in retail price are usually noted on the salescheck covering the transaction. A total of employee discounts, by departments, is compiled by the accounting department for each period and used as a reduction in the appropriate department's book inventory.

Problem

The Smith Brothers Department Store grants its employees a 20 percent discount on all purchases. If a salesgirl buys a dress that is marked $25, what will it cost her?

Solution

$ Discount = $ retail × discount %
$$= \$25 \times 20\%$$
$$= \$5$$

Cost to salesperson = $ marked retail − $ discount
$$= \$25 - \$5$$
$$= \$20$$

Most stores also extend a purchase discount to certain favored groups, such as the clergy, charitable organizations, diplomatic corps, and military personnel. In most cases, this discount amounts to 10 percent.

Problem

A clergyman buys two shirts priced at $3.95 each and when preparing to pay for them presents his 10 percent clergy discount card. What will the salesperson charge him for this merchandise?

Solution

Discount = $ retail × discount %
$$= (2 \times \$3.95) \times 10\%$$
$$= \$7.90 \times 10\%$$
$$= 79¢$$

Cost to clergyman = $ marked retail − $ discount
$$= \$7.90 - 79¢$$
$$= \$7.11$$

Stock Shortage

Stock shortage, or inventory shortage as it is sometimes called, may be defined as the difference between the book inventory and the physical inventory when the former is larger. Shortages may occur through theft, breakage, or careless recordkeeping, but a large part of shortage arises because processes and procedures within the store are not properly followed. Whenever a piece of merchandise goes in or out of the physical inventory, a document representing that action must flow through the book inventory. Only in this way can the level of the physical and book inventory remain in balance. The actual amount of shortage sustained can be determined only when a physical inventory is taken. This amount is usually expressed both in dollars and as a percentage of net sales for the period.

Problem

If a sportswear department has the following figures for the six-month period from February 1 to July 31:

Net sales	$ 65,000
Purchases (at retail)	45,000
Inventory, Feb. 1	100,000
Markdowns	5,000
Employee discounts	1,500
Inventory, July 31	72,000

(a) what was the dollar amount of the stock shortage, and (b) what was the percentage of the stock shortage?

Solution

First, determine the book inventory.

$$
\begin{aligned}
\text{Book inventory} &= \text{beginning inventory} + \text{purchases} \\
&\quad - \text{sales} - \text{markdowns} \\
&\quad - \text{employee discounts} \\
&= \$100,000 + \$45,000 \\
&\quad - \$65,000 - \$5,000 \\
&\quad - \$1,500 \\
&= \$73,500
\end{aligned}
$$

(a)
$$
\begin{aligned}
\$ \text{ Stock shortage} &= \text{book inventory} \\
&\quad - \text{physical inventory} \\
&= \$73,500 - \$72,000 \\
&= \$1,500
\end{aligned}
$$

(b)
$$
\begin{aligned}
\text{Stock shortage \%} &= \frac{\$ \text{ shortage}}{\$ \text{ sales}} \\
&= \frac{\$1,500}{\$65,000} \\
&= 2.3\%
\end{aligned}
$$

Most stores set up monthly reserves, as a percentage of the sales in each department, to cover probable stock shortages. The amount of this percentage, which is called a *retail shortage provision,* varies from department to department and is usually based on the previous shortage experience of each. When a physical inventory is taken, the difference between the actual dollar shortage and the reserve is used to adjust the book inventory figure so that it is brought into agreement with the actual physical inventory.

Other Merchandising Ratios

Aside from the figures reported on the departmental operating statement there are two yardsticks, both involving stock-sales relationships, which give store management valuable information on the merchandising competence of a buyer or department manager. One is stock turnover, or the rate at which the departmental inventory has been turned into sales over a three-, six-, nine-, or twelve-month period. The other is the departmental open-to-buy, or how carefully a buyer keeps his purchases in line with planned sales and stock on hand.

Stock Turnover

Stock turnover refers to the rate, or number of times during any given period, that the dollar investment in inventory has been turned into sales. This is an extremely important merchandising concept because revenue is not realized until actual sales take place. Store management often uses the stockturn ratio as a measure of the efficiency of each of its merchandising operations.

Computing Stock Turnover Stockturn ratios may be computed either on a cost price or a selling price basis, depending on which system a store uses in evaluating its inventory. Since most medium and large retail organizations evaluate inventories on the basis of retail values, the rate of stockturn based on the retail value of the average inventory is more widely used. However, both methods are shown here.

Under the retail method of inventory evaluation the following formula is used:

$$\text{Rate of stockturn} = \frac{\$ \text{ net sales (at retail)}}{\$ \text{ average inventory (at retail)}}$$

In computing stock turnover on a cost basis, the following formula is used:

$$\text{Rate of stockturn} = \frac{\$ \text{ cost of goods sold}}{\$ \text{ average inventory (at cost)}}$$

"Average inventory" is determined by adding together all inventories for a given period, including the beginning and ending inventories, and dividing the sum by the number of inventories used. Average inventories based only on annual or semiannual beginning and ending figures may not be representative of stock levels maintained throughout the period. This is particularly true in fashion departments and other departments handling merchandise of a highly seasonal nature. The more inventories that are used in computing an average inventory, the more representative the figure. Consequently, most retail organizations use monthly book inventories, as well as the beginning and ending physical inventories for a period in computing the rate of stock turnover for each department or the store as a whole.

Problem

A handbag department with net sales of $100,000 for the fiscal year 1970 took physical inventories at retail values every three months during the year with the following results:

Feb. 4, 1970	$15,260
May 5	16,680
Aug. 4	17,520
Nov. 2	18,890
Feb. 2, 1971	14,550

What was the rate of stock turnover for this department during the 12-month period?

Solution

$$\text{Average stock} = \frac{\text{sum of all inventories}}{\text{number of inventories}}$$
$$= \frac{\$82,900}{5}$$
$$= \$16,580$$

$$\text{Stock turnover} = \frac{\$ \text{ net sales}}{\$ \text{ average inventory}}$$
$$= \frac{\$100,000}{\$16,580}$$
$$= 6.03$$

On occasion it may be desirable to compute the unit rate of stock turnover. The formula for arriving at this figure is:

$$\text{Rate of stockturn} = \frac{\text{number of units sold}}{\text{average inventory in units}}$$

Variations in Turnover Rate The rate of stockturn varies both with the type and with the price of merchandise handled. Lower price ranges tend to turn more rapidly than do higher price ranges in the same classification of merchandise. Also, fashion apparel and accessories tend to turn more rapidly than do home furnishings.

Open-to-Buy

Open-to-buy denotes the amount of money available for merchandise purchases in a given period. In stores using the retail method of inventory evaluation, open-to-buy is stated in retail dollars. It is an arithmetic calculation, made at frequent intervals, of the amount of merchandise that can be received during a period without exceeding the planned closing stock for that period.

As discussed in Chapter 12, planned purchases are a balancing figure between planned beginning and ending inventories, planned sales for the period, and planned markdowns. Open-to-buy is also a balancing figure, but related to actual results rather than planned figures. At the beginning of a period, open-to-buy might be identical with planned purchases. But as orders are placed for delivery within that period, planned purchases are automatically reduced by the retail value of such orders. Most stores make weekly or semimonthly computations for each of their accounting units in order to avoid overstocked conditions.

Planned ending stock is the pivotal figure in calculating open-to-buy. Actual increases or decreases from planned figures for sales and stock affect open-to-buy. Increases in sales over those planned increase open-to-buy if stock on hand does not exceed that planned. In the same way, a stock lower than planned, assuming sales occur as planned, automatically increases the open-to-buy for that period. Stock levels that are higher than planned, with sales proceeding as planned, decrease it. If planned sales fail to materialize, open-to-buy is also decreased.

The formula for determining open-to-buy is as follows:

Open-to-buy = planned sales + planned markdowns + planned ending stock − stock on hand − orders placed for delivery during the period

The *Buyer's Manual*[1] illustrates how interim open-to-buy is calculated:

Suppose the following data represent the condition of a department on May 15 (all amounts at retail):

Initial markon percentage	40%
Planned purchases for May	$7,000
Planned stock, May 1	$9,000
Planned sales, for May	$8,000
Actual stock, May 15	$10,500
Actual sales, May 1–15	$4,500
Merchandise in transit	$1,100
Unfilled orders for May delivery	$2,000

Note that the sales are $500 ahead of planned figures, as $4,500 has been sold during the first half of the month, while the plan was for only $8,000 for the entire month. This means that the purchase allotment may be increased $500 at retail. Also note that the actual stock is $1,500 at retail, above the planned amount ($10,500 minus $9,000), and the purchase allotment must be decreased by this amount.

The calculation at retail of the open-to-buy adjustment is:

Planned purchases for May		$7,000
Add variation of sales from plan		500
		$7,500
Deduct variation of stock from plan		1,500
Adjusted planned purchases		$6,000
Minus: Merchandise in transit	$1,100	
Unfilled orders	2,000	$3,100
Open-to-buy, May 15		$2,900

Retail merchants use arithmetic often in the course of their daily work. Students of merchandising would do well to review a fundamental text on business arithmetic in order to acquire greater competence in working with fractions, decimals, and percentages. Such texts also provide shortcut methods for solving arithmetical problems of a repetitive nature which are easily applied to many of the situations found in retail merchandising.

Reference

[1] *The Buyer's Manual*, pp. 438–439.

Glossary

Accessories Articles worn or carried on the person to enhance the apparel and complete the costume. In fashion retailing, the term "ready-to-wear accessories" may include intimate apparel as well as such visible components of the costume as gloves, shoes, and handbags.

Adaptation A design that reflects the dominant features of the style that inspired it, but is not an exact copy.

Additional Markon An increase in the retail price of merchandise above the price placed on it when it was originally received into stock.

Advance Dating Additional time allowed by a vendor in which to pay for merchandise and still earn a cash discount. Such an extension of normal terms of payment is usually arranged for before goods are shipped and invoiced.

Advertising Any paid-for time or space in a medium such as newspapers or television for the purpose of promoting the sale of goods or enhancing the public's opinion of the advertiser.

Advertising Allowance Concession in price or lump-sum payment, given to a store by a resource to help meet the expense of the store's advertising of his product. Usually offered to help launch a new item or brand, or to publicize brands not adequately advertised by other means.

Advertising Credit Mention of a store's name in the advertisement of a producer.

Advertising Plan A forecast for a specified future period of time of the advertising that is planned to attract customers to and business for the store.

Anticipation An extra discount allowed by some vendors to retailers for payment of bills before they become due.

Apparel In its broadest sense, any fashion item that is worn or carried. In fashion retailing, the word "apparel," if used without modification, applies only to outerwear (coats, suits, dresses, sportswear, etc.) for women, misses, and juniors.

Audited Net Sales Total amount of sales for a given period, computed after returns and allowances have been deducted. These totals are usually circulated by the auditing department of a store and credited to the book inventory of each department.

Automatic Reorder A system for replenishing basic stocks without the buyer's decision in each instance. Such systems require the buyer to set minimums and maximums for stock on hand, and require salespeople or assistants to write up reorders for predetermined amounts whenever stock is found to be approaching minimum levels.

Average Markon The markon obtained when the costs and retails of two or more purchases are consolidated.

Basic Stock Merchandise that enjoys such consistent demand that it must be stocked by the retailer throughout a selling season or year and in a reasonably complete assortment.

Book Inventory The value of the stock of a store or department as reflected in its account books. Under the retail system, all additions and subtractions to stock are recorded from day to day as they occur.

Boutique A shop or section of a store devoted to merchandise that is new and unique. In fashion retailing, boutiques usually sell apparel and accessories, carefully coordinated, in limited assortment, and geared to the tastes of narrow segments of the public. The term is broadened to apply also to a shop or section of a store that caters to the wants of a special group of customers but not necessarily those in search of few-of-a-kind items.

Buyer The executive in charge of one or more departments or classifications in a retail store. Responsibilities include, in addition to buying, the promotion, selling, and inventory management of the goods concerned, and the instruction of salespeople in selling points and fashion features of the merchandise.

Buying Office, Resident An organization located in a major market area that represents a number of noncompeting retail stores in the market.

Buying Plan Detailed plan drawn up to guide purchases for a given period. It is based upon quantities currently on hand and on order and anticipated sales.

Cash Discount A percentage off the face amount of an invoice that is offered by the seller to the purchaser as a premium for payment within a specified period.

Central Buying Purchasing that is done for a number of noncompeting stores from a central point, usually a resident buying office, at which market trends and combined store sales experience are analyzed to guide selections.

Chain Organization A group of retail stores that are centrally owned, each handling similar goods, and which are merchandised from a national or regional headquarters office.

Charge-back A document covering merchandise returned to a vendor for credit or exchange, or covering an allowance or rebate to be granted to the store.

Chambre Syndicale de la Couture Parisienne A trade association of Paris haute couture houses.

Check-out A fast-selling item or style; a hot number. Also the cashier's station in a self-service operation.

Classic A particular style that continues as an accepted fashion over an extended period of time.

Classification An assortment of items, all of which are reasonably substitutable for each other to the customer when she is buying for a specific end-use.

Classification Merchandising A system of recordkeeping and planning that guides inventory management and analyzes results in terms of classifications, instead of or in addition to other departmental data, such as price, size, etc.

COD (Cash on Delivery) Terms of sale under which the invoice is due and payable before the goods can be released by the carrier.

Consignment Selling Merchandise owned by the vendor but placed for sale in a retail store during a specified period. At the end of that period, the retailer is billed for such portions of the stock as he has sold or wishes to retain for sale; the unsold or unwanted portions become eligible for return to vendor. Alternate term: *Memorandum Sale.*

Consolidator A service organization that receives deliveries for a store from various suppliers in a large market center. The merchandise is combined into shipments large enough to qualify for lower transportation rates than they would enjoy if they had traveled separately to their destination.

Converter A textile firm that buys "greige goods," or unfinished fabric, from mills and has various finishes and treatments applied to the product, thus converting a basic textile fabric into a salable fashion fabric.

Cooperative Advertising Funds made available to stores by resources to meet all or part of the cost of the retailer's advertising in behalf of the resource's product.

Coordination In merchandising, arranging to present to the customer an assortment of apparel and accessories that are compatible in fashion and price. The term is also used to describe a promotional effort built around an offering of such related apparel and accessories.

Cost of Goods Sold The purchase price of merchandise sold during a given period plus incoming transportation charges. Gross cost includes only these two elements; net cost allows also for cash discounts earned and any workroom (alteration) costs involved.

Cost Price Unit price at which goods are billed to a store, exclusive of any cash discounts which may apply to the purchase.

Costume The sum total of the apparel and accessories worn by an individual at a given time. In fashion merchandising, the term also refers to a two- or three-piece garment produced and sold as a unit.

Costume Jewelry Jewelry that is mass-produced; made from such materials as plastics, wood, glass, brass or base metals (sometimes coated with precious metals) and which uses stones made from clay, glass, or plastic substances.

Couture French term for fine sewing, used in the fashion business to mean the design originators, not necessarily in Paris, and the creative, custom phases of their work. *Couturier* is the male proprietor or designer of a couture house. *Couturière* is the female proprietor or designer of a couture house. *Haute couture* is the literal translation of "fine sewing" applied to high fashion houses whose designers impose their own ideas, rather than those of individual customers, in creating styles.

Craze A fad or fashion that is accompanied by much crowd excitement or emotion.

Cumulative Markon The difference between total delivered cost and total original retail values of all goods handled within a specific period, including the inventory at the beginning of the period.

Custom Apparel made to the order of individual customers, rather than produced and sold as ready-to-wear.

Customer Allowance A reduction from the marked retail price of goods, made to compensate the customer for defects or other causes of dissatisfaction. A special form of markdown.

Cutter A manufacturer who produces apparel by cutting and sewing purchased fabric. The term is more commonly applied to menswear producers than to those in the women's field.

Cutting-up Trades Apparel-producing industries that make garments by cutting and sewing fabric.

Dating A term usually found in conjunction with cash discounts; it refers to the period of time allowed by a vendor for the taking of such discounts.

Delivered Cost The price at which goods are billed to a store, plus transportation charges.

Delivery Date The date by which a vendor is required to ship merchandise to a store in order to comply with the terms of purchase. Failure to meet the delivery date is usually considered cause for cancellation of the order by the purchaser.

Demonstrator In a retail store, a salesperson who devotes his or her efforts to selling and managing the stock of one manufacturer's line. Such persons are usually trained and subsidized by the producer concerned.

Department Manager The executive charged with the operation of a selling department of a store. Usually this is the buyer, but in branch stores the department manager is concerned with stock and sales at his particular unit and may serve in several departments under two or more buyers operating from the main store.

Departmental Operating Statement A detailed financial statement for the buyer, which summarizes the results of his operation over a given period of time, with specific reference to income from sales, cost of goods sold, gross margin, operating expenses, and operating profit. Comparisons with previous year's results and with planned figures are often included in such reports.

Department Store A retail establishment employing 25 or more people; it sells merchandise in each of three categories: home furnishings, household linens and dry goods, and apparel and accessories for men, women, and children.

Design A specific or individual interpretation or version of a style.

Designer The person who gives substance to a fashion idea by expressing it in the form of a style or design for fabric, apparel, or accessories.

Details (of design) Variations in design, such as are achieved through trimmings, skirt lengths, shoulder, waist, or sleeve treatments, etc.

Direct Expenses Those costs of operating a department that are incurred as a direct result of its operations and that would cease if the department itself ceased to exist.

Display A visual presentation of merchandise; in retail stores display takes two forms—window and interior.

Dissection Any portion of a department's merchandise for which sales and inventory figures are separately maintained.

Dollar Merchandise Plan A carefully worked out estimate of anticipated sales, usually over a six-month period, integrated with estimates of inventory levels and purchases compatible with management's sales and profit objectives.

Dummy Invoice A document prepared by the retailer as a temporary substitute for a vendor's invoice if the latter should not be available when the merchandise is to be received, marked, and placed in stock.

Editorial Credit The reference to a specific retail store as a source for a fashion item featured editorially in a consumer publication.

EDP (Electronic Data Processing) The use of computers to record and report information.

Employee Discount A percentage reduction from marked retail prices allowed by retailers to their employees on purchases made within the store.

EOM (End-of-Month) Terms Terms of payment in which the days allowed for the taking of discounts are counted from the last day of the month in which the invoice is dated instead of from the actual date of the invoice itself.

Event A retail "happening"; the exercise of showmanship to draw customers into a store for a show, exhibit, talk, or similar attraction, or for an exceptional merchandise offering.

Extra Dating The granting of a specified additional number of days beyond the regular date on which payment of an invoice would fall due or cash discount can be earned. Usually written "-30x" or "-60x," as the case may be, to indicate that an additional 30 or 60 days are permitted.

Eyeball Control Visual inspection of stock to check for adequacy of supply. In some instances, markers are placed on bins or racks to indicate points at which reordering may become necessary.

Fabric Library Fabric swatches with attached information on where to buy them, their prices, and delivery dates.

Fad A short-lived fashion, usually accepted by only a narrow group within the total population and generally concerned with some unimportant detail of dress.

Fair-Trade Price A retail price fixed by the producer of a branded article, below which retailers are prohibited by law from making sales. Legal in some but not all states.

Fashion A style that is currently accepted by the majority of a group at any given period and place. Also, the force that impels people to continue to seek ever newer expressions of their personalities and way of life in dress, home furnishings, or other respects.

Fashion Bureau An individual or department assigned to collect and assess information on fashion trends from all available sources and make this information available to the store's personnel.

Fashion Business A broad term which embraces both the fashion industry and fashion retailers and also includes auxiliary enterprises, such as publications and services.

Fashion Coordinator In retail stores, the executive charged with the responsibility for keeping abreast of fashion developments, acting as a source of authoritative fashion information to others in the organization, and assisting the merchandising and promotion executives in buying, promoting, displaying, and selling properly coordinated fashion apparel and accessories.

Fashion Cycle The rise, culmination, and decline in popular acceptance of a style. Usually represented visually by a bell or skewed bell curve.

Fashion Forecast Analysis of current fashion trends in the light of what is expected to be accepted by the customers of a store or other firm in a future period.

Fashion Image In retailing, those aspects of a store's image that reflect its position in matters of fashion, such as the degree of leadership it exercises and the stage of the fashion cycle that its assortments represent.

Fashion Industry The various industries that produce apparel and accessories for women, misses, and juniors, and the primary industries that supply the materials of production. Also, in trade parlance, any industry that is markedly responsive to fashion is "a" fashion industry. "The" fashion industry, however, is composed of primary and secondary producers of feminine apparel and accessories.

Fashion Influential A person whose advice is sought by her associates; her adoption of a fashion gives it prestige among the group.

Fashion Innovator An individual who is quicker than her associates to try out a new fashion and is the earliest visual communicator of a new fashion in her circle.

Fashion Merchandising Policy A long-range guide for a store's executives, spelling out fashion aims, standards of quality, price ranges, attitudes toward competition, assortment to be carried and other pertinent factors.

Fashion Trend The direction in which a fashion is moving in its cycle; tendency toward an approaching fashion.

Fine Jewelry The jewelry counterpart of haute couture apparel; it is jewelry made from precious metals and using only gemstones.

Flair Instinctive and intuitive ability to do or use things in an unusual way or in a way favorably stamped with the personality of the individual.

Flash Sales Report Unaudited report of previous day's sales of a department or classification.

FOB (Freight-on-Board) A term which designates the point from which the store is to pay transportation on incoming shipments. "FOB shipping point" means that the store pays all charges from the vendor's shipping point. "FOB store" means that the vendor pays all charges up to the store's receiving dock.

Ford   A style or design that is produced by many different manufacturers at many different prices simultaneously. It is usually widely adopted, widely copied, widely accepted, and soon discarded.

Form   A term often used synonymously with shape. Form denotes the total organization of an object—its external shape as well as its internal nature.

Franchised Store   An independently owned store that sells branded lines of merchandise or services established or manufactured by a franchiser and that pays the franchiser a percentage of sales for use of the name.

Freight Allowed   An arrangement under which the store pays the transportation charges on incoming merchandise but is permitted to charge back all or part of that cost to the vendor.

Good Taste   The ability to make the most artistic and appropriate use of current fashions. Good taste forbids the use of artistically beautiful styles that are not in fashion.

Greige Goods   In textiles, the unfinished fabric as it comes from the loom, before bleaching, dyeing, printing, or the application of special finishes. In hosiery, the knitted product in its undyed and unboarded state.

Gross Margin   Dollar difference between net sales for a period and net cost of goods sold during that period. *Gross margin percentage* is calculated by dividing net sales into this figure.

Gross National Product (GNP)   The market value of the nation's total output of goods and services in any calendar year.

Gross Sales   Total sales for a given period before customer returns and allowances have been deducted.

Harmony   Attribute of any work of art when the plastic elements have been arranged together artistically to produce a look that is pleasing and in good taste.

High Fashion   Those styles or designs accepted by a limited group of fashion leaders, the elite among those consumers who are first to accept fashion change; generally high in price.

Hot Item   An item which demonstrates rapid salability; usually a new style or item capable of generating prompt and strong customer demand.

Impulse Merchandise   Goods susceptible to spontaneous rather than planned purchase by consumers. Such goods, in retail stores, profit from exposure in areas of high customer traffic.

Income, Personal   That money which the individual actually has available to spend, save, and pay taxes with. *Disposable income,* that money an individual or family has left out of personal income to spend or save after having paid taxes. *Discretionary income,* that money which an individual or family has left over after buying such necessities as food, clothing, shelter, and transportation.

Indirect Expenses   Those costs of operating a department that are not directly attributable to its activities and that would remain even if a particular department ceased to exist; overhead shared by all departments.

Initial Markon   The difference between the delivered cost of merchandise and the retail value placed on it when it is first priced and put into stock.

Institutional Advertising   The attempt to sell the store, its services, assortments, fashion image, participation in community events, etc., rather than specific merchandise; seeks to promote goodwill, image, and fashion prestige.

Integrated Operation   A mill or group of mills under one management that performs all processes of textile fabric production from selecting the fiber to finishing the fabric and readying it for sale; characteristic of woolen or worsted fabric production.

Integration *Horizontal* refers to the absorption by one company of other companies functioning on the same level of production. *Vertical* refers to the absorption by one company of other companies engaged in all stages of production from raw materials to sales of the finished product.

Interselling The assignment of salespeople so that each is permitted or required to cover two or more related departments instead of being restricted to a single department or classification.

Invoice An itemized statement of the merchandise, prices, and terms that apply to a vendor's shipment; bill.

Irregulars Merchandise having defects that may affect appearance but not wear.

Leased Department A department that is run ostensibly by the host store, but is actually operated for the store by an outside firm, which pays the store a percentage of sales as rental.

Line The silhouette and details of any apparel style. A collection of designs or styles offered for sale by a manufacturer to retail store buyers.

Line-for-Line Copies A procedure for making exact copies of a style or design, usually a *couture* style, to standard measurements by machine methods instead of being made to individual measurements entirely by hand.

List Price Retail price suggested or fixed by the producer rather than by the retailer. Cost prices, in such cases, are usually stated as percentage reductions from list.

Long-Run Fashions Styles whose fashion cycles extend over more seasons than most.

Maintained Markon The difference between the delivery cost of merchandise and the price at which it is actually sold; allows for markdowns and stock shortages, but not workroom cost or cash discounts earned.

Markdown Reduction from retail price of an item or group of items. *Markdown percentage* for a given period is obtained by dividing the total reductions by net sales for that period.

Markdown Cancellation An increase in the retail price of an item or group of items that had previously been reduced; the increase may be up to or toward the retail price at which the goods were originally placed in stock, but not higher.

Market The potential customers for a product or service. A store's trading area. A city in which the showrooms of producers of a given type of merchandise are concentrated. The period during which producers of a given type of merchandise show their lines to retailers for the upcoming season.

Market Representative In retail parlance, the executive of a resident buying office who gives intensive coverage to a particular grouping of merchandise and makes information obtained about it available to buyers of stores served by the resident office.

Marketing Concept Customer-oriented marketing management.

Markon The difference between the billed cost price and the original retail price of merchandise.

Markup An older term for "markon," still used by some retailers for either the difference between cost and retail prices or for increases in the retail prices of merchandise previously priced and placed in stock.

Mass Fashions (Volume Fashions) Styles or designs that are widely accepted and therefore can be produced and sold in large quantities. Generally these are moderate to low in price.

Memorandum Sale (or Purchase) Consigned merchandise. Title remains with the vendor over a specified period, during which goods are placed on sale in a retail store. At the end of the period, unsold goods are eligible for return to the vendor. The sold or retained portion is billed to the merchant.

Merchandise Manager A major executive charged with supervising the buying, selling, and inventory management activities in a store. If his responsibilities embrace the entire store, he is known as a General Merchandise Manager; if only a section of the store, a Divisional Merchandise Manager.

Merchandise Transfer A report of the transfer of merchandise from one accounting unit of a store to another. Goods may be transferred from one department to another, from parent store to branch department, or from one branch to another.

Merchandising The business of analyzing consumer demand, buying and selling goods to meet that demand, managing inventories, and coping with competition.

Model Stock A unit assortment plan, within budgetary limits, with its components distributed in such a manner as to best satisfy customer demand at a specific time.

Needle Trades Apparel-producing industries; cutting-up trades.

Net Profit That portion of the income from net sales that remains after merchandise costs, expenses, and taxes have been paid. If the income from net sales does not cover these elements entirely, a net loss, rather than a profit, results.

Net Sales Gross sales, less customer returns and allowances, for a given period.

Never-Outs Items that should never be permitted to run out of stock during a year or season.

These are items for which demand is so constant that merchants strive to keep them in stock at all times during their selling season. Their steady, predictable sales make them profitable to handle and cause them to be referred to by stores as "bread and butter" items.

Number The identifying number assigned to a style or design by a producer; industry term for a style or design.

Opening The first showing of a new season's line by a producer or an entire industry.

Open-to-Buy (OTB) The amount of merchandise that a store or department may receive into stock in a given period without exceeding its planned inventory levels.

Operating Statement A report to the management of a store or department, showing net sales, cost of goods sold, expenses, and the resultant net operating profit or loss for the period.

Packing Slip Document accompanying a vendor's shipment and itemizing its contents. Often it is a duplicate, without prices, of the invoice that covers the shipment.

Periodic Stock Control Unit control system in which stock is counted and recorded at regular intervals and sales for the intervening periods are computed.

Perpetual Inventory Control A unit control system in which orders, receipts, and sales are recorded as they occur and stock on hand is subsequently computed.

Physical Inventory The dollar value of stock on hand in a store or department, obtained by taking an actual count, listing all merchandise by number of units, the price of each, and calculating the totals.

Plastic Art Elements Line, form, space, color, and texture. These elements are called *plastic* because it is possible to manipulate them.

Policy A settled, clearly defined course of action or method of doing business deemed necessary, expedient, or advantageous; guidelines established by management for the executives of an organization.

Preferred Resource A resource whose merchandise has achieved a record of success in a store, and with whom the store therefore concentrates a considerable share of its purchases.

Press Release A written statement of news that has occurred or is about to occur, the source of the information, and the date after which its use is permissible.

Prestige Advertising Advertising that attempts to establish the store's reputation for fashion authority, complete selections, general progressiveness, and to build confidence in the store's label.

Preretailing Assignment by the merchant of retail prices to goods at the time the order is placed. This permits the calculation of retail values of merchandise on order and also expedites the checking and marking procedures when the goods arrive at the store.

Prêt-à-Porter French term for ready-to-wear. In fashion retailing, the term is reserved for merchandise produced by the ready-to-wear units of *couture* houses in Paris and other Continental fashion centers.

Preticketing Premarking done by the vendor for the retailer. Usually the vendor attaches a store's own price tickets on which are marked style numbers, selling prices, and other pertinent data. Often such tickets are punched for EDP as well as printed.

Prior Stock Merchandise which has remained unsold in a retail store for longer than the merchant considers acceptable and which therefore has been singled out for special attention directed toward its early clearance.

Private Brand A trademark or brand name owned by a store or group of stores for the retailer's exclusive use in his community. The merchandise may be made up to the brand owner's specifications, or it may be purchased from a vendor's regular stock and specially labeled.

Program Merchandising A procedure whereby a retailer and a key resource jointly make merchandising and promotion plans for the store or department, working as much as a year in advance, in order to facilitate mutual cooperation and profit.

Promotional Advertising The endeavor to create sales of specific items.

Purchase Journal A record maintained for a store or department of all invoices for goods received and all charge-backs to or claims against vendors.

Purchase Order A written, contractual agreement between store and vendor for the purchase of certain specified goods, to be delivered in accordance with conditions written or printed on the face and back of the order form.

Quantity Discounts Special percentage reductions in vendors' selling prices, apart from cash discounts, provided the retailer purchases certain specified minimum quantities.

Rack Jobber Maintains stocks of convenience-type goods chiefly in supermarkets, drugstores, automatic vending machines, and other similar retail outlets.

Rag Business An affectionate name for the industries that produce fashion apparel.

Rayon The first man-made fiber; wood pulp or cotton linters are used as a base, subjected to various chemical and mechanical processes, to produce filaments that can be spun into yarn.

Ready-to-Wear Apparel produced in factories in a range of sizes from which the customer can select her approximate size. Factory-produced apparel, as distinguished from custom-made or homemade apparel.

Receiving Apron A form, often multipart, prepared by the Receiving Department of a store, on which is recorded all pertinent information regarding an incoming shipment. The form is used to identify the shipment for accounting purposes and to record various information regarding the shipment as required by the store.

Regular or Ordinary Dating Terms of sale under which the discount period and the date on which payment becomes due are calculated from the date of the invoice.

Reorder Number A style or item that enjoys a steady or usually fast demand. The term is applied to fashion items that require close watch and prompt reorder action by the merchant, rather than to basics.

Reserve Requisition Control A form of periodic stock count control under which all merchandise in the forward stock (i.e., on the selling floor) is considered sold and counts are made only of the reserve stock (i.e., in stockrooms remote from the selling floor. As forward stock runs low, more is requisitioned from the reserve. Sales are calculated by adding up the requisitions made throughout a given period.

Resource A producer or wholesaler from whom a merchant purchases goods for resale.

Retail Method of Inventory A method of accounting in which all entries relating to an inventory, such as sales, purchases, markdowns, etc. are reported and recorded at their retail values. Purchases are entered also at cost.

Retail Price Price at which merchandise is marked for sale or actually sold.

ROG (Receipt-of-Goods) Dating Terms of sale under which the payment date and discount period of an invoice are calculated from the date on which the merchant receives the goods, rather than from the invoice date. Used where the time in transit is likely to be considerable.

Sale, Average Gross A figure obtained by dividing the net sales of a department or classification throughout a given period by the number of sales transactions that have taken place during the same period.

Sales Plan The merchandise budget. A detailed projection of anticipated sales for a specified period, normally six months, along with the purchases, inventory levels, etc., required to achieve these objectives.

Sales Promotion The coordination of advertising, display, publicity, and personal salesmanship in order to promote profitable sales.

Sales-Supporting Staff Store employees not personally engaged in selling to customers.

Season Letter A code used on retail price tickets to identify goods in stock as to season or month of receipt.

Seconds Merchandise having defects that could affect wear as well as appearance.

Selection Factors The elements that significantly influence the consumer's choice of goods.

Self-Selection Selling Merchandise so displayed and arranged in open stock that customers can make preliminary selections without the aid of a salesperson but need the services of the latter in order to complete the sale.

Self-Service Selling Merchandise displayed and arranged in open stock for the customer to make her own selections without the aid of a salesperson. Selections are then taken to a check-out counter to be wrapped or otherwise packaged and paid for.

Shop Merchandising The setting aside of an area of a store for customers of special types and for merchandise for special purposes. Gathered in such areas are both apparel and accessories, if this is desirable. Decor, atmosphere, and salespeople are selected with the needs of the special customer in mind. Examples include shops for teen-agers or college girls, ski shops, and career-girl shops.

Short-Run Fashion A style that takes fewer seasons than most to complete its fashion cycle.

Shrinkage Another term for inventory shortage.

Silhouette The overall outline or contour of a costume, often referred to as shape or form.

Space The background area on which individual shapes or decorative details are imposed.

Specialty Store A retail establishment that handles primarily merchandise within fairly narrow categories, such as women's apparel, men's apparel, women's accessories, home furnishings, shoes, and so on.

Stock, Age of A summary report of the number of pieces of merchandise in each classification and price line that bear the same season letter identification for purposes of obtaining the value of merchandise remaining in stock that came in during the same period. The purpose of such reports is to call attention to old stock so that steps can be taken to liquidate it.

Stock, Average The average dollar value of a stock maintained throughout a given period. It is obtained by adding to the opening and closing inventories the values of all intervening inventories and dividing this sum by the total number of inventories used. Average stock in units may be obtained by the same procedure, using units of merchandise instead of dollars.

Stock-Sales Ratio A formula used in planning relationships between inventory and sales. It is obtained by dividing sales for a given month into the retail value of inventory at the beginning of that month. This ratio is used primarily in planning beginning-of-the-month inventory in the merchandise budget.

Stock Shortage A condition that exists when the dollar value of an actual physical inventory of merchandise in stock is less than that which is indicated in the book inventory.

Store Image The character or personality that a store presents to the public. The sum total of whatever makes a store individual and different from others in its community.

Style A characteristic or distinctive mode or method of expression, presentation, or conception in the field of some art; a specific design.

Style Number Number assigned to identify a style or design in a maker's line or a retailer's stock.

Target Customers Those customers a store's merchandise, services, and entire atmosphere are planned to attract.

Taste Ability to recognize and appreciate that which is both beautiful and appropriate.

Terms of Sale A statement of the time allowed by the vendor for payment of an invoice, any discounts that are permitted, and any other applicable conditions of sale.

Textile Fabrics Cloth made from textile fibers by one of the following methods: weaving, knitting, braiding, felting, crocheting, knotting, laminating, or bonding.

Textile Fibers Hairlike units of raw material from which textile fabric is made.

Texture The look and feel of all types of material, woven or nonwoven.

Trade Discount A percentage allowance or series of such allowances from the list price of merchandise, in order to determine the cost price that the merchant is to pay. Such discounts apply before cash discount is calculated. Trade discounts differ from cash discounts in that they are not offered as a premium for prompt payment and are deductible whenever the invoice is paid.

Trade Shows, Regional Regional showings of vendors' lines usually held in a single location such as a hotel or merchandise mart in major cities throughout the country. Such trade shows, although not representing the various vendors' complete lines, are held as a service to merchants in adjacent areas who may or may not attend major showings in the major market areas.

Traffic (Customer) Number of persons who enter a store or department and thus are exposed to the appeal of its merchandise.

Traffic (Transportation) Department Executive and staff in a store responsible for executing transportation policies of the store; routing all shipments from vendor to store; tracing or expediting shipments when necessary; filing claims against carriers for loss or damage to shipments in transit; issuing claims against vendors for short shipments and shipments sent by wrong route, etc.

Trunk Show Showing of a vendor's complete line to an audience of consumers assembled for that purpose by a retail organization, so that customers may see and possibly order style numbers, sizes, and colors not stocked by the store.

Turnover The number of times during a period that a stock is sold and replaced. Normally, the figure is calculated by dividing net sales for a given period by the average retail value of the inventory during the same period.

Unit Control A system or systems for recording the number of pieces or units of merchandise bought, sold, in stock, and on order, with further dissections as required.

Variety Store A retail organization that primarily carries limited lines of apparel and accessories for men, women, and children, as well as limited assortments of other goods. Price lines are generally low to medium.

Vendor A wholesaler or manufacturer who supplies a store with merchandise for resale. See Resource.

Vendor Returns Merchandise returned to vendor for credit or replacement. Also called "charge-back."

Vignette A display that shows a product or group of products in actual use.

Want Slips Written reports from salespeople to buyers, which list items requested by customers but not in stock. Some stores or buyers also request such reports from salespeople of items observed to be running low or out, whether or not customers have asked for them that day.

Yarn A continuous thread produced by twisting or spinning fibers together.

Bibliography

Alderfer, E. B., and H. S. Michl, *Economics of American Industry,* 3d ed., McGraw-Hill Book Company, New York, 1957.

American Marketing Association, "Report of the Definitions Committee." *Journal of Marketing,* October, 1948.

Appel, Joseph H., *A Business Biography of John Wanamaker,* The Macmillan Company, New York, 1930.

Arnold, Pauline, and Percival White, *Clothes and Cloth: America's Apparel Business,* Holiday House, Inc., New York, 1961.

Barber, Bernard, *Social Stratification,* Harcourt, Brace and Company, Inc., New York, 1957.

Barker, Clare Wright, Ira Dennis Anderson, and J. Donald Butterworth, *Principles of Retailing,* 3d ed., McGraw-Hill Book Company, New York, 1956.

Beaton, Cecil, *The Glass of Fashion,* Doubleday & Company, Inc., New York, 1954.

Bell, Quentin, *On Human Finery,* The Hogarth Press, Ltd., London, 1947.

Binder, Pearl, *Muffs and Morals,* George G. Harrap & Co., Ltd., London, 1953.

Brenner, Barbara, *Careers and Opportunities in Fashion,* E. P. Dutton & Co., Inc., New York, 1964.

Brenninkmeyer, Ingrid, *The Sociology of Fashion,* Librairie du Recueil Sirey, Paris, 1963.

Brockman, Helen L., *The Theory of Fashion Design,* John Wiley & Sons, Inc., New York, 1965.

Brooke, Iris, and James Laver, *English Costume of the Eighteenth Century,* A. & C. Black, Ltd., London, 1958.

Brown, Lyndon O., *Marketing and Distribution Research,* 3d ed., The Ronald Press, New York, 1955.

The Buyer's Manual, rev. ed., Merchandising Division, National Retail Merchants Association, New York, 1965.

Carlyle, Thomas, *Sartor Resartus,* Doubleday & Company, Inc., Garden City, N.Y., 1937.

CBS/Columbia Group Market Research, *Records and Music, Facts and Figures,* New York, 1967.

Chase, Edward T., "Four Days Shalt Thou Labor," *New York Times Magazine,* September 6, 1964.

Cheskin, Louis, *Why People Buy,* Liveright Publishing Corporation, New York, 1959.

Cobliner, W. Godfrey, "Feminine Fashion as an Aspect of Group Psychology: Analysis of Written Replies Received by Means of a Questionnaire," *Journal of Social Psychology,* Vol. 31, pp. 283–289, 1950.

Copeland, Melvin T., *Principles of Merchandising,* A. W. Shaw Company, New York, 1924.

Cotton from Field to Fabric, National Cotton Council of America, Memphis, Tenn. (undated).

Cundiff, Edward W., and Richard R. Still, *Basic Marketing,* Prentice-Hall, Inc., Englewood Cliffs, N.J., 1964.

Dardis, Rachel, "The Power of Fashion," *Proceedings of the Twentieth Annual Conference, College Teachers of Textiles and Clothing, Eastern Region,* New York, 1966.

Daves, Jessica, *Ready-Made Miracle,* G. P. Putnam's Sons, New York, 1967.

Departmental Merchandising and Operating Results of 1967, Controllers' Congress, National Retail Merchants Association, New York, 1968.

Dunlap, Knight, "The Development and Function of Clothing," *Journal of General Psychology,* 1:64–78, 1928.

Entenberg, Robert D., "Implications of Interfirm Competition at the Retail Level," *Journal of Retailing,* 43 (2):1–8, Summer, 1967.

Escabosa, Hector, "The Heartbeat of Retailing," *Readings in Modern Retailing,* National Retail Merchants Association, New York, 1969.

Facts and Figures on Footwear, National Shoe Manufacturers Association, New York, 1961.

Fischel, Oskar, and Max von Boehn, *Modes and Manners of the Nineteenth Century as Represented in the Pictures and Engravings of the Time,* translated by M. Edwardes, E. P. Dutton & Co., Inc., New York, 1909.

Fitzgibbon, Bernice, *Macy's, Gimbels and Me,* Simon and Schuster, New York, 1967.

Flügel, J. C., *The Psychology of Clothes,* 3d ed., The Hogarth Press, Ltd., London, 1950.

Foley, Caroline, "Fashion," *Economic Journal* (London), 3:458, 1893.

Friedman, Clara H., *The Coat and Suit Survey: An Analysis by the National Board of the Coat and Suit Industry,* New York, 1964, 1965.

Garland, Madge, *Fashion,* Penguin Books, Inc., Baltimore, 1962.

Glove Life, National Association of Glove Manufacturers, Inc., Gloversville, N.Y. (undated).

Gold, Annalee, *How to Sell Fashion,* Fairchild Publications, Inc., New York, 1968.

Greenberg, Allan, and Mary Joan Glynn, *A Study of Young People,* Doyle Dane Bernbach Inc., New York, 1966.

Hansen, Henny Harold, *Costumes and Styles,* E. P. Dutton & Co., Inc., New York, 1956.

Hearn, Lafcadio, *Japan, An Attempt at Interpretation,* The Macmillan Company, New York, 1904.

Hobbs, Lisa, *I Saw Red China,* McGraw-Hill Book Company, New York, 1966.

Hurlock, Elizabeth B., *The Psychology of Dress,* The Ronald Press, New York, 1929.

Jarnow, Jeannette, and Beatrice Judelle, *Inside the Fashion Business,* John Wiley & Sons, Inc., New York, 1965.

Joseph, Marjorie Lockwood, "Changes in Women's Daytime Dress as Related to Other Selected Cultural Factors During the First and Third Decades of the Twentieth Century," unpublished doctoral dissertation, Pennsylvania State University Graduate School, Department of Clothing and Textiles, 1962.

Judelle, Beatrice, "The Changing Customer: 1910–1960," *Stores,* November, 1960.

———, "Classification Merchandising in the Fashion Departments," *Stores,* September, 1965.

King, Charles W., "Fashion Adoption: A Rebuttal to the 'Trickle-Down Theory,'" *Proceedings of the Winter Conference, American Marketing Association,* New York, December, 1963, pp. 108–125.

———, "The Innovator in the Fashion Adoption Process," *Proceedings of the Winter Conference, American Marketing Association,* New York, December, 1964, pp. 324–339.

Kroeber, A. L., "On the Principles of Order in Civilization as Exemplified by Change in Fashion," *American Anthropologist,* 21:235–263, July–September, 1919.

Laver, James, *Dress,* John Murray (Publishers), Ltd., London, 1966.

———, *Taste and Fashion,* rev. ed., George G. Harrap & Co., Ltd., London, 1946.

Leather in Our Lives, Leather Industries of America, New York (undated).

Lester, Katherine M., *Historic Costume,* Charles A. Bennett Co., Peoria, Ill., 1956.

MacSwiggen, Amelia E., "Early Textile Mills," *The Town Crier,* Weed Publishers, Inc., Marblehead, Mass., April 14, 1965.

Metropolitan Life Insurance Company, *Statistical Bulletin,* February, 1965, pp. 3–4.

Morton, Grace Margaret, *The Arts of Costume and Personal Appearance,* 3d ed., John Wiley & Sons, Inc., New York, 1964.

Murphy, Michelle, *Two Centuries of French Fashion,* Brooklyn Institute of Arts and Sciences, The Brooklyn Museum, 1949.

Murray, Anne W., "Four Centuries of Dress in America," *Proceedings of Eastern Region,* College Teachers of Textiles and Clothing, College Park, Md., 1965, pp. 26–34.

NRMA's Standard Classifications, Merchandising Division, National Retail Merchants Association, New York, 1967.

Nystrom, Paul H., *Economics of Fashion,* The Ronald Press, New York, 1928.

———, *Fashion Merchandising,* The Ronald Press, New York, 1932.

Parker, S. S., and L. A. Mayer, "The Decade of the Discretionary Dollar," *Fortune,* June, 1959.

Potter, M. David, and Bernard P. Corbman, *Textiles: Fiber to Fabric,* 4th ed., Gregg Division, McGraw-Hill Book Company, New York, 1967.

Readings in Modern Retailing, National Retail Merchants Association, New York, 1969.

Richardson, Jane, and A. L. Kroeber, "Three Centuries of Women's Dress Fashions: A Quantitative Analysis," *Anthropological Record,* 5(2), 1940.

Roach, Mary Ellen, and Joanne Bubolz Eicher, *Dress, Adornment, and the Social Order,* John Wiley & Sons, Inc., New York, 1965.

Robinson, Dwight E., "The Economics of Fashion Demand," *The Quarterly Journal of Economics,* 75:376–398, August, 1961.

———, "Fashion Theory and Product Design," *Harvard Business Review,* 36(6):126–138, November–December, 1958.

———, "The Importance of Fashions in Taste to Business History: An Introductory Essay," *Business History Review,* 37(1, 2):5–36, Spring/Summer, 1963.

Robinson, O. Preston, Christine H. Robinson and George H. Zeiss, *Successful Retail Salesmanship,* 3d ed., Prentice-Hall, Inc., Englewood Cliffs, N.J., 1961.

Roe, John, *The Sociological Concept of Capital,* The Macmillan Company, London, 1834.

Sapir, Edward, "Fashion," *Encyclopaedia of the Social Sciences,* Vol. VI, The Macmillan Company, New York, 1931, pp. 139–144.

Sharpe, Deborah, "Sociological and Psychological Communications Through Color," *Proceedings of the Twentieth Annual Conference, College Teachers of Textiles and Clothing, Eastern Region,* New York, October 19–22, 1966, p. 10.

Silk: How and Where It Is Produced, H. T. Gaddum & Company, Ltd., Manchester, England, 1961.

Simmel, George, "Fashion," *American Journal of Sociology,* 62:541–558, May, 1957. Reprinted from the *International Quarterly,* 10:130–155, October, 1904.

Spencer, Herbert, *Principles of Sociology,* Vol. II, D. Appleton & Co., Inc., New York, 1882–83.

Survey of Current Business, Office of Business Economics, U. S. Department of Commerce, Washington, D. C., July 1968.

Tarde, Gabriel, *The Laws of Imitation,* Henry Holt and Company, New York, 1903.

Udell, Jon G., "A New Approach to Consumer Motivation," *Journal of Retailing,* 40:6–10, Winter, 1964–65.

U.S. Industrial Outlook, Business and Defense Services Administration, U. S. Department of Commerce, Washington, D. C., 1969.

Veblen, Thorstein, *The Theory of the Leisure Class,* New American Library of World Literature, Inc., New York, 1963.

Wattel, Harold L., *Annual Economic Report,* National Millinery Planning Board, Inc., New York, 1966.

What Is Silk? International Silk Association, New York, 1962.

Wilcox, R. Turner, *Five Centuries of American Costume,* Charles Scribner's Sons, New York, 1963.

Wingate, Isabel B., Karen R. Gillespie, and Betty G. Addison, *Know Your Merchandise,* 3d ed., Gregg Division, McGraw-Hill Book Company, New York, 1964.

Wingate, John W., and Joseph S. Friedlander, *The Management of Retail Buying,* Prentice-Hall, Inc., Englewood Cliffs, N. J., 1963.

Wittkin, Herbert, "An Image Is A Multi-Faceted Thing," *Readings In Modern Retailing,* National Retail Merchants Association, 1969.

Young, Agnes Brooke, *Recurring Cycles of Fashion, 1760–1937,* Harper & Brothers, New York, 1937.

Young, Kimball, *Social Psychology,* 3d ed., Appleton-Century-Crofts, Inc., New York, 1956.

Index

Abraham & Straus, 345
Acceptance of fashion, 6–7, 52
Accessories, 32
    apparel and, 138
    manufacturers of, 138–159
    as short-run fashion, 57–58
Accessory trades, careers in, 354
Account executives, 361
Acrylics, 90
Actresses, 80
Adaptations, 55, 127
Adjustments, customer preference
        determined by, 190
Adrian, 129
Advertisements
    fashion demand and, 25
    institutional, 283
    promotional, 283, 289
    target groups and, 335
Advertising
    by apparel manufacturers,
        131–132
    illus., 128
    careers in, 351, 353, 360–364
    cooperative, 290–292
    by cosmetic industry, 149
    direct-mail, 293
    fashion, 283
        and customer preferences,
            189
        through miscellaneous
            media, 292–294
        newspaper (see News-
            papers)
        plan for, 283, 285–287,
            289–290
    of furs, illus., 117
    by textile fabric industry, 101
    by textile fiber industries,
        92, 94
Advertising agencies, 360–361
Advertising agreement, illus., 291
Advertising request, 286, illus., 287
Advertising results report, illus.,
        289
Age-mix, fashion demand and,
        19–20
Age-of-stock reports, 254–256
Alexander's, 308, 342
Allied Kid Company, 105
Allied Stores, 176, 269
Altman, B., & Company, 178
American Designers Group, 132
American fashions, international
        character of, 349
American Marketing Associa-
        tion, 76, 366

Anticipation, 376
    cash discounts and, 213
Antonelli, 73
Apparel
    accessories and, 138
    definition of, 3
    intimate (see Intimate apparel)
Apparel fashion game, 61–65
Apparel manufacturing industry,
        120–137
    centers of fashion inspiration
        for, 126–127, 129–131
    history of, 120–122
    marketing trends in, 132–134,
        136
    mechanization of, illus.,
        124–125
    merchandising activities of,
        131–132
    operational patterns within,
        123–126
    organization of, 122–123
Apparel trades
    careers in, 351–353
    careers with suppliers to,
        353–354
Archeology, fashion and, 43
Art, fashion and, 12–13
Artists, careers as, 356, 361
Assistant buyers, 355–356
Associated Dry Goods Corpora-
        tion, 177, 269
Assortments (see Merchandising
        assortments)
Average cost, determination of, 373
Average gross sale, 258–259

Baez, Joan, 80–81
Balance sheet, 366–367
Balenciaga, 63, 184
Basic stock lists, 254
Beatles, The, 50, 67, 78
"Beat Last Year" book, 203,
        249–250, 285
Beaton, Cecil, 20
Beau Brummel, 79
Beene, Geoffrey, 130
Bell, Quentin, 16, 23, 79
Belts, 57
Bendel, Henri, 335
Bergdorf-Goodman, 335
Bertin, Rose, 42, 157
Best & Company, 178
Bikini, 5
Blass, Bill, 130
Bloomer, Mrs. Amelia, 44, 48

Boarding, 144
Book inventory, 243, 245
Bookkeeping, 366–380
Boots, 56–57
Bonnie and Clyde, 52
Bosom, the, 63
Boutiques, fashion coordination
        in, 326–328
Bow, Clara, 80
Brands
    fashion policy and, 340
    hosiery, 145
    illus., 145
    style selection and, 184
Brassieres, 146
Brenninkmeyer, 43
Bridal gift registry, 330, 332
Brooks Brothers, 120
Brooks, Donald, 130
Budgets and budgeting, 199–214, 366
    buyers and, 200
Bulletin boards, 316
Burdine's, Miami, 292
Business women, 48
Bustle, the, 48
    Illus., 45, 139
Buyer clinics, 270
Buyers
    and budget planning, 200
    careers as, 356
    clinics, 270
    contact between, 275
    as fashion coordinators, 324
    home-store, exchange of in-
        formation by, 271
    and planning method, 266
    responsibility of, for mark-
        downs, 256
        for selling, 315
    and selection of merchandise
        for resale, 262–281
    training methods used by,
        315–316
    and vendors, 257
    and working the market,
        275–276, 278–279
Buyer's Manual, 380
Buyer's purchase record, illus., 249
Buying motivation, customer
        demand and, 185
Buying offices (see Resident buy-
        ing offices)
Buying plan, 262–266
    illus., 263
Buying power, fashion move-
        ment and, 59, 61
Buying trips, 264–268

California, as fashion center, 129–131
Cancellations, 232
Career girls, customer preference determined through, 196
Career opportunities, 348–365
  in advertising, 360–361
  as consultants, 363
  in manufacturing, 349–355
  in publishing, 361–363
  in retailing, 355–360
  in store ownership, 364–365
  in trade associations, 363–364
Carlyle, Thomas, 31
Carnaby Street, 129
Carson, Johnny, 81
Carson Pirie Scott and Company, 325–326
Cartwright, Edward, 98
Cash on delivery (COD), 375
Cash discounts, 213
Castle, Irene, 80
Casual wear, leisure and, 20
Caution, 127
Cellulose fibers, 90
Chain stores, 169–170, 311–312
  assortment planning and control in, 239
  career opportunities in, 358–360
  fashion coordination in, 326
  fashion image of, 345–346
  merchandising policies of, 170–171
  organizational structure of, 169–170
  training salespeople in, 311–312
Chambre Syndicale de la Couture Parisienne, 126–127
Chanel, Coco, 81, 126, 184
Change
  fashion and, 7–11, 20
    conditions favoring, 37–38
    stability versus, 35–38
    social mobility and, 23
Chaplin, Charles, 81
Chardonnet, Count Hilaire de, 90
Charge-backs, 245
  illus., 231
Charles II, 48
Chemise, the, 5, 23, 58
Chemistry, leather industry and, 105, 110
Cheskin, Louis, 28
China, 16–17
Christmas catalogs, 293
Christmas windows, 295
Classics, 4
  fads and, 5
  as long-run fashion, 58
Classification, definition of, 234

Classification merchandising, 234–237
Climate, customer demand and, 187–188
Clothes, reasons for wearing, 30–35 (See also Apparel)
Club women, customer preference determined through, 196
Cobliner, 82
College boards, 193, 195
Colors
  combinations of, 13
  as short-run fashion, 57
  style selection and, 184
  texture and, 6
Communications media (See also specific type of media, such as Television)
  fashion and, 8
  fashion demand and, 25–26
Comparison bureaus, merchandising and, 174
Comparison shoppers, 174–175
Competition
  in cosmetics industry, 149–150
  fashion cycles and, 56
Conformity, individuality and, 84
Consignment selling, of fur garments, 116
Consultants, fashion, 193
  in industry, 350–351
Consulting services, career opportunities in, 363
Consumer advisory boards, 193, 195–196
Consumer buying, fashion cycle and, 58
  graph of, 59
Consumer preferences, 182
  aids in determining, 188–191, 193, 195–196
  assortment planning and, 219–220
Consumer publications, 272
  career opportunities with, 361–362
Consumers
  and classification merchandising, 234
  fashion cycles and, 56
  and mass production, 81
Contract operations, in apparel manufacture, 123
Convention, rebellion against, 27
Converter, 100
Copeland, Melvin T., 185
Copies of couture models, 127, 171
  advertisement for, illus., 128
Copywriters, 356, 361
Corduroy, 6
Corsets, 139

Cosmetics, 149
  for men, 150
Cosmetics industry, 149–150
Costume jewelry, 152–153
Cotton, 89, 91, 100
  for lingerie, 141
Cotton mills, 98, 100
Counter and window cards, 299
Couture collections
  copies of, 171
  viewing of, 127
Couture houses, 126, 132
Couture model copies and adaptations, 127–128
Craft guilds, 161
Credit slips, 231
Crinoline, 45, 48
  illus., 139
Crystal, David, 121
Cultures, fashion and, 10–11
Current events, fashion trends and, 67
Custom
  fashion movement and, 60–61
  in modern dress, 37
  stability and, 36
Customer demand
  elements of, 184–188
  interpretation of, 182–196
  sales planning and, 203
  seasonal, 187–188, 203
Customer services
  textile fabric industry and, 101
  textile fiber industries and, 95–96
Customer surveys, 190
Customers
  and how-to-wear-it windows, 295–296
  outside information about, 190–191, 193
  store's information about, 188–190
  suburban versus city, 186–187
  target, 334–336
  and trading up, 178
  twentieth century changes in, 183–184

Dacron, 90
Daily News Record, 92
Daniels, Alfred H., 66
Dardis, Rachel, 28
Data
  for buying plan, 264–266
  for classification merchandising, 236–237
  for unit control, 228–232

Dating
    cash discounts and, 213
    types of, 375–376
Daves, Jessica, 83
Davis, Tobé Coller, 193, 363
Decoration, 30–32, 38
Decorative theory, 30–32
    illus., 31
Deitrich, Marlene, 80
de la Renta, Oscar, 73
Demand centers, 235
Demonstrations, 300
Demonstrators, cosmetics, 149
Department stores, 161, 164
    branch-owning, 167, 178
        assortment planning and
            control in, 238–239
    definition of, 164
    fashion coordination in, 322–
        326
    large, organization chart for,
        166
    leased departments in, 115,
        153, 158, 173
    merchandising policies of,
        165, 167
    mergers among, 176–177
    modern, 167
    oldest in the United States,
        illus., 164
    organizational structure of, 165
    staff aids for merchandising
        by, 174–176
Departmental inventory ledger,
    illus., 244
Departmental meetings, 316
Departmental operating reports,
    249–254
Departmental operating state-
    ments, 253
    illus., 252
Departmental purchase journal,
    248–249
Design
    definition of, 3
    new, 55
Design inspiration, sources of, 72
Design piracy, 129–130
Designers
    American, 49, 129–130
    and birth of a fashion, 70–73
    and cosmetics industry, 150
    fabric, 350
    and publicity, 306
    role of, 71–73
Designing, career opportunities
    in, 351–352
Dior, Christian, 9, 63
Dior, House of, 134
Dior's New Look, 49, 65, 73, 82
    illus., 9
Direct-mail advertising, 293

Direct-sell windows, 296–297
Discount stores, 170–172
Discounts
    cash, 213, 374–375
    employee, 377
    quantity, 374
    special, 377
    trade, 374
Display, 294–300
    interior, 297
    window, 295–297
Dissections, 234–235
Diversification
    in apparel manufacture, 133–135
    in jewelry industry, 153
    in shoe industry, 148
Dollar merchandise plan
    basic, preparation of, 200–201
    cash discounts and, 213
    elements of, 200
    gross margin and, 213
    markdowns and, 207–209
    markon and, 210–211
    operating expenses and, 214
    organization of, 199–200
    and purchases planning, 209
    and sales planning, 201–203
    and stock planning, 204–207
    stock shortages and overages
        and, 213–214
    supplemental elements in,
        209–210
Dollar retail, determination of, 371
Doyle Dane Bernbach study,
    77–78
Dunlap, Knight, 34, 35

Economic development, fashion
    demand and, 16–20
Editorial careers, 361–362
Editorial credits, 271–272
Education
    fashion change and, 37
    fashion demand and, 23
    fashion movement and, 59
Egypt, ancient, 30–31, 39
Eisenhower, Dwight, 81
Eisenhower, Mamie, 80
Elizabeth, Queen, 35, 39, 81
Empire period, 44
England, 42–44
    as a fashion center, 129
Environment
    definition of, 16
    fashion cycles and, 56
    fashion demand and, 16–29
Erogenous zones, 61
Escobosa, Hector, 26, 129, 311
Ethnic groups, fashion demand
    and, 20–21

Eugénie, Empress, 8, 45, 79
    illus., 46
Europe, 30 (*See also* names of
        countries)
    as fashion center, 126–127, 129
    history of fashion in, 36–45,
        48–50
    shoe manufacture in, 148
Exclusivity, fashion policy and,
    340
Exhibits, 300

Fabric designers, 350
Fabric librarians, 350
Fabric libraries, 95
Fabric stylists, 350
Fads, 5
    as short-run fashion, 58
Farrow, Mia, 68
Fashion
    acceptance of, 6–7, 52
    as big business, 348
    birth of, 70–74
    changes in, 7–12, 20
    components of, 5–6
    cycling of (see Fashion cycles)
    definition of, 2–3
    as expression of individuality,
        83–84
    intangibles of, 6–12
    misconceptions of, 2
    movement of, 52–69
        accelerating influences on,
            58–60
        retarding influences on, 60–61
    nature of, 2–15
    predicting of, 65–68
    terminology of, 2–5
    varied activities in, 349
Fashion adoption, theories of,
    75–78
Fashion bulletins, 274
Fashion bureaus, 174
Fashion business, scope of, 348–
    349
Fashion calendar, *illus.*, 267
Fashion centers
    foreign, 126–127, 129
    in the United States, 129–131,
        349
Fashion consultants, 193, 303
Fashion coordination, 318–333
    careers in, 358, 361
Fashion coordinators, 174, 304–
    305, 311, 318
    buyers as, 324
    merchandising responsibili-
        ties of, 318–320
Fashion cycle, 54–58
    broken, 56–57

Fashion cycle (*continued*)
   consumer buying and, 58
   definition of, 54
Fashion demand
   economic factors in, 16–17
   environment and, 16–29
   and the individual, 28
   psychological factors in, 26–28
   sociological factors in, 20–26
Fashion distribution center, *illus.*,
   176–177
Fashion experts, 350
Fashion followers, 78–82
Fashion guidance
   for leather industry, 107
   for textile fiber industries,
   97–98
Fashion image
   changing of, 340, 342
   development of, 334–347
   types of, 342–346
Fashion industry
   nineteenth century, 45, 48
   twentieth century, 182
Fashion information, sources of,
   271–275
Fashion innovators, 79
   definition of, 76
Fashion leaders, 70–85, 342–343
Fashion merchandising (*see* Merchandising)
Fashion periodicals, 271, 273
Fashion policy, elements of, 336–
   337, 339–340
Fashion producers, 306–307
Fashion promotion, 282–317
   through advertising (*see* Advertising)
   by demonstrations and exhibits, 300
   by display, 294–300
   fashion coordination and,
   321–322
   fashion policy and, 337, 339
   publicity and (*see* Publicity)
Fashion retailing
   careers in, 355–360
   history of, 160–163
   and merchandising activities,
   174–176
   modern, 163–165, 167–174
   successful, 182
   trends in, 176–178
Fashion shows, 305–306, 312, 316
Fashion trends, 65–68
   data for prediction of, 66–67
   definition of, 65
   evaluation of, 318
   identification of, 234
   information on, 272
   interpretation of, 67–68
   sales planning and, 202

Fashions
   American, international character of, 349
   historical development of, 30–51
   long-run and short-run, 57–58
   men's (*see* Men's fashions)
   new, birth of, 70–74
     testing of, 279–280
     varying rate of response to,
     82–83
   recurring, 52
   retail distributors of (*see*
     Fashion retailing)
   unwanted, promotion of, 182
Federated Department Stores,
   176–177
Fiber
   definition of, 88
   mill consumption of, table, 91
   natural, 88–92, 95, 97
   producers of, 313
   synthetic, 88–91
   trademarked, 97
   unbranded, 97
Field, Marshall, 163, 165
Figure, fashion apparel and, 63
Financial management, 198–199,
   366–380
Financial statements, 366
Fixtures, display, 299
Flash sales report, 249
Flax, 90
Flügel, 34, 61–62, 75, 82–83
Foreign production, in apparel
   manufacture, 134–135
Foreign trade, fashion apparel
   industry and, 134
Form, 12, 32
Forms, display, 299
Foundations industry, 139–141
France, 39, 42 (*See also* Paris)
Franchise, 173
Fruit of the Loom, 134
Fur farming, 111, 114
Fur garments, manufacture and
   distribution of, 115–116
Fur industry
   history of, 111
   marketing trends in, 116, 118
   merchandising activities of,
   116
   organization and operation
   of, 111, 114–116
Fur Information and Industry
   Council, 116
Fur Products Labeling Act of
   1952, 116
Furs, 104, 110–111
   fun, 116, 118
   for hats, 158
   processing of, 114–115
   illus., 112–113

Furs (*continued*)
   sources of, 111, 114–115
   United States foreign trade
   in, table, 114

Galanos, James, 130
Gap-bridgers, 77–78
Garbo, Greta, 80
Garland, Madge, 61–63, 65
Garment factories, 121–122
Gemstones, 151
General stores, 161–162
Genesco, 134, 177
Gernreich, Rudi, 130
Gertz Department Store, 196
Giantism, in textile fabric in-
   dustry, 101–102
Gibson girl, 58, 139
   illus., 47
Gimbel, Adam, 163, 165
Gimbel family, 176
Girdles, 140
Givenchy, 126
Gladding's, 164
Glove industry, 153–156
Gloves
   fabric, 153–154
   history of, 153
   leather, 153–155
   leathers used for, 106
   styles of, *illus.*, 154
Godey's Lady's Book, 48
Greece, 31, 39
Grès, Mme., 184
Gross margin, 213, 369–370
Gross national product (GNP), 17
Gross sales, 369
Group purchase, 271

Hair styles, 31–32, 68, 78, 81
   illus., 80
Halley, George, 130
Hamburger, Estelle, 193, 363
Handbag industry, 156–157
Handbags, 156–157
Harmony, 12
Harper's Bazaar, 52, 73, 158, 193,
   273
Hats (*see* Millinery)
Haute couture, 126
Headwear, 8–9 (*See also* Millinery)
Hess Brothers, 345
Hides, 106
High fashion, 2–3
Hippie fashions, 50
Hips, the, 63
Hobble skirts, 48
   illus., 49

Holidays, customer demand and, 187, 203
Home sewing industry, careers in, 354–355
Horizontal integration, 101
Hosiery, 142–144
Hosiery industry, 142–146
"Hot" items, 266
Howe, Elias, 120

Income, 17–18
Income statement, 366–370
Indians, South American, 36
Individuality
    conformity and, 83–84
    fashion as expression of, 83–84
    millinery and, 158
Industrial Revolution, 44
Industries
    fashion apparel manufacturing, 120–137
    textile fabric, 98–102
    textile fiber, 88–98
Industry
    fashion, 2, 7
    and mass production, 45
Influentials, 79
Interior display, 297–299
International Ladies' Garment Workers' Union, 122
International Silk Association, 92
Intimate apparel, 138–142
Inventories
    book, 243, 245
    forms for, 246
    physical, 245–246
Inventory control, 242–249
Inventory evaluation, retail method of, 199, 242–243
Inventory sheet, illus., 247
Irish Linen Guild, 92
Italy, as fashion center, 129

Japan, 36
Jewelry, 31–32, 38, 150
    costume or fashion, 152
    fine, 151–152
    timelessness of, illus., 151
Jewelry industry, 150–153
Jewelry Industry Council, 152
Jobbers
    definition of, 122
    rack, 145
Jobbing, in hosiery industry, 145–146
Jobs, women's, and spending, 22–23 (See also Careers)

Kasper, Herbert, 130
Kennedy, Jacqueline, 50, 80–82
Kips, 106
Klein, S., 177
King, Charles W., 76–77, 79
Korvette's, 172
Kossuth, Louis, 81
Kroeber, A. L., 52–54, 72

Labels and labeling, 96
    fabric, illus., 93
    fur, 116
Labor unions, garment industry and, 121–122
Lake, Veronica, 80
Lambert, Eleanor, 307
Lane Bryant, 335
Laun, Louis, 97
Laver, James, 4, 32, 35, 43, 48, 55, 58, 61, 63, 75
Lawrence, A. C., Leather Company, 105
Leased department, 173
Leather, 104
    and competitive materials, 110
    glove, 106
    processing of, 106–107
        illus., 108–109
    shoe, 146–147
    sources of, 105–106
Leather industry, 104–110
Legs, 63
Lenglen, Suzanne, 80
Letting-out, 115
Licensing
    in apparel fashion industry, 134
    of textile fiber industries, 97
Lindbergh, Charles, 81
Line, 12, 32
Linen, 90
Lines, fashion apparel, 124–126
    seasonal, de-emphasis on, 133
Lingerie industry, 141
Logan, Jonathan, 122
Looms, mechanization of, 98
Lord & Taylor, 177–178, 295
Louis XIV, 39–40
Louis XV, 35
Louis Napoleon, 44
Lowell, Francis Cabot, 98

MacArthur, Douglas, 81
McCardell, Claire, 129
McCrory chain, 177
Macy's, 162, 175–176, 335, 345
Magazines
    advertising in, 293–294

Magazines (continued)
    customer preference determined through, 193
    publicity in, 303–304
Magnin, I., 311
Mail-order sellers, 163, 169
    career opportunities with, 358–360
Makeup, 31–32 (See also Cosmetics)
Mansfield, Jayne, 80
Manufacturer, definition of, 122
Manufacturers (See also Industries)
    as aid in determining customer preference, 191
    and birth of a fashion, 70, 73–74
    fashion apparel, 120–137
    as source of fashion information, 273–274
Manufacturing, careers in, 349
Marcus, Stanley, 334
Marie Antoinette, 42, 79, 157
    illus., 41
Markdown cancellation, 377
Markdown percentage, 376–377
Markdowns, 245, 376–377
    as aid in determining customer preference, 189
    analyses of, 256
    causes of, 256
    planning of, 207–209
    purpose of, 207
    terminology of, 207–208
Market representatives, 269–270
Market research
    in fashion apparel industry, 136
    by textile fabric industry, 101
    by textile fiber industries, 94–95
Market trips
    itinerary for, 275–276
    reason for, 264
    timing of, 266–268
Marketing concept, 182–183
Marketing trends
    in apparel manufacture, 132–134, 136
    in fur industry, 116, 118
    in glove industry, 155–156
    in handbag industry, 157
    in hosiery industry, 146
    in intimate apparel industry, 142
    in jewelry industry, 153
    in leather industry, 110
    in shoe industry, 148–149
    in textile fabric industry, 101–102
    in textile fiber industry, 96–98
Marketplaces, 160–161

Markets
  fashion coordinator's work
    in, 319
  textile fiber, 91
Markon, 210–211, 370–374
  averaging of, 372–374
  cumulative, 242
  definition of, 210
  formulas for, 371–372
  terminology used in, 370–371
Markon percentage
  average, 373–374
  initial, 371–372
Mass fashion, 2–3
Mass-marketers, fashion image
    of, 343
Mass production, 45, 182
  consumption and, 81
  of intimate apparel, 141
  of ready-to-wear, 123
Mat (matrix), definition of, 289
Materials, 88–119
  fashions and, 88
  fur, 110–118
  leather, 104–110
  style selection and, 184
  synthetic and natural, 88–102
May Department Stores, 176–177
Maxi, the, *illus.,* 50
Men's fashions, 7, 35, 37–38, 42,
    48–50
Men's Wear, 92, 273
Merchandise
  basic or staple, 254
  breakdown levels of, 235–236
  interdepartmental loan of, 245
  knowledge of, and selling,
    310, 315
  nature of, fashion movement
    and, 61
  on order, 245
  selection of, for resale, 262–281
  staple, rate of sale for, 220
Merchandise managers, 356
  as coordinators, 324
Merchandise transfers, 230–231, 245
  form for, *illus.,* 230
  in multi-unit stores, 239
Merchandising, 2, 84
  by apparel manufacturers,
    131–132
  broken fashion cycles and, 56
  careers in, 355–356, 362
  central, 270–271
  by chain stores, 170
  classification, 234–237
  definition of, 366
  by department stores, 165, 167
  by discount stores, 170–172
  fashion adoption and, 76–77
  fashion coordinator's re-
    sponsibilities in, 318–320

Merchandising (*continued*)
  by fur industry, 116
  by glove industry, 155
  by handbag industry, 156
  of hosiery, 145–146
  of intimate apparel, 141–142
  by jewelry industry, 152–153
  by leased departments, 173
  by leather industry, 107
  by retail fashion distributors,
    174–176
  by shoe industry, 148
  by specialty stores, 169
  by textile fabric industry,
    100–101
  by textile fiber industries,
    92, 94–96
  by variety stores, 172–173
Merchandising arithmetic, 366–380
Merchandising assortments
  budgeting of, 216–241
  depth versus breadth in, 340
  display of, 297–298
  expanded, 178
  fashion policy and, 336–337
  good, 216
  management of, 242–260
  planning of, 216–220
Merchandising notes, 278–279
Merchandising operation, evalua-
    tion of, 254–259
Merchandising plan, six month,
    illus., 201, 204, 206, 208,
    210, 212
Mergers
  among department stores,
    176–177
  in leather industry, 110
Miami, 131, 349
Middle Ages
  craft guilds in, 161
  fashions in, 62
Middle class, growth of, 24
Midi, the, 73
  illus., 50, 140
Miller, I., Shoes, 148
Millinery, 157
  fur, 158
  rejection of, 158
Miniskirts, 50, 70
  illus., 10, 50
Minuit, Peter, 104
Mod styles, 50
Model stock planning, 220–221, 266
  table for, 221
Modern dress, custom in, 37
Modesty theory, 34–35
  illus., 35
Mohammedan women, 33
Money, spending of, by working
    women, 22–23 (See *also*
    Wealth)

Monroe, Marilyn, 80
Montgomery Ward, 163, 169, 325
Multi-unit stores
  assortment planning and
    control in, 237–239
  purchase orders for, 229
Murphy, Michelle, 43
Mutation Mink Breeders As-
    sociation, 116, 363

Napoleon, 44
National Association of Glove
    Manufacturers, 155
National Board of the Coat and
    Suit Industry, 191
National Cotton Council, 92, 94
National dress, 16
National Millinery Institute, 158
National Retail Merchants As-
    sociation, 210, 234, 236,
    256, 278, 285, 292, 325,
    349, 362, 363
National Shoe Manufacturers'
    Association, 148
National Shoe Retailers' As-
    sociation, 148
Necklines, 63
Neiman-Marcus, 334, 344
Net terms, 375
New England
  apparel manufacture in, 131
  and costume jewelry indus-
    try, 152
  shoe industry in, 146–147
New Look (see Dior's New Look)
New York City, 308
  department stores in, 335
  fashion advertising in, 286
  as fashion center, 130
  fashion industries in, 141,
    144–145, 148, 152, 155–
    156, 158
  garment industry in, 121–122
    (See *also* Seventh
    Avenue)
  resident buying offices in,
    176–270
New York Couture Business
    Council, 132
New York Times, The, 286
Newberry, J. J., 172
Newsmakers, 79–80
Newspapers
  advertising in, 286, 289–290, 303
  customer preference deter-
    mined through, 193
Night clothes, 48
Norell, Norman, 82, 130
Notice of paid advertising, *illus.,*
    291
Nude-apparel fashions, 58

Number, 3
Nylon, 90, 94
    for hosiery, 143
Nystrom, Paul H., 2, 4, 44, 66, 68, 84, 174

Obsolescence, 56
Ohrbach's, 171, 308, 342
Open-to-buy, 199, 264, 379–380
Open-to-buy reports, 253–254
Operating expenses, 214–370
Operating statement, 253, 366–370
    illus., 252, 368
Order cancellation, illus., 232
Order form, 229, 278
Orders
    outstanding, weekly report of, illus., 246
    writing of, 278
Orient, the, 30, 32
Originals, 55
Orlon, 90
Overstock, 266

Pants for women, 82
    illus., 11
Paris, 39, 42, 49
    as center of fashion inspiration, 120, 126–127, 131
Parker, Samuel, 104
Parrish, Amos, & Company, 363
Patternmakers, 352
Peck & Peck, 168, 335, 346
Peddlers, 162–163
Penney, J. C., Company, 163, 169, 175, 325, 335
Periodic stock count control, 224, 226–227
    record of, illus., 226–227
Perpetual inventory records, 222
    illus., 223
Perpetual inventory system, 222–224
Petit Courrier des Dames, 52
Physical inventory, 245–248
Plastics, 110
Poiret, Paul, 71–72
Polyesters, 90
Polymers, 90
Population, fashion demand and, 18–20
Poverty, 18
    and fashion stability, 35
Press releases, 303
Press Weeks, 132, 303, 307
Pretesting, as aid to determining customer preferences, 189
Preticketing, 237
Price changes, 232, 245
    report of, illus., 233
Price lines, 339–340

Price range, definition of, 339
Prices
    comparative, 340
    fashion policy and, 339–340
    style selection and, 185
Product research and development
    by fur industry, 118
    by leather industry, 110
    by textile fabric industry, 102
    textile fiber industries and, 96
Production methods, new, 38
Profit, 370
Profit and loss statement, 366–370
Promotion plans, manufacturers and, 273
Promotional aids, for apparel manufacturers, 132
Protection theory, 33,
    illus., 34
Publicity
    for apparel manufacturers, 132, 353
    careers in, 351, 353, 362–363
    media used for, 303–304
    methods of obtaining, 302–303
    sources of material for, 304–307
    for textile fabric industry, 101, 351
    for textile fiber industries, 92, 94, 351
Purchase journal, departmental, 248
Purchase orders, 229
    illus., 228
Purchase record, buyer's, 248–249
Purchases, planning of, 209
Purchasing power, dollar, 18
Purses (see Handbags)

Qiana, 94
Quality standards, fashion policy and, 339
Quant, Mary, 129, 325

Rack jobbers, 145
Radio
    advertising on, 292
    fashion demand and, 25
    publicity on, 304
Raw materials industries, careers in, 350–351
Ready-to-wear (See also Apparel)
    manufacturers of, 120–137
Receiving records, 229
    illus., 230
Regency period, 42
Regional variations, 274
    customer demand and, 186
Religion, fashion movement and, 61

Renaissance fashions, 62–63
Reorders, 224
Reporting services, 193
Resale, selection of merchandise for, 262–281
Research departments, department store, 175–176
Research studies, customer preference and, 191, 193
Reserve requisition control, 227
Resident buying offices, 176, 268–271
    bulletin of, illus., 192
    determining customer preference through, 191
    independent, 268
    organization of, 269–270
    store-owned, 268–269
Resource file, illus., 258–259
Resource information, 272
Retail buyers groups, 274
Retail conventions, 274–275
Retail figures, inventory evaluation and, 199
Retail Memo, 193
Retail News Bureau, 193
    report of, illus., 194
Retail reductions, 207, 376–378
Retailers, 94
    and birth of a fashion, 74
    and theory of fashion adoption, 76–77
Retailing (see Fashion retailing)
Returns, 190, 231–232, 245, 256
Richardson, Jane, 53–54, 72
Robinson, D. E., 65, 72–73, 76
Rococo style, 42
ROG, 375
Romans, the, 39
Royalty, 79
Russia, 16

Sack dress, 182–183
St. Laurent, Ives, 72, 82, 126
Saks Fifth Avenue, 163, 178
Sales
    of advertising space, 362
    and evaluation of merchandising operation, 258
    gross, 369
    net, 369
    planning of, 201–203
    stock and, 205–206
Sales events
    customer demand and, 187
    model stock planning and, 220
Sales and inventory report, illus., 225
Sales promotion
    careers in, 356–358
    fashion movement and, 60, 68
    organization of, 282–283

Sales records, 229–230, 366
    buying plan and, 264–265
    fashion movement and, 66
    past, customer preference
        and, 188
    sales planning and, 203
Sales reports, 249–250
    illus., 225, 250, 251
Sales-supporting careers, 358
Salesmanship, personal, 307–308
Salesmen, manufacturers'
    career opportunities as, 353
    customer preference deter-
        mined through, 191
Salespeople
    as aids in determining cus-
        tomer preference, 190
    and individual approach, 310
    and knowledge of fashion
        and merchandise, 310
    personal qualifications of,
        309–310
    training of, 310–313, 315
        fashion coordination
            and, 320–321
Sample maker, 353
Sample-test-recorder technique,
    279–280
Sapir, 37, 75, 82, 84
Sassoons, Vidal, 68
Scarfs, 57–58
Sears, Roebuck & Company, 163,
    169, 325, 335
Season letter, 254
Seasonal variations, customer
    demand and, 187
Seasonality, fashion movement
    and, 60
Self-expression, fashion and, 84
Self-selection, 308
Self-selection racks, 298–299
Self-service, 308
Selling
    buyer's responsibility for, 315
    methods of, 307–309
        fashion policy and, 337, 339
        manufacturers and, 274
    salon, 308
    self-selection, 308
    successful, requirements for,
        309–310
    training for, 310–316
Seventh Avenue, New York City,
    130, 275, 349
Sewing machine, invention of,
    48, 120
Sex, fashion apparel game and, 61
Sexes
    equality of, and similarity of
        dress, 32, 50
    opposite, attraction of, 31
Shape, 32
Sheath, the, 84

Sheppard, Eugenia, 82, 83
Shifts, 84
Shirtwaist dresses, 58
Shoe industry, 146–149
Shoes
    classic, 58
    fashion and, 146, 185
    production of, *illus.,* 108–109
    sizes of, 147
    skirt lengths and, 146, 148
    styles of, *illus.,* 147
Shops
    bridal, 229–332
    fashion coordination in,
        328–330
Shoulders, 62-63
Showroom procedures, 276
Sign order, *illus.,* 288
Silhouettes, 12
    basic skirt, 53–54,
        illus., 53
    definition of, 5
    foundations and, 139–140
    as long-run fashion, 57
    rhythmic changes in, 52–53
    style selection and, 184
    twentieth century, 48–49
Silk, 89–90
    artificial, 90
    for hosiery, 143
    for lingerie, 141
Simmel, Georg, 75, 83
Simpson, Adele, 72, 130
Singer, Isaac, 120
Size, style selection and, 184
Sketchers, 352–353
Skins, 106
Skirt lengths, 49–50, 70, 73
    hosiery and, 142
    millinery and, 158
    shoes and, 146, 148
Slack, Charles W., 77
Slater, Samuel, 98
Social behavior, fashion and, 75
Social freedom, fashion and, 23
Social hierarchy, fashion adop-
    tion and, 75
Social mobility
    fashion change and, 23
    fashion movement and, 59–60
    in the United States, 23–24
Society, fashion and, 11–12
Society leaders, 79
Spain, as fashion center, 129
Spandex, 90
Special occasions (See also
    Holidays)
    buying plan and, 266
    customer demand and, 187
Specialization
    in apparel manufacture, 123–
        124
    in leather industry, 105

Specialty stores, 335
    assortment planning and
        control in, 238–239
    definition of, 167
    individually owned, 168
    merchandising policies of, 169
    organizational structure of,
        168–169
Sports clothes, 20
    illus., 21
Stability, change versus, 35–38
Staff aids in merchandising, 174
Standard Classifications, 236
Stern Brothers, 339
Stevens, J. P., and Company, 98
Stock
    on hand or on order, 264
    model, 266
    planned end-of-period, 265
    planning of, 204–207
    sales and, 205–206
Stock control, visual, 227–228
Stock counts, 224, 226–227
Stock overages, 213–214, 246–248
Stock-sales ratio, 205, 217
Stock and sales reports, 250, 253
    weekly, *illus.,* 251
Stock shortages, 213–214, 246–
    248, 378
Stock turnover, 206, 378–379
    excessively high, 258
    good, importance of, 257–258
    improving of, 257
Store display, fashion demand
    and, 25–26
Store owners, 364–365
    as coordinators, 324–325
Stores
    chain (see Chain stores)
    coordinators in, 323–325
    department (see Department
        stores)
    discount, 170–172
    and fashion image, 334–347
    franchised, 173–174
    general, 161–162
    large, fashion coordination
        in, 322–323
        fashion image of, 344–345
        training salespeople in,
            311-312
    medium-sized, fashion coor-
        dination in, 322
    new, sales planning for, 203
    small, fashion coordination
        in, 322-323
        fashion image of, 345
        training salespeople in, 311
    specialty (see Specialty
        stores)
    variety, 161, 172–173
Style, 2
    acceptance and, 7

Style (*continued*)
    definition of, 3
    rococo, 42
Style number, 3, 276–278
Style selection, factors in, 184–185
Styles
    prophetic, 67–68
    record of sales of, 224
    reoccurence of, 52
Styling, compromise, 72–73
Suburbs
    branch stores in, 178
    customer demand in, 186–187
Sumptuary laws, 61
Swimwear, *illus.*, 4

Taking numbers, 276–278
Tanning and tanners, 104–107
Tarde, Gabriel, 75
Target group, creation of, 334–336
Taste
    canons of, 68
    changes in, 183–184
    conservative, 184
    definition of, 3–4
    salesperson's knowledge of, 310
    style and, 4
Taylor, Elizabeth, 81
Technology
    color and, 6
    fashion movement and, 38, 60
Teen-agers, as target group, 334
Teen boards, 195–196
Telephone calls
    alerting news media by, 303
    selling by, 309
    solicitation by, 293
Television
    advertising on, 292–293
    careers in, 363
    fashion demand and, 25
    publicity on, 304
Temple, Shirley, 81
Terms of sale, 374
Testing bureaus, department store, 175
Textile fabric industry, 98–102
Textile fiber industries, 88–98
Textile Fiber Products Identification Act of 1960, 96
Textures, 13
    color and, 6
    definition of, 6
Ticket
    manufacturer's, *illus.*, 237
    retailer's, *illus.*, 238
Tobé Service, 193
Toile, 127
Toiletries, 149
Trade, fashion and, 2

Trade advertising, 131
Trade associations
    career opportunities in, 363–364
    fur industry, 116
    gloves, 157
    jewelry, 152
    leather industry, 107
    millinery, 158
    and publicity, 307
    shoe industry, 148
    as sources of fashion information, 274
    textile fiber industry, 92
Trademarks, 97
Trade publications, 131
    career opportunities with, 362–363
    and determination of customer preference, 193
Trade shows, as source of fashion information, 262, 274–275
Trading up, 178
Tradition, stability of, 36
Training services, professional, 315
Transactions (*see* Sales)
Transportation methods, fashion change and, 38
Trends (*see* Fashion trends; Marketing trends)
Trigère, Pauline, 130
Trunk shows, 189, 306
Tucker, Beryl, Young Trends, 193
Tuma, Ardelle, 325

Udell, Jon G., 185
Ungaro, 126
Unit control, 221–224
Unit-control bureaus, 175
Unit planning, information recorded in, 221–222
Unit sales plan, *illus.*, 217
United States
    consumer income in, 17
    development of retailing in, 160
    discretionary income in, 18
    eighteenth century, 42
    fashion centers in, 128–131
    fashion industries in, 104–106, 120, 143
    foreign trade in furs by, table, 114
    middle-class growth in, 24
    nineteenth century, 45, 48
    personal income in, 17
    physical mobility in, 24
    population of, estimates and projections of, table, 19
    and fashion demand, 18–20
    purchasing power of dollar in, 18

United States (*continued*)
    retail establishments in, 160
    social fluidity in, 23–24
    textile fabric industry in, 98
    textile fiber industry in, 90–92, 94–98
    textile plants in, table, 99
    twentieth century, 48–50
Utility, style selection and, 184

Vacations, customer demand and, 187–188
Variety stores, 161, 172–173
Veblen, Thorstein, 10, 11, 75
Vendor aids, 299–300
    in training salespeople, 312–313
Vendor analyses, 257
Vendors, and publicity, 306–307
Vertical integration, 100
Victoria, Queen, 8, 45, 48
Vignettes, 297
Villager, The, 133
Vogue, 52, 193, 273

Waistlines, 62
Wanamaker, John, 165
Want slips, 189
    illus., 190
Wars, fashion change and, 37–38
Wealth, stores catering to, 334–335
Weinburg, Chester, 73
Western world, the, 30, 36
    fashion history in, 38–50
Wigs, 58
Wills, Helen, 80
Window displays, 295–297
    vendors and, 299–300
Windsor, Duchess of, 79
Wittkin, Herbert, 339
Women
    status of, and fashion demand, 22
    working, spending by, 22–23
Women's Wear Daily, 25, 66, 77, 82, 92, 131, 134, 273, 362
Wool, 88–89, 91, 99–100
Wool Bureau, 92
Woolen mills, 89, 98
Woolworth, F. W., Company, 172
Workmanship, style selection and, 184
World War II, 8, 9, 54, 65, 73, 84, 100
Worth, Charles Frederick, 45

Yarn, 98
    dyed, 99–100
    for gloves, 154
Young, Mrs. Agnes Brooks, 53–54